An Edinburgh Diary
1793–1798

This sample from the diaries demonstrates how Agnes wrote close to the edge of the page. She was consistent with her record-keeping to a degree which veers close to the obsessive and at no time has any evidence been uncovered that she missed one or more days and then filled in the detail from memory. Her style was unvarying; she rarely made corrections; her handwriting was consistent, but her punctuation was lacking.

An Edinburgh Diary
1793–1798

Agnes Witts

EDITED BY ALAN SUTTON

FONTHILL

Fonthill Media Limited
Fonthill Media LLC
www.fonthillmedia.com
office@fonthillmedia.com

First published in the United Kingdom
and the United States of America 2016

ISBN 978-1-78155-484-5

Typeset in Sabon 10pt on 13pt
Printed and bound by CPI Group (UK) Ltd, Croydon, CR0 4YY

Foreword

I am most grateful to Alan Sutton for bringing before the reader the diaries of my great-great-great-grandmother while she and her family lived in Edinburgh in the 1790s. He has done a remarkable job in his editing, digging out all sorts of obscure bits of information.

My edition of the *Oxford English Dictionary* gives the first use of a flat, meaning an apartment, as 1824 (Walter Scott—*Red Gauntlet*). Agnes Witts used it some thirty years before; OED please note.

I much enjoy my occasional visits to Edinburgh. Indeed I was there last week for a mix of Festival, Fringe and friends. Agnes Witts would have approved.

For future visits I will have a copy of her Diary in my hand.

Francis Witts
Upper Slaughter
August 2016

Preface

The Witts family were originally from Oxfordshire and later relocated to the adjacent county of Gloucestershire. Financial circumstances wrenched them from friends and family to spend the years of 1793 to 1798 in virtual exile; thrown into a new society with which they had little previous connection. From a hesitant start Edward and Agnes Witts soon developed a circle of friends and within short time they were mixing with members of Edinburgh society who were among the most influential in the city, which a few years later—following the exhibition of the watercolourist Hugh William Williams—was to become known as the 'Athens of the North'.

The reason for the family moving to Edinburgh was simply that of domestic economy. Agnes's husband, Edward Witts, had inherited his father's wool stapling business, but due to circumstances which remain unclear his business failed in 1790 and he eventually became bankrupt six years later. The sole income available to Edward and Agnes was the interest on their marriage settlement which Edward's creditors could not gain access to. This income amounted to approximately £300 per year. Family advice—primarily from Agnes's cousin, Susan Charteris, Lady Elcho—recommended Edinburgh as the best place to educate the three boys well, but with economy, it being reckoned that Edinburgh was one third less expensive than England. It was a good choice and served its purpose well for the boys' education until the family wanderlust took them onwards in 1798 seeking further economy, which they found when they ended up in the city state of Weimar.

The introduction for this volume has been limited to a brief summary of the more immediate members of the Witts family. A more extensive family history is provided in an appendix at the end of the book.

The transcription of Agnes Witts's diaries has not been an easy task. Most of the initial typing was undertaken by Carol Boone who performed a work of miracles in translating and interpreting what Agnes was trying to write. Carol understandably left many xxxxx's where she could not make out the words. I have subsequently followed Carol and replaced many xxxxx's with the words (hopefully correctly), but inevitably on numerous occasions Agnes has defeated us both. On several occasions I have spent hours in deciphering; sometimes successfully, but often in abject and frustrating defeat.

Agnes's writing is difficult enough with normal words and her eccentric spelling was not unusual in late-eighteenth-century Britain. When, however, she introduces personal names that raises the problem of interpretation to a new level. The fashion of the day was to leave a *carte de visite*. Such cards, with the correct spelling of a name, were then used by Agnes, but it was not unusual in an initial entry—when a player has just entered the stage—for Agnes to write what she *thought* she had heard, inevitably leading to some name discrepancies.

I have attempted to research as much as was possible in the limited time available to me, but undoubtedly scholars local to Edinburgh will easily pick up my errors, or be able to shine a light where I have seen only darkness. In my defence I can only say that I am a publisher not a researcher, and I merely took on the task of editing the diaries of Agnes and her son Francis after a fruitless search to find anyone else who was willing to take on such a daunting job. This task was begun in 1980, so I have already served 36 years of what appears to be a 50 year sentence! Having said that, we are talking, in total terms, of more than four million words. This Edinburgh diary is only five-and-a-half per cent of the total from the Witts Family Papers which we are publishing.

I have used a vast number of reference sources, too numerous to list, but the publication of this volume may lead to later scholarly study and I can only hope that I have built a sufficient foundation for subsequent resarchers to view this as more than just a stepping stone.

With regard to the illustrations, these are primarily embellishment, but they will at least provide the reader with an idea of the fast-changing fashion of the 1790s where the tricorne was falling out of fashion to be replaced by the bicorne and the beaver hat (the early top hat), and the wig was also fast falling out of favour. As for the fashion for ladies, the ostrich feathers and the illustration of Mrs Smith in 1795 say it all.

I have attempted to keep the illustrations as close to their true chronological relevance as possible, and where I have strayed to using mid-nineteenth century works it is, I hope, fair to say that the scenes portrayed would not have been beyond the recognition of Agnes Witts during her time in Edinburgh. In the captions I have attempted to represent the method of the original source as much as information was available to me. Where I have referred to engravings, unless otherwise mentioned, these are predominantly steel engravings, i.e., using a steel plate to engrave upon as opposed to the earlier use of copper. I have also referred to etchings. For engravings, the artist uses a stylus to draw directly, often very precisely, onto the plate. For etchings, the artist sketches onto the plate, then applies an acid bath to further deepen and broaden (etch) the original lines. As a final word to the illustrations, I must acknowledge the work of my assistants John Kay and Henry Raeburn.

Alan Sutton FSA
October 2016

Contents

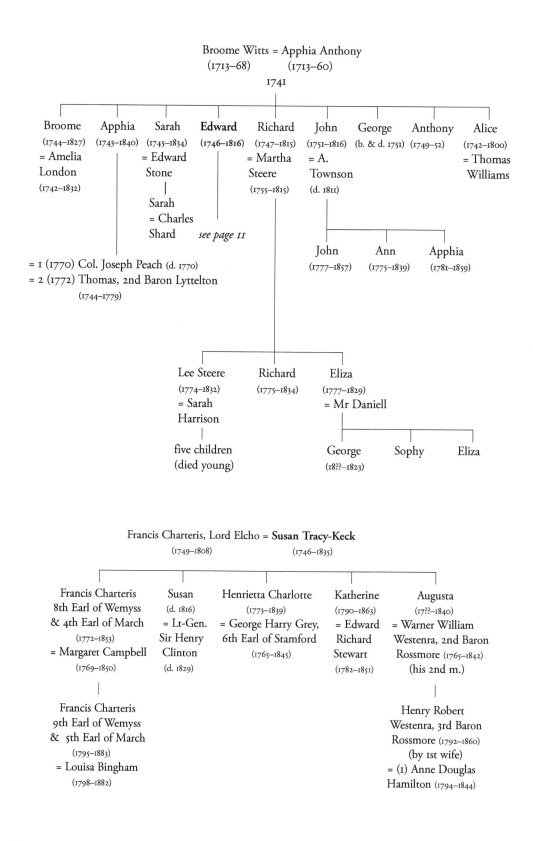

Broome Witts = Apphia Anthony
(1713–68)   (1713–60)
1741

Broome
(1744–1827)
= Amelia
London
(1742–1832)

Apphia
(1743–1840)

Sarah
(1745–1834)
= Edward
Stone
|
Sarah
= Charles
Shard

Edward
(1746–1816)

see page 11

Richard
(1747–1815)
= Martha
Steere
(1755–1815)

John
(1751–1816)
= A.
Townson
(d. 1811)

George
(b. & d. 1751)

Anthony
(1749–52)

Alice
(1742–1800)
= Thomas
Williams

= 1 (1770) Col. Joseph Peach (d. 1770)
= 2 (1772) Thomas, 2nd Baron Lyttelton
(1744–1779)

John
(1777–1857)

Ann
(1775–1839)

Apphia
(1781–1859)

Lee Steere
(1774–1832)
= Sarah
Harrison
|
five children
(died young)

Richard
(1775–1834)

Eliza
(1777–1829)
= Mr Daniell

George
(18??–1823)

Sophy

Eliza

Francis Charteris, Lord Elcho = **Susan Tracy-Keck**
(1749–1808)   (1746–1835)

Francis Charteris
8th Earl of Wemyss
& 4th Earl of March
(1772–1853)
= Margaret Campbell
(1769–1850)

Susan
(d. 1816)
= Lt-Gen.
Sir Henry
Clinton
(d. 1829)

Henrietta Charlotte
(1773–1839)
= George Harry Grey,
6th Earl of Stamford
(1765–1845)

Katherine
(1790–1863)
= Edward
Richard
Stewart
(1782–1851)

Augusta
(17??–1840)
= Warner William
Westenra, 2nd Baron
Rossmore (1765–1842)
(his 2nd m.)

Francis Charteris
9th Earl of Wemyss
& 5th Earl of March
(1795–1883)
= Louisa Bingham
(1798–1882)

Henry Robert
Westenra, 3rd Baron
Rossmore (1792–1860)
(by 1st wife)
= (1) Anne Douglas
Hamilton (1794–1844)

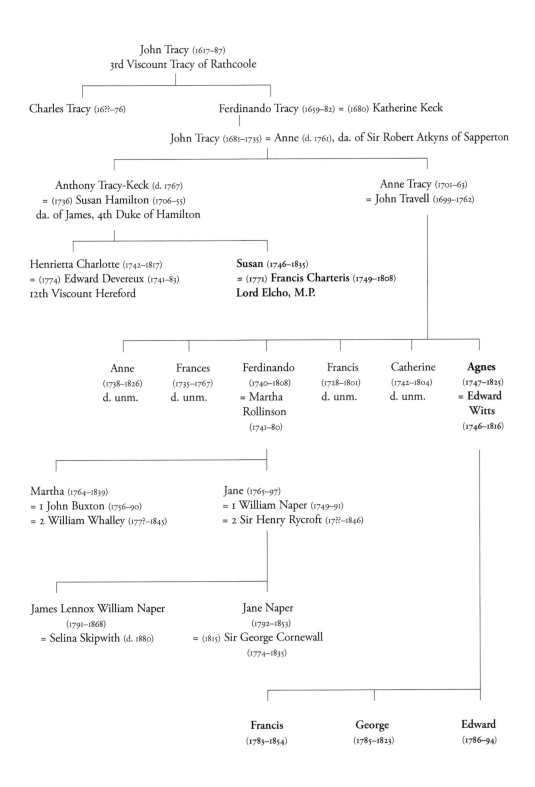

John Tracy (1617–87)
3rd Viscount Tracy of Rathcoole

Charles Tracy (16??–76)

Ferdinando Tracy (1659–82) = (1680) Katherine Keck

John Tracy (1681–1735) = Anne (d. 1761), da. of Sir Robert Atkyns of Sapperton

Anthony Tracy-Keck (d. 1767)
= (1736) Susan Hamilton (1706–55)
da. of James, 4th Duke of Hamilton

Anne Tracy (1701–63)
= John Travell (1699–1762)

Henrietta Charlotte (1742–1817)
= (1774) Edward Devereux (1741–83)
12th Viscount Hereford

Susan (1746–1835)
= (1771) Francis Charteris (1749–1808)
Lord Elcho, M.P.

Anne
(1738–1826)
d. unm.

Frances
(1735–1767)
d. unm.

Ferdinando
(1740–1808)
= Martha
Rollinson
(1741–80)

Francis
(1728–1801)
d. unm.

Catherine
(1742–1804)
d. unm.

Agnes
(1747–1825)
= Edward
Witts
(1746–1816)

Martha (1764–1839)
= 1 John Buxton (1756–90)
= 2 William Whalley (177?–1845)

Jane (1765–97)
= 1 William Naper (1749–91)
= 2 Sir Henry Rycroft (17??–1846)

James Lennox William Naper
(1791–1868)
= Selina Skipwith (d. 1880)

Jane Naper
(1792–1853)
= (1815) Sir George Cornewall
(1774–1835)

Francis
(1783–1854)

George
(1785–1823)

Edward
(1786–94)

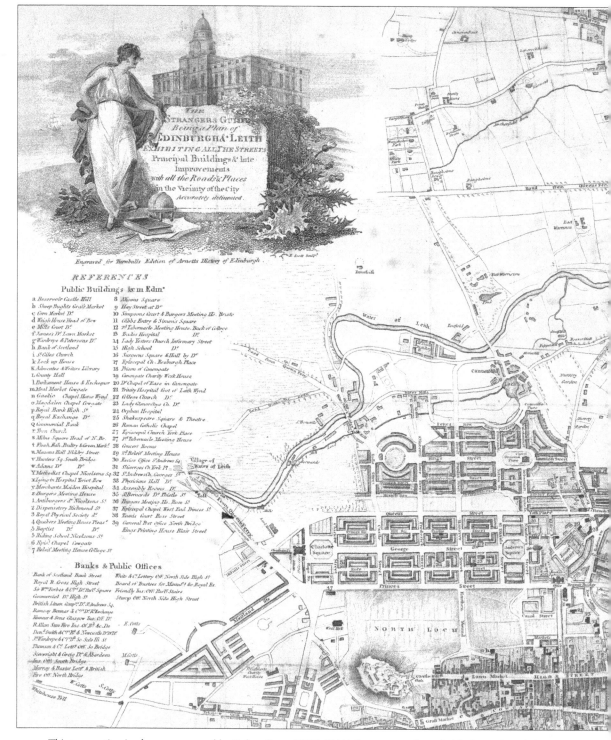

This top portion is of a map engraved by Robert Scott (1777–1841). Scott was eminent in his day and carried on a manufactory in Parliament Stairs, employing many assistants. By his final years he had obtained a prestigious studio at 65 Princes Street and was living at 15 Lauriston Street in the Tollcross area. Both buildings are now demolished.

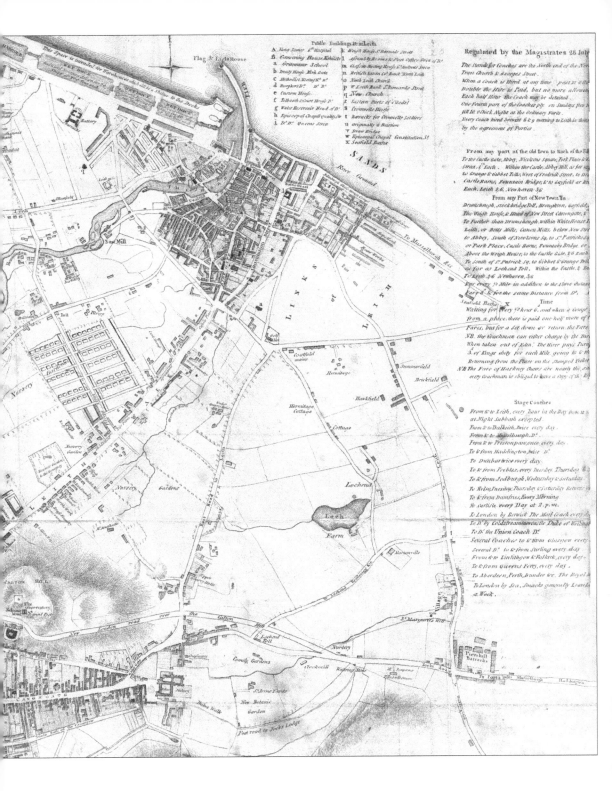

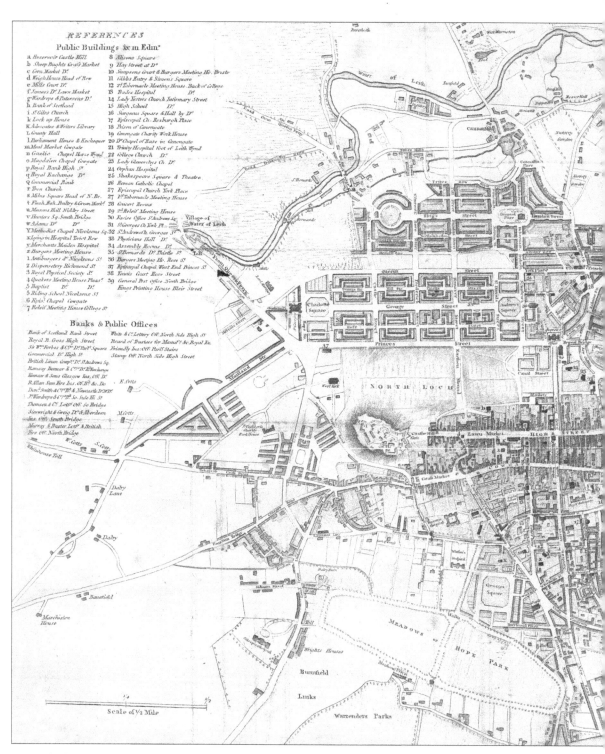

The bottom portion of the same map. It has been reproduced in this manner so that reader may enjoy the maximum size possible for legibility. The original source had the right-hand edge cropped. Scott produced this map in 1817 for the second edition of Hugo Arnot's *History of Edinburgh*. Scott tried to make his map as up-to-date as possible, and construction of the Regent Bridge had only just commenced when he published the map—showing it in anticipation.

Introduction

Part 1: The Witts Family 1746–1854

The text reproduced here is one portion from the complete diaries—1788–1824—of Agnes Witts (1747–1825); a continuous series of notebook diaries with very few gaps. The diaries in this volume are from the years 1793 to 1798 when the family resided in Ediburgh.

The Witts Family Papers contain voluminous diaries written by Agnes's eldest son, Francis Witts (1783–1854), some of whose early diaries overlap with those of his mother. The diaries of Francis Witts—*The Complete Diary of a Cotswold Parson*—which are available in published form elsewhere—are a detailed record of the life and times of a clerical magistrate in Gloucestershire during the first half of the nineteenth century and much of our knowledge of the Witts family is contained in snippet form as flashbacks from his diaries. When an acquaintance, friend or relation dies, Francis Witts has the helpful habit of outlining pertinent facts about the person and the family circumstances at the time. Some of these flashbacks are included as quotations in the family summary below.

A Summary of the Witts Family

The immediate family in Edinburgh during the time of these diaries was Edward Witts, Agnes Witts, and their three sons: Francis, George and Edward. Young Edward died only one year after the family's arrival in Edinburgh.

Edward Witts inherited a wool stapling business in Chipping Norton, Oxfordshire, but seemingly paid inadequate attention to it. His main love in life appears to have been travel. As a youth of sixteen he had been in North Wales and later—wars permitting—he travelled in France, the Channel Islands and Ireland, as well as extensive tours throughout England and Wales. A surviving passport and letters of introduction are dated 1770, and letters survive to his sister Apphia between 1768 and 1773 from his continental tours. After his marriage to Agnes Travell the wanderlust habits continued. He accepted his responsibilities as a country gentleman and was a justice of the peace, a deputy lieutenant for Oxfordshire and in 1779 sheriff for the County, but it remains a fact that his financial affairs were in less than good order.

Coupled with his upwardly mobile interests as an Oxfordshire Gentleman, Edward married Agnes in 1775, bought Swerford Park, became a magistrate and acted as a gentleman of the County.

The diaries of Agnes are mainly a social record, but a few facts do cut through, and the first record of the coming troubles occurs in the summer of 1790 when the house at Swerford was put up for sale and the family moved to Bownham House, Rodborough, near Stroud which they rented. Edward and Agnes quickly formed a strong social set and continued their gentlefolk lifestyle notwithstanding their looming problems.

The family financial circumstances meant that the plans for Charterhouse or Merchant Taylor's School were put aside and Francis went to school at Elmore Court near Gloucester, while the two younger boys, George and Edward remained in the nursery at Bownham.

Edward and Agnes used their carriage and horses in a whirlwind of social visits, local and away, until—to the absolute horror of Agnes—the full extent of their financial position was revealed to her in March of 1793. The next few months are a period of misery as the reality of their predicament sank in. The family removed to Edinburgh to reduce costs, arriving in July 1793.

The life of the family in Edinburgh is covered in Part 2 of this introduction, we therefore fast-track here to the family decision to move on from Edinburgh.

In 1796—possibly as the outcome of Edward's bankruptcy which finally occurred that year—the decision was made to find somewhere even more economical to live, and the place fixed upon was Germany. The opportunity had arisen to take Sir James Riddell's grandson to Germany as a form of guardianship to assist in his education, for which purpose Edward and Agnes would be paid—thus supplementing their income. The planned departure date was March 1797, but unfortunately war on the Continent delayed them, and then the death of Sir James put paid to the project. By the end of the year a substitute had been found. Sir Nathaniel Dukenfield—another well-groomed social contact of the Witts's—decided that Edward and Agnes should take his son Samuel for education and tuition for which they would be paid— thus effectively providing a substitute for the Riddell boy.

Delays in obtaining a passage and other complications held them back until September 1798 when at last they set sail for Hamburg. There they fell in with a Mr Martin, who recommended Weimar—and, as it turns out, it was a good recommendation. In Weimar the family, after another hesitant start, got on extremely well and became favourites at the court of the reigning duke and duchess. After a two-year stay they moved on again and following a short spell in Leipzig, the family settled in Dresden.

While in Dresden a letter arrived from Mr William Drummond, the British minister in Copenhagen reporting that he wished to appoint Frank to be his secretary.[1] Almost immediately the family set out, and after a troubled journey through Germany to Berlin they reached Stettin, and there took passage for Copenhagen, arriving on 8 October 1800. Here they were made welcome by Mr Drummond, but Agnes found herself at an extremely low point, verging on depression.

Unfortunately, the secretarial position lasted less than six months, for a diplomatic crisis with Denmark was heading towards military confrontation. On 22 March 1801 the family together with other British citizens—including Mr Drummond—were evacuated from Elsinore on board a Royal Navy frigate and at sea were transferred to HMS *Kite*, a sloop of war. Eleven days later Nelson destroyed the Danish fleet at the Battle of Copenhagen.

The family was landed at Leith on 1 April 1801 and later in the day arrived at their very familiar Edinburgh where they had friends around them. Francis Witts records the moment:

Wednesday 1 April 1801 Edinburgh

We returned into Great Britain after a sojourn on the Continent of nearly three years. An easterly wind, slight breezes, & considerable exertion of a real British crew belonging to the Kite Sloop of War, Captn. S. Digby, brought us safe into Leith Roads, where we moored about Midday.

---

1.   The appointment was through the influence of Lord Elcho, the husband of Agnes's first cousin, Susan Charteris, Lady Elcho.

After a few days in Scotland with friends and family—including the Elchos—they left for London. Edward and George travelled by sea, and Francis (known within the family as Frank) and Agnes by coach. They all met up in London on 12 May, and began the search for accommodation. Their financial position had worsened, exacerbated by the departure from Denmark where they were expecting to survive on Frank's salary. With this now lost to them, they threw themselves on the mercy of the family, but with little luck. The following years were a mixture of lodgings and descending upon friends or family for free accommodation. Edward and Agnes had a wide circle of good friends and the friends appear to have rallied round. It seems unlikely that friends lent money, but by providing bed and berth they proved their worth. The social whirl continued, and with their income eked out they circled around Cheltenham, Bath and Clifton together with the occasional private home of a friend in the country.

By 1802 Edward and Agnes had taken a tenancy in Clifton—an astute move on their part. They wintered in Clifton and sublet the property during the summer at a much higher rent, during which periods they descended to live free of charge with family, but more usually with friends—of which because of their outgoing nature, Edward and Agnes had plenty. In fact Frank had visited Clifton with his father at the beginning of the year and made notes in his diary:

Friday 1 January 1802

The Houses are good & the rates for letting them moderate 10s. 6d. per Room per week from Lady Day to Michaelmas, & in the other half year at half price. A small addition to this sum procures attendance, cooking, fires &c. The Boarding Houses are on the same footing, the Rates for Boarding at £1.5. per week.

The next problem for Edward and Agnes to solve was the matter of how to fund Francis at Oxford where he had a promise of acceptance at Wadham College. After much negotiation, the family plus one particular friend—John Granville—undertook to provide Frank with the means, and his studies lasted from 1802 to 1805. Apart from John Granville, the family members providing the funds were Edward's brother Broome and Agnes's brother Ferdinando Tracy Travell. As Frank studied, Edward and Agnes continued their visiting habits interspersed with lodgings; widening their watering holes to include Twickenham and Tunbridge Wells.

Back in 1801, the less talented George had been disposed of by putting him to a clerkship in the City through the good offices of Broome Philips Witts, a cousin of Edward's. George spent a miserable year working for Messrs Price and Darlot, Hamburg Agents and two more years working for Mr Solly. In 1805 he rebelled and left, determined to join the Army. This created more uproar in the wider family with the intimation that Edward and Agnes had spoiled their children and had little control over them. Later that year, through the influence of Lady Lyttelton, his aunt, George successfully entered the Royal Artillery at Woolwich and the crisis passed almost at the same time that Frank had completed his studies. As usual Francis provides the family information in flashbacks:

Tuesday 5 July 1825

We drove to Dropmore, the seat of the distinguished statesman, Lord Grenville ... As a private individual, Lord Grenville merited my gratitude and support, by the friendly assistance, which, at the request of Lady Lyttelton, and as a connexion of that family, he gave to my brother, when he wished to enter into the Artillery, even when he might well have excused himself from making an application to Lord Chatham, then Master General of the Ordnance, on the score of political disagreement. That application was successful …

During 1805 and early 1806 Frank continued his attempts at obtaining a Government position and also tried to gain entry to the legal profession, but all to no avail and he fell back on the Church. In the summer of 1805 the family trio (the quartet minus George who was now in the Army) went to Buxton following a stay with their friends the Granvilles at nearby Calwich Abbey. The purpose of the visit was for Frank to take a course of waters to ease his rheumatism. Here they met the Backhouses, mother and daughter. In the following months letters went backwards and forwards between Agnes and Mrs Backhouse. In December 1805 Frank went north to Yorkshire to meet the young lady again, a stay of one month, covering the Christmas and New Year period. From this point on detailed negotiations took place and in 1808, a family friend, Revd William Burslem united Francis and Margaret in Bath.

Previous to the marriage Frank had entered the curacy of Urchfont in Wiltshire. Edward and Agnes lived with him for several months in a cottage at Urchfont. Following Frank's marriage to Margaret, Edward and Agnes moved to Cheltenham and set up home there.

On 27 September 1808, Agnes's brother, Ferdinando Tracy Travell, rector of Upper Slaughter, died at Cheltenham where he had been staying with another sister. Agnes had been prepared for this moment, for back in the summer of 1805 she and Edward had made contact with a Mrs Timbrell, who, with her sisters, owned the advowson of the living of Upper Slaughter and by careful nurturing and negotiation paved the way for Frank to succeed his uncle to the rectory of the parish. Following his entry to the living of Upper Slaughter Frank then spent the best part of six months in Yorkshire with Margaret at her home, Beck House, while his new living was placed in the hands of a temporary curate, an old college friend, William Dowell. In the summer of 1809 Frank and Margaret finally settled into the rectory at Upper Slaughter, to be home for the remainder of their lives.

Edward and Agnes continued their nomadic life, but it concentrated on the four points of their home in Cheltenham; Upper Slaughter with their beloved Frank; Stanway House—(the country home of Agnes's cousin Lady Hereford) and Calwich Abbey, the home of their good friends the Granvilles. In 1811 Edward and Agnes had a particularly good year, for having sub-let their house in Cheltenham to save money, they spent the whole year as guests at one or other of these refuges interspersed with an occasional few days elsewhere.

As for Francis and Margaret, country life went on as normal. They suffered a major disappointment on 10 May 1811 when their first born child, Jane Margaret Witts, died only twenty-one days after her birth. In January the following year Francis made his debut appearance at the Quarter Sessions as a magistrate for the county, a position he was to hold for the remainder of his life.

In the following years Frank and Margaret made frequent visits to Yorkshire. In 1812, during one of these trips Frank went back to Buxton to try the waters once more for his complaint. The following March the couple had the joy of a son—Edward Francis—their only surviving child.

For some reason Francis either did not keep a diary between 1808 and 1820, or they have been lost. It seems that the former is more likely. There are a few travel diaries for trips made in 1812 and 1818, but beyond that all we know of the day-to-day activities of the young family are snippets from the diary of Agnes.

In late 1816 Edward declined and after a short illness he died on Christmas Day 1816. Agnes records the event:

Wednesday 25 December 1816

Wonderful fine weather for Xmas day, but all gloom in our truly distresst family, as all possible hope of the life of my beloved Husband was fled I was alone supported under such a trial by witnessing his pious resignation to the approach of Death his senses perfect, & his power of joining in the sacred Duty of receiving the Sacrament from the hand of his Son truly edifying, My Sister, Anne Margaret & myself forming the congregation round the sick Bed, poor Dear Soul he lay perfectly at ease throughout the rest of the day, giving to all around him a noble Pattern of the last hours of a true Christian.

Edward's death resulted in one of Agnes's infrequent gaps in her diary which she did not recommence until 1 February 1817. That same year Agnes's cousin, Lady Hereford, died leaving Stanway to her nephew Francis Charteris, now styled Lord Elcho. Agnes occasionally took up residence again at Stanway, staying with her other cousin, Susan, Lady Elcho, the young Lord Elchos' mother. Apart from this, and Calwich visits mixed with the whirl of Cheltenham social life, little appears to have happened. In the summer of 1818 Frank and Margaret had an extended stay in the north including a trip to the Lakes.

In January 1820 Francis Witts appears to have made a New Year Resolution to recommence his diaries, for on 3 January he starts a new record and with occasional gaps continues it until the end of his life. The new record starts with concerns for the health of Margaret and they go to Bath seeking some form of cure. In fact, Margaret continued in a more or less poor state of health for the remainder of her life.

The diary in 1820 is different, stylistically, from earlier journals and is much given over to reporting what was in the newspapers and current affairs and then peters out with an account of a holiday with Margaret. After this there is a gap of two years, and then in September 1822 he commences once more, but this time there is a totally different style. The news reporting continues, but now there is more comment, and more to do with magisterial duty and the events of the locality. With a few changes here and there, this is the style that he follows for the next thirty years with the exception that in later diaries, the news reporting falls away and the entries increase in length.

In 1823, at the age of forty, Francis learned of the death of his brother George. He had been mainly posted abroad, his later years being in Malta. He became very ill and was sent back to England but died on board during the voyage on a Falmouth packet. Francis recorded the event:

Wednesday 13 August 1823

The suspence, in which we have been plunged for so long a time respecting my unhappy brother, is now closed in a most painful manner by the receipt of letters from Falmouth, giving intelligence of his decease on the 8th. inst. GOD rest his soul!.... It seems, that he died on the morning of the 8th. about 8 o clock, of extreme debility, but he expired without pain, & appeared sensible of the sympathy and attention, which he experienced from all on board, & particularly from the Surgeon of the Packet. From the expressions in the letters I conclude, that his mental alienation subsisted to the last, but that he was more tranquil & composed, before he left the Island, and indeed, at all times was perfectly manageable. What a wreck was there of fine talents, an ardent mind, diversified acquirements, and manly disposition!…

One-and-a-half years later he loses his beloved mother and in a rare moment of reflection he comments on being alone:

Sunday 9 January 1825

Thus am I at length bereft of Father, Mother & Brother! GOD's will be done! GOD be thanked for the blessings still left to me, an excellent wife & promising child. Great reason have I to speak well of my departed Parent. She was a most affectionate wife & mother, a well principled Christian, warm in her friendship, strong in point of judgment, well informed, had an extensive knowledge of life, and in her best days, even to a late period, shone in society & conversation.

Agnes Witts had been an amazing mother and Francis felt his loss deeply. From now on, until his own death almost thirty years later he steadfastly built the fortune of the family and consolidated his position. Until the end of his life he remained in the same rectory, remained the pastor of the parish, a magistrate and a pillar of society.

In 1850 Margaret died after a long illness, and Francis lived alone. Francis loved his son, daughter-in-law and grandchildren much and longed for their presence which he received far less frequently than he would have wished for. In later life he picked up long-lost family contacts and busied himself as much as he could—including an extended trip to London to travel numerous times to the Great Exhibition, but he knew his days were numbered and he was aware of a heart condition. He eventually took a curate to ease his workload and to provide a little company. He wrote his entry for 17 August 1854 in full as usual, ending with the words: *Received from C. J. Geldard a present of two brace of Moor game.* He never lived to eat them. The following day, at lunchtime, in the presence of his young curate he had a heart attack and died.

Diary tradition in the family was begun by Agnes and her diaries amount to almost 900,000 words covering the period April 1788 to Christmas Day 1824. She died at her home in Cheltenham just two weeks later—Sunday 9 January 1825. During the 37 years of diary keeping there are few gaps, and these are of short duration usually marked by periods of illness such as the gap of 8 to 15 April 1797 when she miscarried.

The diary tradition was carried on by her son Francis—much the favoured son. His juvenile jottings commence in 1795 with a *Journal of a Tour in Scotland*. Written up in 1796 when he was a mere 13 years old, this is the result of notes he took in August 1795 when the family visited friends and acquaintances outside of Edinburgh. This was clearly under the encouragement of his mother Agnes. However, his diary keeping continued, and although gaps in his diary are significant, he eventually left a record of the years 1798 to 1854 amounting to a more than 2.3 million words. These diaries have been published in 10 volumes under the title *The Complete Diary of a Cotswold Parson*.

Part 2: Agnes Witts and the Edinburgh Years 1793–1798

Agnes Witts is an interesting person. Her family was of the gentry, but rather than the landed gentry it was of the mercantile gentry—a breed which polite society found interesting but perhaps a little *bourgeois*. Although this was not a term in use in later eighteenth-century Great Britain, it was, nevertheless, the case that land was seen as the proper source of wealth with commerce coming a long way below in the prejudiced perceptions of the first families. Perhaps to make up for this perceived shortcoming the family was not shy to parade the Tracy connection—Lady Elcho and Lady Hereford, first cousins to Agnes—and the Lady Lyttelton connection—the elder sister of Edward. It is clear from Agnes's diaries that she and Edward mixed in the best of society in Oxfordshire and Gloucestershire or when further abroad in London, Margate, Bath or any of the other fashionable gathering places. Typical of the high connections was Elizabeth Bentinck, née Cumberland, the daughter of Richard Cumberland the playwright. For some reason which is obscure, Edward and Agnes were close to Cumberland and effectively 'fostered' and brought up Elizabeth (±1761-1837), who married, 1782, Lord Edward Bentinck (1744-1819), second son of the Duke of Portland and brother of William Henry Cavendish Bentinck who was Prime Minister twice; first April to December 1783; secondly 1807-1809. Agnes and Elizabeth were very close and during the Edinburgh years more than 70 letters go back and forth, but then in July 1798 the letters suddenly stop, and no more is ever heard of Lady Elizabeth; what led to the cessation of correspondence remains a mystery. Clearly a serious breach occurred between the two.

Without doubt Agnes was extrovert and popular. As her son Francis said at her death 'she shone in society'. With great zest for life she required constant amusement which she found in stimulating conversation and cards. To be left alone at home was referred to as 'a great jail evening'. Edward and Agnes were popular with a wide circle of friends and their social life was always busy, and this proved to be especially the case during her Edinburgh years.

In terms of her religion she was devout, and a regular and committed Anglican. Even so she was not bigoted and had numerous Catholic friends not least of whom was Principal Gordon, of the Scots College in Paris, who had—by circumstance of the French Revolution—found himself exiled back to his native Scotland. Among other Catholics Agnes was to meet was Vincenzo Labini, an archbishop who served as Bishop of Malta from 1780 to 1807 who was in the company of Nathan Erskine, a Scottish Catholic who made little secret of his Jacobite preferences. In fact it seems that Agnes found it intriguing to learn more about the feeling and sensibilities of those in her temporarily adopted home. Agnes was well-educated, well-read and well-informed; her conversations not have lacked stimulation or interest.

To provide a background to the Edinburgh years we have to travel back in time to August 1789. Agnes had received a series of letter from Edward who was on business in London. Each letter added to the gloom as the shock finally hit home. The consequence was that the serious problems with Edward's business resulted in them having to sell their beloved Swerford Park. Their son Frank makes an interesting diary note in 1805. At the time he was studying at Wadham College, but went for a stay of a few days with his uncle and cousins who also had property at Swerford:

Saturday 23 March 1805

A fine clear day, hard frost in the morning after a cold meat & ale breakfast, took my knapsack & steered my Course towards my Uncle's at Swerford at ½ past six o clock reached his house before one: about 19 miles.... Walked with Mrs. Travell & Martha Buxton to my Father's very pretty old place of his own creation Swerford Park, the most romantic Dell, I have seen in Oxfordshire; now occupied by a Mr. & Mrs. Chinner, people unworthy of so nice a place. Our dinner party besides my Uncle & Aunt consisted of Mrs. Whalley & Martha & Jane Buxton. Read Hayley's 3rd Volume of Cowper aloud to the Ladies & played two Rubbers at Family Whist.

The uncle was Ferdinando—a widower—one of Frank's benefactors for his college fees and expenses. His uncle, as well as having the living at Upper Slaughter in nearby Gloucestershire also retained a family home in Oxfordshire. The aunt would have been one of his maiden aunts from Cheltenham. Frank had been only six years old in 1789 when Agnes and Edward were forced to move, and their re-location took them to Rodborough in Gloucestershire where Agnes had friends—Sir George Onesiphorus Paul and his sisters the Miss Snows—and Edward had business connections in the area. They took a tenancy on a spacious mansion, Bownham House, and proceeded to build a new coterie which included Stroud valley mill-owners and gentry. They also maintained other friendships and had the benefit of being near their family in Cheltenham.

Agnes with her vibrant personality became a virtual queen of the Stroud valleys and she and Edward were viewed as being somewhat more than gentry. Her young family were of great importance to her, closely followed by her social life. It appears that she did not see the storm clouds building or perhaps Edward shielded her from the worst, for although she knew that the business was undergoing problems, she had no idea of the severity.

As part of the social whirl, Bath was a much favoured centre. On 25 February 1793 Agnes went with her brother Ferdinando to Bath while Edward went to London on business. Edward joined his wife in Bath on 7 March:

Thursday 7 March 1793

Very much the same kind of weather only rather better from the sun now & then making its appearance for a short time, my Dear Husband arrived after breakfast in the Mail Coach from Town much fatigued & harrass'd, & the joy of our meeting greatly damp'd by cruel perplexities, persuaded him to go to Bed for two or three hours to make up for sitting up all night, & enable him to go with me to Dine at Mr. Wiltshires at Bath ford whither we went with Miss Wiltshires & Miss Western in a Coach meeting both my Brothers, Mrs. Buxton & Mrs. Naper & Mr. J: Wiltshire, not very brilliant, by being detaind at Cards, did not get back to Bath till ½ past nine, when Mr. Witts & I went to the Ball at the lower rooms to join Mrs. Chollet by appointment as well as Balls usually are at those rooms but I was truly low & uncomfortable. rec'd a Letter from Miss Anne Snow.

Agnes was so taken up by her social life she paid little heed to Edward. At last, the following morning, he was forced to break the news:

Friday 8 March 1793

A very severe cold day for the time of year being violent high N: east wind, & tho the sun was constantly shining it was very difficult to keep ones self warm while moving ever so fast; the Day past very manfully by the recapitulation of many dismal events from Mr. Witts's detail of his London bussinesses which terminated far worse than I expected & gave me little powers of supporting myself, walk'd miserably about with him in the Morning, & was very ill all the evening with Hysterics.

Family conferences followed and the decision was taken to move to Edinburgh. Advice had already been received from Lord and Lady Elcho, for Susan Charteris, Lady Elcho was Agnes's first cousin. The tenancy at Rodborough was given up and immediately plans were made for the exodus. The question remained, would any of Agnes's personal attendants travel with her?

Thursday 4 April 1793

Still a frost but very mild air & constant sun which made the snow nearly depart I was much too busy to think of stirring out pack'd up two very large Boxes. my mind much agitated by Molly Braxtons Parents writting a Letter of refusal to her going with me into the North, greatly relieved by Catherine Newmans not objecting to attend one, most thoroughly overcome with fatigue little able to do anything at night.

From 10 April 1793 the family spent time at Upper and Lower Slaughter—a mixture of being with her brother at Upper Slaughter and other family who had property at adjoining Lower Slaughter. Agnes penned a rather sad entry a few days later:

Friday 19 April 1793

Very sad weather till noon, being violent & frequent storms of hail & snow, & most bitterly cold, which we felt at Church attending the service & duty of the day being a public Fast appointed, a very excellent well adapted sermon from Mr. Nicholls the Curate, Mrs. Naper & I went in the chaise to Upper Slaughter, rather a doleful visit being the last time I was to see my Bror. Ferdinand perhaps for ever, a day of much bussiness & conversation being the last of our stay at Lower Slaughter.

After finally vacating Bownham House the family headed to Calwich Abbey, Derbyshire, the home of their good friends the Granvilles. From here in a letter of Friday 14 June 1793 to her sister-in-law, Apphia, Lady Lyttelton, Agnes pours out her heart:

... Mr. Witts had left me here with our good & kind friends, while he went into Oxfordshire, in the vain hope of concluding his unfortunate affairs in some measure to his satisfaction, but the very harsh & cruel treatment we continue to meet with leaves us little hope of a speedy, or happy conclusion, & has so much depress'd my spirits that I have had no power to attend to any thing ... all our property which we had packe'd up before we left Bownham House, under the eye & permission of an official Man, empowerd by the Comissioners to superintend our removal & sent them up to London in readiness to be put on board a vessel for Scotland have been for the last week unpacke'd & ransacke'd by one of the Assigne's by orders from the commissioners under the false idea we had removed more than we were allow'd, how it will all end I know not, but I have little doubt we shall unfairly be the sufferers ... the various difficulties I have to struggle with one who has not suffer'd in a similar manner can form any idea, to which the very small assistance have met with except from my own Brothers & Sisters & Neices & the very hospitable friends are now & have been so long with, has not a little contributed) to encrease, till cruel experience has taught me the contrary, I thought that to be unfortunate was a certain claim to compassion from those who term themselves friends but we have found it otherwise, our sole trust is in the Almighty who I doubt not will give us equal power to our inclination, "to strive for, & protect our beloved Boys …

The tragedy in this letter was not reflected in the matter-of-fact way in which Agnes recorded events of that day in her diary:

Friday June 14th. An intire bright fine Day, with rather a cold wind but I had small enjoyment of anything our boy from being extremely low & unwell, the morning much broke by archery & a visit from Mr. Wright & Miss Frances Berresford, and some packing of mine, all but Miss Cardin and the 4 children went to dine at Mrs. Milles at Snelson, a sociable friendly visit, a table at whist & casino not at home till near eleven o'clock. Wrote to Lady Lyttelton.

The reference in the extract to 'our boy' is interesting. Agnes had suffered several miscarriages before giving birth to Francis Edward in 1783. After this successful birth she safely bore two more sons: George in 1785 and Edward in 1786. Notwithstanding the fact that the children numbered three, Agnes often behaved as if there was only one—her beloved Francis.

From the letter of 14 June it is possible to witness the emotion she *withholds* from her diary entries. In general, her passion and her emotions were poured into her letters with her diary entries being very 'matter of fact'. It is therefore most unfortunate that so few of her letters survive.

On Monday 17 June the family left their friends the Granvilles and take a short holiday in the Lakes, eventually reaching Scotland on Sunday 14 July. Two days later they were nearing Edinburgh, but Agnes was low in spirits, and the early experiences of Scotland were not encouraging:

the first stage was 15 miles to Bild a miserable lone ale House where we could get a tolerable pair of Post Horses, & just enough bad food to call it a wretched bad Dinner, as bad or worse accomodations than ever I met with even in Wales … we only went a stage of 19 miles to a very poor Inn call'd Noble House before we arrived there the country rather mended upon being not quite so hilly & rather better planted & cultivated, & roads smoother. Here our accomodations were very moderate & our attendants worse, without shoes or stockings, short Petticoats & Jackets, & dirt & filth of every kind very intolerable to my feelings however we got a good nights sleep all 5 in one room, for security.

The following day, Wednesday 17 July they finally arrived in Edinburgh and put up at Walkers' Hotel as a temporary billet while they searched for accommodation. They soon settle on an apartment in No. 2 George Square, quite close to 25 George Square where 22-year-old Walter Scott lived with his parents.

Edward and Agnes Witts were ably assisted in their first few days in Edinburgh by James Stormonth, a solicitor who was agent to Lord Elcho, and Lord Elcho had already asked

Stormonth to assist his family connections. By 25 July the family were already settling and Dr Adams called at George Square:

> … in the evening Dr. Adams,16 Rector or Head Master of the High School was here for an hour or two, to talk over the subject of the Boys going to the School, much pleased by his manner & behavior & highly gratified by his approbation of our Dear Francis's School knowledge after his undergoing an accurate examination.

Agnes and Edward sought somewhere better and some six weeks later they identified a house in the fashionable area of Hanover Street, just off Princes Street.

> *Friday 6 September 1793*
> … at noon made myself a little fit to be seen & walk'd up to North Hanover Street to look at a Flat up two pair of stairs w.ch Mr. Witts had seen & was much pleased with & so indeed was I. We still wished we might be able to continue to purchase it Mr. Witts went there again in the afternoon taking Mr. Stormonth with him on a consultation.

By 1 October the purchase price had been settled but apparently the purchase was not fully completed and the family could not yet move in, and it may have been that they committed to a lease in George Square for they were still there in February when tragedy occurred. Young Edward became ill early in February 1794 with much coughing. By the 14th Agnes realised the severity of his condition.

> *14 February 1794*
> My Edward being still worse & the result of another Medical consultation was its being pronounced he had a Dropsy on his Chest w.ch by its very rapid advances allow'd of no hope, & probably our loss & regret would but too soon be compleated, & Dear little Creature he was so bad in the evening we thought every hour would be his last, of course past a most wretched night.

Two days later it was all over:

> *14 February 1794*
> Dry but cold without sun & rather gloomy too well corresponding with our miserable situation which alas this day ended in the most fateful manner. my sweet little Edward breathing his last a quarter before 9 in the Morning, he had been dying in a manner the whole of the night, his poor Papa up with him many times in the night as excepting at short intervals he was sensible to the last & wish'd to have us all about him of which I was little capable but took a last leave of him not a quarter of an hour before I lost him for ever, our distress & confusion beyond conception....

> *19 February 1794*
> Dry but lowering in the Morn: & at mid.day a severe shower which made it damp the remainder of the day & was very cold. My feelings tried to the utmost, by preparing to leave the House for the day with my poor remaining Boys, to avoid the wretched spectacle of seeing my little Angel carried to the Grave whither his affectionate Father would follow him in compliance to the trying custom of this Country, which ever make a great parade of funerals …

By May, spring had arrived and with it Agnes's spirits began to recover and she made more friends. Also, the long delayed completion of the purchase was coming to a conclusion.

Friday 16 May 1794
… in the afternoon Mr. Witts went to a Coffee House to meet the different Agents & People concernd relative to compleating the absolute purchase of the house in Hanover Street a great & useful event …

By 27 May the family at last moved into their new home and life could settle down. From here on the social circle widened as new friends were made, visiting cards were exchanged and the social etiquette is carefully followed. It was not long before invitations were extended, and such was Agnes's popularity that this included summer visits to friends' homes in the country, for in the summer of 1795 the family quartet made a peripatetic tour from 21 August to 28 September.

By 1796 the world was a whirl for Agnes. Her circle had widened further, the boys were becoming friends with French emigrés, most notably the sons of the Comte d'Artois' mistress and together with theatre going, novels, dancing lessons for the boys and unceasing visiting and receiving visitors Agnes's life was extremely busy. The late summer of 1796 was also busy with visits to the Army camp of the volunteers followed by another peripatetic itinerary, and yet something was not right. During the course of the year Edward had finally been declared bankrupt. A notice appeared in newspapers in April:

THE Commissioners in a Commission of Bankrupt, awarded and issued forth against EDWARD WITTS, of Bownham-House, in the Parish of RODBOROUGH, in the County of Gloucester, Woolstapler, Dealer and Chapman, intend to meet on the 24th Day of May instant, at Eleven o'Clock in the Forenoon, at the White-Lion, at Banbury, in the County of Oxford, in Order to make a Dividend of the Estate and Effects of the said Bankrupt, when and where the Creditors who have not already proved their Debts, are to come prepared to prove the same, or they will be excluded the Benefit of the said Dividend; and all Claims not then proved will be disallowed.

Agnes remains silent in her diary, her social and family life dominates everything, and yet there must have been undercurrents which may be in now lost letters. Happily a few letters from Edward to Lady Lyttelton survive in the *Witts Family Papers* and a letter from Edward to his sister, as early as 26 April 1795 shows that there already plans for the continent very early on (see Appendix 2).

From the diary one single fact us revealed, that by January 1797 Agnes is seeking information about Germany:

Monday 16 January 1797
… rec'd an early visit from Count Purgstall to gather German instructions afterwards went on bussiness into the old Town …

In April 1797 there was a shock as the fifty-year-old Agnes had a miscarriage, stopping her social activities in their tracks while she slowly recuperated. A little later Edward makes clear that the cost of living was getting beyond his means. On 10 July 1797 he wrote a long letter to his sister which contains the following interesting information:

Lord Elchos wish was to prevent us sinking our own Income for the £200: which after all, is not sunk, but that it is absolutely necessary to prepare that Sum beforhand when we go to the Continent, in case of any Contingencies—and in settling all our affairs here next May, I hope & trust I shall accomplish my wishes—in the mean time my Dear Sister you may do me a very sincere kind office if you would apply to my Brother Richard seriously to return the £50 & the Int. due to my Sons for to assist us in the plan we have formed which he has no right either in honesty or Justice to detain from them any longer as it is consists entirely of the accumulated Guineas & half Guineas collected from their Relations—& can never be so well disposed of as in the finishing of their Education—I am very glad to gather from your Letter that no individual distress—more than the Times have occasioned the pressures you complain of.—certainly in our small Scale, we feel them less—as we have no Luxuries that come under the great Taxes—& thank God in the plan proposed for the next 4 years we shall be wholly exempt from all Taxes: The price of Butchers meat is now our greatest grievance.

By November 1797 with the German plan temporarily disrupted by the unfortunate death of Sir James Riddell, Edward wrote to his sister Lady Lyttelton on the 17th and more of the family plans become clearer, with their initial proposed destination in Germany being Leipzig:

The University Classes are just begun & Francis fully employd in Mathematicks—& French, Greek & German Languages—besides being an Assistant in the French to his Mother who take three Lesson a week from a Master, & in our own intercourse at home, she comes on much beyond our Expectation—but steadyness & perseverence will generally overcome large as well as small difficulties. That George may have time—to finish his Latin Classic's well & acquire french, he does not begin Greek till he goes to Leipsic—where he will plunge at once into Greek & German ...

By May Edward and Agnes burned their boats by selling the Hanover Street house and their furniture and many belongings. It is not clear what came of the proceeds, and indeed it may have been that the house was on a large mortgage, unfortunately paucity of records mean we are unlikely ever to know. What is known is that by 1800 Lord Elcho's agent James Stormonth was living in the house and he remained therefore numerous years. Perhaps he owned it all along as a beneficiary on behalf of Edward and Agnes Witts. Agnes provides the details of the exodus:

Tuesday 8 May 1798
Still bright fine weather but so very much hurried in quitting our poor favorite Mansion that I could little enjoy that or anything else, accomplished all tolerably. & got into our Lodgings in South St Andrews Street to a late Tea finding them pleasant & comfortable...

Wednesday 9 May 1798
A cloudy but dry Morning, & very bright afternoon, went early back to Hanover Street to arrange things for the Sale, on return busy in setting Lodgings in order went late to Cards & Supper at Lady Sinclairs, a large party, many Gentlemen but sadly late.

And so the five years' residence in Edinburgh came to an end and the majority of friends faded away. The remaining 'quartetto' of the family as Agnes referred to them left Leith safely on Sunday 5 August 1798 on their onward voyage to Germany. After more than two years in Germany followed by six month in Denmark, they arrive back at Leith on Wednesday 1 April 1801, evacuated from war-troubled Denmark, on board the Royal Navy sloop of war HMS *Kite*, and quickly caught up with friends in Edinburgh, plus family in Lord and Lady Elcho. This enforced return to Edinburgh ended on 3 May for Edward and George who sailed on a Berwick smack for London, and 8 May when Agnes and her eldest son Francis finally said 'good bye' to her cousin Susan, Lady Elcho at Branston, their home near Haddington, and also headed for London. Agnes was never to return to Scotland, although she did maintain contacts by letter for many years, most notably with Mrs Eleanor Brougham whom she also met later, receiving her with great joy on a visit to England, 10 June 1809.

The last diary entry made by Agnes Witts was Christmas Day 1824—eight years to the day from the death of her believe husband Edward. She died at her home in Cheltenham just two weeks later—Sunday 9 January 1825.

Witts Family Papers F185

1793

Sunday May 26th.

Something of a wetting fog early in the Morning but as usual, was a prediction of a hot fine Day, & the evening beautiful to a great degree, church not beginning at Ellason till two o'clock, we 4 Ladies went to visit Mrs. Bingham at Norbury, & return'd to Church where the service was very moderately perform'd by a Mr. Shipley, came home but little before Dinner & took a most pleasant walk in the evening.

Monday May 27th.

A remarkably clear fine Morning, & as remarkable, a thick foggy air at noon, which made it gloomy hot for the time, but it became quite cold in the evening; Mrs. & Miss Hodgson & a Miss with them made a visit in the Morning, & Mr. Vennour came to Dinner to stay a week, it was too hot to walk much in the morning but we went for a little while on the water which was pleasant, drank Tea out of the Door & saw the Cows milk'd, & afterwards all took a most wonderful long walk more than three miles, which tired all the party & me compleatly. wrote to Mrs. Catherine Thornton.

Tuesday May 28th.

Cold & stormy, & tho sometimes the sun shone bright, yet there was a strong appearance of rain, imediately after breakfast the whole party excepting myself & Louisa Port, went to Ilam, some on business others on pleasure, & returnd to a late Dinner she & I read, work'd, conversed, & walk'd for an hour we were all well contented without an evening walk & a long bout at Quadrille. rec'd a Letter from Mrs. Buxton

Wensday May 29th.

Quite a winter instead of a summer day dark black clouds & strong wind, but no rain came till quite evening, but it was so bitterly cold we had fires like winter, Mrs. Granville & the gentlemen rode to call on Mrs. Unwin, the Ladies & I walk'd, Mr. & Mrs. Wheeler & Miss Berresford Dined & supt here, much lively converse some good music, & Cassino. liked Mrs. Wheeler much.

Thursday May 30th.

Wonderful to tell, some Snow had fallen in the night, & was visible on Weaver even at mid. day, a fine bright day, tho with a strong cold wind Mrs. Port & her two eldest Daughters went away after breakfast, the Gentlemen rode, & Mrs. G. & I had a fine chatty Morning, with only the interruption of a visit from the two Mrs. Binghams not pleasant enough to walk in the evening, inlisted Mr. Venner into the Cassino party. wrote to Mrs. Tyrwhitt. —

Friday May 31st.

Rather a gloomy cold day, but dry & very suitable to exercise, which induced even us Ladies to walk both Morning, noon, & Night, the two former walks principaly to Turney the quick movements of the Gravel Carts drawing it out of the River Dove for the purposes of covering the new road, after our evening walk a smart game at Cassino at which we were successful. wrote to Mrs. Buxton.

Saturday June ye. 1st.

Lowering cold & stormy, but little or no rain fell, Mr. Witts set off early in the Morning on horseback to meet the Coach at Uttoxeter, in which he purposed to fight his way into Oxfordshire, whether he was going on so much painful & anxious bussiness that doubled my regret at parting with him, we walk'd as usual to the Gravel Pitts at noon, Miss Mills call'd in the Morning & Mr. Vennour, went away in the evening when we took our walk, after which, Mrs. Granville & I play'd at Picquet. wrote to Mr. Burslem[1] & rec'd a very kind Letter from my Sister Travell.

Above, left and right: John Dewes Granville (1744–1826) and Harriet Joan Granville, née Delabere (1754–1825). This couple were probably the closest friends of Edward and Agnes Witts. Harriet's sister, Anne, married John Granville's brother, Bernard Dewes. John and Harriet lived at Calwich Abbey in Staffordshire, and the Witts's were frequent visitors there. They also arranged to meet in fashionable watering places, generally Cheltenham and Bath. John Granville was one of the patrons of Agnes and Edward's eldest son Francis, to meet the cost of him attending Wadham College, Oxford during the years 1802 to 1805.

---

1.   William Burslem (1746–1820). William Burslem was born at Market Drayton and educated at St John's College, Cambridge. In 1793 he was rector of Hanbury, Worcestershire. He was an old friend of Edward and Agnes.

Sunday June y^{e.} *2*^{d.}

Dark, stormy, & Lowering in the Morning, & in the course of the Day frequent showers tho such small misty rain it was of little service to the fruits of the earth which much required it, Mr. G. on horseback & Mrs. G. & I in the chaise went soon after breakfast, to call on Mrs. Mills &'c at Snelson & return'd to Church at Ellaston at 2 o'clock where Mr. Shipley again did the Duty, & came here to Dinner, soon after which Mrs. G. & I set forth again to Ashborn to Drink Tea at Mrs. Berresfords, the younger part of the family visiting out in the Town but soon join'd us; we did not return home till 9 o'clock. very low all Day.

Monday June 3^{d.}

Warm & cloudy in the Morning but little or no rain fell tho it look'd very threatening, at mid day it clear'd up & was very bright the remainder of the Day, which shew'd off to great advantage, Mr. Binghams place at Norbury, where we dined, meeting M^{r.} & Mrs. Gisborne of Wooten Hall pleasant young people, a nice entertainment, & pretty chearful visit, a long pool at Commerce which prevented our return home till quite supper time. a sweet evening.

Tuesday June 4th.

Very hot & gloomy & somewhat like Thunder but none came, & it grew bright towards even^{g.} much too close & hot for walking in the Morning tho we were drawn as far as Norbury ware to Survey the new Gravel Pit; & walk'd again in the evening at the top of the West field, & home over the new road, where we were much surprized to be overtaken by Mr. B. Dewes's[2] his Daughter & Miss Cardin in their Chaise who were come unexpectedly to stay. play'd 2 rubbers at Cassino. wrote to Mrs. Savage & rec'd a Letter from Lady Lyttelton.

Wensday June 5th.

Dark & Lowering in the Morning, small rain or rather mist at Noon, but very fine & pleasant in the afternoon, the Gentlemen the greater part of the Day out fishing, we Ladies walk'd in the evening much the same way as the former evening. rec'd a Letter from Mr. Witts.

Thursday June 6th.

Wet, windy & showery the chief of the day & got much colder, no going out, my Dear Husband return'd at Noon having walk'd from Uttoxeter where the coach had dropp'd him in the preceeding Night, most happy to see him return but much agitated by hearing the painful result of his Journey;[3] Mrs. Mills Mrs. Furnavel & Miss Mills dined here, a party at Whist & Cassino. rec'd a Letter from Mrs. Tyrwhitt.

---

2.   Bernard D'Ewes (±1742–1822). Bernard D'Ewes (usually spelt Dewes) was descended from the Granville family and his great-grandfather, Sir Bevill Granville, was killed at the battle of Lansdowne, Bath, in 1643. His uncle, Bernard Granville of Calwich, was a close friend of George Friedrich Handel who spent much time at Calwich Abbey. Dewes' aunt was Mary Delany, an interesting woman and close friend of George III and Queen Charlotte. Bernard Dewes does not feature much in the diaries. His uncle Bernard Granville, who died in 1775, passed him over in regard to the inheritance of the Calwich estate in favour of the younger brother John; one of the conditions being that John should change his name to Granville.

3.   The business was in respect of his pending bankruptcy. He was trying to sort out his affairs to try to forestall and avoid the bankruptcy, but it was not to be.

Friday June 7th.

Remarkably fine & pleasant in the Morning, but wet in the afternoon, M^{r.} & Mrs. Gisborne here in the Morning, the Gentlemen fishers had an early cold Dinner, to pursue their sport with more vigor & did not return till near dark, Mr. Witts row'd us Ladies for a little while in the Morning Cassino as usual. wrote to my Sister Travell.

Saturday June 8th.

Dry tho very cloudy in the Morning but very hard rain, in showers at Noon, fine again in the afternoon, the Gentlemen again had an early Dinner to pursue their fishing with greater vigor Mrs. Granville & I went in the Morning to Ashborn more 2 or 3 visits. all but myself walk'd before Tea. rec'd a pleasing long Letter from Mrs. Naper.[4]

Sunday June 9th.

Rain in showers the greater part of the day, & very cold & uncomfortable, as glad of fires as in Winter, went to Ellaston Church in the Morning where Mr. Pickford did the Duty, a long day on the whole survey'd drawings &'c, wrote to Mrs. Guydickens & rec'd a Letter from Mrs. J. Pettat.

Monday June 10th.

Quite a beautiful & very pleasant Day from Morn: to night we walk'd a good deal in the Morning, dined very late to accomodate the fishers, Mr. Venour call'd here in the Morning as did Miss Mills who also dined here, & so did Mr. Hodgson who had been of the fishing party all Day wrote a very long Letter to Mrs. Naper. Georges Birthday

Tuesday June 11th.

After having been a frost in the night was a delightful clear Morning, but there was a very severe hard shower at Noon which made a damp evening. as soon as we had breakfasted Mrs. Granville & I went in the Chaise to give me pleasure of walking over Ilam, which appeard in peculiar high beauty, we return'd home thro Ashborn for the purpose of bringing back Miss Berresford to Calwich to stay, & while she was preparing we went to survey Sr. Brooke Boothbys Plants & Hothouses[6] & were much amused caught there by the rain, return'd home only to Dinner much Cassino in the evening as well as Music but I was miserably low & wretched from awkward Letters rec'd I could enjoy nothing & had a shocking Night.

---

4. Jane Naper (1765–1797). Jane was Agnes's niece, the daughter of Ferdinando Tracy Travell (1740–1809) and Martha, née Rollinson (1741–1780). Jane married, first, William Naper (1749–1791), and they had two children: James Lennox William Naper (1791–1868) and Jane (1792–1853) who married, 1815, George Cornewall, 3rd Baronet of Moccas Court, Herefordshire.

5. This was Martha the wife of John Pettat of Stonehouse, Gloucestershire. She was the eldest daughter of Howe Hicks, 6th Baronet. The family had been friends of Edward and Agnes Witts during the Witts family's residence at Bownham House, Rodborough, Gloucestershire (1790–1793).

6. Brooke Boothby, 6th Baronet (1744–1824). Brooke Boothby was a linguist, translator, poet and landowner, based in Derbyshire. He was part of the intellectual and literary circle of Lichfield, which included Anna Seward and Erasmus Darwin. In 1766 he welcomed Jean-Jacques Rousseau to Ashbourne circles. Ten years later, in 1776, Boothby visited Rousseau in Paris, and was given the manuscript of the first part of Rousseau's three-part autobiographic *Confessions*. Boothby translated the manuscript and published it in 1780. In 1784 he leased Ashbourne Hall from his father and began the restoration using his wife's dowry to renovate the structure, remodel the parkland, purchase rare plants and obtain works of art.

Wensday June 12th.

Dark & gloomy, tho mild & fine excepting a shower at Noon which, did not hinder us from walking out a great while near home surveying the Gentlemen fishers, dined at a very late hour, M^{r.} & Mrs. Gisborne came to Dinner & staid supper, a long & tedious pool at commerce.

Thursday June 13th.

Still quiet tho rather gloomy weather no rain, & much finer in the Afternoon than Morning, the Gentlemen spent the whole of the day at Mr. Hodgsons at Crakemarsh on a fishing party & did not return till a late hour we Ladies strove to amuse ourselves by various means in their absence, walk'd before Dinner to Ellaston to fetch Mr. Manswarings children,[7] walk'd again in the evening, & play'd at Cassino. rec'd a Letter from Miss Louisa Lee, & wrote to Lady Edwd. Bentinck & my Sister Travell.

Friday June 14th.

An intire bright fine Day, with rather a cold wind but I had small enjoyment of anything or body from being extremely low & unwell, the Morning much broke by Archery, & a visit from Mr. Wright & Miss Frances Berresford, & some packing of mine, all but Miss Cardin & the 4 Children went to dine at Mrs. Mills's at Snelson, a sociable friendly visit, a table at Whist & Cassino not at home till near eleven o'clock. wrote to Lady Lyttelton

Saturday June 15th.

A very fine pleasant Morning, but changed at Noon to be thick & stormy, with flying Mist or rain the whole afternoon, the morning fully occupied by packing & many other things tho we did not dine till a very late hour to accomodate the fishers Mr. Witts rode to Ashborn, & M^{r.} & the two Mrs. Binghams dined with us, Whist & Cassino in the evening. wrote to Miss Anne Snow.

Calwich Abbey in Staffordshire, close to Ashbourne in Derbyshire.

---

7. James Eyton Mainwaring (1750–1808). James was the fifth son of Edward Mainwaring of Whitmore Hall, Staffordshire and Sarah, née Bunbury. He was vicar of Ellaston, Staffordshire 1783–1808.

Sunday June 16th.

Quite a stormy disagreable Morning & bitterly cold, & at times hard showers of rain, & in the afternoon constant small rain & very uncomfortable alltogether, as our Spirits were all much depress'd by the idea of our parting trial the next day, most of us went to Church at Ellaston at 2 o'clock where Mr. Pickford did the Duty. Mr. Port & one of his Sons dined with us.[8] Music in the evening. rec'd a Letter from Mrs. Guydickens & Lord Edward Bentinck.

Monday June 17th.

Very stormy in the Morning but dry & as the day advanced it grew much finer & there was much sunshine as well as shade tho the wind remain'd extremely high; left Calwich, & our worthy Friends with infinite regret, & much depression of spirits between 8 & 9, all five in the chaise having dispatch'd Catherine in a Coach to Manchester, Mr. Granvilles Horses took us to Leek 14 miles, by Wooton Ramson commom &'c, most disagreable rough road for the first 8 miles till we came into the great London road, the Town of Leek stands prettily in a rich fertile & well planted vale surrounded both by barren & cultivated Hills, & is distant from Macclesfield our next stage 13 miles, of a charming rich & diversified Country rather hilly road excellent, & the cultivation of the land & the look of the country in general most neat & beautiful the river Sale[9] divides the Counties of Stafford & Chester & is about the midway of this stage. Macclesfield is a large Manufacturing Town, both in Copper, Cotton & silk but all at a lower ebb than formerly, Nothing very striking in the Town in which are two Churches & one very bad Inn the Angel where we got a moderate Dinner, & went 9 miles of a very good & pretty road to a small Inn in a village calld Bullocksmithie where we changed Horses & went 10 miles to Manchester before we reach'd Bullocksmithie, we pass'd Peyton a fine large place of Sr. George Warrens, with extensive plantations, & very large piece of bad colour'd water, Stockport thro which we pass'd is a very large disagreable Town, & the 7 miles from thence to Manchester being an intire paved road made it horridly shaking & disagreable & tired me sadly, a prodigeous large Town, of which we could see but little as we pass'd to our Inn the Star in Deansgate, which we found very moderate in all respects.

Tuesday June 18th.

A very bright shewey Morning but soon changed to dark & stormy & became quite cold, & an extreme high wind & in the evening thick misty rain quitted Manchester between 11 & 12, finding so little worthy observation that we walk'd very little about found it 11 very disagreable miles to Hilton Lane an alehouse Inn where we changed Horses, the road being in part heavy sands or rough paved road which shook one abominably, & the country very dreary, cultivation bad, & trees which in general were oak miserably blasted by sea breezes, from Hilton Lane to Chorley is 11 miles more the greater part still the same horrid pavement, & the views no better, 2 miles before we reach'd Chorley, is Dunberry Hall the Seat of Sr. Frank Standish rather a dismal old place, situated low & yet barren, we got but a poor Dinner at the

---

8. John Port (birth and death unknown) had been born John Sparrow, the son of Burslem Sparrow, an Iron Master from a Staffordshire family, but originally a Welsh family and Frances, née Newell. He took the surname of Port on succeeding to Ilam on the death of his uncle George Port, formerly Newell. John married Mary D'Ewes, daughter of John D'Ewes of Wellesbourne, Warwickshire and Anne Granville (1707–1761) of Buckland, Gloucestershire.

9. This is very unclear and Agnes Witts may be referring to the River Dane. The landscape has changed much since the building of the Macclesfield Canal, 1826–31.

Bulls Head at Chorley a miserable old Inn, & afterwards proceeded 10 miles to Preston, the last 3 or 4 of wch the Country mended, & the situation of the Town was striking on a good eminence, & appear'd large & the streets wide, we took up our quarters at the Black Bull a very good Inn, where we found Catherine had been arrived several hours by a Coach.

Wensday June ye 19th

A beautiful fine shewey Morning, & so it continued with but small intervals of clouds & cold wind the greater part of the day, when we had eat our Breakfast, we took a walk attended by a conductor to survey the beauties of the Town, which principaly lie on a good gravel walk, planted on each side & commanding a sweet view of the River Ribble much wood & many Hills & several Gentlemens Seats, the principal of which was Sr Harry Houghtons & Mr Starkies, quitting Preston at 11 we arrived at Black Pool 20 miles distant between 2 & 3, stopping only at Kirkham a small market Town halfway for Hay & water as we had the same Post Horses all the way & another chaise for Catherine & the Boys we had only just time to appoint our apartments which were comfortable enough before Dinner, which being a general ordinary was at 3 o'clock, where we found a Mr Holm & 2 Daughters & a Mrs Leigh & 2 Daughters pretty young Women, & to them came in the evening a M^r & Mrs Leycester Bro^r to Mrs Leigh, walk'd & dawdled, unpack'd & set our <u>house</u> to rights, & sup'd so early as to finish with^t candles, & went to Bed at 10 o'clock. had the joy of receiving Letters at Preston, from Lady Edward Bentinck, Mrs Naper, & my Sister Travell —

Thursday June 20th

Dry but very cold & stormy, tho sometimes warm'd by a little sunshine which was very necessary, as it was bitterly cold in this exposed situation, which is the most exposed Sea Bathing place I ever was at, being quite open to the Western Ocean, opposite to Ireland & the Isle of Man which is sometimes visible at the time of the setting Sun, & bounded on one side by the Welch Mountains & on the other by those of Westmoreland & Cumberland, & by being a shallow, & at the same time rather a rocky coast, is very seldom visited by any Vessels, which makes it a dull scene for the land views are desolate & miserable, we walk'd about a little in the Morning, visited the Library, Shop &'c, but I had too much of a cold to walk in the evening a sociable working party in the afternoon, finding my Lady companions very agreable, particularly the Leigh & Leycester party our party enlarged by the arrival of a Mr Starkie a Man of fortune near Preston, & a M^r & Mrs Taylor from Manchester awkward people wrote to Mrs Granville.

Friday June 21st

Weather worse rather than better being extremely cold & stormy & very much like rain but none fell till quite night, but in the evening there was a most tremendous storm of wind both at land & on the Sea, it ran quite Mountains high I never before saw the Ocean in so perturb'd a state such a violent noise it quite disturb'd our rest; walk'd in the Morning with Mr Witts & the Boys for an hour or two on the Sands, got compleatly wet thro' in my feet. Dined for the first time in the Great Room, & being impossible to walk out play'd two rubbers at Whist. Mr Campbell a Gentleman from one of the other Lodging houses added to our party at Dinner.

Saturday June 22^d

Still cold & stormy, but dry, & at times some sunshine, which was very acceptable, to give some degree of warmth to the air, our 5 Dear Selves took a walk in the fields to a little village call'd Layton & home by the Preston road, our party diminish'd by the departure of Mr. Starkie & M^{r.} & Mrs. Taylor, I was fearful of walking again in the evening my cold being indifferent, had a working party & for an hour in the evening. play'd at Cassino with the Boys in our own room. rec'd a Letter from Miss Anne Snow & wrote to Miss Louisa Lee.

Sunday June 23^{d.}

In the Morning a much milder air & but little wind but towards mid.day it became cold & stormy tho constant sunshine; being no church within 3 or 4 miles, we had service very well perform'd by Mr. Leycester in the great room, after which our own party walk'd to a place call'd Gym about a mile distant, where is a Lodging & boarding house for the benifit of the lower kind of people that require bathing, our party increased at Dinner by Mr. Campbell & a Friend of Mr. Holmes for one Day only, much writting & agreable conversation. fill'd up the evening wrote to Mrs. Naper & my Sister Travell.

Monday June 24th.

Severely wet & windy all the former part of the day, & tho dry in the evening was very cold & stormy part of the Morning spent by the Ladies in a general working party some in battledore & Shuttlecock & other sports in the great room, & the rest alone in my little own observatory, our party increased at Dinner by Mr. Walmsley & his Daughter who arrived the night before & decreased by the departure of Mr. Holme in the Morning.

Tuesday June 25th.

A very happy change in the weather & in the feel of the air being both mild & pleasant, enough so to make sitting out of Doors pleasanter than walking much bathing when the tide served at noon, among the rest my three Boys who I attended in the Machine; after Dinner amused by some itinerant muscians who were brought into the great room, & the young people danced; after tea, walk'd in a party about a mile to a small farm to see a neat old man & his Wife; a Dr. Dawson added to our set at Supper.

Wensday June 26th.

Cold & stormy again, which very little induced me to walk much, & in the evening several showers no addition this day to our party, walk'd only in the evening to Cromer much Billiard Playing in parties & working after Supper rather a long Day alltogether so much sameness, but my spirits being peculiarly low gave a dullness to everything. A remarkable high sea.

Thursday June 27th.

Some very trifling showers early in the day but became very bright & fine, & was pleasant walking as well as sitting out, Mr. Witts rode out with Mr. Walmsley upon one of his Horses, the evening tho rough & boisterous to make walking at all elegible & after dark extreme hard rain, play'd at Cassino to teach Mrs. Leycester; our party increased by the arrival of a Clergyman & his Wife M^{r.} & Mrs. Davies from Macclesfield, much mirth after Supper. rec'd Letters from Mrs. Granville & Mrs. Buxton. Edward bath'd.

Friday June 28th.

Rather inclined to rain in the Morning, but clear'd of & tho it was dry till quite evening was very cold & stormy, tho at times some sunshine, walk'd in the fields before Diner with Miss Thodosia Leigh added to our family set & play'd at Cribbage with the Misses in the evening being prevented going out with Mr. Leycester in his Phaeton from fear of rain. our party increased by the arrival of a Miss Johnson Mrs. Leycesters Sis^{r.} a very pleasant Woman & a M^{r.} & Mrs. Blackburne new married people & her Mother Mrs. Sherfoot.

Saturday June 29th.

Very wet in the Morning, & tho it ceased raining before Noon became a most violent tempestous Day, & the Sea ran Mountains high, I only walk'd out for ½ an hour before Dinner to blow myself, Mr. Witts took a long ride with Mr. Leycester, some <u>private</u> working & reading in the evening; I was miserably low & wretched all day principaly owing to a most melancholly Letter I rec'd from my Sis^{r.} Travell

Sunday June 30th.

Quite dry the whole day, tho very windy, it was pleasant all the early part of the day from constant sunshine, but in the evening it was so very stormy it was miserably cold & uncomfortable Mr. Leycester perform'd the Morning service to a congregation of between 30 & 40, after which he took Edward & myself in his Phaeton on the sands 2 or 3 miles where we got out, to scramble up a high sand bank very curious as cover'd with a kind of long grass which makes it a strong boundary, & cover'd with a variety of pretty plants, on my return walk'd about till time to dress for Dinner, staid in the House all the evening & wrote to Miss Anne Snow.

Monday July 1st.

Wonderful disagreable weather for the day of the month, being very cold & stormy, yet drying so soon, I was able to walk a little, but it was far from pleasant, much mortified by not receiving any Letters; our party increased in the evening by a Mr. Hulton a friend of many of the party a lively young man, play'd at Cassino mostly with the Blackburne family.

Tuesday July 2^{d.}

Still very windy but so I apprehend it always is at Black Pool, walk'd at noon through the fields about a mile to Mr. Barleys Kitchen Garden where we eat Strawberries, M^{r.} & Mrs. Davies walkd with us, mild & pleasant at a distance from the Sea attempted to walk in the evening with the whole party on the walk, but it was so very windy we were glad very soon to return & play both at Whist & Cassino.

Wensday July 3^{d.}

Quite a beautiful looking & feeling Morning but before noon became dark & lowering, & so gloomy not as strongly to portend rain if not thunder; began some little packing, after which walk'd on the Sands for an hour picking up shells, Mrs. Davies, Miss Th. Leigh & Miss D. Holme with us, began raining hard before Dinner & so continued the whole of the evening which was spent in work, much laughing & talking & some Cassino. Mr. Campbell drank Tea & supp'd wrote to Lady Edward Bentinck

Thursday July 4th.

A very comfortable Day in point of weather, being both wet & stormy, excepting for two or three hours at mid.day, & at night still violent wind & high sea as was seldom known, Mrs. Leigh & her two sweet Daughters took their leave of Black Pool which made a sad gap in our society felt much at their departure, Mr. Hulton went away also. I never stirr'd out of the house all Day had enough to do preparatory to our departure sent Catherine off on a double Horse in the evening 2 or 3 miles to be in readiness to go early the next Day in a Cart to Lancaster; play'd much at Cassino. rec'd Letters from Miss Snow & Miss Louisa Lee

Friday July 5th.

A most unpleasant Morning, being a thick wetting fog, of course very close & damp no very promising appearance for our Journey but it fortunately clear'd off in some degree before we set out, & we had little or no rain the whole of the Day & it was clear & fine in the afternoon, & a very mild pleasant air; we left Black Pool soon after breakfast with small regret, excepting taking leave of Mr. & Mrs. Leycester & Miss Johnson, who we liked so much & had rec'd so much civility & attention from a very indifferent pair of Post Horses & a Boy driver took us in three hours & a half to Garstang 16 miles over rather a desolate disagreable country excepting plentiful corn fields, however it was so small gratification to our eyes, to behold some trees & good hedgerows of which we had been deprived while at Black Pool, the road was very shaking & bad, being very narrow & intirely paved like a causeway which in many places was much broken, it lay in general very near the Sea of which we often got views; Garstang is a poor little market Town nothing to recommend it, either in buildings or situation, made more lively by the Cumberland Militia being there on their march, we got a good Dinner at the Royal Oak for which we were charg'd shamefuly high; from this place to Lancaster 11 miles we improved in every respect, having good Horses, the roads quite smooth & good, & the weather so good that Papa & his Son Francis went in the Chair, & the general face of the country pleasing & varied, much Mountainous some woody & some cultivated highly, 3 miles from Lancaster on the left we were shewn the plantation surrounding Ashton Hall the seat of Lord Archibald Hamiltons the House not visible; the first view of the Town of Lancaster with its Castle & Docks is very striking, but not so much so on the Spot, appearing dark & dull, & in some places the grass growing in the Streets, which are not paved for walking, the Castle is appropriated for the use of the County Goal to which great aditions are now making, the large Church stands close to it, & from the church yard their is a good view of the adjacent country & the Sea at a distance, into which the River Lune flows which surrounds the Town: the chief Trade of which is in West India goods, some Vessels are building on the Docks. we walk'd about in the evening & found the Kings Arms a very good Inn more civility than is customary at Inns in the south.

Saturday July 6th.

Rather thick & foggy in the Morning but became a very pleasant warm Day, with much light & shade for the near views, the more distant & mountainous, more invellop'd in fog & clouds than could be wish'd, the afternoon was peculiarly bright & fine tho we both heard & saw there had been very considerable rains in the countries thro' w.ch we went. after a very good breakfast we walk'd through the several markets, the Butchers one particularly neat &

Lancaster Castle from the River Lune.

Lancaster, from the Aqueduct Bridge; a later view; an engraving after J. M. W. Turner, 1827.

well fill'd tho' we found provisions in general at a high price, being obliged to wait till the Post came in we could not leave the Town till near twelve by that Mail Coach we dispatch'd Catherine to Kendal by the near road going ourselves, a more distant one 6 miles about for the sake of a more beautiful country, the first stage 9 miles to Hornby, the view of the Town of Lancaster in general on quitting it is very fine the situation & elevation both of the Castle & Church is very fine, & that of the Bridge of River Lune beautiful, which meanders in a very bold stile for many miles, & its banks very woody as well as rocky, within 3 miles of Lancaster you discern Hornby Castle once in the possession of Lord Weym's but now of a Mr Marsden, on a very bold eminence & behind it at a very considerable distance Ingleborrow Mountain in Yorkshire which is much famed for its height & indeed appears to touch the clouds, the whole road is fine having perpetual views of the river, & very rich ones of corn & wood lands, with many gentlemens Seats the hedge rows are very peculiarly fine in this part of the world, & more fill'd with flowers & sweets[10] than I ever saw before, the bridge over the Lune at Hornby is a very striking view on the left to the country we had pass'd & to the right to Hornby Castle, the descent from which being all a Haymaking scene render'd it far more beautiful while we were changing Horses wch we found a tedious business we walk'd up to the Castle wch is undergoing <u>an entire</u> repair, it does not appear to such advantage on a near view, a modern fronted House being attach'd to the old Castle of which little remains but a Tower with a kind of Cupula Steeple we went up to the top of the Tower 120 steps from whence the view is fine; to Kirkby Lonsdale is 7 miles, of a very pleasing & raised road, rather rough & stoney, 2 miles from the Town is a handsome old place but apparently ill kept, belonging to a Mr Stanwich call'd Borough Hall, the approach to Kirkby Lonsdale is uncommonly fine, over a Bridge of two arches that before you come to it is wonderfully striking & where you enter the county of Westmoreland this Bridge is over the River Lune which here tho not navigable is very rapid & beautiful, & its banks still highly dress'd; the Town is dirty & ill paved, & very little Trade in it what there is of Blankets, but many good looking houses the Royal Oak is but a sorry looking Inn but excellent accomodations, while our Dinner was preparing we went into the Church Yard & to a walk beyond wch commands a beautiful view having dined most comfortably we set forwards 13 miles to Kendal, the views fine on first leaving Lonsdale, afterwards very Mountainous but by no means barren forms being frequent & cultivation good the most striking features pointed out to us, were Fasltown Rock by travellers compared to the Rock at Gibraltar & Whitbarrow cragg a noble promentery the road is rough, shaking, & rather hilly, the first view of the Town of Kendal is fine, its almost demolish'd Castle stands on a fine eminence opposite, the streets are wide, & clean tho not well paved, we arrived so near dark that we saw little else than that the Kings Arms was a good Inn. rec'd a Letter from my Sis^r Travell that gave me much pleasure from its very kind & amusing contents.

Sunday July 7th

A very close hot Morning with strong fog remaining on the surrounding Mountains, & very oppressive to ones feelings so as to make me quite ill, after Breakfast we walk'd to the great Church almost at the end of the Town we enter'd, & more than ¼ of a mile from the Inn, a

---

10. This is an archaic use of the word for scents as given by roses or wild flowers.

A slightly later engraving of Lowther Street, Kendal.

very large old structure & without one Gallery which proves the size of its ground plot, as we conjectured there was nearly 2000 people compose'd the congregation, the reader a very indifferent one, the preacher a Dr. Baylis better but in the old stile, Sunday schools appear to be singularly well conducted at least the numbers prove it so, which march with great regularity to & from Church, under the inspection of 10 Masters to both Boys & Girls, there is also a Blue Coat School who form the choir to accompany the organist; Dining very comfortably at 2 o'clock we were enabled to set forth at ½ past three having dispatch'd poor Catherine by a Mail Coach to Carlisle to wait our arrival there while we made the Tour of the Lakes for which purpose we went the road to Low wood by Bowness which is 9 miles, the view of the Town of Kendal & its bridge as we left it is very fine but we soon became so intirely lost among the Fells, that it was intirely a Mountain scene, the road in general was good rather rocky & rough with perpetual rises & falls, & some considerable steps which the Driver magnified into Mountains & doubled the powers of his Horses to draw up our heavy Carriage[11] but he was more affraid than hurt & we got with much safety & infinite pleasure to Bowness having been well pleased with the wonderful misshapen promontorys, from which frequently issue the most beautiful limpid sheams, & are many cover'd with heath in full blossom; a mile & half from Bowness on leaving the road to Hawkeshead you have the first striking view of the

---

11. The Witts family brought their own heavy carriage with them, and this was pulled, from inn to inn by the local teams of post horses, driven by the inn postboys. It seems that the postboy (a term which could accompany all age ranges from boys to old men) persuaded Edward Witts that it would be necessary to double the team of horses to cope with the gradients.

noble Lake of Windermere, which is far beyond my powers of discription & greatly exceeded even my raised imagination, the first sight of it is imediately opposite to Mr. Curwins House & Island call'd Bella Island, the road to Bowness runs nearly by the side of the lake, here we changed Horses & went 5 miles more to Low wood Inn where we purposed making our station, it is the ᴬmost beautiful road that can be conceived chiefly passing thro' a wood with frequent openings to the Lake, shaded by the noble Fells that surround it, the evening was bright & clear to so eminent a degree that shew'd all the scenery off to the utmost advantage & the road as excellent as a walk in a Garden running at the back of Mr. Flemmings place at Rayrig, & the Bishop of Landuffs (Dr. Watson's) at Calgarth, & to our right hands fine corn & grass lands in good cultivation, Low wood Inn commands a most beautiful view of the Lake, probably a mile & half from the head, in the whole it is 14 miles in length & at the widest part a mile & half over which is nearly at the Bishop of Landaffs which is a new built handsome stone house. we found the Inn neat & comfortable & the accomodations very comfortable, we were so charm'd with the views, & the evening was so truly summer we could hardly bring ourselves to go to rest. wrote to Mrs. Granville from Kendal.

Monday July 8th.

The most delightful fine Morning that could be conceived & so it continued the whole day quite summer, very hot, tho there was at timed charming light & shade to shew off the great variety of beauties, & at noon a few heat drops from a passing cloud. we were impatient to get a first view of the charming Lake on whose banks we were situated & it appear'd in all its splendor early in the Morning, after Breakfast we went in a boat with one rower provided by the Master of the House at 5 shillings expense to go on the Lake as far as the ferry Island, 7 miles, which is a little farther down than Mr. Curwins Island nothing could exceed the pleasantness of the whole expedition, the water was so clear that at many places where it was not shallow you might discern the bottom, & in it was reflected in the most perfect & beauteous stile all the land views; It is impossible to discribe particularly the number of names of the numerous Fells which at the Ambleside end of the Lake are more peculiarly intermingled, the Bishop of Landaff, & Mr. Flemmings houses on the Banks are great ornaments, & so is Sr. M: Flemmings[12] at Rhydal tho at a much greater distance, the boat was a clever one, & being allow'd the comfort of an elbow chair in it I sat in as much state as an Indian Princess, we landed on Bella Island where Mr. Curwins Gardiner rec'd us & sent in our names, & conducted us all round the Island wch. in size is 42 acres, & is near two miles in circumference, in many parts but narrow, in others a considerable width. the House is situated nearly in the centre, & of a form that has an admirable good effect being circular, with a dome roof, & all the chimnies collected in the centre of the Dome, & a Portico in front, we were inform'd there is three excellent rooms on the first floor & many bedchambers, but the family being now resident the house is not shewn the Island is occasionaly divided by hurdles for the purpose of Sheep pastureage, being never mown; a good gravel walk surrounds the whole at a very small distance from the edge of the Lake, & for the greater part runs by the side of the Shrubbery, besides which there is some fine oak & ash Timber happily disposed & a large clump of high Scotch firs on an eminence. Vessels of various

---

12. Michael Fleming (±1745–1806), 4th baronet, of Rydal Hall.

kinds & sizes are station'd near for the convenience & pleasure of the family, in all respects it appear'd quite a second paradise, & we left it with regret after having spent an hour & ½ in it. the Gardiner was a sensible Scotchman from whom we obtain'd much useful knowledge, on our return to our Vessel we row'd to our most distant point we intended viewing w.ch was the Ferry Island here we again landed & after having got some bread & cheese & ale to enable us, went to a rocky cliff at some little distance from the Ferry house, for 20 or 30 yards it is bad climbing but repaid us amply by shewing off the Lake in a much fine manner, our row back was equaly pleasant, tho a small wind having arisen, curved the water more beautifully. There is several little wooded Islands or Holmes on various parts of the Lake chiefly near the great Island, after being 6 hours out we were not sorry to return to a very good dinner of a Pike out of the Lake & a Leg of Mountain Mutton. We drank Tea on the bowling Green which lies on the Lakes edge after which we walk'd a quarter of a mile to a small Gentlemans House that stands on a sweet Wooded eminence with a fine grass Knoll in front call'd the Doves Nest, which commands a noble view of the Lake & Fells, on our return a small Cannon was fired off on the bowling Green for the purpose of hearing the wonderful reverberations of the report among the Mountains which continued for the space of a minute.

Tuesday July 9th.
A wonderfull clear fine Morning but from 9 to 12 became rather gloomy & hazzy which made it so oppressively hot it was miserable to move, but the remainder of the day & evening clear again & broiling hot, left Low:wood Inn rather before nine, felt hurt at turning our backs on so delicious a spot, pass'd thro Ambleside 2 miles distant, a miserable old little Town, a mile or less from the head of the Lake & surrounded by Fells, from thence to Rydall Sr. M: Flemmings

Lake Windermere from Lowwood.

… left Low:wood Inn rather before nine, felt hurt at turning our backs on so delicious a spot, pass'd thro Ambleside 2 miles distant, a miserable old little Town, a mile or less from the head of the Lake & surrounded by Fells …

is about a mile farther, a wonderfull fine romantic spot, surrounded by everything to fullfil that idea the house is fitting up improving, from it is it stands on an eminence you see a part of Windermere & its surrounding fells, & behind it in a thick wood is two fine Water falls, w.ch in a wet season must be stupendously fine as even now they were most pleasingly noble ducking over & amongst imense rocks, & the shade by which they were invellop'd much favor'd the scenery, you approach them by a neat gravel walk winding among the woods the lower one has a very good effect by apparently running thro the arch of a bridge which is the way to the upper one, our road also lay close by Rydall water, a small Lake within a very small distance of S.r M: Flemmings it is a quiet pretty piece of water & has two small wooded Islands on it, about 2 miles from it is Grasmere Lake much spoken off by tourists as beautiful in its way, but we were not so very much struck with it, it is two miles in length of the Vale thro which it was rich for the general stile of the country, & the viliage & church of Grasmere are great ornaments Lays Water or Thalmere Lake we were better pleased with which is two or three miles farther after having past Dunmail Race which is a strong rising ground for three miles between imense high Mountains, at the end of which you enter the county of Cumberland at which spot is a wonderful large collection of rock stones piled up in a monumental form & said to be raised as a memorial of the last King of Cumberland, near to this the wonderfull Mountain of Hellvelyn rears its lofty head the highest cragg of which is said to be three miles high of this I have great doubts but I am most sure, I never saw any to compare to it, indeed the whole stage of 18 miles to Keswick is one continued chain of Mountains from w.ch in wet seasons rush torrents in Cascades, there was now sufficient to judge what it might be than one wooded Mountain we were peculiarly struck with call'd the Hough, feather'd down with Wood from its top to the base, under which were the richest meadows & corn fields possible the roads were excellent tho rather shaking & being so very hilly we were 4 hours & ½ performing it tho we were obliged to have 4 Horses, before you came in sight of Keswick you discern the bold Skiddaw, from the top of the Hill as you descend to the Town the view of the vale is excessively rich & fine its own Lake to the left hand & on the right, but at 4 miles distance the small Lake of Bassenthwaite, we found the Queens Head a very comfortable Inn, & after a good dinner tho almost broiled with heat, we set forth to survey the Lake of Keswick or Derwent water as it is sometimes call'd, but being near a mile from the Inn I found the walk to & fro a sad fatigue being far from well, the boat is larger & row'd by two Men & not near so pleasant a one as that on Windermere, neither were we by any means so much pleased with it alltogether it is much smaller & more in a circular form being nearly as wide as Windermere but very short, its Mountains are certainly very stupendous & fine, those of Skiddaw & Saddleback at the bottom of the Lake, & those of Borrowdale & many others on the left hand & upper end: a Mr Packlington has the chief property on the Lake but has shewn little tact, as on the longest Island wch has but 5 acres he has continued to place as many buildings, one of them a house for himself & another an imaginary Church he has also another residence on the Lake on the Borrowdale side far superior, near to Lodawr Water Fall,[13] where we landed & which must be a very fine thing in rainy seasons the rocks being extremely high & yet woody we landed likewise at the end of the Lake, on which & its environs we remain'd till near dark.

The lake at Keswick; an engraving from 1784.

---

13.   Lodore Waterfall.

Wensday July 10th.

A most uncommon hot Day such broiling sun, it was hardly possible to keep even tolerably cool when keeping quite quiet which I was obliged to do all morning in order to re-exist a little after the heat & fatigue of the former Day pack'd & departed in the Morn: in order to send the large Trunk by a Carrier to Edinburgh to prevent having 4 horses in this hilly country, had a very good Dinner at an early hour & set out for Penrith between 4 & 5, extremely hot for the first hour but pleasant after when we got on high ground, but so hilly a stage of 18 miles that we were better than 4 hours going it, quitting Keswick you leave the Mountain Saddle Back or St. John on your left hand under which runs the vale of St. John, which is fertile & quiet, after that the Country is dull till within 3 or 4 miles of Penrith the road lying much more over barren heath of 3 or 4 miles in length & the road but rough & stoney at 3 miles from the Town to the right you leave the Lake of Ulswater with its stupendous Mountains & sweet vale of Rotterdale so highly spoken of, but which we gave up seeing, as it took us so much out of our route & I fear'd the fatigue; much fine Corn & grass around Penrith the Town appears inconsiderable on first entrance but is large in itself, stands in a bottom, but being built of such ill colour'd stone that it appears like bad brick, which makes the old ruin of a Castle at the back part of the Town have a strange & ill effect; the Crown is an excellent Inn in point of accomodation, & was very full of company, a new one is building close by, the Church appears to be large & handsome but we did not go into it said to be frequently 3000 assembled in it on a Sunday, night so violently hot we could scarce get any rest. wrote to my Sis^{r.} Travell.

Thursday July 11th.

Nearly if not quite as hot much oppress'd by it & heartily glad we had no farther to go than 18 miles to Carlisle, & of as bad stoney rough road as ever I desire to go & very dull into the bargain lying chiefly over barren baggy heather the first mile or two from Penrith is tolerable over the Race ground, & commanding a good view of the country we had left, of Lowther Hall the seat of Lord Lonsdale, it was so hilly as well as rough that we were near 4 hours performing this tedious stage & almost over come with heat & dust; which made us very glad to find ourselves at the Buck Inn in Carlisle; which stands in a wide street, with a charming opening into a Garden wch shews you the distant country; the Town stands on an eminence in a vale & appears very old, Gates at all sides of the Town & walls nearly round it but much broken, the Suburbs are very mean & the inhabitants have a wretched appearance; we found the Inn in sad confusion the stables having been burnt down that Morning with a considerable loss, but we got pleasant airy apartments & found poor Catherine rejoiced at our arrival. much taken up in the evening by reading & considering many interesting Letters rec'd, walk'd out late when it began to be cooler to survey the Bridge leading to Scotland the Cathedral & many parts of the Town. rec'd a delightful long Letter from Mrs. Naper.

Friday July 12th.

Not near so oppressively hot as there was a most considerable wind & that turn'd to the North but still the sun was scorching hot, so busy all the Morning in answering difficult & interesting Letters that we never went out of the house before Dinner which we had at an early hour to permit us to go to evening prayers at 4 o'clock at the Cathedral shock'd to see it so ill attended both in point of congregation, ringers, & readers, of course very little gratified, after

Carlisle, from the bridge; a later view; an engraving after J. M. W. Turner, 1827.

tea walk'd to the Castle & survey'd it accurately under the direction of a Gunner, of which there is 4 that are dependant on the Castle & a Town Major, the Castle is in good repair at this time, several Cannons mounted, which are fired on the saluting Days about six times in a Year. there is also a store house for Powder & Balls we were shewn the rooms when Mary of Scots was confined for the first 14 months she was Prisoner in this Kingdom, from the leads over which there is a fine view of the adjacent country, M^r. Howards of Corby Castle & the Scotch Hills, & Cumberland Mountains, the River Eden the bridges, & fine meadows fill'd with Cattle beneath. wrote to M^rs. Tracy, my Sis^r. Travell, & M^r. Leake.

Saturday July 13th.
A beautiful fine day, being a clear north wind which prevented its being violently hot, tho the sun was scorching, soon after breakfast we walk'd thro' & about the Market making our remarks, the rest of the Morning, work'd a little & alter'd some of our packages preparative to our departure next Day, in the afternoon after we had drank Tea, walk'd by the broken Walls down to the Race ground meadow sat for sometime on the stand to rest not at home till near dark wrote to L^d. Edwd. Bentinck

Sunday July 14th.
A charming fine Day for travelling not being much too hot there being a fine air till the sun became low which made it unpleasant being full in our eyes or else our Days Journey would have been very pleasant we set out at 9 o'clock leaving Cath to follow us in the evening in a dilligence to Dumfries our first stage 10 miles to Long Town, rather a shaking road but the country pleasant,

Dumfries, an engraving by W. Miller after a painting by Clarkson Stanfield R.A.

several good plantations & some gentlemens seats in view, Long Town is a new built Town & a smart looking Inn where we only changed horses, & proceeded on 13 miles to Annan; 4 miles from Long Town on crossing over a Bridge over a small stream we enter'd Scotland which occasion'd me a strange contrasiety[14] of feelings & ½ a mile farther we pass'd thro the viliage of Gretna Green renderd so famous for being the place where english couples under age go to be married we were shewn the Alehouse where the service is usualy perform'd, never in the parish Church which is a handsome one more like in appearance a Town Hall having neither Tower nor Steeple not by the regular Clergyman of the Parish. We were much struck in passing thro a viliage call'd Durnay to see a large congregation assembled in the Church Yard where divine service was perform'd by a Minister standing in a kind of Centry Box, the Kirk being rebuilding was the cause, the roads were excellent, Horses the same, & for the greater part of the way to the left we had a view of Solway Firth which flows into the sea, the country was rather wild, but yet much good Grass & Corn growing, Annan is a small Market Town, the Kirk at the entrance, where the service is only perform'd in the Scotch language, we got a very decent good Dinner at the Queensberry Arms, after which we went 16 miles to Dumfries, the greater part of the road excellent, rather Mountainous in point of views, but some good corn land & fine plantations particularly within a mile or two of the Town, which is visible 6 or 7 miles before you get to it & cuts a great figure with its many steeples it is no great proof of the beauty or fertility of the soil when it is related that the great quantities of Peat for burning that are stack'd

---

14. Contrasiety is clearly written; and appears to be a word made up by Agnes Witts.

Above: Dumfries, an engraving looking towards Devorgilla Bridge.

Right: The appearance of this print by John Kay in 1795—at the time the Breadalbane Fencibles were stationed in Edinburgh—created no small sensation among the fair portion of the higher circles. Though unaccompanied by any other explanation than what is given on the Engraving, the parties represented were generally supposed to be Lord and Lady Breadalbane.

up on each side of the roads are quite astonishing; it is no pleasing sight to look on the fair sex chiefly walking without either shoes or stockings, being not in favor of delicacy or the beauty of their Limbs. we were much struck with the beauty of the chief street in Dunfries in which the Kings Arms Inn stands, being wide, neat & on a declivity, the Town was rendered much more lively by a regiment of 700 men & 20 Officers, Fencibles just raised by the Earl of Breadalbane in the Highlands, which cut a humorous appearance, being all in their native Plaid Dress with Jackets short Petticoats & round caps. We walked about the Town that evening as much as the heat would permit, there is a beautiful River runs by the side of the Town which has likewise a fine view & appeared to be the Town Mall for the Sunday evening Promenade

Monday July 15$^{th.}$

Quite a cruel scorching hot Day hardly possible to keep cool on any terms, but grew cooler in the evening, somewhat cloudy & many evident signs of rain; as soon as we had breakfasted rec'd a visit from D^r. Burnside, a Minister of the Town to whom we had a Letter of recommendation, for his advice relative to the schools in Dumfries which proved to be decidedly against fixing our Boys there, but much in favor of Edinburgh which determined us to lose no time in getting there, M^r. Witts & the Boys walk'd about a good deal but I was too much oppress'd by the heat to be able to stir much; after a very bad Dinner we set out to go to Moffat 21 miles all in one stage, leaving Catherine to come on in a dilligence:— the road in general pretty good & very hilly which made it so tedious we did not arrive till near dark nothing very striking in the road the first 3 or 4 miles from Dumfries, very large plantations chiefly of Scotch Firs, & rather better than half way, imence ones, many very young, of Lord Hopetouns, & a large castle like house call'd Raghill very gloomy looking among the Mountains, the habitations in general very wretched, even Farm & ale houses no better than huts, Moffat is a small Town standing in a hole surrounded with Hills, the Inn pretty good. sign I forget. wrote to M$^{rs.}$ Naper.

Above left: Three officers of the Hopetoun Fencibles. The centre figure is Francis, 7th Lord Napier (1758–1834). The figure to the right is Major Pilmer and to the left Major Clarkson. An etching by John Kay.

Above right: James Hope (1741–1816), 3rd Earl of Hopetoun and the Hopetoun Fencibles. An etching by John Kay, 1795.

Tuesday July 16th.

Having been a hard shower in the night attended with Thunder & lightening the air was much cool'd, it was very damp, & during the course of the Morning, many flying storms, & in the afternoon almost perpetual rain, left Moffat at 10, 2 miles from the Town a most tremendous Hill of near three miles in length call'd Alexdra Brae, a most wretched road & so indeed was the whole of the stage, but there is hopes of some amendments in it a new road being making w.ch at present only serves to make it worse the Country is in general most dreary & mountainous, not a tree to be seen but now & then some Scotch firs, & very very few houses excepting sad wretched mud Cottages, now & then some few small cornfields & flocks of bad looking small sheep, & Oxon trying to feed on the Moor Lands, the first stage was 15 miles to Bild a miserable lone ale House where we could get a tolerable pair of Post Horses, & just enough bad food to call it a wretched bad Dinner, as bad or worse accomodations than ever I met with even in Wales here Catherine join'd us in her Fly or diligence which was suitable to the Inn & in which she proceeded on that night to Edinburgh, we only went a stage of 19 miles to a very poor Inn call'd Noble House before we arrived there the country rather mended upon being not quite so hilly & rather better planted & cultivated, & roads smoother. Here our accomodations were very moderate & our attendants worse, without shoes or stockings, short Petticoats & Jackets, & dirt & filth of every kind very intolerable to my feelings however we got a good nights sleep all 5 in one room, for security.

Wensday July 17ᵗʰ·

Fine & dry early in the Morning, but soon became stormy, & many very hard showers in the course of the Morn: with very high wind but none fell after we reach'd Edinburgh where we arrived between 1 & 2 it being only a 16 mile stage, the road very shaking & indifferent the whole of the way, the country much mended from the yesterdays Journey tho Mountainous till within 3 or 4 miles of the Town, in some degree so the whole way, as parts of it stand on a Rock but the views become fine & cultivated, & the first sight of the Town & Castle & Sea beyond very striking. we drove to Walkers Hottel in Princes Street where we found Catherine who had arrived the night before it is a large House in a high stile, where we had a very excellent apartments paying high for them, eating far from good; the first step we took even before we could get any Dinner was to introduce ourselves to Mʳ· Ainslie the Sadler, to whom we had a note of recommendation from Lord Elcho & found him a very useful obliging Man, walk'd with him for 3 hours in the evening in various parts of the Town to seek out a Lodging for our imediate residence much disgusted by the dirt & disageableness of all we saw excepting an unfurnish'd one at Nº· 2 in Georges Square, return'd home most heartily tired.

Thursday July 18ᵗʰ·

Still showery, but not sufficiently so to keep me much in the House; Mr. Stormonth[15] Lord Elcho's Agent came to us after breakfast, & went out with us on the search, much approved of our fixing upon No 2 in Georges Square in consequence of which he began taking steps for us for that purpose & attended us to several Upholsters in order to hire & procure furniture to put into it a very perplexing & anxious business in the afternoon went to several shops to buy many necessary things, & hired a very little maid by the name of Kitty at 4 Pounds a Year rec'd Letters from Lady Edwᵈ· Bentinck Mʳˢ· Buxton & Miss Anne Snow & wrote to Miss Snow.

A view of the Old Town viewed from Princes Street, taken from a painting executed some 21 years after the time that the Witts family were living in the area. An engraving by J. Clark from a painting by A. Kay.

15. James Stormonth (1768–1846) was a 'writer' (solicitor) of 9 St James's Square, he also acted as an agent for Lord Elcho. Interestingly by 1800 he was the owner of 18 North Hanover Street, this was the house that Edward Witts bought in the New Town, so presumably James Stormonth bought it from Edward Witts in 1796.

Friday July 19th.

Quite a disagrable damp wet Day from morn to night, in the afternoon such violent & frequent showers that it might be call'd perpetual rain, in the Morning in spite of it I puddled about & was a dirty as might be, trying all possible to hurry everything on at the Lodgings to get in the next Day. Mr. Witts out all the evening on the same purpose. Mr. Stormonth sat an hour with me in his absence. wrote to Lady Edward Bentinck & Miss Gorges.

Saturday July 20th.

A much better day, for tho now & then cloudy, very little if any rain fell, after an early breakfast our whole party trudged to the Squ^{re.} To overlook work people, to so good a purpose that we determined to remove to it after Dining at the Hottel; which we accomplish'd Mr. Witts going with our luggage in a hackney Coach, drank Tea at home, & endeavor'd all I could to feel happy. I once more <u>had</u> a home, tho on many accounts it was likely to be so barren of comforts got however a very restless poor night in my new habitation. in the Morning the Boys & I had explored the walks in the Meadows just below the Square.

Sunday July 21st.

A very fine Day throughout, constant sunshine, but rather a cool air, got ourselves ready to go to Morning church, by every recommendation instead of going to the large English church in Cowgate, found ourselves in a small non fancy Chappel, very dirty & a strange looking congregation three Clergymen—officialy, supplied the place of a parish Clerk no Surplices worn wch is universal in Scotland, tolerable singing but very moderate reading & preaching, & we were glad to find we were got into a situation we did not mean, after service walk'd up to the new Town & about, till it was time to go to evening service wch we did at Dr. Websters new Chapel near to the new College, a pretty building but the seats sadly narrow, Mr. Webster a dull reader his sermon on benevolence quite an essay came home to Dinner at 4 o'clock, a good Leg of Mutton was the opening of our housekeeping, but I felt far from tired or in good spirits. before Tea walk'd on the meadow & Herriott walks & had some conversation about the different parts of the Town with a variety of people we met. the Boys happy in making an acquaintance & playing with some Boys in the Square.

Monday July 22^{d.}

A fine Day, quite dry tho at times thick & rather gloomy, Mr. Witts out early at Market, after Breakfast we again both went out in search of various things but I was so low & indifferent all Day I was little able to encounter all the difficulties I had to surmount, went out again in the afternoon on some errands, Mr. Stormonth here for an hour in the evening. rec'd a Letter f^{m.} L^{dy.} Edwd. B.

Tuesday July 23^{d.}

Quite a beautiful fine warm Day till evening when after a small shower, it became a wonderful thick fog so much so, as not to be able to discern very near objects, Mr. Witts out the greater part of the Morning with Mr. Stormonth, visiting Mr. Oliphant at Leith &'c. I busy all the Morning at home in spite of the fog as it was dry under foot, walk'd into parts of the New Town we had not before seen rec'd Letters from Mrs. Granville & my Sis^{r.} Travell

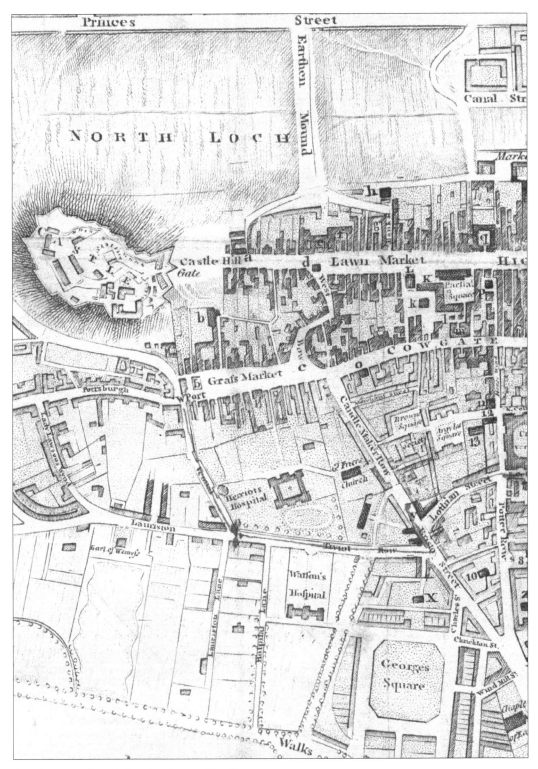

An enlargement from Robert Scott's map of 1817.

Holyrood House and Chapel from Calton Hill. An engraving by William Miller after a painting by Clarkson Frederick Stanfield.

Wensday July 24[th.]

Another fine clear warm Day, again a small shower in the afternoon, & a little tendency of fog quite late in the evening, at home all the Morn[g.] M[r.] Oliphant call'd & found him both obliging & pleasant M[rs.] Aucheleck & M[r.] Stormonth both call'd in the evening, the latter accompanied us in our evening walk conducting us to Holyrood House Cannongate &'c not at home till nearly dark. rec'd an obliging message from the Lady Charteris's with a presant of fruit.

Thursday July 25[th.]

Very fine in the Morning quite hot & indeed the whole of the Day, till quite evening when there was hard rain for an hour or two which pleasantly laid the dust. M[r.] Witts & I walk'd late in the Morning calling on the Lady Charteris's but not admitted,[16] at an upholsterers & other useful errands, in the evening D[r.] Adams,[17] Rector or Head Master of the High School was here for an hour or two, to talk over the subject of the Boys going to the School, much pleased by his manner & behavior & highly gratified by his approbation of our Dear Francis's School knowledge after his undergoing an accurate examination. at night wrote to M[rs.] Granville.

---

16. Agnes's first cousin, Susan, née Tracy-Keck (1744–1835), was married to Francis Charteris, Lord Elcho (1749–1808). His sisters were Frances Charteris (d. 1835), married William Traill (1746–1831); Henrietta (b. 1747); Catherine (d. 1812); and Anne (d. 1793). It is not precisely clear who these sisters were, but probably Henrietta, Catherine and Anne.
17. Alexander Adam (1741–1809); head master of the Edinburgh High School.

Alexander Adam (1741–1809); headmaster
of the Edinburgh High School. An engraving
from a portrait by Henry Raeburn.

Friday July 26th.

An intire clear fine Day, & extremely pleasant after the rain, I never went out the whole of
the Morning & was far from well either in Mind or Body, spirits not mended by the strange
conduct of our new under Maid who took it into her head to run away without any provocation
just before Dinner & was heard of no more, such conduct shew'd she was no loss but the
inconvenience was great & caused us to be out & about the whole evening searching out for
another but in vain. a Major Elves, Fort Major at the Castle & a Friend of Lord Elcho's call'd
here a most singular character rec'd a very interesting & important Letter from my Sister
Travell, another from Miss Hughes. & wrote to M^rs. Buxton.

Saturday July 27th.

Another very beautiful fine Day, constant sun, but such a clear North air it was none too hot.
went out to Market M^r. Witts with me before 8 o'clock neither amused by it. A M^r. Noble here
twice in the course of the day a kind of Scholastic Tutor to whom Francis was to be sent for
an hour in the Day till after the vacation was over & he could be sent to the High School, M^r.
Stormonth also here, & a M^rs. Morrison an opposite Neighbour & the Wife of an Advocate
call'd here in the evening before Tea took a long walk under Salisbury Craggs &'c attended
by M^r. Guthrie the Bookseller, in whose shop we chanced to go, by the way & he obligingly
offerd himself to shew the way, & entertained us much by a recital of many customs & forms
of the general face of the Town & country. no tidings of any other servant wrote to M^rs. Tracy
of Sandywell.

A view of Edinburgh
from Salisbury Crags.
An aquatint by
Robert Havell junior,
from a painting by
E. Crawford, 1828.

Sunday July 28th.

Quite as delightful weather, tho the air rather cooler particularly towards evening; went to
Morning service at the large English Chappel in Cowgate sitting both in Mr. Ainslies & Mr.
Guthries seats close together service very well perform'd, a most excellent sermon by an English
stranger, hardly time to walk home, & get a sandwich before it was time, to set out again for
evening service where Mr. Witts & I went to the High Kirk St. Giles principaly to hear Dr. Blair
preach,[18] indeed he did the whole of the service, which appeard to us very singular quite unlike
the english disenting meetings, singing good it is a large handsome Parish church originally,
but fitted up in the stile of a meeting house, rather disappointed in Dr. Blairs preaching matter
certainly excellent, his manner not pleasing & his voice very unintelligible as well from its
natural tone as his broad Scotch idiom walk'd before Tea all round the walks, & upon the
heath land beyond which commands a fine view.

Monday July 29th.

A very fine Day till quite evening when it became stormy & rather inclined to rain Mr. Witts on
several bussiness in the course of the Morn: when I was much engaged in household employs
one part hiring a new under Maid I hope with better prospects of success than the former
one, walk'd out before Tea chiefly in the new Town, & making enquiries after a writting &
arefmetec school for George & Edwd. Francis went for the first time for an hour to a Mr. Noble
a private Tutor under whom he was to learn till after the vacation. rec'd a Letter from Mrs. Hyett

---

18. Hugh Blair (1718–1800). Hugh Blair attended Edinburgh High School and Edinburgh University, graduating MA in
1739. He was licensed to preach in 1741 and by 1760 had become minister to the High Kirk, St Giles. From 1762
onwards Blair also held the Chair of Rhetoric in Edinburgh University. His lectures on taste won him wide fame. It
was Blair who encouraged James Macpherson to proceed with the collection of his *Ossianic* Fragments, and Blair who
wrote the introduction to the first edition which appeared in 1760.

Above left: Hugh Blair (1718–1800). Hugh Blair attended Edinburgh High School and Edinburgh University, graduating MA in 1739. He was licensed to preach in 1741 and by 1760 had become minister to the High Kirk, St Giles. From 1762 onwards Blair also held the Chair of Rhetoric in Edinburgh University.

Above right: Dr James Graham going along the North Bridge in a high wind. An etching by John Kay.

Tuesday July 30[th.]

Fine early in the Morning, but before noon turn'd to mild gentle rain, & was a damp air the whole Day till quite evening, of course I never stirr'd out till seven in the evening when we strolled about the walks & adjacent parts of the Town to the Square, the two younger Boys went at several different parts of the Day to Mess[rs.] Pator & Gordons school on the North Bridge. very busy at accompts all the Morn: & wrote to my Sister Travell.

Wensday July 31[st.]

Weather still good & dry, tho rather more cloudy & stormy than some days, with a high cool wind, M[r.] Witts went early to Leith to breakfast with M[r.] Oliphant, & concern'd me much on his return by informing me of the death of Lady Anne Charteris, I call'd in the Morning on M[rs.] Morrison to return her visit, & we all 5 went to dine with M[r.] Stormonth in S[t.] James's Square, up three pair of Stairs a dirty dwelling, but a fine view from the back windows, a good Dinner & a hearty welcome, & we met a M[r.] Adamson & young M[r.] Maconochies, very fine lads I walk'd before Tea with the Boys in S[t.] Andrews Square &'c, & we did not come home till nearly dark, when M[r.] Simpson, one of the Gentlemen in the House visited us, a Clergyman of the Town Kirk as agreable Man. wrote to M[rs.] Guydickens.

Allan Maconochie, Lord Meadowbank (1748–1816), advocate, academic jurist, judge and agriculturalist. The 'fine lad' Agnes refers to was probably his son, Alexander Maconochie, (1777–1861), Lord Meadowbank after 1816. He went on to be an MP and had a distinguished legal career.

Thursday Aug[st.] *1*[st.]

Quite fine, constant hot sun & clear cool air, M[r.] Witts & I went early to a Market, & at mid. day I sallied forth again to visit M[rs.] Auchenleck, up 5 pairs of stairs in the Land Market, where I only found one of her Sisters, perform'd several little bussinesses besides in the afternoon M[r.] Witts read to me in D[r.] Shebbeares old Novel of Lydia,[19] before Tea walk'd with Francis on the walks & on Bruntsfield Lynn[20]

Friday Aug[st.] *2*[d.]

Most delightful continuation of weather rather warmer than some Days, & in the evening a thick close air, I was far from well the whole day, & my spirits low to a wretched degree, much occasion'd by receiving no Letters from Dear England, my Dear Francis rather unwell also in his head & stomach, I never stirr'd out till quite evening when M[r.] Witts & I walk'd up to the Castle & home over the Mount by the new Town.

Saturday Aug[st.] *3*[d.]

A hotter day than many former ones, yet there was a strong wind, & dust quite intolerable, & in the evening a hard shower of rain, all of us but Edward were by appointment to dine with

---

19.　John Shebbeare (1709–1788). *Lydia, or Filial Piety*: first published 1755; a third edition was published in 1786.
20.　Bruntsfield Links, not 'Lynn' as Agnes Witt inadvertently first noted it. The Links are 35 acres of open parkland in Bruntsfield, immediately to the south-west of the adjoining Meadows. Unlike the Meadows, which formerly contained the Nor Loch, drained in the eighteenth century, Bruntsfield Links had always been dry ground.

Edinburgh Castle, by Alexander
Nasmyth.

M[r.] Oliphant of Leith the Sea Port belonging to this place & at two miles distance, walk'd
to the Bridge end, where M[r.] Stormonth join'd us & we went in a Hackney Coach, w.[ch] had
not carried us a quar[r.] of a mile before one of the fore Wheels came off; very fortunately we
were not overturn'd, got out & the matter was soon repair'd M[r.] O being a comissioner of
the Customs, his residence is at the Custom House, good Rooms but a dismal place standing
in a narrow street w.[ch] all at Leith appears to be, a very hearty reception; tho an odd very odd
Dinner, after which two Boys that live with him went with my Boys to see all the glories of
the place after a large repast of Coffee, Tea & sweetmeats we walk'd to the Pier & about just
escaped rain no Hackney Coach being to be got M[r.] S. myself & Boys came home in a Post
Chaise & M[r.] Witts under the shelter of an Umbrella.

Sunday Aug[st.] 4[th.]

Quite a fine Morning & Noon, a cloudy afternoon & a wet evening, went to Church in the
Morning to S[t.] Peters Chappel, D[r.] Websters, where a M[r.] Allen did the Duty staid the Sacrament,
the administration of which is rather different from the English churches, went to evening
service again at S[t.] Giles's Kirk, to hear M[r.] Greenfield, very well pleased both with Sermon &
Prayers, staid at home all the evening, a severe thick fog succeeding to the rain rec'd a Letter
from Miss Anne Snow & wrote to Miss Louisa Lee.

Monday Aug[st.] 5[th.]

Most charming clear fine Day, bright sun & brisk wind, but again lowerd at 6 o'clock & was
more or less small rain & damp all the evening M[r.] Witts out the greater part of the Morning
at Leith &'c, Francis & I took a pleasant strole on the walks &'c, only went out in the evening
to S[t.] Peters Chappel to make some enquiries about renting a Pew. rec'd a delightful informing
Letter from M[rs.] Naper of 11 sides.

Tuesday Augst. 6th.

Nothing could be more charming than the weather still continued, we went to Market before Breakfast, & I did not stir out the rest of the Morning but in the afternoon all the Boys walk'd with us on the Leith walk, went to two or three shops there & to the Physic Garden on the opposite side, a spot of 4 Acres much planted with tall trees to keep off cold winds & sea breezes, which draw up all the plants sadly there is hot Houses & Greenhouses, in which Botanical lectures are read by Dr. Rutherford the Professsor which causes the Garden to be more in that stile & medical, than in flowers. wrote to Mrs. Witts at Nibley

Wensday Augst. 7th.

One of the hottest Days I had been sensible of since I came into Scotland, being burning sun & little wind, rather cloudy in the evening, but no rain, I walk'd at mid.day with Mr. Witts & Francis to some useful Shops & we all drank Tea with Mr. Simpson up stairs, & his two Daughters shy Girls of 17 & 15, & 2 Sons younger, great favorites & Playmates of our Boys, Mr. S. being a very considerable & good converser the visit went off well wrote to Miss Anne Snow.

Thursday Augst. 8th.

After having been some rain in the night it was a cloudy Morning early, & soon began raining hard & lasted till Noon, when it became clear & dry till evening when it was again cloudy but dry I staid at home all Morn: but deny'd myself to Miss Halkett, Miss Walmseleys Friend who civilly call'd, Father, Mother & Son, walk'd in the evening about the Streets & engaged for a Seat in Dr. Websters new English Chappel. wrote to Mrs. Tyrwhitt.

Friday Augst. 9th.

Had been much rain in the night & continued wet till 8 or 9 o'clock when it became fine & remain'd extremely so all the day, again lowering in the evening, Mr. Witts breakfastead up stairs with Mr. Simpson for the fathers & Sons to attend each other to the examination at the High School, annualy perform'd at the commencement of the vacation a very gratifying meeting of all parties, Mr. Witts dined by invitation with, the Mayor & heads of the Town, who preside over the Schools, the Masters & many other Gentlemen & came home much pleased by the great invitation that had been paid him as an English Stranger I was very low & poorly & never stirr'd the whole eveng. read in Dr. Shebbeares Lydia a great deal of low humour wrote to Mrs. Hyett.

Saturday Augst. 10th.

Wet early in the day, but was dry, tho still remain'd damp & rather cloudy till towards afternoon when it became fine, Mr. Witts out & about much of the Morning, I full of many little bussinesses walk'd in the new Town in the evening as far as to see Charlotte Square the new one that is building came home well tired. rec'd a Letter from my Sister Travell ever a great comfort, & wrote to Miss Hughes.

Sunday Augst. 11th.

Very fine Day, only too windy to be quite pleasant & in the evening rather stormy & the air sharp, went to Church in the Morning to St. Peters, Dr. Websters Chappel & took possession of our new rented Pew service well perform'd by Mr. Webster, the Boys went there again in the afternoon & we to the new Kirk to hear Dr. Blair very well pleased with him this time sat by desire in Commissioner Grieves seat; before Tea went again to the Chappel firstly kept a tedious long time by a most wretched methodistual Preacher a very beggarly congregation. wrote to Mrs. Naper

Monday Aug^{st.} 12th.

A most charming fine hot Day till toward evening when it grew cold & cloudy, after mid. day I made myself smart, & walk'd with Mr. Witts to Frederick Street to return Miss Halketts visit, much pleased by the reception she gave us, & thought her very agreable in her manner, walk'd very little in the evening in & about the Square, Mr. Stormonth sat with me while we drank Tea & indeed till after dark.

Tuesday Aug^{st.} 13th.

Wet in the Morning which prevented my going to Market & was showery all the fore part of the day, dry in the evening but cold & windy, I read a great deal in Lydia, much amused by the wit in it but provoked at the indecency. in the afternoon took so long a walk with Husband & Boys that I was tired to Death quite to the farther end of Queen Street & into several Lodging Houses. wrote to Miss Mary Sheppard.

Edinburgh gentlemen, Edward Innes and James Cooper, 1792, an etching by John Kay.

Wensday Aug^{st.} 14th.

Fine in the Morning, but a most tremendous shower at Noon, Mr. Witts out on some visits which detain'd him long for shelter, but it became so dry by the evening that I walk'd out in the streets first to the Library in Parliament Close & then apartment hunting in Leith Street; bitterly cold & windy which brought on Rhumatism in my head & face.

Thursday Aug^{st.} 15th.

Rather a showery day with damp air but no hard rain, but sufferd so much so much pain in my head &'c that I never stirr'd out the whole day; finish'd reading Lydia, & Mr. Witts begun reading in Charlotte Smiths new Novel of the Old Manor House[21] well pleased with it, & it made my work go on well. Mrs. Auchenlech call'd in the evening. rec'd a Letter from Miss Snow.

Friday Aug^{st.} 16th.

Very fine & clear in the Morning, but before Dinner became cloudy, & wet & so continued more or less the whole of the evening, Mr. Witts & Francis walked to Leith imediately after breakfast to call on Mr. Oliphant on their return I walk'd into the New Town, over taken by a hard shower, return'd home in a Hackney Coach fearful of increasing my rhumatism which was much worse at night much amused by the Manor House rec'd a Letter from Mrs. Granville & wrote to Mrs. Travell

Saturday Aug^{st.} 17th.

Showery many parts of the day, damp & cold the whole of it, & I was so thoroughly low & wretched that it pass'd very miserably with me & my rhumatism was so bad I was fearful of stirring out at all, my amusement solely arose by our Book.

Sunday Aug^{st.} 18th.

Quite dry, & in every respect a much finer day, but still the air very cold & unlike Aug^{st.} went to Morning Church at St. Peters Chappel where Mr. Allan read Prayers, & a stranger preach'd, went to evening service at the new Kirk where instead of Mr. Greenfield, a stranger officiated, & extremely well, sat in Comiss^{r.} Grieves seat Francis walk'd with us before Tea round Carlton Hill for the first time much pleased with the view towards Leith &'c from it & with the whole of the walk, distrss'd to find on our return poor George quite ill both in his head and stomach, sent for Mr. Wood the younger Apothecary wth whose manner I was pleased, & his remedy soon relieved the d^{r.} Boy

Monday Aug^{st.} 19th.

A tolerably fine Day, but a small shower or two in the course of it, George happily much recoverd & able to go to School, Mr. Stormonth here for an hour in the Morning, walk'd a little before Tea to the circulating Library &'c more & more amused by the Manor House.

Tuesday Aug^{st.} 20th.

A very windy disagreable Day, with some very trifling foolish showers, which did not lay in any degree the dust, which was much horrid from the wind being so high; Mr. Witts & I were out the

---

21.   Charlotte Turner Smith (1749–1806). *The Old Manor House* was published in 1793.

greater part of the Morn: house & upholstery hunting, went on the Leith road to one bought several articles of furniture too much tired to go out again in the afternoon rec'd Letters from M^rs. Chollet & my Sis^r. Travell who ever takes all opportunities of writting to one.

Wensday Aug^st. 21st.

Quite an unpleasant day, being a very high cold wind & yet so thick & damp an air that it often look'd like small rain, I made myself easy to sit at home the whole day full employ'd by writting, reading & working M^r. Witts a good deal out on various bussinesses wrote to M^rs. Charles Western. began reading the Card, a humorous old Novel.

Thursday Aug^st. 22^d.

In the Morning very much the same kind of weather, but in the afternoon became clear & realy quite warm & pleasant; at noon I walk'd out with M^r. Witts house hunting & call'd on M^r. Stormonth on that subject not at home till quite Dinner time much pleased by a Flat we had seen in S^t. Andrews Square M^r. Stormonth

Francis Braidwood, Edinburgh Cabinet Maker, an etching by John Kay *c.* 1790. Braidwood's Upholstery warehouse was No. 4 South Bridge, West Side.

call'd here in the evening to go with M^r. Witts to visit Professor Playfair,[22] the former return'd here again & staid chatting away for an hour or two.

Friday Aug^st. 23^d.

A fine Day excepting a long & violent storm of hail & rain before noon the afternoon was bright clear but windy & very cold M^r. Witts out a great deal in the Morning, finding out the possession of the favourite house we had seen in S^t. Andrews Square, which was thought most eligible by Messrs. Stormonth & others, walk'd in the evening to take another survey of it, & in several parts of the Town. rec'd a most pleasing Letter from Lady E: B: & wrote to M^rs. Granville.

Saturday Aug^st. 24th.

A good deal of rain & much boisterous wind at many parts of the Day which made staying at home more preferable to me than going out, engaged in many employs much entertainment from the Manor House.

---

22.   John Playfair (1748–1819). In 1785 John Playfair became joint professor of mathematics with Adam Ferguson in the University of Edinburgh, where each session he taught three courses, two of which focused on geometry and trigonometry.

Sunday Aug^{st.} 25th.

No rain the whole Day, & tho at times the air was thick & the wind in the east it was doubtless a fine Day. went to Morning service at our own Chapel Mr. Oliphant call'd on us between the churches, in the afternoon went to St. Andrews Kirk in George Street a very light handsome building, disappointed in not hearing Mr. Maddie the usual good Preacher, but a stranger perform'd the service well, before Tea with all the 3 Boys walk'd round the Carlton Hill felt on my return I had walk'd 5 miles in the course of the Day. rec'd a Letter fr^{m.} Mrs. Buxton

Monday Aug^{st.} 26th.

Still stormy weather, a prodigious hard shower after breakfast but dried soon enough for me to take a walk about the Town before Dinner on some necessary domestic bussinesses, little or no rain in the evening but I kept within hard at work.

Tuesday Augst. 27th.

Dry tho cold & windy, till quite evening, when it was very hard rain & to appearance continued so the greater part of the night: Mr. Professor Playfair here for an hour pleased with his behaviour & manner tho his looks are not prejudiciary,[23] he was very obliging in his attention to Francis's School knowledge. Mr. Witts having a bad cold, Francis & I went to Market in his stead, in the afternoon, we all walk'd over the Mound to the New Town, & attempted in vain to get into our future destined House in St. Andrews Square the Woman not being at home to make up for our disappointment walk'd into the Gardens opposite to Queens Street surprized at their size, got home only just in time to save a wetting, finish'd reading the Manor House, like most books of its kind, it concludes unnaturaly & not well wrote to Mrs. Parsons.

Wensday Aug^{st.} 28th.

Again clear & dry all day but wet & very wet in the evening, Mr. Witts & Francis out in the Morning speculating on many things, & we all went after Dinner, admitting Catherine of the party to make a survey of the house in St. Andrews Square such violent rain came on we were necessitated to come all 6 in a Hackney Coach in our absence a Mrs. Hamilton & one of her Sons, Inhabitants of the Flats[24] under us made us a first visit, work'd & Mr. W. read in the Card a humorous old Novel. wrote to L^{dy.} Ed^{d.} Bentinck[25]

---

23.   It is unclear what Agnes Witts was trying to write here.
24.   The term 'Flat' originated in Scotland. The *Oxford English Dictionary* states that the first recorded use is listed as 1827; this therefore antedates the other first recording by 34 years.
25.   Elizabeth Bentinck, née Cumberland, was the daughter of Richard Cumberland the playwright. For some reason which is obscure, Edward and Agnes were close to Cumberland and effectively 'fostered' and brought up Elizabeth (±1761–1837), who married, 1782, Lord Edward Bentinck (1744–1819), second son of the Duke of Portland and brother of William Henry Cavendish Bentinck who was Prime Minister twice; first April to December 1783; secondly 1807–1809. Agnes and Elizabeth were very close and during the Edinburgh years more than 70 letters go back and forth, but then in July 1798 the letters suddenly stop, and no more is ever heard of Lady Elizabeth; what led to the cessation of correspondence remains a mystery. Clearly a serious breach occurred between the two.

Thursday Aug^{st.} 29th.

Quite a charming Day, the air being mild & soft, with little or no wind, had not been sensible of such pleasant weather for some time; made an unsuccessful visit to our Neighbour Hamiltons they not being at home, walk'd & Francis with us in the Town to several Upholsterers shops &'c, on our return found Mrs. Hamilton very civilly, waiting for us in our parlour as she was leaving Edinbro' tomorrow a hearty, chatty old Gentlewoman. In the evening walk'd over & about Brunsfield Lynn & home a new way by Brunsfield Castle once the residence of Mary of Guise Mother to Mary Queen of Scots & Herriott Hospital. rec'd a charming, long Letter from Mrs. Naper.

Friday Aug^{st.} 30th.

A very rainy Morning, & so continued with much violence till after 12 o'clock & tho not much of any consequence the remainder of the day; it was too damp & wet for one to like to go out; as soon as it at all held up M^{r.} W sallied forth to Leith, as our Letter promised a speedy arrival of our long expected packages where he learnt they must arrive in a very few Days & after dark play'd with the Boys at Cassino. rec'd Letters from Mrs. Witts of Nibley & Miss Louisa Lee, both very pleasing in their different ways.

Saturday Aug^{st.} 31st.

Tolerably fine in the Morning, but began raining by ten o'clock, & continued steadily for 2 or 3 hours & after a very little interruption, a violent Thundershower fell between 3 & 4, tremendous black clouds, very loud claps of thunder, & the most violent rain accompanied by some hail I almost ever saw, the Square was nearly under water tho little more rain fell, it was miserably damp & uncomfortable all the Morning, the Boys & I made ourselves easy to stay at home, much reading & working & wrote to Miss Snow

Sunday Sepr. 1st.

A damp dull looking Morning, & became raining just before church time, which made me go in a Chaise to St. Peters Chappel, Mr. Witts & Francis contrived to get there pretty dry & clear, the service dully performd by Mr. Allan, I staid the Sacrament Father & Son went to evening service at Mr. Cleenes English Chappel in the new Town came back delighted. Rather a long dull Day the evening being so wet & damp there was no stirring out.

Monday Sepr. 2^{d.}

Dry & very fine early in the day, stormy & cloudy with a very disagreable high wind at noon & wet extremely wet in the afternoon & all night. Mr. Witts went to Breakfast with Mr. Oliphant at Leith, where he learnt the Vessel that contain'd all our packages was landed in safety a Joyful hearing, on his return I walk'd with him & Francis to Trotter & Young Warehouse great Upholsterers on a survey well pleased. play'd a little at Cassino with the Boys in the evening.

Tuesday Sepr. 3^{d.}

A very fine dry bright Day, but the wind very disagreably high & boisterous, Mr. Witts & Francis went directly after breakfast to Leith in the hope of finding our 13 cases of packages all landed, which happily was well founded, & after placing them on two Carts they arrived safe at mid. day in Georges Square & much rejoiced was I to see them once more, while they were unloading,

Francis walk'd with me to the fishmarket to buy some for Dinner, as busy as possible all Day with unpacking all we could. Mr Witts wth Mr Stormonth in the afternoon, where he learnt our hopes of the house in St. Andrews Square were all blackd. much vex'd about it.

Wensday Sepr 4.th
Weather much finer being little or no wind, & perfectly dry from Morning to night, as busy as possible getting things to rights hanging pictures &'c, went out at Noon for an hour or two, to Trotters Warehouse about press beds &'c in our absence unfortunately Mr Charteris[26] call'd accompanied by Mr Graham of Fintry & Mr Brown work'd very hard all the afternoon. rec'd a very obliging Letter from Mrs Savage.

Thursday Sepr 5.th
A bright fine Morn: but cold & very autumnal feeling, but soon became very cloudy, & continuing so almost all the Morning prevented the power of seeing the eclipse of the Sun which was to have been visible at noon, more than by being a very dark gloomy Day & in the

An unnamed Edinburgh oyster lass. An etching by John Kay.

afternoon mild quiet air for an hour or two Mr Witts out the greater part of the Morning returning visits, I as busy as possible trying to arrange all our baggage: Mr Stormouth here in the afternoon.

Friday Sepr 6.th
Quite a beautiful bright fine day, tho certainly out of the sun cold air & very autumnal feeling, began early in the day much continued bustle & unpacking, too much in the rough to admit Mr Charteris who call'd again, at noon made myself a little fit to be seen & walk'd up to North Hanover Street to look at a Flat up two pair of stairs wch Mr Witts had seen & was much pleased with & so indeed was I. We still wished we might be able to continue to purchase it Mr Witts went there again in the afternoon taking Mr Stormonth with him on a consultation. wrote to Mrs Naper.

Saturday Sepr 7.th
Rather a stormy day, upon the whole more clouds than sunshine, & at mid.day small rain but dry again in the afternoon, more & more hard work in setting things in order never ceased all Day, remaining from Morn: to night a deshabile Mr Witts admitted Mr Comiss.^r Grieve who call'd in the Morning, heartily glad in the evening to lie down to rest myself on my charming easy new Sopha.

---

26. Francis Charteris, 8th Earl of Wemyss and 4th Earl of March (1772–1853). Francis was the son of Francis and Susan, Lord and Lady Elcho. Agnes Witts's first cousin, Susan Charteris, née Tracy-Keck (1745–1835), married Francis Charteris, Viscount Elcho of Amisfield (1749–1808). Lord Elcho died on 20 January 1808, and his father, Francis Charteris 7th of Wemyss (1723–1808) died on 24 August 1808; he was succeeded by his grandson, Francis—the visitor on the occasion of this diary entry.

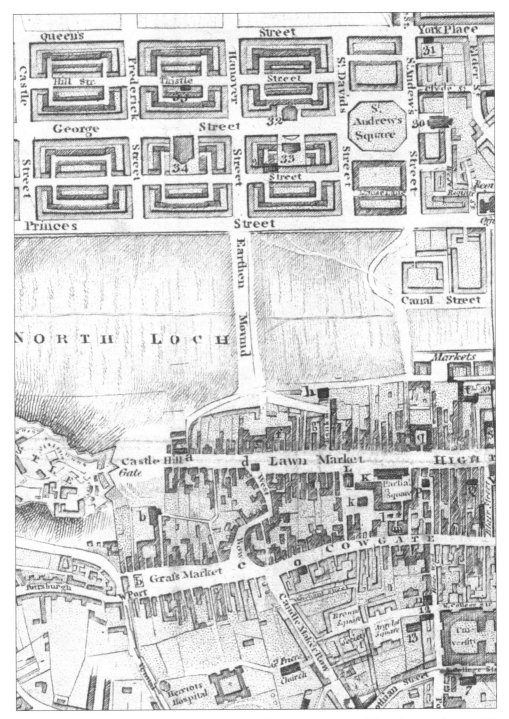

An enlargement from Robert Scott's Map. The Mound in Agnes's time would have been unobstructed. It was formed by dumping around one-and-a half million cartloads of earth excavated from the foundations, cellars etc., of the New Town into the drained Nor Loch. The construction of the Earthen Mound, as it was originally called, commenced in 1781 and continued until about 1830.

Sunday Sepr 8th.

Upon the whole a fine Day, being dry & some sunshine but the wind was so high, it was far from pleasant moving about, went to Morning Service at the New North Kirk to hear M^r. Hardie with whom we were not very highly pleased, & the service very singular, a strange old miserable dirty church & very much crowded, on our return home Miss Halket call'd, I attended her to every service at the new Kirk to hear D^r. Blair all the Boys going with us. M^r. Witts went in a hired chaise with M^r. Professor Playfair to dine at M^r. Grahams at Fentry 5 miles off to meet M^r. Charteris & others & returnd home well pleased with his visit at 9 o'clock neither the Boys or I walk'd out in the evening, but talk'd, read & wrote recd Letters from Mrs. Guydickens, & my Sis^r. Travell & answerd the latter.

Monday Sepr 9th.

A very damp disagreable Day from Morn to night no stirring out for me all day & little pleasure to those that did, I was very indifferent & extremely low in spirits, not able to enjoy the real pleasure I had in receiving a visit from M^r. Charteris who sat an hour with me & was very free open & pleasant & a nice young man in all respects. full of many little bussinesses all day.

Tuesday Sepr 10th.

Quite a delightful change in the weather, being a warm air & constant sunshine. extremely busy till after mid.day with a continuance of unpacking & settling many things, when Mr. W. Francis & I took a short pleasant walk to Queen street &'c not at home ourselves till near Dinner time, in the evening the Boys walk'd alone & we still much engaged.

Wensday Sepr 11th.

Nearly as fine a Day, only rather more clouds & stronger wind, much employment as usual all Morning among the rest, both of us had our hair cut walk'd from two till near 4 part in old & part in new Town, for some little bussiness & some air, in the afternoon, finish'd putting up & framing book shelves.

Witts Family Papers F186

1793

Thursday Sep.ʳ 12ᵗʰ·

A fine mild quiet day without either sun or wind, but I made very little use of it, but going in a Chaise to dine at Mʳ· Comissioner Grieves in Princes Street to meet a large party, consisting besides Mʳ· & Mʳˢ· Grieve of two Miss Kinneurs. Dʳ· Blair, Mʳ· Graham, Mʳ· Oliphant, Mʳ· Clang & a Mʳ· Murhall, a large Dinner & setting out & much civil hospitality, I sat agreable at Dinner between Dʳ· Blair & Mʳ· Graham, two very conversible neighbours & it was upon the whole a pleasant visit returnd home between 8 & 9. rec'd Letters from Miss A: Snow & Miss Forrest.

Friday Sep.ʳ 13ᵗʰ·

Weather still more tame, being so thick an air that it might almost be deemd a fog, & in the evening became small rain or wet mist I never went out of the House the whole day spent chiefly in assisting Mʳ· Witts making paper cases to boxes &c Mʳˢ· Auchinlek call'd in the Morn: while the Boys were gone to pay their devoirs to Lᵈʸ· Cath: Charteries. rec'd a Letter from Miss Louisa Lee.

Saturday Sep.ʳ 14ᵗʰ·

Thick fog quite early in the Morning; but a beautiful bright warm day, from nine to 12, when it again became thick, & so remain'd all day with frequent small rain & mists, I was never out all the day but to Market in the Morning with Mʳ· Witts, very busy making a finish of all our paper works. rec'd a Letter fᵐ· Miss Sheppard.

Sunday Sep.ʳ 15ᵗʰ·

The most intire Day of violent hard rain from Morning till night I ever saw, of course very damp & uncomfortable & quite impossible to stir out even to church Morning or evening, Mʳ· Witts went to our own chappel in the Morning, while I read the service to Boys & Catherine, much reading, some talking & a little sorting of papers &'c to rights. wrote to Lᵈʸ· Elcho & Mʳˢ· Buxton

Monday Sep.ʳ 16ᵗʰ·

A happy change in weather being a very clear fine Day with much sunshine & mild air, tho in the evening there was some errands both in old & new Town, among the rest call'd on Mʳˢ· Anchenlek & invited them to come & drink Tea with us next Day

Tuesday Sep.ʳ 17ᵗʰ·

A mild pleasant Day without any wind & tho there was very little sunshine the light & shade was beautiful to shew off the country that much pleased our eye as we took our walk attended by

Francis Garden (1721–1793),
Lord Gardenstone. An etching
by John Kay.

Francis to Lord Gardinstons Roupe at Morningside,[1] which is about a mile beyond Bruntsfield Linn, where there was to be a sale the next day; we return'd back in part a quite different road & was well pleased, the two M^rs. Auchenleks drank Tea with us, & proved themselves sensible tho singular women, & I hope were well pleased with the visit

Wensday Sepr. 18th.

Very foggy in the Morning & never well clear'd off till after mid.day, at 12 o'clock Papa, Mama & Francis went again to Lord Gardenstons house long before it began, & a strange groupe of purchasers made their appearance, & made it amusing, made a few very trifling bargains, not at home till near 4 much to our surprize M^rs. Home & 2 Daughters from over our heads, made us a visit between 8 & 9, in hopes to teach them better manners to break in at such unseasonable hours, which put a stop to the pleasures of our domestic circle. began reading at least M^r. Witts to me Stewarts History of Mary of Scots.

Thursday Sepr. 19th.

Rather foggy in the Morning early but soon became a charming fine Day till Dinner time when it again grew thick & hazy, accompanied by small trifling rain. very busy the early part of the Morning with arranging some stores not before settled, went out between two & three M^r. Witts with me to survey the High schools to give me an idea of their situation before they again met, well pleased with it, went afterwards into the New Town on some errands. evening spent very pleasingly as usual writting, reading, & working, & conversed with the Boys on a new eligible plan that of each preparing a subject to be thoroughly discuss'd & explain'd by the elders. wrote to Miss Louisa Lee.

---

1. Francis Garden (1721–1793), Lord Gardenstone. Francis was the second son of Alexander Garden of Troup, Banffshire, and Jean, eldest daughter of Sir Francis Grant. A roup was a sale by auction.

Friday Sepr. 20^(th.)

Thick small rain till mid.day when it became dry but was thick & Hazy the remainder of the Day tho tolerably fine tho not enough so to make me have a wish to stir out, but busied myself in many things, Mr Witts (& Francis with him) went to pay some unsuccessful visits. wrote to M^(rs.) Chollet.

Saturday Sepr. 21^(st.)

Quite a fine Day from Morn to night, after being rather foggy early in the Morning, I went with Mr Witts & Francis to Market, the former went to Leith with an idea of breakfasting with Mr Oliphant but he was not at home, much business of various kinds all the Morn & all 5 walk'd before it was near dark to Drink Tea with M^(rs.) Auchenleks, a new Sister introduced to us & also a Mr Steele a Gentleman Friend, a great talker & therefore amusing, the evening being fine & Moon clear by no means dislik'd our walk home at 8 o'clock. rec'd a Letter from Miss Snow.

Sunday Sepr. 22^d.

Having been rain in the night, it was a damp unpleasant Morn: & wetted so much just at Church time that I went in a Chair; but it was dry enough to walk home the Chappel very thin Service perform'd but very moderately by a Stranger, tho it remaind very cold & stormy, & the wind tremendously high I returned to the New Kirk to hear a most excellent sermon from Dr Blair quite delighted with it. wrote to M^(rs.) Savage.

Monday Sepr. 23^d.

After a night of very hard rain it was a pretty fine Morning, but was cloudy at many different periods of the day, & at times small rain or fog fell, which with having a great variety of work to do with my needle took from me the wish of going out the whole Day; spent the evening as usual in I hope a rational way & certainly improving to the Boys.

Tuesday Sepr. 24^(th.)

A visible appearance of having been some thing of a frost, but was a charming bright fine Day, tho when absent from the Sun the air was cold & indeed wind high but when is it not so in Edinburgh; at mid.day I made a short visit to M^(rs.) Home upstairs, nothing striking to trace down to rememberance, after which accompanied by Mr Witts & Francis made an unsuccessfull visit to Miss Hacket after which went into several houses to look at for purchase, not at home till near 4. great pleasure from receiving Letters from M^(rs.) Granville & both my Sisters. wrote to Miss A Snow.

Wensday Sepr. 25^(th.)

A very fine Day, tho not a very clear air & at times quite hot nay even <u>Sultry</u> for Scotland, much a day of disagreable bustles chiefly arising from the illness of Kitty our under Maid, who had been complaining for some Days & now seriously ill with a fever & other complaints; Mr Witts Francis & I took a pleasant walk at Mid.day, on the Dalkeith road as far as Newington, where we went to survey a large place New House, & handsome Kitchen Garden, making by Mr Creighton, The Coachmaker, Hot houses, & Walls, & all in a grand stile, the situation pleasing, & the view beautiful.

Thursday Sepr. 26th.

Much pleasanter day, being a very clear air & uninterrupted sunshine, nothing could be pleasanter, Kitty being very little better, went into a Lodging, hoping soon to be recover'd & return to her place, having poor Catherine sole performer of all offices; accompanied by my two Dear & usual companions, I went to make a call of enquiry on Lady C Charteris & very unexpectedly had an half hour audience to her Bed side, she was wonderfully obliging, & tho a poor emaciated looking Creature from always being in Bed, has been I daresay well looking, the room so dark I could but very little discern her countenance; from John Street we returned over the Carlton Hill, a disagreable climbing road up to it, from Cannongate, the view to the North clear & beautiful. wrote to M^rs. Granville

Friday Sepr. 27th.

Quite an uncommon fine & warm day for walking & nothing about us I did for three hours at mid.day, & before breakfast went to see poor Kitty at her Lodgings who was no better at all; M^r. Witts, Francis & I walk'd thro the Corn Market, round the base of the Castle Rock entering the new Town at the West Church, across Charlotte Square & home by Queen Street &'c looking into several new houses by way of observation, having certainly walk'd 4 miles I was down dead tired when I came home to Dinner. rec'd a great treat in the Morning, by receiving by the Post 20 sides of paper in Letters from Lady Elcho Lady Edward Bentinck & M^rs. Naper. all very interesting at night wrote to my Sister Catherine.

Saturday Sepr. 28th.

If possible a still more charming Day the air being more clear & therefore not so sultry hot, the most constant sunshine, fortunately were not set out on our Noon tide walk when M^r. Charteris call'd on us & was very pleasant, the usual happy trio then set out on their rambles just calling on M^r. Frasier the under Master at the High school, & at M^r. McKeans where all the Boys in future were to learn to write, well pleased with the appearance of both, afterwards walked down the road to Leith, & all round Richmonds Nursery Garden, & return'd home across the Fields by Holyrood House & Cannongate. not a small walk this.

Sunday Sepr. 29th.

Very moderate weather which has unfortunately been the case for many past Sundays, wetting fog early in the day, which never clearly went off, tho it became dry, but was cold & unpleasant, went to Church at our own Chappel in the Morning, service as usual very dully perform'd by M^r. Allan, in a very different manner by M^r. Cleeve, to whose small Chappel we went in the afternoon, his manner is rather too theatrical, but very devout, & strongly commanding attention, & his Sermon most excellent. at night wrote to M^rs. Guydickens.

Monday Sepr. 30th.

Dry & bright, but very cold & windy very busy all the early part of the Morning the Boys went for the first day to M^r. McKeans writting School, on their return we all walk'd, first to take another look & our <u>favorite</u> House in North Hanover Street, which grew more in favor on another survey then to Queen Street new Chappel, to see how it went on & home, evening as usual, domestic, quiet, & pleasant.

South Hanover Street looking towards Princes Street and the Mound. The imposing building facing, the Royal Institution, now the Royal Scottish Academy, was built in 1826, and during Agnes's time in Edinburgh this was presumably open space on the Mound leading to the Old Town.

Tuesday Oct[r.] 1[st.]

Upon the whole a severely tempestuous day, in great measure wet, after mid.day tho chiefly in showers attended by uncommon high wind, I never went out the whole Day, M[r.] Witts sat most part of the Morn. transacting the important bussiness, of almost agreing on the purchase of the house in Hanover Street, a very interesting event; the Boys had all colds Francis a very bad cough.

Wensday Oct[r.] 2[d.]

Again extremely stormy & cold, but in general bright sun, & rain only in very fleeting showers, but I thought it more prudent to keep within all day not being quite stout or well; a memorable Day to the Boys being their first entrance into the High Schools, Francis in the 5[th.] class, the Rectors own, where he gained the 15th seat from the Desk, & the 2 others in the 1st. class M[r.] Frasiers all as happy as possible, & in such spirits with the hope of getting forwards it was delightful to see them. rec'd a pleasing Letter from M[rs.] Parsons.

Thursday Oct[r.] 3[d.]

Weather no better still very cold & stormy no sun but thick air amounting at times to small rain, yet not having been out for two Days I ventured to walk into the New Town, call'd at Mess[rs.] Trotter &'c to order the Boys Beds &'c, rather caught in rain before we could get home, a chearful evening from the mirth of the Boys recounting their school adventures; continued to be amused by Stewarts History of Queen Mary of Scots rec'd a Letter from Miss Snow.

Friday Oct. *4th.*

The same stormy unpleasant weather, thick air but no rain, M.[r] Allan the Minister (one of them) of S.[t] Peters Chappel call'd here in the Morning, after which M.[r] W. & I walk'd confined ourselves mostly to the streets to be shelter'd from the wind, went into Canongate Church, a fine old building much remains of royal grandeur. no variety in spending the Evening.

Saturday Oct. *5th.*

Again very stormy but rather a more mild air & at mid.day a hard shower for half an hour I went to Morning Service (previous to the Sacrament) at our own Chappel a very small congregation of all females afterwards M.[r] W. & I call'd on M.[r] & M.[rs] Thornton in our new House in Hanover Street, by way of introducing ourselves as their Landlords, only she at home from whom little could be learnt, overtaken by the rain & so wet before I could get home, I was obliged to change much of my dress a tiresome business. wrote to Miss Forrest.

Sunday Oct. *6th.*

A much better day the wind still high & cold, but constant sunshine & of course clear air, went to Church in the Morning to our own Chappel where M.[r] Webster did the Duty I staid the Sacrament, went to evening service at S.[t] Andrews Kirk again disappointed in not having M.[r] Maddie, service but moderately performed by a Stranger

Monday Oct. *7th.*

A very indifferent day being both cold & stormy tho dry, at times the wind so very high as to make a most wearing tiresome sound, M.[r] Witts went to Leith in the Morning early meaning to breakfast wth M.[r] Oliphant who not being at home he broke his fast with Captain Ritchie whose Vessel brought our baggage from England I never thought of stirring out having much of the Rhumatism & sadly out of spirits into the bargain rec'd a Letter from M.[rs] Buxton.

Tuesday Oct. *8th.*

A thick wetting fog or small rain early in the Morning, which in some degree clear'd of before Noon, but still remain'd damp the whole day, & very windy again at night, I was fearful of venturing out, but employ'd myself well in working, reading, & writting. M.[r] & M.[rs] Thomson <u>our</u> <u>new</u> Tenants in Hanover Street call'd on us found him a very pleasant Man much of a Gentleman. wrote to M.[rs] Naper.

Wensday Oct. *9th.*

Not much better weather in the Morning enough so at Noon to lend me to go out having been shut up for two Days but it was damp & unpleasant & dirty to a disagreable degree M.[r] Simpson call'd on us in the Morn. & when we walk'd we only stroll'd into the New Town & when we could find it most clear & dry. evening as usual wrote a very long Letter to Lady Edward Bentinck

Thursday Oct. *10th.*

Bright & fine early in the Morning, but soon became cloudy, yet it remain'd dry, mild & pleasant at Noon I sallied forth, first to call on M.[rs] Morrison in Bucclugh Place just return'd to Town & afterwards to call on Lady Catherine Charteris, with whom I found her Nephew a pleasant half hours visit afterwards by way of exercise walk'd in the New Town in our absence Comissioner & Mrs. Grieve call'd here

Friday Octr. 11th.

A very moderate Day being for the greater part of it extremely damp & foggy & at others hard rain, no kind of temptation to me to think of stirring out, busy in arranging the Boys new Beds & other domestic bussiness & evening spent as ever.

Saturday Octr. 12th.

Very fine Day after a Night of hard rain quite mild, nay almost oppressively hot for the season, after a variety of bussiness early in the Day, being half holiday we took the Boys out with us to walk, & finding it very dirty, contented ourselves with merely strolling in Queen Street & in the Nursery Garden there; a chearful evening by making our Boys happy by inviting three of their friends Oglevie, Horner, & George Simpson to drink Tea & spend the evening in a variety of sports, in wch we join'd.

Sunday Octr. 13th.

A very pleasant clear Day, with a mixture of sun & shade & clear & dry, went to Service in the Morning at our own Chappel, very ill perform'd by an affected Stranger walk'd in the Square & its vicinity the greater part of the time between the Churches, went to the Town Church to the evening Service, attended by Miss Simpson & her Brother George to hear their Father Preach & sat in their Seat. a good useful discourse & prayers, but not a happy manner a handsome Church & very well attended.

Monday Octr. 14th.

A dry fine Day but extremely windy & rather cold. went out rather early in the day drawn by the hearing of a Roup at a House in Princes Street but so bad a collection of things were not tempted to stay a minute, found it not pleasant enough to stay out very long. Miss Browns visited here in my absence.

Tuesday Octr. 15th.

Not so good a day being damp & cloudy as well as windy, which but too well accorded with my feelings which were low & miserable, very much arising from receiving a very unpleasing Letter from Mrs. Tyrwhitt who I little thought capable of wishing to give pain walk'd all round the walks which did me good, with Mr. Witts & all the Boys who as usual read to us in the German Gil Blas, rather humorous. rec'd a Letter from Mrs. Tyrwhitt.

Wensday Octr. 16th.

Something of the same kind of weather only rather more of a drying air, walk'd at mid.day as usual into the New Town, going into two or three large Houses in St. Andrews Square wch with their Furniture were on Sale, were but just return'd home when we were visited by a Mr. Maitland, Son of General Maitland, & residing in West Lothian 9 miles distant recommended to our acquaintance by the Lee's of Totteridge a very pleasant agreable Man. M^{r.} & Mrs. Home their Son & eldest Daughter from above Stairs drank Tea with us queer people but the Men better than the Women.

Thursday Oct[r.] 17[th.]

A very uncommon fine Day for the time of Year, quite mild nay indeed hot with constant sunshine at Noon I went to visit M[rs.] & Miss Brown in the Square w.[ch] answer'd wonderfully, the Mother being quite an agreable Woman & very polite & obliging. M[r.] Witts join'd me in making unsuccessful visits to Comissioner Grieve & M[rs.] Grieve, & to Lady Catherine Charteris who was too indifferent to receive us.

Friday Oct[r.] 18[th.]

Much change in the weather, being dark, stormy & very cold, and at times much appearance of rain, being busy writting all Morning we did not go out till two o'clock when we walk'd to the very end of Princes Street quite to the Turnpike, & home by the back part of the Town thro Westport Street Corn Market &'c quite a new round wrote to M[rs.] Callander[2] & M[rs.] Witts, Nibley House.

Saturday Oct[r.] 19[th.]

Much such another Day but still dry breakfasted early & afterwards attended M[r.] Witts to Market, a busy Morn: but found time before Dinner to walk with the Boys on the walks almost blown away. M[r.] Witts dined up stairs with M[r.] Simpson meeting 4 other Gentlemen not very gay & he was at home quite early. began reading a singular Book call'd Allexanders History of Women.[3] well amused by it.

Sunday Oct[r.] 20[th.]

Still cold & stormy, & wet between 3 & 4 & so remain'd the greater part of the evening, Went as usual to Morning Church at our own Chappel where M[r.] Webster did the Duty well walk'd in the Square before we went to the New Kirk, where instead of D[r.] Blair the Service was perform'd by a M[r.] Macnight a Preacher at Leith who both in Prayers & Sermon was most extremely good & to be liked caught in the Shower before we could get home, obliged to get into a Chair in the Street M[r.] Witts taken so suddenly ill in his stomach & bowels imediately after Dinner as sadly to alarm me, evening spent wholly in attendance on him. rec'd a Letter from my Sister Travell long expected.

Monday Oct[r.] 21[st.]

Quite a Winterlike day, hard rain attended by a constant thick fog from Morn to Night, fit for nothing but sitting by the fireside & attending my poor Husband who continued very far

---

2. John Callandar (1739–1812), of Westerton, Stirling and Preston Hall, Edinburgh. John's younger brother, Alexander (1741–1792) had made a fortune in India, and bought Preston Hall in 1789. Alexander died unmarried, and John inherited the property. John Callandar had served in the army, but his military career came to a halt at the end of the American war. He was MP for Berwick-on-Tweed, 1795–1802 and again 1806–07. He married, 1783, Margaret, née Romer of Cherwick, Northumberland, widow of Bridges Kearney.

3. *The History of Women. From the Earliest Antiquity, to the Present Time; Giving Some Account of almost every interesting Particular concerning that Sex, among all Nations, ancient and modern.* William Alexander MD in Two Volumes. 1779.

from well; luckily arrived to our aid the new Novel of Rosina written by Lady E: Butler which interested us much,[4] the Boys wet sops going & returning from school. wrote to M^rs. Buxton.

Tuesday Octr. 22^d.

Very little change in the weather being alike confining, less rain but more fog, which made it both damp & cold, thank God M^r. Witts better but not quite convalescent. much enlivened by a very propitious Post receiving Letters from M^rs. C: Western, Miss Louisa Lee & a most delightful one from M^r. Burslem which did owed it to the goodness of his heart as much as it pleased me. wrote to Miss Snow.

Wensday Octr. 23^d.

A very fine Day to make amends for 2 such gloomy ones, constant sunshine &, as usual brisk wind, which help'd in some degree to dry up the extreme dirt; went out rather early, first to Lady C. Charteris with whom I sat an hour realy pleasantly as she was peculiarly chearful & always most obliging, her Nephew there a little while afterwards walk'd in the new Town for air & cleanness M^r. Witts dined at M^r. Herris in this Square meeting the same party & others he had met at M^r. Simpsons, as thank God he was got quite well again. found Rosina begin to grow dull & tiresome. rec'd Letters from M^rs. Callander & Miss A. Snow.

Thursday Octr. 24th.

So very indifferent a day, of fog, small rain & high wind I had no wish to go out of the House & always find enough to do & employ myself in much reading working & writting, writting a very interesting one to M^rs. Tyrwhitt, & a very long one to my Sis^r. Travell.

Friday Octr. 25th.

Tolerably bright & fine early in the day but soon became absence; & as wet & disagreable a one as any of the former this week, prevented an engagement at the House in Hanover Street about some proposed alterations, & I thought myself scarce of being by the fireside all day, but on M^r. Witts's return from St. Georges new Chappel in Queen Street where the Seats were this day to be set & appropriated, he judged it necessary for me to go up in a Chair to determine which I did, I found it a fine long swing & was pretty well satisfied with our destination

Saturday Oct. 26th.

Fine early in the Morning wet & stormy till Noon, when it became very bright & fine till between 2 & 3 when a violent & long storm came on & was afterwards fine again: It being so fine I was tempted to accompany M^r. Witts & Boys on a walk to Calton Hill, the storm overtook us just as we got to the Bridewell, but we took shelter in a House upon the Hill before it became very hard so was little the worse, very hospitably rec'd by an old Woman who offer'd us a dram to comfort us, obliged to return home in a Hackney Coach the torrents

---

4. *Rosina: A Novel* by the Author of *Delia, an Interesting Tale*, in five volumes. 1793. Mary Pilkington, née Hopkins (1766–1839). This is probably the novel Agnes and Edward were reading. It is not clear why she believes it to be by Lady E. Butler. Novels at that period did not usually carry the names of the authors; the fashion was for the authors to remain anonymous.

Princes Street with the commencement of the building of the Royal Institution. A painting by Alexander Nasmyth, 1825. This view would not have been that unfamiliar to Agnes and Edward Witts. Nelson's monument would not have been on Calton Hill, but apart from that there would not have been vast change.

both above & below were so great. Mʳ· Professor Playfair drank Tea here, & by much agreable conversation made the evening pass very pleasantly. expected Mʳ· Simpson & his family but they were prevented.

Sunday Octʳ· 27ᵗʰ·

A very fine Day excepting extreme high wind, & a very small shower after evening service which frightened us to take shelter in a Hackney Coach on the Bridge tho it brought us home by sunshine. went to Morning service at our own Chappel where Mʳ· Allan was more than ordinary dull, which made Mʳ· Cleeve appear peculiarly brilliant in the afternoon where we all went, a most capital Sermon. rec'd a Letter fᵐ· Mʳˢ· Naper.

Monday Octʳ· 28ᵗʰ·

Having been something of a frost in the night it was bright & very fine till past Noon when it became cold & stormy, with strong appearance of rain but none of any consequence fell, being kept off by the violence of the wind. It proved a Morning of much visiting & many engagements commencing with a civil call from Mʳˢ· Auchenlek, to whom succeeded Major & Mʳˢ· Callander from Preston Hall in their smart Post Chaise & four whose behaviour was as obliging as ever to me, & promised to be still more so in future; when they went an unexpected visit from Mʳˢ· Craggie commenced, who came to acknowledge the civilities shewn to her Son on account of his accident a lively pleasant mannerd Woman & bid fair to prove an agreable acquaintance. Mʳ· Witts & I then set forth accompanied by Mʳ· Simpson to see our new House in Hanover Street where we were engaged to survey an intended alteration, found Mʳ· Thompson obliging & pleasant on our return home shew'd Mʳ· S Sᵗ· Georges Chappel & return'd only just before Dinner, blown almost away Mʳ· Simpson & his Son George drank Tea here, altogether I was compleatly knock'd up by the events of the day.

Tuesday Octr 29th.

Wet in the Morning, dry at Noon, & wet again in the afternoon. Mr Witts out a little in the Morning, I was glad to keep quiet to make up for the hurries of yesterday heard much of Rosina which began to be very interesting & did a great deal of work.

Wensday Octr 30th.

Wet & foggy in the Morning, but clear'd at Noon & there was a little sunshine, but still it was so damp & chill, that it was most bitterly cold & very dirty moving, I returnd Mrs Craggies visit, & went afterwards with Mr Witts to Lord Eliocks[5] sale in St Andrews Square a great crowd of people bought nothing return'd home quite starved much working, reading, & talking in the evening.

Thursday Octr. 31st.

Rather a moist Morning, tolerably dry at Noon, but cold & windy, Mr Stormonth here for an hour or more in the Morning quite glad to see the old creature again after his long absence, walk'd in the New Town look'd in again at Ld Eliocks sale bought an old fashioned slate Table for the Boys, drank Tea up Stairs with Mrs. Home, no one there excepting a Miss Field but their own large family an odd visit, bad singing, some reel dancing, & much strange conversation.

Friday Novr 1st.

A very sharp frost for one night & very cold indeed tho much sun, went out early to accompany Mrs. Auchenleks to the Roman Catholick Chappel All Saints being a great festival in their Church. a long uninteresting Sermon from their Bishop, High Mass, & the communion service of Sacrament administerd to four persons only, by a Priest much decorated in shewey vestments, the service lasted 2 hours, & did not raise my ideas of the Popish Religion laying so much stress on ceremony; return'd home to eat, & set forth again to walk, which we did on Princes Street parade for the sake of sun, all drank Tea w.th Mr Simpson up stairs quite an impromptu, friendly, chatty, & pleasant.

Saturday Novr 2^{d.}

Another frosty night & was a bitter cold day tho by change of wind it became a damp thawing air & in the evening wet, very wet. I went to Morning Prayers at our own Chappel, call'd on Miss Browne afterwards a lively visit afterwards walk'd in the Town with Mr Witts & Francis to have a tooth pull'd out for him by Mr Spence concluded the evening by accompts.

Sunday Novr 3^{d.}

After a night of hard rain, it was a tolerable bright fine Day one only shower at Noon, but very wet again in the afternoon or rather evening, went to Chapel as usual, afterwards went in Mrs. Craggie's Coach, attended by two of her Sons & our own three to Leith to see a Whale that had been caught & kill'd in the Firth of Forth near Queenferry, three were seen at the same

---

5.   James Veitch (1712–1793), Lord Eliock. James Veitch was a well-respected judge, with a scholarly bent. He was appointed a commissioner for the forfeited estates in 1767, a deputy governor of the Royal Bank of Scotland in 1776, and appointed the following year as commissioner for fisheries and manufactures.

place the other two escaped, this was call'd a very small one only 32 feet long, a very wonderful object to look on being nearly high water we were unable to examine it so minutely as could be wish'd. return'd just in time for evening service which we attended at a new Seceeding Chappel near the new College, Mʳ Struthers a very popular Preacher. a prodigeous crowd or else should have been well gratified. rec'd a Letter from Miss Snow & wrote to Mʳˢ Naper.

Monday Novʳ 4th.

Clear & fine till after mid.day when it became lowering & some small pretensions to rain, which were fullfill'd in the afternoon, Mʳ Witts walk'd to Leith to Breakfast with Mʳ Oliphant & take a last look at the Whale. Francis remain'd at home with me being unwell in his Stomach I was fearful of his going to School. Miss Browns call'd here, extreme well behaved young Women, when they went I went out to walk in the Town on some errands accompanied by Husband & Son

Tuesday Novʳ 5th.

Quite a sharp frost, & very bitterly cold, the fog never well going off, the whole of the day tho the Sun made strong efforts, very busy all Morning in preparing to go to Coll: Calanders at Preston House 10 miles distant, &, 4 from Dallkeith, where we set off for in a hired Chaise at 2 o'clock, was excellent, & country fine much astonish'd to see it so good, Dalkeith a pretty town standing on an eminence, close to which is the Duke of Bucclugh & we went within view of a Seat of the Marquess of Lothians & all so of Lord Somervilles, Preston Hall is a prodigeous fine place in embryo House not enough finish'd to be habitable, our friends residing in a Cottage at ½ a miles distance, but never Cottage exhibited more splendor of mind hospitably, they rec'd us with much friendship, a Mʳ & Mʳˢ Dewar, & a Miss Rait with them, dined there lively going people, supt also & staid till a late hour, play'd at Bragge with some success.

Wensday Novʳ 6th.

After having been a severe night of rain it clear'd off to be a chearful fine Day with constant sunshine quite uncommonly fine for the season, after an excellent Breakfast, we sallied forth on a walk to survey Preston Hall,[6] but so great was the wet & dirt, I was soon compleatly wet thro my feet but was amused & pleased with the view of the place & the expectation of what it would be much interesting conversation with Mʳˢ Callander during our walk. a Morning visit from a Mʳˢ Keir & to Dinner came Lady Dalrimple Sʳ Johns wife Sister & Daughter,[7] a Mʳ & Mʳˢ Falconer, Capᵗⁿ Maitland Broʳ to Lord Lauderdale an uncommon agreable Man & Mʳ Dewar again sumptious Dinner & &'c as is always. Bragge playing to a few, with bad success to me, the whole party supt, much pleasant singing afterwards not in Bed till between 2 & 3.

---

6. Alexander Callander hired London-based architect Robert Mitchell to design a replacement house at Preston Hall and the foundation stone was laid on 18 March 1791. Alexander Callander died the following year, and the house was completed in 1800 by his brother John (later Sir John Callander, 1st baronet).

7. John Dalrymple (1726–1810), 4th baronet, baron of the Court of Exchequer 1776–1807. He married, 1760, his cousin Elizabeth Hamilton.

Thursday Novr. 7th.

An open day without frost but not so fine as the former one, being cold & stormy & some trifling showers. Left Briesey Back between 12 & one after having seen much solicted to extend our visit & attend our Friends to Dine at Mr. Dewars but we had order'd our Chaise & wanted to be at home with our Boys, was much pleased with our drive home, the country appearing to advantage; found the Boys well & happy. rec'd a delightful affectionate Letter from Lady Edward Bentinck.

Friday Novr. 8th.

Foggy damp & cold but no rain, busy early in the day, at Noon attended by the two eldest Boys the Preachings occasioning some Days holidays, I went to call on Lady C: Charteris who I found kind & obliging as ever & presented me with a very pretty pink Latten Letter case of her own making, & introduced the two Sons of her next Door Neighbor Mrs. Moray to my Sons, extended our walk a little into the New Town. at night wrote to Lady Elcho.

Saturday Novr. 9th.

Much such another day still dry but very very cold went with Mr. Witts at 2 o'clock to the New Kirk, there being general service throughout the whole Town, it being the preparation for the general communion the next day. the service perform'd by Mr. Macnight who we had heard before, & was again much pleased with him, his Sermon masterly, & his last prayer peculiarly fine did not return home till almost dark. the Boys went to our own Chappel wrote to Miss Louisa Lee

Sunday Novr. 10th.

One of the most violent & severe days of rain from Morn: to Night I ever saw in my life attended by a tremendous high wind blowing a constant storm, went in a Hackney Coach to the Town Church, where Mr. Simpson had engaged Seats for us in the Marquess of Tweedales Loft that we might be Spectators of the administrating of the Sacrament according to the mode of the established Church of Scotland, a most crowded Church very good Prayers & Sermon from Mr. Simpson, who was assisted in the Ceremony by Dr. Hunter & three other Ministers; the whole of the ordinance was perform'd in a very Serious & elevating manner, & to a number far beyond expectation as before we left the Church at 2 o'clock 500 had rec'd the Communion; evening spent as most Sundays are I trust not improperly. rec'd a Letter from Miss Anne Snow & wrote to Miss Sheppard.

Monday Novr. 11th.

Quite a perfect dry day, having been a frost in the night, & a sharp North wind, a little sun but a great tendency to fog & very cold, I never went out, having much to do & to think on, my spirits very low & much agitated, by the confirmation of Mrs. Eliza Tracys death,[8] & receiving all the particulars of it in a Letter from Betty Guydickens. rec'd a Letter also from Mrs. Granville, wrote to Miss B. Guydickens & Mrs. Parsons.

---

8.   Eliza Tracy was a maiden maternal aunt of Agnes Witts who lived at Sandywell Park, near Cheltenham.

Tuesday Novr 12th.

Again Frost attended with some fog, which never clearly went off, tho the Sun made strong efforts, it was excellent walking tho rather cold; at mid.day I as usual walk'd with M^r. Witts, call'd at some shops & went into a poor Roup on the Leith Walk; an unusual Fair held in Queen Street at the Corner of S^t. Andrews Square, a great crowd but apparently little bussiness some Cattle to be traficked for. very busy getting my Black cloathes in order. at night severe rain & wind again rec'd a Letter from Miss Gorges.

Wensday Novr 13th.

A very miserable day of wind & rain, little better than Sunday last of course an intire Stay at home day, not ill suited to my numerous employs went into Mourning for my much valued Friend & Aunt M^rs. Elizabeth Tracy, of whose Death, Funeral & Wite^9 I had a very particular account in a long informing Letter from my Sister Travell. the Boys getting thro their eveng. lessons in good time we treated them with a Game at Cassino. wrote to Miss Anne Snow –

Thursday Novr 14th.

Foggy, damp & disagreable in the Morn: tolerable at Noon, but wet very soon after I went to call on M^rs. Craggie to congratulate her on her recovery then went with M^r. Witts & Catherine also, to shew her the House in Hanover Street, & survey the alterations that had been making, did not find M^r. or M^rs. Thomson at home, severely caught in the rain but with the help of an Umbrella & Boots, braved both rain & extreme dirt.

Friday Novr 15th.

Nearly as bad a day in the Morning frost, but grew rather less foggy & damp towards Noon, the eldest Miss Brown sat here an hour, & shew'd herself to be a well inform'd interesting well behaved young Woman, when she went we attempted to walk, pick'd up two of the Boys on their return from School & walk'd them to the New Town not at home till near Dinner. wrote a very long Letter to my Sister Travell.

Saturday Novr 16th.

Of this Day little can be said in any respect, at least in praise, for it was wet & foggy with high wind, my spirits were not very high, & of course I had no idea of stirring from the fireside but as usual much employ'd & at night wrote to M^rs. Granville.

Sunday Novr 17th.

After a most tremendous night of Wind & Rain the Morning wore a very unpromising appearance but not absolutely raining we sallied forth on foot accompanied by the two eldest Boys, to the New Chappel in Queen Street which was open'd this day overtaken by rain before we got there; a very beautiful building & very suitably fitted up in the inside, it was not very full & before the service begun at the Communion Table, M^r. Cleeve read a kind of conservation Prayer or address in which he was join'd by 4 of the principal proprietors Lord

---

9. Wite — an archaic word defined as: 'to go away', 'to depart', 'to perish'.

Aboyne one, no Sermon after Church made an unsuccessful visit to Miss Halkett & pass'd the rest of the time till evening service at M^rs. Thomsons in North Hanover Street, much pleased with a peculiar well adapted Sermon from M^r. Cleeve on the opening of the Chappel expressive of much grateful feeling, stump'd home as fast as possible when it was nearly dark M^r. Witts again attack'd by a complaint in his bowels which made him quite ill for some hours.

Monday Novr. 18th.

Thick & foggy & rather wetting in the Morning, dry & more clear at Noon, & afternoon but I had had enough of wet & dirt the day before to have any desire to stir out of the House M^r. Witts got pretty well again & went out a little M^r. Charteris here in the Morning for a few minutes.

Tuesday Novr. 19th.

Very much the same kind of weather only worse being at times hard rain & miserably damp & uncomfortable, no idea of going downstairs some gratification by receiving from Preston hall some Game & a roasting Pig in Col: Callanders Cart. work'd hard at plain work & wrote to Lady Edward Bentinck

Wensday Novr. 20th.

Again the same gloomy damp weather but grew rather better at Noon the sun making some faint attempts to shew itself, quite tired of confinement I made a trial of encountering the dirt, but first & M^r. Witts with me went to call on M^rs. Brown where we met a M^rs. Dundas, afterwards call'd on L^dy. Catherine Charteris who as usual was full of kindness & then walk'd in Princes Street in the hope of being clean but in vain. my Dear Francis had so very bad a cold and cough that he was obliged to come home from School at Noon to be Nursed.

Thursday Novr. 21st.

No change of weather, only the air some what more drying but still equally gloomy & in the afternoon the fog wonderfully thick & dark to a very uncommon degree; my Dearest Boy rather better but yet it was necessary to keep home from School & nurse him incessantly with warm liquids. M^r. Stormonth here in the Morning. at Noon M^r. Witts & I walk'd on the Walks in the Square & adjacent streets for an hour & took a survey for the first time of the Assembly room at night play'd at Cassino with the Boys.

Friday Novr. 22^d.

Little or no difference in the weather, hardly quite so gloomy a sky as some past days, & rather drier walking but still a most unpleasant thick air Francis better consequently able to go to School, M^rs. Auchenlek here in the Morning, M^r. Witts & I walk'd late on the old Parade, Princes Street, I was very indifferent in the evening & my spirits much hurried.

Saturday Novr. 23^d.

Rather a damper air & of course a more unpleasant Day yet still I braved it, & walk'd in the streets & with the Boys on several errands tho very far from well in the Morning, better in the evening which was spent in the accustomed manner; had the delight of receiving a Letter of 11 sides from M^rs. Naper rich in events & interesting anecdotes.

Sunday Novr. 24th.

Again thick air, but tolerably dry tho as usual dark & gloomy, all 5 went to our town Chapel in the Morning, & the service was very dully perform'd by M^r. Allen, quite otherwise by M^r. Cleeve at S^t. Georges Chappel where M^r. Witts & I went in the evening a large congregation, & a most clever & well adapted Sermon for the purpose of a collection to raise Money for flannel Waistcoats for the soilders[10] abroad, the collectors Lord Aboyne & 3 or 4 others.

Monday Novr. 25th.

More disagreable weather than ever being at times small rain & constant thick fog which made it so dark even at mid.day I could scarce see to work & had no of temptation to stir from the fireside had it it been a better day my Dear Companion being gone to take his long intended ride to call on M^r. Maitland at Clifton Hall in West Lothian, 10 miles off which took up the whole of the Morn: but being most obligingly rec'd it was well spent. I was very low & poorly the whole day.

Tuesday Novr. 26th.

No rain or else very much the same kind of uncomfortable confining day, even M^r. Witts went out very little, kindly reading much to me in the Trial of the poor Queen of France & other things, this of all subjects did not tend to raise my spirits which were at a sad low ebb indeed. got no Letters from England.

Wensday Novr. 27th.

Something of a clearer & better day in the early part of it but very little, & in the evening & Night hard rain. M^r. Charteris call'd in the Morning to settle about only being introduced to the Duchess of Atholl, I walk'd in the New Town merely for exercise being quite house sick, & in the evening went to Cards & Supper at M^rs. Browns, a party of 16 as many Gentlemen as Ladies lively & pleasant enough a Table at Vingt'un & whist at which I play'd several rubbers, not at home till between 12 & one strange raking for us.

Thursday Novr. 28th.

Weather very similar still damp & foggy & very dirty from the rain, M^r. Charteris here again in the Morning on the same bussiness as the former Morning. We walk'd on the Walk, & in the Square merely for exercise late, M^r. Simpson join'd us. prevented going to the Abbey as was engaged by the Dutchess of Atholl's being ill not sorry.

Friday Novr. 29th.

Rather a clearer air than some past Days, but yet damp & dreadfully dirty moving about yet being more tolerable overhead, I sallied forth accompanied by M^r. W. to call on L^dy. C: C. who was too unwell to receive us, we stroled into the New Town in quest of adventures & cleanness but rather barren in either & came home quite tired in our absence Lord Adam Gordon & M^r. Charteris call'd leaving a Card for the Duttchess. wrote to M^rs. Naper.

---

10. *Sic.*

A watercolour, dated 1827, attributed to Samuel Dukinfield Swarbreck, after a drawing by John Wilson Ewbank.

Saturday Novr. 30th.

Still thick air & very uncomfortably damp so much so I had no temptation to stir out; had full bussiness with my usual occupations, added to which the Nursing of Francis with a very bad cough & cold which kept him from School, the eruption that appeard upon George the night before declared by Mr. Wood to be the Chicken Pox but he was so well it was needless to keep him at home at night Francis had also some spots come out. Mr. Witts & I at seven in the evening went in a Hackney to fullfil our engagement at the Abbey, met with a most gracious reception from the Dutchess of Atholl & Lord Adam Gordon[11] with whom besides Mr. Charteris we found a small but agreable party a Table at Cribbage at wch I play'd 4 rubbers, returnd home well pleased between nine & ten rec'd Letters from Lady Ed^{wd.} Bentinck, Miss Anne Snow Mrs. Buxton & Miss Elizabeth Guydickens.

Sunday Decr. 1st.

Happily a hoar Frost, with a clear North air in the Morning, but soon the fog got the better of the sun, & at night it raind a little, poor Francis very unwell with a severe sprinkling of the

---

11. Adam Gordon (±1726–1801). Adam Gordon was a younger son of Alexander Gordon, 2nd Duke of Gordon and Lady Henrietta Mordaunt. He entered the army, fought in the Seven Years War and was MP for Aberdeenshire 1754–1768 and Kincardineshire 1774–1788. In 1767 he married Jean Murray, née Drummond (d. 1795), Dowager Duchess of Atholl. Adam Gordon was appointed Commander-in-Chief in Scotland in 1789 and promoted general in 1793. Following his resignation from Parliament Gordon became closely connected with Henry Dundas and the Duke of Gordon in Scottish politics.

disorder George likewise confined by a dose; We went to our own Chappel in the Morning & staid the Sacrament before our return M^rs. Macqueen, M^rs. Craigie, & M^r. Oliphant call'd here, went to Evening service at the New Church, service dully perform'd by M^r. Grenfield a very quiet spiritless evening from my having a very bad cold & cough & the Boys but moderate.

Monday Decr. 2nd.

No frost but a tolerable fine day till past noon when it became a thick foggy rain & at night hard rain, my Cough so bad I breakfasted in Bed my two <u>most</u> beloved companions attending upon me Francis very full indeed of the disorder. George return'd from School the happiest of Boys having become Dux[12] of his class; rising 92 the number he was drawn, in a day more than a fortnight.

Tuesday Decr. 3^d. Wensday, Decr. 4th. & Thursday 5th.

So little pass'd from my being quite ill with a violent cough & cold attended by a little fever & several unpleasant symptoms that I never rose till mid.day, & was little able to be off the Sopha afterwards, of course nearly incapable of employing myself; my Dear Companions anxiously kind & attentive to me; Francis so well recoverd that on Thursday he went to School for the first time, the first Day damp & foggy the two next trifling frosts, which produced bright fine Days with constant sunshine

Friday Decr. 6th.

The Morning set in much like the two last but became cloudy & damp at noon & raind in the evening I was considerably better owing to a medicine of M^r. Woods & began to think better of myself attempted to take an airing in a Hackney Coach, but it proved a mere attempt as for half a Crown the Man would take us little more than an half hours drive, & that in & about the Town M^r. Witts receiving a most unpleasant Letter from my Bro^r. Ferdinand spoilt our tranquillity

Saturday Decr. 7th.

Miserable change in the weather being again very thick fog, & small rain, which made me feel much less well yet still I purposed going to the Abbey[13] to dine where we had been engaged for a week tho the preparation for it, & going in a damp Hackney Coach almost overset me & much increased my Cough yet we made a most pleasant easy visit met there besides themselves M^r. Charteris, & the three other Military attendants, a M^r. & M^rs. Hamilton & with them a Miss Scott, & also a Miss Imrie, an entertainment in a very handsome stile, & yet with a great degree of comfort & pleasantry, & much kind & painted civility shewn to us, a Table at Whist & Cribbage both sixpences, at home soon after nine; our Boys had drank Tea with some school fellows & friends of the Simpsons. rec'd Letters from M^rs. Savage & my Sister Travell

Sunday Decr. 8th.

Quite a miserable day in all respects the weather being dreadful, almost uninterrupted rain the whole day attended by a thick, & so dark it was difficult to see at mid.day, & my Cough

---

12. Dux—the head pupil in a class.
13. The Abbey of Holyroodhouse.

&'c so much worse I was little able to set up or of course employ myself, which did not mend my Companions not one of whom stirr'd out of the House the whole Day. wrote to Miss: B. Guydickens

Monday Dec.ʳ 9ᵗʰ· & Tuesday Dec.ʳ 10ᵗʰ·
Were both so much alike in thick damp & wet dark weather, & in the continuance of my bad Cough & other uncomfortable symptoms they are by no means worth seperating & nobody calling the scene was in no respect varied but that happily I was so far better as to be able to work & employ myself & on Tuesday wrote to Sisᵗ· Travell.

Wensday Dec.ʳ 11ᵗʰ·
Very small change in any events the weather continuing, damp, wet, & gloomy, & my cold little if any better, no one call'd, Mᵗ· Witts walk'd a little in the Morning, & spent two hours in the evening at the Abbey, having obtain'd a copy of a Chaplains License for the Dutchess of Atholl. wrote to Miss Snow.

Thursday Dec.ʳ 12ᵗʰ·
A wretched day, being mostly hard rain as well as thick fog, if anything I was less well than the day before & begin to be heartily sick of my long confinement, my Dear Francis not quite well in head & stomach hoped to cure him by an Emetic. rec'd a very long Letter from Miss Snow & wrote to Lady Edward Bentinck.

Friday Dec.ʳ 13ᵗʰ·
If possible a worse day than any former one being severe rain the greater part of the day, in the evening the wind rose & the Moon was clearer like the weather grew worse rather than better happily Francis quite well Mᵗ· Witts out calling on Mʳˢ· Halket &'c. Mᵗ· Simpson call'd on me. wrote to Mʳˢ· Granville.

Saturday Dec.ʳ 14ᵗʰ·
Somewhat a better day, being dry, & the air not quite so thick but rain again in the evening, my feelings were likewise somewhat better the Boys much employ'd themselves by having leisure to take a long walk, Miss Margaret Brown here for an hour in the Morning recd a Letter from Mʳˢ· Granville melancholly yet pleasing.

Sunday Dec.ʳ 15ᵗʰ·
Rather more dry owing to a sharp cold wind but rain again in the afternoon, I was very low & poorly, perhaps owing to the loss of my Dear Companions all the day almost, going to Sᵗ· Peters Chappel in the Morning, & Sᵗ· Georges in the evening where Mᵗ· Cleeve kept them till after dark. Mᵗ· Brown sat ½ an hour with me. wrote to Mʳˢ· Charles Western.

Monday Dec.ʳ 16ᵗʰ·
A clear bright fine day, tho with so violent cold high wind that it was not thought prudent for me to venture to go out. Mᵗ· Simpson call'd in the Morning & we were also agreably surprized by a visit from Mᵗ· Pennington of Nottingham who was come to reside here the Winter to take

his degrees & he had brought his Wife with him.[14] M[r.] Stormonth call'd late in the evening, & staid till 11 o'clock so deep in chat.

Tuesday Dec[r.] 17[th.]

Equally clear & dry, & a much finer day the wind being neither so high nor cold, indeed a very fine Day for the time of year; which tempted me to go out in a Hack Charriot a little way on the Leith road concluding my airing by visiting M[rs.] Pennington in South James Street, & found her very pleasing but looking ill return'd home better for my expedition, tho my cold in my head & eyes so bad in the evening I was <u>forc'd</u> to play at Cassino with the Boys.

Wensday Dec[r.] 18[th.]

Not quite so bright & fine a day, but dry & tolerable till after mid.day when it rain'd very hard but fortunately not till I had performed my little walk & made 4 visits in the Square, to M[rs.] Macqueen & M[rs.] Brown without any success, to M[rs.] Craigie meeting her on the steps of her own Door going to walk I join'd her & walk'd with her on the pavement pleasurable for ½ an hour concluded my round by calling on M[rs.] Hamilton, who not being at home I introduced myself to her Daughter who I found an agreable pleasing young Woman, my Cold was so very indifferent at night that not being able to see to work much we play'd at Cassino with the Boys.

Thursday Dec[r.] 19[th.]

A very fine Winter day, being quite dry without frost, & yet constant sunshine, the wind was both high & cold, yet being very low & languid I ventured to brave it by walking & realy was the better for it. first to sun myself in Princes Street & on my return call'd on L[dy.] C: Charteris, who gladly rec'd me & admitted M[r.] Witts also a wonderful exertion & favor

Friday Dec[r.] 20[th.]

The same dry fine weather still pleasanter being no wind, which induced me to take my usual walk in the New Town, & I was certainly better than for sometime past, much employ'd & tired with hunting for a new Maid our Servant wanting to leave us unhandsomely in haste to be married but thought her no loss on the whole Cassino at night.

Saturday Dec[r.] 21[st.]

Not near so fine a Day, for tho still dry it was foggy dark & gloomy & suited quite to the shortest day, M[r.] Noble here in the Morning, we walk'd to call on M[rs.] Pennington taking all the Boys, a very chatty easy visit; great pleasure to converse with an English acquaintance or indeed any one, situated as I now am. wrote to M[rs.] Buxton

Sunday Dec[r.] 22[d.]

Something of a frost & rather a brighter day but still the sun could never well dispel the fog which made me affraid to venture to Church but in a Chair which I did to our own Chappel

---

14. Pennington.

the two eldest Boys going with me, Mr Witts having so bad a cold he was glad to lye a bed & nurse it, I was very far from well all day, my Cough, oppression, & defluxion being again increased. Francis attended Mr Pennington in the afternoon to St Georges Chappel.

Monday Decr 23.^d

A miserable wet, damp foggy Day & so dark it was difficult to see at mid.day. Mr Witts's cold still very bad, & my complaints increasing which made Mr Wood order me fresh medicine & begin drinking asses milk. Mr Pennington call;d in the Morning, heartily glad when the Dear Boys came home from School to enliven us; at night play'd at Cassino; our under Maid left us & Johanna Murray a new one began xxxxxx in her stead

Tuesday Decr 24.th

Again damp & foggy but no rain tho as unpleasant as it could be without it, Mr Wittss cold a little mended which induced him to go out but I think he was the worse for it; I was very indifferent & low even to a degree of misery. Could see to do nothing at night but play at Cassino. began drinking Asses milk.

Wensday Decr 25.th

Rather a better day being a dryer air much lighter & for an hour or two at noon real sunshine a great rarity. I felt much better in the Morn. wch tempted me to go to Chappel in a chair, detaind there between 3 & 4 hours from the great number of communicants, certainly 200 at least.

'The Social Pinch'; a well-dressed man pays for the sedan chair, an etching by John Kay. This Etching is represented at the east corner of the Parliament Square, with a partial view of the Parliament House, as it existed at that time. Donald Kennedy—seated on the pole of the sedan, and presenting his 'mull'—was a native of Perthshire. Donald Black, the other figure, came from Ross-shire, and was a bachelor. The Chairmen of Edinburgh, chiefly Highlanders, were at one time a numerous and well-employed body, and some of them were known to amass large sums of money. The later introduction of hackney-coaches, however, changed the habits of fashionable life.

Thursday Decr 26th.

Wet dark & gloomy but too well corresponding with my feelings as I was sadly ill both in health & spirits the whole day, & Mr Witts's cold as bad or worse than ever yet he went out a little, it becoming more drying at Mid.day. had the happiness of receiving a long Letter from Mrs. Naper.

Friday Decr 27th.

A tolerable day being a drier air yet still remaining dark & gloomy neither of our colds very famously well, yet Mr Wood encouraged our going out which we did not till late waiting for Mrs. Pennington in which we were disappointed, walk'd only in the Square. wrote to Mrs. Callander.

Saturday Decr 28th.

Quite a happy change in the weather being a sharp frost, a clear air & constant sunshine from rising to setting , which tempted me first to walk on Princes Street parade, & afterwards to make a long visit to Mrs. Pennington while Mr Witts went to Leith calling on me on his return. the Boys drank Tea at Lady C. Charteris's to meet Master Morays. wrote an anxious Letter to my Brother Ferdinand.

Sunday Decr 29th.

Again a trifling frost, but very early in the day it became dark & foggy & unpleasantly cold, went to our own Chappel, a moving, tho at the same time uninteresting Sermon from Mr Webster. Mr Pennington sat with us in our Pew, Mr Witts & I went to evening service at the old Grey Friars a dull Sermon from a dull preacher.

Monday Decr 30th.

Something of a frost, with a strong cold wind but no sun & in the evening rain. a busy Morning from several visitors, Mrs. Callander & Miss Rutherford, the former so very obliging as to be term'd quite kind, M.^r & Mrs. Pennington & Mr Stormonth, when they were all gone, walk'd for sometime in the Square; the Boys very happy in this being the first day of three holidays out & about all the Morning & Cassino at Night

The Greyfriar's Church. An engraving by
T. Stewart from a painting by Daniel Wilson.

Tuesday Dec.ʳ 31.ˢᵗ

A comfortless kind of day, fine in the Morning Foggy at Noon & wet in the afternoon, which did not tempt me to go out at all, Lord Adam Gordon & Major Imrie call'd in the Morning as did M.ʳ Graham my cold &c very indifferent at night play'd at Cassino again & much interested in the new Novel of Selima.[15]

rec'd 185 Letters
wrote 191 Letters

1794

Wensday Jan: 1.ˢᵗ

A very bright fine day to open the new Year with, something of a frost, but the sun had much power that it had made it quite dirty, yet I walk'd a great deal first to sun myself in Princes Street, & afterwards to call on L.ᵈʸ C. Charteris to wish her a happy new year, a point much regarded in Scotland she was particularly well & lively & always kind giving not only Parents of Boys a new years gift but also Catherine.

Thursday Jan 2.ᵈ

Frost again but a cold tame day being no sun & a sharp wind, walk'd only in the Square & on the walks but the better for that. Miss Hamilton made a late Morning call was very pleasant, & kind to the Boys about their drawings; more & more interested in Selima rec'd Letters from Miss Louisa Lee, Miss B. Guydickens & my Sis.ʳ Travell, the latter much less pleasing than usual.

Friday Jan: 3.ᵈ

Had been a sharp frost, & was fine in the Morning, but soon began thawing, grew stormy, & was wet before evening, so I contented myself with staying at home, M.ʳ Simpson sat an hour with me, & was friendly & pleasant as he ever is; much work & a great deal of reading in Selima.

Saturday Jan: 4.ᵗʰ

Quite a fine Day for the time of Year, being a dry & yet mild air, equally without fog or sun – M.ʳ Pennington here early in the Day, & at mid.day I went to sit an hour with her having first taken a little promenade in Princes Street. rec'd a Letter from Miss Anne Snow, & wrote to M.ʳˢ Naper.

Sunday Jan: 5.ᵗʰ

Pretty much a similiar day, only neither so clear or so mild but very dry, went to our own Chappel in the Morn: a dismal dull Sermon f.ᵐ M.ʳ Allan, a very different one & excellent Prayers from D.ʳ Blair in the afternoon in the New Kirk rec'd a tiresome Letter from my Bro.ʳ Ferdinand & wrote to my Sister Travell.

---

15. *Selima, or the village tale, a novel, in a series of letters, by the authoress of Fanny* in six volumes; Margaret Holford (d. 1834).

Monday Jan: 6th.

Very much the same weather, only rather more foggy after mid.day, but perfectly dry Mr. Witts went early into the Court of Justiciary to hear one of the ringleaders of the convention tried where he staid near 6 hours, in the meantime I went an airing with Mrs. Pennington in a Post Chaise in which we united going to Leith & driving on the sands, on our made an unsuccessful visit to Mr. Oliphant at the Custom House; Mr. Simpson call'd before Dinner, & the Mrs. Auchenlecks drank Tea with us.

Tuesday Jan: 7th.

Quite a beautiful fine day, bright sunshine & quite dry being somewhat of a frost Mrs. Pennington walk'd here early & sat an hour or two, we attended her home & walk'd a little more on our return rec'd a visit fm. Col: Callander who came to fix for our going to Preston Hall very busy all the evening. wrote to Miss Anne Snow.

Wensday Jan: 8th.

Not so good a day tho still dry, being a most violent high cold wind & little or no sun went out early to call on Ldy. C: C: introduced by her to Mrs. Moray call'd on Mrs. Pennington, Mrs. Brown very agreably & without success on Mrs. Hamilton, had my Hair cut the Penningtons drank Tea here, were very pleasant & play'd at Cassino.

Thursday Jan: 9th.

Wet in the Morning but turn'd out a brilliant fine day, very busy in the Morn: in preparing for our little excursion to Preston Hall to stay some days, the only regret parting from the Dear Boys. Mr. & Mrs. Callendar call'd on us in their Coach to convey, us, a fine drive but realy dark before one got there no company, a lively game at Whist & much free & pleasant converse.

Friday Jan: 10th.

Another charming day, constant sunshine & air so mild it was like spring, the Gentlemen rode, & we walk'd for a great while but only in the Garden it was so dirty; Baron Norton dined here (his Lady too ill to come) & a major Wallers; the Gentlemen sat late over their bottle, & were very merry when they join'd us at Whist Major W. staid all night.

Saturday Jan: 11th.

Such a day was scarce ever known at this Season, mild as May, little or no wind & constant sunshine the two Gentlemen out a hunting, & Mrs. Callander confined to her Bed with a bad head ache till Dinner time, Mr. Witts & I walk'd to the Mauseleom &'c the pleasant Major returnd with the Col:, & we had a very merry & to me a successful Game at Whist wrote to to Miss Gorges.

Sunday Jan: 12th.

Not quite such fine weather, being colder more wind & no sunshine, no going to church, nor any employment the whole Day but conversation which made the day appear long, tho it was well supported; walk'd for sometime in the Garden, a Mr. & Mrs. Lascelles & Mr. Dewar here in the Morning & all the three Gentlemen dined at Baron Nortons, did not return till past ten, but perfectly <u>well behaved</u>.

Monday Jan: 13th.

Still dry & pleasant, but very windy & cold, the Gents gone a Hunting from whence the Major did not return, Mrs. C. was fearful of walking so far but my Husband & I walk'd to & all over Preston Hall house, most pleased with the increased improvement; a strong contest at Whist in the evening. had the pleasure of receiving a Letter from Dear <u>Francis</u>.

Tuesday Jan: 14th.

The same fine weather, only a trifling appearance of rain at Noon which came to nothing we all walk'd to Preston Hall, but return'd home in the Coach frighten'd at the appearance of rain, Mr. & Mrs. Fisher he the Clergyman of the Parish, dined here very well behaved pleasant people after they were gone in the evening we play'd our own party at Whist & <u>we</u> were worsted.

Wensday Jan: 15th.

An uncommon bright fine day, perhaps had been something of a frost in the night, but the air was mild & the sun constant, soon after breakfast our agreable Friends both attended us in their Coach to Edinbro' I believe mutually sorry to part, their behavior to me & reception of us, most kind, drove home to land our baggage & then went with Mrs. Callander into the New Town & walk'd home; most happy to find all the Dear Boys well when we all assembled at Dinner time

Thursday Jan: 16th.

Quite as fine & bright a day only the Wind was both higher & colder, I was busy the early part of the Morning in setting things in order after my little absence, & then escorted by my usual companion went to call on Mrs. Pennington, & from there on Ldy. C: C: who was, too unwell to receive me. working & having reading &'c in the evening. fearful I had got a fresh cold.

Friday Jan: 17th.

A Fine pleasant looking dry day, but very windy & rather cold as the day advanced, which made me find it very cold walking about in a smart visiting garb having made 4 calls all unsuccessful, to Mrs. Hamilton the Birds, Mrs. Craggie, Mrs. Macqueen, & Mrs. Halkett Craggie, came home half cross, quite blown & starved & very much of an increased cold. heard Mr. Witts read in a stupid new Book Philip Waldgrave by name.[16] wrote to Miss Sheppard.

Saturday Jan: 18th.

An appearance of having been a little rain in the night but turn'd out a pleasant mild day, tho the wind was unpleasantly high for walking Mrs. Pennington made an early visit here, I return'd with her home by way of a walk, having first stopp'd at a Painters to see some Pictures, in the evening I went in a Chair to the Abbey hoping to visit the Dutchess of Atholl, but she was indisposed & could see no one, so return'd home disappointed having taken so much pains for nothing, drank Tea at home & play'd at Cassino. rec'd Letters from Lady Edward Bentinck & Miss Snow & wrote to Miss Louisa Lee.

---

16. *The History of Philip Waldegrave*. Joseph Towers (1737–1799).

Sunday Jan: 19th.

Very fine & pleasant in the Morning, much sun & tho rather windy the air was quite mild, in the afternoon there was a short trifling shower more like a mist. Frans. being unwell both in head & stomach never stirr'd out all day the rest of us went to our own Chappel in the Morning a dreadful dull reader & preacher a stranger; in the evening M^r. Witts & I went to S^t. Georges Chappel, where M^r. Sandford preach'd as well as M^r. Cleeve read, so wet & damp I was forced to come home in a Chariot.

Monday Jan: 20th.

Not a pleasant day being an extreme high wind & yet damp, & in the evening a little rain I walk'd a very little late in the day merely to a Shop. having made an engagement with M^r. & Mrs. Pennington to go with them to the Ball always held on the Queens Birth day, dress'd wholly after Dinner & went to the assembly rooms in George Street, spacious handsome rooms but much unfinish'd. pretty well amused but chiefly by the novelty of the scene, knowing so very few of the company literaly not one Lady to speak to, tho a large meeting, a great many Military all in their uniform. at home about 2 o'clock.

Tuesday Jan: 21st.

A mild fine Day, tho it grew rather foggy after noon, but was still dry, & good walking, got up rather late & felt somewhat fatigued after my raking walk'd to call on Mrs. Pennington but did not find her at home, walk'd in Princes Street &'c. much mortified at never getting any Letters from England.

Wensday Jan: 22^{d.}

Quite a beautiful day, warm, still & constant sunshine, more like May, Mrs. Auchenlech call'd as did Frank Charteris to take his leave on going to England Mrs. Pennington sat an hour with me & I walk'd home with her taking her thro' the old town & over the mound. wrote to Miss B. Guydickens.

Thursday Jan: 23^{d.}

Weather very much changed tho not as seasonably, pretty fine in the Morning, but before noon turn'd to very stormy, with violent tho short showers of Hail or small snow, & at night very severe wind & real snow tho not much; I intended walking to see L^{dy.} C: C: but put it off in hopes of a better Morn: M^r. Witts walk'd & I went in a Chaise to drink Tea at M^r. Penningtons no one there but our own Quartetto, beat them thoroughly at 3d. Cassino, did not much like slipping home. wrote a long Letter to M^r. Burslem owed a considerable time

Friday Jan: 24th

Not much more snow had fallen but it was a miserable confining day, being quite undecided whether it would be a thaw or frost, but at night began snowing hard, attended with a such a severe wind that it blew quite a tempest. M^r. Witts attended M^r. Pennington to a Chemical Lecture by D^r. Black well entertain'd, the day spent as usual in a variety of employs wrote to Lady Edward Bentinck.

Above left: The foot of the West Bow, off Grassmarket. An engraving by T. Picken after a painting by George Cattermole.

Above right: Dr Joseph Black (1728–1799), Professor of Chemistry in the University of Edinburgh. An etching by John Kay.

Saturday Jan: 25th.

After a most tremendous night of Wind & Snow we waked to see a most dismal Morn of prodigeous deep snow, & most bitterly cold, very little more snow fell in the course of the day, but it blew most terribly & made our Chimnies smoke at a very uncomfortable rate all methods of moving seem'd most difficult great exertions in the Square & streets to make it safe for people to walk, could not let the Boys go to School, the London Post the only one that arrived & that not till many hours after its time. began to be quite sensible what severe weather <u>could</u> be in Scotland; the three Master Cragies unexpected & undeterred spent two or three hours here in the evening, I was far from well & more out of spirits. but pleased with having Mr. Witts read in the Secret History of Charles the Second.

Sunday Jan: 26th.

A severe frost, so of course little if any snow gone but it was bright sunshine all day to make the piercing wind supportable, I went in a Chair, & my companions walk'd to St. Peters Chappel, bitterly cold even there, not much elevated by Mr. Websters dull manner.

Monday Jan: 27th.

Frost quite as severe if not still more so, but was a bright fine Day from constant sunshine but still so very cold the thermometer was down to 14, & the snow was judged to be a deeper one than for seven years past, Mr Witts walk'd to see Mrs Pennington &'c & in the meantime to my great surprize Miss Halkett walk'd to call on me, & was so agreable I felt sorry we had not met more frequently. rec'd Letters from Mrs Granville Mrs Buxton & my Sister Travell.

Tuesday Jan: 28th

Pretty fine & frosty in the Morning, but before noon it became dark & cloudy, & at intervals there was most violent showers of Snow during the whole day such huge flakes I never before saw, but still the air was milder this quite prevented my intention of walking out read & work'd much, cut the Boys Hair, wrote to Mrs Granville & rec'd a Letter from Mrs Witts of Nibley.

Wensday Jan: 29th

Still a hard frost, of course the Snow very little decreased tho at mid.day it was somewhat of a ground thaw, but being no sunshine it melted slowly, I never stirr'd from the fireside & Mr Witts out but little, so reading & working flourish'd well & at night Cassino with the Boys Mr Simpson here for a few minutes in the Morning.

Thursday Jan: 30th

Had been a very severe frost in the night & was if possible colder than ever in the Morning, but happily before noon began thawing fast & so continued the whole of the day & at night small rain, which brought the frozen Snow & Ice off the tops of the houses with such violence that it sounded like the report of a Gun, Mr Pennington here in the Morning, & also Mr Kingslake & Mr Palmer who conducted themselves better than expectation[17]

Friday Jan: 31st

The most constant & rapid thaw ever known for the Snow deep as it was, was all melted away before the evening & the rain was very short & trifling but of course the streets were quite in a flood, as usual I was quite confined, Mr Witts out the greater part of the Morning on a variety of bussiness.

Saturday Feb: 1st

A mild damp Morning but before Noon became most violent hard & settled rain without any abatement till evening, I began sensibly to feel the ill effects of my constant confinement both on my health & spirits, which was more than ordinarily below par to which getting no Letters from England was a great increase. wrote to Mrs Buxton.

Sunday Feb: 2^{d}

Prodigeous hard rain in the Morning & to appearance had been so the whole night, but fortunately gave over before it was time for Church, but remain'd a dismal thick fog & damp & dirty to a most unpleasant degree, went to our own Chappel where Mr Allan shone more

---

17. Messrs Wapshott, Palmer, Matthews and Palmer of Chipping Norton were Edward Witts's bankers, and this visit was in relation to the bankruptcy. Robert Kinglake (1765–1842), was a surgeon and apothecary of Chipping Norton, but he was also a Burgess for the town. Kinglake had studied at Edinburgh for a considerable time, and this may partially explain his presence there, to give local advice to Mr Palmer.

than usual I staid the Sacrament & went to evening service at the old Grey Friars, where we were surprized & much entertain'd by an excellent Sermon from a very old Minister M^r. Erskine, in a most strong energetic manner & prayers excellent.

Monday Feb: 3^d.

Constant hard soaking rain with hardly any interruption from Morn till night, & very disagreably dark & damp, even M^r. Witts went little out & the poor Boys had little pleasure in their Candlemas Holiday; I was miserably out of spirits & very far from well. rec'd a Letter from Lady Edward Bentinck & wrote to Miss Snow.

Tuesday Feb: 4th.

again hard rain in the Morning, but held up for some hours at Noon, & was little rain again in the afternoon, M^r. Witts out the greater part of the Morning on various bussinesses & calls, I was still very low & poorly, not the better for writting a trying & painful Letter to M^rs. Naper on account of her long silence.

Wensday Feb: 5th.

Dry, mild & pleasant, & realy not very dirty in the streets tho there had been so much rain far from being easy uncomfortable about poor Edward who had visibly been growing thin for some little time, had a cough & several other complaints that alarm'd me, had M^r. G. Wood to him, who order'd him not to go to School till he was better, walk'd in the Square a little while early at one o'clock set forth to call on L^dy. C: Charteris who rec'd me if possible with more than ordinary kindness, from her went to call on M^rs. Pennington not at home till near Dinner time & well tired, but still it did not procure one Sleep, which I much wanted having had several bad nights, & this one of the worst from several combining causes.

Thursday Feb: 6th.

Very much the same kind of weather till 3 or 4 o'clock when it became rainy for a short time; My mind a good deal agitated by much conversation both with M^r. G: Wood & M^r. Pennington seperately about Edward who continued very much the same, walk'd out from one to three so luckily escaped the storm, in Princes & Queen Street quite pleasant. Edwards complaints rather increased at night. play'd at Cassino.

Friday Feb: 7th.

A very stormy unpleasant day throughout hard rain for some hours in the Morning, warm & damp tho the wind was so tempestuous, M^r. Witts was far from well Edward worse rather than better myself again coughing & very much deranged in all respects, happily for as our pleasant friends the Penningtons were engaged to drink Tea to meet M^r. Kinlake[18] & M^r. Palmer but they being preengaged we spent our evening pleasantly between conversation & Cassino; our own party.

---

18. Agnes continually misspells names, even people known to her such as Robert Kinglake.

Saturday Feb: 8ᵗʰ·

Dry & not unpleasant the wind being mild tho still very high, Mʳ· Witts attended a Lecture of Dʳ· Blacks, I staid at home till two o'clock for Mʳ· Wood who thought poor Edward somewhat better tho for my own part I saw little change, we then walk'd with the elder Boys, first to see Dightons Painting & then on the old accustomed Mall Princess Street. Cassino as usual at night. wrote to my Sister Travell

Sunday Feb: 9ᵗʰ·

Again dry but very windy with a good deal of sunshine till quite evening when small rain came on, ventured to let Edward take a few turns in the Square, as he certainly was not worse, yet a blister was recommended to be put on at night to assist his breath; went to our own Chappel in the Morning a Mournful Sermon from Mʳ· Webster, on our return home Mʳ· & Mʳˢ· Pennington called & went with me to evening service at the Grey Friars, much pleased with Mʳ· Finlayson, a most capital Sermon on Death, full both of pathos & energy, very affecting & at the same time consoletary, a very pleasant looking man & Gentlemanlike.

Monday Feb: 10ᵗʰ·

A dismal bad day in all respects being very severe storms of hail, rain, & snow, tho none to remain on the ground, & wind quite tempestuous, My little boy not at all better tho the blister had risen well, alltogether I was quite miserable & very far from well Mʳ· Witts out a little in the Morning merely on business. rec'd a Letter from Miss Anne Snow.

Tuesday Feb: 11ᵗʰ·

Weather better being tolerably dry, yet still something of a damp wind consequently sadly Nervous, and poor little Invalid worse rather than better, both the Mʳ· Woods visited him, & my hopes about him were not raised by some friendly & interesting talk with Mʳ· Pennington who likewise call'd in the Morning terribly apprehensive about him. walk'd to call on Mʳˢ· Callander who had sent us word they were in Town for 2 or 3 days for the purpose of chusing furniture for Preston Hall, went with her to two Upholsterers, afterwards call'd on Mʳˢ· Pennington. rec'd a Letter from my Sisʳ· Travell

Wensday Feb: 12ᵗʰ·

Dry & cold from a very sharp & high wind but a good deal of sun & therefore a fine Day but I was thoroughly unhappy from the increased illness of my poor Edward, at least apparent danger, which led the Mr. Woods to wish for further advice to be call'd in to him. Mʳ· Witts went early in the day to call on Coll: Callander on some little bussiness, during which Mʳ· Simpson call'd on me, late in the day we walk'd on the walks & found them quite dry. unable to employ myself in anything, but wish & talk. play'd at Cassino at night

Thursday Feb: 13ᵗʰ·

Quite a disagreable day in point of weather being damp & wet & the Wind so high as quite to blow as former were most miserable on our Dear Childs account whose disorders appeard to yeild to nothing that could be devised, Dʳ· Hamilton attended with the Mʳ· Woods in the Morning & oder'd an Emetic which like everything else appeard useless. Mʳˢ· Callander & Miss Rutherford here in the Morning, shewing every possible mark of tender sympathy. M^r. Pennington & M^r. Simpson here scarce able to employ myself in any one thing wrote to Lady Edward Bentinck.

Friday Feb: 14th.

Weather as bad or worse being decided & eventual steady rain which would not admit of a possibility of getting a breath of air, however much in need I stood of bracing, My Edward being still worse & the result of another Medical consultation was its being pronounced he had a Dropsy on his Chest wch by its very rapid advances allow'd of no hope, & probably our loss & regret would but too soon be compleated, & Dear little Creature he was so bad in the evening we thought every hour would be his last, of course past a most wretched night. rec'd a Letter from M^rs. Naper & wrote to my Sis^r. Travell

Saturday Feb: 15th.

Had been a trifling fall of Snow in the night, wonderfully damp, rain & sunshine wth wind fill'd up the Day; My poor Child miserably bad with his breath & his weakness so increased we did not attempt to get him out of Bed, but he was more composed till quite night, & most interesting in manner & expression. M^rs. Pennington came early & spent the greater part of the Morn: with me, all the three medical Gentlemen here at different times, & M^r. Simpson both Morn: & evening, D^r. Adam made a most kind & consoling visit, & grand M^r. Pennington spent the whole evening here, I much wanted his aid as well as the dear little suffering Angel wrote to Miss Anne Snow.

Sunday Feb: 16th.

Dry but cold without sun & rather gloomy too well corresponding with our miserable situation which alas this day ended in the most fateful manner. my sweet little Edward breathing his last a quarter before 9 in the Morning, he had been dying in a manner the whole of the night, his poor Papa up with him many times in the night as excepting at short intervals he was sensible to the last & wish'd to have us all about him of which I was little capable but took a last leave of him not a quarter of an hour before I lost him for ever, our distress & confusion beyond conception, M^r. Simpson came down to us instantly & M^r. Pennington as soon as possible & staid the whole of the day, writting Letters & shewing every possible act of friendly kindness, M^rs. Pen: came before Dinner & M^r. S. again in the evening, but all consolation to me however kind was deem'd useless in such poignant distress for a time. had a most wretched sleepless & painful Night.

Monday Feb: 17th.

Very much the same kind of weather only the air rather more damp, our agonizing distress only palliated by having so great a variety of things to do, order & think on, M^r. Simpson here several times in the day, M^r. & M^rs. Pennington both also, & Miss Brown for an hour in the evening most feelingly friendly. sent the poor Boys out to walk in the fields as some kind of relief to them in the Morning. rec'd a most pleasing & informing Letter from Miss Snow. M^r. Playfair here in the Morn:

Tuesday Feb: 18th.

Rather a clearer air & some little sun but still of course all melancholly & gloom within but ill able to attend to the various & necessary occupations I was obliged to be ingaged in. felt it right to send to request to see M^rs. Craigie who had offer'd her services to me in the most friendly manner, she & Miss Macdonald sat more than an hour with me, our kind friends M[r.] S & M[r.] P. call'd & also a M[r.] Rowley from London hard at work all the evening.

Wensday Feb: 19[th.]

Dry but lowering in the Morn: & at mid.day a severe shower which made it damp the remainder of the day & was very cold. My feelings tried to the utmost, by preparing to leave the House for the day with my poor remaining Boys, to avoid the wretched spectacle of seeing my little Angel carried to the Grave whither his affectionate Father would follow him in compliance to the trying custom of this Country, which ever make a great parade of funerals, 20 Gentlemen were ask'd to attend, 16 of whom came, M[r.] Allan of St. Peters Chappel perform'd the service, part in the House, the remainder over the Grave in the burying ground belonging to the Chappel of care to the West Kirk, where the dear remains were deposited, I trust to rest in peace; an hour previous M[r.] Simpson was so kind to go with me & the Boys to M[rs.] Pennington where M[r.] Witts join'd me when all was over, & we staid with them till quite night receiving every proof of tender attention. rec'd a Letter from M[rs.] Callander

Thursday Feb: 20[th.]

A sad damp Nervous Day, being flying rain or mist constantly, & unnatural warm, having had a sad night I felt worse rather than better but by employment strove to recover myself the Boys return'd to School, M[r.] Simpson M[r.] Pennington & M[r.] Allan call'd here, & Miss Halket late in the day who would take me an airing for an hour in her Chaise in the hope of doing me good & was most obligingly kind; Miss Brown call'd in my absence. rec'd Letters from from M[rs.] Hyett, Miss Sheppard & from both my sisters very gratifying.

Friday Feb: 21[st.]

Very much the same kind of weather only early in the afternoon there was a very heavy shower of rain, M[r.] Witts walk'd a little late, no one call'd but good M[rs.] Auchenleck who fell into the general custom of coming in Mourning to visit the afflicted, my health & spirits both very moderate & my dear companion not much better, tried to amuse ourselves, I by much necessary work & him by reading to me in Geralds well written but ill judged Pamphlet

Saturday Feb: 22[d.]

Again rather a damp relaxing day, & so mild it was rather unpleasant warm, & at night hard rain, M[r.] Maitland, M[r.] Cleeve, M[r.] & M[rs.] Pennington, & Miss Brown all here in the course of the Morning, the Boys happy in making a lively use of their half holiday. I began to find how much I wanted both air & exercise being miserably low & Nervous finish'd our Book. much entertain'd by it.

Sunday Feb: 23[d.]

Very wet in the Morning with violent high wind, & continued so in frequent showers the greater part of the day with bright enlivening Sun between, we all went to S[t.] Peters Chappel in the Morning I in a Chair being anxious, to attend divine service before we went or saw any one els, but alltogether we were so much affected the early time was almost too much for either of us, & went out of the house no more the remainder of the day. rec'd Letters from Miss Louisa Lee & Lady Edward Bentinck answerd the latter & wrote to M[rs.] Callander.

Monday Feb: 24th.

A miserable & severe wet Day almost from Morn: to night, very little stirring out even for M.r Witts, & the Boys only to & fro from School, I was full of useful employs, but very indifferent both in health & spirits. recd a very affectionate & acceptable Letter from M.rs Naper.

Tuesday Feb: 25th.

Dry early in the day but soon became wet & gloomy for 2 or 3 hours, & then again dry & fine but not sufficiently so to tempt me to go out, M.r Witts made many necessary visits, M.r Kenlake sat an hour with me & was very entertaining talking of Oxfordshire, M.rs Graham at last made me a visit & the two Miss Browns a most kind long & friendly one later. M.r & M.rs Pennington drank Tea & play'd at Cassino here. wrote to my Sis.r Travell

Wensday Feb: 26th.

Most memorable from being my sweet Francis's birth day when he enter'd into his twelfth year of age, a pretty fine day being clear & with some sun tho the Wind was boisterous, I walk'd from 11 to 12 w.h Mr. Witts in the Square & on the walks, then dress'd for the day & was ready to receive a pleasant friendly visit f..m M.r G: Wood & a very agreable long one from M.rs Craigie M.r & M.rs Homes & two Daughters from above stairs drank Tea here not disagreable.

Thursday Feb: 27th.

Dry, cold & without wind till mid.day when it became very stormy, & a little misty rain now & then but very trifling, being the general Fast day went to Morning Service at S.t Georges Chapel, where the service was well read both by M.r Cleeve & M.r Sandford but no Sermon spent the intermediate hour between the churches at M.r Penningtons, & went with them hear D.r Blair, a very fine practical Sermon, & so very large a congregation, that the crowding was more like a Theatre. rec'd Letters from Lady Edward Bentinck & Miss Anne Snow.

Friday Feb: 28th.

Very wet in the Morning clear'd in a degree at Noon, & was fine in the afternoon. I never went out in the Morning being busy writting, only D.r James Hamilton call'd a visit of compliment we went to drink Tea at M.r Penningtons meeting Captain & M.rs Swindell[19] & her Father M.r Neville, D.r Treat, & a M.r Brown a student a

Hugh Blair (1718–1800). Hugh Blair was licensed to preach in 1741 and by 1760 had become minister to the High Kirk, St Giles.

---

19. Captain J. Colby Swindell of the 55th Regiment of Foot.

Table at Whist & another at Back Gammon I play'd at both with success. wrote to M^rs. Naper & Miss Anne Snow.

Saturday Mar: 1st.

Rather an unpleasant cold Morning something of a frost, but grew stormy at Noon, I was much distress'd by seeing my Dear Husband very far from well, being feverish, chilly & thoroughly deranged all over, persuaded him to take our good Friend M^r. Penningtons advice, he grew worse towards night, & of course most sadly unhinged our little party rec'd Letters from my Sis^r. Travell, M^rs. Buxton & Miss Betty Guydickens

Sunday Mar: 2^d.

A most delightful bright Morning but before Noon more clouds, & several severe storms of hail &c & very cold; M^r. Witts bad had but a very moderate night & was quite ill all day, his good Doctor here in the Morning, I found him on my return from S^t. Peters Chappel where I staid the Sacrament & the remainder of the day fully taken up in attending my beloved Husband. M^r. Oliphant & Miss Macdonald here in the Morn:

Monday Mar: 3^d.

A trifling fall of Snow on the ground which soon melted away & it was a bright fine day excepting 2 or 3 short showers & very mild. My Dear Man, had had a dreadful bad night, having a strong fever on him & many unpleasant symptoms so of course he was very ill early in the Day but grew better rather towards evening, M^r. Pennington & M^r. Simpson both here Morning & evening. I walk'd for near an hour in the Square & walk'd before Dinner & was better for it; being very uneasy about M^r. W.

Tuesday Mar: 4th.

Rather a dark gloomy looking Day with high wind & very black clouds but dry till near dinner time when there was very severe rain & most tremendous high Wind all the evening. My Dear Husband having had a tolerable good night was certainly better but very weak & languid, his spirits quite low & never much irratated; his kind Medical Friend here in the Morning as usual; happily M^rs. Gunnings new Novel of the Memoirs of Mary[20] which I read much aloud, dissipated some dismal moments & still more dismal thoughts. rec'd a Letter from M^rs. Granville

Wensday Mar: 5th.

Wet in the Morning, & thro the early part of the day was alternate showers & sunshine but very fine in the afternoon; M^r. Pennington having been himself ill did not come till late, but rejoiced to find his dear Patient quite without fever & very much better which permitted me after he was gone to venture out so long from home to go in a chair to call on L^dy. C. Charteris, the meeting both affectionate & moving an own Sister could not have treated me with more tenderness & she sent me back loaded with good things for M^r. W. wrote to M^rs. Buxton.

---

20.   Elizabeth Gunning (1769–1823). *Memoirs of Mary*, 1793.

Thursday Mar: 6th·

Still very blustery but the air mild & the showers so transient it could not be esteemd rain tho the clouds were very lowering, My mind much more at ease about my Dear Nursery who had slept sound & easy tho under the power of Opiate, & his Doctor allowd him to eat Meat for the first time. I walk'd to call on Mrs· Pennington for a few minutes & to some shops, & found it very pleasant did a good deal of work in the course of the day & was much amused by Mary. rec'd Letters from Miss Forrest & my Bror· Ferdinand. very pleasing

Friday Mar: 7th·

Too damp & foggy a Morning for to make it pleasant for me to think of walking out, much more my Dear invalid at Noon settled rain wch· continued for some hours, Mrs· Auchenlek here in the Morning, Mr· & Mrs· Pennington came to Dinner & Mr· Simpson, his two Sons & youngest Daughter drank Tea here: Mr· Witts tho greatly better rather over done with so many friends at one time. wrote to Lady Lyttelton.

Saturday Mar: 8th·

Very wet the greater part of the day & quite damp the remainder, much business all the Morning making up Medicines, & many other employs & the evening working & reading, Mary very entertaining but the receipt of a Letter from Mrs· Naper much more so & better than all Mr· Witts was far better than on any past day.

Sunday Mar: 9th·

A very fine Day throughout, tho now & then clouds gave an alarm of rain but none fell & there was as much sunshine as there was wind, the Boys & myself went to Church in the Morning to St· Peters Chappel, Mr· Webster performed the service & at the close of it, collected near twenty young people round the altar to say their Cathecism which he asked & explaind in a very singular manner a few of us Parents &'c attending. on my return home found my Dear Husband who was got comfortably better out on his first walk, to pay his first compliment to his best Friend & Physician, & was not fatigued by it. Frans· went to evening service to St· Georges Chappel taking S. Simpson with him & George attended me to the New Kirk where I was delighted by a feeling sermon from Dr· Blair. rec'd Letters from Lady Edward Bentinck & Mrs· C. Thornton & wrote to my Bror· Ferdinand.

Monday Mar: 10th·

Quite a damp unpleasant day having been much rain in the night, frequent small showers in the day & most strong wind, Mr· Witts a little out just for air I got myself exercised, Mr· Simpson here early in the day, & Miss Halket later. wrote to Mrs· Witts. Mr· Allan drank Tea here.

Tuesday Mar: 11th·

A cold stormy day, with now & then flying showers & alternate sun, but a constant and tremendous high wind, Mr· Stormonth was here exactly after breakfast on business, Mr· Pennington likewise call'd, & advising me to walk, I was indeed to take so unpleasant a draught but well expected it was so dreadfully unpleasant could find no shelter even on the side walks. rec'd a Letter from my Sister Travell. finished hearing Mary, the end less pleasing & well written but I was very unwell therefore perhaps was difficult to please; My Husband quite xxx.

Wendsay Mar: 12[th.]

A tolerable bright fine Day, tho wind very cold & high with stormy black clouds which after noon let out some trifling showers, went out to walk soon after Breakfast to made sure of sunshine first to the Fish Market & other errands in the Town & afterward in the Square & on the walks, M[r.] & M[rs.] Pennington again dined here, she coming an hour or two before Dinner, & M[r.] Brown a Medical student an acquaintance of theirs drank Tea, & play'd several rubbers at Whist.

Thursday Mar: 13[th.]

Day much pleasanter tho still cold as the wind was not so high & the sun more constant, & no rain to speak on, went our early first calling to see the much talk'd of Picture of Louis the 16[th.] taking leave of his Family previous to his execution better pleased w.[h] it than expectation, afterwards went a string of visits to M[rs.] Maitland, M[rs.] Halkett Craigie, M[rs.] Graham, M[rs.] Thomson, M[rs.] Pennington, & M[rs.] Hamilton, finding none at home but M[rs.] Halkett, a pleasant large old Gentlewoman. began reading Delia writ by Lady — Butler

Friday Mar: 14[th.]

Excepting a very strong wind quite a pleasant day being a mild air & some sun, went to Morn[g.] prayers at S[t.] Peters Chapel, a sad thin congregation, afterwards M[r.] Witts join'd me & we both made a visit to Lady C: Charteris no interruption from Lady Francis from thence walk'd the back way by the Gardens to the Leith Walk, call'd on the Penningtons only him at home who refresh'd us with cold mint &'c as I was heartily fatigued. wrote to M[rs.] Naper

Saturday Mar: 15[th.]

Very wet & stormy, such frequent showers tho neither long nor violent. There was no going out for me, & I thought rather imprudent for my Husband tho he was grown so stout & well. M[r.] Charteris made us a very dull visit, & Miss Margaret Brown a very lively one; much working & reading in Delia rec'd a Letter from Miss Snow & writ to my Sister Travell.

Sunday Mar: 16[th.]

A very bright fine Morning tho cold but at Noon grew stormy, & in the afternoon there was not only tempestuous wind but showers of hail, we all went in the Morning to S[t.] Peters Chapel as usual where the Boys were again Catechised. M[r.] Witts & George staid at home in the evening, the former being afraid of the damp, & the latter having a bad cough Fran[s.] & I went to the Town Church to hear M[r.] Simpson & brought S. Simpson home to Dinner with us. wrote to Lady Edward Bentinck.

Monday Mar: 17[th.]

A fine & quite dry day with much sun but still high cold wind, probably had been somewhat of a frost in the Country; M[rs.] Pennington call'd here we walk'd back with her to the New Town, & took her & M[r.] P. to see our House in Hanover Street, M[r.] & M[rs.] Thomson not at home on my return sat an hour agreably with M[rs.] Brown before Dinner; M[r.] Pennington coming the evening to see my poor George who had got so bad a Cough that he was quite an invalid. much amused by Delia.

Tuesday Mar: 18th.

Dry tho rather foggy in the Morning a sharp shower at Noon & fine in the afternoon. George no worse but staid at home from School & required much nursing & many cockering[21] to be made for him, his good Dr call'd early, & so did Mr Simpson in the course of the Morning. walk'd late when it became dry on the Walks & Square, far from well & miserably out of spirits.

Wensday Mar: 19th.

A fine day upon the whole much so in the Morning, but grew cloudy & a little stormy at Noon Mr & Mrs. Pennington came together soon after breakfast his dear little patient not at all better his Cough & head being both very troublesome, walk'd home with Mrs. P & did some errands in the New Town wrote to Miss Elizabeth Guydickens.

Thursday Mar: 20th.

Quite a brilliant fine day, much like a Spring day the sun was so hot & so constant, in spite of a cold air, poor Georges disorder imagined by Mr P to turn out at last the measles as some eruption appeard & towards evening, Francis grew restless & unwell & shewd the probability of his falling also. walk'd a good deal in the forenoon on Bruntsfield Lynn &c, & went to dine with Mr & Mrs. Maitland of Clifton Hall at their Lodgings in Princes Street a party of 12 consisting of Mrs. Swinton, her 2 Daughters & a Son Lord Swintons family[22] a Major & Mrs. Campbell, a Mr Durham & a Miss Gibson, very agreable, handsome entertainment & polite reception home at 9 o'clock no cards not much to be done after Dinner. recd a Letter from Mrs. Buxton

Friday Mar: 21st.

Very nearly as fine a day, only the wind rather more cold Mr Pennington made us a very early visit, George being extremely full of the Measles he judged it best to keep him in bed the whole day. Francis was too indifferent to go to School tho failing but slowly, pretty fully employ'd in the Morning in attending upon them poor fellows, got a fine walk almost to Morning side went to dine at Mr Penningtons where we met Mr James Rose & in the evening Mr Arnold; play'd one rubber at Whist & home early

Willison David Esq. No 7. St Ninian's street
Willison Mifs, Lourifton
Willison David printer, Craig's clofe
Winter William officer of excife, Livingston's yards
Winton George builder, No 1. Charlotte street
Wife Alexander grocer, No 2. south Caftle street
Wifhart James fpirit dealer, foot of New street, Canongate
Wifhart Patrick writer, No 1. head of Scott's clofe
Witchell John grocer, No 1. Nicolfon's street, weft fide
Witts Edward Efq. No 18. north Hanover street
Wordie Mrs, No 2. Queen's street
Wordfworth Samuel riding mafter, academy Circus
Wood Walter, No 6. St James's fquare
Wood John folicitor at law, and furveyor of window duties
 for the county of Edinburgh, foot of Allan's clofe
Wood Alexander furgeon, No 37. St Andrew's fquare
Wood Andrew furgeon, foot of Horfe wynd
Wood George furgeon, No 6. St Andrew's fquare
Wood John Efq. of excife, Leven lodge
Wood Mrs, Bucclengh street
Wood Mrs, eaft end of Hope park
Wood Thomas furgeon, No 14. Nicolfon's fquare
Wood John leather merchant, Pleafance
Wood Lady, No 55. Prince's street
Wood Alexander cork cutter, Crofscaufeway
Wood John drawing academy, No 6. Hunter's fquare
Wood   fhoe and lafting fhop, No 20. Terrace
Wood William bookfeller, Luckenbooths
Wood John staymaker, St Mary's wynd
Wood Mifs, Britifh Linen Company's clofe, Nether bow
Woods William of the Theatre Royal, No 1. e. Regifter ftr.
Woodhead Anthony folicitor at law, Richmond place
Wright John Efq. advocate, new Affembly clofe
Wright Thomas of Greenhill, George's fquare, w. fide
Wright Malcolm meichant, Gosford's clofe
Wright Alexander wine merchant, Gow's land, Ramfay gar-
 den
Wright,Dr William phyfician, No 2. eaft Regifter street
Wright Mrs fpirit dealer, Pleafance
Wright John woollen draper, head of Stevenlaw's clofe
Wright Robert builder, Tobago street
Wright James cart and plough wright, Caftle wynd
Wright William tool maker, Nicolfon's street
Wright George staymaker, Potter-row
Wright George auctioneer, foot of meal market ftairs

The page from Thomas Aitchison's *Edinburgh Directory* for the year July 1797 to July 1798 lists the residence of Edward Witts being 18 north Hanover Street.

---

21. The writing is unclear here, but if 'cockering' it is in the sense of pampering a child, to treat with excessive tenderness and care.
22. John Swinton of that Ilk, the twenty-seventh Laird, became a member of the Supreme Court in 1782, taking the title, 'Lord Swinton'.

Saturday Mar: 22ᵈ·

So fine a day was seldom or ever seen at this season of the Year, mild air without wind quite clear & uninterrupted sunshine, & so warm all aditional cloathᵍ was troublesome when out Mrs. Clerk the Lady who is to succeed us in this House with her Sister call'd to make observations & were civil & obliging, afterwards we walk'd first to call on Lady Catherine Charteris, kindly rec'd as usual had a silent encounter with Lady Francis as she was getting out of a Carriage, call'd at the Abbey to make an enquiry after the Dutchess of Atholl, & walk'd home over & round Calton Hill; My poor Boys very middling in their different stages of the disorder, Georges as evidently declining, as Francis's was coming on who could do little but lye on a Sopha, George sat up two hours in the evening. rec'd a Letter from my Broʳ· Ferdinand & wrote to Miss Louisa Lee & Miss Snow.

Sunday Mar: 23ᵈ·

A very fine dry Day, but not so pleasant the wind being cold & in the East which made it thick & hazy; the Measles coming out most kindly on Francis he was kept in Bed the whole day, & tho George was up the greater part, he was very languid & poorly & his eyes much affected, their kind Doctor call'd between the churches. We went both Morning & evening to the New Grey Friars, being disappointed in the former of hearing Dʳ· Baird, Mʳ· Dixon from Leith performing the service in his stead but very well tho in a Singular stile, sat both times in a good seat in the Gallery with very civil people, & much pleased with Dʳ· Baird in the afternoon, a Masterly Sermon both in point of matter & manner, on the Story of Cain & Abel. wrote to Mʳˢ· Granville.

Monday Mar: 24ᵗʰ·

Still more of a easterly wind which made it far from pleasant, tho it was dry & a good deal of sunshine, Francis extremely full of the disorder so of course in Bed but for a quarter of an hour in the evening, but well & in fine spirits, poor George much the reverse, having a good deal of Fever much weakness & debility, & his eyes so bad he could not open them nor bear the light, was blooded & was better towards evening when Mʳ· P. call'd a second time; we walk'd for air & exercise to the very end of Princes Street where we were join'd by Mʳ· & Mʳˢ· P. return'd home over the mound Mʳ· Thomson here for an hour in the evening on the subject of the Hanover Street house

Tuesday Mar: 25ᵗʰ·

Such an intire Fog from Morn: to night that it was perfectly disagreable & tho the perfectly dry, I had as little walk as time to stir out having enough to do between by two Dear invalids Francis not quitting his Bed except for half an hour after dark, but pure well & merry & the eruption apparently dying away, Georges eyes still so bad & himself in so torpid & uncomfortable a state that Mʳ· Pennington put on two Leeches on each temple the attendance on w.ᶜʰ was a tiresome bussiness but certainly beneficial & he spent the rest of the day in Bed to recruit. Mʳ· Simpson here in the Morning & Charles Craigie²³ drank Tea.

---

23. Charles Craigie was the son of Charles Halkett (1715–1774), a colonel in the Dutch service and Governor of Namur. Charles senior had married Anne, heiress of John Craigie Esq. of Dumbarnie one of the Lords of Justiciary in Scotland by Susan eldest daughter of Sir John Inglis baronet of Cramond and Lady Susan Hamilton his wife, daughter of the

Wensday Mar: 26th.

Somewhat a better day being less of a fog & some sunshine, but the wind was bitterly high & cold My Dear Boys were both so much better that they got up before Noon & had a happy meeting in the parlour & able to pursue a great variety of pastimes; we went out merely for exercise, went into a very extraordinary large empty house in Hill Street, concluded our walk by calling on Mrs. Pennington who was not well C: Craigie again drank Tea here.

Thursday Mar: 27th.

The wind being still in the same unpleasant quarter; no very good weather was to be expected some sun early in the day but damp & cold afterwards my first Morning exploit, was visiting Mrs. Hamilton the first time I ever was successful, found her both pleasant & agreable & a large circle of Ladies with her afterwards. Mr Witts & I went into Princes Street to call on Mrs. Clark our future successor in this house rec'd a very polite reception, found it too cold & comfortless to walk more & glad to return to the Boys who wanted society, Francis pauly,[24] but George coughing much; Mr Allan here when I came home.

Friday Mar: 28th.

A much better day than several former ones, the air being less thick & cold & the sun more powerful, but a wonderful thick fog again in the afternoon, the Dear Boys well enough to get up to prayers as soon as ever their Dr had paid his visit we sallied forth going thro the Fish Market a wonderful fine sight visited Mrs. Auchenlecks, then Mrs. Pennington where we met a Mrs. Roget, & from thence went down the Leith walk & across the Fields to the Cannongate to call on Ldy. C: C: who being too indifferent to receive we return'd home the back way heartily tired. attempted to play at Connections after Dinner but thought either it or ourselves very stupid. the two eldest Cragies drank Tea here wrote to my Bror Ferdinand.

Saturday Mar: 29th.

Rather a Moist Morning & the wind out at the eastern corner but the wind rose & dispell'd the rain & at Noon blew quite a storm, to our constant visitor Mr P succeeded Miss Margaret Brown, Mr Simpson & Dr Adam to enquire after Francis who grew better & better every hour, not so Dear George who at best stood still & continued coughing sadly, not happy about him I was low unwell & completely wretched tried to disipate it by walking for an hour before Dinner on the walks almost blown away & very uncomfortable.

---

fourth Earl of Haddington. By the deeds of settlement her husband, Charles Halkett, and their successors were obliged to assume the name and arms of Craigie in addition to those of Halkett. Charles was a major in the army and he later died in India. Miss Halkett was Isabella Cornelia Craigie Halkett, (1768–1858), the daughter of Charles and Anne. Isabella married Robert Blair, Lord Avonton.

24. Pauly—paulie, pawlie, paullie, paley and other spelling derivatives—a poor weakly child, also applied to an under-sized lamb.

Witts Family Papers F187

1794

Sunday Mar: 30th.

A mild pleasant Morning but tho it continued dry & tolerably fine it changed at Noon to be colder & rather stormy, went to Morning Service at our own Chappel where M[r.] Allan was dull as usual on our return home M[r.] P. call'd as usual on his Dear Patients who both were much the same, M[rs.] Craigie likewise call'd & was lively & agreable M[r.] Witts & I went to evening service to the New North Kirk to hear D[r.] Hardie with whom we were very well pleased. George Simpson dined here & soon took himself off, wrote to M[rs.] Savage.

Monday Mar: 31st.

Quite an unpleasant day being tho much milder & the wind turn'd to the South, very stormy, flying showers of rain & excessive high wind yet M[r] P thought George might venture to walk for half an hour in hope it would mend him as he was very indifferent indeed Francis kept in by a Mercurial[1] dose; I was quite ill with Hysterics or convulsive spasms, only walked on the walks to accompany my poor Boy & so much worse in the evening that M[r.] P. was sent for who made me up a con-pasing[2] draught but I had a most wretched night.

Tuesday Ap: 1st.

Comenced like itself being very showery with a mixture of sunshine, but so damp it was little fit for the dear invalids to go out tho George was much better which assisted at least to raise my spirits & make my mind easier, M[r.] & M[rs.] Pennington both here in the Morning as kind as possible, I was full of spasms all day, walk'd a little late with M[r.] Witts chiefly in the Town to shops on speculation of Furniture.

Wensday Ap: 2d.

Quite a beautiful fine Morning but soon grew cloudy, & some trivial showers felt, we were <u>all</u> rather more convalescent of course our minds not so gloomy, walk'd first in the Square, & afterwards again on speculation, & wonderful to relate both went in the evening to the Play, on an invitation from M[rs.] Maitland to sit in her Box very well entertain'd tho the acting was

---

1. Mercurial—mercury in various compounds was used as a medicine, it is not clear what is happening here, but it may have been a mercuriate which would have been a further variation.
2. It is not clear what Agnes Witts means by con-pasing, but presumably she means something to compose herself; relaxing.
3. *Rosina* was a comic opera, in two acts written by Mrs Frances Brooke [née Moore] (±1724–1789). It was first performed at Covent Garden in 1782 and enjoyed wide popularity. This farce may have been a variation from the original. The Theatre Royal was built in 1768–69 and lasted sixty years before being substantially altered in 1830, but it closed thirty

below even mediocrity, the Play Douglas & the Farce Rosina,[3] the latter pretty well perform'd, the House a better one than I expected & full & smartly fill'd.

Thursday Ap: 3[d.]

A most charming day, mild air, much sun very little interrupted by clouds, M[r.] Witts out & busy the greater part of the Morning planing repairs for the house in Hanover Street, M[rs.] Pennington came early to spend the day, & join'd Father, Mother, & Sons in a walk to Bruntsfield Links, late in the Morning; M[r.] G. Robinson coming unexpectedly from Bamff, & M[r.] I. Rose join'd M[r.] & M[rs.] Pennington at Dinner, & play'd a lively game at whist; I was unhappy about George thinking him not so well M[rs.] Auchenleck call'd in the evening rec'd a Letter from my Sister Travell.

Friday Ap: 4[th.]

In the Morning a thick fog accompanied by small rain, which afterwards turn'd out hard showers a confining Day to me & My Boys, George somewhat mended by having taken an Emetic early in the Morning M[r.] Pennington & M[r.] Simpson our only visitors rec'd a Letter from M[rs.] Naper.

Saturday Ap: 5[th.]

Upon the whole a dry fine day, tho the wind was sharp & cold, but the sun hot, in the evening a trifling shower, went out early in the day with M[r.] Witts on some furniture speculation which carried us into various shops at several different parts of the Town after having call'd on M[rs.] Pennington she accompanied us on the Leith Walk to the Chair Manufactory I was well tired on my return home, having been out near 4 hours. Boys tolerable indeed Francis quite so.

Sunday Ap: 6[th.]

A thick foggy Morning which before the hour of Church turn'd to small rain, & in the afternoon was very severe rain & wind, too damp for either of the Boys to be ventured to go out, not even Francis to church we went to S[t.] Peters Chappel in the Morning & to M[r.] Strothers's in the afternoon, but disappointed in not hearing him himself but a stranger, went in M[rs.] Craigies Coach in the Morning & back, & in the evening in a Chaise rec'd a Letter from Miss Anne Snow & wrote to M[rs.] Catherine Thornton.

Monday Ap: 7[th.]

Severely wet from Morning to night no interruption & at times prodigeous hard rain, I was very far from well, M[r.] Witts out some part of the Morn: on useful bussiness & to call on our good friend M[r.] Pennington who was not well. much work & some reading. George still hoarse & coughing sadly. rec'd a Letter from M[rs.] Granville

Tuesday Ap: 8[th.]

Wet again in the Morning, but tho it soon became dry, the wind was so tremendously high & cold, it was by no means fit for Francis to make his first entrance into School or for George

---

years later when it was demolished to make way for a Post Office in 1859. In style and size it resembled the theatre in Bristol, and in 1780 the tickets were three shillings, pit and boxes; two shillings the gallery; and one shilling the upper gallery, providing the proprietors £140 on a full house.

or myself to stir out indeed the latter had taken a Mercurial Dose, much business in receiving new & sending away old Furniture, M^r. Simpson made a short call in the Morning. rec'd a Letter from my Brother Ferdinand, & wrote to M^r. Richard Witts & my Sister Travell.

Wensday Ap: 9th.

Very severely cold & windy accompanied by short hail storms, but ventured Francis to school, M^r. Pennington call'd on his Patient & was far from clear whether his Cough would not turn out the Hooping Cough I walk'd no more than to call on M^rs. Brown where I spent an hour & half most agreably, dined by invitation <u>below</u> <u>stairs</u> with M^r. & M^rs. Hamilton a party of 13, 8 of them Gentlemen, a handsome entertainment & very pleasant, ourselves & 2 or 3 more staid Supper, play'd at Whist much ease, like M^rs. Hamilton much. wrote to M^rs. Parsons

Thursday Ap: 10th.

Quite a happy change in the weather, being mild & very pleasant, some sunshine & wind much subsided, George much the same sent him out on the walks with Cather for the benefit of both while we went & sat an hour with the Penningtons from thence to Lady C; Charteris by the Leith Walk & back Lanes, being late in the day made her but a short visit, rather dull on both sides & I came home much fatigued. recd a Letter from Lady E: Bentinck

Friday Ap: 11th.

Again cold & stormy, but tho the showers were both short & transient, they were enough to keep me within all day, & George also, about whom Mr. Pennington was so doubtful he wish'd for further advice which for a time I parry'd, as he certainly appeard better tho perhaps it was more decided he had the Hooping Cough. wrote to Lady Edward Bentinck

Saturday Ap: 12th.

A most charming day, mild air, much sun, & little wind, Papa, Mama, & Francis, went out to walk leaving George & his <u>Nurse</u> Catherine to perambulate nearer home; call'd first on M^rs. Pennington, who we found alone & so miserably out of spirits, it was most distressing, & naturaly infect'd me; from her went to see Raeborn the Painters Portraits pretty well entertaind by them found out some strong likenesses; then to survey the new Bridewell on Calton Hill a very well designed building & charming situation. George lively & gay tho Cough'd rather more, recd a Letter from Miss Snow & a short one from Miss Sabine in one of her Fathers from Pisa in Italy. wrote to M^rs. Granville

Sunday Ap: 13th.

A very brilliant charming Day, tho it grew rather more cold & a little stormy towards evening, George certainly much better & able to go out a great deal in the air. we went to Morning Service as usual, at S^t. Peters, where the length of the service detain'd us till we were almost too late at S^t. Georges Chappel a very fine Sermon from M^r. Cleeve.

Monday Ap: 14th.

Weather quite as dry & fine, which tempted us to let George be more out than did him good set out on our Morning or rather Noon walk with an intention of going to see M^rs. Pennington

Libberton Wynd, Cowgate. An engraving by T. Picken after a painting by George Cattermole. Libberton Wynd was demolished in 1834 to make way for the George IV Bridge.

but meeting with her in Street made our visit walking I came home quite fatigued, tho with little exertion but I was knock'd up by hearing of the death of poor M[r.] R. Cumberland.[4] rec'd a long Letter from Miss Louisa Lee, & wrote to Lord Edward Bentinck & Miss Anne Snow.

Tuesday Ap: 15[th.]
Had been hard rain in the Night, & was rather wet & damp, in the Morning, but soon clear'd & was dry & fine with abundance of sunshine the remainder of the day, & the finest night imaginable a bright full Moon walk'd out first with George, on the walks & Square & then went into Cowgate &'c with M[r.] Witts speculating at Brokers but bought nothing. drank Tea up stairs wth the Home family not very lively, no one but their own family. rec'd a Letter from L[d.] Edw[d.] Bentinck with the melancholly news of the death of M[r.] R. Cumberland in the Island of Tobago of the Yellow Fever much hurt & distress'd by it.

Wensday Ap: 16[th.]
A very fine day, tho with considerable Wind which made it less pleasant, & in the afternoon a sharp shower but very short; My poor little Boy not so well but I thought more in consequence

---

4. Richard Cumberland (d. 1794). Richard was the eldest son of the dramatist Richard Cumberland (1732–1811); and the sister of Agnes's close friend, Elizabeth Lady Bentinck. Richard had married Albinia (1759–1850), eldest daughter of George, 3rd Earl of Buckinghamshire. Richard died in Tobago in 1794 and his body was brought back to England where he was buried at Hampton Court. Albinia lived on as a grace and favour tenant at Hampton, with four servants for more than another half century.

A view of Heriot's Hospital towering in the distance, viewed from the Old Town. An engraving from a painting by J. M. W. Turner, 1822.

of a severe emetic he took fasting, very uneasy about him, & very low & quite unwell the whole day. after walking with him, went to Herriotts Hospital,[5] a very fine building for the purpose of a most beneficial charity, finely situated, the Chappel a beautiful room newly fitted up & the Stucco work very beautiful, by accident found M.ʳ Com: Brown there, intended to have met the Penningtons there but they were unpunctual & we were tired of waiting for them & walk'd home where they join'd us at Dinner, & staid late enough in the evening to play at Cassino.

Thursday Ap: 17.ᵗʰ

A most extraordinary warm fine day for the season, indeed for any period of the year, George very much better, but still M.ʳ Pennington was so urgent that D.ʳ Gregory might see him that we complied; M.ʳ Witts & I walk'd first to see Lady Catherine, where I heard some intelligence that was very interesting, from thence into Queen Street, to Lady Janet Dundas, to look at some hanging Book shelves, afternoon so wonderful fine I walk'd after Dinner with Francis on the walks w.ᶜʰ were brilliant M.ʳ Simpson drank Tea quite en" famile pleasant.

---

5.   Heriot's Hospital was built in the early seventeenth century using a bequest from George Herriot, and opened in 1659, with thirty sickly children in residence; its finances grew, and it took in other pupils in addition to the orphans for whom it was intended. In the 1880s, it began to charge fees; but even to the current time continues its charitable object of providing free education to fatherless children.

Friday Ap: 18th.

Weather so peculiarly warm & fine it was quite astonishing, tho the air was rather thick, but probably from heat, the thermometer being up to 64' at a North Window, My Dear George continuing to grow better & better Dr. Gregory & Mr. P. visited him before our return from Morning Church, & the former found so little cause to prescribe that they had left him before we came home but with a promise of coming the next day. went to Morning service at St. Peters the service perform'd jointly by Mr. Allan & Mr. Walker, the Chappel extremely full,[6] went to evening service at Mr. Sandfords Chappel, where we met & sat with the Penningtons. walk'd in the evening on the walks, not so warm as the evening before

Saturday Ap: 19th.

Again very warm but not so pleasant being a very thick air & at noon a small shower, Dr. Gregory & our Friend met here at 12 o'clock, & gave the utmost satisfaction in regard to George who was wonderfully well all Day , liked the Dr. far better than I expected, walk'd back with Mr. P. to his own house, where we eat cold meat & went with them to look at Masters Pictures, well pleased & found out several likenesses, being too late to go to Prayers, call'd on Mrs. Thomson in Hanover Street but was not admitted. rec'd Letters from Mrs. Parsons & Mr. Delabere.

Sunday Ap: 20th.

Another most charming day, perhaps a better than any, being a clear air & equally warm seldom such an Easter Day known, fires quite useless went to St. Peters Chappel both parts of the Day, a great crowd, no Sermon in the Morning, so great a number of communicants that service was not over till past two, had only just time to run home & eat some cold meat before we went again, equally full & a vast deal of imaginery fine singing. Dined at Commissr. Browns quite unexpectedly being ask'd only at Morning church, sat down 12 to Dinner, very pleasant, many of the Dundas family,[7] Mrs. Dundas the recent Widow, very interesting Woman. Dr. Gregory added to the party at Tea. rec'd a delightful long Letter from Mrs. Burslem.

Monday Ap: 21st.

Still dry & warm but not so pleasant as some of the former days, the air being very thick close & of course oppressive. Mr. Witts went early to Breakfast with Mr. Oliphant at Leith, & did not return till Noon when we walk'd first to call on Mrs. Pennington who was not well, & afterwards into some Houses in Frederick street to see furniture, in the evening walk'd a little in the Square with Francis George much the same as usual at night wrote to Mrs. Buxton.

Tuesday Ap: 22d.

An extreme fine hot day, tho somewhat oppressive the air being still rather thick, but in all points like summer, no fires & open Windows quite necessary George very ill poor fellow

---

6.   St Peter's Episcopal Chapel, Roxburgh Place, built 1790.
7.   Commissioner Brown. George Brown Esq. (±1722–1806), of Lindsaylands and Ellistown was one of the Commissioners of His Majesty's Board of Excise for Scotland and was known as a gentleman of amiable temper and suavity of manner. He lived in George Square, and later St James's Square. He married Dorothea, née Dundas, and the couple had two sons and three daughters; Viscountess Hampden. Lady Wedderburn of Ballendean and the Hon. Lady Alexander Hope.

the greater part of the day principally owing we hoped to the effects of an Emetic he had taken the night before, much fever, & his breath sadly labor'd. Went to Morning Prayers at S:. Peters Chap. afterwards went to a Roupe in New Street Cannongate where we bought several odd things & bid for several more. on my return rec'd a more pleasing visit than ordinary from M:. Charteris he being more free & easy went in a Chair to dine at M:. Penningtons, meeting D:. Freer & M:. Arnold, & M:. Race in the afternoon, play'd at Cassino & walk'd home finding it quite warm & pleasant happy to find my poor Boy rather better on our return rec'd Letters from Lady Edward Bentinck & Miss Betty Guydickens, the former most affectionate as well as most interesting melancholly being an accurate detail of her poor Bro:. Cumberlands death.

Wensday Ap: 23.d

By no means a pleasant day, being a most boisterous high wind which made the dust intolerably troublesome, & at the same time an oppressive thick air. in the evening a sharp shower of rain a great comfort. poor George very indifferent indeed, much fever & oppression on his breath a blister laid on at night, D:. Gregory as well as M:. Pennington here went late in the day to Trotters' Upholstery Warehouse to order some furniture. very low in spirits. —

Thursday Ap: 24.th

Still a prodigeous high Wind, but being a clear air & constant sunshine it was much pleasanter & warm enough tho a North wind, in the evening again some useful showers, D:. Gregory & both M:. & M:rs. Pennington here in the Morn: poor George better but still feverish & moderate, tho his blister had perform'd wonders. when we went out went furniture Calico hunting & some other little bussinesses & call'd on Lady C: Charteris who was more than ordinary indifferent all but George drank Tea agreably up stairs with M:. Simpson, M:. Balderston being added to their own family party – rec'd Letters from my Sister Travell & M:rs. Buxton.

Friday Ap: 25.th

A most unpleasant day being a dreadful cold high wind, which occasion'd the dust to be so very troublesome, that one was blinded when out, call'd on M:rs. Pennington, & went to give final orders at Trotters Warehouse about the furniture, glad to get home again under the Shelter of my own house, D:. Gregory gave George a friendly call, & pronounced him in so safe a state he should not see him again for a time. wrote to M:. John Delabere.

Saturday Ap: 26.th

Most happy change in the weather for tho the air was still cold, the wind was much subsided & most constant sunshine M:. Witts took an early Breakfast, then to Market, & afterwards went with M:. Pennington both to D:. Gregorys, & D:. Blacks concluding Lectures, M:. P. call'd here, after which we took a most pleasant, but very long walk crossing Queen Street, & over the fields to the Villiage of Stockbridge opposite to S:. Barnards Well, where we went to look at a large old House to be let, & now occupied by Lady Diana Scott, a very diserable House & premises, & most elegantly & comfortably furnish'd imagine we had walk'd more than 5 miles but being better than usual bore it well. wrote to M:rs. Hyett.

Sunday Ap: 27ᵗʰ·

Again dry & fine, but cold & rather windy went as usual to Morning Service at Sᵗ· Peters, from whence Mʳ· Witts went to return Col: Cas: Gordons visit & found him at home, in the meantime I rec'd one from the English Mʳ· Brown, went to evening service at the New Grey Friars sat in Mʳˢ· Irvines seat an excellent Sermon & Prayers from Dʳ· Baird. All but poor George who was but moderate went to drink Tea at Mʳ· Penningtons, meeting Dʳ· Rotheram, Mʳ· Brown & a Mʳ· Foster & 2 Ladies dropp'd in accidentaly a pleasant converseable evening, walk'd home between 9 & 10 Francis sooner. Bob: Brown with George in our absence

Monday Ap: 28ᵗʰ·

Very wet till Noon when it became partialy so, being in heavy showers accompanied with prodigeous high wind, but sunshine between whiles, I was compleatly unhappy by my Dear Husbands having been taken extremely ill in the night with a bilious complaint, which brought on so considerable a degree of fever that he was very much reduced & kept his Bed almost the whole of the Day, & poor George but indifferent & took an Emetic in the Morning my time fully employ'd between the two. Mʳ· Pennington with us in the Morning & under his sanction I ventured to give Mʳ· Witts many different things & he was better at night in consequence, but his complaint was but too familiar to his recent one Francis a most animated happy being by going to a young Ball at Mʳ· Morays, not at home till between 11 & 12. rec'd a Letter from Miss Gorges.

Tuesday Ap: 29ᵗʰ·

Again wet stormy & cold, but far from perpetual & dried fast between, Mʳ· Witts had had a tolerable good night & was evidently better tho a poor weak creature all day & looking sadly, Mʳ· P here early, my only walk to call on Mʳˢ· Craigie & Mʳˢ· Brown found only the latter at home, Mʳ· & Mʳˢ· Pennington came to eat their last Dinner here which made us all Dull as they were to leave Edinbro' the next Morning, of course much interesting conversation & I was as low as death but from too many causes. George happily better than usual rec'd a most affectionate but melancholly Letter from Lord Edward Bentinck.

Wensday Ap: 30ᵗʰ·

Very much the same kind of weather only the Storms were rather more heavy, & it was bitterly cold, our dear & worthy Friend paid us a very early visit before he set off, & hoped he left my Dear Husband purely as he had had a good night but appearances were deceitful, & he had a very languid poor day, total loss of appetite & inability of doing anything but lye on the Sopha, luckily Dʳ· Gregory call'd to see George, & enter'd much into Mʳ· Witts's case which gave me both courage & confidence as he approved of all that had been done for him. Mʳ· Simpson likewise call'd. I workd hard, tried to be as comfortable as my situation would admit & in the evening was amused by Francis reading in the Packet a Novel written by Miss Gunning.[8]

---

8.   Elizabeth Gunning (1769–1823). *The Packet* was published in 4 volumes, 1794.

Thursday May 1[st.]

In the Morning dry & fine tho cold at noon some showers, after which it was more mild & pleasant; my Dear Husband very indifferent the greater part of the day, quite uneasy about him, tried to hope his uncomfortableness was much increased by a medicine he was obliged to take. went late out in the Town on some necessary errands, on my return walk'd out for ½ an hour on the walks with George. much fatigued with the labours of the day but more by anxiety of Mind.

Friday May 2[d.]

Cold & windy, but dry & with much Sunshine my Dear Husband after rising tolerably well, grew suddenly so much worse being taken with severe shivering fits, that I was greatly alarm'd & imediately sent to D[r.] Gregory who came instantly & happily quietted my fears, sent M[r.] Witts to Bed & order'd him some little medicine but more regermen,[9] his behavior & attention quite charming he came again late in the evening & found his Dear patient better even beyond his hopes. before Dinner I walk'd into the Town on Some necessary bussiness, & before Tea took a <u>run</u> with Francis <u>all</u> round the Meadow walk for exercise; the rest of the day wholly spent in Nursing &'c nearly worn down wrote to M[rs.] Pennington at Carlisle.

Saturday May 3[d.]

Still extremely cold & stormy, had been much rain in the night, & some trivial showers in the morning, M[r.] Witts had had a pretty good night & the D[r.] when he made an early visit thought him much better & fit to be trusted to my care alone for some days, but yet he was miserably weak & languid & required much care & attention. George happily got almost well, he & I walk'd round the walks after Dinner when it was become finer than in the Morning but shockingly cold. Francis dined by invitation at Admi[l.] Duncans M[rs.] Auchenleck call'd in the Morning & M[r.] Stormonth was here in the evening on some bussiness wrote a long Letter to my Sister Travell.

Sunday May 4[th.]

Nothing to boast of in point of weather being still cold & windy, & very cloudy with strong show of rain tho very little appeard, my Dear Man tho in a very gradual manner certainly mending, but I could not consent to his venturing out even in a Carriage Francis & I went to Morning Service at S[t.] Peters Chapel where was a stranger did the whole Duty but in a very moderate way, & to the evening service at the Town Church, where D[r.] Hunters manner displeased me much, a Sermon of an hour long all but 5 minutes not at home till more than a quarter after 4 rec'd a most affectionate long Letter from L[dy.] E: B.

Monday May 5[th.]

A much better day the air being more mild & not near so high a wind, with sufficient sunshine to make pleasing light & shade, which we were much gratified by in taking an airing of a few miles in a Post chaise for the benifit of my Dear Invalid in which George as well as myself had no

---

9. Regermen—regimen—a particular course of diet and treatment for the unwell.

objection to go also went 4 miles or more on the road to the Queens Ferry, returning home the Linlithgow road thro the villiage of Corstorphine having gone a pleasant drive of 8 or 9 miles, over a Country that in many parts was pleasing & some rather triste & barren, my Dear Husband much revived by the air & not fatigued. Mr Palmer call'd in the Morning. in the evening read a great deal in the packet.

Tuesday May 6th.

On the whole a pretty fine day tho still a high cold wind, but continued sunshine made it pleasant Mr Witts ventured to walk out being realy very tolerably well, & was none the worse for it, going to Mr Stormonth on bussiness & to 2 or 3 Roupes in St James Square, where I quitted him & went to sit an hour with Lady C: Charteris, who was both affectionate & pleasant & sent me home loaded with fruit & flowers & other proofs of her kindness, I never see her but with grateful pleasure. rec'd Letters from M^rs. Pennington & Miss Snow.

Wensday May 7th.

Very much the same weather little more stormy & had been since in the night, Dr Gregory call'd here in a most friendly pleasant manner we walk'd late on

Dr Andrew Hunter (1743–1809). In 1786 Dr Hunter was translated by the Magistrates to the Tron Church. An etching by John Kay.

various parts of the Town where it was most shelterd, & to many shops & Roupes the day made vexatious & tiresome by Catherine being both ill, helpless, & hopeless. in the afternoon drank Tea ourselves & Sons with Mr Simpson & his Sons, a friendly pleasant visit. wrote to Lady E: B. & Miss Snow.

Thursday May 8th.

No change in Weather, much wind some sunshine, & some trifling hail storms, My Dear Husband to appearance quite convalescent, & Dear Georges Cough & all complaints almost flown away; Francis at home for near a weeks holidays being the first day of the Preachings, consequently a very serious day all over the Town, we went to Morning service at the Tolbooth Church for the first time, which is handsome & newly fitted up, Dr Kemp, only read prayers, a Mr Dixon preachd & good singing more than two hours in the Church which was extremely full, afterwards walk'd in Princes Street, sent home from fear of hail storm. English Mr Brown call'd me finish'd the Packet & read a fine sermon of Dr Hardies preach'd on last Fast Day a very fine composition. wrote to Miss Elizabeth Guydickens.

Friday May 9th.

By no means a good or pleasant Day, being wet in the Morning, & appeard likely to be showery after tho but little fell. but it was disagreably cold & windy; I made three visits in my Morning

Revd John Kemp DD (1745–1805), one of the ministers at the Tolbooth Church. An etching by John Kay, 1792.

Walks, first to M^rs. Duncan merely one of form, for many civilities but she not home, the same ill success in one to M^rs. Maitland who was on a short visit to her Mother M^rs. Gibson, afterwards had better luck in calling on M^rs. Halkett Craigie who is always very conversible & pleasant, the evening proving fine M^r. Witts & I tete tete walk'd all round the Meadow walk, while the Boys went to see the Birds & Beasts. on our return found M^r. Stormonth, afterwards call'd M^rs. Auchenleck, to there succeeded, M^rs. Hume from up Stairs for a short visit wrote to Miss Sheppard.

Saturday May 10th.

The Morning had a wonderful appearance the ground being coverd with snow & more falling which soon turning to rain, it quickly disappeared & by Noon was quite dry, tho damp & cold, notwithstand^g. the sun. went out late first to look at some Household furniture in a House in Bristol Street that was soon to be Rouped, & afterwards to Church at the old Grey Friars, where the service was so tediously performd by the same Gentleman we had heard on Thursday we did not get home to Dinner till ½ past 4. Miss Brown sat an hour or two with us after Tea

Sunday May 11th.

A fine shewey Morning early, which soon turn'd to Misty & small flying rain, which obliged me to go to Chappel in a Chair, mended at Noon, but was another hard shower in the afternoon & was very cold. at S^t. Peters in the Morning, & in the Cowgate Chappel in the afternoon, which undoubtedly is a very handsome one a very fine toned Organ, the Service very moderately perform'd by two clergymen, we sat on a charming seat in the Gallery; Bob: Brown dined here, too cold to go out in the evening. wrote to M^rs. Pennington.

Monday May 12th.

Upon the whole a very good day, being quite dry & almost constant sunshine, tho the air was very cold, went out early & Francis with us being still holidays, went to Hanover Street, to make many observations & take measures of many things preparatory to our speedy removal there, went to Survey the furniture of a House or two going to be Rouped & many other similar bussinesses which kept us out near 4 hours, & were out again on the same design for an hour in the evening. alas! no Letters from England

Tuesday May 13th.

A dry good day, air milder but not so much sun, Morning chiefly taken up in attending Roups spent nearly 4 hours at a large good one in George Street not unentertaining, from such a

French Ambassador's Chapel, Cowgate. An engraving by T. Stewart from a painting by Daniel Wilson.

number & variety of company, & very well repaid for our trouble by purchasing a handsome Wilton Carpet, at a very cheap rate, not at home till quite Dinner time; walk'd round the Meadow walks before Tea, grown cold & Windy. wrote to Miss Louisa Lee.

Wensday May 14th.

By no means a pleasant day, being a cold high wind, with flying small showers, but not enough to lay the dust which was quite intolerable, busy again at Roupes, & also in overlooking our furniture making at the Upholsterers, I afterwards went & spent a friendly & therefore very pleasant hour with Lady C: Charteris; late in the evening Miss Georgiana Brown call'd.

Thursday May 15th.

A dark gloomy Morning & rather cold but before Noon, turn'd warmer, bright & pleasant, & so was the whole of the day & a remarkable fine clear evening soon after breakfast M.ʳ Witts Francis (being holiday) & I went with Commissioner Brown & his Son & youngest Daughter to see the sight of the Day, the Earl of Leven, Lord High Commissioner of the Church of Scotland walk in Procession to the New Kirk, M.ʳ Brown & M.ʳ Witts walk'd with many others in his Suite, the young people & I were station'd at Windows in a House in the High Street, where we well saw as much as was to be seen, w.ᶜʰ was not so much as had been represented, M.ʳ W. did not return till after Tea dining with his <u>Grace</u> & a large Party, where he was <u>pleasantly</u> noticed, when my curiosity was gratified, I went to a Roupe in Bucclugh Place, made an unsuccessful visit to M.ʳˢ Hamilton, one more to M.ʳˢ Craigie finding her at home; Francis a most entertaining companion in the absence of his father, late in the Morning M.ʳ & M.ʳˢ Hamilton made me a very chearful easy visit when M.ʳ Witts came home in the evening walk'd in the Square, meeting some pleasant people made it lively

David Leslie, 6th Earl of Leven and 5th of Melville (1722–1802). In 1774 Leslie became the Lord High Commissioner to the General Assembly, a position he held for nearly twenty years.

Friday May 16th.

Windy & unpleasant; tho dry & not at all cold, Mr. Simpson call'd in the Morning after which, we walk'd to two or three Roupes, & to see Watsons Portraits in the Exchange moderate painting but strong likeness, in the afternoon Mr. Witts went to a Coffee House to meet the different Agents & People concernd relative to compleating the absolute purchase of the house in Hanover Street a great & useful event,[10] small flying showers prevented any going out. wrote to Mrs. Buxton & rec'd a Letter from my Sister Travell.

Saturday May 17th.

A Moist Morning & showery at times several parts of the Day, Francis confined by a very bad swell'd face owing to an accident, I never went out in the Morning, pretty employ'd in much useful bussiness but walk'd part round the walks with Mr. Witts between Dinner & Tea finding it very cold & windy. rec'd Letters from Mrs. Granville & Miss Anne Snow.

Sunday May 18th.

Very steady mild rain till 12 o'clock when it became dry, bright & warm till the evening when it was a very great mist & wonderfully damp, judging it too wet to attempt going to Church, employ'd the time in some useful preparations for our moving, went to evening service at St. Andrews Church, sat in the Lord Provosts Seat who had given us a general entrée then the service pretty well performed by a Stranger walk'd on the walks before Tea, accompanied by Mrs. Craigie & Miss Macdonald, poor Frans. confined the whole day.

Monday May 19th.

Mild & pleasant in the Morning tho rather gloomy, & soon became cold & stormy tho remain'd dry & at night the wind was boisterously high. My Dear George went to School for the first time after his confinement w.ch had been 9 weeks, his Cough having nearly left him, Francis still kept at home by his face; I went about two, a walking with Mr. Witts first to call on Mr. Webster at Spittalfield House a strange miserable Place, then to several brokers in search of odd bargains w.ch we made, after Dinner walk'd quite round the Walks, almost blown along & on our return went over Dr. Adams, new bought House in this Square. wrote to Mrs. Callandar.

---

10. Although Edward was bankrupt, there was some separate money from the marriage settlement which the assignees were unable to touch. This provided a modest annual income, and it was presumably from this money that the Hanover Street house was purchased.

Above: View of the High Street
Edinburgh and the Lawn Market by
Alexander Nasmyth, 1824.

Right: John Knox House, Netherbow,
High Street, Edinburgh. An engraving
by T. Stewart from a painting by
Daniel Wilson.

Tuesday May 20ᵗʰ·

A tolerable pleasant day a mixture of sun & clouds & quite dry till evening when there was a
shower that prevented going out. attempted in our Morning walk a visit to Lady C: Charteris
but she was too indifferent to admit me, call'd on Mʳ· & Mʳˢ· Allan & were alike unsuccessful,
went afterwards to Mʳ· Young the builder in Thistle Street to talk our intended alterations to
our house in Hanover Street. in the evening began a new Novel call'd Ellen Countess of Castle
Howel.[11] wrote to Mʳˢ· Granville at night.

---

11.   Anna Maria Bennet (d. 1808). *Ellen Countess of Castle Howel*, 1794.

Wensday May 21ˢᵗ.

A miserable cold uncomfortable day being a thick air, & at the same time a very cold wind went out rather early to Mʳˢ· Clerks sale in Princes Street where we staid the greater part of the Morning & bought a few things, a great crowd some genteel people there in expectation of Mʳ· Simpson & all his family & Mʳ· Balderston to drink Tea, disappointed in all but Miss Simpson & her Brothers found her a very conversible sensible Girl. Francis able to return to School a very hard shower of rain & hail in the evening.

Thursday May 22ᵈ·

Still a thick air but neither so cold or windy as the preceeding day, very cloudy in the evening & some trifling rain fell. Very busy for some hours in the Morning packing up Books, Medicines & many other things, at noon went again to see Lady C: C: who I sat an hour with, on my return into Georges Square made a fruitless visit to Mʳˢ· Brown, & an odd one to Mʳˢ· Home & her Daughters upstairs. walk'd a little on the walks before Tea sent home by rain. wrote to Mʳˢ· Travell.

Friday May 23ᵈ·

A blowing boisterous Morning tho dry till three o'clock when heavy rain came on & so continued in great measure the whole of the evening, I was so busy packing I never stirr'd out all Morning. drank Tea at Mʳ· Balderstons meeting the Simpson family, conversible & pleasant, & handsome entertainment.

Saturday May 24ᵗʰ·

Quite a fine dry day, very cold tho some sunshine, but very well calculated for the removal of some of the lightest of our baggage by Porters went up to Hanover Street in the middle of the Morn. to arrange some matters, after which Mʳ· Stormonth call'd, busy all the afternoon again rec'd a Letter from Mʳˢ· Savage.

Sunday May 25ᵗʰ·

Without doubt as cold a day as ever was known at the season of the year, without sun & very thick air, Mʳ· Witts went to Church twice & dined with the Lord Commissioner, Francis attended me in the Morning to Sᵗ· Peters Chappel, after which visited Mʳˢ· Duncan & Mʳˢ· Macqueen both at home & very gracious, went to evening service at the old Grey Friars conducted into a good Gallery by Mʳˢ· Carre; the Boys dining at Mʳ· Browns for a wonder I eat my Dinner by myself at 6 o'clock went to sit for an hour with Mʳˢ· Craigie by way of take leave, & drank Tea & staid till past nine at Mʳ· Browns quite in a friendly family way.

Monday May 26ᵗʰ·

Quite a brilliant fine day, only still very cold for the season in the wind & out of the Sun but perfectly well suited to our grand bussiness of flitting to use a Scotch phrase, which commenced very early & continued with much spirit till quite night Mʳ· W. backwards & forwards all day till he was tired to death, I went up to Hanover Street at mid.day returnd to Georges Square to Dinner having first call'd on Mʳˢ· Hamilton who rec'd me in a most friendly stile return'd to the New Town in the afternoon in a Hackney Coach to prevent fatigue & convey some choice things & walk'd back at night to our old home; tired down

Tuesday May 27th.

Very much the same sort of weather only a trifling shower about breakfast time which gave some alarms for the safety of the removal of the last of our baggage, a most bustling Morning, Mr. Witts & I finally got away before Noon, only to be engaged in a still greater in our new house, but all things went on prosperously, & little or no damage, dined in a kind of scrambley way, but still it was in a dwelling of our own which gave a double relish, work'd as hard as possible all the evening assisted by the Boys, & got both the Parlour & our bed chamber in good order. rec'd a very kind Letter from Mrs. Callander

Wensday May 28th.

A most tremendous wet day without interruption from Morn to Night, attended by a good deal of wind, which made us rejoice all our goods were safe & well deposited, the poor Boys almost wet to the ~~school~~ going to school did not let George return there after breakfast very full of bussiness the whole day, as tired as dirty.

Thursday May 29th.

Most pleasant reverse in point of weather, being a clear fine day & constant sunshine; Mr. W. out for 2 or 3 hours in the Morn: on several calls & business I had full employment at home, principally in attending upon a Cabinet maker, putting up comforts, all four walk'd before Tea on Leith Walk to Chair & Canab[12] maker at night wrote to Miss Anne Snow.

Friday May 30th.

Dull & gloomy, being a thick air from east Wind & no sun, never stirr'd out from Morning to night being very busy, & thoroughly persecuted with workmen off all Descriptions, & the house most comfortless by the staircase & passages being both white wash'd & colord Mr. Simpson call'd in the Morning. in the evening work'd & heard Ellen.

Saturday May 31st.

As fine a day as can be with east wind cold air but hot sun, not much more clear or tolerable in point of comfort than the day before, went out late in the Morning to the South end of the Town on several errands, & in the evening with the Boys walk'd to St. Bernards Well a very pretty spot not a mile from the Town. rec'd Letters from Miss Snow & Mrs. Naper much agitated & surprized by the latter informing me she was going to be married to Mr. Rycroft not highly gratified by the intelligence.[13] wrote to her at Night

Sunday June 1st.

The wind still in the same point, but much sun & extremely pleasant till afternoon when it became a thick misty air & most sultry hot, went both to Morning & evening service at St. George's Chapel Mr. Cleeve peculiarly eloquent in his Sermon, after Morning service walk'd

---

12. This is very unclear, presumably a rushed contraction for 'cabinet'.
13. Jane Naper, Agnes's niece had been widowed in 1791. Her proposed husband, Henry Rycroft (±1770–1846) was about five years her junior and perfectly eligible. He was the younger brother of a baronet, Sir Nelson Rycroft, and later (1816) was knighted himself as Knight Harbinger to the King. It is not clear what objection Agnes Witts can have had.

the whole length of Queen S$^{t.}$ in the afternoon attempted to walk again, but it was so very hot & was so very indifferent & fatigued it ended in nothing. much astonished by a note from Lady C. Charteris informing us M$^{r.}$ Charteris was married to Miss Margaret Campbell the night before, having no idea it was to have taken place so soon.[14] rec'd a Letter from M$^{rs.}$ Pennington.

Monday June 2$^{d.}$

An extreme fine warm air, rather too hot at mid.day for much moving, but in the evening a most wonderful thick fog came on quite suddenly amounting almost to small rain & quite damp & cold. M$^{r.}$ Ferguson & M$^{r.}$ Thomson here in the Morning finally settling all matters relative to the House, I never went out in the Morning all 4 went in the afternoon to call on Lady C: Charteris to wish her joy returned home to a late Tea cold & damp

Tuesday June 3$^{d.}$

Another very fine Day, very hot sun, but cool wind, a continuation of much settling bussiness & many workmen about, till after mid.day when we went into Georges Square to call on M$^{rs.}$ Hamilton to wish her joy of her Sisters Marriage,[15] made a long & pleasant visit, found Miss Elphinston there, M$^{rs.}$ Auchenleck call'd in the Morning, & M$^{r.}$ Stormonth in the afternoon after Tea walk'd again into the South Town on some errands & the Boys with, again cold & rather inclined to be foggy.

Wensday June 4$^{th.}$

Rather cloudy in the Morning, extremely fine all day, & again close & gloomy in the evening, day made disagreable, by perpetual Cannon firing, Bell ringing, Squibs flying, little Bonfires in every street, all in honor of the Kings birth-day, which allow'd me only to go out late in the evening with M$^{r.}$ Witts & the Boys in Queen Street & thereabouts, after he return'd home from spending two hours in the Parliament House, at a large meeting of the Lord Provost & all the principal people in & about town to celibrate in a Loyal manner this <u>happy</u> day, by drinking health & eating a <u>desert</u>, a new way of wishing long life to King; it was likewise a holiday to the Boys, but from fear of accident I kept them mostly at home.

Thursday June 5$^{th.}$

A most glorious fine warm Day from Morn to night, tho still the wind was in the east, never went out all Morning, busy in many things, & having my hair cut, & I went to Dine at D$^{r.}$ Gregorys, where we met M$^{r.}$ & M$^{rs.}$ Brown & 3 Daughters & a large company, beside, amounting to 7 Ladies & 8 Gentlemen, a very handsome entertainment, & a lively pleasant visit; before I return'd home went across the street & sat ½ an hour with Lady C: Charteris who as ever was friendly & most kind.

---

14. Francis Charteris, 8th Earl of Wemyss and 4th Earl of March (1772–1853); the son of Francis and Susan, Lord and Lady Elcho. Francis married, 31 May 1794, Margaret, 4th daughter of Walter Campbell (1741–1816) of Shawfield.

15. Mrs Harriet Hamilton was the elder sister to Margaret Campbell. She was the eldest daughter of Walter Campbell (1741–1816) of Shawfield and married Daniel Hamilton of Gikercleugh.

Friday June 6th.

Had been much rain in the night was showery all the forenoon, & a smart continued rain in the afternoon which kept one within the whole Day, & not very pleasantly employ'd, being waiting all Day for Upholsterers & other workmen who never came & made the Day tedious & tiresome.

Saturday June 7th.

Quite a fine Day, tho still a cold air, but very hot sun, the Workmen coming got the drawing room in great measure finish'd, walk'd both Morning & evening & Francis with us George having got a very bad swell'd face, about the Town on various roads. Mr. Cleeve call'd in the Morning rec'd a very informing Letter from my Sisr. Travell.

Sunday June 8th.

A dry day, but till quite evening most stormy & tempestuous when the wind sunk & it was quite bright & pleasant, went to both Morning & evening service at St. Georges Chappel & being Whit Sunday rec'd the Sacrament. Mr. Robert Hamilton sat with us in the evening Service; Mr. Brown (Student) call'd between Churches, & after Tea all but George who was still confined with his face walk'd thro Georges Square to the walks where we had pleasure in seeing several of our old Neighbours who met us most lively & cordially indeed, & sent us home pleased by attention,

Monday June 9th.

By no means a pleasant day tho quite dry, being a gloomy sky, & wonderful high wind which made the dust intolerable sinking towards evening it was pleasant; Went to Church in the Morning, not out afterwards, but busy in many things: George still a prisoner from his face, the rest of us walk'd after Tea in the fields round & about St. Bernards Well &'c.

Tuesday June 10th.

Very much the same kind of unpleasant weather till afternoon, when it became small rain in showers; went to Morning service again at St. Georges Chappel nearly blown away, & never out again the whole day; engaged in the Morning putting up bookshelves &'c, & in the evening putting many things in order. wrote to Lady Edward Bentinck.

Wensday June 11th.

Rather a stormy day, but warm some showers at noon but very fine in the afternoon & evening I never went out in the Morning, Mr. Witts walk'd to Leith &'c, after Tea we all walk'd to Fountains Bridge[16] & round under the Castle home. wrote to Lady Elcho a Letter of congratulation

Thursday June 12th.

Very warm & close, no wind but very heavy clouds & some sunshine, evening finer than the Morning, I walk'd at Noon late only to call on Mrs. Halkett Craigie always a pleasant visit &

---

16. Fountain Bridge, now Fountainbridge, was part of the old Glasgow road, just over a quarter-of-a-mile south-west of the castle.

Detail from a painting of
1825 of Edinburgh from
Calton Hill by Alexander
Nasmyth.

to some shops on the bridge in the afternoon went alone to drink Tea with Lady C: Charteris,
who I found most friendly & frank, my Gentlemen call'd to walk home with me, which we
did over Calton Hill wrote to M^rs. Pennington.

Friday June 13th.

A hot wind of course not very pleasant, & being myself but very indifferent with strong flying pains
all over me & a violent Symptom of an approaching cold I by no means found the day pleasant
in any respect went out late at Noon, into Georges Square, when we call'd on M^r. Simpson, M^rs.
Clerk now situated in our old house & M^r. Hamilton, she being dressing, in the evening walk'd
in the Nursery Gardens out of Queen Street & on that pavement; rec'd a Letter from M^rs. Buxton

Saturday June 14th.

A particular clear fine day & such a delightful evening is seldom seen at any season of the year,
I kept within all Morning & thought myself the better for Nursing, M^r. Witts out & about, &
leaving famous accounts of the great Naval Victory gaind by Lord Howe over the French,[17]
for which the Cannon at the Castle fired 21 Volleys, & by order of the Lord Provost &
Magistrates the whole Town were orderd by beat of Drum to illuminate their House for which
great preparations were necessary, after Tea we walkd to the end of the South Bridge thro' ^a
concourse of People to see what was going forwards & return'd home to light our own when
the beat were at 9 o'clock; we put up six Candles in each of our front windows & among them

17.   The Glorious First of June, of 1794, was the first and largest naval battle between The Royal Navy and the fleet of
      the First French Republic. The British Channel Fleet under Admiral Lord Howe attempted to prevent the passage of
      a vital French grain convoy from the United States, which was protected by the French Atlantic Fleet, commanded by
      Vice-Admiral Louis Thomas Villaret de Joyeuse. The two forces clashed in the Atlantic Ocean, some 400 miles west of
      the French island of Ushant on 1 June 1794.

The Glorious 1st of June; the victory of Admiral Richard Howe, 1st Earl Howe, in the first and largest fleet action of the naval conflict between Great Britain and the First French Republic during the French Revolutionary Wars. The two forces clashed in the Atlantic, some 400 miles west of Ushant on 1 June 1794. A contemporary engraving.

a Bouquet of flowers, we afterwards paraded the streets with the Boys, principally in George Street, Andrews Square, & Princes Street, & a beautiful sight it was. The streets being full of well dress'd people & others, unfortunately it was not only a peculiar light Night, but nearly a full Moon, but some of the principal Houses shops & Hottels were very prettily light up we return'd home soon after ten, but could not go to Bed till near 12 not wishing to leave our illumination burning. wrote a very long Letter to my Sister Travell, & rec'd one from Miss Anne Snow.

Sunday June 15[th.]

Perfect fine weather, sun extremely hot but fine air or rather wind to counterbalance & clear from Morning to Night, M[r.] Witts & I went to Morning service at Lady Glenorchys Chappel[18] for the purpose of hearing M[r.] Jones whose manner was even more violent & extraordinary than we had expected, his Sermon an hour & 25 minutes long, with only a short Psalm between to give him break & time to recover strength not highly pleased on the whole. M[rs.] Jones so civil to wait to convey us into her Seat, went to evening service at S[t.] Georges where M[r.] Cleeve shone most peculiarly both in reading & preaching to a very large congregation, my cold was so very bad I staid within all the evening, M[r.] Witts & the Boys walk'd late. rec'd a Letter from Miss L. Lee

Monday June 16[th.]

No change in the weather, but still as delightful as ever, but my cold was so very indifferent I had no other engagement of it but in the house not going out till quite evening for an hour. two M[rs.] Auchenlecks drank Tea, our friend, but not her usual companion civil sensible Woman but odd, when they went we all walk'd on Queen Street &'c &'c. rec'd a Letter from M[r.] Delabere & wrote to Miss Snow. began reading Herman of Unna[19]

---

18. Lady Glenorchy's Chapel had been built next to Trinity College in 1772. Both the Church and the College were cleared away in 1848 to make way for the marshalling yard, now part of the area taken up by Waverley Station.

Tuesday June 17[th.]

Lovely weather still, & my cold some what better, went out at Noon walk'd M[r.] Witts to some shops, & after having drank Tea early walk'd to Dicksons Nursery Garden on the Leith Walk, where we were induced to stay a great while from the variety of nice plants we had & the excellent order in which it was kept, went the cross lanes to Cannongate for the sake of calling on Lady C; C: who regaled me with W. & Water[20] not at home till late. rec'd a Letter from M[rs.] Naper informing me she was to be married to M[r.] Rycroft on Thursday next. — very interesting. —

Wensday June 18[th.]

The same truly summer season so very busy all Morning arranging some Green house plants Lady C: C: had sent us we neither of us ever walk'd but amply made up first by walking near 6 miles in the evening & the Boys with us, were out more than three hours, not at home till past

Dr Thomas Snell Jones (1754–1837), Minister of Lady Glenorchy's Chapel, Edinburgh.

ten, having been to New haven, a small fishing Villiage on the shore of the Firth, a mile from Leith by which way we returnd, call'd at M[r.] Oliphants to rest a few moments tho he was not at home a very beautiful walk, & I less tired than could be thought.

Thursday June 19[th.]

Everlasting soft air & hot sun, but sad troublesome dust, so bad as even to make me wish for rain I went out late at Noon to some shops & home over the Mound.[21] in the evening M[r.] W. & Francis walk'd with me to the Dean a house where Lord Swinton resides a Dull old Place, a mile N: W: of the New Town & tracd our way back by Stockbridge: my thoughts much turn'd all Day upon my Nieces Wedding. rec'd a Letter from Lord Edward Bentinck. very melancholly

Friday June 20[th.]

Not quite so hot a day, the Morning & Noon being cloudy, in the afternoon the air was more clear & the sun shone & was a most pleasant evening I staid within all Morning, & was hard at work being about to change my Mourning in the evening walk'd to Georges Square & the Walks, in the former we stumbled upon M[r.] Charteris, who I had not before seen since his Marriage & had some talk, on the latter join'd M[r.] & M[rs.] Hamilton.

---

19. Benedikte Naubert, Karl Gottlieb Cramer, *Herman of Unna: A Series of Adventures of the Fifteenth Century*, 1794.
20. Presumably whisky and water.
21. The earthen mound traversing the Nor Loch was commenced in 1783; 800 feet across with a maximum height of 92 feet. It was filled from excavations for cellars in the New Town, and at the height of work some 1,800 cart-loads a day were tipped and by 1816 it had been estimated that 435,250 cubic yards of material had been tipped.

Saturday June 21ˢᵗ

Prodigeously hot being both very close & broiling sunshine, toward afternoon it became cloudy, & while we were at Dinner a very sudden & hard shower fell, & several more in the course of the evening which effectively kept me within as did the heat in the Morning, but I was fully employd & very agreably in receiving a visit in the Morning from Mʳ Professor Playfair always a treat. Francis drank Tea at Mʳ Broughams in George Street with his Schoolfellow & friend.[22] rec'd an agreable Letter from Mʳˢ Granville & wrote one of congratulation to Mʳˢ Ryecroft. —

Sunday June 22ᵈ

A very fine shewey Morning but soon became wet, but held up sufficiently to suffer us to go to Morning Service at Sᵗ Andrews Church; the service well perform'd by Mʳ W: Moodie, in the afternoon to Sᵗ Georges where Mʳ Cleeve was very eloquent small rain the greater part of the evening which made it quite stay at home & permitted me to write two long Letters to Mʳˢ Buxton & Miss Forrest.

Monday June 23ᵈ

Had been a great deal of rain in the night, & was damp, close, & hot, & raining at intervals all day, better suited to home employments than going out, amused by hearing a great deal of Herman of Unna; Mʳ Stormonth sat an hour in the evening

Tuesday June 24ᵗʰ

Much rain had again fallen in the night & was wet early in the Morning but turnd out a dry & fine day, tho very hot in spite of much wind, I did not go out till 2 o'clock when I call'd on Mʳˢ Halkett Craigie, who was at home & on Mʳˢ Brown now in James's Square who was not at home after Tea went to Lady C: Charteris, & while I paid my visit my Gentlemen walk'd & call'd for me to return which we did over the Mound, having all eat abundance of strawberries.

Wensday June 25ᵗʰ

Rather inclined to be showery tho warm & some trifling rain fell more than once in the course of the day but nothing of consequence, Mʳ Witts went after Breakfast for the first time to Leith to Bathe in the sea in his absence Mʳ Oliphant call'd but being dressing I was prevented the pleasure of seeing him, Mʳˢ Moray wonderful to tete, made her long expected visit accompanied by the eldest Miss Brown, the former stiff & formal such visits no pleasure, after Tea all 4

---

22. Francis was at school with James (1780–1833) and Peter; James was two years older than Francis, Peter a year or more younger. Peter died tragically in a ship-board fire off the coast of Brazil in 1800. Francis later became friends with the elder brother of the family, Henry Brougham (1778–1868) who later became Lord Chancellor and 1st Baron Brougham and Vaux. James was educated at Edinburgh High School and later took Hume's course in Scottish Cuo law in 1798 and joined the Speculative Society with his maverick brother Henry, 16 months his senior. Eschewing early ambitions to become an army agent or serve in the East or West Indies, he attended the Court of Session as a trainee advocate, before accompanying his friends Francis Horner and William Murray to London in 1803, where he studied English law. He acted as agent for his father's Brougham Hall estate near Penrith and devoted himself to furthering Henry's political and legal career. He was an MP from 1826 up to his death. Henry was educated at Edinburgh High School (1785–1791) and then at Edinburgh University. He was an advocate in Edinburgh (1800–1803), after which he moved to Lincoln's Inn, London. His illustrious parliamentary career began in 1810 when he became MP for Camelford. He became Attorney-General to Queen Caroline in 1820 and Lord Chancellor in 1830.

walk'd to Loch Hern, crossing both Leith roads & home by the Mussel burgh road & all the way up Cannongate a long pull of more than 4 miles, but amused by new & romantic scenery

Thursday June 26th.

Very much the same kind of Day only rather more Sun between the little showers, & the air being clear made it very pleasant late at Noon I walk'd for an hour to some shops on the bridge &'c, & in the evening only in Queen Street & other streets near having had enough the evening before of a very long walk. rec'd a <u>most</u> interesting Letter from Lady Elcho & wrote to Mrs. Granville.

Friday June 27th.

Quite a fine day, & warm tho there was little sun till the evening which was an uncommon beautiful one I never went out in the Morning & was not very well, Miss Margaret Brown call'd here as did our Neighbour below stairs Mr. Jones, a singular, but seem'd as if he would be amusing & entertaining, after Tea walk'd to Leslies Nursery Gardens, & spent sometime surveying plants, & brought home many flowers. wrote to Miss Gorges.

Saturday June 28th.

A hotter day than most of the past ones, tho there was a considerable degree of wind & but little sun till evening, Mr. Witts went to bathe, in his absence I rec'd a visit from young Mr. Brown after which I walk'd into John Street first to return Mrs. Morays visit, & afterwards to Lady Catherine to whom I had much interesting conversatioon, returnd home almost broil'd & did not go out again till near sun set & then only walk'd in the cool adjacent streets.

Sunday June 29th.

Quite as hot a day if not more so, be thick & gloomy till quite evening when it was more clear Mr. Witts & I went to Mr. Sandfords Chapel for the Morn^{g.} service, which was perform'd in a pleasing pious manner & a very good & useful sermon, a remarkable full congregation in the evening at St. Georges Chapel, & a prodigeous fine sermon from Mr. Cleeve, after Tea walk'd to Georges Square & on the walks nothing interesting in any degree occurr'd almost dead with heat.

Monday June 30th.

Still hot as ever, unable to keep cool tho perfectly quiet till after sunset, much bussiness of various sorts all day, quite late walk'd to St. Bernards Well &'c rec'd pleasing & very informing Letters from Lady Edward Bentinck & my Sis^{r.} Travell.

Tuesday July 1st.

As hot as ever if not more so, and at mid.day so cloudy & oppressive as much to portend rain but none came, & it was as fine again as ever in the afternoon; Mr. Witts went to Leith to bathe Mr. Simpson call'd here in the Morning, & M^{r.} & Mrs. Allan drank Tea here not very lively or brilliant when they were gone we walk'd in Queen Street &'c rec'd a Letter from Miss Snow.

Wensday July 2^{d.}

No cooler at all, towards evening, most wonderful dark gloomy clouds & very high Wind & at 11 o'clock at night a very hard Shower which however did not cool the rain as the Night was peculiarly sultry, I kept house all Day as usual after Tea walk'd & sat on the Calton Hill & then ended our walk by a half hours call on poor Lady Catherine & had much talk with her. wrote a long Letter to Mr Burslem. long owed.

Thursday July 3^d.

Just the same fine warm weather, only rather too much so, not being able to keep oneself tolerably cool even sitting quite still; Francis kept from going to School after breakfast by having a rash & unwell in his Stomach, but walk'd with us in the evening to Georges Square where we call'd on Mr Hamilton for a quar^t of an hour to enquire after her, who was ill & confined, walk'd afterwards on the walks, when we join'd Mrs Craigie & her eléive. rec'd a Letter from Miss B: Guydickens, & wrote a mellancholly one of condolence to Miss Louisa Lee, on the death of her poor Sister Mrs Fiott.[23]

Friday July 4th.

Still a hotter day than ever, such a clear broiling evening I never before saw, Mrs Auchenleck call'd here in the Morning, & at two o'clock I absolutely crawld to St James's Square to see Mrs Brown & sat with her till quite Dinner time under the shade of a Tree in the Excise office Garden most pleasantly in the evening went into the Town on some errands, return'd over the Mound & walk'd in Queen S^t in the hope of being cool but in vain.

Saturday July 5th.

Quite as hot as ever if not more so & in the afternoon such a thick oppressive air that made it very intolerable to bear, I never stirr'd in the Morn^g but was almost overcome with visitors first Col: Cas: Gordon then Miss M. Brown, & last tho not least in pleasure Col: & Mrs Callandar, just return'd from London, very much pleased to see them; 6 Boys drank Tea with the Boys, Broughams, Craigies & Simpsons, after we had presided Mr Witts & I went to the Play to join the Brown family & several others, to hear Incledon & Miss Pool sing in Lone in a Villiage,[24] who were just arrived from England, very well entertain'd & not near so hot as might have been supposed, after the Play went to Mr Browns to eat a cold Supper, a party of 15 more Gentlemen than Ladies, very lively, some singing not at home till near one; a fine walk but not cool

Sunday July 6th.

No kind of change in the weather, only toward evening rather more Wind springing up made the heat less intense, went to Morning service at St Peters for the sake of hearing Dr Webster preach which he did very well, but perhaps I had raised my ideas too high & was therefore rather disappointed & hardly thought my very hot walk was compensated for, in the evening to St Georges, where Mr Morris Lord Folchistones Tutor did the whole Duty, Mr Cleeve not

---

23. The connection with the Lees and Fiotts came about from Agnes Witts's friendship with Louisa Lee (who married Edward Arrowsmith in 1802). They lived at Totteridge Park in Hertfordshire, where effectively the head of the household was Philadelphia Lee, née Dyke, Louisa's mother. Louisa's sister, Harriet (d. 1794) married, 1782, John Fiott (1760–1799), a merchant, of London.

24. William Boyce; Charles Benjamin Incledon; Maria Dickons; Bartholomew Cooke: *Love in a Village*. The favourite duet 'Together let us range' was sung by Incledon and Miss Pool. Charles Incledon (±1763–1826) was one of the most famous singers of his age. The identity of Miss Pool is unclear.

being well, & very well, after Tea walk'd to Calton Hill, & all about it strolling on the Grass, & enjoying the bracing air very much. wrote to M^rs. Savage

Monday July 7th.

Literaly much hotter than ever, not even a possibility of keeping even tolerably cool with all the Windows & Doors open & in the evening such a thick Mist as amounted to a fog, but cleard off after sun set, I never moved till that time & M^r. Witts very little, working, reading & writting a great deal, between 8 & 9 went to sit in Finlaysons gardens till it was cool enough to walk in Queen Street wrote to my Sister Travell.

Tuesday July 8th.

Not quite so sultry a day the wind being turn'd to the West, & a good deal of it, as well as clouds & while we were at Dinner a trifling shower tho but of little consequence, at home all the Morning late, rec'd a visit from M^rs. Jones & found her a pleasant conversible Woman; after Tea walk'd round Calton Hill in our way to see Lady C. C. who was too indifferent to admit us. wrote to Lady Edward Bentinck.

Wensday July 9th.

Very much the same kind of weather not very hot in the Morning but so again in the afternoon, M^r. W kept house in the Morning as well as myself, having been very unwell in his Stomach & bowels. M^r. Charteris calld on us with whom we had some very interesting converse too soon terminated by the arrival of M^rs. Macqueen who was easy & pleasant; M^r. Brown came early in the afternoon drank Tea with us, & attended us to the Botanic Garden where we spent an hour very pleasantly Francis drank Tea at M^r. Simpsons.

Thursday July 10th.

Certainly the weather much cooler the wind being higher & in a clearer point, a very quiet Morning, not very high in spirits tho M^r. Witts was much better; after Tea went to call on the Browns in S^t. James's Square sat ½ an hour there, meeting the agreable D^r. Gregory, afterwards walk'd on Leith Walk & Queen Street with Maria Georgiana & Robert Brown as well as our own Sons. wrote a very long letter to Lady Elcho.

Friday July 11th.

Again the weather was more sultry than was almost ever known, a very thick & oppressive air in the afternoon w.ch grew clear as the evening advanced. M^rs. Callander & Miss Rutherford call'd for an hour at Noon & I afterwards broil'd with them to some shops, but declined attending her to Stranges Children Ball at the George Street Assembly Rooms, being engaged to go with Miss Brown to the Play, & took Francis with me, the Play Hamlet, that part astonishingly well perform'd by a young Tradesman of 19,[25] the second time of his acting so well as to be quite

---

25.   The 19-year-old tradesman was Henry Erskine Johnston (1775–1845). His first performance in this part had been just two days earlier, 9 July 1794. He was born in Edinburgh on 3 August 1775, the son of Robert Johnston, barber and wigmaker, and his wife Elizabeth. He made his début in Edinburgh in 1794 reciting Collins's 'Ode on the Passions', which impressed Stephen Kemble sufficiently to engage him to appear as an amateur in the part of Hamlet in the city. His success was immediate and enthusiastic: he was extravagantly fêted, and dubbed the Scottish Roscius—the 'boy wonder'.

entertaining, the farce of the Son in Law in which Miss Poole & Incledon Lucy & she had acted Ophelia, a full house of Gentlemen, the Play not over till near 12, when Miss Brown & I were bold enough under the sanction of 2 Gentlemen to look in for an hour at Stranges Ball well amused. not at home till one, what a Rake. wrote to Miss A: Snow.

Saturday July 12th.

Not quite so hot in the course of the Day but terribly so in the evening, being again thick & close, when late a violent blast of wind came on & strong appearance of rain; I only went out in the Morning to make an unsuccessful Visit to my next Door Neighbour Mrs. Jones, after Tea walk'd to the end of the Town of Leith & over the Lynn to the other road, purposing to visit Lady C: C: but found it too late came home much tired with the Heat & dust which was extreme.

Sunday July 13th.

Had been some rain in the night but it had had no effect in clearing or cooling the air being insufferably hot & close, tho a violent wind & many clouds at 6 o'clock in the evening after tremendous clouds & darkness. There was hard rain for 2 hours or more. went to St. Andrews Church in the Morng. where the service was moderately perform'd by a young Stranger, & in the afternoon to St. Georges as usual. reading, writting, & conversing fill'd up the evening rec'd a Letter from Miss Louisa Lee very melancholly.

Monday July 14th.

Weather considerably cooler being a great deal of wind & scarce any sun many clouds but no rain at Noon ventured for a wonder to go out, taken in at Mr. Grieves finding them on the Street coming to see us, to some Shops on the Bridge, & call'd on our poor Friend in John Street. It was the first day of the Race, but the Town appeard as thin of company, as their was want of sport on <u>the Sands</u>, Mr. Stormonth & Mr. Brown here in the evening, the latter staid till near dark. rec'd a Letter from Miss Forrest.

Tuesday July 15th.

Dry & warm, but such an excessive high wind that made all moving unpleasant, & such ark clouds particularly towards evening that look'd much like rain but none fell; Mr. Witts & George accompanied Mr. Brown at an early hour in the Morning to a Botanical Lecture & all walk'd together to the Leith Sands to the Races, where they stood in the Lord Provosts stand & were well amused. Mrs. Callander & Miss Rutherford call'd on me, & I return'd with them to their Lodgings for an hour. sat at home all the evening

Wensday July 16th.

A prodigeous fine Day, remarkable clear air some wind & much sun., Mr. Witts took his Son Francis in the same walk to the Race Mr. Brown again going with them, I went with Mrs. Callander in her Chaise & enjoy'd it very much there being great sport, much company & a very lively scene call'd on Mrs. Brown before Dinner, expected the Callanders to Tea, but they were prevented, Mr. & Thompson call'd late in the evening after which the Boys walk'd on a message to Lady C: C:, & me in Queen Street &'c.

Thursday July 17ᵗʰ·

By no means a pleasant day being such an extreme high wind there was no going out of the house with any pleasure, the dust being so very disagreable when it sank in the evening it was more pleasant I only call'd on Mʳˢ· Callander & walk'd a little just before Dinner, their party drank Tea with us, & we Ladies walk'd on Queen Street till a late hour.

Friday July 18ᵗʰ·

Very hot & close early in the day, but when the sun appeard & the wind arose, it was a very agreable day in the evening, strong signs of rain but very little fell, very busy in the Morn: early negotiating with Dʳ· Gregory to attend poor Miss Rutherford, join'd him at their Lodgings & much concern'd to hear her opinion of her case. went to the Race with old Mʳˢ· Grieve in her Chaise who proved a pleasanter escort than I had expected, the sport so good I was well amused. Mʳ· Brown accompanied Mʳ· W. & Francis to the Races, & return'd with them to Dinner, his obliging manner, & easy converse made the day pass lively, after Tea attempted to walk on Calton Hill, sent back by fear of rain.

Saturday July 19ᵗʰ·

A hot brilliant Morning, grew cloudy about 2 o'clock, after which some gentle showers fell, & after dark very hard rain indeed but most seasonable. Mʳ· Witts & I sat an hour here with Mʳˢ· Brown in the Excise Office Garden. much interesting talk caught in the rain before I got home, the Boys drank Tea there & afterwards Mʳ· Stormonth call'd on us, & walk'd with us in Queen Street between the showers did but just save our distance in getting home before the violent rain began. wrote to Mʳˢ· Callandar.

Sunday July 20ᵗʰ·

Wet early in the Day, dry the middle & again damp & misty in the evening, I did not go to Morning Church my Gentlemen did to Sᵗ· Georges Chappel & just as I was setting out to go to the evening service there was prevented by a summons from Mʳˢ· Callandar to join her at Mʳ· Higgins's in Queen Street to be presant at a Meeting between Dʳ· Monro & Dʳ· Gregory on Miss Rutherfords account, staid there more than two hours much agitated & perplex'd about it, which made me quite ill & very nervous all the evening attempted to walk out prevented by wet.

Monday July 21ˢᵗ·

Several very severe showers of rain in the course of the Day which fell chiefly in the Morning & noon the evening being dry tho the wind was most extremely high & realy cold, I only went out in the Morning to call on Mʳˢ· Halkett Craigie when the rain <u>luckily</u> detain'd me for more than an hour after Tea went over the Calton Hill to see Lady C: C: who as ever was most friendly & pleasant

Tuesday July 22ᵈ·

A very fine day throughout, peculiarly so in the evening, when the sun was bright, the air cool & no wind, attempted to see Mʳˢ· Charteris by making an unsuccessful call on her at Mʳˢ· Hamiltons in Andrews Square but did not find her at home, instead visited Mʳˢ· Thomson in the same

Square much pleased with their new House, after Tea walk'd to Georges Square, where we were introduced by M.ʳ Hamilton to M.ʳˢ Charteris, visited M.ʳ Simpson for a quarter of an hour, met many acquaintance there & to & fro which made it a pleasant walk.

Wensday July 23.ᵈ

A very bright shewey Morning which soon changed to cloudy & at noon was some trifling showers but in the afternoon & night, there was most violent & constant rain for many hours more useful than pleasant; M.ʳ & M.ʳˢ Charteris made an early call here, before they set off for the West Country, much pleased with them both their behaviour being both aimable & affectionate. George drank Tea with Bob: Brown & the two Broughams here & staid afterwards with Frank while we went to the Play in M.ʳˢ Browns Box which like every other corner of the House was stuff'd as full as possible being Johnstons the Scotch Luminarys benifit,[26] when he acted in Douglass Petruchio, & spoke Collins's Ode on the

Henry Erskine Johnston (1775–1845). An etching by John Kay.

Passions, Drydens Ode out of Alexanders Feast, all wonderfuly well in their different way, but not so capital as he was in Hamlet tho professedly a great rising genius not at home till near one in the Morning thro torrents of rain in a chair. wrote to M.ʳ Delabere & Miss B. Guydickens.

Thursday July 24.ᵗʰ

A pleasant day neither hot nor cold, quite dry, more wind than was agreable, Miss Margaret Brown here in the Morning, I walk'd out at Noon into the old Town on some errands found M.ʳ <u>Brown</u> here on our return to Dinner, who we ask'd to join us, & very soon after it he took Frans. with him to a Lecture on Natural History from whence he went to drink Tea at M.ʳ Simpsons, George walking with us to Lady C: C:, & while I conversed with her they walk'd on the Craigs. M.ʳ Stormonth being here prevented our going early. rec'd a Letter from my Sister Travell.

Friday July 25.ᵗʰ

A very bright Morning, but soon changed to dark & gloomy & continued so all the day, tho dry & was realy turn'd quite cold, staid at home all Morning & saw no one, work'd much & heard the beginning of Miss Gunnings new Novel of Lord Fitzhenry, after Tea with the Boys walk'd quite a new walk in the Meadow under the Craigs beyond the Abbey quite to the Musselburgh road & home over Calton Hill

---

26.   Johnston's first appearance in London took place at Covent Garden, as 'H. Johnston from Edinburgh', also in *Douglas* (23 October 1797). He was praised in the *European Review* for his figure, countenance, and voice. He went on to have a distinguished career, but his performances in the capital came to an end as a result of his having horsewhipped George IV when the latter was Prince of Wales for an insult to Johnston's wife. He remained in London and last performed in 1830. He died in obscurity in Gillingham Street, Belgrave, London, on 8 February 1845.

Saturday July 26th.

Weather much changed being dark & cloudy & rather cold, tho no rain, but towards evening strong signs of it & much did fall in the night, at home quite quiet all Morning, in the afternoon the 2 young Morays, Steward Bremner, & John Brougham drank Tea here, the only disengaged Boys of many that were ask'd, when the Lads all walk'd by themselves & Mr. Witts & I in some close adjacent lanes & fields for shelter from the wind

Sunday July 27th.

Wet & very wet early in the Morng. but cleard off & was quite dry the remainder of the day, but with a strong cold wind, went to Morning Service at St. Andrews, where a stranger preach'd a good Sermon in a bad manner, Mr. Cleeve very great in the afternoon at St. Georges, Mr. Brown sat in the seat with us, not pleasant enough in the evening to walk anywhere but in the Streets at home early & wrote a long Letter to my Sister Travell rec'd a short one from Miss Anne Snow with an alarming account of the health of her Sister Mrs. Paul.[27]

Monday July 28th.

A very pleasant warm day being more sunshine & tho the wind was high it was very mild soon after breakfast Captain Maitland call'd & join'd our visit to Clifton Hall. We walk'd to Georges Square call'd on Mrs. Hamilton who was enough recoverd to receive me heartily glad

The Fleshmarket Clock. An engraving by T. Picken after a painting by George Cattermole.

27. Frances Paul, née Snow. (1755–1794). Frances was the daughter of Robert Snow and Valentina Paul; she married John Paul in January 1775.

to see her once more but shock'd at the great alteration in her Miss Ramsay with her, call'd likewise on M^rs. Clerk, after Tea call'd on M^rs. Brown, with whom was only her Daughter Maria & Mr D. Erskine, but the conversation was kept up so briskly it was near dark before we thought of moving. so only walk'd home

Tuesday July 29th.

A very Sombre day in all respects a very gloomy Sky & cold high wind, before Dinner began raining & continued hard all the evening, Mr Jones call'd here in the Morning. we read so much in Lord Fitzhenry that we finish'd it without being much amused. between Tea & dark play'd at Cassino rec'd a Letter from Miss A Snow with an account of poor M^rs. Pauls death & answer'd it

Wensday July 30th.

Wet in the Morning, dry tho dark & gloomy all Day & very wet in the evening I ventured to walk to Drink Tea with Lady C: C: Mr Witts also of the party she was particularly lively & agreable I was oblig'd to come home in a Chaise it rain'd so hard loaded with fruit & flowers. wrote to M^rs. Callandar & Miss Louisa Lee.

Thursday July 31st.

A dismall day in all respects being wet more or less constantly, & having rec'd a most painful Letter from my Brother Ferdinand, my spirits were sunk even below comfort. Mr Stormonth here in the evening for an hour on business. rec'd Letters from Lady Edwd. Bentinck & M^rs. Granville.

Friday Aug^st. 1st.

A damp misty Morning which before Noon became violent hard rain, & continued without interruption all day & night, the poor Boys almost drowned returning home from School; we had nothing for it but to read & work as hard as we were able entertain'd much by the secret History of Charles the 2^d.

Saturday Aug^st. 2^d.

Wet & damp in the Morning, very wet at Noon, but dry, very windy & cold in the evening but still having been so much confined in the course of the week Mr Witts & I walk'd a considerable way on the Leith walk & back again both the Boys drank Tea at Mr Broughams & just before their return home poor George was flung down by a Boy in the street, & had his collar bone broken which sadly alarm'd us sent first for Mr Wood to put it in a proper situation who gave us hope it was likely to go on very well but it made a sad bustle & kept us up very late rec'd a Letter fr^m. M^rs. Callandar

Sunday Aug^st. 3^d.

Cold & stormy tho some sunshine, & no rain till quite evening, George had an excellent night & was going on as well as possible but we none of us left him in the Morning to go to church. M^rs. Brougham very obligingly call'd to see him, & spent an hour here found her a most pleasing Woman Mr Brown likewise call'd we took him with us to Dinner he walk'd with us in the evening attempted to go to Georges Square but it look'd too lowering to venture. rec'd a Letter from Mrs Pennington.

Monday Aug^{st.} 4th.

A very good Day, much sunshine no rain, & tho there was some wind it was much warmer poor George going on as well as could possibly be hoped for Mr. Riddel the Father of the Boy who had been the cause of his accident call'd, & behaved in a very polite & proper manner, I made an unsuccessful visit to Mrs. Hamilton finding with her Miss Elphinston, & a talkative agreable Gentleman but of the Country & best of all herself very much recoverd Mr. Stormonth drank Tea here after which I went & sat with Mrs. Brown till past nine Dr. Gregory most agreably interupting our tete tete

Tuesday Aug^{st.} 5th.

A moderate kind of day, gloomy & rather cold but no rain I walk'd out late at noon on some errands on the Bridge, John Brougham drank Tea here, I was low & miserable, from wrong conduct of one who knew far better,[28] only stroll'd a little about in Queen Street &'c in the evening. Mr. Brown had call'd in the Morn: rec'd a Letter f^{m.} Miss L Lee

Wensday Aug^{st.} 6th.

A very unpleasant day being small mist or rain in the Morning, dry but gloomy all day & inclined to be wet again in the evening, Mrs. Callander here for an hour in the Morning; George going on as well as could be expected from his accident I went for an hour Francis attending me after Tea to Lady Catherine Charteris, came home nearly in the dark, & as near in the rain.

Thursday Aug^{st.} 7th.

A very pleasant day, much sun & very clear air, but a very hard shower in the evening Miss M: Brown here later in the Morning, we went out with her, & her Father to see some Pictures, Mrs. Brown drank Tea here, a great treat as well as wonder her conversation always pleasing.

Friday Aug^{st.} 8th.

Rather a cloudy Morn: but turn'd out a very fine day, at 10 o'clock Mr. W. & I walk'd over the Mound &'c to Bruntsfield Linx, to see the Reg^{t.} of Argyle Fencibles review'd by Lord Adam Gordon, which had collected together a great concourse of people of all ranks, some very genteel & smart we stood by Admiral & Miss Duncan,[29] & walk'd back with Mrs. Browne & Capt. & Mrs. Gray, stopp'd to refresh ourselves in Georges Square invited into Mrs. Craigies House by Miss Macdonald; M^{r.} & Mrs. Jones, Miss & Master Simpson, their father as usual disappointing us & Mr. Brown drank Tea here. walk'd a little in Queen Street after they were gone. a full day.

---

28. This is a form of code that Agnes Witts used for domestic disharmony.
29. Adam Duncan, Viscount Duncan of Camperdown (1731–1804). After a successful career, Admiral Duncan found himself on dry land. He was promoted rear-admiral of the white on 21 September 1790, vice-admiral of the blue on 1 February 1793, and just over a year later, on 12 April 1794, vice-admiral of the white. Despite the outbreak of the French Revolutionary War in 1793 he was not employed until February 1795 when he was appointed commander-in-chief in the North Sea. He became a national hero after his success leading the fleet against the Dutch at the Battle of Camperdown, 11 October 1797. From an Edinburgh society point of view, Duncan had married into the Dundas family. He married, 1777, Henrietta Dundas (1748–1832), third daughter of the Rt Hon. Robert Dundas of Arniston, Edinburghshire, lord president of the Court of Session, and his first wife, Henrietta Carmichael. She was the niece of Henry Dundas, the political manager of Scotland, and eighteen years Duncan's junior

Saturday Aug^{st.} 9th.

A dry fine Day tho not very pleasant the wind being very high & not much sun & towards night quite cold, I was not well & much out of spirits with complicated vexations, before Dinner walk'd on the Bridge to some Shops, & after Tea Francis & I tete tete walk'd to the Cannon Mills, & a long round, some part quite new to me.

Sunday Aug^{st.} 10th.

Very far from an agreable Day tho it was perfectly dry & much sun, from the wind being so extremely high, it was hardly possible to stand, went to Morning service at St. Georges Chappel, & to evening at St. Andrews Church, whither we accompanied Miss Halkett & sat in her seat, having previously call'd on her, on her return from Harrowgate. Mr. Moodie perform'd the service extremely well but in some measure disappointed my raised expectations Bob: Brown dined here, in the evening we went to St. Peters Chappel to have a Rehearsal of church music not much gratified with it. rec'd a Letter from Mrs. Ryecroft long expected & one from Miss Snow.

A caricature of William Moodie (1759–1812), by John Kay. Moodie was a Scottish Minister, Moderator of the General Assembly of the Church of Scotland, philologist, and Professor of Hebrew and Oriental Languages in Edinburgh University.

Monday Aug^{st.} 11th.

A dry fine Day neither much sun or wind, I pass'd it mostly alone & therefore not in a very chearful manner, it being the examination Day at the Schools, where Mr. Witts early took his Boys, & Mr. Brown with them that George might be better guarded from any hurt to his arm, they never return'd till 4, having both gain'd much credit in their examination & George the gratification of being 2nd of his class for which he gain'd a handsome premium & poor Francis thro a mistake like other Boys of his class a very indifferent one, Mr. Witts & Mr. Brown dined with the magistrates & did not return home till between 9 & 10 the Boys & I walk'd over the Bridge &'c meeting numbers we knew. Miss Macdonald sat an hour with me in the Morning & by her sensible conversation pleased me much wrote to Lady Edward Bentinck.

Tuesday Aug^{st.} 12th.

A most glorious fine summer Day without being oppressively hot, soon after Breakfast Papa, Mama, & Sons took a most pleasant walk into the Corn Fields surrounding the Cannon Mills &'c, where the promising signs of a plentiful harvest were very gratifying & the chearful busy faces of the reapers very pleasing came home at 12, rec'd long & very agreable visits from M^{rs.} D: Hamilton, & Miss Halkett at different times in the Morning, & all 4 drank Tea by invitation at Mrs. Clerks in Georges Square, where we met her Bro^{r.} & Sis^{r.} M^{rs.} & Miss Irvine & a Miss Rattasay, & 2 Master Duncans to meet the Boys, a very chearful visit & delightful pleasant walk home.

Wensday Aug^{st}. 13th.

Another very fine Day, tho not so much brilliant sun & towards evening rather gloomy, M^r. W. & Francis went to bathe in the Sea to the great delight of the latter M^{rs}. Auchenleck call'd here I never went out till after Tea when our own party & J: Brougham added walk'd by the Abbey, & thro the Meadows to the Musselburgh road almost to the barracks that are building & home over the Calton Hill well tired & very hot. wrote to Miss Snow.

Thursday Aug^{st}. 14th.

Rather a dull gloomy day but yet oppressively hot, I did not go out till late when I call'd on the Browns to see the Invalid party & according to custom outstaid my own Dinner here met an agreable English Gentleman there a M^r. Phillips, after Tea walk'd to Ramsay Garden & the Castle Hill, taken in to see the large Water Reservoir there, by M^r. Kerr & M^r. McEliear a very polite manner as the two Bailles. rec'd a long entertaining Letter from M^{rs}. Buxton

Friday Aug^{st}. 15th.

Still close & hot, dark & gloomy with strong signs of rain but scarce any fell, I went to Morning Service at S^t. Georges, preparatory service to the Sacrament on my return home rec'd a visit from M^{rs}. Major Sandys a pleasing well bred Woman Daughter of M^{rs}. Halkett Craiggie, M^r. Brown call'd before Dinner & M^r. Stormonth late in the evening I went George attending me with an intention of drinking Tea with Lady C: C: but found her so indifferent only staid a short time & return'd home to a second Tea drinking. wrote to M^{rs}. Granville

Saturday Aug^{st}. 16th.

Stormy & disagreable in the Morning with strong tendency to rain but very little fell, & in the evening it was pleasant enough tho still lowering I was at home all Morning, much reading in Zimmerman on Solitude[30] a very entertaining & well informing book we had here some days engaged in after Tea walk'd to Georges Square & a little on the walks, M^r. Brown attending us, who we had pick'd up.

Sunday Aug^{st}. 17th.

A very fine Day, after a wet night & early in the Morning, much wind at mid.day but remarkably pleasant in the evening, went to S^t. Georges Chappel to both services, receiving the Sacrament in the Morning, went out to Walk early in the evening, sitting for an hour in one of the Queen Street Garden, & afterwards walking there, with many others till quite dark attaching ourselves to M^{rs}. Brougham, who we found very conversible & agreable.

Monday Aug^{st}. 18th.

An uncommon clear fine day from Morn to Night, but I was much out of spirits by getting no expected Letters from England & from much vexatious plague from Catherine, went late in the forenoon to call on M^{rs}. Sandys, who I found at home & most obliging & pleasant, M^r. Stormonth call'd on us while at Tea, after which I went to call on the Brown's where I found a

---

30. Johann Georg Zimmermann (1728–1795). *Solitude.*

pleasant small circle, M^r. Witts coming to fetch me home we were so press'd to stay to eat a family cold Supper that we consented, D^r. Gregory added to their own family. wrote to M^rs. Buxton.

Tuesday Aug^st 19th.

Quite an uninterrupted fine day, & most pleasant not being oppressively hot, but I kept within all Morning, proposing an afternoon walk to Leith which M^r. Witts & I perform'd drinking Tea wth. M^r. Oliphant, with whom we had much very interesting conversation as he was recently return'd from England he walk'd back great part of the way with us, to & fro the back way, the Boys in our absence drinking Tea with young Sandys by his Mothers invitation.

Wensday Aug^st. 20th.

Another fine day excepting a small shower in the Morning & another in the evening, being but indifferent I staid within all Morning & only walk'd in the adjacent streets after the shower which made it damp, intended to have gone to Lady C: C to communicate some pleasing intelligence but she was too ill to see me. alas! no Letters from England.

Thursday Aug^st. 21st.

Wet in the Morning but chiefly in Showers which disipated at Noon, & was dry the rest of the Morn, tho a hot air & very gloomy sky, I never went out, we finish'd reading Zimmerman's Man^l. & I went to drink Tea with Lady C: C: were well & most graciously rec'd, a prodigeous deal of talk M^r. Witts walk'd home with me.

Friday Aug^st. 22^d.

A remarkable bright & fine hot Morning, lower'd at Noon was wet in showers all the afternoon & evening, I made an unsuccessful visit to Mrs. Jones, & one very pleasant to M^rs. & Miss Halkett, where I was detain'd beyond bounds by a shower, we <u>all</u> went to drink Tea with M^rs. Auchenbecks, a very dull stupid bussiness, & so wet I was obliged to come home in a chair. began reading the life of Petrach.

Saturday Aug^st. 23^d.

Very wet early in the Morning but soon clear'd & was a very bright fine day tho with most considerable high wind, M^rs. Brougham made a long tho late noon visit, & proved herself both sensible & agreable after she went walk'd in the Streets till near Dinner, Masters Sandys & Peter Brougham drank Tea here we walk'd a little in the Streets in the evening, while the young Jack went farther, & when we all met again, we play'd with them both at Goose & Pope Joan rec'd Letters from Miss Louisa Lee & my Sis^r. Travell the latter cruelly long delay'd by the Post.

Sunday Aug^st. 24th.

Quite a fine day, tho by no means pleasant from very high wind & extreme dust & towards evening grew very lowering, & before dark it rain'd. we went to Morning service at the New Kirk where we were much gratified by a peculiar fine Sermon from M^r. Greenfield, to S^t. Georges Chappel to evening Service, & never went out afterwards, the weather not tempting a great deal of reading & serious talk with the Boys.

Monday Aug^(st.) 25^(th.)

Wet in the Morning but soon clear'd up to be not only dry but remarkably bright & fine tho it rain'd again in the evening, I was very low & indifferent all day, only went out just before Dinner for a quarter of an hour on Queen Street to view the fleet of 10 Russian Men of War arrived in the Firth a very fine sight Miss Brown both dined & drank Tea here as a take leave visit, previous to her leaving home for a long time rec'd a Letter from M^(rs.) Charles Western

Tuesday Aug^(st.) 26^(th.)

A fine day, with much sun & wind a sharp shower in the afternoon, & misty rain before dark we all went soon after Breakfast taking M^(r.) Brown with us to the Botanic Garden, to select some plants out of the hot house we had, had a promise of very pleasant employment & very civil Gardiner. We drank Tea at Mr. Jones's 2 odd Ladies there, most civil reception but a droll visit alltogether.

Wensday Aug^(st.) 27^(th.)

The most constant & violent hard rain I almost ever saw from Morn to night no interval of cessation, of course quite stay at home M^(r.) Brown being engaged to eat his Morsel with us enliven'd the day in some degree staying till after dark

Thursday Aug^(st.) 28^(th.)

A happy contrast in point of weather being dry, warm & remarkably pleasant after the violent rain, I went out rather early & Francis with me to say Lady C: C: pleasant as usual, I afterwards call'd on M^(rs.) Brown always entertaining, between Dinner & Tea which we drank late the evenings shutting in so soon, we took our walk, to Georges Square & a little round.

Friday Aug^(st.) 29^(th.)

Another very fine day, but I had very little power of being out or enjoying it being much taken up by the arrival of M^(r.) Broome Witts,[31] who coming to Edinburgh on a Journey, became an inmate with us for the time of his stay, & unfortunately came very far from well with a fever & sore throat unable to get any Medical person to him till night, all our own being out of Town, M^(r.) Law officiated for M^(r.) Wood. I call'd on M^(rs.) Brougham for an hour before Dinner, very agreable. M^(r.) Brown here in the evening. rec'd a Letter from Lady Edw^(d.) Bentinck.

Saturday Aug^(st.) 30^(th.)

Quite a cold disagreable Day being a thick air & realy a sharp unpleasant wind & towards Night small rain much taken up with attendance upon M^(r.) B: Witts who continued but very indifferent & was advised by the Medical people, who call'd several times in the day upon him to keep his Bed till quite evening M^(r.) Witts Francis & I walk'd in the Morning, but was not tempted to go farther than in the streets on some errands. wrote to Miss Forrest. B. Brown drank Tea.

---

31.   Broome (1744–1827), was Edward's eldest brother.

Sunday Aug^st. 31st.

Still cold, but dry & much more pleasant till quite evening when the wind was again quite piercing M^r. Witts so much recoverd as to sit up the greater part of the day to have abundant conversation with him; My Husband & I went to the New Kirk, taking D^r. Brown with us to hear D^r. Blair who was great even beyond himself, in the evening to S^t. Georges Chappel the Boys drank Tea at M^r. Browns, & we walk'd a little on Queen Street before Tea. rec'd a Letter from Miss Betty Guydickens.

Monday Sep^t. 1st.

A very thick unpleasant Morning but was little more than a Mist till Noon, when it began raining very hard & so continued the whole of the day. no resources but from work, reading, writting & talking & in the evening Cassino M^r. Witts so well as to be visited for the last time by the Medical Gentleman. writ a very long Letter to M^rs. Pennington.

Tuesday Sep^t. 2^d.

Constant rain from Morning to night & in general very hard, of course quite confining, but our agreable friend & inmate made the hours pass chearfully & to Dinner we had M^r. Brown, & to Tea we had M^r. Stormonth & Peter Brougham, quite a party of Gentlemen; play'd at Pope Joan for the amusement of the Youngsters & sat up till a late hour conversing. wrote to Lady Edwd. Bentinck.

Wensday Sep^t. 3^d.

A dull quiet Morning which however turn'd out a brilliant & very pleasant day, my two Gent. pass'd the greater part of the Morning in the Court to attend Watts trial for High Treason,[32] Francis out with some young friends & George attended me over the Calton Hill, to visit Lady C: C: on our return fell in with M^r. B: Witts with whom we walk'd to Georges Square & its environs, my Husband & I walk'd in Queen St^r. before Tea

Thursday Sep^t. 4th.

Dry & fine, tho not very brilliant, being but little sunshine, M^r. B: Witts went out to Breakfast M^r. W. & Francis to Bathing, & I never went out at all staying at home from the expectation of seeing M^rs. Callandar who at last never came. M^r. Brown drank Tea here coming to give us a full account of Watts trial & condemnation where he had staid the whole time 23 hours. rec'd a Letter from My Sis^r. Travell & wrote to M^rs. Rycroft.

Friday Sep^t. 5th.

A gloomy close Morning, & at noon some loud claps of thunder, accompanied by a trifling shower our friend again breakfasted out, on his return we all 5 went to survey the Castle with

---

32. The trials at large of Robert Watt and David Downie, for high treason, at the session of *Oyer* and *Terminer*, at Edinburgh, 27 August, 3 & 5 September 1794 at which they were both found guilty and sentenced to be hanged, drawn, and quartered, on 15 October 1794. Robert Watt was a political radical who was found guilty of high treason by the Edinburgh authorities in 1794 after a revolutionary plot to capture the capital cities of Scotland, Ireland and England was uncovered. Watt and Downie were both found guilty, the jury recommending mercy. In the case of Downie, this was agreed to, and the death sentence was commuted to permanent transportation to New Holland.

Archibald Gilchrist (1766–1804) as one of the Edinburgh Volunteers. Gilchrist was an eminent haberdasher and had retail premises in the High Street on the corner of Hunter Square. He was elected a member of the Town Council in 1796, held the office of treasurer in 1797–98 and by 1801 had become one of the Magistrates.

which we were well amused return'd home by Herriotts Hospital wch we likewise survey'd & were entertain'd, quite tired when we came home the Boys in the evening at M^r. Browns. wrote a very long Letter to my Sister Travell.

Saturday Sep^t. 6th.

A most determined wet Day almost from Morn: to night, which effectively locket one up My two Gentlemen dined out at M^r. Gilchrists & my two Boys drank Tea at M^r. Broughams, & M^r. Brown drank Tea with me, coming to give a minute account at Downies Trial who was condem'd as well as Watt altho recommended to mercy by the Jury. rec'd a melancholly Letter from Miss Anne Snow.

Sunday Sep^t. 7th.

Most cruelly wet early in the day accompanied by violent storms of Wind which continued the whole of the day, tho with rain stopp'd so as to permit us to go to S^t. Andrews Church where M^r. W. Maddie gave us an excellent discourse went to Evening Service to D^r. Blair, M^r. Brown dined here, & our worthy friend, M^r. B: Witts quitted us late in the evening, to sleep at an Inn, to go by a Coach in the Night.

Monday Sep^t. 8th.

Cold & very stormy, tho but little rain fell but the Wind was tremendous, M^r. Witts & his Boys went to the Sea in the hope of bathing, but found it too rough to safely venture. at

LK.fecit 1794

DAVID DOWNIE.

David Downie, a goldsmith of Edinburgh, was tried for High Treason in 1794 along with Robert Watt. Watt was executed, but Downie was pardoned on condition that he banish himself from the British dominions and he died in exile.

Noon I went to sit an hour with M[rs.] Brown, in the afternoon walk'd in the old Town to some shops. rec'd Letters from M[rs.] Buxton & Miss Sheppherd & wrote to Miss Anne Snow. M[rs.] Auchenleck calld

Tuesday Sep[t.] 9[th.]
Again rather stormy, but quite dry, tho with little sun; M[r.] Witts walk'd with me to Lady C. C's & back thro the South Town on some little bussinesses in the evening another walk a round by the Cannon Mills the evenings now become social & pleasant from much work reading, & pleasant converse with the Boys

Wensday Sep[t.] 10[th.]
A pretty fine day tho with a thick easterly wind, & in the evening small rain; M[r.] Witts & both his Sons bathed, M[r.] Simpson & his eldest Son call'd here, as did Miss Halkett, after which I walk'd a little on the bridge &'c meeting several pleasant people much entertain'd by hearing Petrach, play'd a little at Cassino, & wrote to Miss Louisa Lee.

Thursday Sep[t.] 11[th.]
Quite a delightful Day, being constant bright sun, & very mild air. we made good use of it by walking in the fore noon to see Lord Morays Place at the West end of the Town where M[r.] <u>Brown</u> join'd us & where we rec'd very good civilities from his Lordship who sent us the Key of the Shrubbery, & gave us the offer of looking into the House to see the view to greater

High Street from Head of West Bow, Lawnmarket. An engraving by T. Picken after William Leighton Leitch.

advantage, which indeed is very beautiful, the Firth no where appearing to the eye in a nobler stile, the Boys drank Tea with Mr Brown, & Mr W. & I walk'd to Georges Square & its vicinity on some errands. rec'd a Letter from Mrs Callander & answer'd it.

Friday Sep^t 12th

A dull sombre day being a thick easterly wind & realy cold, Mr Witts went to Breakfast with Mr Brown, previous to going with him to the College to be present at the Physical examination, when 12 students got their diplomas. Miss M: Brown sat an Hour with me, on my Husbands return walk'd a little with him, very busy in the afternoon, potting some Hot House Plants we had rec'd from the Botanic Garden

Saturday Sep^t 13th

A quiet mild day, without either sun or wind, My Gentlemen all went to Bathe, Mr Brown sat an hour with me in their absence, I went out late with an intention of paying some visits, intercepted on my road by Mrs Callandar so I carried on to see Miss R. at Miss Callandars, wch detain'd me till near Dinner time Miss Margaret Brown dined with us, & staid till near ten at night but was so lively & agreable the visit appeard by no means long.

Sunday Sep.^{t.} 14th.

Not so pleasant a day, the air being more thick & rather inclined to small rain & realy quite cold, the Boys & I went to St. Andrews Church, an odd stranger perform'd the Service & not in a very satisfactory manner between Churches went to call on Mrs. Halkett Craigie Mr. Brown went with us to St. Georges Chappel & returnd home to dine with us.

Monday Sep.^{t.} 15th.

Bright & shewey early in the day, cloudy at mid.day again fine but rather windy, my companions again at the Sea, I went to see L.^{dy.} C: C: who I found more than ordinary chearful on my way home visited Mrs. Brown always agreable. work & Petrach in the evening & the Boys drawing.

Tuesday Sep.^{t.} 16th.

Quite a dull gloomy Morning, & very cold & began raining at Noon & so continued more or less the whole of the day very unpropitious for our long expected visit to Preston Hall, where we went in a P. Chaise arriving there between 4 & 5, found no company & poor Miss Rutherford confined to her Bed being more ill than usual, no amusement but conversation of which there was a very large share. rec'd Letters from Mrs. Granville & Miss Snow.

Wensday Sep.^{t.} 17th.

Little or no rain, but violent wind, & in the middle of the day much sunshine I went with Mrs. Callandar in the Chaise to the Hall to take a Survey of the improvements in the House, which were very great she very ill all the afternoon with a violent headache & her poor Niece tho not so bad as the former day little able to keep up; so on the Gentlemen I depended for amusement

Thursday Sep.^{t.} 18th.

The most violent & uninterrupted Day of rain I ever saw, Mrs. Callandar so ill as to be in Bed till Dinner time, the Gents at Preston Hall all Morn: I conversed pleasantly with poor Miss R. & work'd very hard. much conversation in the evening. no company nor no Cards.

Friday Sep.^{t.} 19th.

A brilliant fine Day constant sunshine & very mild air, return'd to Edinburgh early in the Day all 5 in the Coach, the poor Invalid to consult Dr. Monro, the Country appeard in high beauty, walk'd about shopping &'c with Mrs. C. till three o'clock quite tired down heartily glad to return to my beloved Boys who were well & happy. rec'd Letters from Mrs. Savage & Mrs. Pennington.

Saturday Sep.^{t.} 20th.

A shewey fine Morning, a cloudy Noon & a very wet afternoon, Mr. Witts & his Sons went to Bathe Miss M. Brown call'd here, & I went to see Lady C: C: such violent rain while there I was obliged to return in a Chair; in the evening began reading the Mysteries of Udolpho.[33] rec'd a Letter from Mr. Delabere.

---

33. Ann Radcliffe (1764–1823); *The Mysteries of Udolpho*, 1794.

Daniel Sandford (1766–1830), founder of the Charlotte Chapel congregation, was the first Bishop of the reunited Scottish Episcopal Diocese of Edinburgh.

Sunday Sept. 21ˢᵗ·

Quite a clear beautiful Day, a very mild air, little Wind & much sunshine, went to morning service at Mr. Sandfords Chappel, & to the evening as usual at St. Georges, Mr. <u>Brown</u> dined here on Preston Hall game.

Monday Sepᵗ· 22ᵈ·

Very wet & stormy in the early part of the day, but dry the remainder, tho continued a gloomy sky I spent two hours in the forenoon in Messʳˢ· Young & Trotters Warehouse looking over what of Col: Callanders furniture was finish'd to send them an accurate account by no means an unpleasant employ. Mʳ· Witts & George bath'd Francis drank Tea with S. Simpson who had call'd in the Morng. & confirm'd the report his father was going to be married to Miss Kerr. wrote to Mʳˢ· Callander

Witts Family Papers F188

1794

Tuesday Sep.^t 23.^{d.}

Quite Wet in the Morning, & tho it ceased raining before Noon it became a most disagreable tempestuous Day, totally unfit for Women to stir out of the House & not pleasant for either <u>Men</u> or <u>Boys</u>, the latter went to School for the first day for two hours, & brought home some Playmates, M^{r.} <u>Brown</u> call'd here. wrote to M^{rs.} C: Western.

Wensday Sep.^t 24.th.

No rain, but still strong wind as well as sun, I again kept house fearful of exercising the Rhumatism in my head, Mr. Witts & Sons went to Leith in the hope of Bathing but disappointed, M^{r.} <u>Brown</u> again here as also Miss M. Brown, & Mr. Principal Gordon[1] lately arrived from London happy to see him & much conversation with him much interested in hearing the Mysteries of Udolpho.

Thursday Sep.^t 25.th.

Rather a cold gloomy day but quite dry Mr. Witts & I went to Georges Square to make quite a string of visits Mr. Simpsons, Mrs. Clerks, Mr. Balderstons & Mrs. Graigie found some of every family at home, call'd on M^{r.} <u>Brown</u> to see him in his new Lodgings on South <u>Bridge</u> Street much surprized on our way home to stumble on the Miss Nevilles who had arrived the Night before at Walkers Hottel after a Tour to the Highlands; Mr. Principal Gordon dined here & was most agreable, Miss Nevilles drank Tea, & we play'd a most talkative rubber at Whist.

Friday Sep.^t 26.th.

A very cold day. with a raw air tho some sunshine, & at Noon strong signs of rain tho none fell of any consequence, all 4 of us attended by <u>Mr. Brown</u> started at 12 o'clock to go to Dr Herriots Hospital to see the Edinbro' Volunteers receive their Colours from the Hands of the Lord Provost call'd by the way in James's Square when Mr. Brown, Margaret, & Georgiana

---

1. Principal Gordon is something of a mystery. He is presumably the Principal Gordon who was the head of the Scots College in Paris from 1777 to 1793. The Scots College—Collège des Écossais, 65 rue du Cardinal-Lemoine, was founded in 1326 and until 1793 the College was part of the University of Paris. In August 1792 the Scots College was twice invaded by an armed crowd. Alexander Gordon was marched off by four National Guards to the local revolutionary committee in order to be confronted with the new clerical oath. He refused, but shaken, he applied for a passport to leave France and left for England in September. There was much controversy at that time, and later, as to whether Alexander Gordon had done all that was possible to have saved the College records. He appealed to William Pitt for help in 1789, but without success.

accompanied us, such an immense crowd assembled, it was not easy to force our way on the ground, all ranks of people shew^{d.} an eagerness to view the Loyal shew, 3 Hundred Men made their appearance, tho the Corps consists of thrice that number all either Gentlemen or respectable tradesmen the uniform neat & simple; the Principal perform'd a Prayer of a considerable length on the occasion, Lord Adam Gordon as Commander in Chief & his suit added to the shew which was very smart when it was over ourselves & party adjourn'd to Miss Nevilles apartments at the Hottel to see the Ceremony finishd by the colours being deposited at the Lord Provosts House in Princes Street. Miss Nevilles drank Tea with us as did Mr. Brown & we play'd a laughable rubber at Whist rec'd a Letter from my Sister Travell.

Saturday Sep^{t.} 27th.

Quite a clear fine day tho still a very sharp air, but well suited to a very long Morning walk with our English Ladies call'd on them early where we were soon join'd by Miss Crawford & Mr. Dugald Stewart[2] the former declined being of the party but most politely before she left us, invited us to dine with her to meet our friends in the plan of our walk first saw the Register office then over the Calton Hill to Holyrood House where we were fortunate enough to have interest to see the only thing worthy of observation, a Picture of Vandyke of Charles the 1st. & his Queen going a Hunting, all the other sights are mere trash; much entertain'd by the sight of the College as far as it is finished & met with much civility at Mr. Dalziels House where we sat a quarter of a Hour pleasantly, much entertaind by many curiosities In Dr. Monro's anatomical class & by several ancient curiosities both in the Library & Museum, & perhaps as much as anything by Mr. Stewarts agreable manner if judicious remarks home only in time to get dress'd before Dinner time where we found Lady Cathcart, M^{r.} & <u>M^{rs.}</u> <u>Stewart</u> Dr. Blair, & Mr. Wood, a very elegant entertainment both Dinner Tea & Supper, much lively & agreable conversation & much very much pleased with my new acquaintance. rec'd a Letter from Mrs. Rycroft.

Sunday Sep^{t.} 28th.

Dry & not unpleasant tho still a very cold air, went to St. Andrews Church in the Morning Miss Nevilles attending us, where Dr. Hardie performd the Service in a very capital style, walk'd afterwards about the South & old Town with them & I attempted tho without success to call on Mrs. Gray, went to even^{g.} Service at St. Georges Chappel, from whence our Friends return'd with us to Dinner & staid with us to late in the evening I was both tired & sleepy.

Monday Sep^{t.} 29th.

Quite a pleasant change in the weather being quite warm with much sunshine & little wind Mr. Witts went early to Miss Nevilles to carry them to some yet unseen shews, at Mid.day I joind

---

2. Dugald Stewart (1753–1828). Stewart was professor of mathematics at the University of Edinburgh (1747–1772) and in 1785 succeeded Ferguson in the chair of moral philosophy, which he filled for twenty-five years, making it a centre of intellectual and moral influence. Young men were attracted by his reputation from England, Europe and America. Stewart's course on moral philosophy embraced—besides ethics proper—lectures on political philosophy or the theory of government. He spent the summers of 1788 and 1789 in France, where he met Suard, Degérando, and Raynal, and came to sympathize with the revolutionary movement. His political teaching after the French Revolution drew suspicion on him.

A sleepy congregation. An etching by John Kay.

them to see Gardiners Manufactory for Weaving Damask & Diaper Linnen, much entertain'd by it, after shewing the Herriots Hospital I left them to see the Botanic Garden without me, & sat the meanwhile with my very pleasant Friends the Browns; & join'd the party at Walkers Hottel again, as we were all 4 to Dine with the good Ladies, & a large good entertainment we had, play'd at Cassino in the evening, & parted w.th some regret, little knowing when we might see an English friend or acquaintance again.

Tuesday Sep^{t.} 30th.

An equal mild, nay warm Day tho not so pleasant, being a thick air & little or no sun Mr. Witts & Francis bath'd, & I went late to see poor Dear Lady Catherine from whom I had been seperated so long, we <u>all</u> went to drink Tea at Mr. Browns to meet Sir & Lady Wedderbourne[3] & Coll: Riddel play'd a merry game at Whist & supp'd very chearfully not at home till near 12.

---

3.   John Wedderburn (1729–1803). John served as a seventeen-year-old along with his father in Ogilvy's Regiment at Culloden. He escaped capture and lived for many years in Jamaica. The baronetcy was forfeited, but despite the attainder Wedderburn *assumed* its legitimacy and became *de facto* 4th baronet in 1746. He married, first, 1769, Margaret (d. 1769), daughter of David Ogilvy, who, but for attainder, would have been Earl of Ainslie. He married secondly, 1780, Alicia, 2nd daughter of James Dundas of Dundas.

The Lawnmarket. A watercolour by John Skene, 1822. On the right is the West Bow, descending steeply to the Grassmarket.

Wensday Octr 1st.

Very much the same kind of warm close weather the air only rather more thick & later rain imediately after breakfast we walk'd for a little while in the adjacent streets to see the Volunteers vesting their colours in the possession of the new Lord Provost Miss Crawford, Mr Brown, & Mrs Callander here in the Morning, with the latter I was drawn to dawdle in the Streets for 2 hours work'd much & heard a great deal read in the Mysteries of Udolpho.

Thursday Octr 2^{d.}

Again a gloomy close Day but dry & certainly very fine weather for the time of year, Mr Brown call'd here early in the day, to bring interesting news Paper intelligence half of which turn'd out false he attended us in a walk to the old Town on some errands; Mr Witts & dined at Mr Browns invited to partake of a Haunch of Venison Red Deer 5 Gents besides their own family who all departed before Tea, we alone staid Supper & had much agreable & chearful converse. rec'd a Letter from Miss Louisa Lee.

Friday Octr 3^{d.}

Another dull looking day, & towards afternoon a small shower of rain Mr Witts & Frans.^s went to Bathe but previous M.^r C: Brown sat an hour here I visited Mrs Halkett Craigie & Mrs Major Sandys found both at home & very pleasant rain prevented my doing several little bussinesses. heard a great deal in the Mysteries of Udolpho much interested by it. wrote to Mrs Buxton.

The West Bow; entrance to Major Weir's House. An engraving by T. Stewart from a painting by Daniel Wilson.

Saturday Octr. 4th.

Almost constant steady rain till Dinner time, of course quite a quiet domestic day in which many useful things were done, & such rapid reading in Udolpho that we finish'd it before we went to rest wrote a very long Letter to my Sister Travell.

Sunday Octr. 5th.

A very brilliant shewey Morning after somewhat of a frost in the Night, which produced stormy clouds at Noon, & a shower in the afternoon. went to Morning service to S^t. Andrews, where a Stranger performd in rather an uninteresting manner, walk'd in Princes Street before we went to S^t. Georges Chappel to evening service from whence I was obliged to come home in a Chair. went out of Mourning for my poor lost Edward.

Monday Octr. 6th.

Wet & very wet the greater part of the day, more suited to a variety of bussiness & employs than to pleasure, poor Boys almost drown'd going to & from School, sat in the whole day in the study enjoying a fire. in the evening began reading Charlotte Smiths Banishd Man[4]. wrote to M^rs. Granville.

Tuesday Octr. 7th.

Dry with a good deal of bright sunshine but very cold & stormy, M^r. Witts & I went to visit M^r. & M^rs. Allan, Lady C: Charteris, & ended with M^r. Browns always gay & lively, in the evening the Boys read as usual one in Miltons Paradise Lost, the other in D. Chesterfields Letters. rec'd Letters from M^rs. Parsons & Miss Anne Snow, & wrote to Miss Snow.

---

4.   Charlotte Turner Smith (1749–1806). *The Banished Man*, 1794.

Wensday Oct.ʳ 8ᵗʰ.

Very wet till Noon, & very stormy the remainder of the day, which gave me not a wish to stir out employ'd myself much in work & many building bussinesses, reading & some accounts in the evening

Thursday Oct.ʳ 9ᵗʰ.

Bright & fine the whole day but such a cold wind as boded more rain; at mid.day I went out to visit & Shop, unsuccessful in not meeting with M.ʳˢ Crawford at home, sat more than hour with M.ʳˢ Brougham, more & more pleased with her sense & candour. M.ʳ Brown dined here as did Georgina & Robert Brown. recd a Letter from Lady Edw.ᵈ Bentinck

Friday Oct.ʳ 10ᵗʰ.

Such a day of violent & constant rain I had seldom seen, the poor Boys quite drench'd going to & fro to school, well suited to work & reading of w.ᶜʰ I did much. M.ʳ Brown here in the Morning. wrote to M.ʳˢ Pennington.

Saturday Oct.ʳ 11ᵗʰ.

A damp thick close Morning, which was very soon succeeded, by a very high wind & tho some sunshine was alternate showers, & in the evening the Wind was so tempestuous as to be

Above left: General Sir Ralph Abercromby (1734–1801). An etching by John Kay.

Above right: William Craig, Lord Craig (1745–1813). An etching by John Kay, 1799.

quite alarming. M[r.] Brown call'd here early to go a Lodging Hunting in George Street & I for M[r.] Pennington but find on none we dined at M[r.] Browns to eat another Haunch of Venison & met Lord Abercrombie,[5] Lord Craig,[6] Sir William Forbes Coll:[7] & M[rs.] Abercrombie & D[r.] Rotheram, declined supping tho much press'd. Bob: Brown dined with Boys.

Sunday Oct[r.] 12[th.]

Certainly a fine Autumn Day tho still cold & windy but in the sun quite delightful, went to Morning Service at S[t.] Andrews much gratified by having M[r.] Moodie, who perform'd all the service in a most masterly & pleasing manner, walk'd on Princes Street before we went to Chappel in the afternoon spent the evening in much reading &'c with the Boys.

Monday Oct[r.] 13[th.]

A still pleasanter Day being as much sun & far less wind, M[r.] Brown brought his friend M[r.] Foster who is to be M[r.] Penningtons Colleague on the matter of Lodgings soon after breakfast at noon we went with them to see one in xxxxxxxxxx Street w.[ch] was determined on, I then calld on M[rs.] Grey & ended by spending an hour with good Lady C: C: M[r.] Witts read a whole volume of the Banish'd Man George dined with Bob: Brown. rec'd a Letter from Miss Gorges.

Tuesday Oct[r.] 14[th.]

A tolerable bright fine Morning but soon overcast, & became violently stormy, blowing quite a tempest & very early in the afternoon began to rain & so continued all the evening yet with all these unpromising appearances of weather I wrapped myself up, & ventured to walk to Leith with M[r.] Witts to call on M[r.] Oliphant in consequence of a Letter rec'd from M[r.] Principal Gordon, but did not find him at home returnd within 2 hours, tho we stopped at several places, just saved a wetting. at night wrote to Lady Edward Bentinck & M[rs.] Rycroft.

Wensday Oct[r.] 15[th.]

Wet early in the Morning but was bright & fine before Noon, but still very stormy, being to day the wretched Watt was to be executed for High Treason, I had no wish to stir out, & kept the Boys at home after the first school hours, but everything was so well conducted there was no kind of riot or much bustle. M[r.] Brown came here to Tea & to give us a very particular account of the execution. Peter Brougham also drank Tea.

---

5. There was no Lord Abercrombie; the title had died out in 1681. Agnes is mistaken in his title, and she was probably referring to Ralph Abercromby (1734–1801). General Sir Ralph Abercromby was a distinguished soldier, fighting in the wars against Republican France, and commanded the British forces that captured Trinidad and Tobago. He died in Egypt, 1801. Ambercromby was prominent in Edinburgh society and married, 1767, Mary Anne, daughter of John Menzies and Ann, daughter of Patrick Campbell. They had seven children. Abercromby was a Freemason, a member of Canongate Kilwinning Lodge No. 2 in Edinburgh. He twice served as MP for Clackmannanshire, and was appointed Governor of Trinidad.

6. William Craig, Lord Craig (1745–1813). In 1787 Craig became Sheriff-depute of Ayrshire; and on the death of Lord Hailes in 1792, he took his seat on the bench as Lord Craig.

7. Sir William Forbes Coll does not make sense, the writing is unclear, but this may be William Forbes (1739–1806), 6th baronet. He succeeded to the baronetcy in 1743 and was apprenticed to Messrs Coutts & Co., Bankers, Edinburgh, in 1754, becoming a partner in 1760. That firm became known as 'Forbes, Hunter and Co.,' and began to issue bank notes in 1783.

Thursday Octr 16th.

Wet almost incessantly the whole Day much plagued & vex'd by the disappointment in a Maid servant I imagined myself to have engaged but found I was mistaken; M^{r.} & Mrs. Brown drank Tea here very chatty & pleasant indeed, tho quite unexpected.

Friday Octr 17th.

Dry & pleasant enough tho little sun & rather thick foggy air in spite of some apprehensions of dirt I sallied forth accompanied by Mr. W. to make our Wedding Visit to M^{r.} & Mrs. Simpson in Georges Square of course found them at home setting up for Company & some we found there, we likewise visited Mrs. Clerk & went to several shops on our return home, after which walk'd in Queen Street till near 4 o'clock.

Saturday Octr 18th.

Wet early in the day, dry & with sunshine the remainder of the day, but with such a violent & cold high wind that it was very unpleasant. Being out M^{r.} <u>Brown</u> call'd before Noon & tempted us to go with him as long talk'd of to examine the anotomical museum attach'd to Dr. Monro's Class in the College so much gratified by what we saw as to stay near two hours, after which went to see Lady C: C: the Boys drank Tea at Mr. Broughams. rec'd a Letter from Miss Snow & wrote to Mr. Delabere.

Sunday Octr 19th.

Bright & very fine in the Morning, not quite so much so either at Noon or afternoon but continued dry, went to Morning service at the Cowgate Chappel, the usual performers as moderate as ever a stranger read Prayers & very well at St. Georges in afternoon & Mr. Cleeve preached evening pass'd as usual. wrote to Miss Sheppard.

Dr Alexander Monro (1732–1817), Professor of Anatomy in the University of Edinburgh. An etching by John Kay, 1790.

Monday Octr 20th.

Very fine early in the Morning cloudy at Noon, & was a very severe shower of rain from 2 till 3 o'clock, which kept me at M^rs. Halkett Craigies where of course I made a very long chatty visit after having made an usuccessful call on M^rs. Naysmith to enquire the character of a Servant. rec'd a very long & pleasing Letter from my Sister Travell.

Tuesday Octr 21st.

Thick unpleasant air, but dry, M^r. Witts took a very long & distant walk; while I made a pleasant visit to M^rs. Brown where I met M^rs. Douglas & D^r. Gregory, & before I came home call'd on my very near Neighbours M^rs. Jones which turn'd out as different as the Women are different. much reading & work in the evening.

Wensday Octr 22^d.

Very much the same kind of dull looking weather but of which I could never judge, not going out at all M^rs. Callander & the two Miss Browns calld on me at the same time which made each visit less pleasant. M^r. Witts out all Morning shewing M^r. Terrel a young Barbadoes Student, & a recommended protegee of the Browns some of the glories of the Town & brought him back to Dinner, where also M^r. <u>Brown</u> dined & we had a very conversible evening. wrote to Miss B: Guydickens

Thursday Octr 23^d.

No change in the weather excepting being a colder as well as higher wind, M^r. Witts walk'd to Leith with M^r. Terrel, & call'd on M^r. Oliphant on bussiness in his absence I went to call on M^rs. Charteris, whom I found at home & was introduced to her <u>Step</u> Mother M^rs. Campbell, afterwards I made an unsuccessful visit to Lady Dumfries & Miss Gordon & walk'd in the street by way of exercise. Fran^s. drank Tea with B: Brown.

Friday Octr. 24th.

By no means a bad Autumnal day, being dry & with sunshine at intervals, I made good use of it by paying a comfortable long visit to the worthy L^dy. C: C: where I met her Nephew, & on my return walk'd a turn or two with him & his Wife in S^t. Andrews Square evening as usual much working & reading.

Saturday Octr. 25th.

Tolerably dry & fine in the Morning but at mid.day became wet, & very wet indeed which quite put a stop to every idea of going out, always propitious to useful employment, in the evening M^r. W delighted us <u>all</u> by reading a part of Shakespears King Lear having finish'd the Life of Petrach.

Sunday Octr 26th.

Wet in the Morning, & very stormy, damp, cold & uncomfortable the rest of the Day, went to S^t. Andrews church where we were much gratified by M^r. Finlaysons performing the Service in his excellent manner walkd for a short time in Princess Street before we went to S^t. Georges Chappel, where we were much affected by M^r. Cleeve preaching a funeral Sermon on the occasion of the Death of M^rs. General Douglass's Son the family appearing there for the first time since their severe trial John Brougham drank Tea here a very nice Boy.

Monday Octr. 27th.

A dry but very sharp air in the Morning a severe shower at Noon, which was but of short duration & the streets dried quick enough, for me to go to sit an hour or two with M^rs. Brown in her widowed state & walk a little in the streets afterwards. recd a Letter from Miss Anne Snow & wrote to my Sis^r. Travell.

After being a frost in the night, it was a clear fine Day with much sun, M^r. Brown call'd early, M^r. Witts walk'd with me to see Lady C: C: & we took a round both before & after, & when we got home found M^rs. Brown who staid chatting with us till Dinner time, began reading D^r. Blairs Rhetoric.

Wensday Octr. 29th.

Another much the same kind of fine Autumn Day, M^r. Witts went out early to breakfast with M^r. Brown for the purpose of going with him first to D^r. Gregorys opening Lecture & afterwards to D^r. Monro's, I met him on his return & we walk'd for more than an hour. finish'd reading King Lear — wrote to Miss Louisa Lee.

Thursday Octr. 30th.

Rather wet in the Morning, but the wind being high it soon dried, & was very good & pleasant walking at Noon met a large part of the world on Princes Street Parade, made a late & unsuccessful visit to M^rs. Brown. Fran^s. obliged to return from school being so indifferent from the coming on of a cold, much nursing of him. M^r. W. began Shakespears Winter Tale.

Friday Octr. 31st.

Lowering in the Morning, & wet, small rain the far greater part of the Day, so that even M^r. Witts never went out of the Door & Francis staid at home to such good purpose to nurse his cold that it was near well by night. much reading & work & wrote to M^rs. Tracy of Sandywell.

Saturday Novr. 1st.

A bright fine day tho cold, excepting one sharp shower at Noon, D^r. Kinglake sat with us two hours in the Morning & entertain'd very much with an account of his Summer Tour, 3400 miles all on foot accompanied by M^r. Palmer, walk'd late & call'd on M^rs. Brown. a pleasant ½ hour.

Sunday Novr. 2^d.

Quite an unpleasant day, being very cold & damp, & frequent severe showers, but continued to get tolerably dry in the Morning to S^t. Andrews Church & in the evening to S^t. Georges Chappel where M^r. L. Moodie & M^r. Cleeve both shone.

Monday Novr. 3^d.

After hard rain in the night it was a Morning frost accompanied by a fog, which the Sun never completely disipated, tho on the whole must be calld a fine winter day tho very cold; M^r. Palmer here for a long visit in the Morning & was agreable enough, after which M^r. W. & I walkd on the Leith Walk for an hour coming home compleatly dirty. rec'd a Letter f^m. Miss Snow

Tuesday Novr. 4th.

Quite a sharp hoar frost & wonderfully cold, in spite of much sunshine had a sad slippery walk to John Street, where I staid longer with Lady C than usual, M^rs. Brown I visited for a few minutes on my return, she drank Tea with us, as did M^r. Foster & M^r. Brown the latter having previously dined here rec'd a pleasant Letter from M^rs. Granville & wrote to Miss Anne Snow.

Wensday Novr. 5th.

After a most severe night of violent rain & high wind it continued with unabated force the whole of the day, to my remembrance I never knew a more desperate day, the poor Boys almost wash'd away going to & fro to School, I spent it very busily in some necessary employs.

Thursday Novr. 6th.

Almost as violent & continued rain till two o'clock, when it ceased but was miserably damp, cold & uncomfortable, being the first Day of the Preachings, we went to evening Service at S^t. Andrews nothing very eminent in the manner or matter of M^r. Grant the performer. M^r. Brown went with us to Church & we brought him home with us to Dinner but he went away imediately after.

Friday Novr. 7th.

Something of a Frost, & upon the whole a tolerable fine Day, tho the sun could never quite get the better of the fog & was dirty walking. went to Morn: Prayers at S^t. Georges Chappel, afterwards visited M^rs. Brougham, M^rs. Thomson (a lying in visit) & M^rs. Brown found all at home & company with the latter. the Boys in the Morning went to see Lady C: C:

Saturday Novr. 8th.

A very fine Winter day being clear & bright & yet not very cold, busy & Being busy in the Morning, & went to Service at the New Church at 2 o'clock, where the whole was admirably perform'd by M^r. Macnight Junr. from Leith, not at home till past 4. M^r. W. finish'd Cymbeline, wch we had been reading for a night or two before.

Sunday Novr. 9th.

Another charming day, sun quite warm & little or no wind, went both to Morning & evening service at S^t. Georges Chappel it being a Sacrament in which M^r. Cleeve was assisted by a stranger as he was in the evening prayer, M^rs. Brown & her Son Robert went to Church in the afternoon with us & return'd home with us to Dinner, & M^r. Brown brought to Tea a M^r. Cooper, lately arrived out of Lincolnshire to graduate for a Physician, who brought regards &'c from M^r. & M^rs. Chaplin, rather a pleasant Man & a chatty evening.

Monday Novr. 10th.

Wet in the Morning & very damp & stormy the remainder of the day, which did not give me any encouragement to go out having much of the Rhumatism in my Head. much working & reading, began Shakespears Julius Caesar. never any Letters.

Tuesday Nov.ʳ 11ᵗʰ·

Again fine having been a frost. Boys return'd to School after the holidays of the Preachings made a very long visit to Lady C: C: where, I just saw Lord Weyms[8] who was much alarm'd at the sight of me, call'd on Mʳˢ· Brown where as usual I met a circle

Wensday Nov.ʳ 12ᵗʰ·

Another fine day with a mixture of Sun & fog, Mʳˢ· Auchenleck call'd in the Morning, I went late to call on Miss Halkett who had been ill, & afterwards walk'd on Princes Street, Mʳ· Stormonth drank Tea with us, which put a stop to our usual literary evening employments; & I was low & far from well.

Thursday Nov.ʳ 13ᵗʰ·

Being more constant sunshine it was a still finer Day, which tempted me to walk to Georges Square to call on Mʳˢ· D. Hamilton lately returnd home, a pleasant visit as ever, afterwards made 3 unsuccessful calls on Mʳˢ· Duncan, Mʳˢ· Macqueen, & Mʳˢ· Brown in Sᵗ· James's Square, rec'd Letters from Miss Louisa Lee & my Sisʳ· Travell & wrote to Mʳˢ· Callander

Friday Nov.ʳ 14ᵗʰ·

An unpleasant day, being a damp cold high Wind no sun & strong appearance of falling weather much like Snow I walk'd a little to call on Mʳˢ· Charteris who was too ill to receive me, & to go into Sᵗ· Georges Chappel with Mʳ· Cleeve in regard to our Pew. Mʳ· Brown dined w.ᵗʰ us & Mʳ· Cooper joind him at Tea, & we play'd a lively Game at Whist.

Saturday Nov.ʳ 15ᵗʰ·

Weather less pleasant, being small rain & for the greater part of the Day no going out for me. in the evening arrived without being particularly expected on that day Mʳ· Pennington from England & became an inmate with us till he could settle himself comfortably in Lodgings, rejoiced to see him & pleasure much interesting conversation rec'd from him Letters from Mʳˢ· Pennington & Mʳˢ· Buxton

Sunday Nov.ʳ 16ᵗʰ·

A fine Day being clear air, little wind & much sun, Mʳ· Brown visited us while we were at breakfast to see Mʳ· P. went to Morning service at Sᵗ· Andrews where Mʳ· L. Moodie as ever performd the service admirably, walk'd between churches, & our friend join'd us at Sᵗ· Georges Chappel, much friendly & interesting conversation all the evening.

---

8. Francis Charteris (1723–1808). But for the attainder of his elder brother, David Wemyss, Francis would have been 7th Earl Wemyss, but he assumed the title anyway, basing his argument under the erroneous impression that, as he did not deduce his claim through an attainted person, the forfeiture of his later brother did not affect such claim. Francis was the father of Francis Charteris (1749–1808), Lord Elcho, who married Agnes's cousin, Susan Tracy Keck (1746–1835). Their son, Francis Charteris (1772–1853), was successful in having the attainder reversed in 1826 and succeeded as 8th (6th) Earl Wemyss. It is not clear why the elderly man should have been 'alarm'd' at the sight of Agnes.

Monday Novr 17th.

Still dry but very cold, being a thick air & no sun yet I ventured into John Street to see my worthy friend who I found kind as ever but in more spirits than common, on my return call'd on M^rs. Brown; only saw our Friend Pen: at breakfast as he was engaged out all the day; in the evening finish'd Julius Caesar

Tuesday Novr 18th.

Much the same weather only still more cold & disagreable quite wretchedly so yet I walk'd in the Town on several little bussinesses wth M^r. Witts for two hours, on our return found our dear guest returnd home to us with a very bad head ache M^r. Charteris call'd in the Morning, M^r. J: Rose dined with us & M^r. Cooper & M^r. <u>Brown</u> drank Tea & play'd at Whist chearful enough. the Boys both dined at M^r. Browns. rec'd a most charming Letter from M^r. Burslem 12 sides of paper.

Wensday Novr 19th.

A still more unpleasant Day from the wind being so extremely high, & the cold very intense, as not to give me an idea of stirring out of my own House. M^r. Law call'd on me when he came to visit M^r. Pennington, the latter brought his Niece Miss Robinson to introduce her to me, our worthy friend dined & spent the evening with us, much talk & a little Cassino with the Boys. wrote to M^rs. Parsons.

Thursday Novr 20th.

Very much the same weather but tho the wind remain'd quite as high, it was not so severely cold. M^r. P: quitted us after breakfast to enter upon his own Lodgings much to our regret, M^r. Witts & I braved the weather & walk'd to Georges Square & all round the Meadows. drank Tea at M^r. Browns & supt also invited to be introduced to M^rs. Mure, & there was also Miss Abercrombie, Miss Oliver & M^r. Erskine a pleasant visit play'd at Whist rec'd a Letter from M^rs. Rycroft.

Friday Novr 21st.

From the wind being changed, the weather was quite alterd, being wet & foggy the whole of the day, M^r. Pennington sat an hour with me in the Morning while M^r. W. was out the only event worthy of remark excepting my writing a long Letter to my Sis^r. Travell.

Saturday Novr 22^d.

Quite a mild open fine Day, tho at times very cloudy & strong appearance of rain, but upon the whole a wonderful fine Day for the time of year & very fortunate for the grand review of the Volunteers on Brunsfield Lynn by the Duke of Bucclugh as L^d. Lieutenant of the Country, where such a concourse of people of all descriptions were assembled that is past all belief we went with M^r. Com: Brown & his Daughter Mar: M^r. Pennington & some others & tho I was almost tired to death with being on my feet from 4 to 5 hours I was much amused & gratified the Mid Lothian Fencibles attended & upon the whole it was a grand Gala it being half holiday the Boys were so fortunate as to be there

Ensign Charles Johnstone in the Hopetoun Fencibles.
An etching by John Kay, 1795.

Sunday Nov.ʳ 23ᵈ·

By no means a pleasant Day being so thick an air that it almost amounted to a wetting fog & very cold, Mʳ· Cooper call'd on us & attended us to Sᵗ· Andrews church where the service was sadly performd by an absolute Stranger, between churches I made a pleasant visit to Mʳˢ· Mure & an unsuccessful one to Miss Robinson, Mʳ· Pennington went with us to Church in the evening at Sᵗ· Georges, & returnd to Dine as also Miss M: Brown to do Honor to my Birthday, Mʳ· Cooper & Mʳ· Brown drank Tea.

Monday Nov.ʳ 24ᵗʰ·

Weather worse rather than better being at times literaly a wetting fog, but still I ventured to go to see Lady C: C: encouraged by Mʳ· Cooper & Mʳ· W. going so far with me, but came back dirtied up to my knees Mʳ· W. out with Mʳ· Cooper the greater part of the evening at Dʳ· Gregorys &'c. rec'd a Letter from Miss Sheppard & wrote to Mʳˢ· Pennington.

Tuesday Nov.ʳ 25ᵗʰ·

A little better weather & not much still rather foggy, but dry walking in the new Town, Mʳ· P. call'd here & we walk'd back with him over the Bridge to a Shop or two on our return visited Mʳˢ· Brown, & when we got home found we had miss'd of several visitors. rec'd Letters from Miss Anne Snow & Miss B. Guydickens & wrote to Mʳˢ· Granville

Wensday Novr. 26th.

Rather wet in the Morning, but the wind becoming high it was clear & much dryer but was too tempestuous to incline me to go out, but I was glad as Mr. Brougham sat near two hours with me Mr. Com: Brown likewise call'd at the same time Mr. Witts read a good deal in Blairs Rhetoric.

Thursday Novr. 27th.

After having been frosty in the night it was dry & bright in the Morning with a very sharp cold air at noon grew stormy & from 2 to 3 there was a severe shower of rain & sleet. Mr. Witts having borrowed Mr. Coopers Mare took a long Ride to Roselin &'c having first call'd on Mr. Charteris at White House, I went to call on M^{r.} & Mrs. Hamilton in their new house in Ramsay Gardens without success, made afterwards a long & pleasant visit to Mrs. Sandys detain'd by the shower met other company there Mr. Cooper dined with us, we play'd Poole at B: Gammon & he staid till quite late.

Friday Novr. 28th.

A most tremendous day of hard & continued rain & very violent wind, a worse day could not be, neither of the Boys went to School, indeed Francis was quite ill with one of his bad colds & Coughs attended by a slight fever, full employ to nurse him in the Morning, Dined at Mrs. Mure's, meeting M^{r.} & Mrs. Brown Miss Halkett & 2 other Ladies, a very pleasant easy visit, much Whist playing & staid Supper.

Saturday Novr. 29th.

Another very boisterous unpleasant Day, tho very little rain fell, but such shocking high wind in the night that we were sadly disturbed, I walk'd a little at Noon well wrap'd up, but only in the Street to some shops, Mr. Pennington call'd here late in the Day & found our Dear Boy somewhat better but still indiff. wrote to Mrs. Buxton

Sunday Novr. 30th.

Weather much better wind being subsided a tolerable clear air & some sun but very cold, were mortified by having a very dull preacher at St. Andrews in the Morning, as usual went to St. Georges in the even^{g.} Mr. Pennington & Mr. Brown dined with us Francis's Cough very so so & did not go out. wrote to Miss Anne Snow.

Monday Decr. 1st.

Again wet & very stormy in the Morning but grew dry enough to permit me to venture down to my worthy Friend in John Street, with whom I sat an hour or two, & concluded, by spending a chearful ½ hour with the Browns Fran^{s.} greatly better but still kept within, went to Tea & Supper, at Mrs. Mures, remarkably agreable, a party of 12 two thirds Ladies, Whist & Cassino at both of which I won to admiration.

Tuesday Decr. 2^{d.}

Wet early in the Day, dry at noon but very wet in the afternoon, ventured Francis to School at 12 o'clock the poor fellow he came home dripping wet but did not seem the worse for it; much work & reading & some writting wrote to Miss Louisa Lee.

Wensday Dec.ʳ 3.ᵈ

Rather wet & stormy in the Morning, but clear'd as the day advanced, & was dry & fine, but I never went out being full of employs w.ᶜʰ prevented my letting any one in that call'd; We went to Tea & Supper at Miss Abercromby's, in a Coach with the Brown Family, where we met several others in all 7 Gentlemen & 6 Ladies a pleasant evening, 2 Tables at Whist an excellent Supper & the Honors of the meeting better perform'd than is usual wrote to Lady Edward Bentinck.

Thursday Dec.ʳ 4.ᵗʰ

Dark & foggy in the Morning, which tho it never quite went off, turned out a tolerable fine Day & quite dry, it proved quite my Levee Day receiving visits from M.ʳˢ Maitland, M.ʳˢ Mure, M.ʳ & Miss Hamilton & Miss Halkett, the two first staid a very considerable time at all their departure we walk'd in Princes Street, & ended by making a lively call on the Browns.

Friday Dec.ʳ 5.ᵗʰ

A most cruel Day of almost constant rain & strong wind, so little could be seen or done but much reading & working, even M.ʳ W. never stirr'd out & the Boys were well soak'd going to & fro to School.

Saturday Dec.ʳ 6.ᵗʰ

Dry, but foggy the greater part of the Day, the sun trying in vain to overcome the gloom hoping it would be clearer walking than I found it I went to make a string of calls in the South Town, first in full Mourning to call on M.ʳˢ Gray her Father being just dead an unsuccessful call on Miss Abercromby, found M.ʳˢ Hamilton at home & also M.ʳˢ Craigie call'd on M.ʳ Pennington, who we met afterwards. The two Broughams drank Tea here & we all play'd at Pope Joan.

Sunday Dec.ʳ 7.ᵗʰ

Dark & foggy in the Morning, but became wet very wet before church time & so continued the whole of the day without ceasing, yet I ventured to S.ᵗ Andrews Church each time, & much gratified by hearing excellent discourses from the two M.ʳ Moodie, M.ʳ Brown & M.ʳ S: Rose call'd here between churches M.ʳ Pennington dined here, & Principal Gordon & the Reverend M.ʳ Sandford drank Tea & we had much agreable conversation from such sensible men. wrote to M.ʳˢ Rycroft.

Monday Dec.ʳ 8.ᵗʰ

Thick fog & rain at intervals the whole of the Day, which made it miserably close & uncomfortable tho I was hardy enough, to fullfil an engagement I had made with the Principal, to walk down to Lady C: C: but the wet & dirt were intolerable but it gave her pleasure & I did not mind it, He went with me afterwards to visit M.ʳˢ Brown where I staid till Dinner time. rec'd a Letter from Miss Snow.

Tuesday Dec.ʳ 9.ᵗʰ

Apparently a frost early in the Morning but very soon became wet & severely wet the whole day, yet M.ʳ Witts was wise enough to take a long ride & getting completely wet through never returnd till near dark. I had a bad Headache. M.ʳ Cooper the Clergyman dined here a very pleasant Man & much of a Gentleman. M^r. & M^rs. Jones & Principal Gordon, drank Tea here, after the former were gone we play'd 2 rubbers at Whist, & did not part till near ten, the Principal was so lively & agreable rec'd Letters from M^rs. Tracy & my Sister Travell.

Wensday Decr. 10th.

A very beautiful day, dry clear & much sun & little wind, such a treat after so many bad days that it was most enjoyable, & set the whole world moving. M^r. Witts out the whole Morning on bussiness & errands I only moved in the new Town, made many unsuccessful visits, rec'd one from M^rs. Callander, walk'd with her on Princes Street. we dined at M^r. Browns & Francis with us much in a free pleasant way meeting only M^r. & M^rs. Erskine of Cambo, play'd at Whist, & staid Supper.

Thursday Decr. 11th.

Dry tho gloomy in the Morning, but soon became wetting & stormy, & the afternoon & night was dreadful both for wind & rain, the weather prevented my intention of walking to see M^rs. Charteris, but walk'd a good deal in the streets & to call on M^r. Cooper in the afternoon to Tea we had a <u>fine</u> party at home, M^r. & M^rs. Brown M^rs. & Miss Mure, M^r. Principal Gordon & his two young Friends the M^rs. Laws & M^r. Cooper, M^r. Riddel, M^r. Pennington & Miss M: Brown join'd us, but, it went off pleasant & comfortable & every one seemed to like it, a Table at Whist & another at Cassino.

Friday Decr. 12th.

Dark & lowering in the Morning, & dirty to an extreme degree, but mild & dry at mid.day, when I went out over the Bridge on some errands, made two or three unsuccessful visits, much working & reading in the evening but I was unwell & very very low, on several accounts.

Saturday Decr. 13th.

A mild fine Morning with a little sunshine trifling rain at noon & very violent high wind at night went early in the Day to see Lady Catherine & made her a peculiar long visit, we dined at M^r. Riddells, where we met only S^r. James & Lady Riddell[9] & M^r. Mill of Fearn at Dinner, but in the evening came M^r. & M^rs. Belcher, M^r. Maitland & Miss Macartney, M^rs. Oliphant, Major Mellville, & M^r. Campbell, 3 Card Tables, & a good Supper certainly an agreable visit

Sunday Decr. 14th.

A cold but dry pleasant Day with a good deal of sunshine, went to Morning Service at M^r. Sandfords Chappel a most delightful Sermon I visited M^rs. Brown between churches, a very moderate Sermon from M^r. Lawson in the afternoon in S^t. Georges Chappel M^r. Pennington drank Tea with us; & staid late. wrote to M^rs. Pennington.

---

9.   James Riddell (1728–1797), 1st baronet of Ardnamurchan and Sunart. James and his second wife, Sarah (1731–1817), became close friends with Edward and Agnes Witts. James's first wife was Mary Milles, daughter and heir of Thomas Milles of Billockby Hall, Norfolk. They had five children including two sons, Thomas Milles Riddell (1756–1796) of Larbert, Stirling, 'lord of the manor of Billockby in Norfolk', whose son, James Milles Riddell (1787–1861) would inherit James Riddell's title and lands, and George James Riddell (1759–1783) of Loddon Stubbs, Norfolk, who after a military career was killed in a duel by Mary Milles' nephew, David Cuninghame. In years to come, Francis Witts, Agnes's son, maintained the friendship when Lady Riddell lived at Bath.

Monday Dec. 15*th.*

Wet & very wet with violent wind the greater part of the day, quite a stay at home Morning
drawn out in the evening by an invitation to Tea & Cards from M^rs. Maitland, where we made
a party of 14, 3 Card Tables at which we <u>worked</u> with great perseverance till near 12, with
only the interval of a chearful scrambling cold Supper.

Tuesday Dec. 16*th.*

After having been something of a frost in the night it was a clear fine Day, in the early part a
good deal of sun, but grew rather cold & stormy but remaind dry, I went early to call on M^rs.
Charteris at White House found them both at home & realy very pleasant staid more than an
hour on my return home visited M^rs. Clerk in George Squ^re. M^r. Pennington & without success
M^rs. Mure at night wrote a very long Letter to my Sister Travell.

Wensday Dec. 17*th.*

Again dry & tolerably fine in the early part of the Day, but grew very stormy at mid.day M^r.
<u>Brown</u>, Lady Riddell, & M^rs. Macqueen, visited here all at seperate times in the Morning, after
which quite late I just went out for air, & to call on M^rs. Brown for half an hour.

Thursday Dec. 18*th.*

Dark but dry in the Morning but soon became wet & very stormy, & in the evening tremendously
windy, quite a stay at home day even M^r. Witts never stirr'd out & we busied ourselves among
other employs in making a fire screen, poor Boys well soak'd going & coming from School.

Friday Dec. 19*th.*

A dry pleasant day on the whole a good deal of wind, but it was mild, Miss M: Brown call'd
early M^r. Witts & I walk'd to Stewart: field to call on M^rs. Stewart but did not find her at home
return'd home by the Leith Walk, call'd on M^r. Pennington, well tired by the time I got home,
went to Tea Cards & Supper at Sir James Riddells, the party besides them & oursleves were
S^r. James Colquhoun, M^rs. Maitland, M^rs. Oliphant & her Son, M^r. Riddell, & M^r. Campbell a
great deal of Whist playing, & a very elegant small supper. wrote to Miss Charteris —

Saturday Dec. 20*th.*

Still dry, but rather dark & gloomy from a very foggy air, & very cold at mid.day. I went out early
to call on L^dy. C: C: to whom I made an interesting visit & return'd home likewise early, by which
means I rec'd a pleasant visit from M^rs. Clerk, M^r. Cooper dined here, & staid till near ten o'clock, in
which time we had the power of judging that he was both sensible & agreable taught him Cassino

Sunday Dec. 21*st.*

A pretty considerable frost, wch. made it dry & comfortable walking, but being no sun &
much wind it was very very cold, much pleased by M^r. Moodie at S^t. Andrews Church in the
Morning, after my return Miss Mure call'd in a fine easy way for ½ an hour & did the same
on M^rs. Maitland & Miss Macartney, M^r. Cooper & M^r. Pennington, were with as at S^t. Georges
Chappel at evening service the latter dined with us & staid till nine o'clock Fran^s. dined at M^r.
Browns. rec'd a Letter from L^dy. Ed^d. Bentinck

Monday Decr 22^d

Had been much rain in the night, & tho not a confirm'd wet Day, was perfectly stormy, cold & disagreable, violent wind & great inclination to snow having something of a cold I had not a wish to go out Principal Gordon here for two hours in the Morning, his conversation always pleasing, & improving

Tuesday Decr 23^d

Dry tho cold & gloomy in the Morning with much wind, but at Noon it changed to be misty wch made it perfectly disagreable to be out, Mr Witts went out early on Mr Coopers Horse to make a visit at Preston Hall, & returnd late, in his absence I had two excellent escorts at different parts of the Morning in Principal Gordon & Mr Pennington the latter going with me to Goring & Trotters Warehouse, & the former to attend me in a long visit to Lady C: C: I visited Mrs Brown also, & the Principal return'd to Dine with us & staid till near ten o'clock & we spent a most chatty evening

Wensday Decr 24th

Yet dry but very thick air much like snow, & most bitterly cold; I went to Morning prayers at St Georges chappel a very large congregation; afterwards made an unsuccessful visit to Mrs Brougham, a long & pleasant one to Miss Mure & one to Mrs Stewart, on the bussiness of Lord & Lady Elcho, rec'd in a most obliging manner. rec'd a Letter from Mrs Granville.

Thursday Decr 25th

Very miserable in point of weather & yet not unsuitable for Xmas Day having been a pretty considerable fall of Snow in the night & kept on Snowing the greater part of the Day but chiefly in showers attended by violent wind & most intense cold obliged to both go & return to St Georges Chappel in a Chair, the Service perform'd by both Mr Cleeve & Mr Lawson, a very large number of communicants, such a battle for want of Chairs many of us were obliged to retire into Mr Cleeves House to wait for them, prevented going to evening service by being engaged to Dine at Dr Gregorys where besides himself & Miss Ross we met Mrs Brown a M^r & Mrs Stacey from Oxford & their Daughter, Dr Rotherham, Mr Pennington, & Mr Creech, an excellent Dinner, & a very pleasant rational visit not at home till near ten tho the evening was wholly passt in conversation. before Dinner I call'd for a few minutes on Lady C: C: rec'd a letter from Mrs Pennington.

Friday Decr 26th

Wretched weather again, being a mixture of Snow, hail, & rain, but still it melted away fast, my Cold very indifferent & Francis returnd home very early from School having a very bad cold & cough which made him quite ill Mr Witts out much of the Morning on various bussinesses. I wrote to Mrs Witts at Nibley House.

Saturday Decr 27th

A very raw unpleasant Day, but thawing fast the Snow of course was nearly gone & towards evening there was a drying air, a very busy Morning in many useful employs, Mr Cooper & Mr Pennington dined here most pleasantly & Mr Principal Gordon, the two Mr Laws, Mr Brown & Mr Stacey were all added to our party at Tea & we made two Tables at Whist, quite gay & lively Francis's cold as well as mine much better. wrote to Miss Snow.

James Gregory MD (1753–1821),
Professor of the Practice of Medicine
in the University of Edinburgh. An
etching by John Kay.

Sunday Dec.ʳ 28ᵗʰ.

A Dry pleasant Day tho without sun as being no wind it was quite mild & nice walking George only attended me to St. Andrews Church for Morning Service where Mr. L. Moodie as usual was very pleasing, between services I visited Mrs. Erskine of Cambo & Mrs. Stacey taking the latter as well as him & their little Girl to St. Georges Chappel for evening service. Mr. P: Gordon & Mr. Pennington each visited us for a few minutes before Dinner.

Monday Dec.ʳ 29ᵗʰ.

Again dry & fine, certainly something of a frost as it was very cold tho no wind, but towards afternoon grew thick & foggy, Mrs. Brougham, Mrs. Erskine of Cambo, & Mrs. Stewart & Mrs. Mcdougal Grant call'd on me, at three seperate times w.ᶜʰ so filld up the Morning I never got out till three o'clock just to call on Mrs. Brown, we drank Tea & Suppd at St. James Riddels, meeting a party of 12, the greater part Ladies, 3 card Tables & a very elegant Supper

Tuesday Dec.ʳ 30ᵗʰ.

A very decided hard frost, & very cold, but a clear air & some sunshine, made it pleasant & very seasonable weather, I did not go out at all in the Morn. hoping to nurse my continued bad cold, but rec'd visits from Mrs. Mure, Miss Halket & Miss McCartney w.ᶜʰ scarce allow'd me time to dress to dine at White House with Mr. & Mrs. Charteris, whither we went in a Chariot with Principal Gordon, no other Company, an easy & much pleasanter visit than we expected, a good Dinner play'd 2 rubbers at Whist & home by the light of a clear Moon between 9 & 10 o'clock write to Miss Gorges.

Wensday Dec.ʳ 31ˢᵗ.

Continued Frost, but bright & fine & charming walking, Mr. & Mrs. Stacey here early went with them to see their new taken Flat, & Trotters xxxxxxx to hire furniture for it,[10] call'd to take leave of poor Mr. Pennington before he set off in the Mail Coach for Nottinghamshire, & on good Lady Catherine to give her a full & true account of our visit the day before Mr. & Mrs. Stacey drank Tea here quite in a free way to settle more about their Lodgings.

Rec'd 135 Letters
wrote 113 Letters

10. The Trotter Family were associated with the Edinburgh Merchant Company since 1691, and the esteemed William Trotter (1772–1833) established himself in his sole right, after various partnerships, in 1805, in Princes Street. He was the most important, and successful Cabinet Maker in Scotland, and his extensive premises were described in Thomas Dibdin's *Tour in the North Countries of England and Scotland*, quoting, in part 'The locality of this great warehouse is rather singular. It is on the ground floor, lighted by a skylight. Of great length, and vistas filled with Mahogany and Rosewood objects of temptation. Of all styles, including the modern form'.

1795

Thursday Jan: 1ˢᵗ·

The Year open'd by a remarkable bright fine frosty Day & the New Town made very lively by the Volunteers being all assembled in Sᵗ· Andrews Church to hear a Sermon from Principal Baird w.ᶜʰ was a very excellent one, & very well adapted a Psalm, an Anthem, & God save the King by an aditional band concluded the whole to the general satisfaction of a numerous audience. I afterwards visited Lady Riddle & Mʳˢ· Stewart but did not find them at home, more fortunate in meeting Mʳˢ· Erskine of Cambo & Mʳˢ· Halket Craigie, drank Tea & sup'd at Mʳ· Browns meeting a large Party few of which staid Supper.

Friday Jan: 2ᵈ·

Very much the same pleasant frosty weather, but my Cough being very indifferent I staid within to Nurse it, & rec'd visits from Mʳ· Noble, Mʳˢ· Major Sands, & Miss M: Brown; & in the evening Mʳ· Cooper came in unexpectedly to Tea & staid late playing at Piquet.

Saturday Jan: 3ᵈ·

Again fine & pleasant till toward afternoon when it grew extremely cold & stormy, Mʳ· Cooper call'd on us at noon to walk with us to Leith to see the Glass Manufactory Mʳ· <u>Brown</u> join'd our party on our return call'd on Mʳˢ· Brown the Boys drank Tea at Mʳ· Broughams a day of pleasure having gone with us to Leiᵗʰ·   rec'd a Letter from my Sisʳ· Travell & wrote to Lady Edᵈ· Bentinck.

Sunday Jan: 4ᵗʰ·

Still dry the greater part of the Day but extremely cold & the wind so violent it was but just possible to stand in the afternoon some showers of hail, went to Morning service at Sᵗ· Andrews heard Mʳ· Moodie, afterwards visited Mʳˢ· Stacey in her new Lodgings, & Mʳˢ· Mure. went to Mʳ· Sandfords chappel in the afternoon, Mʳ· Cooper dined here & Principal Gordon came late in the evening. the Boys went at 6 o'clock to a charity Sermon & Music appointed for the relief of the indigent blind at Sᵗ· Georges Chappel

Monday Jan: 5ᵗʰ·

Wet & stormy in the Morning, but grew fine before Noon & was very mild & pleasant, quite lucky for our little Jaunt to Preston Hall, could not well get ready to start before ½ past two, but arrived there just before it was dark, a very large party we met there, sat down 19 to Dinner, only Lady Dalrimple & her family staid to Supper, the Drawing lighted up in all its splendour, a most beautiful room, & so are everyone in their different ways throughout the House no Cards w.ᶜʰ made the evening long. rec'd Letters from Lady Elcho & Miss Anne Snow.

Tuesday Jan: 6ᵗʰ·

After having been a hoar frost in the night, it proved a most bright delightful Day with constant sunshine & no wind, which made it warm & mild like Spring, after Breakfast survey'd every part of the House above & below, & then I walk'd w.ᵗʰ the Col. & Mʳ· W. all over the home premises, Mʳ· Dundas call'd in the Morning & Mʳ· Higgins came to Dinner & staid all night, having no employment but forced conversation it seem'd a very long Day

Wensday Jan: 7th.

Foggy in the Morning, but soon clearing off it became a mild pleasant day, with light gleams but little Sun left Preston Hall at Noon our friends kindly sending us home in their Chaise, tho anxious to keep us longer, found our Dear Boys quite well & had the pleasure of receiving a Letter from Mr. Pennington with a very good account of both him & his Dear Wife. Mr. W. began reading in Measure for Measure

Thursday Jan: 8th.

Quite a damp disagreable Day, & so dreadfuly dirty in the Streets it was miserable walking & yet I ventured to walk thro' all difficulties to see Lady Catherine, the Principal & Mr. Witts both being at her Levee, visited Mrs. Brown on my return. we went to drink Tea & Sup at Mrs. Mures, a singular odd party, but it was rather a dull bussiness, most of the set going away early, much bad whist playing & no very famous Supper. rec'd a Letter fr.m Miss Louisa Lee & wrote to Mrs. Granville.

Friday Jan: 9th.

A strong inclination to frost, with such a sharp wind that it was bitterly cold in spite of much sunshine, but I never went out the whole day being very much engaged in writing, Margaret Brown brought her Friend Jane Wedderbourne to see me a very fine young Woman Mr. Witts at night again reading Shakespeare. wrote to Mr. Pennington & my Sisr. Travell

Saturday Jan: 10th.

Quite a severe Frost but bright & seasonable, I had such a succession of Morning callers that I never got out for a walk till near 3 o'clock, first Mrs. Auchenleck, then Mr. McDougal Grant, Capm. & Mrs. Gray, Mrs. Robinson Scott[11] & Miss Maccdonald, Mr. Playfair, & Principal Gordon, could have time only to take a turn in Princes Street coming home to Dress to Dine at Mrs. Stewarts, where we met a very pleasant party of 14 to Dinner & 25 to Supper the better half Gentlemen, the whole party smart & agreable, excellent entertainment, much mirth & good humour, 3 Whist Tables & a large set at Vingt'un not at home till one o'clock Mr. W. later.

Sunday Jan: 11th.

A very severe frost & extremely cold tho much sunshine, the wind being wonderfuly cold, went both to Morning & evening service at St. Georges Chappel this being the first Sunday Mr. Cleeve began his Morng. sermon, which was the introduction to a course of Lectures on the gospel his evening discourse ended by a most elaborate en logium on the late Ld. Aboyne spent the time between churches with Mrs. Brown.

Monday Jan: 12th.

No change of weather, but it was an uncommon pleasant Day being constant warm sunshine & no wind but towards even. it became intensely cold & the frost very severe Mr. Principal Gordon & I perform'd a very pleasant tete tete walk to White House where we found Mrs. Charteris at home, & very obliging found other company, returnd home thro' Georges Square

---

11. Throughout the diaries Agnes switches between spelling the name as Mrs Robinson Scott and Mrs Robertson Scott. In fact the latter spelling was correct. George Robertson Scott was an advocate living at 44 George Street.

the Principal dined here as did M[r.] Stormonth, & M[r.] Playfair & M[r.] Cooper came to Tea after playing one rubber at Whist I went to my evening engagement at M[rs.] S. Farqussons, M[r.] Witts joining me as soon as his Gentlemen went where we met a party of 23 most the same we had met at M[rs.] Stewarts, 4 Card Tables much good singing some reel dancing an excellent cold supper & upon the whole a very pleasant bussiness. not at home till near one.

Tuesday Jan: 13[th.]

Not near so fine a day tho still a sharp frost, as it was a thick fog early in the day, which brought on a rhyme which made it very slippery & unpleasant. M[r.] Rowley from London made as early visit to him succeeded M[rs.] Stewart to accompany me, to be introduced to Lady Cath: Charteris, but first we went to call on M[rs.] Brown another on M[rs.] Erskine of Cambo, & an unsuccessful one on Lady Riddell, instead of a joyous evening of our own Quartette, it was interrupted by M[r.] Richards Brown who drank Tea & sat an hour or two

Wensday Jan: 14[th.]

Still frosty & very cold & unpleasant being much the same sort of Day as yesterday with a strong inclination to snow tho none fell to speak on having determined to stay at home all day, I received visits from D[r.] Rutherford, Lady Rothes,[12] & M[r.] Cooper in the evening M[r.] Witts read Measure for Measure wrote to Miss Sheppard.

Thursday Jan: 15[th.]

Some little snow had fallen in the night, & perpetualy during the course of the day, there were short showers of Snow & hail which made it very unpleasant & very dirty disagreable walking yet have determined so to do, I made several visits in the Morning, Lady Rothes, M[rs.] Major Sandys, M[rs.] Halkett Craigie, M[rs.] Graham, & M[rs.] Robinson Scott all at home but the latter, work'd much in the eveng. & heard the conclusion of Measure for Measure. rec'd a Letter from Lady Edw[d.] Bentinck & wrote to my Bro[r.] Ferdinand a very tiresome bussiness.[13]

Friday Jan: 16[th.]

Very much the same sort of weather, only there appear'd a stronger inclination to thaw, which made it still worse walking yet I braved it having promised to go to poor Lady Catherine, who had quite a fever, from her went to call on Miss Ross at D[r.] Gregorys, & on our return call'd on M[rs.] Stacey in S[t.] Andrews Square. M[r.] Cooper dined here, & at 8 o'clock we carried him with us to M[rs.] Maitlands route & Ball which turn'd out extremely pleasant, from 60 to 70 people, 4 Card Tables, 15 Couple of Dancers frequent reels, & at the conclusion some fine singing, not at home till between 1 & 2.

Saturday Jan: 17[th.]

Again, Snow & hail in frequent showers very cold & had been a sharp frost in the night tho melting in the Day, I was very busy at home all Morning, late I rec'd a visit from M[rs.] Callander

---

12. Jane Elizabeth Leslie (1750–1810). Jane succeeded *suo jure* Countess of Rothes, 1773. Her second husband was Dr Lucas Pepys, MD, FRS, physician to George III. Dr Pepys was created a baronet in 1784.

13. The 'tiresome business' was probably in relation to money, and income from Edward and Agnes's marriage settlement.

who was come into Town for a few Days, Mr. Witts dined at Dr. Rutherfords, between 5 & 6 the Boys went to a Dance at Mrs. Halkett Craigies, & I follow'd them in an hour to be present at the gay little scene 18 Boys & Girls & near as many grown Spectators, a very pretty display'd entertainment, of Tea & Cakes, & frequent application of fruits & xxxxxx at home about ten rec'd Letters from Mrs. Hyett & Mrs. Buxton.

Sunday Jan: 18th.

Had been a considerable fall of Snow in the night, & continued snowing thro the Day in frequent showers, & was miserably cold & comfortless yet I went twice to church at St. Georges Chappel where Mr. Cleeve cheated us of our Morning Lecture because there was a small congregation very shabby wrote to Miss Anne Snow.

Monday Jan: 19th.

If possible the weather more severe, at night a most tremendous storm of snow & hail I never thought of moving in the Morn: busy preparing to go to the Queens Assembly at night Mr. Cooper drank Tea with us before & went with Mr. Witts I went with Mrs. Callander, a very full & genteel Ball, many Volunteers & such a variety of Military the uniforms from their variety made a great shew at home soon after one.

Tuesday Jan: 20th.

Quite a deep snow, & yet snow'd more or less, & very hard sometimes the whole day, neither Mr. W. or myself thought of stirring from the fireside & the Boys return'd from School like Millers, to our agreable surprize Principal Gordon came in for an hour or two in the evening. wrote to Mrs. Thos. Leigh & Miss B: Guydickens

Wensday Jan: 21st.

So very little change in the weather it was hardly to be remark'd excepting not being so many showers of snow, no one here but Miss Stacey, & Mr. W. went very little out any more than myself of course read, work'd, & wrote much, & at night heard part of All's Well that ends well. wrote to Lady Elcho.

Thursday Jan: 22^{d.}

A much sharper frost than ever, of course more intensely cold, tho no Snow fell & there was some sunshine, Miss M: Brown & Mr. Cleeve here in the Morning & Mr. Witts visited Lady Catherine & some others, we dined at Mr. Erskines of Cambo, 15 at one Table & 4 young Ladies at a side Table, the Brown family, & M^{r.} & Mrs. Robinson Scott, the most agreable of the Party, at home at nine o'clock no Cards. rec'd Letters from Mrs. Witts of Nibley & Miss Snow.

Friday Jan: 23^{d.}

Very much the same weather, little or no snow fell, but no sunshine which made it intensely cold, Mr. W. having a little of a sore throat never went out any more than myself, our only visitors the two Mr. Coopers, Mr. John having returnd the day before went on with our Shakespears Play in the evening. wrote to Lady Edwd. Bentinck

Saturday Jan: 24ᵗʰ·

Weather unchanged, till near Dinner time when the wind turning Westerly it became a thaw for an hour or two but at night froze again. being quite house sick I ventured out for a couple of hours visiting, made six finding only Mʳˢ· Mure & Mʳˢ· Brown at home, walking very indifferent indeed, Principal Gordon here for a few minutes before Dinner, the 2 Mr. Coopers Dined here & we play'd 3 lively rubbers at Whist. my Poor Francis kept from School, by a bad head ache & little fever.

Sunday Jan: 25ᵗʰ·

A very miserable day tho no falling weather, as the frost had been again very sharp, w.ᶜʰ made it slippery like glass from the previous little thaw, & was colder than ever being a sharp wind, we never attempted going to Morning Service anywhere but went to the evening at Sᵗ· Andrews where Mʳ· Moodie was very charming. a long day. Franˢ· better.

Monday Jan: 26ᵗʰ·

More & More miserable weather being early in the Day very severe wind as well as frost & at mid.day & all the evening hard snow too bad for Francis to venture to school from whence George came back with a bad cold; Mʳ· J. Cooper here in the Morning. rec'd a Letter from Miss B: Guydickens

Tuesday Jan: 27ᵗʰ·

A most tremendous bad Day throughout being incessant storms of snow & dreadfully cold & gloomy Francis' cold terminally in a rash & Georges too bad to venture to school. We went to drink Tea & sup at Lady Riddels, meeting only a Miss Macfarlin & Sir James Coloquhon, much odd Whist playing, but more odd Highland conversation very amusing.

Wensday Jan: 28ᵗʰ·

Still severe frost but a clear air & much sunshine, tho as cold if not colder than ever Mʳ· Stacy here in the Morning, we dined & supt very agreably at Lord Justice Clerks, meeting a large & good party of 6 Ladies & 10 Gentlemen excellent entertainment, much mirth & some card playing dreadful long Journey to & fro in a chair not at home till one almost starved.

Thursday Jan: 29ᵗʰ·

Still as severe as ever, but being clear & much sunshine it was more bearable, & being quite tired of using no exercise, I sallied forth to walk guarded by a pair of Shetland Hose over my shoes, walk'd over the Bridge to some shops, visited Mʳˢ· Brown & Mʳˢ· Erskine the latter not at home, on my return home admitted Mʳˢ· Brown of Castle Street dined at Mʳ· Coopers, meeting Principal Gordon, & Dʳ· Gregory, extremely pleasant so much clever conversation, a very good Dinner & hearty welcome, play'd at Whist home between 10 & 11. rec'd a Letter from Mʳ· Pennington with the happy news of his Dear Wives being safely brought to Bed of a Son.

Friday Jan: 30ᵗʰ·

Very much such another Day, so out I set again upon my rambles first to the Browns in James's Square to Lady C: C: for a long visit & ended with calling on a Mʳˢ· Hewar, in whose party I was to go to the concert in the evening, which I did at Seven, the Room in the Cowgate is a handsome Oval Room with a Dome & Sky light, the Music was all sacred in honor to the late Earl of Hadinton,[14] who had been Governor, & all the Company appear'd in slight Mourning as a compliment the Band very insufficient for the sublime performance & the Vocal part very miserable, the Room full but chiefly of Ladies, wretched getting away, wet & dirt inconceivable at home between 10 & 11. wrote to M.r Pennington. M.r Cooper went with M.r Witts to the Concert.

Saturday Jan: 31.st

A truly uncomfortable cold Day being still a very severe frost accompanied by a very thick foggy air & at night, another considerable fall of snow, I never went out at all & M.r Witts very little as he had much of a cold, the two M.r Coopers dined here, & M.r Brown also drank Tea by some mistake disappointed in seeing Principal Grodon & M.r Law also, playd many rubbers at Whist the Gentlemen staying late as did the Boys till 11 at a Young Ball at M.rs. Cumins rec'd a Letter from my Sister Travell.

Sunday Feb: 1.st

No sign of a thaw, but on the contrary more cold & miserable than ever the sun attempting to make its appearance early in the day but was soon succeeded by a fog, M.r Witts kept his Bed till Noon for his cold, the Boys & I went to S.t Georges Chappel in the Morning between services I spent with M.rs. Brougham lamenting over the sad illness of her Son John Francis went with me to evening service at S.t Andrews a sad dull stranger preacher.

Monday Feb: 2.d

A much milder air, & at noon such warm sun that it produced quite a temporary thaw, but alas froze again at night, it was quite pleasant being in the air, I was out near three hours making

Cardinal Beaton's House, foot of Blackfriars Wynd, Cowgate. An engraving by T. Stewart from a painting by Daniel Wilson.

14.   Charles Hamilton (1721–1795), 7th Earl of Haddington.

Lord Rockville, Dr Adam Smith (author of
The Wealth of Nations) and Commissioner
Brown, drawn by John Kay, 1787.

many near visits, as M^rs. Maitland, M^rs. Brown Castle Street M^rs. G. Fergusson, M^rs. Halkett Craigie & M^rs. Oliphant & M^rs. Stewart all visible but the latter who was ill M^r. W. again kept home for his cold. George in the even^g. with John Brougham. rec'd Letters from Miss Anne Snow & Miss Forrest. & wrote to my Sis^r. Travell.

Tuesday Feb: 3rd.

A wretched day being a thick air & perpetual snow in kind of storms, some wind & miserably cold, by no means fit for M^r. Witts to go out nor did I, till evening when I went to a party at M^r. Commissioner Browns, of not more than 13, many disappointing from illness, 3 Card Tables however, & a smart Supper but not very lively or brilliant. rec'd a Letter from Miss Neville

Wensday Feb: 4th.

Quite a similar Day being a very moist air, & frequent falling snow, M^r. Witts tho yet pretty well affraid to go out & so was I, M^r. Erskine of Cambo our only visitor much reading in the evening, some working & writing wrote to Miss Louisa Lee

Thursday Feb: 5th.

A much better Day, for tho the frost was yet as severe, yet it was a clear air, no snow fell & much sunshine, which made M^r. Witts venture out without fear, we first call'd on M^r. Cooper, who went with M^r. W. to visit the Principal who was ill, while I visited M^rs. Simson in Georges Square, afterwards Miss Abercrombie very agreably, & ending with M^r. Browns in James's

Square, M^r. Coopers & M^r. Stacy drank Tea here & play'd several merry Games at Whist. wrote to M^rs. Hyett

Friday Feb: 6th.

Quite a comfortless day, being more cold than ever, yet a thick gloomy sky which infected ones spirits not an idea of stirring out, not even M^r. Witts, no one here to enliven but Lady Riddel for an hour in the evening who by her singular manner amused for the time. wrote a Letter to Miss Snow.

Saturday Feb: 7th.

Again a comfortless day, tho not so cold & rather a melting air, & Appearance of the frost being on the go, which made it wretched bad walking, yet still I went to see poor Lady Catherine who as well as myself, was but in very moderate spirits, went no where else, glad to get home safe without any pelts off the roof of the Houses, the snow tumbles off, like the report of a Cannon. heard part of Shakespeare's King John read in the evening.

Sunday Feb: 8th.

A very miserable Day, tho a decided slow thaw, being still extremely cold, & damp in to the bargain, wretched walking even to S^t. Andrews Church where we went to both services, which were each perform'd by strangers & only moderately well, I was very indifferent, & extremely low all Day.

Monday Feb: 9th.

Continuation of thaw, with sharp showers of rain at intervals, nothing could be more unpleasant, & M^r. Witts dining at M^r. Coopers to meet M^r. Phillips, & not coming home till near 10 at night did not make it much lively, tho the Boys were as good companions as they could began a new novel the Vicissitude of genteel Life[15] rec'd a Letter from M^rs. Granville.

Tuesday Feb: 10th.

A continued thaw with a vengeance as from ten o'clock in the Morning, to the same hour at night it raind extremely hard & without ceasing, the poor Boys came from School like drown'd Rats, & the two M^r. Coopers, who came to Dinner not much better, heartily glad of their chearful company & we play'd many merry Games at Whist, they not leaving us till near 11 o'clock.

Wensday Feb: 11th.

Had been a fall of Snow in the night & kept snowing on the whole Day without interruption, accompanied by a moist driving wind, yet still my Dear indefatigable Boys chose to go to school & return'd coverd as white as Millers much working & reading were all we had for it.

---

15. Alethea Lewis (1749–1827), *Vicissitudes in Genteel Life*, 4 volumes, 1794.

Thursday Feb: 12ᵗʰ·

A most tremendous severe Day the Snow being deeper than any former one, the Wind having been so high it was drifted wonderfully, & the accounts wonderful of its depth, the frost continues being severe it was likely to remain with us Mʳ· Witts out a great part of the Morning, paying visits & giving some intelligence, I was so much affected by the weather, & so heartily house sick I was able to do little but read my Novel, & at night hear reading from my Gentlemen.

Friday Feb: 13ᵗʰ·

From a clear air & much sunshine the weather appeard much improved, tho the frost was as sharp as ever I ventured out & even down to see good Lady Cath: who I found tolerable & rather lively, on my return call'd on Mʳˢ· Maitland where I was so long detain'd by a serious chat that I was scarce at home in time to be ready for Dinner to receive Principal Gordon, who dined with us the 2 Mʳ· Laws the 2 Mʳ· Coopers, & a Mʳ· Bancroft came to Tea, & we had a pleasant lively evening; playing at Whist & Cassino. rec'd a Letter from Mʳˢ· Leigh & a strange short one fᵐ· my Bʳ· Ferdinand.

Saturday Feb: 14ᵗʰ·

Again a clear air & much sunshine, but the wind being turn'd Westerly was of course much milder & an evident thaw commenced even in the Shade. attended by my Husband I visited Mʳˢ· Mure who was still confined to her Room by a severe Cold, Lady Riddell who was very lively & agreable, & Mʳˢ· Brown with whom as usual we found other company. much work & reading in the evening

Sunday Feb: 15ᵗʰ·

Quite a confirm'd thaw being a mild air & some sunshine, quite pleasant being out being tho very bad walking the Snow melting so fast, went to Sᵗ· Georges Chappel to both services between which the two Boys attending me I went to visit Mʳˢ· Brougham & to see her Son John, & Mʳˢ· Erskine of Cambo. wrote to Mʳˢ· Buxton

Monday Feb: 16ᵗʰ·

Much such another Day, perhaps the thaw still stronger from more Sun, which made the streets wet & dirty to so great a degree, that I enjoyd the change of weather in my own house, seeing no one but Mʳ· Charteris who paid me a short visit. rec'd Letters from Lady Edward Bentinck & Miss Gorges.

Tuesday Feb: 17ᵗʰ·

Had been again a sharp hoar frost in the Night, but the day being clear with much sun it melted very fast, Lady Riddell here before I went out to take my walk, which I did as far as the College merely for exercise, but it was miserable going, on my return visited Mʳˢ· Stewart in George Street we all went to drink Tea at Mʳ· Staceys, where we only met a Mʳ· Gibbs play'd many rubbers at Whist w.ᵗʰ great success

Wensday Feb: 18th.

Very far from a good day for tho there had been as usual a frost in the night, there was no sun but on the contrary a thick air wch made it very dirty & unpleasant walking. Mr. Cooper call'd quite early for him, & accompanied us in our walk as far as L^{dy.} Catherines who we made very happy as ever by our presence, as we were by the good Principals company for 4 hours in the evening, much charming conversation.

Thursday Feb: 19th.

Quite a comfortless Day being very very cold & stormy & tho frosty in the night jeopery[16] in the Days, so dirty I never stirrd out, Mr. Witts went to Leith the two Mr. Coopers dined here & we had a great deal of Whist playing. wrote to L^{dy.} E: Bentinck

Friday Feb: 20th.

Weather not at all mended on the whole rather worse tho at times the Sun shone as the wind was high & most intensely cold & so stormy it look'd much like snow, no one here but the Principal just before Dinner, Mr. Witts read in the evening in Gays Works, wrote to Mrs. Granville & Mrs. Callander a Letter of condolence on Preston Hall having been on fire but happily no very great damage done.

Saturday Feb: 21st.

Had been some more Snow in the night and continued falling more or less the whole of the Day, but melting as it fell it did not increase the severeness, but an evident thaw commenced, tho in a very mild manner, I never went out & Mr. Witts but little.

Sunday Feb: 22^{d.}

Continuation of a thaw, but a very gentle one, more aided by constant sunshine than anything Fran^{s.} having a pain in his face kept house the rest of us went to both Services at St. Georges Chappel where Mr. Lawson read Prayers in the Morning, Mr. Cleeve gave a very fine Lecture, & we staid the Sacrament & he gave a very excellent Sermon in the afternoon Mr. Brown dined here & staid late.

Monday Feb: 23^{d.}

Still thawing but not very fast & at times showers of Snow & Sleet, a very comfortless morn^{g.} but clearer at mid.day Mr. Charteris call'd to inform us of the Death of the Duchess of Atholl, & in the evening we had a Tea drinking party consisting of Sr. James & Lady Riddell Mr. Stewart & Mrs. M. Grant, Mr. Riddell, Principal Gordon 2 Mr. Coopers, Mr. Bancroft, & M^{r.} D: Erskine, disappointed of Misses Wedderburne & Brown by illness much whist playing, all went off well, & every one Seem'd pleased Mr. Coopers Man acted as Butler.

Tuesday Feb: 24th.

A remarkable fine Day as mild as Spring but dirty walk to an extreme, I first in my walks visited Lady Rothes & Mrs. Brougham finding both at home & then went with Mr. Cooper to

---

16. Jeopery—this is difficult to interpret, but seems to be what she wrote—in the sense of jeopardy/jeopardous—dangerous to venture.

be introduced to M^rs. Phillips in S^t. John Street, when so near went for a quarter of an hour to L^dy. C: C:, my Companion attended me as far as my road home as M^rs. Browns, where I was introduced to her sister Miss Dundas.

Wensday Feb: 25th.

Still mild & thawing fast, but not near as pleasant a Day being no sun & rather foggy, & if possible still dirtier walking. I visited M^rs. McDougal M^rs. Mure M^rs. Stacy & M^rs. G: Fergusson all visible but the latter. was very ill myself all the evening rec'd a Letter from M^r. Pennington from Newcastle

Thursday Feb: 26th.

A very miserable day of Storm & snow wind, & cold, & to one still more miserable for instead of enjoying my Dear Francis's birth day, or going to church being Fast Day, I again went to Bed as soon as I had eat my Breakfast having to my great surprize miscarried sent instantly for M^r. John Cooper, who attended me, as carefully & kindly, the greater part of the Day rec'd Letters from Miss Louisa Lee & my Sis^r. Travell

Friday Feb: 27th.

Again Snow & frost accompanied by wind & storm, rather better at mid.day but wretchedly bad altogether I had had a very sleepless night & was very ill indeed, my good Doctor with me both Morn & Night, & M^rs. Brown & Principal Gordon also calld on me, I got up at night just to have my Bed made but bore it very ill. rec'd a Letter from Miss Anne Snow

Saturday Feb: 28th.

Severe Frost, thermometer below as down at 22 but much sun shine in the course of the Day having got some sleep from an opiate I was rather better, both M^rs. Brown & her Daughter M. with me in the morning & many callers on M^r. Witts. I sat up for 3 hours in the evening, spent pleasantly M^r. Pennington Drinking Tea here who had arrived in the Morning.

Sunday Mar: 1st.

Again sharp frost & extremely cold tho continued sunshine as all those said who were going about M^rs. Brown sat by my bedside for 3 hours in the forenoon M^rs. Mure also for sometime, & I had no less than 4 Gentlemen visitors at my bedside besides, many with M^r. Witts that I did not admit, got up at 5 o'clock & sat till 10, my Doctor John here for an hour late, the Boys at church both times at S^t. Georges chappel

Monday Mar: 2^d.

Still frost but apparently not so hard being a blacker dismal looking Day to which my feelings did but too well correspond, as I was not near so well being extremely weak & languid & full of complaints tho I got up before Noon, M^r. Cooper, M^r. Pennington M^r. Law & Miss Stacy, my visitors. could do nothing but read in the Weird Sisters[17] a New Novel & play B: Gammon

---

17. *The Weird Sisters* a novel, in three volumes, by the author of *A Butler's Diary*, 1792, and *Waldeck Abbey*, 1795. Published by William Lane (1746–1814), of the Minerva Press. Eighteenth-century authors were often anonymous. In this instance the true author is not apparent.

Tuesday Mar: 3ᵈ·

Again dark & gloomy, scarce any frost & at mid.day wetting fog, & small rain, I was very indifferent & good for nothing the whole Day, Mʳ· John Cooper here for 2 hours in the Morning making Bark & striving to get me better. Miss M: Brown my other guest.

Wensday Mar: 4ᵗʰ·

Much the same kind of weather in the Morning, but at noon was charming Sunshine, of course it melted very fast, with great joy I ventured into the Drawing Room, finding myself much better for the change, Mʳ· W went to make his mournful visit at the Abbey & some others, while I rec'd visits from Mʳ· Pennington Miss Mar. Brown, Mʳ· Cooper & Mʳ· Cleeve Principal Gordon & the 2 Mʳ· Laws drank Tea & play'd at whist. very pleasant.

Thursday Mar: 5ᵗʰ·

Quite a confirm'd thaw, being a steady rain the greater part of the Day, of course no intercourse with any one in the Morning, but the two Mʳ· Coopers dined here, & Principal Gordon & Mʳ· Pennington came to Tea & we had much Whist & conversation as they staid late.

Friday Mar: 6ᵗʰ·

A thick oppressive Day, & part of it severe rain, having had a bad night I was a miserable poor Creature the whole of the Day, Mʳˢ· Brown & Lady Riddell each made long visits at seperate parts of the Morning & Mʳˢ· Mure drank Tea with us in a most friendly way playing at 3 handed Cribbage. wrote to my Sisʳ· Travell.

Saturday Mar: 7ᵗʰ·

A beautiful day, having been clear air & much sun but so dirty in the streets that those that were able to move could have but small enjoyment in it, Mʳˢ· M. Sandys & P: Gordon here in the Morning, Mʳ· Pennington to Dinner & the good Principal join'd us in the evenᵍ· & we had a lively talkative Game at Whist. the Boys dined at Captain Lockharts & spent the evening at Mʳ· Browns being Bob's birthday. wrote to Miss Anne Snow.

Sunday Mar: 8ᵗʰ·

A cold comfortless sort of Day, & in the evening sharp rain, Mʳ· Witts & Boys went to both services at Sᵗ· Georges Chappel, Mʳ· Bancroft spent a very conversible hour with me in their absence, Miss G. Brown call'd, & poor Mʳ· Cooper pass'd an hour late in the evening with us but we were all so low, because it is, was his last visit, that we had little enjoyment rec'd a Letter from Mʳˢ· Savage.

Monday Mar: 9ᵗʰ·

Damp & wet all the Morning but was a clear fine afternoon, Principal Gordon here for two hours in the Morning, to him succeeded Mʳ· Stacey for as from a great jail evening quite alone,[18] but cheerful, being much better in the evening than since I was ill

---

18. Jail evening was not a common term and appears to be an Agnes invention, but for a social animal such as Agnes Witts its sentiment is obvious enough.

Tuesday Mar: 10ᵗʰ·

A clear mild day, with little flying storms at times but at mid.day fine with bright sun, Mʳˢ· Brougham & Mʳ· J. Cooper my only Morning Visitors at 2 o'clock I ventured out in a chair, as was my Duty went to Mʳ· Browns in Sᵗ· James's Square, happy to be once more there & as usual found a large circle did not come home till 4 Principal Gordon spent the whole evening with us wholly taken up with conversation on business in which he proved himself most friendly & kind.

Wensday Mar: 11ᵗʰ·

But a moderate kind of a day being damp, & foggy, & being disappointed in going out in a Coach I could not venture out at all. Mʳ· Pennington, Mʳˢ· Oliphant & her Daughter & Principal Gordon my guests in the evening our home party uninterrupted. wrote to Miss Neville.

Thursday Mar: 12ᵗʰ·

A very cold, stormy Day in spite of some sunshine, & in the evening sufficient snow again to cover the ground, I went out in a Chair to make some <u>grateful</u> visits, as to Mʳˢ· Stewart, Mʳˢ· Mure Mʳˢ· Sandys, Mʳˢ· Brougham, & Mʳˢ· Erskine of Cambo Principal Gordon (who likewise call'd in the Morning) & Mʳ· Oliphant from Leith dined here, & in the evening came Mʳ· Mʳˢ· & Miss Stacy, Mʳ· Gibbs, Mʳ· Bancroft & Mʳ· Rose, wᶜʰ form'd two merry Whist Tables. the Boys dined with Mʳ· J: Cooper, who took them to the Circus.

Friday March 13ᵗʰ·

Quite a bitter cold Day & the earth coverd by a snow of 3 inches deep, some sunshine but very stormy all this shut me up all Morning, Miss Mure & Mʳ· Pennington my guests, we dined at Sʳ· James Riddells, where we met Col: Stewart, & Principal Gordon an excellent Dinner & very lively & pleasant, in the evening came, Mʳˢ· Douglas & her Sister Miss Scott Sʳ· James Colquhin & a Mʳ· Dalrimple all staid Supper but the Ladies.

Saturday Mar: 14ᵗʰ·

A very sharp frost & severely cold, tho much sunshine & perfectly dry & good walking which tempted me to make my first attempt to move out without a Chair, as was my Duty, made my first visit to Mʳ· J. Cooper, meeting Mʳ· Pennington there declined going to see him as I had intended & both Gent: walk'd home with us, we all 4 Dined at Mʳ· Stormonths, where we met Sʳ· William Ramsay[19] & Principal Gordon, a queer odd Dinner & not a very famous visit tho the Baronet was very polite & made it pleasanter, came away directly after Tea, when Mʳ· W. & I went to Mʳ· Sam Browns where we spent the remainder of the evening only the 2 Men & their Wives playing at Whist eating a cold Supper, & much talk after

---

19. William Ramsay (d. 1807), 7th baronet. William Ramsay's date of birth is not known, but as his father died in 1783 aged 76, and as he was third son, we may assume he was born in the 1740s. His eldest brother John succeeded as 5th baronet in 1782, but died the following year. The next brother, George, died from a duel with Captain Macrae near Musselburgh in 1790. William married, 5 August 1796, Agnata Frances, daughter of Vincent Hilton Biscoe of Hookwood, Surrey.

Sunday Mar: 15ᵗʰ·

Literaly the very coldest Day of all the many cold in the course of the Winter, incessant small showers of snow & a high wind which made the cold intense, I yet venturd to Church both times to Sᵗ· Andrews in the Morning where there was a dull stranger preach'd, & to Sᵗ· Georges in the evening, where Mʳ· Lawson read prayers & Mʳ· Cleeve preachd almost starved to death with cold made realy quite ill with it. between churches visited my up stair Neighbour Mʳˢ· Trotter to return thanks for the loan of an easy chair when I was ill.

Monday March 16ᵗʰ·

Still cold & very cold with a sharp wind & in the afternoon hard rain, I prudently staid at home all Morning, Mʳ· Pennington & Mʳ· J: Cooper dined here & the Principal, & Mʳ· Bancroft came in the evening & we play'd many rubbers at Whist myself with wonderful success. Mʳˢ· Syme, Mʳˢ· Maitland & Mʳ· Charteris here in the Morning rec'd a Letter from Miss Snow.

Tuesday Mar: 17ᵗʰ·

A most cruel severe Day of driving hard snow & wind, realy more intensely cold than almost I ever felt no keeping warm even by the fireside my only guest the Principal who came to attend Mʳ· Witts to Dine with Mʳ· Oliphant at Leith & he likewise call'd again when they returnd in the evening. wrote to Miss Forrest.

Wensday Mar: 18ᵗʰ·

Upon the whole a fine Day being a clear air & warm sun & the snow melted away very fast, which made it so dirty I was constraind to take a chair to make a train of needful Morning visits, first to Lady C: C: whose joy was great to see me once more, to Mʳˢ· Phillips, to Mʳˢ· Dundas, to Mʳˢ· Clark to Mʳˢ· Macqueen & Mʳˢ· Calderwood Denham call at home,[20] but the latter & very pleasant calls they were, in the eveng. Mʳ· W. read in Cumberlands new Novel of Henry.[21]

Thursday Mar: 19ᵗʰ·

A Stormy but dry Morning with some sun at Noon a sharp shower & again fine, Mʳ· Witts went early to white House to see the Charteris's accompanied by the Principal, who sat here half an hour on his return & was our only visitor in the course of the Day when we were much entertained by Henry. rec'd a Letter from Lady Edward Bentinck

Friday Mar: 20ᵗʰ·

Realy a tolerable fine Day, for tho the wind was high it was not cold & there was much sunshine I only walk'd to make some visits, as Mʳˢ· Mure, Mʳˢ· Maitland, Mʳˢ· Stacy & Mʳˢ· Syme, all at home, the good Principal dined with us, & Mʳˢ· Brown & Miss Margaret & the Mʳ· Laws came to Tea & we play'd both at Whist & Cassino.

---

20. Mr Calderwood Denham was presumably the son of Thomas Calderwood of Polton, who married, 1735, Margaret Steuart, née Denham (1715–1774). In 1756 she and her husband embarked on a journey through England and the Low Countries, which she documented in a series of articulate and opinionated letters to her daughter, later published as *A Journey in England, Holland, and the Low Countries*, 1842.

21. Richard Cumberland (1732–1811), *Henry*, 1795.

Saturday Mar: 21ˢᵗ·

Much such another Day rather more fine, I No otherwise avail'd myself of it, than by walking to the Assembly Rooms to see Strange the Dancing masters practising previous to his Ball, 8 or 900 people assembled, some good dancing, interspersd with martial Songs of music, staid there till 4 o'clock Mʳ· J: Cooper went with us; play'd Cards & supt at Mʳˢ· Hamiltons in Ramsay Garden rather a hetrogenous party 8 Ladies 10 Gentlemen, Whist & Vingtun not very lively yet staid late. rec'd a Letter from Mʳˢ· Ryecroft.

Sunday Mar: 22ᵈ·

No change in the weather only rather colder, went to both services at Sᵗ· Georges Chappel 2 very excellent sermons that in the evening quite a masterly composition. Mʳ· Pennington call'd first & went w.ᵗʰ us there, as did Mʳ· Bancroft. Mʳˢ· Muse came in the afternoon & staid 3 or 4 hours. wrote to Mʳ· B. Witts.

Witts Family Papers F189

1795

Monday Mar: 23ᵈ·

A dry wholesome day but not very pleasant being a strong wind & no sun, went out late visited Miss Oliphant in the absence of her Mother, & Mʳˢ· Brown who as ever was most agreable, Mʳ· Pennington & Mʳ· John Cooper dined here, & Mʳ· Gibbes join'd us at Tea, & we had a very pleasant evening; Cards & conversation well blended.

Tuesday Mar: 24ᵗʰ·

Quite a good day being mild & much sun Mʳ· Witts took a ride to Inveresk to look at Mʳ· Charteris future House there, I went & made a comfortable long visit to good Lady Catherine, but was much fatigued by the great exertion of the walk. Mʳ· Principal call'd on us late in the evening, just before we went to Cards & Supper at Mʳˢ· Oliphants, where was a very pleasant party of 20 tho unfortunately the far greater part Ladies, but it was an extreme genteel party, much Whist playing.

Wensday Mar: 25ᵗʰ·

Another clear fine Day, tho the air was rather sharp & frosty, the greater part of the Morning spent in attending Mʳˢ· Brougham to Madame Rosignols Dancing School practising, met many there I knew, & well pleased with the manner of teaching & the performance in general, went to the Play in the evening to see Johnson in a new Line, Don Felix in the wonder in which He by no means shone, & a very stupid Farce, our set Mʳˢ· Stacy, Mʳ· Gibbs, Mʳ· Bancroft, Mʳ· J: Cooper, Mʳ· W. myself & Francis, the latter in the place of Mʳ· Pennington who was prevented by illness

Thursday Mar: 26ᵗʰ·

Having been a sharp frost in the night it was very cold in the shade & hot in the sun Mʳˢ· Craigie from Georges Square, Mʳˢ· Stewart & Mʳ· Simpson all here at different times in the Morning, & we went to make a friendly visit to Mʳ· Pennington who we found somewhat better, Principal Gordon drank Tea with us & staid till so full of friendly & pleasant chat. much delighted with Henry as we advanced on with it.

Friday Mar: 27ᵗʰ·

Weather tolerably good, dry cold & windy with some sun, Miss Halkett & Mʳˢ· Auchenlech my visitors, I went late to walk for a short time on Leith walk & ended my peregrinations by calling on Mʳˢ· Brown. Francis went in the evening late to Madame Rosignols Ball great delight to him not at home till between one & two

Saturday Mar: 28ᵗʰ·

A cold comfortless sort of Day tho quite dry, which made me stay all Morning at home & for a wonder not one caller, Mʳ· Pennington dined with us drank Tea & staid till he went to a Party, & we also to one at Mʳˢ· Grahams, where we met Com. Browns family & besides a party of 11, a dull very dull thing all together, 2 Tables at Cards & a good Supper. wrote to Mʳ· Burslem a letter very long owed.

Sunday Mar: 29ᵗʰ·

Another cold unpleasant Day, dry but extreme cold wind, went to both services at Sᵗ· Georges Chappel, where Mʳ· Cleeve shone much walk'd a little in Princes between churches very indifferent & very low all day wrote to Lady Edward Bentinck & Miss Snow.

Monday Mar: 30ᵗʰ·

Foggy & not very pleasant in the Morning & at noon small flying rain in showers, which made it very dirty & unpleasant out altogether, yet having agreed to take Mʳ· Pennington with me to Lady Catherines I kept my apointment, found her as usual, but less terrified by a new face than I expected. Principal Gordon call'd on my return & kept him to Dinner, Mʳ· Bancroft came in the evening & we had a very merry Game Whist

Tuesday Mar: 31ˢᵗ·

Much the same sort of unpleasant weather being thick air & damp, & sometimes small rain I was far from well & much worried in point of spirits somewhat relieved by airing with Mʳˢ· Brown in her Sisters Carriage in & about the Town. went very early in the evening, to the Georges Square Assembly, which as usual being the last was dedicated to young People among which my Sons made some a very pretty sight, & meeting many I knew was very pleasant not at home till one o'clock. rec'd a Letter from Anne Snow.

Wensday Ap: 1ˢᵗ·

An exceeding pleasant day, being a mild but clear air no wind & some sunshine, went to Church at Sᵗ· Georges Chappel, was visited by Mʳˢ· Pennington & Cooper, Mʳ· Witts & Sons being a holiday to them went to White House to see Mʳ· Charteris who was not well, I walk'd with Lady Riddel, by Fountains Bridge & Lauriston to Georges Square visited Coll: Riddell who was not at home more fortunate in finding Mʳˢ· Craigie & Mʳˢ· Douglass of Cavers who we visited;[1] I ended my Morning Tour by making a very pleasant visit to Mʳˢ· Erskine of Cambo not at home till past 4; the Principal & Mr. Laws came to Tea, & play'd much at Whist.

Thursday Ap: 2ᵈ·

Not so fine a day being more of a fog Mʳ· Witts went to Clifton Hall to see Mʳ· Maitland I again went to Church, after which call'd on Mʳˢ· Mure, Mʳˢ· Halkett Craigie & Mʳˢ· Brown,

---

1. This is possibly Lady Grace, daughter of the 10th Earl of Moray, who married 10 July 1789, George Douglas 18th of Cavers (d. 1815). George and Lady Grace Douglas had two sons, James Douglas (b. 9 August 1790), and another son (b. 28 September 1796). The attribution is tentative because Agnes was usually very particular about the use of titles and of form in general.

on my return home was visited by M^r. R. Brown a very quiet Stranger. deep in work of Henry all evening

Friday Ap: 3^d.

No change of weather excepting being rather colder, Chappel most exceedingly full being good Friday, M^rs. Pennington & Cooper sat with us there, & return'd home with us to eat sandwich's, & we return'd over the Bridge with them going to M^r. Bells the Surgeon to enquire after M^r. Charteris about whom we were very anxious but could gain no account went to evening service. Peter Brougham drank Tea.

Saturday Ap: 4th.

A fine pleasant Day, tho rather a cold air perfectly dry, & very well suited for walking, went to Chappel Morning Prayers, M^r. Witts also after which we both walk'd thro Georges Square to White House being anxious to see M^r. Charteris, who we found better a more chatty visit than usual, return home by the Lothian road. Principal Gordon here for a quarter of an hour in the evening. finished Henry well pleased with it. rec'd a Letter from M^rs. Buxton & wrote to my Sis^r. Travell. —

Benjamin Bell (1749–1806). Bell was a member of the Royal College of Surgeons and practised in Edinburgh. An etching by John Kay, 1797.

Sunday Ap: 5th.

Quite a bright fine Easter Day, but very cold in spite of constant sunshine spent many hours of the forenoon at S^t. Georges Chappel, where M^r. Stacy assisted M^r. Cleeve in the Morning & M^r. Lawson in the afternoon; walk'd in Princes Street between churches & after Dinner walk'd with M^r. W. to M^r. Bells to learn his decided opinion about M^r. Charteris, very favorable the Principal drank Tea here, & we had charming conversation till between 10 & 11.

Monday Ap: 6th.

Not so pleasant a day being, a thick air & very cold, M^r. Witts took a long ride, & I went to Lady C: C: accompanied by the Principal, call'd also on M^rs. Moray & M^rs. Phillips, the latter only at home, on my return call'd in S^t. James's Square, found only Georgina visible, & on M^rs. Stacy

Tuesday Ap: 7th.

A gloomy thick Morning, which soon turnd to rain & so continued the whole Day, at times very hard, Lady Riddell sat an hour with me, M^r. Cooper & Mr. Pennington dined, M^r. Comm:^r Brown & M^r. Rose came to Tea & Whist at which we had a merry game as well as at Back Gammon. wrote to M^r. B: Witts.

Wensday Ap: 8ᵗʰ·

Not a <u>whit</u> a better Day being rain or wetting fog the whole of it & miserably cold & comfortless not even Mʳ· W. went out having something of a cold, no Morning callers, but Principal Gordon came to Tea & made one of his charming 3 or 4 hours visits wrote to Mʳˢ· Pennington & Miss Louisa Lee.

Thursday Ap: 9ᵗʰ·

A very moderate kind of a day, being a thick gloomy sky tho no absolute rain, Mʳ· Witts went to White House & some other distant visits, I alone saw Sir James Riddell as a Morning caller, we went to Cards & Supper at Mʳˢ· Mure's not unpleasant, but rather odd & droll, tho only one other Gentlemen besides Mʳ· Witts Tables both at Whist & Cassino at the latter of which I won.

Friday Ap: 10ᵗʰ·

Very much such another comfortless day dry but a horrid cold easterly wind & of course thick air, Mʳ· Witts staid at home intirely to nurse his cold which was worse & was visited by Mʳ· Jones, I went & made two or three unsuccessful calls & concluded by sitting an hour with Mʳˢ· Brown. rec'd a Letter from Lady Edward Bentinck & wrote to Miss B: Guydickens

Saturday Ap: 11ᵗʰ·

Weather very much worse being the greater part of the Day, hard rain as well as dreadful thick fog most totally confining till night when we went to Cards & supper at Capᵗⁿ· Brown's, a large & smart party of 23 tho the proportion of Ladies much too great, 3 Whist Tables & a large round one for the young People, two Tables at Supper a very elegant setting out, much mirth & some singing kept is till a very late hour. very agreable

Sunday Ap: 12ᵗʰ·

Dry in the Morning, but lowering, & there was a very severe shower during evening service & was rather wet all the evening, we went to Morning service at Sᵗ· Georges, & to evening at Sᵗ· Andrews where Mʳ· Moodie was most pleasing, Principal Gordon sat a couple of hours in the evening, taking leave as he was going for a short time into the Country rec'd a Letter from Mʳˢ· Granville. between churches visited Mʳˢ· Maitland & Mʳˢ· Stacy

Monday Ap: 13ᵗʰ·

Very thick fog in the Morning, clear'd & was tolerably pleasant at Noon but rain'd again in the afternoon & continued more or less all the evening; I went to Mʳˢ· Erskines of Cambo to look over her house for Lady Riddell then to make a long visit to my good Lady C: C: from whence I did not return till very near Dinner time. in the evening there was a general illumination, in honor of the Prince of Wales's Marriage, & in spite of the bad evening we sallied forth for more than hour to see the infinite variety, to the great delight of the Boys.

Tuesday Ap: 14ᵗʰ·

Severe wind & rain till quite Noon with a gloomy thick air & easterly wind, I was very busy all Morning but never stirr'd out of the House, dined at Mʳ· Erskines of Cambo, very agreably, meeting all the Brown family, Capᵗⁿ· & Mʳˢ· Dewar &'c, staid till 9 o'clock all conversation, when we adjourn'd to Mr Browns & Miss Carnegie with us to eat a merry family Supper there.

Wensday Ap: 15th

A most unpleasant day, being a most violent high wind, yet hot & gloomy, with now & then showers, I went to meet Lady Riddell at Mr Erskines to assist her in the survey of it, made several visits none at home but Mrs Mure, with whom I went to see Raeburns Pictures. Mr W. & I went to an early Tea drinking to Mrs Maitlands who was ill, where we met Lady Riddell & Mrs Macdowal, & Mrs G. Fergusson came in also for a short time, play'd rubbers without count at Cribbage, & staid & eat a cold meat Supper the Boys both at Mad^e Rosignols Public.

Thursday Ap: 16th

Dry with much sunshine, but not very pleasant the wind being still extremely high again made many visits, but found none at home but Mrs Stewart & Miss Cranford, both very pleasant. went to tea Cards & Supper at Lady Riddells, taking Mr J. Cooper & Mr Bancroft with us, & meeting M^rs & three Miss Baileys, Mrs Davis, Mrs Mure, Miss Bruce & Mr Baron Gordon, very lively & agreable not at home till one, I play'd at Whist, Cassino & backgammon lost at all.

Friday Ap: 17th

Again very stormy, with an intermission of showers & sunshine, Mr Cooper & Mr Bancroft call'd here, to attend Mr Witts to visit the East Indians which they did without success, & all join'd me at Mr Browns, from whence we went to see Stewarts minature Pictures. In the evening we had quite a rout, Lady Riddell, Mrs Mure, M^rs & Miss Graham, Miss Carneggie, & Miss M. Brown, Mr Riddell, Mr Cooper, Mr Bancroft, Mr Rose & 2 Mr Laws, a Table at Whist, & a large round one for the young people, every one appear'd pleased & did not seperate till between 11 & 12. wrote to Lady Edward Bentinck.

Saturday Ap: 18th

Perfectly dry the whole Day but very windy & cold, I went out early with Lady Riddell to see several House likely to suit her in George Street then with her visited Mrs Davies Miss Macartney enquiring after Mrs Maitland, Lady Betty Cunningham went home with the former to eat Steack Pie, visited Mrs Erskine & her young friends most pleasantly, found Mr Pennington at home on my return dress'd in haste to dine at Mrs Mures, where we met M^r & Mrs Kerr of Blackshiels[2] his Sister Mrs Herries,[3] & a Miss Murray, a handsome & cold Supper, a Table at Whist & Cassino, but not very lively no other company coming in. at home early rec'd a Letter from Miss Snow.

---

2. James Kerr (1751–1820). James was admitted, to the Speculative Society of Edinburgh, 1 December 1772 with an essay—*Toleration of Religion*. He was appointed Manager of the Leith Bank at its institution in 1801, and was well known in Edinburgh as a liberal patron of the fine arts. Kerr was an apprentice with William Forbes, banker, but inheriting a fortune from his wine merchant father, Alexander, he spent a considerable time on the Continent. He was a member of the Catch Club, one of the oldest and most celebrated associations of musical amateurs in Edinburgh and was himself an excellent flute player.

3. Miss A. Kerr appears to have married William Herries, a merchant at Ostend.

CONNOISSEURS

The first figure is William Scott, plumber, who is looking through his glass at a print of the 'Three Graces'. The next figure is James Sibbald, bookseller. Third, with spectacles is George Fairholme of Greenhill, near Edinburgh. The fourth is James Kerr of Blackshiels. The two remaining figure are either unknown, or imaginary. An etching by John Kay.

Sunday Ap: 19ᵗʰ·

Rather a showery Day but drying up quick was by no means unpleasant, went to both services at Sᵗ· Georges Chappel, where Mʳ· Witts attended at the Door to receive the contributions, brought home by Mʳˢ· Stewart in her Carriage in the evening in a shower, between services visited Mʳˢ· Stacy. rec'd a Letter from my Sister Travell.

Monday Ap: 20ᵗʰ·

An exeeding pleasant Day quite mild & spring like, went to see Lady C: C: particularly poorly but ever most friendly, visited the Browns, & staid sometime at Stewarts the Painter waiting in vain for Mʳ· Cooper, very busy all the evening consulting on difficult Letters of bussiness & wrote to Miss Gorges & Miss Anne Snow.

Tuesday Ap: 21ˢᵗ·

Still more mild & pleasant weather went out early, first call'd on Lady Riddell, then on Lady & Miss Sinclair made a very pleasant chatty visit, afterwards walk'd to Georges Square, visited Mʳˢ· Douglass Cavers &'c, Mʳˢ· Simpson both at home, Miss Gordon at Sʳ· Hew Dalrimples, Mʳ· Pennington, & ended by an enquiring call on Miss Macartney. went at 9 o'clock accompanied by

Mess.rs. Cooper & Bancroft to a Ball at M.rs. Baillies, about 60 people very gay & smart a prodigious fine Supper everything admirably well conducted not at home till near 4 in the Morning.

Wensday Ap: 22.d.

A very showery Day tho short ones & very soon drying up, did not get up very early, my first call to see M.rs. Erskine, who carried me in her chaise to see M.rs. Brown, whence as usual I met a large & lively party, went in the afternoon on foot to Drink Tea with M.rs. Stewart quite in a free way, as I thought but it terminated in a circle of eleven, 2 Tables at Whist & a very good Supper from which we were allow'd early to depart many of us being glad to take to our Bed.

Thursday Ap: 23.d.

Quite as dripping a day if not much perfectly April weather, but mild & growing, some Cookery with nursing Francis, who was detain'd from School by one of his little fevers & coughs for which we solicited the aid of M.r. Pennington who came at noon, I went late to visit M.rs. Baillie where met M.rs. McDowall she carried me in her chaise to visit M.rs. Davies who we likewise found at home, went to Dine at Lady Riddells, where we met M.r. & M.rs. Riddell Col: Riddell[4] & M.rs. Carr & M.rs. Mure, & to Cards & Supper were added M.r. Bancroft & M.r. Cooper very lively & pleasant. brought home by M.rs. R. in her chaise.

Friday Ap: 24.th.

A clear fine Day, with only sufficient rain just to swear by M.r. P. made an early visit to his patient who was better M.r. Witts attended me in several visits in the new Town, joind Lady Riddell by accident, we accompanied us in some, we then went into S.t. John Street principaly to see M.r. & M.rs. Charteris who were there, who joind us at L.dy. C: C: bedside where I pass'd a chearful Hour, call'd in St. James's Square on the Browns, & with difficulty evaded their persuasions to stay and eat a family Dinner, but I quite long'd to be at home in quiet which I much enjoy'd

Saturday Ap: 25.th.

Again very showery, tho short & trifling till late at night when it was most severe rain, my Morning or rather noon walk was only to call on M.rs. Erskine M.rs. Oliphant, & M.rs. Stacy the two latter of whom I found at home, M.r. Witts dined at D.r. Gregorys with a party of Gentlemen, I with Lady Riddell, where was M.r. & M.rs. Riddell & Miss Graham, after Coffee we went to the Play where our party was much enlarged, M.r. Cumberlands new Play of the Wheel of Fortune, which was so ill acted, it had to merit a very stupid miserable Farce returnd home with Lady Riddell to Supper, & came home after twelve in torrents of rain; Francis tho better did not go to school, but went to a Boy party at M.r. Broughams

Sunday Ap: 26.th.

A very cold stormy Day, wind both bitterly cold as well as high, & some trivial showers, went both to Morning & evening service at S.t. Georges chappel between churches rec'd visits from

---

4. Thomas Milles Riddell (1756–1796).

Dr James Gregory in the uniform of the Royal
Edinburgh Volunteers. An etching by John Kay, 1795.

Miss: B. Mure & the Principal who we were rejoiced to see return'd, Mʳ˙ Pennington & Mʳ˙
Cooper dined here, Mʳ˙ Bancroft here for a little while late in the evening.

Monday Ap: 27ᵗʰ˙

A tolerable fine Day, air much milder, wind not so high, & the showers few & short went out
early on some Shopping bussiness for Mʳ˙ Cooper & Mʳ˙ Bancroft, who both call'd to settle
with me & indeed to take their leave both being on the move for England. the Principal met
them. I afterwards visited Miss Graham in Queen Street, & Mʳˢ˙ Brown Sᵗ˙ James's Square.
drank Tea & supp'd quite in a free way, not even dressing with Lady Riddell, meeting Miss
McFarlan Sʳ˙ James Coloquhoun⁵ Mʳ˙ M. Ridddell & Mʳ˙ Bancroft, walk'd home at past 12.
lively & pleasant, play'd at several different Games.

Tuesday: Ap: 28ᵗʰ˙

Thick & misty in the Morning, a very severe shower at noon, & very showery all the Day
after, which prevented my going out tho prepar'd so to do in the evening had a large rout at
home; as Lady Riddell, Mʳˢ˙ Erskine & Miss Carnegie, Mʳˢ˙ Robinson Scott Miss Graham, Mʳ˙
Mʳˢ˙ & Miss Stacy, Sʳ˙ James Coloquhoun Principal Gordon Mʳ˙ M. Riddell & Mʳ˙ Pennington,
it went off very pleasantly. wrote to my Sisʳ˙ Travell.

---

5.   James Colquhoun (1741–1805). James was an Advocate, 1765; Sheriff Depute of Dumbartonshire, 1775; and a Principal
      Clerk of Sessions, 1779. He succeeded as 2nd baronet in 1786. He married, 1773, Mary (d. 1833), youngest daughter
      of David Falconer, 5th Lord Falconer of Halkerton.

Wensday Ap: 29ᵗʰ·

Very stormy in the Morning, the wind blowing quite a tempest but dry till Noon when their was many & very violent storms of hail & rain, I went out early with Lady Riddell to see a house after w.ᶜʰ went to see good Lady C: C: to whom I made a very long visit on my return thro Andrews Square call'd on Mʳˢ· Erskine, almost blown away by the time I came home, went to Tea, Cards, & Supper at Mrs. Mᶜ·Dowells where was rather a grand & formal set of 13, only 4 Gentlemen, play'd much at Whist, large Supper & not at home till near one. rec'd a Letter from Mʳˢ· Pennington

Thursday Ap: 30ᵗʰ·

Still the same stormy unpleasant weather with frequent hard storms of hail & rain but fine between with sun, Mʳ· Pennington made me a very friendly call I went only out in Queen Street to taste the air in the hope of curing a headache but soon sent home by a shower went to Tea, Cards & Supper, quite in a walkley free way to Mʳˢ· Oliphants, a party of 12, lively & pleasant enough wrote to Mʳˢ· Witts of Nibley.

Friday May 1ˢᵗ·

Much unlike the Day in point of weather the wind being most boisterously high & very cold, but mostly dry & much sunshine, went out early with Lᵈʸ· Riddell House hunting for her, visited with her Mʳˢ· Mure & Lady Rothes, & then to several shops on the Bridges, before I returnd home sat ½ an hour with Mʳˢ· Brown; Principal Gordon here for 2 or 3 hours late in the evening, his conversation more than ordinary agreable & delightful.

Saturday May 2ᵈ·

A most heavenly day, quite mild & summer like, no wind & much sun, visited my next Door Neighbour Mʳˢ· Hay, went an airing with Mʳˢ· Brown first to Bruntsfield Linx to see the Volunteers & then a few miles into the Country; much delighted with both the sight & smell of vegetation not at home till near 4 when I rec'd a parting visit from Mʳ· & Mʳˢ· Stacy, the Principal dined here, & went with us in the evening to Mʳ· M. Riddells to Cards & Supper a party of nine Lady Riddell one.

Sunday May 3ᵈ·

Again most tremendously stormy but dry the whole of the Day at Sᵗ· Georges Chappel both services between them was admitted to Mʳˢ· Maitlands Bedside, who I found better visited Mʳˢ· Stacy for the last time. I went & drank Tea with Mʳˢ· Erskine in a most pleasant free way. liked it much.

Monday May 4ᵗʰ·

Quite an unpleasant Day being an extreme high wind, & at the same time a degree of damp heat that made it very oppressive, I went out early to some Shops in order to return home to receive Mʳˢ· Erskine & Miss Carnegie who came to take leave the Principal likewise call'd & we kept him to Dinner, as he was to join us in a Tea drinking party at Lᵈʸ· Catherines who received us most pleasantly, I returnd home tired to deaᵗʰ· rec'd a Letter from Miss Louisa Lee. wrote to Mʳˢ· Granville

Tuesday May 5th.

Very little change in the weather being still dreadfuly windy tho not so oppressive, I went out to make some calls first on Miss Bruce with whom I spent a pleasant ½ hour, then on Mrs. Stewart to wish her joy of M^{rs.} Mc.dowall Grants safe delivery & on Mrs. Syme in the absence of Mrs. Brougham; went at 9 return to Mrs. Davies's party which consisted of 17 Ladies & 13 Gentlemen, her House very elegant & well adapted, I play'd 2 rubbers at Cassino, a most sumptuous Supper not at home till two in the Morning.

Wensday May 6th.

Still very windy but a finer Day being constant sunshine, I went out early unsuccessful in my first call on Lady Riddell, found Mrs. Brown at home as also Mrs. Robinson Scott, & very agreable, made 2 more unsuccessful calls & three more with success, to Miss Maccartney, Miss Sinclair & Mrs. Jones dined at Mr. Com: Browns, a party of 14 Principal Gordon & Mr. Laws Sons & Mrs. Mure all 4 of whom walk'd home with us, & playing several rubbers at Whist staid till near eleven o'clock.

Thursday May 7th.

Again very tempestuous, & at noon a smart shower, afternoon bright sunshine but no decease in the wind, & at night wet again, no other event happend in the Morning, but receiving an agreable long visit from Mrs. Brougham went at an early hour, & quite in a free undresst way to Lady Riddells where we met Principal Gordon & Mr. M. Riddell, a chearful little Supper.

Friday May 8th.

Wind not quite so high, a good deal of sun & the air most remarkably clear, rec'd a visit from Miss Halkett, before I went out, when I call'd on Miss Graham & her Aunt Campbell, Mrs. Baillie, & Mrs. Graham of Fintry,[6] finding all at home, went to Tea Cards & Supper at Lady Rothes's where we met a very lively pleasant party of 16 or 17 quite in a free way play'd seven rubbers at Whist won considerably & was brought home by Mrs. Christie of Durie[7] in her Coach

Saturday May 9th.

A universal wet Day from Morn to night sometimes very hard accompanied by severe wind, a fine Morning for home bussiness, having no interruptions, went to Tea, Cards & Supper at Lady Riddells, where we met a party of 14, but somehow it was peculiarly dull & stupid & losing my money at Cards did not make it more gay or brilliant.

Sunday May 10th.

No rain tho very strong appearances of it but such a miserable cold & high wind, it was dreadful walking about, went to both services at St. Georges Chappel between which I carried

---

6.   Robert Graham (1749–1815), of Fintry in Forfarshire, was a descendant of Sir Robert Graham of Strathcarron, ancestor of the Grahams of Claverhouse. In 1780, he sold his estate, of which he was the 12th laird, but retained his designation. He married Margaret Elizabeth Mylne of Mylnefield, by whom he had four sons and ten daughters. Robert Graham was appointed a Commissioner of the Scottish Board of Excise in 1787.
7.   Mary Christie, née Turner Barclay-Maitland. Mary married, 1783, James Christie of Durie (d. 1803); they lived at Durie, Fife, and had eleven children.

my Sons to introduce them to M^rs. Davies, whom we found at home M^r. Erskines Niece Miss Charlotte Stewart dined & drank Tea here, & the Principal came late in the evening & staid till near eleven. much interesting conversation.

Monday May 11th.

Not quite so high a wind, but still very cold & stormy, but no further wet than from short & trifling hail storms. I rec'd a visit from M^rs. Baillie before I went accompanied by both the Boys to see L^dy. C: C: on my return call'd on M^r. Pennington whom we found very triste, & on M^rs. Brown who was too ill to see me concluded by calling on Miss Macartney as an enquiry after her Aunt Maitland; a pleasant quiet evening of home employments & enjoyments.

Tuesday May 12th.

As usual very Windy cold & comfortless & so very dark it made it quite unpleasant walking at night late very hard rain. M^r. Witts much taken up all Morn: with receiving L^dy. Riddells Friend Count Gorzenski just arrived from England, I walk'd over the Bridges to some shops, visited M^rs. Brown brought home by M^rs. Oglivie in her Chaise; my spirits hurried by Franks coming home from School in a Chair, having severely hurt one of his Knee's, wch M^r. Pennington attended, he dined here, but could not be persuaded to go with us to Tea & Supper at Lady Riddells, where was a pleasant party of 8 equal number of each sex the Dear Principal one. wrote to M^rs. Ryecroft.

Wensday May 13th.

Still extremely cold, & rather stormy but no absolute rain tho looking very lowering, at 11 o'clock, we accompanied Lady Riddell, & Count Gorzenski in her Coach, to Leith, where we suvey'd the Battery, Glass Houses &'c, returning home by the Abbey which we survey'd & got home only just before Dinner, very glad to spend a quiet evening at home. Franks Leg mending.

Thursday May 13th.

A cloudy Morning but dry & very cold but, at Noon turn'd to rain, which continued hard & unabated the whole Day & night, yet notwithstanding we attended Lady R. & her Gent: on an airing, to Dalkeith driving thro the Duke of Bucclughs Park & plantations & home thro Inverish Musselburgh &'c had the Day been finer nothing could be more pleasant not at home till just 4 Cards & supper at M^rs. Oliphants a party of 20 made in Honor of the Count lively & pleasant enough rec'd a Letter from my Sister Travell

Friday May 14th.

Quite a wet Morning, but clear'd in some degree at Noon, but was wet in storms & violent wind & cold all Day, went at Noon with M^rs. Oliphant & her youngest Daughter in their Coach, to call on her Niece M^rs. Ridd then to some shops in the old Town & afterwards aird to Leith, in the evening we had a grand party of 16, 9 Gentlemen & 7 Ladies 3 Card Tables which were kept up with spirit till 12 o'clock.

Saturday May 15th.

Dry & a better day, being much sunshine but still bitterly cold, poor Francis's Leg mending fast went out with Lady Riddell made many visits seperately & together, found none at home but my Neighbour Mrs. Jones, M^{rs.} G: Fergusson, Mrs. Halkett Craigie, & Mrs. Craigie in Georges Square from thence took a transient view of the Volunteers on Bruntsfield Linx, & drove to White House which we walk'd over & returnd home by the Lothian road went to the Play in Mrs. Davies's Carriage, wth Miss A Baillie & sat in Mrs. Baillies Box, highly charm'd with Mrs. Siddons in Lady Randolph,[8] left the house as soon as Douglass was over, & join'd Mr. Witts at a small Supper party of 8 at Lady Riddells.

The first Theatre Royal was in Shakespeare Square; a long-gone corner of Edinburgh on what is now the east side of North Bridge Street at its junction with Princes Street. This theatre was opened in 1769 by actor-manager David Ross. It was rebuilt in 1830 and finally demolished in 1859. The statue on the top is that of William Shakespeare.

Mrs Woods; Sarah Siddons (née Kemble); Mr Sutherland (active 1782–84) in Hume's *Douglas*. An etching by John Kay. Interestingly, posterity has not recorded Mr Sutherland's forenames. Sarah Siddons played the part of Lady Randolph.

---

8. Sarah Siddons (1755–1831). Sarah was the elder sister of John Philip Kemble, Charles Kemble, Stephen Kemble, Ann Hatton and Elizabeth Whitlock, and the aunt of Fanny Kemble. In 1773 Sarah married a fellow actor, William Siddons. Over the next few years the couple had seven children, two of whom died in infancy. She was most famous for her portrayal of the Shakespearean character, Lady Macbeth, a character she made her own. The character she played in 1795 was also exactly the same as she played on her last stage appearance on 9 June 1819 as Lady Randolph in John Home's *Douglas*.

Sunday May 17th.

Very wet all the Morning, tolerably dry excepting Showers the rest of the Day but very cold, & unpleasant, Mr. Witts went alone to Chappel in the Morning, after which Lady R. call'd upon me in her Coach & took me to Lady C. Charteris to enquire the character of a Servant for her, in the meantime she & Mr. Witts visited Mrs. Phillips on our return visited Mrs. Maitland for a few minutes & then went to St. Andrews Church where Mr. Moodie much pleased us. at 6 o'clock went to call on the Browns in St. James's Square, rejoiced to find Maria just arrived staid to drink Tea & walk'd home just as it grew dark thro small rain. wrote to Mrs. Buxton.

Monday May 18th.

Another very indifferent Day, being still cold & stormy & at times trifling showers, went out at mid.day in the Coach with Lady R. & Compte Gorzenski, made several visits & calls, but found only Mrs. Oliphant & Lady H Dalrymple at home, on my return call'd at the Browns for a short time with some of whom Mr. Witts squeezed into the Pit to see Mrs. Siddons perform Mrs. Beverly in the Gamester,[9] I had an almost equal squeeze, in Mrs. Dewars Box up stairs, her acting as charming as it was affecting. Francis's Leg well enough recover'd to permit his going to school.

Tuesday May 19th.

Upon the whole a milder, & much better Day than any we had been accustom'd to for a long time, tho there was several short showers in the forenoon, yet our usual Coach party ventured to go to survey Roselin Castle, about seven miles distant but it was too wet & dirty to walk much about it but the scenery was beautiful & the road thither both good & pleasant winding thro cornfields in sweet verdure, made a good cold repast & did not return till 4 when the Principal dined with us, & we play'd Cards & Supper at Lady Riddells a party of 10, Mr. & Mrs. Belches, Mrs. Dalrymple & 2 Daughters the Count & Mr. Pennington. rec'd a Letter from Anne Snow

Wensday May 20th.

A great change in the weather being become almost oppressively hot, tho with a considerable wind & but little sun, such a rapid change made me almost ill & able to enjoy nothing I went about made 4 visits in & about George Street, none visible but Mrs. Macdowal Grant, who was sitting at the receipt of unction after her lying in, afterwards walk'd with Mr. Witts a little way on the Leith walk, & returning home by the Cambrick Manufactory, sat with one of the Proprietors a sensible old Woman for a great while, Lady Riddell, Miss Bruce, Compte Gorzenskie, Principal Gordon & Mr. M: Riddell here to Tea & Cards, Francis went to see Mrs. Siddons in Belvedera[10]

Thursday May 21st.

Again very gloomy & unpleasant with so high a wind that made the Dust quite intolerable went out early with Lady Riddell & her Count, to see the Lord Commissioner walk in whose moving both He & Mr. Witts made a part & Dined with him & we Ladies got a window to

---

9. *The Gamester*, 1753, a play by Edward Moore (1712–1757). Mrs Beverley was a character in the play.
10. This was probably *Venice Preserv'd*, an English Restoration play written by Thomas Otway, and the most significant tragedy of the English stage in the 1680s. The play enjoyed many revivals through to the 1830s; one of the main characters is Belvidera. In 1774, Sarah Siddons won her first success as Belvidera; this brought her to the attention of David Garrick.

see the procession, & afterwards. Coach'd it about with her Ladyship all the Morning made 5 visits in Georges Square none visible but M^rs. Clerk; the two Miss Browns call'd on me before Dinner, in the evening Lady Riddell ourselves & the Count went to Tea Cards & Supper at M^rs. Douglass Cavers, where besides herself & 3 Sisters, we met Miss E: Cummins, Miss Duncan & M^r. Simpson, a Table at Whist & Cassino, & alltogether a pleasant visit, & home properly early.

Friday May 22^d.

Much such another Day but not quite so wet, I went & made a long visit to good L^dy. C: C: who much wanted the comfort of a Friend & returnd home after visiting M^rs. Brown, we went to Cards & Supper at Lady Riddells meeting M^r. & M^rs. Baillie, & M^rs. Spiers & 2 Daughters & M^r. M. Riddell a Table at Whist & Cassino nothing very lively or brilliant brought home by M^rs. Baillie in her Coach.

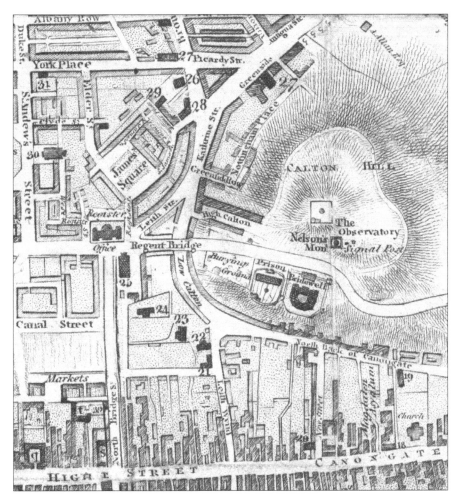

An enlargement from Robert Scott's map. Shakespeare Square and the Theatre is marked as 25, at the right-hand side of the junction of Princes Street and North Bridge Street. Obviously during Agnes's time in Edinburgh Regent Bridge and Nelson's Monument would not have existed, but apart from these differneces the landmarks would have been familiar.

Sarah Siddons as *Isabella*. Sarah Siddons with her son, Henry Siddons, an engraving by J. Caldwell, 1785, from a painting by William Hamilton RA.

Saturday May 23^{d.}

A very brilliant warm fine Morning but at Noon the wind turn'd to the East, & it became as cold & disagreable with a great tendency to rain Principal Gordon Margaret Brown, Mr. Pennington & M^{rs.} & Miss Dalrymple visited here in the Morning I went to make several calls all relative to Stage Tickets excepting one to Mrs. Syme, in the absence of Mrs. Brougham, I went to see Mrs. Siddons in Isabella,[11] accompanied by Compte Gorzenski & my Husband, having got by favor of L^{dy.} Dalrymple in a front row of a side Box, highly pleased & pack'd for acting being quite inimitable

Sunday May 24th.

Quite a bitter cold Day, as necessary to have good fires as if the depths of Winter, realy cold even at Church, where we went both times to St. Georges Chappel, staying the Sacrament in the Morning between Services I call'd on Mrs. Coll: Dalrymple who I found at home; Mr. Witts Dined with Lord Adam Gordon to meet the Compte, & supp'd at Lady Riddells the Principal & Mr. Pennington dined with me & staid till past nine, both most conversable companions

Monday May 25th.

Not quite so severely cold, the wind being less high, & some sunshine, visited Mrs. Erskine & Lady Riddell, & Mrs. Hamilton Ramsay Gardens the latter not at home, walk'd with Lady

---

11.   On this Edinburgh tour of Sarah Siddons, the playhouse proprietors were obviously trying to draw in the crowds, as this was one of her most famous successes. On 10 October 1782, she was an immediate sensation playing the title role in Garrick's adaptation of a play by Thomas Southerne, *Isabella, or, The Fatal Marriage*.

R & the Compte about the streets, & meet them & a large party to the tune of 18 but alas chiefly females at M^rs. Spiers, 3 Card Tables handsome hot Supper, & all very well; some pleasant agreable people.

Tuesday May 26th.

Still cold & unlike the time of Year, but clear & dry & well enough moving for just walking call'd first on the Browns in S^t. James's Square, then went to Lady C: C: who I pleased by a long visit, on my return call'd on M^rs. Robinson Scott, to settle with her about joining her at the Play, & when I got home rec'd visits from M^r. & M^rs. Simpson & Principal Gordon went to see M^rs. Siddons in Jane Shore a great treat.[12] Francis there also in the Gallery.

Wensday May 27th.

Very much the same weather, very cold & unlike the end of May, call'd on Lady Riddell where meeting the Count, we took him a walk, to see M^rs. Scotts at Bell vue, a very pretty place walk'd in the Gardens & Hothouses &'c went to Tea & supper at Lady Riddells meeting the Count the Principal & M^r. M. Riddell very chearful, easy, & pleasant.

Thursday May 28th.

A gloomy Morning which early turnd to rain, & continued being hard the greater part of the Day & was very cold & miserable, M^r. W. went with the Count to pay their Compliments to the Lord Commissioner at his Levee I wrote hard all Morning & in the evening went again to Lady Riddells the same party excepting M^r. Riddell, the parting evening with the poor Count. wrote to M^rs. Pennington & my Sis^r. Travell

Friday May 29th.

Weather still very similiar, cold & comfortless, & a short shower or two at mid.day engaged the early part of the Day, in bussiness with Principal Gordon which made me deny myself several callers, admitted none but Col: Riddell, went out rather late, first calling on M^rs. Erskine then on Lady Betty Cunningham neither at home, afterwards on M^rs. Jones to see her children, picked up M^r. W. & took a short walk driven home by a shower, went see M^rs. Siddons in Isabella in Measure for Measure,[13] my Party Miss Riddell, 2 Miss Macfarlans, my Son George & 2 other Boys M^rs. S. if possible greater than ever. Join'd my Husband in a Supper party at Lady Riddells, where was M^rs. & Miss Macdougall & M^r. M. Riddell.

Saturday May 30th.

No change for the better in the weather still thick & gloomy & much like rain tho scarce any fell, made many visits in the Morning, all I found at home was M^rs. Mure, Miss Spiers, M^rs. M. Sands, & M^rs. Maitland staid quietly & comfortably at home all the evening a great treat because uncommon

---

12. *The Tragedy of Jane Shore*, by Nicholas Rowe (1674–1718), first performed in 1715.
13. Another character of Isabella was in Shakespeare's *Measure for Measure*.

Sunday May 31st.

Rather a lowering Morning but kept dry till mid.day when there was a hard & long shower, & rain'd again violently just as the evening closed, went to Morning church at St. Georges, detain'd in Mr. Cleeves House till a chair came, went to evening service at St. Andrews heard a most excellent sermon from a young stranger Mr. W. & I went to Drink Tea with Mrs. Mure who was ill returnd home before dark, Principal Gordon here for an hour quite late in the evening.

Monday June 1st.

Quite a compleat wet Morning, only xxxxxx xx 6 hours at mid.day & very wet again in the eveng. quite a stay at home Morning no interruption, but a very pleasant visit from Mr. Erskine walk'd from 6 to 7 in the streets by way of exercise. wrote to Mrs. Witts

Tuesday June 2d.

Rather a bright promising Morning but soon overcast, & there was such perpetual hard showers the whole of the Day that it might almost be call'd constant rain; I was detain 3 or 4 hours at Lady Riddells in the Morning by it, but not unpleasantly found the 2 Miss Mc.Farlans there who we also met again in the evening there, as also Sir James & Coll. Colquhoun, a very agreable Man just arrived from England which made the evening peculiarly pleasant.

Wensday June 3d.

A universal fine Day more like true summer than any Days past, went with Lady Riddell to a Sale of Pictures on the South Bridge, afterwards visited with her to several places, Mr. Stormonth sat with us while we drank Tea, after w.ch our own Quartette walk'd all round & over Mrs. Scotts domain very pleasantly, & on our return calling on the Browns in St. James's Square were detain'd to supper.

Thursday June 4th.

Again very unpleasant weather after having been a night of severe rain. such a thick damp air, & quite oppressively hot being the Kings Birthday were plagued to death by squibs & xxxxx of every kind,[14] I only went in the Morning to call on Mrs. Erskine poor little Anna being alarmingly ill, the Principal & Mr. Pennington call'd here, Mr. Witts went soon after Dinner, to join the Royal Party at the Parliament House to drink the Kings health I drank Tea & again sat an hour with Mrs. Erskine & then went to Lady Riddells where the Principal & Mr. W. soon join'd us & we spent a chatty evening

Friday June 5th.

Very much the same kind of strongly oppressive weather, thick air & no sun, but dry till noon, when there was several loud claps of Thunder which were succeeded by most violent & long showers of rain w.ch continued more or less the whole evening fortunately went out early enough, to make a long visit to poor Ldy. C: C: who I had not seen for 10 Days on my return made an unsuccessful call on Ldy. Dumfries & went to see Anna Inglehart where the rain came

---

14. Squibs in the sense used here probably refers to low people or beggars. The other word has not been deciphered.

on so furiously I was forced to get home in a Chair in the evening went to a very large Party at Lady Sinclairs, wch unexpectedly turnd out a Ball, 20 Gentlemen & 25 Ladies a very genteel party, a very handsome Supper & on the whole very agreable & pleasant. at home by three.

Saturday June 6th.

Wet & very wet in the Morning, held up & got a little dry at mid.day but wet again in the evening, late in the Day I visited Lady Riddell, Mrs. Erskine, & Mrs. Brown, went to Tea & Supper with L^{dy.} R. meeting only Miss Bince & Principal Gordon.

Sunday June 7th.

Very wet in the Morning, clear'd up at Noon, & was a bright fine evening, tho a sharp east wind I did not go to Church in the Morning, but in the evening to St. Georges, Mr. Pennington call'd here between services after Dinner I went to see Anna Inglehart Mrs. Erskine not at home, after Tea walk'd w.^h Husband & Boys on Queen Street where was quite a crowded Mall. rec'd Letters from My Sister Travell & Mr. Delabere, & wrote to Lady Edward Bentinck & Miss Louisa Lee.

Monday June 8th.

A very fine shewey Morning which soon grew cloudy & became miserably cold & comfortless tho quite dry, Lady Riddell call'd on me to attend her in our Mournfulls to call on Mrs. Belsches who had lost a Brother, we then seperated, when I made seven or 8 visits finding only Mrs. Macdowell, Mrs. Oliphant, & Mrs. Brougham at home, concluding with Mrs. Erskine the Principal call'd on us before Dinner, & we went to Tea & Supper at Mrs. Mures meeting only Lady Riddell, & Mrs. Frances Lovatt, almost tired out with a mixture of Cassino, Cribbage & loud talking, starved to Death walking home. wrote to Miss Anne Snow.

Tuesday June 9th.

Still high east wind but being much sunshine was more bearable, yet having something of a cold I did not go out in the Morning, My only company M^{r.} & Mrs. Spiers, walk'd out with the Boys before Tea went to a Nursery Garden & Hot Houses, work'd by Steam, 2 Miles West of Edinbro well entertain'd tho much tired with the length of the walk & quite starved the Principal sat with us 2 or 3 hours late in the evening. rec'd Letters from L^{dy.} Edward Bentinck & Miss B. Guydickens

Wensday June 10th.

Very much the same kind of clear cold weather, perhaps not quite so starving a wind Mrs. Mcdowall Grant call'd on me before I went out wch I did at Noon, first call'd to take a last leave of Mrs. Erskine who was going away, on L^{dy.} C: C: who I found chearful & made happy, & ended with Mrs. Brown w.^h whom I sat so long I was but just at home in time for Dinner to meet the Principal, who attended us to Tea Cards & Supper at Miss Bruce's, where we form'd a party of 8 Ladies & 4 Gentlemen moderately agreable, but I was very successful at Whist.

Thursday June 11th.

Still miserable east wind, & sharp high wind but such strong sunshine that in it it was quite warm. we walk'd between two & three to St. Barnards Well in which shelter'd vale it was comfortably warm; went to Cards & Supper at Mrs. Macdowalls, a party of 13 nothing

Calton Hill from the Old Town. An engraving by William Home Lizars from a painting by John Wilson Ewbank.

peculiarly lovely much Card Playing, & a very good Supper rec'd a long entertaining Letter from Miss Snow.

Friday June 12th.

Much such another Day, went out at mid.day on some shopping odd bussinesses in the old Town & when there call'd on old Mr. Auchenlechs, wallk'd again in the evening, around & home by St. Barnards perfectly starvd with cold. rec'd a Letter from Mrs. Granville.

Saturday June 13th.

The Wind yet in the same unpleasant corner but a prodigeous fine bright fine Day, & in the forenoon realy quite oppressively hot, Lady Riddell made an early call here, & at one we went accompanied by Mar: Brown & some young men to Bruntsfield Linx to see the Volunteers review'd by Lord Adam Gordon w. had collected together on the ground it was supposed more than 20,000 Persons, of various ranks & discription which turn'd a very beautiful scene & the Corps made a very fine appearance, I was very glad to be brought home by Mrs. Oliphant in her Coach being well tired went to Tea & Supper at Lady Riddells meeting Sr. J. Colquhoun & Mr. M. Riddell, much conversation as well as Cards.

Sunday June 14th.

No change of weather materialy, as much sun & as dry as yesterday, but not near so warm. went to Morning Church at St. Georges & in the evening attended Ldy. Riddell to St. Andrews to hear Mr. Moodie who as ever was charming Principal Gordon dined & drank Tea here, &, between 8 & 9 when he went, Mr. W. & I went to call for ½ an hour on the Browns in St. James's Square a bitter cold night. Francis again confined w.th a Cough.

Monday June 15th.

A very bright fine pleasant Day for the wind still in the same cold point; set out between 11 & 12 in Mrs. MacDowall Grants Chaise which she had kindly lent us taking Francis with us,

Lord Adam Gordon reviewing the Volunteers. An etching by John Kay, 1796.

hoping the Country air would do his Cough good, to Invereck to see M^rs. Charteris,[15] who we found alone, she rec'd us not only politely, but realy very kindly, the place very pretty & the drive to & from (6 miles each way) extremely pleasant close to the Sea went to Tea Cards & Supper at Lady Riddells, meeting M^rs. Douglass Cavers & her Sisters Miss Scotts, Baron Gordon, Principal Gordon, S^r. James Colquhoun & M^r. M: Riddell & M^rs. Macdougall, very lively & pleasant. much Cards.

Tuesday June 16th.

Perpetual east wind, gloomy & cold in the Morning some sun at mid.day & very cold again in the evening. went out early with Lady Riddell into the Court of Session, the first time I ever was there & fortunately most of the judges were on the Bench, & tho there was no very material cause brought on, I was well amused for the two hours we staid far better than I was the two succeeding hours dawdling about with her Ladyship to several shops & watching poor M^rs. Maitlands funeral pass. went to a very small Card & Supper Party at M^rs. Oliphants, L^dy. Riddell, M^r. B. Maitland & ourselves all the company. rec'd a Letter from my Sister Travell.

Wensday June 17th.

Very similar weather not a bit like summer, went at mid.day, to see L^dy. C: C: to whom I made a long & pleasant visit, after having walk'd & chatted much with M^rs. Phillips in S^t. John

---

15.   Inveresk. The Charteris home was Stoneyhall House, at Stoneyhall, a hamlet in the parish of Inveresk, county Edinburgh, near Musselburgh.

Hugh Montgomerie, 12th Earl of Eglintoun (1740–1819). Montgomerie was a distant cousin to Lady Betty Cunningham.

Street went again in the evening to Lady Riddells, meeting another pleasant party of 10, quite agreable much whist playing, more talk & an excellent Supper.

Thursday June 18th.

Very wet, & constantly so till near afternoon, & still bitterly cold no warmer in the evening when it cleard up & was bright & fine, a charming Morning for a variety of both sitting & bustling bussiness never stirr'd out the whole Day, having much of the Rhumatism, Lady Riddell call'd for a few minutes before she went to her evening party. rec'd a Letter f^m. Miss Neville

Friday June 19th.

Again dry but no better weather being still the same cold point of wind, went accompanied by M^r. Witts to make the Mournful visit to Miss Macartney on her Aunt M^rs. Maitlands death but she did not receive us, went on the same account to M^rs. Stewart to whom we made a most rational & pleasant visit we then seperated & made more visits, finding only M^rs. Dalrymple of Fordel & M^rs. Brown at home, in the evening we had a party to Tea & Cards at home L^dy. Riddell, Lady Betty Cunningham[16] M^rs. Douglass Cavers her Sister Miss Scott M^rs. Mure, S^r. James & Col: Colquhoun Principal Gordon, M^r. M. Riddell & a M^r. Crigthon, all very chearful & lively. wrote to my Sister Travell.

---

16.   Lady Betty Cunningham. This is probably Elizabeth Cunningham, née Montgomerie (1706–1800); daughter of Alexander Mongomerie, 9th Earl of Eglinton (*c.* 1660–1729). She had married, 1749, John Cunningham (1696–1777), 3rd baronet.

Saturday June 20th.

Wind changed for the better, of course a pleasanter Day but my visits were so oppress'd by the discovery of very ill conduct of one most dearly beloved by me,[17] I could enjoy nothing the Principal here both in the Morning & again to Tea, M^{rs.} D: Hamilton here for a wonder in the Morning accompanied by one of his Brothers[18] I walk'd a little in Queen Street before Dinner to disipate a bad headache, & late in the even. walk'd some part of the way home with the Principal rec'd a charming long Letter from Mr. Burslem.

Sunday June 21st.

Tho the wind was turn'd Westerly it still was a cold dull comfortless day & very little like mid. summer went to St. Georges chappell to both services, between which rec'd visits from M^{rs.} & Miss Baillie & Miss B. Mure, the Principal here for an hour or two in the evening, rec'd a Letter from Miss Anne Snow.

Monday June 22^{d.}

Miserably wet in the Morning but clear'd up at mid.day, but was most dreadfuly cold, so much so I was happy to sit all Day by a good fire, being very rhumatic & unwell, but work'd, wrote & heard much read in Coxe's Tour into Switzerland,[19] did not see a Creature all Day nor did Mr. Witts go out at all. wrote to Mrs. Savage.

Tuesday June 23^{d.}

Dry early in the Morning, but soon became wet, & remain'd so more or less the whole Day & no warmer, the Principal here in the Morning, for hour, & we went to Tea Cards & Supper at Lady Riddells meeting a pleasant lively party of 11, much Card Playing & a very handsome Supper.

Wensday June 24th.

Wet & most miserably wet almost from Morning to night with little or no cessation the good Principal dined with us & we took him to Tea & supper in a private way to Lady Riddells where was only besides, Mrs. Mure & the two Miss Macfarlans wrote to Lady Edward Bentinck.

Thursday June 25th.

A moist close Morning but not hard rain, dry for several hours in the middle of the day & wet again in the evening, happy to be able to catch a dry hour to get out walk'd with Lady Riddell to some shops &'c visited Lady C: C: as also Mrs. Brown on my return, & Mr. Stormonth drank Tea here wrote to Mrs. Granville.

---

17. This is a coded expression used by Agnes in relation to domestic disharmony. Unfortunately because Agnes's correspondence no long exists, only vague guesses might be made to cause of the unrest. Usually it appears to have been financial matters concealed from her.
18. This does not appear to make sense, it is clearly written <u>Mrs</u> D: Hamilton.
19. William Coxe: *Travels in Switzerland. In a Series of Letters to William Melmoth, Esq.* (3 volumes 1789).

Friday June 26th.

Wet & very wet for some hours in the Morning cleard at Noon & became a very bright fine Day I did not go out in the Morning but rec'd visits at seperate times from M^rs. Belsches, Miss Graham, & Principal Gordon, D^r. Brown drank Tea here for a very great wonder, & walk'd with us afterwards to the Botanic Garden, on our return the Principal came again, & we sat by the light of the Moon till near 12, conversing on very interesting subjects wrote to M^rs. Tracy

Saturday June 27th.

For a wonder dry the whole day, tho at times it look'd very lowering & like thunder the air being much warmer; M^rs. Mure call'd late in the Morning after she went, I went into the old Town to some shops & returnd over the Mound, in the evening it look'd so like rain we only walk'd in Finlaysons Gardens & on Queen Street where was a very full Mall.

Sunday June 28th.

Very severe rain the greater part of the forenoon, when in clear'd off & became a pleasant warm evening tho dull, I did not go to Church in the Morning & to evening service was obliged to go in a Chair to S^t. Georges chappl. Principal Gordon dined with us & we sat chatting till between 8 & 9, when we call'd but Lady Riddell for ½ an hour who was very ill & then walk'd on Queen Street till near 9, among a large number. wrote to Miss Snow.

A depiction of the High Street of Edinburgh in the eighteenth century. A water-caddie carrying a barrel on his back can be seen in front of the well head towards the right of the image. A lithograph by W. and A. K. Johnston, 1852.

Monday June 29ᵗʰ·

Another very wet dismal morning, but clear'd much earlier than the former Day & was a fine Day, I went out at Noon accompanied by Mʳ· W. & made our <u>Mournful</u> visit to Mʳˢ· & Miss Oliphants & Mʳˢ· Read in the evening we had a Party at home Lᵈʸ· Sinclair & Miss Sinclair, Mʳˢ· Macdowall, Mʳˢ· Davies Comissioner & Mʳˢ· Brown & 2 Miss Browns, Dʳ· Gordon Mʳ· Riddell & Mʳ· B. Maitland very chearfull & pleasant

Tuesday June 30ᵗʰ·

Dry but very cold east wind, & in the evening a strong inclination to small rain, my first call in Sᵗ· James's Square after Mʳˢ· Brown who had been unwell the night before, & then to Lᵈʸ· C: C: drank Tea & eat a pleasant Sandwich Supper with Lady Riddell who was better, meeting Dʳ· Gordon & Mʳ· M. Riddell. rec'd a Letter from Miss Louisa Lee & one from Mʳ· Pennington from Glasgow.

Wensday July 1ˢᵗ·

A thick misty Morning but not positive rain, at Noon became pleasant enough all but cold east wind very uncommon for the day of the month, as fires were not only pleasant but almost necessary, I went to call on Dʳ· Pennington first <u>come</u> for Glasgow, & <u>going</u> to Newcastle to fetch his Wife afterwards went to make visits in Georges Square none at home but Mʳˢ· Hamilton & Miss Scotts, dined at Mʳ· M. Riddells myself the only Lady, meeting P. Gordon & 2 other agreable Men, went to drink Tea with Lᵈʸ· Riddell where my <u>own</u> set of Gents soon join'd me we had a chearful evening, much Whist but more talk.

Thursday July 2ᵈ·

Dry but not pleasant all Day, being still easterly wind & very thick air, wᶜʰ towards evening turn'd out small misty rain, Miss Browns call'd at Noon to accompany me to visit Mʳˢ· Davies, after which I made some more visits equaly unsuccessful. Principal Gordon dined here & we went to drink Tea with Lᵈʸ· C: C: where Mʳˢ· Moray join'd us obliged to go to Lady Riddells in a Hackney Coach it was so wet, where we met Mʳˢ· Fraser Lovatt & Mrs. Capᵗⁿ· Brown, much Whist playing & a sandwich Supper. rec'd a Letter from Lᵈʸ· E: Bentinck

Friday July 3ᵈ·

Very similar weather, if possible still colder & less like summer, but dry, P: Gordon made a short but painful take leave call Miss Sinclair & Mʳˢ· Brougham seperately made long visits, wᶜʰ prevented my going into the old Town to some shops so went from 6 to 7 in the evening taking the Boys with us, on our return, as <u>usual</u> went to Tea Cards & Sandwiches where was only Sir James Colquhoun, & Miss Macartney & the poor Principal for a little while.

Saturday July 4ᵗʰ·

Somewhat a pleasanter Day being clearer & a little sunshine; poor old Mʳˢ· Auchenleck made an early call, Mʳˢ· Davies & Miss J: Baillie a very pleasant visit, & Lady B. Cunningham so long a one I had only time for a very short walk before Dinner, went at an early hour again to Lady Riddells where we met Sʳ· James Colquhoun Mʳˢ· Dalrymple Mʳ· M. Riddell, & Mʳ· Crichton.

Sunday July 5th.

Much warmer the wind being turnd to the South, but still gloomy & a very thick air went to Morning Service at St. Peters Chappel (where the service was as usual very dully perform'd by Mr. Allan) for the sake of being near Drummond Street, where afterwards we visited Mrs. Pennington who arrived the night before, astonish'd to see her grown so very fat, only just in time to get to St. Georges Chappel for the evening service: Miss J. Baillie & Mrs. Davies's 2 eldest Boys drank Tea here, she prevented by illness, walk'd till a late hour on the Queen Street Mall, with the Beauty.

Monday July 6th.

An uncommon warm close morning w.ch was succeeded by a brilliant hot day quite summer at last, was call'd upon by Miss J: Baillie in Mrs. Davies's chariot to go to the review of the Volunteers on Bruntsfield Linx, in Honor of Mr. Dundas who was that Day enterd into the Corps, a lively fine sight, but the heat was insufferable there, came only home just in time to meet Mr. & Mrs. Pennington at Dinner who staid with us till near nine when we went to Mr. Com: Browns to Supper meeting quite in a free way Mr. & Mrs. Calderwood Denham & Mrs. Fyffe very chearful & pleasant quite a full Day.

Tuesday July 7th.

A very fine Day, not near so sultry hot, being a clear air, but I was a good deal oppressed by my long walk to St. John Street found my good friend much as usual, glad to get home without more exertion; went to Tea, Cards, & Supper at Captn. Browns, a smart & very pleasant party of 10 Gents & 8 Ladies much card Playing & a very elegant Supper came home late in Mrs. Davies's Chariot.

Wensday July 8th.

Another clear fine Day but by no means hot, the wind being still in the old eastern point I never went all Morning being busy in much work, & had no other visitor but Mr. Charteris at a late hour, Mr. W. Francis & I went to Drink Tea at Dr. Penningtons no other company, rather Dull & sombre she being ill with a cold came home before it was near dark. George confined by two black eyes from a pitch battle.

Thursday July 9th.

No change of weather dry, cold wind & hot sun went at mid.day to call on Mrs. Pennington to take her to introduce her to Lady C: C: found her but indifferent yet still she went when the good Lady rec'd us as might be expected, on my return I paid a long visit to Mrs. Brown. we went to Tea, Cards & supper at Lady Sinclairs a pleasant lively party of 7 Gentlemen & as many Ladies, walk'd home near one in the Morning. wrote to Mr. Delabere.

Friday July 10th.

Still dry cold for the season, & in the evening very uncommonly so indeed went at Noon to call on Mrs. Pennington whose indisposition we found so much increased as to confine her to her Bed which made our visit the shorter, return'd to the New Town over the Mound & visited Mrs. Davies & Mrs. Mure who were both at home, at ½ past ten we went out an airing w.th

Lady Riddell in her Coach Sr James Colquhoun making the 4$^{th.}$ went to Lord Abercorns at Dudingston[20] a handsome place out of repair walkt a little about the grounds returnd home a different road by Leith play'd one rubber at whist & eat sandwichs with the good Lady

Saturday July 11$^{th.}$

Hot sun & still cold east wind from Morn till night, went out again with Lady R. an airing at 11 o'clock Miss M. Macfarlan making the 4th went the Seaside road to Musselburgh got out to survey the Camp on the Linx, & call'd on Cap$^{tn.}$ & M$^{rs.}$ Gray at their Lodgings returnd home a very pleasant road thro' cornfields quite new call'd on M$^{rs.}$ Pennington for a few minutes as I came back & found her better, went to Tea Cards & supper at Lady Riddells, meeting Lady & Miss Sinclair Sr James & Col: Colquhoun, & Mr M. Riddell play'd at Cassino with great success. rec'd a Letter from my Sister Travell

Sunday July 12$^{th.}$

Wind turn'd to S. West, which made it much warmer, but still the air remain'd very thick & rather oppressive. went to Morning service at St Georges chappel where Mr Lawson did the service went afterward with Lady R. to call on poor Lady B. Cunningham, & afterwards in her Coach to M$^{rs.}$ Penningtons where she dropp'd me to pay my take leave visit which made it very triste indeed, I join'd Mr W. at the new church where Dr Blair gave us an excellent sermon, Miss Charlotte Stewart dined & drank Tea here & late we walk'd on & about Queen Street as usual.

Monday July 13$^{th.}$

Quite a pleasant dry day with so much sun as to make it quite warm tho the wind was yet in the east, I never stirr'd all Morning being full of employs, after Tea walk'd with the Boys to the South Town & into the Meadow walks wch sent me home compleatly tired wrote to my Sis^r Travell

Tuesday July 14$^{th.}$

The wind being changed it was a broiling hot Day, tho their was not constant sunshine but a thick gloomy air wch made it quite oppressive Mr Riddell made an early call here, when I went to some shops, to visit Lady C: C: & to sit with M$^{rs.}$ Brown on the excise office Garden dined & supt with Lady Riddell, meeting M^r M$^{rs.}$ & Miss Macdonald Cap$^{tn.}$ Gray, & the two Mr Riddells very chearful & agreable except being fill'd with extreme heat.

Wensday July 15$^{th.}$

Still easterly wind but a very clear fine warm Day till quite evening, when it became damp & cold, I sat within all Morning, my visitors Dr Brown & M$^{rs.}$ Davies dined rather earlier, to go with Lady Riddell in her Coach to the Camp at Musselburgh, Miss Sinclair making the 4$^{th.}$ in the Coach where we drank Tea in Captain Grays Tent with a large Party very lively & pleasant at 8 o'clock the two Regiment perform'd their evening Manoveurs with the Music playing, not in Town till 10 o'clock when we supt with Lady R. & play'd afterwards at Cassino. wrote to Lady E: Bentinck

---

20.   John James Hamilton (1756–1818), succeeded as 9th Earl of Abercorn, 1789.

Thursday July 16[th.]

East wind as usual, & a good deal of it but on the whole a fine Day, I kept within all Morn: my only caller Lady Riddell, imediately after Tea join'd her in a walk the Boys also to M[rs.] Scotts Policy & home by the Queen Street Gardens, play'd <u>Cribbage</u> & supt with her, M[r.] Belsches & M[r.] M. Riddell also. rec'd a Letter from M[rs.] Tracy; & wrote to M[rs.] Erskine.

Friday July 17[th.]

Very much the same kind of weather only rather less rain & a thicker air did not go out till past two when I visited Lady Sinclair & Miss Oliphants finding both at home spent the evening at M[r.] Belsches meeting a party of 13 most of our acquaintance, 3 Card Tables, a good Supper & a very handsome House.

Saturday July 18[th.]

Dry, but cloudy looking, with strong symptoms of rain but none fell, & towards evening it became very cold, I only went out in the Morning to make an unsuccessful call on M[rs.] Com: Brown, in the evening went into Finlaysons Garden at an early hour with our Sons to join Lady Riddell & some young people w.[h] her, to whom she gave a treat of Strawberries under the Tent, when concluded we return'd to her House where M[r.] M. Riddell join'd us & we play'd inumerable rubbers at Cribbage & eat sandwiches

Sunday July 19[th.]

Quite a mild fine Day, tho with little sun but towards evening, the wind became very high & quite cold, went both Morn & evening to S[t.] Georges chappel where M[r.] Lawson perform'd both services, between them I made an unsuccessful call on Miss Macartney & her relatives & a pleasant long visit to M[rs.] Brougham, M[rs.] Auchenleck drank Tea here, & the evening look'd so lower[g.] we staid home

Monday July 20[th.]

Much hotter day than we had been used to & fortunate for those interested in the Races which this Day began, I visited Lady C: C: & M[rs.] Brown, & we Drank Tea supt &'c at Captain Browns meeting a party of 16, a very mixt party but else pleasant enough, tho rather too much card playing & too late home, walk'd back wth M[rs.] Belsches

Tuesday July 21[st.]

Another very broiling day, quite oppressively hot, & late in the evening, hard rain attended by thunder & lightening, M[r.] Witts & his Sons went to the Race w.[ch] was a miserable one, I attended L[y.] Riddell to the Play House to see the annual meeting of the Pipers well amused by the oddity of the scene, when over call'd on M[rs.] Callander at Walkers Hottel, went to the Play in M[rs.] Grahams Box with her & some of the Browns to see John Kemble in Penruddock in the Wheel of Fortune much pleased with his performance,[21] a full House, went to sup. at M[r.] Browns with several others where M[r.] Witts join'd me. forced to come home in a Chair it was so wet

---

21.   John Philip Kemble (1757–1823). John was the brother of Sarah Siddons. He was famous in his portrayal of Penruddock in Richard Cumberland's play *The Wheel of Fortune.*

Wensday July 22ᵈ·

A close lowering Morn, which became absolute violent rain, which continued for 3 or 4 hours & well soak'd all the attendants of the race when it was bright & fine the rest of the day but bitterly cold in the evening, Mʳˢ· Captn. Brown & Coll Callander at seperate times my only Morning callers; we made a <u>voluntary</u> Tea drinking visit to Mʳˢ· Oliphant,[22] where we met an agreable Mother, Son, & Daughter of the name of Drummond relations, staid till nine o'clock taking a run in Queen Street by the way.

Thursday July 23ᵈ·

Much such another Morning in point of weather, & terminated in a still more violent wet manner, beginning raining at 12 & never ceased pouring torrents the whole of the Day & even. Mʳ· Macartney sat sometime in the Morning, & Mʳ· W. only went out just to call on Lady Riddell, I work'd prodigeously, & heard much of a very entertaining fact Dʳ· Moore on the French Revolution rec'd a Letter from Mʳˢ· Erskine of Cambo.

Friday July 24ᵗʰ·

Wet in the Morning, showery at Noon but tolerably dry in the evening, at home all the Morning, & without any visitors, but a large share of anxious vexation from F——'s improper conduct went to Tea Cards &'c at Lady Riddells meeting Mʳˢ· Carr & Col: Riddell, Mʳ· M. Riddell & Miss Bruce very pleasant. wrote to Miss B. Guydickens

Saturday July 25ᵗʰ·

A dry & very fine Daẏ, & a peculiar pleasant evening, made a long call on Mʳˢ· Davies another on Lady B. Cunningham & a very long one on Mʳˢ· Com: Brown, drank Tea for a wonder at home when Lady R. call'd on us to walk & Boys with us to Dixons Gardens bringing home a profusion of flowers all 4 supt at my <u>Ladys</u> & Mʳ· M. Riddell also, playing at Cribbage after Supper rec'd a Letter from Miss Snow.

Sunday July 26ᵗʰ·

A most brilliant warm fine day perfect summer, I went with the Boys to Sᵗ· Georges Chappel, after which I joind Lady Riddell, & went w.ᵗʰ her in her Coach to visit Mʳˢ· Oliphant, Mʳˢ· Phillips Lady C: C:, & thro Georges Square, over Bruntsfield Linx, by Muscarts & Fountains Bridge home where I did not arrive till near 4, & at 6 I went to Tea with Mʳˢ· Davies for the purpose of attending her & Sister to Musselburgh Camp by the way we went to Inveresk for me to leave a message at Mʳ· Charteris's, at <u>Camp</u> Col: Leighton gallants us about, & we sat a little in his Tent, & were not at home till past 10 but a beautiful light evening; spent very pleasantly.

---

22. Mrs Oliphant was Mary, née Stirling (d. 1847), third daughter of William Stirling (±1730–1799), 4th baronet of Ardoch and Christian (d. 1788) daughter of John Erskine of Carnock. She married, 1790, Ebenezer Oliphant, seventh of Condie and they had at least five sons, Laurence (1791–1862), who succeeded as eighth of Condie in 1806; William (who died in India); Anthony (b. 1793); James (b. 1796); and Thomas. The Drummond connection goes back to Laurence Oliphant Esq., the fifth of Condie, who dying early in life, his widow married the last Drummond of Invermay, who bequeathed a considerable fortune to his wife's son, Laurence Oliphant.

A watercolour, dated 1827 attributed to Samuel Dukinfield Swarbreck, after a drawing by John Wilson Ewbnk.

Monday July 27th.

A lowering Morn: which terminated before Noon in a very wet day, & only clear'd at even. fit for nothing but keeping within & pursuing many employs. did not see one Creature but each other rec'd a Letter from Mrs. Pennington.

Tuesday July 28th.

Quite a strong wind, but on the whole a warm fine Day, tho enough clouds to fear more rain but none fell. kept house till two when Mr. W. & I went in Mrs. Davies's chariot to dine at Inveresk with M^{r.} & Mrs. Charteris a fine pleasant drive both there & back, & met such a reception as made it quite pleasant, Miss Ainslie only there, return'd at nine to Cards & Supper at L^{dy.} Riddells, where we met Mrs. Mure, M^{r.} & M^{rs.} & Miss Macartney & Mr. M. Riddell.

Wensday July 29th.

Very much such another day only twice in the course of it there fell 2 sharp showers, at Noon went with Lady Riddell in her Coach a most pleasant drive to Sir James Foules's at Colleton, much charm'd with the romantic Scenery & came home quite burden'd with flowers, Tea Cards & Supper at Mrs. Douglass Cavers in Georges Square, a party of 11, much <u>very</u> much whist playing, but agreable from extreme hearty civility not at home near one

Thursday July 30th.

Dry & fine in the Morning, some showers at noon & afternoon & dry again in the evening, busy all Morning in preparing to go to Clifton Hall for two Days, for which purpose Cap^{tn.} Maitland arrived in his Curricle to convey us out to Dinner,[23] the drive would have been very

---

23. Alexander Charles Maitland (1755–1848). Alexander was the eldest son of General the Hon. Sir Alexander Maitland, a younger son of the sixth Earl of Lauderdale, by Lady Elizabeth Ogilvie, daughter of the Earl of Findlater and Seafield.

pleasant but for a sharp shower the Country being fertile & agreable the distance nine miles, the place old & not in very high repair but the reception was hospitable & therefore pleasant 4 fine hearty children 3 Boys & a Girl. rec'd a Letter f^m. M^rs. Buxton

Friday July 31st.

A fine Day with only the interruption of a few short showers till quite evening when it became settled rain, the Gentlemen out on their walks all Morn: M^rs. M. & myself a little in the home domaine M^rs. Dundas of Dundas & Miss Erskine dined there which varied the Country scene.

Saturday Aug^st. 1st.

An extreme wet Morning, cleard off before Noon, but more or less was showers the whole of the day, and at night, an extreme hard thunderstorm which lasted for two hours or more; left Clifton Hall at 11 in the P. Chaise & M^rs. M. with us, the drive pleasant & found our Dear Boys quite well, busy on my return setting the House to rights, having had the drawing room furniture taken down, the Boys following their own inventions in the evening, we after Tea took a walk in Queen Street, & then went to call on the Browns in St. James's Square, who kept us to Supper. came home in a chair.

Sunday Aug^st. 2^d.

A dark lowering Morning a violent thunderstorm at Noon & a most prodigeous wet evening, went to Morning service at S^t. Georges from whence we return'd with Lady Riddell, & took shelter from the Storm at her house, & eat <u>Luncheon</u> & paid our respects to S^r. James, call'd on Lady Sinclair & went with her into her seat at S^t. Andrews church where M^r. L. Moodie gave us a very fine Sermon. M^rs. Davies & Miss J. Baillie drank Tea & spent 3 very chatty hours. wrote to M^rs. Pennington

Monday Aug^st. 3^d.

A fine Day with a very strong wind the evening peculiarly pleasant, some law bussiness in the Morning with M^r. Stormonth after which I call'd on the Macartneys & on Lady C: C: much fagg'd with my walk there & back, after Tea join'd S^r. James & Lady Riddell in a walk to see S^t. Bernards Well &'c return'd home to Cards & Supper with them, & M^r. M. Riddell also

Tuesday Aug^st. 4th.

Another warm fine Day tho without much sun M^rs. & Miss Macartney made me an appointed call, after which I went & sat an hour with M^rs. Davies, & another with M^rs. Com: Brown Cards & Supper again with Lady Riddell, meeting Miss Macfarlan & M^r. M. Riddell, won 21 Games at Cribbage rec'd a Letter from my Sister Travell

---

He was an army officer and had a distinguished career in the American Revolutionary War, being present at the battles of Bunkers Hill and Long Island. Towards the close of the war, on his passage home with dispatches, he was captured by a French privateer, and conveyed to Tours, where he was detained for about a year. He married, 1786, Helen (d. 1834), daughter and heiress of Alexander Gibson Wright of Clifton Hall. Alexander was first cousin to Rear-Admiral Sir Frederick Lewis Maitland, who took the surrender of Napoleon Bonaparte while he commanded the *Bellerophon*, in July 1815. Alexander succeeded as 2nd baronet in 1820.

Wensday Aug^(st.) 5^(th.)

Quite a true hot summer Day & tired myself to death in the Morning, by going to several shops, & visits in Georges Square, just to M^(rs.) Carre, then to poor M^(rs.) Craigie where I only saw Miss Macdonald, & to M^(rs.) Simpson went to Cards & Supper at Lady Sinclairs a party of 10 chearful enough.

Thursday Aug^(st.) 6^(th.)

Dry & hot tho not very pleasant being a gloomy skie & a very high wind, I staid within all Morning & rec'd 2 take leave visits, one from Lady B. Cunningham the other Miss Julia Baillie, went to Tea Cards & supper at Lady Riddells, meeting Lady B. Cunningham & M^(r.) M. Riddell. wrote to Miss L. Lee

Friday Aug^(st.) 7^(th.)

Again dry in the Morning, but very unpleasant, being an extreme high east wind which terminated in violent hard rain about 3 o'clock for 4 hours. M^(rs.) Trotter & M^(rs.) Brougham here in the Morning I never stirrd out all Day being prevented an evening airing with Lady Riddell from hard rain. wrote to Miss Anne Snow.

Saturday August 8^(th.)

Oppressively hot, but not pleasant being a gloomy sky & yet a high wind, not well & more out of spirits which made me keep at home and lament over the ill conduct of others Francis dined at Lord Palkannits, after Tea we did some errands on the Bridge & visited Lady C: C: late. rec'd a Letter from Miss Anne Snow.

Sunday Aug^(st.) 9^(th.)

The same sultry, & not pleasant weather, a trifling shower while we were at Chappel at S^(t.) Georges, where the Boys only accompanied me both Morning & evening, M^(r.) W. being ill with a bad cold & little fever. D^(r.) Brown dined & drank Tea here I walk'd alone a little on Queen Street, after having made an unsuccessful call on Lady Riddell who was ill. wrote to my Sis^(r.) Travell

Monday Aug^(st.) 10^(th.)

A Cruel wet Morning, w.^(ch) did not abate till noon, & tho little rain fell afterwards it was a damp close disagreable Day. M^(r.) W. being better accompanied his Sons & the young Broughams in their Coach, to the public examination at the Schools where are Boys got good stations & Premiums of xxxxx & Francis much credit from speaking admirably a speech out of Virgils Enead. I had a long busy Morn: to myself, went to Tea Cards & Supper in a chair to M^(rs.) Carre's in Georges Square, a good rather elderly party of 9 at home by twelve.

Tuesday Aug^(st.) 11^(th.)

An entire unpleasant Day being thick & damp, & altho not absolute rain was so moist it was unpleasant to be out, tho Francis enjoy'd a long ride on D^(r.) Browns Poney. I went into Thistle Street to Lauries Dancing school & to make a useless call on Lady Riddell, & came home soon to much business.

Wensday August 12th.

One of the most oppressive hot Days I almost ever remember, at noon a most tremendous Thunder Shower, in which I was caught & obliged to take shelter in a Shop in the Cannongate in my way to Lady C: C: where I made a long visit, on my return went to several Shops & came home tired to Death dresst & went to dine at Mr. Com: Browns to eat Solan Goose,[24] & to meet Major & Mrs. Dewar chearful & pleasant enough, at ½ past eight call'd at Lady Riddells where we were detaind to Cribbage & Sandwiches meeting Miss Macartney & Mr. M. Riddell her Ladyship very indifferent indeed having been confined for near a week.

Thursday Augst. 13th.

An extreme hot broiling Day so oppressive it was scarce possible to move about & after dark some Thunder & lightning & violent heavy rain. at noon I went with the Boys to their first lesson with Madame Rosignoli the Dancing Mistress, did some shopping bussiness & visited Mrs. Macdougal, & Mrs. Dewar the latter only at home Tea Cards & Supper at Lady Riddells where were Mr. M. Riddell & Miss Bruce, our comfort sadly interrupted by a fright of Francis's not returning home from his evening walk, found at last at Supper at Provost Stewart terrified to death.

Friday Augst. 14th.

Very hot again but more bearable the air being clear, went at Noon with Lady R & Miss Macfarlan in the Coach to Colleton, puddled about at Sr. James Foulis's[25] & brought away many flowers, then visited Dr. & Mrs. Walker at the Parsonage a sweet romantic spot, did not return home till past 4 well tired down, spent the evening again at Lady Riddells the party Mr. M. Riddell Miss Macfarlan Major Melville & one of his Daughters. very happy to hear Mrs. Charteris was safe in her Bed with a Son[26]

Saturday Augst. 15th.

A most disagreable Day from Morn: to night being a perpetual wetting Fog, as thick as if November no stirring out for me any part of the Day, rec'd a visit from Mrs. Captn. Brown, did much work & heard much read in Montalbert. wrote to Mr. Charteris & Mrs. Buxton.

Sunday Augst. 16th.

Another very unpleasant Day, being hard rain in the Morning, & a thick disagreable mist the greater part of the Day went to Tea & Supper at Lady Riddells, where Mr. Riddell & Mr. M. Riddell were also. much settling of our approaching Tour.

Monday Augst. 17th.

Very wet indeed in the Morning, but cleard before Noon & was a very bright warm till evening when their was another hard storm which made it very cold. accompanied the Boys to the Dancing School from thence join'd Major Mellville & Mr. M. Riddell at the Abbey when the former attended us to survey Lord Adam Gordons new Kitchen Garden well pleased with,

---

24. Solan goose—an archaic name for the gannet.
25. James Foulis (d. 1825); succeeded as 6th baronet of Colinton, 1791. He married, 1791, Margaret, née Dallas.
26. Francis Wemyss-Charteris, 9th Earl of Wemyss (1795–1883).

afterwards visited Lady C: C: where came M^r. Charteris much wishing of joy, ended my Morning career by visiting M^rs. Brown went to Drink Tea Cards & Supper at M^rs. Mures, Lady Riddell with us a dull party of 6 Ladies & 2 Gentlemen much Cassino.

Tuesday Aug^st. 18th.

As usual very wet in the Morning but clear'd before Noon, but was not pleasant the west wind being tremendous, made many visits found 4 at home, went to Tea Cards & Supper at Lady Riddells, Miss Bruce, Major Melville, & M^r. M. Riddell 2 or 3 callers besides not at home till past 12 o'clock

Wensday Aug^st. 19th.

A dry but lowering Morning & at noon wet for several hours, but dry again in the evening I went out at 12 with the Boys to Madame Rosignolis but check'd in any farther progress from the rain — went again in the evening to Lady Riddells to meet the same party as the former evening.

Thursday Aug^st. 20th.

Dry the whole of the Day but such a violent west wind that made it very unpleasant but I had little time to be out, being so busy in preparing for our next Days Journey, late in the Morning I call'd on M^rs. Brougham & on M^rs. Com. Brown, & in the evening Maria Brown call'd on me, very busy all the evening writing: rec'd a Letter from M^rs. Callander & wrote to M^r. Burslem & M^rs. Granville

Friday Aug^st. 21st.

A dark thick Morning, a clear Noon, a lowering afternoon, & a wet night. set out between 8 & 9 all 4 of us in the Lanark fly, 1 Gentlemen & 2 Ladies our Companions, the former obliging & full of information, the Country rich & beautiful for the first 5 or 6 miles, afterwards little could be said in its praise, being a continuation of bleak Hills & Barren Moor Lands our first stop at Revelrig Toll about 10 miles from Edinburgh, to bait the Horses, the House such an Hovel I preferd sitting at the Door & eat eggs, seven miles farther we changed Coaches, on the Highway there being no House to stop at, the change was much for the worse it being a small uneasy Coach & so old & ruinous I expected it would break down every step, at Carnwath 25 miles from Edinbro' we stopt again for a hour, a miserable Inn where the Boys eat Bread & cheese. here we lost 2 of our companions it is dignified by the name of a Market Town but is like a dirty stragling viliage. 6 miles more brought us to Lanark of a jumbling hilly road, & over a Country at once Dreary & dull in spite of large plantations of Fir & Larch, & some fine corn land but more heath & morass, Lanark is rather a miserable looking Town, but large & apparently populous, the New Inn a good & comfortable Inn, having so late a Dinner, we could only move out while it was getting ready, saw the situation of Lord Justice Clerks House at Braxfield less than a mile from the Town to whom & M^rs. Macqueen we sent a note of enquiry & rec'd a very friendly invitation to Dinner next Day.

Saturday Aug^st. 22^d.

A dry but lowering looking Morn. which however before Noon terminated in a clear beautiful fine Day, with much sun & brisk wind & a true fine summers evening with strong dew & a glowing sky, between 11 & 12 we sallied forth on foot with a guide to survey the falls of the Clyde, which are situated about two miles from the Town, a very pleasant walk of strong Hill & dale, at the end of the two miles we arrived at Bonninton the Seat of Lady Ross,[27] a Handsome House standing with a fine drop of ground below it, & large old plantations of forest Trees after passing over the Lawn we enter'd into the Woods, & walks, which pass over the tops of the rocks between which the River Clyde flows with most impetuous torrents, the first fall (or Lynn) we came to was call'd Corhouse, & dashes over large & craggy Rocks from 50 to 60 feet high, & from the late rains was stupendously full & beautiful, on the bank close to it, is a handsome House of the same name belonging to Miss Edmonstones. the fall of Bonninton is about ½ a mile higher up the river the same varied & charming walks continuing all the way, extremely well kept, & the great variety of shrubs, & smaller plants very gratifying to the eye the chain of Rocks some bare, others well cloathd with wood, continue uninterrupted from one fall to the other, & in some places, are majesticaly high, the fall of Bonninton is totally different from Corhouse being one large grand sheet of Water of considerable width but not very high, we returnd by different walks all beautiful & varied, to the great Cotton Works, founded by a M^r. Dale[28] & which are in a great stile larger than those near Matlock in Derbyshire which having seen we pass'd by these to Braxfield Lord Justice Clarks,[29] whose domain is not a quarter of a mile distant where we met with the most friendly, pleasant reception, the only company there a Miss Mackenzie. Braxfield is a comfortable but irregular built house, well furnishd; after Dinner M^rs. Macqueen & I walk'd in their premises which are woody romantic & very pleasant, had a merry game at Whist from Tea to Supper, soon after which we walk'd up the Hill to the Inn, attended by the Footman with a Lanthorn the Boys having gone 2 or 3 hours before. wrote to M^rs. Callander.

Sunday Aug^st. 23^d.

Not so fine a Morn: or indeed Day in general as might have been expected from the previous evening, being dark & lowering tho scarce any rain fell, the Town full of people of all ranks & descriptions, going to the several places of Worship of which there was three the great Kirk of the Town a Secceding Meeting House, & a temporary Pulpit erected a stones throw from the end of the Town, round which a large congregation were assembled some standing & others of temporary seats, the whole together presented a most irreverend sight, a quarrel with the Minister of the great church has thus seperated the congregation but still there is remaining a very large one which we attended, The Lord Justice & M^rs. Macqueen calling upon us to take us with them to their seat in one of the Lofts the Church is very large & form'd to contain a numerous congregation, the Minister nothing very striking in his performance, but

---

27. Bonnington, the seat of Elizabeth, née Dundas, dowager Lady Lockhart-Ross.
28. David Dale erected his Twist Mill in 1784–1785. Later there was legal action between Miss Edmonstone and Mr Dale, because a dam-dyke had been built across the river and Miss Edmonstone complained that 'lazy people made use of the dyke as a means of passing over and trespassing on her land' at Corehouse.
29. The Lord Justice Clerk was Robert MacQueen (1722–1799), from the small estate of Braxfield, near Lanark. In 1776 he became a judge and was created Lord Braxfield. He was often referred to as 'the hanging judge'. Braxfield's statement 'let them bring me prisoners, and I will find them law' was his legal theory. In 1788 MacQueen was promoted to Lord Justice Clerk. He has been viewed as the inspiration for the character Lord Weir in Robert Louis Stevenson's unfinished novel *Weir of Hermiston*. Agnes and Edward Witts had become acquainted with the MacQueens in Edinburgh.

Robert MacQueen (1722–1799), Lord Justice Clerk, 'the hanging judge'. An etching by John Kay.

extremely long winded. We were prevented returning with the Braxfield family to spend the Day as we intended being obliged to xx Lanark on that Day no horses being to be obtain'd on the Monday we therefore got a hungry Dinner at the Inn, & set off in a Post Chaise for Hamilton, 15 miles of a good & very beautiful road winding by the side of the Clyde & never at any distance from its Banks. a mile & a ½ from Lanark we got out of the chaise & went down a steep Hill to the River to survey another fall at a Mill call Stone Byre, & which would in my opinion be far superior to either of the others were it possible to get a compleat front view of it but that it is not except to very <u>daring</u> spirits who would xxxx to run the risk of breaking their necks by descending the Rocks, there is in fact 3 seperate falls, tumbling over very tremendous broken rocks, the noise & spring of all which makes it both an aweful & rather a fearful sight. The Country thro' which we went is on the whole rich & fertile, many Gentlemens seats, well planted, the most considerable one Molsley a new built House in the Castle stile belonging to Lord Hyndford. we reached Hamilton between 6 & 7, the only Inn of any note in the Town is the Duke's Arms a moderate House but well attended we preferd inhabiting the Assembly room to a small stuffy parlor drank Tea walk'd out of the Town on the Glasgow road. to Bed early.

Witts Family Papers F190

1795

Monday Aug.st 24.th

A wet Morning but soon clear'd off to leaving warm fine Day, tho for a hour or two early in the afternoon it became lowering & a few heat drops fell as soon as we had finish'd our breakfast in our splendid sitting room we walk'd to the Palace of Hamilton which is situated close to the bottom of the Town from where it is so well shelter'd as not to be any material objection it was built in the Year 1591, but having been newfronted & undergone much repairs, does not appear so ancient it stands upon a great deal of ground but has not a great many habitable apartments, the Park ground & Lawns around are rich & well laid out, & the distant views of the adjacent Country pleasing but not very extensive. The Principal room is the Gallery, which occupies the whole Front up one pair of stairs & is a 101 feet long, it contains a great variety of pictures chiefly family portraits both ancient & modern; the two most celebrated Pictures are Daniel in the Den of Lions by Reubens, a most striking painting, & the portrait of an Earl of Denbigh the Master doubtful whether Reubens, Vandyke or other, but unquestionably a most charming Picture. there is a wonderful large collection of Pictures of various kinds & by numerous Masters, & many well worthy of minute observation, the Palace alltogether was a very gratifying sight to me bringing to my ideas many anecdotes of old times. the House Keeper a very civil intelligent Englishwoman, who indulged me by very informing answers to all my questions. returning to the Inn to rest a little while, we set forth again to visit the Castle of Chatelherault, which is a mile & a ½ from the Town, & is the termination of the domain & stands in the Deer Park, upon a very fine eminence, commanding a very extensive view, & a most pleasing near one the River Avon flows close by its side, running thro a narrow glen, with woody rocks on each side. It was built merely for a pleasure house, being only 2 or 3 sitting rooms, furnish'd & those very indifferently, there is a small flower garden at the back of the Castle the old Gardiner & his Wife having the care of the domain the latter was a very sensible well behaved Woman from whom I gaind much entertaining knowledge we had a very excellent Dinner after which we strolled a little about the Town, & went over the large Church, which is very inferior in the inside to what it appears to be, being a handsome looking building.

Tuesday Aug.st 25.th

An extreme fine Day, almost without interruption, very hot in the Morning but rather cloudy in the evening. we left Hamilton between 8 & 9 the first 5 or 6 miles the Country was rich & cultivated, after which by degrees it became very dreary the road lying over barren moor land from which very little distant view could be got; the first stage was 16 miles, & we changed both Horses & Chaise very much for the worse at a miserable looking lone Inn call'd Kings Wells, w.ch carried us 8 miles farther of very much the same kind of country, to Kilmarnock,

221

where the face of the country begins greatly to improve, it is a large populous Town, with very miserable narrow streets here M^r. Baillies Coach met us & carried is in great comfort to his House at Newfield 5 miles further,[1] where we met with a very pleasing reception from all the family. the House stands on a rising ground, & commands an extensive & very beautiful view, well diversified with rich objects, the rooms are comfortable tho not large & on the whole it is a very chearful agreable spot. between Dinner & Tea we walk'd over the domain, & in the evening play'd at Cassino; Miss L. Baillie a Neice the only company besides ourselves.

Wensday Augst. 26th.

Quite a wet Morning, but the wind rising it soon clear'd off & was a tolerable fine Day, M^r. B. & M^r. W. went in the Chaise to Irvine, we Ladies amused ourselves seperately as we liked, a M^r. M^{rs}. & a Miss Read dined here, we walk'd a little after Dinner but it was too wet & dirty to be pleasant evening spent as the former. wrote to Lady Riddell & rec'd a Letter from Miss Louisa Lee

Thursday Augst. 27th.

Rather a showery Morning, & at times continued so the whole of the Day, at Newfield but M^r. Baillie M^r. Witts & I were more fortunate in a drive to Ayr in the post Chaise, not having one shower but constant sunshine it is a very pretty drive of 10 miles, in general charming road & very pleasing views, Ayr is a large handsome Town, standing close to the Sea, I first attempted a visit to Lady Dumfries who was not at home & then accompanied the Gentlemen in a walk on the sands & about the Town, & went into an Inn & got some excellent cold meat &'c, returnd home a little different road much pleased with our excursion; evening passt in Music & Cassino. wrote to Lady C: Charteris.

Friday Augst. 28th.

An exceeding pleasant day, quite dry & tho much sun none too hot, the Gentlemen went in the chaise to Irvine, & to make a call on Lord Eglington[2] at Eglington 2 miles farther M^{rs}. Baillie & I walk'd in their own domain, an odd but entertaining Gentleman of the name of Cruikshank dined at Newfield, evening spent as the former ones. rec'd a Letter from Miss Snow.

Saturday Augst. 29th.

Another very clear & most pleasant day, I accompanied the Gentlemen again in a drive to Irvine & while M^r. Baillie was transacting some bussiness there, we drove on towards Killmellin, passing by Eglington & returnd again to Irvine, which is a chearfull small Market Town with some shipping Trade the River of the same name connecting the Town with the Sea which is not distant a mile. from M^r. Baillies 5 miles we took a pleasant walk after Dinner & in the evening as usual play'd with success at Cassino

---

1. Hugh Baillie (±1732–1813). Hugh was the son of Hugh Baillie of Monckton and married Anna Pearce, the daughter of the Chief Judge of Calcutta. Hugh Baillie served in a senior position with HEIC and in 1795 had not long since returned to Scotland.
2. Hugh Montgomerie (1739–1819), 12th Earl of Eglinton. Hugh Montgomerie had entered the army in 1756 and had served through the American Revolutionary War. He was Lieutenant Governor of Edinburgh Castle 1794–1798. He married, 1772, his cousin, Eleanor Hamilton, 4th daughter of Robert Hamilton of Bourtree Hill, Ayrshire.

Sunday Aug$^{st.}$ 30$^{th.}$

Not near so pleasant a day, being dark & lowering with strong appearance of rain tho hardly any fell went in the Coach to Morning service at Dundonald Church about a mile distant, where a large congregation were assembled, many genteel People, three Carriages there at least but so miserable a church I was never in before M$^{r.}$ Duncan by no means a bad performer but very long went to his House afterwards, & eat Bread & cheese & drank Ale the evening rather a long one conversation being our whole employ.

Monday Aug$^{st.}$ 31$^{st.}$

A cloudy Morning which produced a very dry & pleasant day excepting being too strong a wind, we bid adieu after breakfast M$^{r.}$ Newfield & our many pleasant friends there, M$^{r.}$ Baillie sending us in his Coach to Kilmarnock from whence the same chaise carried us to Glasgow 22 miles stopping for a short bait at Kings Wells, from whence the road continued equaly barren & hilly for 4 or 5 miles but not quite so dismal in its appearance, it then very much improved & became rich in scenery as well as cultivation & the road excellent, Glasgow is visible 6 or 7 miles before you arrive at it & cuts a very handsome figure for more so we thought than when we got there, for tho the principal streets are many of them both long & wide, yet the buildings are so irregular, & the streets kept so abominably dirty they disgust rather than please the eye we arrived at the Bucks Head Inn between 4 & 5 & soon got a moderately good Dinner, & other tolerable accomodations, tho certainly it is but a second rate Inn. after Dinner we went to explore the New Town in which we were much disappointed, there being no kind of similarity either in the streets or houses

Thursday Sep$^{r.}$ 1$^{st.}$

An oppressive hot day, most broiling sun, & a thick air being an easterly wind, & the heat & dirt of the Town made one more sensible of it, added to wch I was far from well & nearly overcome by so much walking about in the heat of the Day, as imediately after breakfast we set off first to secure a Chaise & Horses to carry us the whole Tour to the Highlands, & then to see the College the High Church & the Infirmary, the first were it better situated would be a fine old building but the High Street is dirty & narrow not even paved, it is built much in

The Buck's Head Hotel, a watercolour by Thomas Fairbairn. *Glasgow Museums*

the stile of some of the Colleges in Oxford & was founded early in the Sixteenth Century, we saw the Hall, the room for graduation & the Libraries the chief use of the College is not for the accomodation of students, but for the use of the Professors & their seperate Classes. the High Church stands upon a fine eminence at the North west end of the Town & is a wonderful large ancient Pile of Building, said to be 500 years in building, & begun 11 Hundred Years ago, & the only Romish Cathedral remaining in North Brittain, there is now three seperate places of Worship in it, one of them in a manner underground in the vaults the most extraordinary situation for public service that can be imagined; the church yard is a very large spot of ground, & almost wholly coverd with flat grave stones; The Infirmary stands close to it, & appears a very fine building, but we made no other survey of it but of the outside. after making a very miserable Dinner, we walk'd out again to see St Andrews Church, which stands in a Square of the same name, but which, like all the other buildings is in an unfinish'd state, & is chiefly inhabited, by considerable Merchants & their warehouses from thence we walk'd to the Green, & by the River side the former exhibited a very novel scene there being hundreds of Women employ'd in Washing Linnen, for which purpose their is a public work House erected on the Green which is nearly coverd by the cloaths bleaching on it. a wonderful sight to a southern eye.

Wensday Sepr 2d

Quite a thick foggy Morning but terminated in a beautiful fine Day, quite a clear air & much sunshine very fortunate for all the fine scenery we had to pass thro left Glasgow at seven, & went to Paisley 2 miles in a chaise & pair of Horses we had hired for the whole Highland Tour at 17/6d pr Day paying no other charges Paisley was 4 miles out of the road to Dumbarton but for the sake of seeing that Town we passed it & came into the Glasgow road again 5 miles from that Town; the road was good & the country rich & beautiful, abundance of fine corn land, on which harvest was advancing fast, & ever appearance of the many advantages arising from trade & commerce; Paisley is a large Town, full of manufactory the chief thing to commend it for in truth there is very little to be seen in it; we went to see some Looms weaving Muslin, & to see the remains of the old Abbey church one end of which has been recently repaird, & is a very handsome church. the Town stands in the County of Renfrew, the County Town of that name which we pass'd thro just before we reach'd Kingsinch Ferry,

Glasgow and the River Clyde published by Thomas Kelly in London around 1816. A copperplate engraving.

Dumbarton Castle, an engraving by William
Miller after J. M. W. Turner.

appears more like an old dirty Villiage. This Ferry is over the River Clyde, & was errected by
Mr Spiers who has a handsome House & place call'd Elderslie not ½ a mile from it, the River
is here very wide & its banks beautiful, it is a very commodious mode of passage & quickly
accomplishd & imediately after we fell into the road from Glasgow when we had 9 miles to
Dumbarton of as beautiful a country as possible, never out of Sight of the River, very unequal
ground, much corn & woodland & many Gentlemens Seat in view the most material one on
the opposite side the River, Ershine House belonging to Lord Blantyre; a Canal reaching from
the Clyde to Falkirk improved the view, the Castle at Dumbarton visible several miles before
you reach the Town is a noble object, the Rock on which it stands is wonderful & in indeed
the principal point of View, the buildings now on it being inconsiderable, its situation is fine
standing on the conflux of both the River Clyde & Leven; the bleachfields on the banks of
each have a pleasant appearance from the busy scenery they present, Dumbarton is rather a
small Town about a mile from the Castle, & has little to boast of but its situation, here we
enjoy'd eating some good cold meat at a tolerable Inn, & rec'd an obliging invitation from
Sir James Colquhoun to make his House at Rosedae our Inn while we remain'd on the Banks
of Lock Lomond which first shew'd itself about 5 miles from Dumbarton the remaining 6 we
pass'd within the constant view of it & never at any distance, it has been so often & so well
described I shall not attempt it satisfying myself with the knowledge it far more than answerd
my expectation; the roads were excellent, much to the credit of the County, as their is not
one Turnpike. We were rec'd in the most hospitable manner by the Baronet[3] with whom we
found his agreable Brother Col: William[4] Rosedae[5] is an excellent House & stands beautifully

---

3. Edward and Agnes had first met Sir James Colquhoun at the Riddels', 19 December 1794.
4. Colonel William Colquhoun was an army officer, the second son of Sir James Colquhoun, 1st Baronet (1714–1786).
    Colonel Colquhoun remained unmarried.
5. Rosedale, Dumbarton.

Rob Roy's Cave, Loch Lomond.

fronting the widest part of the Lake, which is judged to be 8 miles wide, & in the view of the chief Islands, but neither the House or environs are kept in the stile that might be wish'd; we had very good plain entertainment & the best of all which an apparent hearty welcome we walk'd a little both before & after Dinner, & finish'd the evening with Tea, Supper, a Game at Whist & much conversation.

Thursday Sep.ʳ 3.ᵈ

A sombre Morning, which terminated in a very fine warm Day, with at intervals much hot sun which produced very disirable light & shade, imediately after a social breakfast, the whole party got into a Boat with 4 rowers & went on the Loch, we landed on one of Sir James's Islands, which is large & much wooded tho very rocky & call'd Inchtavannach, it was a long & steep climb to the top, but when we arrived there were well rewarded by a most glorious view not only of the Lake & its numerous as well as beautiful Islands but of the distant country, as well as its own sweet quiet shore the descent was rugg'd & difficult, on our return to the Boat we row'd to different parts of the Lake for an hour or two, & when we landed, went to a very pretty Hill on the opposite side of the Lake, which Sʳ James here ornamented with a Shrubbery thro w.ᶜʰ there is walks & from the top of which in my opinion is one of the finest views of the Lake &'c we had an early Dinner at which were added to our party a Clergyman of the name of Stewart an odd but entertaining Man, at 5 o'clock we set off for Arroquhar, hoping to perform the 11 miles with ease before it was dark, but that was far from being the case, the road being so rough & so very hilly we were an hour & ½ in the dark w.ᶜʰ I more regretted from losing some of the many beauties we had to pass, the road lying wholly on the banks of the Lake excepted when removed by the ascent of stupendous hills to a greater distance, till we reach'd Tachet, which is a mile from Arroquhar, when we left this wondrous fine piece of water to our right hand & it extends 8 or 9 miles farther being 30 english miles in leng.ᵗʰ we were much disappointed in our accomodations at the Inn which having other company in it reduced us to the necessity of sitting in our miserable bedchamber, & the Boys to repose in a sad Garret.

Glencoe, an engraving by William
Miller after J. M. W. Turner.

Friday Sep.ʳ 4ᵗʰ.

Rather a cloudy stormy Day, but no rain fell excepting in very trifling short showers, in the
forenoon & the evening was very fine. day light shew'd us the peculiarity of the situation of
Arroquhar[6] being a lone House seated in the very centre of high & rocky Mountains, a very
craigie one imediately opposite to the Inn from its uncommon form on its summit has gain'd
the name of the Cobler,[7] which however I could not easily find but its resemblence. Loch
Long commences at this place & is an arm of the Sea, we pass'd by the Side of it for a mile or
two, it has no singular beauty to speak on the part we went by, being narrow, & by not being
shaded with wood loses much merit, we quitted it abruptly & enterd the Vale of Glencro,[8]
thro which the roads runs for several miles & is a wonderful scene of Mountainous rocks,
& rude barreness literaly not a tree visible, & the resemblence of a house or rather hutt most
rare, some small cultivation is to be observ'd at different places in the vale, but the far greater
part, is such stones & heath, & down the sides of the Mountains perpetual torrents of water,
which gave a fine variation to the view, the road is narrow & very stoney; after ascending a
long & steep Hill, we turn'd into another vale call'd Kinloss nearly as long, & somewhat in
the same stile but wider & not near so rocky & grotesque after a very long drive of 14 miles
we found ourselves at Cairndow, here we baited in a very comfortable small Inn on the Banks
of Loch Fyne, one of the largest estuaries of N. Brittain. It is more than 30 miles in length, &
communicates with the open Sea on either side of the Isle of Arran, it is a noble water varied
in its outlines by creaks & promontories & is at certain Seasons of the Year the crowded resort
of Herings & those engaged in the Fishery, as we saw at Inverary, where the salting & sending
them off to a distance is a great trade Cairndow is 10 miles from Inverary, all the way by Loch
Fyne, which presents many views very picturesque, about ½ way the stupendous plantations of
the Duke of Argyle begin to appear & every step till you arrive fresh beauties shew themselves,
within a mile the Loch forms itself into a kind of circular Bay which presents an infinite fine
scene as well to the Town as to the Dulmer domain, in a very conspicuous part of which stands

6.   Arrochar.
7.   The Cobbler.
8.   Glencoe.

Loch Long.

the Castle a noble building but not very ancient; we found the Inn an excellent one & after a very good Dinner, took the Chaise to drive thro the plantations, which are fine & extensive of a variety of kinds, the Beeches the most superior; at 6 we got permission to see the House, which is an an extreme good plan & very well furnish'd, the drawing room superbly so with Gobelin tapestry, but no pictures throughout the House, we were taken to the Leads on the top of the house which afforded a very fine view. Miss E: Mure who was on a visitation walk'd about with us. return'd to our Inn well tired & wrote to Lady Riddell & Mrs. Brown.

Saturday Sepr. 5th.

Very wet for 2 or 3 hours in the Morning, but clearing up became a very fine brilliant Day, with much light & shade; the rain prevented our setting off till between 10 & 11, when we pursued our road to Dalmalie[9] a most beautiful stage of 16 miles, for the first hour & ½ our road lay wholly thro the Dukes glorious plantations, soon after leaving which our attention was attracted by the sweet quiet beauties of Loch Aw,[10] which opend upon us in a very enchanting style with the Mountain of Cruachan on its N. eastern extremity, there is several small Islands, one with a small Ruin on it apparently of a Church alltogether I have seldom been more struck than with this Loch & its adjacent environs, the roads are very rough & bad & the Hills up & down perpetual, Dalmalie is situated in the Vale of Glenorchay[11] which must be esteem'd rich & beautiful, here we join'd M^{r.} & Mrs. J. Mure & Miss E: Mure in our Dinner party & afterwards went 12 miles to Tyndrum, a very tedious stage, from the incessant hills & very ruggd roads, the Mountain scenery more wonderful than pleasing; the Inn unquestionably the worst in point of accomodation that we stopt at but the civilities of the people made amends.

Sunday Sepr. 6th.

A fine but rather stormy Morning, the wind continued very high all day, but very bright & fine till afternoon, when there was a sharp shower which produced unfortunately a cloudy evening; Tyndrum stands in a most wild spot, surrounded by unnumber'd as well as by unmeasurable

---

9.   Dalmally.
10. Loch Awe.
11. Glenorchy.

Mountains, the prospect around us was alike dreary for the first 2 or 3 miles after we quitted it, which we did early in the Morning, & remain'd more or less so the whole of the 14 miles stage to Tynluit[12] where we stopt to bait the Horses; the vale of Dochart thro which we passt is rather more rich & cultivated & the Loch of its name tho small, has yet an Island with a ruin on it which was a pleasing variation our eyes were perpetualy attracted by the torrents that rush'd down the sides of the Rocks, which at times are so tremendous as to wash down the Bridges on the road, as we found experimentaly passing on this Days Journey at least 4 or 5 in this dismantled state, but the streams being then shallow we forded them with safety, but by no means with satisfaction, from Tynluit to Killin is 7 miles more, of a very hilly but more pleasant country, the approach to the Town is very striking, the River Tay by which we had travell'd for several miles, here begins to form itself into a wide & very rapid stream, & close to the Town rushes over a rocky cliff in a fine stile, at Killin likewise Loch Tay commences & reaches 16 miles to Kenmore; before Dinner at Killin we found the Mures & M[r] Gyles who was added to their party in a walk a mile & ½ from the Town to a burying ground of the Bradalbane Family, w.[ch] by no means requited us for the fatigue of so hot & so long a walk, our return was made more amusing by meeting many of the congregation returning from the Kirk, the neat simplicity of their dress & manner was attractive & we held conversation with some that could understand us but the far greater part spoke in the Erse language. we all dined together very tolerably, & proceeded to Kenmore the whole road presented us with charming views, Lock Tay being a constant object on our right hand, nay indeed the road lay so near the edge of the precipice that hung over it & in many places being no defence it was rather alarming. Kenmore is a small Town beautifully situated rather on an eminence overlooking the Loch & surrounding Hills some cloath'd with Wood others barren, the Church is a great ornament standing aloof from any other building, & is of a pretty design, the Bradalbane Arms is a tolerable good Inn, where we were early glad to go to our Beds being heartily tired with so long a Journey in such very rough roads.

Monday Sep[r] 7th

Rather a lowering Morn: inclined to rain but none fell of any consequence, & the afternoon was peculiarly fine, after an early breakfast, we went in the Chaise 2 miles by the side of the Loch to see the Waterfall from the Hermatage, which well repaid us for a miles walk up a steep ascent the Hermatage is well designed, the entrance to it being thro an arch'd rock w.[ch] lends you abruptly to the sight of the Fall which is 240 feet high, but not wide but rushed in a fine natural stile over jutting rocks it is call'd the Water of Archan[13] the Hermatage is fitted up suitably to its name with Moss shells, dry'd Fowls & small beasts of various kinds stuff'd & well disposed, on our return to Kenmore, we walk'd into the pleasure ground of Taymouth ordering our Carriage to meet us on the other side the place, with a view of which we were indeed very highly gratified, so much so that all description must be vain, the River Tay is one of its finest ornaments it is kept in a noble stile & does credit to Lord Bradalbane it was not easy to quit this enchanting spot, but necessity having no law we proceeded 14 miles to a miserable little Inn call'd Balliguard the only baiting place between Dunkeld or rather Inver. a more delightful country I never pass'd through, than the strait of Tay, never losing sight of its

---

12.   Taynuilt.
13.   Acharn. The 'Hermitage' was a new build; erected in 1790.

noble river, & for several miles within sight of the stately Mountains of Benlaws, & Strehallen or Maidens Pass, supposed to be the 2 highest in Scotland; the fields rich I glowing with corn, & some fine Meadow land well sprinkled with Cattle, the road rough & bad made us a tedious time before we got to our poor Inn w.ch could afford us nothing better for our Dinner than eggs & Bacon & Potatoes, fortified with these we set forth again to go 10 miles to Inver, the roads getting worse & the Country more hilly tho still as beautiful, it was nearly dark before we got there but could discern the lofty plantations of the Duke of Atholl at Dunkeld which lay on the other side of the river. Lord Stonefield having previously taken up the best apartments in the Inn, we fared but very moderately, but fatigue made us rest well & & forget all wants.

Tuesday Sep.r 8th.

Wet & very wet till 11 o'clock, which compel'd us to remain in our very sorry Inn, sorely against our Will, when in spite of dirt & damp we went to see the waterfall from Ossians Hall, & the Day afterwards turn'd out beautifully bright & fine, & were well rewarded for our trouble, it being an exceeding fine fall of its kind not high, but a strong force of water, & the rocks it tumbles over strong & nobly shapen, the Woods, plantations & shrubbery around as well as the walk are in a very good stile & the Room from whence it is seen very elegantly fitted up, but not at all in the stile of a Hermatage w.ch it is sometime unjustly calld having much looking glass so constructed & plac'd as to reflect the Water fall even from the very ceiling & elegant paintings of various devices on the walls; it is situate on the same side the River as Invar, consequently we cross'd over the Ferry to Dunkeld, where a delightful gravel walk close to the noble River Tay for a considerable way is the chief thing worthy notice excepting some very fine Trees of various kinds & more particularly Larches, & the fine old ruin of the Cathedral of Dunkeld one of the six at this time remaining in Scotland, it is large & in many parts very intire, but standing in a very confined situation & so very near to the House is impossible to be viewd to advantage; the House is old & not by any means magnificent in its outward appearance, & standing so very near to the Town which is by no means a small one, carrys in its appearance a very small idea of grandeur. while we were walking by the rivers side were as unexpectedly, as very agreably surprized by overtaking our good friends D.r & M.rs Pennington who were like ourselves surveying the place, it was soon determined we were to dine with them at their Inn at Dunkeld which proved a far better than that we were at Inver; & afterwards we all proceeded to Perth 16 miles Francis going with them in their chaise, it is a new made Turnpike road & in the general a very good one, the Country wore the face of cultivation & of course plenty but tho very pleasant is certainly not very rich in point of scenery it was so nearly dark when we got to Perth that for that night I could form little opinion of it but that the Kings Arms Inn was tolerably good & very quiet, had a comfortable Supper with our friends & I was gratified by a charming Letter from L.dy Edw.d Bentinck

Wensday Sep.r 9th.

Very wet again till noon & extremely clear & fine the remainder of the Day. M.rs Pennington being ill with a bad head ache lost me much of her company, which precious as it was to me I could not but much regret; but getting better she & all of us walk'd a little before Dinner in the Town but being a Fair Day it was less desirable; Perth is without question a good Town & stands remarkably pleasant, the Bridge both as an object in itself & the veiws from it are quite delightful

The Hermitage sits on the banks of the River Braan in Craigvinean Forest. The Hermit's Cave was built around 1760 for the third Earl of Breadalbane who unsuccessfully advertised for a permanent hermit.

got a very indifferent Dinner & would have been most comfortable with our friends but for the cruel xxxxx we were so soon to part, & when to meet again so doubtful. went to M[r.] Oliphants at Rossie[14] in the even[g.] made it 7 miles there to avoid a very deep water, met with a very pleasant reception from the family, walk'd before Tea, music after. wrote to Lady C: Charteris.

Thursday Sep[r.] 10[th.]

A fine Day tho not much sunshine; the rest of the party either walk'd or went on horseback while M[rs.] Oliphant[15] & I went an airing in the Chaise to survey the outward beauties of Dupplin Lord Kinnouls which appeard to be good old House situated upon the sight of a Hill very well planted, afterwards took a circuit round the adjacent country home. Lady Lucy Ramsay, M[r.] Oliphant of Conti[16] & the Dear Principal who had long been staying with him at Newton dined here, such agreable additions to the party could not fail of making the Day pass pleasantly which concluded by a Rubber at Whist & some Music.

Friday Sep[r.] 11[th.]

Another good Day very brilliant in the Morning, a little cloudy at Noon w.[ch] produced a trifling shower. M[rs.] Oliphant & I again left the rest of our party to follow their own inventions while we took a long airing thro' Perth (on the road to w.[ch] I met my travelling friend M[r.] Gyles & had a long chat with Him) to the view of Elcho Castle about 4 miles distant & to M[r.] Hays of Seggieden[17] just on the other side of the River Tay who is building a handsome new house, not finding M[rs.]

---

14.   James Stuart Oliphant (1767–1847), 5th of Rossie Hill. James was the son of Robert Oliphant (1717–1785), 4th of Rossie Hill and Marion Buchanan (b. ±1740).

15.   This is presumably the dowager, Mrs Marion Oliphant, as James did not marry until 1809.

16.   Ebenezer Oliphant (d. 1806), 7th of Condie and Newton, married, 1790, Mary, 3rd daughter of William Stirling, baronet, of Ardoch.

17.   James Hay (1771–1838), of Seggieden. James was the son of James Hay of Seggieden (1739–1781), and Jean née Donaldson. James senior built Seggieden House in the Adam style, which was supposedly finished in 1789, but this diary for 1795 shows that work was still in progress. James junior inherited the estate in 1781. He pursued a military career and had many commissions including the Eastern Battalion of the Royal Perthshire Local Militia; he was also a deputy lieutenant of Perthshire. He married, 1801, Margaret Richardson, daughter of John Richardson of Pitfour. The Mrs Hay referred to is the dowager Mrs Hay.

A later engraving of Smeaton's Bridge at Perth, built 1766–1772.

Hay at home, her servant entertain'd us with Oatcakes & Cheese while the Horses were baiting, w.ch kept us so long that we did not get home till between 5 & 6, having completed a drive of near 20 miles, the Principal drank Tea with us rec'd a Letter from Miss Betty Guydickens.

Saturday Sep.ʳ 12th.

A most glorious Day, much hot sun & most perfect clear air, Mʳˢ. Oliphant & myself in the Chaise, Mʳ. O. & Mʳ. Witts on horseback, went to see the Palace of Scone, which is two miles from Perth & stands on a noble elevated situation commanding a most rich & extensive view of the fine vale around Perth the Palace is now in the possession of Lord Mansfield & was anciently the residence of the Kings of Scotland & where they were crown'd. the remains of the old Palace are in high preservation & many of the rooms well & modernly fitted up, the entrance is into a long Gallery of 140 feet long with a carved ceiling curiously painted near to the Palace is a new Dairy fitted up in the most elegant stile I ever saw one; the Gentlemen here quitted us to go to Dine with a Mʳ. Grant & came home late. wrote to my Sister Travell.

Sunday Sepr. 13th.

Quite a hot Day tho the wind was very high, a small shower in the afternoon, walk'd about & about in the fields & home premises for 2 or 3 hours in the forenoon, in which walk the Principal join'd us, Miss Grace Oliphant Sister to Contie dined here, as also Mʳ. Grant & his Nephew & another Gentⁿ. & Miss Oliphant staid Supper.

Monday Sep.ʳ 14th.

A most extraordinary warm fine Day uninterrupted sunshine, at 12 o'clock bid adieu to our agreable Friends at Rossie with much regret & went 16 miles to Col: Morays at Abercairny[18] a cross country road rough but very safe, country rich & very beautiful with Gentlemens Seats innumerable & the scenery much improvd & enliven'd, by the noble prospects of a plentiful harvest

---

18. Charles Moray (d. 1810), jointly inherited the Moray estate with his brother Alexander. Colonel Charles Moray married the eldest daughter of Sir William Stirling of Ardoch, and they had three sons and five daughters. The eldest son, James, succeeded him in 1810.

Elcho Castle, and ancient property of the Earl of Wemyss. An engraving of 1803 by James Fittler after a painting by John Claude Nattes.

cutting down fast. Abercairny is a very handsome old Place lying quite low, many improvements making, the most material a handsome piece of Water. met with a most pleasing reception the first time we ever saw the Colonel who we found far from well, M^r. Oliphant of Contie, Captain John Murray & 2 or 3 other Gentlemen there, walk'd before Tea & play'd at Cassino afterwards.

Tuesday Sepr. 15th.
A most uncommon hot Day quite oppressive, much sun & little wind, after breakfast walk'd for 2 or 3 hours about the Place with Col: & M^rs. M. surveying many improvements both past present & to come, many different Gentlemen call'd, at noon we went in the Chaise accompanied by M^rs. M. to Sir Willm. Murrays at Ochtertyres[19] a most romantic pretty place six miles distant, a good & beautiful road came home so late there was no dressing, no company at Dinner, afterwards saw the house & offices, play'd Cassino pleasantly in the evening.

Wensday Sepr. 16th.
Quite as broiling a Day if not more so, walk'd very little about, trying to keep cool as we were to Dine & sleep at Ochtertyre, where the Family were as pleasant as they were numerous a most agreable visit play'd at Cassino in the evening. wrote to Lady Riddell.

---

19. William Murray (1746–1800), 5th baronet of Ochtertyre. He was the son of Patrick Murray, 4th baronet and Helen, née Hamilton. He married, 1770, Augusta, née Mackenzie, daughter of George Mackenzie, 3rd Earl of Cromarty and Isabel Gordon.

Drummond Castle, an engraving by J. T. Smyth after a painting by J. C. Brown.

Thursday Sepr. 17th.

If possible still hotter being a thick foggy air, which prevented us the power of walking much about this sweet place, as from the great inequality of the ground it would have been most fatiguing, return'd to Abercairny between 2 & 3. well pleased with our visit & very grateful for the many civilities we had rec'd. Miss Jane Campbell from Monzie, & with her Miss Robinson, & Col: Cunningham & Miss Oliphant dined here, very chearful & lively.

Friday Sepr. 18th.

No kind of change in the weather still as hot as possible, left Abercairny after breakfast with equal respect & gratitude, went 4 miles to Crieff in Col: Morays Chaise, when a hired one carried us 21 miles to Sterling,[20] in general a rough & very indifferent hilly road; the first 5 miles thro' a rich fine Country thro the Villiage of Muthill, & in sight of Drummond Castle, a fine old Place on a wooded eminence, after which all good scenery ended till we reach'd Dumblaine, the road mostly lying over dreary barren heaths; at Ardoch we stopt to give the Horses Meal & water & went to see the remains of a large Roman Camp, very intire in its form & on a fine rising ground from whence we saw S^r. Willm. Sterlings new built House Father to M^rs. Moray. Dumblaine is a large old Town standing in a Valley, while our Dinner was preparing at a tolerable good Inn we went to see the ancient Cathedral, which is a fine old ruin, the West end of which is now use'd for the[21] of Divine service it is 6 miles to Sterling of a good but winding road & thro' a rich & very pleasant country lively diversified by Water & Wood, unequal ground & many Gentlemens Seats, the situation of Sterling is very fine, & its Castle on a noble commanding Rock very similar to that of Edinbro' is a prodigeous fine object. The Golden Lyon is an excellent Inn, large good rooms. before it was dark we walk'd a little about the Town, which tho large is by no means handsome the streets being in general long & narrow & not paved.

Saturday Sepr. 19th.

A thick close Morning very oppressive at Noon some fleeting showers wch alarm'd us for a

---

20. Agnes Witts repeatedly spells Sterling for Stirling.
21. This was a change of page and in turning overleaf Agnes omitted the word 'performance'.

The ruins of Dunblane Cathedral, an engraving after a painting by William Radclyffe. A mixture of eleventh to fifteenth century architecture, the building was restored 1889–93.

wet Day, but no rain of any consequence fell, walk'd up to the Castle, the air so unfortunately thick could see little of the fine view which is the principal object worthy of observation, the Castle buildings tho large & numerous being chiefly occupied either as Barracks for Soilders or a Riding House for Cavalry; the windings of the River Forth are as wonderful as beautiful & was indeed the only prospect we could clearly discern Mr. Witts & his Sons extended their walks while I return'd to the Inn to write, & after eating a good Dinner, went 9 miles to Mr. Riddells at Mount Riddell on the Falkirk road, the Country would I am convinced have appeard charming, had the fog permitted us to see it to advantage. Mr. Riddell was at Edinbro, but Mrs. Riddell rec'd us with much friendly politeness, besides her 6 fine children, she had a Miss MacKenzie a relation w.th her, & after Tea came Miss Bruce the Daughter of Sr. M: Bruce to Cards & Supper, an agreable fine Woman, very chatty, Mr. Laird the Tutor very stupid indeed. wrote to Miss Snow.

Sunday Sepr. 20th.

Another thick close Morning, very fine for 2 or 3 hours at Noon but lowering again in the afternoon, walk'd with Mrs. R. until it was fine to survey their own premises, which command a most rich as well as extensive view, it is a new built House, indeed new formd place altogether, & were it not seated on rather too high an eminence would be very desirable the House is neat & comodious & those parts that are furnish'd completed in taste. dined <u>very</u> late Mr. R. returning from Edinbro'. evening by no means dull or heavy from much pleasant conversation. wrote to Lady C: Charteris.

Monday Sepr. 21st.

Again lowering & very foggy, but turn'd out a broiling hot Day, our 4 noble selves & little James Riddell in the Chaise, Mr. R. on horseback went to see the Carron Works which are at about 2 miles distance,[22] & on many accounts are well worth the dirt, fatigue & noise it is necessary to undergo to see them properly; from thence we went to see Mr. Forbes's place at

---

22. The Carron Company was an ironworks established in 1759 on the banks of the River Carron near Falkirk. The company was at the forefront of the Industrial Revolution, and prospered through its development and production of a new short-range and short-barrelled naval cannon, the carronade.

Original caption: *Copper Bottom's Retreat, or a View of Carron Work!!!*
    One night in autumn, during the militia riots, in 1797, a great band of colliers, aided by a few of the town's lads, went out with a drum, and parading round the house, so alarmed Mr Forbes and his brothers that they fled by a back door, and ran up through the wood. Looking round, from among the trees, they beheld the flickering blaze of Carron Works, and imagining that Callendar House was in flames, proceeded with all speed by the village of Redding to Linlithgow, from whence they posted to Edinburgh, where, applying to Lord Adam Gordon, the Commander-in-Chief, they caused a troop of the Lancashire Dragoons to be sent out to Falkirk, who inflicted their unwelcome presence on the inhabitants for nearly half a year. It is to this affair the caricature of *Copper Bottom's Retreat* alludes. An etching by John Kay.

Calander which is about a mile from Falkirk fine wooded Place,[23] an old standing in a low bad situation, & a very large expensive new Kitchen Garden well situated abounding with fine fruit some of which he brought to M. Riddell where he this Day dined as also his Brother, singular Men, who went away before we began Cribbage.

Tuesday Sepr. 22[d.]

Another heavy Morning, which produced a sharp shower at Noon, but it was very fine again in the afternoon, & so uncommonly bright & clear as to shew off the view remarkably, which indeed is as superlative a one as I ever saw from any house. our own party walk'd after breakfast

---

23.   William Forbes (1756–1823), 1st of Callendar. William Forbes of Callendar was a prosperous coppersmith and landowner who lived in Callendar House in Falkirk. Forbes was a self-made man. The son of an Aberdeen merchant, he began work as a coppersmith and won a government contract to sheath ships' hulls in copper. With a vast fortune he purchased the estates of Callendar and Linlithgow near Falkirk, which had been forfeited by the Jacobite Earl of Linlithgow after the 1715 Jacobite Rising.

to see S.ʳ Michael Bruces at Stenhouse, 2 miles distant near Carron were disappointed in seeing the old baronet as he was not well, but met with a most obliging reception from his Daughter, & saw the Portraits of our old ancestors Cornelius De Wit & his Wife by Vandyke which were in such bad preservation they gave little pleasure, but from the connection. returnd home in the Baronets old tumbril of a P. Chaise the rain being severe; the House & all in & about it were ancient in all points suitable to its present possessor who is more than fourscore; none but our own home party at Dinner, a very chatty pleasant evening.

Wensday Sep.ʳ 23.ᵈ

Inclined to be showery in the Morning & the air much colder, but at Noon became as fine again as the former Days. left M. Riddell after breakfast with many invitations to renew our visit at some future period, went 7 miles of a cross country but most pleasant road to Dunmore Park M.ʳˢ Speirs's, who with her 4 Daughters we found all at home & very obligingly happy to see us. the Place is the property of the Earl of that name, & was originaly the house appropriated to the Steward of the family but now the Family Mansion, the old one in the Park being pull'd down all but an ancient Tower in which there are some very pleasant apartments. M.ʳˢ Speirs's House stands literaly on the banks of the Firth of Forth which in itself is a most beautiful scene being constantly lively & diversified by the number & variety of Vessels on it & from the changes of the Tide, but the Counties of Fife & Clackmannan on the opposite shore, present the most varied & beautiful scenery imaginable, being enrich'd by numerous fine Places & different objects. we walk'd before Dinner into the Park & Gardens which are at some distance from the present House, the Park is rich land & well stock'd with fine Trees of various kinds, the Gardens are extensive & before they went out of repair I daresay abundant. play'd at Whist in the evening rec'd Letters from M.ʳˢ Hyett & Miss Anne Snow.

Thursday Sep.ʳ 24.ᵗʰ

By no means a pleasant Day, being for the greater part of the Day thick misty rain & cold wind which never went cleverly off, but we spent the Morning most satisfactorily by going to M.ʳ Bruces at Kinnard about 4 miles distant,[24] M.ʳ Witts, Francis & one of the young Ladies on Horseback the rest in the Coach neither the House or place worthy observation, both being dull & at presant the residence of Lord Doun but the Library in itself is a delightful study for many hours & the Librarian very well calculated for his office, it containing a great variety & number of the late M.ʳ Bruces collection of curiosities made in his long Tour & residence in Abissinia Egypt &'c &'c admirably well class'd & arranged the Drawings of Birds, Fishes, & Flowers most beautiful, & the many Manuscript Books as valuable we did not return home till late & pass'd the evening as the former one.

---

24.   James Bruce (1730–1794), of Kinnaird, was a Scottish traveller and travel writer who spent more than twelve years in North Africa and Ethiopia, where he traced the origins of the Blue Nile. Bruce returned to Britain in 1774 and was elected a fellow of the Royal Society. His arrogance and temperament made him difficult to bear and his tales hard to credit. He retired to Kinnaird, in 1776, and married Mary (1754–1785), the daughter of his neighbour Sir Thomas Dundas and Lady Jane Dundas, née Maitland, with whom he had two sons and a daughter. After such an illustrious career his end was more prosaic; he died after falling down the stairs at Kinnaird.

James Bruce of Kinnaird with Peter Williamson. The latter was kidnapped as a child from the quayside in Aberdeen and sent to plantations in America as a slave. Suffering numerous vicissitudes including capture by Cherokees, he eventually returned to Scotland and published his life story. He died in 1799.

Friday Sep.[r] 25.th

Rather a stormy Day but quite dry, a mixture of wind, clouds & sunshine, after breakfast accompanied by two of the Miss Speirs's, we went across the Water in a very comfortable Boat, & landed just opposite to Clackmannan Castle, up to which we had near a mile to walk & thro the Town w.[ch] has little the appearance of a Capital to a County, the Castle stands on a fine eminence a small part of it is habitable, the Tower which we mounted with some difficulty is high & commands a most glorious view of the Forth & the adjacent Country with many varied objects, that side that looks towards Stirling Castle at a distance and Alloa in front view is most pleasing, we had a very pleasant voyage back & were well pleased with our Jaunt, M.[r] Bruce of Kennet & his Brother,[25] & Mr. Logan the Librarian at Kinnard dined here, but going away early our evening past as the former.

Saturday Sep.[r] 26.th

A most delightful Day, bright warm sun, & clear air from Morn: to night, I walk'd for several hours with two of the young Ladies, wile the other rode with M.[r] Witts & Sons, in the Park, Woods &'c no company, reading as well as Cards in the evening. rec'd a Letter from M.[rs] Granville.

Sunday Sep.[r] 27.th

Another equal fine Day, went in the Coach to Morning Service to Airth Church about 2 miles off a most beautiful situation, where M.[r] Ure the Minister gave us a very good plain discourse, afterwards took a short airing, which was concluded by a walk in the Park, & going into the Tower in which there are such pleasant apartments, & the view so delightful I quite wish'd to inhabit them; Young M.[r] Bruce of Kinnard & Miss Ure dined.[26] I read one of D.[r] Blairs sermons for the benifit of the public in the evening. rec'd a long lost Letter from my Sister Travell.

---

25. Alexander Bruce (1755–1808), of Kennet. Bruce married, 1793, Helen, 1768–1851, daughter of Hugh Blackburn, of Glasgow. Alexander had five brothers, Lawrence-Dundas, James, Thomas, Ralph, and Burnet. It is not clear which of these brother accompanied him to dinner. They were distant cousins to James Bruce the explorer.

26. This is presumably James Bruce, the eldest son. The three children of the explorer are thrown into the shadows by the fame of the father and little is known of them.

Edinburgh from the west by Alexander Nasmyth. As the Witts family headed east home to Edinburgh they must have witnessed a similar view—minus Nelson's Column.

Monday Sep.ʳ 28.ᵗʰ

A cloudy suspicious Morning, flying mist & cold wind, grew somewhat better at Noon & fine bright & fine in the afternoon. left Dunmore Park after an early breakfast, 7 miles to Falkirk & having very bad Horses there changed them to go to Linlithgow 8 miles farther, the Country advancing to it is rather thin & barren the Town is large & old, the Castle a faux of complete modern ruins burnt in the rebellion in the year 1745, got a moderate early Dinner, & having good Horses, went the 16 miles to Edinbro' very quickly, the even.ᵍ being very brilliant, the road appeard remarkably pleasant, & so did our own neat comfortable dwelling Principal Gordon call'd late in the evening. rec'd another Letter from my Sis.ʳ Travell.

Tuesday Sep.ʳ 29.ᵗʰ

Quite a thick gloomy Morning, which became rain between 3 & 4 & continued 2 hours very hard but was afterwards fair, very busy all the forenoon unpacking & settling, call'd late on M.ʳˢ Syme to wish her Joy of M.ʳˢ Broughams being safe in her Bed, then with M.ʳ Witts went to M.ʳ Commissioner Browns detaind there to Dinner by the hard rain where were also M.ʳ & M.ʳˢ James Brown & Miss Abercrombie very chearful & agreable, call'd at home to see the Boys & went to Tea Cards & Supper at Sir James Riddells in their new House no one there rec'd a Letter f.ᵐ Miss Snow.

Wensday Sep.ʳ 30.ᵗʰ

Another gloomy kind of Day from a very thick fog but extremely hot & oppressive at Noon went with the Boys to the Dancing School & then to visit Lady C: C: who was rejoicd to see me once more went to Tea Cards & a sandwich supper at Miss Bruces meeting S.ʳ J. & Lady Riddell & M.ʳ M. Riddell, Miss Ord, Miss Ross, & Lady Hay dull & stupid enough.

Thursday Octr 1.st

Seldom so bright & warm a day at this season, more like July, my Gentlemen all went to Bathing I intended to keep close at home, to write & do much other bussiness but being call'd on by Mrs. Brown in a Coach to go an airing, I could not resist the pleasure of her company, & went a short one on the Lothian road &'c a pleasant quiet evening at home enjoying our Dear good Boys. wrote to L^{dy.} Ed^{d.} Bentinck

Friday Octr 2.^d

In point of weather as different a day as possible having been hard rain in the night, & thro' the whole of the Day so intire thick & wetting a fog there was no seeing across the Street. Mr. W. out on various bussinesses most of the Morning, expected the Principal to Dinner but by a mistake he never came evening as pleasant as the former one. wrote to Sis^{r.} Travell.

Saturday Octr 3.^d

a dry day & in general a very pleasant one, much disagreable domestic fuss & bustle before I could attempt to get out when I attempted to make several visits, but found none at home but Mrs. Mure & Mrs. Campbell & Miss Graham, the Principal Dined & drank Tea with us, after which we went to Cards & Supper at Mrs. Mures, to see M^{r.} & M^{rs.} J: Mure before they return'd to England; a party had been at Dinner but a very small one staid to Supper.

Sunday Octr 4.th

A most glorious fine Day quite like summer went to both services at St. Georges Chappel visited Lady Sinclair between services Mr. M. Riddell here in the afternoon to take leave wrote much in the evening to Mrs. Erskine of Cambo & Miss Louisa Lee

Monday Octr 5.th

Very wet all the Morning & forenoon but dry in the afternoon & wet again to a great degree at night, quite a stay at home Morn. the Principal dined with us again & went with us to Tea, Cards & Supper at Lady Riddells to meet the Dutchess of Gordon & 2 Daughters, Lady & Miss Sinclair,[27] much Card playing but more entertaining, & singular conversation, the Dutchess shewing off in a great stile.

---

27. Alexander Gordon (1743–1827), 4th Duke of Gordon. Alexander married, 1767, Jane (1748–1812), the daughter of William Maxwell, 3rd Baronet of Monreith, and, Magdalen, daughter of William Blair. Jane was described by the diarist Sir Nathaniel Wraxall, as a celebrated beauty. From 1787 she was the social centre of the Tory party and was described in the Female Jockey Club of 1794, as possessing 'an open ruddy countenance, quick in repartée, and no one excelling her in performing the honours of the table, her society is generally courted'. It went on to say that 'The Duchess triumphs in a manly mien; loud is her accent, and her phrase obscene.' She resided for some years in Edinburgh, but eventually refused to renew her residence at George Square, Edinburgh, because it was 'a vile dull place'. The Duke and Duchess's marriage was tempestuous from the start and neither made any particular effort to be faithful to the other. The couple had seven children: Charlotte (1768–1842), married, 1789, Charles Lennox, 4th Duke of Richmond; George (1770–1836), 5th Duke of Gordon; Madelaine (1772–1847), married first, 1789, Robert Sinclair, 7th Baronet; Susan (1774–1828), married, 1793, William Montagu, 5th Duke of Manchester; Louisa (1776–1850), married, 1795, Charles Cornwallis, 2nd Marquess Cornwallis; Georgiana (1781–1853), married, 1803, John Russell, 6th Duke of Bedford; and Alexander (1785–1808).

Tuesday Oct.ʳ 6ᵗʰ

A tolerable fine Day tho cold & very autumnal feeling, went early with Francis to the Dancing School, afterwards made a long visit to Lady C: C:, & instead of visiting Mʳˢ· Brown as I intended air'd with her in a Hackney Coach chiefly in the Streets. In the evening went again to Lady Riddells to meet Mʳˢ· Riddell who was that Morn: come to Town, no one there but Principal Gordon besides Mʳˢ· Mure call'd just before we went to Dinner.

Wensday Oct.ʳ 7ᵗʰ

A dry pleasant Morn: & indeed whole Day went a string of visits, began with Miss Crawford, where I very pleasantly met Mʳˢ· W. Palmer who had arrived the night before & I found her Husband visiting mine at my return home, calld also on Lady Hay, & the Dutchess of Gordon neither at home, but made an agreable long visit to Mʳˢ· Sandys. Mʳˢ· Riddell call'd here after Tea & took us away with her to Sir James to Cribbage & Supper, Miss MacFarlan likewise of the party.

Thursday Oct.ʳ 8ᵗʰ

A very cold disagreable thick Day strong east wind, & extreme hard rain all the afternoon & night, in the Morning sat an hour pleasantly with the Palmers who were resident in Lord Dumfries House, visited Mʳˢ· Syme, pick'd up by Lady Riddell in her Coach, & carried a Shopping on the Bridge & to call on Mʳˢ· Buchan Hepburn at Mʳˢ· Craigies in Georges Square. a home evening rec'd Letters from Mʳˢ· Buxton & Mʳˢ· Rycroft, & wrote to Mʳˢ· Davies

Friday Oct.ʳ 9ᵗʰ

A wet Morning & very moderate forenoon, which made staying at home more pleasant finish'd making a Screen long begun, & many other things; Principal Gordon call'd, before we went to Tea Cards & Supper at Lady Riddells Maria Brown call'd no one at Lady R's, but Mʳˢ· Riddell & Mʳˢ· Cameron not very lively & so extremely wet a night glad to come home in a Chair

Saturday Oct.ʳ 10ᵗʰ

A very cold comfortless Day being a strong east wind, at mid.day very damp, & in the evening very wet again, went early with the Boys to the Dancing school for practising, & to visit Lady C: C:, on my return call'd on Mʳˢ· Brown a comfortable home evening, began reading Guthries History of Scotland wrote to Mʳˢ· Buxton.

Sunday Oct.ʳ 11ᵗʰ

A dry & therefore far better day, cold wind but much hot sun, went to Morning service at Sᵗ· Georges, afterwards visited the Palmers & Mʳˢ· Mure went to evening servcice at Sᵗ· Andrews, where a stranger performed the service tolerably, the Principal dined here & we had a most interesting eveng· of conversation

Monday Oct.ʳ 12ᵗʰ

Wet at intervals the greater part of the forenoon, dry but not pleasant the remainder of the Day, never went out all Morning nor recd any callers, went to Dine & to spend all the evening at Mʳˢ· Mures, meeting the Palmers, Mʳˢ· & Miss Ross & 2 Gentlemen, some Cards much conversation and realy agreable enough.

Tuesday Octr. 13th.

Prodigious hard rain till 11 o'clock when it clear'd up & became an extreme warm & fine Day, no wind & much sun, Miss Sinclair calld one me to visit Mrs. Palmer, who was not at home any more than several others I visited excepting Mrs. Brougham who I visited for the first time since her lying in. went to Tea, Cards & Supper at Lady Sinclairs meeting Sir J: & Lady Riddell, M^{r.} & Mrs. Palmer, Principal Gordon & 2 other Gentlemen very agreable indeed.

Wensday Octr. 14th.

Extreme hard rain for 2 or 3 hours in the Morning but went off & was pretty fine tho not clear Mr. W. & Francis went to Bathe, I never stirr'd all Morn^{g.} nor saw anyone, in the evening we had one of our little parties, Lady Riddell, Lady & Miss Sinclair, M^{r.} & Mrs. Palmer, Miss Bruce, Principal Gordon & Mr. Robinson all went off pleasantly. wrote to Mrs. Granville.

Thursday Octr. 15th.

Quite an intire wet day from Morn to night at times thick fog at others boisterous wind & storms, fit for nothing but home employments to me, my Dear Francis made his first entrance into the Humanity Class in the College great delight to him. rec'd Letters from Mrs. Pennington & Mrs. Savage, & wrote to Miss Anne Snow.

Friday Octr. 16th.

As usual a very wet Morning but cleard about 9 o'clock, but was wet again at Noon, & indeed very showery the remainder of the Day, I went early with Francis to the Dancing School & afterwards to see Lady C: C: who I found very indifferent as she had been quite ill, Mr. W. join'd me & went to several shops of the Bridge, ending by a very long & pleasant visit at the Browns where we found Lady Wedderburne detain'd there by the rain. Tea, Cards, & Supper at Lady Riddells meeting Miss Bruce & the Principal.

Saturday Octr. 17th.

A damp foggy Morn, wch proved a warm & very pleasant day, Mr. Witts went early with the Principal to dine with Mr. Oliphant at Lei^{th.} I went to make visits in Georges Square accompanied by Francis found only Mrs. Douglass, Mrs. Simpson, & Mr. Duncan at home, went in the evening again to Lady Riddells the same party as the former night only Miss MacFarlan added. rec'd a Letter from Miss A Snow.

Sunday Octr. 18th.

A most horrible wet Morning, indeed very little cessation of rain till near evening service declined going to Church in the Morning, after which Mr. Palmer call'd, Frank & I went St. Andrews Church to evening service, to hear Mr. Geenfield not highly gratified Bob: Brown dined here & we went to Drink Tea at Mr. Palmers, meeting Mrs. Palmers Nieces Mrs. Farquharson & Miss McCloed. wrote to Mrs. Rycroft.

Monday Octr. 19th.

Dry but rather cloudy looking in the Morn & even before Noon turn'd to hard settled rain & so continued all day but we had several pleasant visitors in the Morning, as Mrs. Palmer, M^{rs.}

Douglass Cavers M^r. Playfair & the Principal, a fine day for work & wrote to M^rs. Pennington.

Tuesday Octr. 20th.

No rain of any material consequence in the Morning tho it was very stormy & the wind quite tremendous, but in the evening it raind without ceasing in the Morning I visited M^rs. Palmer, M^rs. Brougham & Miss MacFarlan & 3 others I did not find at home M^r. Witts engaged in attending Francis for the first time to the Greek & French Classes a quiet evening rec'd a Letter from M^rs. Davies & answerd it.

Wensday Octr. 21st.

Tolerably dry in the Morning, flying showers at Noon, & very wet in the afternoon went early with Frank to the Dancing School, & as usual visited Lady C: C:, afterwards went a shopping & then call'd on M^rs. Palmer, & took her to the Register Office to see M^rs. Damers Colosal Statue of the King by no means pleased with it, from thence went to Stewarts Minature Painter & ended very pleasantly by taking M^rs. Palmer to call on M^rs. Brown, another quiet home evening.

Thursday Octr. 22^d.

Much alteration in the weather being a little frost & a cold east wind in spite of much hot sun which made it fine walking, M^r. Witts & I were out for several hours in the Morning, going into empty new houses in Hill Street & Charlotte Square, & to Raeburn the Painter, & to Naysmith & Walker Drawing Masters at home & alone all the evening.

Friday Octr. 23^d.

Another dry & clear day & not near so much wind, I staid all day within & rec'd visits at seperate times from M^rs. Sandys, M^rs. Dugald Stewart & M^r. Robinson. Principal Gordon here in the evening much fighting at Back Gammon. rec'd a Letter from my Sister Travell & wrote an interesting one to L^dy. E: B.

Saturday Octr. 24th.

A most disagreable wet & stormy Day, such a wind it was hardly possible to stand on ones Legs, yet I braved it & went to Madame Rosegnols practising which turn'd out a sad dull bussiness scarce any one being there but Lady Duckenfielld & her family from thence to Lady C: C: & very glad to get home young M. Riddell dined here, & to Tea 4 more Boys.

Sunday Octr. 25th.

Tolerably dry & clear in the Morning but at & before Noon became very showery & so continued the whole of the Day, & the wind very cold went both to Morn. & even. service at S^t. Georges terrible wet walking to & fro. P. Gordon & M^r. Lewis Law dined & spent the evening here till a very late

Monday Octr. 26th.

Quite a bright dry day tho a sharp cold wind, a long conversation with a Tutor for M^rs. Davies in the Morning, after which made 2 or 3 unsuccessful visits, look'd at some houses for M^rs. Davies & to see Woods the drawing Master ending by a visit to M^rs. Brown who was very ill.

Tuesday Octr 27th.

Constant rain, attended with most violent high wind a perfect stay at home Day, the Principal here in the evening to back Gammon and Oysters. wrote to my Sis^r. Travell

Wensday Octr 28th.

No change for the better in the weather being nearly as wet & quite as stormy, M^r. Witts not well in his stomach, so staid at home all day as well as one much reading in Guthries Scotch History very entertaining, the Principal again for the same sports in the evening. wrote to Miss B: Guydickens.

Thursday Octr 29th.

If possible a still worse Day, the wind being quite tremendous, & having the rhumatism very bad in my head, I could ill stand its disturbance notwithstanding Col: & M^rs. Callander came into Town & made us a long Morning visit wch furnish'd matter of conversation.

Friday Octr 30th.

Quite as dreadful weather till afternoon when the extreme wind carried off the rain, we went to Dine at M^r. Commissioner Browns, meeting Lady Duckenfield, Lady Wedderburne, & Miss Jane, S^r. Willm. Forbes, M^r. G: Cranstoun, & M^r. D. Erskine, not so lively as such a party might indicate at home early.

William Forbes (1739–1806), 6th baronet, a banker in Edinburgh. An etching by John Kay.

244

Saturday Oct.r 31st.

Very much such another Day in point of weather, not quite so much rain, but wind so dreadfuly high it was quite distracting, no power of stirring out of the house, in the evening another party of Boys, 3 Blairs, Brown 2 Morays & John Brougham, & among the <u>rest</u> Principal Gordon, who was pleased with such a novel party. recd a Letter from Miss Louisa Lee.

Sunday Nov.r 1st.

Somewhat a better day, being dry & the wind moderate, till quite evening when it was again wet and stormy, went to both services at S.t Georges, between visited & eat with Lady Riddell who we were happy to welcome home again; a quiet & proper home evening.

Monday Nov.r 2d.

A happy change in the weather being dry cold, tho exceedingly so, being a sharp frost. went at Noon to Dancing school meeting the Baronets Lady & family with good Lady C: C:, return'd home thro the old Town shopping & over the Mound, spent the evening at S.r James Riddells where was only the Principal

Tuesday Nov.r 3d.

Another very similiar Day being quite a sharp frost but not quite so cold a wind, famous good walking, before I set out on a string of visits rec'd good Master Mellville, & Lady Wedderburn & Maria Brown found only Miss Cranfurd & Miss Mellvilles at home, walkd over the Bridge, & met such numbers of my acquaintance it was quite amusing.

Wensday Nov.r 4th.

A very unpleasant cold Day being a thick foggy air in the Morning which at noon amounted to small rain or mist, & became hard rain at night, on my first out going visited M.rs Hamilton in Ramsay Gardens then went to Madame Rosignolis where I met a large party & ended my Morning peregrination by a visit to M.rs Brown, the Principal dined here & in the Carriage came M.r Henry Brougham[28] to Tea who much pleased us all by his sensible conversation. the Principal finishd the evening by Oysters & Back Gammon.

Thursday Nov.r 5th.

Upon the whole a tolerable fine Day tho as usual a wet evening, the Boys went at Noon being holidays on account of the preachings to dine & spent the Day with the young Dukenfields near Leith Bob: Brown accompanying them M.r Witts & I walk'd to Georges Square & a little in the Meadows while we were sitting comfortably tete tete at night an express arrived from Lady Riddell saying we were expected there, & tho reluctantly at a late hour & after a second message we were obliged to go, where we met Miss Bruce & a M.r Porterfield, a lively chatty Man.

---

28. Henry Brougham (1778–1868). Henry was educated at Edinburgh High School (1785–1791) and then at Edinburgh University. He was an advocate in Edinburgh (1800–1803), after which he moved to Lincoln's Inn, London. His illustrious parliamentary career began in 1810 when he became MP for Camelford. He became Attorney-General to Queen Caroline in 1820 and Lord Chancellor in 1830. Francis went to school with his younger brothers, James and Peter.

Friday Novr 6th

A clear fine Day with much sunshine but a clear sharp air, went to Morning prayers at St Georges & visited afterwards in several houses those I found at home were Miss MacFarlans, Mrs Brougham, Mrs Campbell, & Mrs Belches, before Dinner rec'd P. Gordon & Mrs Hay, the Principal came again to Tea Backgammon & Oysters. Frank at Mr Balfours. met again in the evening

Saturday Novr 7th

A very disagreable Day of some rain & constant high wind no going out, the Principal call'd in the Morning & came again in the evening, the Boys both at Lady Hunter Blairs. rec'd a Letter from Miss Snow & wrote to Mrs Davies

Sunday Novr 8th

A very fair pleasant Winter Day, being a little frost which produced clear air little wind & much Sunshine went to both services at St Georges Chappel, a Sacrament at which were great numbers, walk'd between churches in Princes Street with Lady Riddell evening spent as other Sundays — wrote to Mr Witts of Friday Street.[29]

Monday Novr 9th

Very much such another Day but not so fine being at times a damp foggy air but dry walking on first going out at Noon visited Lady C: C: on return went to some shops, made an unsuccessful in St James's Square, & a successful one on Mrs Mure who I had not seen for a month spent the evening agreably at Sr James Riddells meeting Sr James & Coll: Colquhoun, Mr Riddell & Principal Gordon a Table at Whist & Cribbage.

Tuesday Novr 10th

Still a frost & somewhat foggy, tho the sun sometimes did the favor to appear, we set out with Mr W. first to call on Mrs Halkett Craigie just returnd to Town, & on L^{dy} Mary & Mr Murray on Leith walk none at home, more fortunate in finding Lady Dukenfield to whom I extended my walk her presant House being at the end of Leith Walk almost in the Town, came home late & tired but not too much. rec'd a Letter from Mrs Davies

Wensday Novr 11th

Very far from a pleasant Day being the greater part of it a thick fog which made it very damp & sad walking, yet I braved it alone & walked to the Dancing School to meet Francis, & where I met the Windsor Forrester Ladies,[30] on my return made a long visit to Mrs Brown, the Principal here till a late hour in the evening.

---

29. Broome Philips Witts (1767–1845). Broome was a first cousin once removed to Edward Witts; the eldest son of his cousin Broome Witts (1738–1769). He was in business in Friday Street, London as a silk merchant.

30. The Royal Windsor Foresters was a regiment of Fencible Cavalry, consisting of 6 troops. The Regiment saw much service in Scotland during the invasion scare of 1797 and was disbanded in 1799/1800. The regiment was raised by Charles Rooke (174?–1827). Colonel Charles Rooke saw service in the American Revolutionary War. Charles and his family became close friends with Edward and Agnes Witts while in Scotland. It appears that Charles was on good terms with King George III, and this may have been a factor in the name and formation of the Regiment. Charles was later allowed to reside in the 'Stone Tower' of Windsor Castle where he died 1827. The Windsor Forrester ladies were the wives of some of the senior officers.

Thursday Novr 12th.

No rain but not a pleasant day being a damp high wind which determined me to stay within wch gave me the power of receiving a long visit from Mrs. Callander & Miss Rutherford. much interested by a new Novel Robert & Adela.[31] wrote to Miss Anne Snow.

Friday Novr 13th.

A mild & very pleasant Day for the time of Year, made an early call on Lady Riddell who I persuaded to go a walk with me first going to the Dancing School where Francis had been obliged to give us the slip & go to the Greek Class, we then visited Mrs. Phillips & Lady C: C: & on my return home call'd on George at the Drawing class. the Principal here in the evening.

Saturday Novr 14th.

Not so fine a Day tho perfectly dry being a very cold & high wind tho much sun, Mr. W. & I went early to Lady Riddells with whom we eat a nice Lunchon, & then walk'd with her over the Mound to George's Square to visit Lord Justice Clerk & Mrs. Macqueen not at home, we then seperated we to make our first visit to Miss Robinsons, & afterwards to Madame Rosignolis practising where there was quite a crowd wch kept me late, Sr. James & L^{dy.} Riddell, Miss Bruce, Major Mellville, Principal Gordon here to Tea & Cards & staid late. Mr. Crichton also.

Sunday Novr 15th.

Another very cold Day less sun & therefore more severe, went to both Services at St. Georges Chappel where Mr. Witts stood at the Plate I visited between churches Mrs. Mure & Mrs. George Fergusson unsuccessfully, & Miss Graham nearly recover'd from her Surgical operation pleasantly. the 2 Boy Dukenfields Dined here & Bob: Brown added to the party at Tea. their Tutor calling to take them home

Monday Novr 16th.

Still very windy but more mild & very damp I kept the House my only visitor Mr. Cleeve Mr. Witts walk'd to Leith &'c. wrote to Mrs. Davies a very long Tutor History. the Principal here at night to his usual feasts, backgammon & Oysters.

Tuesday Novr 17th.

Such an extreme high wind that it might be term'd quite tempestuous, at times small showers wch were kept off by the great wind, no temptation to me to go out & Mr. Witts hardly, we both went quite en famille to Sir James Riddell, no one there, much conversation & more Cribbage.

Wensday Novr 18th.

One of the most dreadful Days ever known, such violent rain as well as wind, that it was difficult to say which was the most tremendous, at Noon it turnd to Snow, & at night was hard frost, fit for nought but home employments, & almost too dark even for that we went to Cards &

---

31. *Robert and Adela: Or, the Rights of Women Best Maintained by the Sentiments of Nature,* in Three Volumes, anonymous, first published 1795.

Supper to M^rs. Mures, meeting Sir James & Lady Riddell, M^rs. Fraser, Miss Plendarleith much card playing at a variety of Games.

Thursday Novr. 19th.

A severe hard frost for one night & most extremely cold, & as perfectly dry as if there had been such torrents the previous day, I went to a variety of shops on & about the Bridge, sat by poor M^rs. Browns bedside for ½ an hour & visited M^rs. Syme in the absence of M^rs. Brougham, the Principal, & Henry & James Brougham drank Tea here, a mixture of conversation & back gammon.

Friday Novr. 20th.

Continued sharp frost, but a much pleasanter Day being less wind & more Sun, I went early to the Dancing School from thence to see Lady Dukenfields future habitation in the Cannongate, & thence on Lady C: C:, & ended my Morning peregrinations, by sitting a chearful ½ hour with Lady Riddell drank Tea & supp'd at Miss Bruces, meeting the Riddells, a M^rs. Cunningham, Major Mellvill & the Principal who had dined with us. rec'd a Letter from Miss Snow.

Saturday Novr. 21st.

Quite a disagrable Day, the frost being on its departure accompanied by small snow & rain, & at night tempestuous wind & storms all this a perfect impediment to stirring out excepting in the evening to Tea & Supper at Major Melvills where we met the Riddells & Miss Bruce, Sir Robert Anstruther & his Daughter M^rs. Campbell, 2 Tables at Cards, a good Supper & pleasant evening.

Sunday Novr. 22^d.

A Cruel bad Day incessant rain till after mid.day, M^r. W. only went to church in the Morning all of us to S^t. Georges in the afternoon. rec'd Letters from M^rs. Davies & my Sis^r. Travell & answerd the latter.

Monday Novr. 23^d.

Had been a frost in the night, but the air was damp & disagreably cold all Day, & wet again in the evening. I made a string of visits in the Morning, finding only the Speirs's M^rs. Robinson Scott, & M^rs. Halkett Craigie at home, went to Tea & Supper at Sir James Riddells, M^r. General Campbell, M^r. Crichton, & M^r. Campbell Junr. of Ashness pleasant enough.

Tuesday Novr. 24th.

Quite a wretched Day of wind & rain so incessant M^r. Witts was scarce ever out, & the darkness so great that it was almost aweful, a full Morning of work &'c, the Principal here in the evening.

Wensday Novr. 25th.

A happy change in point of weather being a sharp frost which had dried the streets compleatly & made it delightful walking. the sun making the great cold bearable, accompanied by M^r. W. made a Wedding visit to M^rs. Hugh Robinson, & another to Lady Dukenfield neither at home more sure with the two next Lady C: C: & Lady Riddell, the latter sitting at home Wensday

Patrick Crichton, Colonel of Edinburgh Volunteers, an etching by John Kay, 1794. He is inspecting the 'Awkward Squad' of volunteers, who march in the background.

mornings to receive a Levee, met several people then concluded my visits by a long one to M^rs. Brown in S^t. James's Square , at night began teaching the Boys Cribbage & wrote to M^rs. Davies.

Thursday Novr. 26th.

Still a severe frost & most bitterly cold, & by no means a pleasant Day, for after mid.day it became damp & thick & some sharp showers of snow fell but fortunately I was return'd home from going to the Dancing School & to some shops.

Friday Novr. 27th.

Not quite so cold & miserable a Day, but yet perfectly confining, being stormy & inclined to falling Snow, yet M^rs. Mure thought fit to puddle about & call'd here to late we were just going to Dinner. wrote to Miss Louisa Lee

Saturday Novr. 28th.

Still sharp frost & most exceedingly cold went to the Dancing School practising at mid.day, where as usual there were great numbers, here M^r. Witts joined me & accompanied me to call on Lady C: C: who had much to say to us, we Dined for a wonder alone the Boys Dining at Commissioner Browns & concluding the evening at the Broughams. rec'd a letter from M^rs. Witts.

Sunday Novr. 29th.

A damp & very disagreable Day, Frost apparently on its departure, & yet extremely cold, went to Morning Service at S^t. Georges, & to the evening at S^t. Andrews where M^r. Moodie was very great indeed on the pathetic subject of Dea^{th.} between services Lady Dukenfield, & Principal Gordon here.

Monday Novr. 30th.

A very disagreable Day, of wind rain & extremely damp. Mr. Witts little out, & I not at all, but full of many bussinesses & the Principal here in evening

Tuesday Decr. 1st.

No better weather, not quite so much rain but equally damp & stormy, all which persuaded me easily to remain at home the Principal dined here & Henry Brougham came to Tea. wrote to Mrs. Hyett.

Wensday Decr. 2^{d.}

Not much improvement in the weather being still damp & very windy & at times sharp showers Mr. Witts out good part of the Morning, & while I was deliberating Mrs. Brougham came & made me a long & to me very pleasant visit, which decided my staying at home. Mr. Carson drank Tea, after heard a final arrangement from Mrs. Davies. playd at Cribbage with the Boys rec'd a Letter from Mrs. Davies.

Thursday Decr. 3^{d.}

A dry & very cold wind, with some sun but tho not very pleasant, was good dry walking which tempted me to be out several hours in the Morning first to Lady Riddell, & from thence Mr. Witts with me, to make many visits in Georges Square & its vicinity, found only at home, poor Mrs. Craigie the first time of my seeing her, Miss Robinsons, & Miss Abercrombie visited Mrs. Brown on my return with whom I found a large & very grand circle, very low & poorly all the evening. rec'd a Letter from Miss Louisa Lee.

Friday Decr. 4th.

A similar dry Day to the former only more pleasant from not being such a high wind I made good use of it by being out from 11 to three, first to the Dancing School then a pleasant visit to L^{dy.} Dukenfield another to Lady C: C:, & afterwards paid six in the new Town finding only Mrs. Halkett Craigie at home; Tea & supper at Sir James Riddell no creature else. Francis at a Ball at Miss Paisleys.

Saturday Decr. 5th.

Quite a mild Day for the Season of the Year, but damp & therefore not pleasant & so dirty in the street I was not tempted to walk neither had I any visitors went to Cards & Supper at Mrs. Stewarts, a pleasant & smart party of 9 Ladies & 7 Gentlemen

Sunday Decr. 6th.

A particular unpleasant Day being close & foggy to so great a degree as almost to amount to small rain & cruelly dirty, Francis confined all Day w.th one of his bad Coughs, Mr. W. & George went to both services at St. Georges Chappell, where from Mr. Cleeves illness a disagreable stranger did the Duty. I went to St. Andrews in the Morning where Mr. Moodie was most excellent & to St. Georges in the evening

Monday Dec.ʳ 7th.

Rather a better Day the air being clearer but still close & uncomfortable, Francis yet too indifferent to be let out, Lady Riddell, Mʳˢ· General Campbell, & Miss MacFarlan my visitors I never went out but work'd hard & at night play'd at Cribbage. rec'd a Letter from Mʳˢ· Granville.

Tuesday Dec.ʳ 8th.

Very much the same weather, warm damp & therefore uncomfortable, went at Noon to see Lady C: C: to several shops & to see Mʳˢ· Brown, Tea Cards & Supper at Sir James Riddells, rather a large drawing room party tho not very lively sat down 13 to Supper. rec'd a Letter from Mʳˢ· Pennington.

Wensday Dec.ʳ 9th.

Still mild & damp & very warm tho so intirely without sunshine, but to me not pleasant I went out at Noon, first to Lady Riddells Levee where I met but a few having miss'd of those I most wanted to have seen, then to Mʳˢ· Major Sands where I paid a pleasant visit & afterwards 2 unsuccessful ones in St· Andrews Square. went to Tea & Cards at Lady Dukenfields an odd sort of a visit, meeting several of the Windsor Forresters & their Ladies, Mʳ· Brown & his Daughter Mary but the Military Gents chose to sit so long over their bottle we had little of their company. play'd at whist & Cassino.

Thursday Dec.ʳ 10th.

Something better Day the air being rather more clear in the early part of it with a little sun but the fog returning & having something of a cold I staid within & rec'd visits from Principal Gordon Mʳˢ· Halkett Craigie, & Mʳ· M. Riddell the Principal dined here & we had much back gammon. rec'd a Letter from Miss Anne Snow, & wrote to Mʳˢ· Davies.

Friday Dec.ʳ 11th.

A most sombre day in all respects the weather being so wet & bad there was neither going out nor seeing any body but the Principal in the evening when Back Gammon flourish'd abundantly as usual wrote to Mʳˢ· Witts Nibley House

Saturday Dec.ʳ 12th.

Not quite so thick & wet in the Morn. but after mid.day much more so being incessant hard rain, I continued to walk down to the Dancing Practising where there was a large Company but obliged to come home in a Coach. both Dined & Supt at Sʳ· James Riddells a grand entertainment & large party of 9 Gentlemen & 6 Ladies 3 Card Tables & staid till a late hour.

Sunday Dec.ʳ 13th.

Another very wet & wretched Day tho falling more in showers were able to huddle twice to church in the Morning I went to St· Andrews St· Georges in afternoon. Mʳ· J. Rose call'd between services.

Monday Dec.ʳ 14th.

Dry till after mid.day, tho still damp & gloomy, but very hard rain the remainder of the Day

& evening, this made me give up all thoughts of stirring out & saw no one but the Principal for a short time in the Morning. rec'd a Letter from Miss B: Guydickens

Tuesday Dec.ʳ 15ᵗʰ·

Still thick & foggy but not quite so damp & no rain, yet very moderate walking went early to see Frank dance, where I made a long stay w.ᵗʰ Lᵈʸ· D. afterwards visited Lᵈʸ· C: C: where I met others & ended by a long visit to Mʳˢ· Brown where as usual I met a pleasant circle. in John Street visited Mʳˢ· Phillips

Wensday Dec.ʳ 16ᵗʰ·

Such an uncommon mild yet dry fine Day as is seldom known so near Xmas; which made a string of visits very pleasant in the New Town, just made one at Lᵈʸ· Riddells Levee where I met several, afterwards made some more visits finding none at home but Mʳˢ· Campbell & Mʳˢ· Halkett Craigie. Mʳ· Witts breakfasted with Sʳ· Nathˡ· Dukenfield[32] to accompany him to the Barracks to visit Col. Rookes Miss Browns drank Tea with us & were very pleasant wrote to Mʳˢ· Savage.

Thursday Dec.ʳ 17ᵗʰ·

Very hard rain till after 12 when it ceased but continued dark damp & uncomfortable & quite confining the Principal Dined & spent the evening here, much back gammon. wrote to Miss Snow & rec'd a Letter from Mʳˢ· Buxton.

Friday Dec.ʳ 18ᵗʰ·

Dry tho gloomy in the Morning, but turn'd at Noon to violent & incessant rain, but being engaged to go with Lᵈʸ· Dukenfield both to the Barracks & to Innvereck her Carriage call'd for me at 11, made pleasant visits to each particularly so to Mʳˢ· Charteris as I had great delight in seeing her fine little Boy, the Principal here in the evening to Tea &'c.

Saturday Dec.ʳ 19ᵗʰ·

No change in the weather being again a dark & damp Morning & a most dreadful wet remaining part of the Day, w.ᶜʰ permitted us to have no callers but the Principal we all 4 went to Dinner at Sʳ· N. Dukenfields, meeting Mʳ· & Mʳˢ· Longden & a Captain Wilkinson & in the evening by the arrival of Beaus & Belles of various ages there was a smart little Dance of 9 Couple, which did not end till nearly Sunday Morn:

Sunday Dec.ʳ 20ᵗʰ·

Wet & very wet in the Morning, but as we were none of us disposed to rise very early that alone did not prevent our going to Morning Church, after which it became more clear & was a dry air, I visited Mʳˢ· Col: Dalrymple & then went to Sᵗ· Georges Chappel which was crowded. rec'd Letters from Mʳˢ· Parsons & my Sisʳ· Travell, answerd the latter & wrote to Mʳˢ· Tracy

---

32. Nathaniel Dukinfield (1746–1824), of Sulham, Berkshire, later of Standlake House, Berkshire. Dukinfield succeeded as 5th baronet on the death of his cousin, Samuel Dukinfield (1716–1768). He was a captain in the 7th dragoons, exchanging into the 32nd foot. He married, 27 February 1782, Katherine Warde (d. 1823) sister of John Warde of Squerries. He was closely acquainted with Charles Rooke and became a senior officer in the Windsor Forresters.

Monday Decr 21st.

All hope of any fair weather seem wholly at an end as it was a most wretched Day, at night quite pour'd & blew in perfect hurricane, saw no one in the Morning but the Principal for a few moments before Dinner; went to Cards & Supper at Mrs. Speirs's a mix'd set of 14 the Riddells came, not very gay or brilliant.

Tuesday Decr 22^{d.}

Rather a better Morning being tolerably dry being considerable wind tho still very mild, went to Lady C: C: some shops & Mrs. Browns, & at 8 o'clock went a P. Chaise to the Ball at the Barracks given by the Windsor Forresters a most gay pleasant meeting & most admirably conducted in all respects, the number assembled. some very gay but of course the company must be a mix'd one; Supper in fine small rooms, my set a very lively one returnd home at ½ past three. a most dreadful wet & windy evening both to go & return.

Wensday Decr 23^{d.}

In general a much better day being dry till quite night, the air clearer & more cold, not visible very early and soon after went to Lady Riddells Levee where I met many & staid a great while, afterwards made a pleasant visit to Mrs. Brougham; went to Cards & Supper at Mr. Robertson Scotts a party of 11 pleasant enough, whist & Cassino

Thursday Decr 24th.

Very wet early in the Morning, but did not continue tho it was a damp & very unpleasant Day wch gave me no temptation to go out & saw no one till the Principal came to Dinner, & staid late at night with back gammon & talk^{g.} wrote to Mrs. Granville

Friday Decr 25th.

Certainly fine for a Xmas Day being quite clear & dry with a little sun, & moderately cold were kept long at Morning Church, between services walk'd on Princes Street & visited Miss Melvilles & went again to St. Georges Chappel where a stranger assisted Mr. Cleeve as he did in the Morning.

Saturday Decr 26th.

Tolerably fine with a clear air in the Morning, but grew foggy & damp at afternoon on my first going out call'd for a few moments to speak to Mrs. Brougham, walk'd to St. Georges Square to visit Mrs. Douglass Cavers then to the Dancing School practising & from thence to L^{dy.} C: C: the Boys spent the even at L^{dy.} H: Blairs & the Principal did the same with us.

Rec'd 94 Letters
wrote 101 Letters

Witts Family Papers F191

1795

Sunday Decr. 27th.

Dry early in the Day, but a severe wind which increased at Noon quite to a Storm, accompanied by frequent showers & at night the wind was so very violent as to be quite alarming, & flew down chimney Pots &'c in abundance & one of ours among the numbers went with difficulty to Morning Service at St. Georges Chappel, from thence to Mr. Browns where we visited till time to go to evening Service at Mr. Sandfords chappel wrote at night to L^{dy.} Edwd. Bentinck & Mrs. Parsons

Monday Decr. 28th.

Somewhat calmer tho still windy, & dry tho cold, with some sunshine, but at night the wind was as violent as the last night, with hard rain & hail most dismal, got up literaly by candle light to get dress'd & breakfasted to accompany L^{dy.} Dukenfield at ½ past nine to the Court of Justiciary, to hear an interesting Trial that was expected to come on, but being put off were disappointed & was not half an hour in the Court, after which went into the Advocates Library till the Carriage came much entertained by the Sight of some fine Prints, on my return sat an hour with L^{dy.} Riddell visited some others but found only Mrs. Speirs at home

John Kay, a self-portrait.

Tuesday Decr. 29th.

Tempestuous Wind somewhat abated, but it still continued very stormy & much rain fell in the course of the Day which proved quite stay at home & sombre till we went to S^r. J: Riddells in the evening, where we met S^r. J: Colquhoun & Major Melville, very pleasant

Wensday Decr. 30th.

A much better Day being dry & clear w.^h some sunshine, & probably had been something of a frost went with Francis to the Dancing School, & from thence visited L^dy. Dukenfield & L^dy. C: C: both pleasant because friendly, went afterwards to some shops & home late, when we found a profusion of name Tickets,[1] the Boys went to a little Dance, at Sir James Grants.

Thursday Decr. 31st.

A most tremendous Day of wind & hard rain no possibility of stirring out & saw only the Principal for a few minutes in the Morning; of course a most sombre Day to conclude the old year wit^h.

1796

Friday Jan^y: 1st.

The new year set in a most tumultuous manner by severe storms of wind, & now & then rain & hail & towards afternoon became Snow, & a most dreadful night it proved of snow & rain Francis breakfasted with the young Dukenfields & went with them to see the Barracks, George & he both went wth us to Lady Riddells to Tea, where we met a stupid party of 9, made rather more lively by M^rs. Walter Riddell the Boys got a early supper. wrote to Miss Neville.

Saturday Jan: 2^d.

A more wretched Day than even any of the former being very hard rain in the Morning, severe snow at Noon & appearance of frost at night the Boys spent 3 hours in the forenoon with M^rs. Walter Riddell the only memorable event in the course of y^e. Day

Sunday Jan: 3^d.

Very hard rain in the Morning which with the help of thick air & fog so disipated the Snow that had fallen but left it most damp & disagreable, I did not go to Morning church my Gents did before I went to evening service at S^t. Andrews Church I call'd on M^rs. Walter Riddell, a stranger perform'd the service moderately, the Principal dined here & staid late & M^r. Henry & John Brougham drank Tea. wrote to M^rs. Buxton.

---

1. Name tickets were visiting cards. Visiting cards became an indispensable tool of etiquette, introduced into England from France in the eighteenth century. 'Visite Biletes', literally 'visiting tickets' began during the reign of Louis XIV as redundant playing cards with names written on them. The system developed with sophisticated rules governing their use. The essential convention was that one person would not expect to see another person in his or her own home (unless invited or introduced) without first leaving his or her visiting card for the person at his or her home. Upon leaving the card, he or she would not expect to be admitted at first, but might receive a card at his or her own home in response. This would serve as a signal that a personal visit and meeting at home would not be unwelcome. On the other hand, if no card was forthcoming, or if a card was sent in an envelope, a personal visit was thereby discouraged.

Monday Jan: 4th.

A pleasant day, being a dry air & some sunshine, at mid.day went with Mrs. Riddell in a Coach to the Dancing School to take her little Girl to be a Scholar, then visited Ldy. C: C: & afterwards Mrs. Brown. went to Tea & Supper at Miss MacFarlans a party of 11 very pleasant & good entertainment.

Tuesday Jan: 5th.

Another fine dry day only too windy for comfort, Lady Dukenfield concluded her breakfast here & we went to the Parliament House in the hope of being much amused by the trial, which being put off we were again disappointed, & I returnd home when Mrs. Riddell sat an hour here, Mr. W & I then went to make visits in Georges Square, finding Mrs. Macqueen, & Mrs. Craigie only at home a quiet pleasant evening at home

Wensday Jan: 6th.

A very uncommon fine Day for the time of year, being mild clear, & much sunshine. rec'd early visits from Mrs. Stewart, & Miss Dalrymples, & then to join a very large circle at Lady Riddells Levee, where every tongue was loud in the expectation of Compte D'Artois who arrived that Day at Noon,[2] & was seated in the Abbey quite incog afterwards made a visit or two & then went to Dine in a free way at Mr. Com: Browns no one there excepting their own family but Mrs. Mure & Miss Napier return'd home at an early hour.

Thursday Jan: 7th.

A thick gloomy Morning tho yet dry but early in the afternoon the fog became such & sent me home from a string of visits near home in a Chair went to Cards & <u>had</u> sandwiches at Mrs. Dalrymples a dull tiresome party of 10, & only one Card Table no fun

Friday Jan: 8th.

Another foggy day but no rain but a shower at Dinner time, went early to meet Francis at the Dancing School, then visited Ldy. Dukenfield & Ldy. C: C: ending as usual with Mrs. Brown. Mr. & Mrs. Walter Riddell, Principal Gordon, & Mr. Crichton drank Tea here & Mrs. Dalrymple her Son & 2 Daughters came in late from Moyes Lectures when there was a Whist Table.

Saturday Jan: 9th.

Again most wonderfuly fine & quite warm at mid.day went to call on Lady Sinclair just returnd home, & from thence to Madame Rosignolis practising in George Street where I staid till 4 o'clock when I brought home three young Dukenfields to Dinner, the Boys went with ours to a young party at Lady Hays, we went to Tea & Supper at Mr. Macdougalls a party of 14 very pleasant rec'd Ler. Miss Snow

---

2. Charles Philippe (1757–1836), comte d'Artois. Charles was the younger brother to reigning Kings Louis XVI and Louis XVIII, and an uncle of the uncrowned King Louis XVII. Charles escaped to Britain in 1792 where George III gave him a generous allowance. Charles lived in Edinburgh and London with his mistress Louise de Polastron. Charles supported his brother (later Louis XVIII) in exile and eventually succeeded him as Charles X. His rule of almost six years ended in the July Revolution of 1830 which resulted in his abdication and the election of Louis Philippe, Duke of Orléans, as King of the French. He reigned as King of France and of Navarre from 16 September 1824 until 2 August 1830.

Agnes Witts, née Travell
(1747–1825), by Joseph Wright of
Derby; painted at Bath *c.* 1776.

Edward Witts (1746–1816), by
George Romney, 1779.

Witts family group by John Hamilton Mortimer, *c.* 1769. From left to right: Richard Witts (1747-1815); Broome Witts (1744-1827); Edward Witts (1746-1816); Apphia Witts, afterwards Mrs Peach and later Baroness Lyttelton (1743-1840).

Above left: Ferdinando Tracy Travell (1740–1808), favourite brother to Agnes, but a relationship combined with sibling friction. Ferdinando was the father of Jane (1765–1797), who married first, William Naper (1749–1791), secondly Sir Henry Rycroft (*c.* 1771–1846); and Martha (1764–1839), who married first, John Buxton (1756–1790), secondly William Morgan Whalley (1772–1845).

Above right: Francis Travell (1728–1801), elder brother to Agnes. Little is known of 'Beau' Travell. Francis never married and lived between the family home in Swerford and Cheltenham. Although unmarried, Francis fathered two illegitimate sons with Elizabeth Hitchman; Francis Hitchman (1763–1790) and George Hitchman (1767–1808). Although this was shocking by the mores of the day it seems to have been accepted by the family and Agnes frequently referred to her nephew 'Frank'. It appears that Francis was not helpful to Agnes and Edward during their financial crisis, and when he died Agnes hints at the past problems in her diary entries.

The Rectory, Upper Slaughter, Gloucestershire *c.* 1820. The original part of the house dates from the seventeenth century. It was the home of Agnes's eldest son, Francis, from 1809 to 1854.

Above left: A miniature of Agnes's eldest son, Francis Edward Witts, by Charles Jagger, Cheltenham, 1808.

Above right: A miniature of Broome Philips Witts (1767–1845), by Thomas Hargreaves, *c.* 1809. Broome was first cousin once removed to Edward Witts. He was a wealthy silk merchant in London and was of much assistance to Edward when the family were abroad in Germany and also afterwards on their return to Britain. *Collection of Stephen Lloyd*

Francis Charteris, Lord Elcho (1749–1808), pastel by Archibald Skirving, Rome, 1790. Lord Elcho was the son of Francis, 7th Earl of Wemyss; and father of the 8th Earl of Wemyss and 4th Earl of March. He was the husband of Agnes's first cousin, Susan, née Tracy-Keck. *By kind permission of the Earl of Wemyss and March*

Francis Charteris, 8th Earl of Wemyss and 4th Earl of March (1772–1853), by Archibald Skirving; drawn in Rome, 1790. Francis was known to the family as 'Pear-face'. He was the son of Lord Elcho (1749–1808), and grandson of Francis, 7th Earl of Wemyss (1723–1808). He inherited Stanway in Gloucestershire from his aunt, Henrietta, Viscountess Hereford. Henrietta had inherited it from her Tracy forebears back in 1773. In 1813, Henrietta—who like her sister Susan—was close to Agnes Witts, gave the living of Stanway to Agnes's son, Francis. *By kind permission of the Earl of Wemyss and March*

Right: Comte d'Artois 1798, by Henri-Pierre Danloux (1753–1809). Charles Philippe (1757–1836) was King Charles X of France from 16 September 1824 until 2 August 1830. In 1792, Charles escaped to Great Britain, where King George III gave him a generous allowance. Charles lived in Edinburgh and London with his mistress Louise de Polastron. For most of his life he was known as comte d'Artois. He was uncle of the uncrowned King Louis XVII, and younger brother to reigning King Louis XVI (guillotined 21 January 1793, Place de la Concorde, Paris) and King Louis XVIII (d. 1824). He supported the latter in exile and eventually succeeded him. His rule of almost six years ended in the July Revolution of 1830, which resulted in his abdication. Exiled once again, Charles died in 1836 in Gorizia, then part of the Austrian Empire. He was the last of the French rulers from the senior branch of the House of Bourbon. *Palace of Versailles*

Above left: Marie Louise d'Esparbès de Lussan, by marriage vicomtesse then comtesse de Polastron (1764–1804). Marie Louise was a member of the Esparbès de Lussan family and the mistress of the comte d'Artois, who later reigned as Charles X of France.

Above right: Another portrait of Marie Louise, comtesse de Polastron. Her son, Louis de Polastron (1785–1804), lived with her in Edinburgh. On 1 May 1796 Agnes's sons Frank and George visited the young comte de Polastron. He came to the family for tea on 9 May, and on 15 May the boys dined with Madame Polastron and Louis.

Above left: A later portrait (*c.* 1804) of Richard Cumberland (1732–1811) attributed to Joseph Clover. The playwright was an acquaintance in the coffee house circle with Goldsmith and Garrick. He was well known to Johnson, Boswell and many others of great influence. He was an old friend of Agnes and Edward Witts and in later life he lived at Tunbridge Wells where the Wittses caught up with him 2 October 1805, and young Frank was introduced to him for the first time. *Tunbridge Wells Museum and Art Gallery*

Above right: Children of Elizabeth née Ridge and Richard Cumberland, by George Romney. Richard Cumberland was one of the best-known writers of the day and friend to leading painters, poets, and actors. Here, his daughters, Elizabeth and Sophia, read his latest play. *Portrait of Two Girls. Museum of Fine Arts, Boston*

Left: Lady Edward Bentinck, née Elizabeth Cumberland by George Romney. Elizabeth Bentinck, née Cumberland, was the daughter of Richard Cumberland the playwright. Edward and Agnes were good friends with Richard Cumberland and for some obscure domestic reasons effectively 'fostered' and brought up Elizabeth (*c.* 1761–1837), who married, 1782, Lord Edward Bentinck (1744–1819). Agnes and Elizabeth were very close and during the Edinburgh years more than 70 letters go back and forth, but then in July 1798 the letters suddenly stop, and no more is ever heard of Lady Elizabeth; what led to the cessation of correspondence remains a mystery. Clearly a serious breach occurred between the two. Agnes could be outspoken and it is quite likely that Agnes was the cause of the breach, possibly through comments in a letter to which Elizabeth took some offence.

Above left: John Sinclair (1754–1835), 1st Baronet of Ulbster and Thurso Castle, Caithness. John Sinclair was MP for Caithness, President of the Board of Agriculture 1793–98, 1806–14; Privy Councillor 1810; cashier of excise (Scotland) 1811–30. Colonel of the Rothesay and Caithness fencibles 1794; Lt-Col. and Commandant of the Caithness volunteers 1803. Lady Sinclair features extensively in Agnes Witts's diaries, being mentioned no less than 89 times, the last time just a day before the Witts family's departure for Germany. It seems likely that she was Diana Jane Elizabeth née Macdonald, daughter of Alexander, 1st Baron Macdonald. She married, 1788, John Sinclair as his second wife. *National Galleries of Scotland: Scottish National Gallery*

Above right: George Hay (1753–1804), 7th Marquess of Tweeddale, by Jean-Laurent Mosnier (1743–1808). Hay married, 1785, Hannah Charlotte, fourth daughter of James Maitland, 7th Earl of Lauderdale. Earlier in his life he was an officer in the naval service of the Honourable East India Company and was Lord Lieutenant of Haddington 1795–1804. In 1802 he and his wife went to France for the benefit of his health. They were detained by Napoleon and imprisoned at Verdun where they both died two years later. *Private Collection*

Right: Lieutenant-General John Campbell, 1st Marquess of Breadalbane (1762–1834), known as John Campbell until 1782 and as The Earl of Breadalbane and Holland between 1782 and 1831. He was a great-grandson of Colin Campbell of Mochaster, younger son of Sir Robert Campbell, 3rd Baronet, of Glenorchy, and uncle of John Campbell, 1st Earl of Breadalbane and Holland. Lord Breadalbane and Holland raised the Breadalbane Fencibles Regiment, in which he served as a lieutenant-colonel. See diary entry 14 July 1793. *Angelica Kauffmann*

Above left: Reverend Robert Walker (1755–1808) skating on Duddingston Loch c. 1800. Agnes and Edward Witts visited Henry Raeburn's studio, presumably to meet him, on 22 October 1794, and this may have been with a view of commissioning a painting. It is interesting that the studio exhibition Agnes attended on 27 April 1798 should feature paintings by Raeburn and Henri-Pierre Danloux. There is an on-going controversy relating to this famous painting, better known by its shorter title The Skating Minister. The official attribution is to Henry Raeburn but some experts believe it to be the work of Danloux. *National Galleries of Scotland; Scottish National Gallery*

Above right: Portrait de jeune homme en buste, by Henri-Pierre Danloux (1753–1809). Born in Paris, Danloux emigrated to London in 1792 to escape the French Revolution. There he was influenced by fashionable portrait painters Thomas Lawrence, John Hoppner and George Romney. In 1793, he exhibited at the Royal Academy which resulted in commissions from a number of British patrons. It is not known what brought him to Edinburgh for a short time, but the commissions to paint the Comte d'Artois, Admiral Duncan and Lord Adam Gordon may have been the reason. Danloux returned to Paris in 1801, presumably after the preliminary treaty signed at Paris on 9 October 1801.

Left: Adam Duncan, 1st Viscount Duncan (1731–1804) defeated the Dutch fleet off Camperdown (north of Haarlem) on 11 October 1797. This victory was considered one of the most significant actions in naval history. Battle scene action portrait by Henri-Pierre Danloux, 1798. *National Galleries of Scotland, Scottish National Portrait Gallery*

Above left: Lord Adam Gordon (*c.* 1726–1801), by Henri-Pierre Danloux. Gordon was MP for Aberdeenshire in 1754 and Lt-Col. of the 3rd Foot Guards in 1756. In 1767 he married Jean, Dowager Duchess of Atholl. He left Parliament in 1768, but returned again as MP for Kincardineshire in 1774. Unhappy with the terms of the Treaty of Paris after the American War of Independence and the fate of the Loyalists, he supported the new ministry of Pitt in 1783. He left Parliament in 1788. Gordon was appointed Commander-in-Chief, Scotland in 1789, promoted general in 1793, and made governor of Edinburgh Castle in 1796. He was replaced as Commander-in-Chief in 1798. *National Galleries of Scotland, Scottish National Portrait Gallery*

Above right: William Forbes of Callendar (1756–1823), by Henry Raeburn. Forbes was a prosperous coppersmith and landowner. He won a government contract to sheath ships' hulls in copper. With a large fortune he purchased the estates of Callendar and Linlithgow near Falkirk, which had been forfeited by the Jacobite Earl of Linlithgow after the 1715 Jacobite Rising.

Sir Brooke Boothby (1744–1824), 6th Baronet, by Joseph Wright of Derby, 1781. See the diary entry for 11 June 1793. Brooke Boothby was a linguist, translator, poet and landowner, based in Derbyshire. He was part of the intellectual and literary circle of Lichfield, which included Anna Seward and Erasmus Darwin. In 1766 he welcomed the philosopher Jean-Jacques Rousseau to Ashbourne circles. Agnes and Edward Witts were acquainted with Boothby through their friendship with the Granvilles of Calwich Abbey which was nearby. *Tate*

Isabella Cornelia Craigie Halkett (1768–1858), *c.* 1795 by Henry Raeburn. Isabella was daughter of Charles Craigie who himself was the son of Charles Halkett (1715–1774), a colonel in the Dutch service and Governor of Namur. Charles senior had married Anne, heiress of John Craigie Esq. of Dumbarnie one of the Lords of Justiciary in Scotland by Susan eldest daughter of Sir John Inglis baronet of Cramond and Lady Susan Hamilton his wife, daughter of the fourth Earl of Haddington. By the deeds of settlement her husband, Charles Halkett, and their successors were obliged to assume the name and arms of Craigie in addition to those of Halkett. Charles was a major in the Army and he later died in India. Isabella married Robert Blair, Lord Avonton. Miss Isabella Halkett was a favourite with Agnes Witts.

Henry Brougham, (1778–1868), a later portrait by Sir Thomas Lawrence. The Witts family were on very friendly terms with the Broughams, (at least, that is, with Mrs Brougham—Eleanora—and her three sons). Agnes remained a life-long friend to Eleanora. Francis was at school with James (1780–1833) and Peter; James was two years older than Francis, Peter a year or more younger. Peter died tragically in a ship-board fire off the coast of Brazil in 1800. Francis formed a friendship with Henry who later became Lord Chancellor. In later life Francis (a Tory) was optimistic about a clerical advancement when Henry (a Whig) was in government, but the fall of Lord Melbourne's administration in November 1834 finally put paid to that ambition.

Henry Erskine Johnston (1775–1845), in the title role of *Douglas* in the play by John Home. He made his début in Edinburgh in 1794 reciting Collins's 'Ode on the Passions', which impressed Stephen Kemble sufficiently to engage him to appear as an amateur in the part of Hamlet in the cian. His success was immediate and enthusiastic: he was extravagantly fêted, and dubbed the Scottish Roscius—the 'boy wonder'. Agnes saw him on 23 July 1794 in a benefit performance.

Sir Ralph Abercomby (1734–1801), by John Hoppner. General Abercromby was a distinguished soldier, fighting in the wars against Republican France and commanded the British forces that captured Trinidad and Tobago. Ambercromby was prominent in Edinburgh society and married, 1767, Mary Anne, née Menzies. Agnes met him on Saturday 11 October 1794: *we dined at Mr. Browns to eat another Haunch of Venison & met Lord Abercrombie...* National Portrait Gallery

Sir John and Lady Clerk of Penicuik by Henry Raeburn, 1792. John (d. 1798) married Rose Mary, daughter of Joseph Dacre Appleby of Kirklington, Cumberland. Agnes and Edward visited Penicuik on 16 May 1798, shortly after the death of Sir John. The new baronet—6th baronet—was eleven-year-old George Clerk (1787–1867). *National Gallery of Ireland, Dublin*

William Baillie, Lord Polkemmet (d. 1816), by Henry Raeburn. Lord Polkemmet, was the son of Thomas Baillie of Polkemmet and Isabel Walker. He married, first, 1768, Margaret Colquhoun (b. 1751), daughter of Sir James Colquhoun of Luss, 1st Baronet and Helen Gordon. He married, secondly, 1803, Janet Sinclair, daughter of George Sinclair. Janet was the sister of John Sinclair of Ulbster (1754–1835), 1st Baronet. The Witts family were on very friendly terms with Lord and Lady Polkemmet and dined with them frequently.

The Lord Justice Clerk, Robert MacQueen (1722–1799), by Henry Raeburn. In 1776 Macqueen became a judge and was created Lord Braxfield. He was said to be the best lawyer in Scotland, an expert in intricate legal questions arising out of the 1745 Rising. His later fame owes more to his reputation as a 'hanging judge'. Reactionary in politics and a hard drinker, he was notorious for uttering such memorable phrases as 'Hang a thief when he's young, and he'll no steal when he's auld'. Raeburn painted Braxfield when he was dying, and little more than a shadow of the man described in his prime as being like 'a formidable blacksmith'. The Witts family were on very friendly terms with Lord and Lady Braxfield.

Henry Mackenzie, by Henry Raeburn. Mackenzie was the author of *The Man of Feeling*, a sentimental novel published in 1771. In November 1833 Francis Witts returned to Edinburgh—the first time in 32 years. In George's Square he reminisced: 'Here resided in days of yore the Solicitor general, afterwards Lord President, Blair, the naval Hero, Duncan, whose splendid battle of Camperdown, in the early period of the wars with France and its revolutionized allies, earned him the well-deserved honours of the peerage. With the veteran Admiral I was well acquainted having been the playmate of his sons. Here too resided the acute, broad Scottish, and very learned Judge, Macqueen of Braxfield, near Lanark, Lord Chief Justice Clerk, with whom our family was in intimacy, and whom we visited at his country seat. Here too was the house of the talented author of the *Man of Feeling*, Mackenzie'. Agnes Witts was on friendly terms with Henry Mackenzie's daughter, and Agnes and Francis bumped into her on 9 May 1801 when Agnes and Francis were travelling south from Edinburgh to London and she was heading north.

'The Archers' by Henry Raeburn. Robert Ferguson of Raith (1770–1840) and his brother Ronald Craufurd Ferguson (1773–1841). Robert Ferguson was the eldest son of William Ferguson of Raith, Fife, and Jane Crauford, daughter of Ronald Craufurd of Restalrig, (sister to Margaret, countess of Dumfries). General Sir Ronald Craufurd Ferguson was his brother. He was educated at the High School in Edinburgh, 1777–1780. He was also privately tutored by John Playfair. He then studied Law at Edinburgh University. He qualified as an advocate in 1791. Robert and Ronald Ferguson became members of the Royal Company of Archers in 1792 and 1801 respectively. The two brothers are shown in a striking and complex arrangement of contrasts. Robert is lit from the left, while Ronald behind him is shown entirely in shadow, gazing out at the viewer while framed in the tautened bow of his brother. The Fergusons were a family of Fife landowners. And Edinburgh lawyers and it was one of the Ferguson family that attended Agnes and Edward on 2 June 1794. *National Gallery, London*

John Playfair (1748–1819) by Henry Raeburn. In 1785 John Playfair became joint professor of mathematics with Adam Ferguson in the University of Edinburgh, where each session he taught three courses, two of which focused on geometry and trigonometry. On 22 August 1793 Agnes recorded: 'Mr. Stormonth call'd here in the evening to go with Mr. Witts to visit Professor Playfair'. On the 27th Agnes wrote: 'Mr. Professor Playfair here for an hour pleased with his behaviour & manner tho his looks are not prejudiciary, he was very obliging in his attention to Francis's School knowledge'. They dined and 'drank tea' together on several occasions and on 21 June 1794 Agnes says: 'I was fully employd & very agreably in receiving a visit in the Morning from Mr. Professor Playfair always a treat'. *National Portrait Gallery, London*

Right: Vincenzo Labini (1735-1807). Labini was an Italian archbishop who served as Bishop of Malta from 1780 to 1807; he was also titular Archbishop of Rhodes from 3 March 1797. It appears that Agnes was anticipating the event when she met him with Erskine of Cambo on 8 February 1797. Through her great friendship with Principal Gordon, she was in contact with several high-ranking members of the Church of Rome.

Above left: Robert William Elliston (1774–1831), by George Henry Harlow. Elliston was an actor and later became a theatre manager. *The Mountaineers* was a play by George Coleman, first performed at the Haymarket Theatre, London, on 3 August 1793. Elliston played Octavian, and this was a famous part for him. In 1798 Elliston was still very much at the beginning of his theatrical career.

Above right: John Philip Kemble (1757-1823), by Sir William Beechey, *c.* 1798. John was the brother of Sarah Siddons. He was famous in his portrayal of Penruddock in Richard Cumberland's play *The Wheel of Fortune*. Agnes Witts saw him perform in this rôle on 21 July 1795.

Sarah Siddons (1755–1831), by William Hamilton as Isabella from *The Tragedy of Isabella* or *The Fatal Marriage*. She was the elder sister of John Philip Kemble, Charles Kemble, Stephen Kemble, Ann Hatton and Elizabeth Whitlock, and the aunt of Fanny Kemble. She was most famous for her portrayal of the Shakespearean character, Lady Macbeth, a character she made her own. Agnes Witts saw Sarah Siddons on numerous occasions, and particularly in the part of Isabelle on 23 May 1795. *University of Bristol Theatre Collection*

John Quick as Tony Allspice and John Fawcett as Dashall in *The Way to Get Married* by Thomas Morton. Samuel De Wilde, born and died in London, was a portrait painter and etcher of Dutch descent famous for his theatrical paintings. He was the leading painter of actors and actresses between 1770 and 1820.

Henry Moyes (1750–1807). Moyes was blind from the age of three from smallpox, but he became well educated and mixed with the greatest engineers and scientists of the day.
In 1766 he was befriended by Adam Smith, when the latter was in Kirkcaldy writing his *Wealth of Nations*. The boy showed precocious aptitude and, as well as teaching Moyes himself, Smith secured the patronage of David Hume and Thomas Reid in the young man's education. During 1784–86, Moyes toured the United States giving successful lectures in Boston, Philadelphia, Baltimore, Princeton and Charleston.

Sunday Jan: 10th

A tolerable fine Day being dry & mild tho a foggy air went to both services at St Georges Chappel between visited Lady Hay; the Principal came to us late in the evening for a large portion of conversation.

Monday Jan: 11th

A better Day tho the sit still thick but it was not so damp, went at 11 to the Dancing School where Lady Riddell join'd me to go on various peregrinations into the Cannongate & Georges Square those we found at home were Miss Grant, Miss Scotts, Mrs Duncan & Mrs Carre & Miss Robinsons, brought home by Mrs Belsches in her Coach went to Tea at Mr Riddells meeting St James & my Lady, the Principal & Mrs Allen but for singing it would have been a dull bussiness.

Tuesday Jan: 12th

A very wet & stormy Morning but at Noon clear'd off & became a windy bright day, sufficiently so to encourage me to go out went first to Mrs Browns where on the arrival of the Misses from Dalkeith Ball a sad confusion took place relative to the clashing of our intended Dance & the Charity Ball in Georges Square. walk'd down to Ldy Dukenfield in consequence & tired to death all evening writing Cards of alteration.[3]

---

3. It appears that Agnes had sent invitations to a ball she was putting on, partially explaining the dancing lessons for Francis. She discovered that her proposed event clashed with a charity ball and postponed it to the 20th.

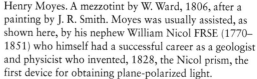

Henry Moyes. A mezzotint by W. Ward, 1806, after a painting by J. R. Smith. Moyes was usually assisted, as shown here, by his nephew William Nicol FRSE (1770–1851) who himself had a successful career as a geologist and physicist who invented, 1828, the Nicol prism, the first device for obtaining plane-polarized light.

Wensday Jan: 13ᵗʰ·

A mild but rather foggy Morning, but quite dry till one o'clock when it began raining & continued without interruption accompanied by violent wind we went early with Miss Sinclair & Col: Fullerton to the Court of Session to hear a cause he was much interested in, were there a very short time as it was only just open'd, walk'd back with Miss Sinclair & made several visits in George Street, finding Mʳˢ· Bruce, Mʳˢ· Mure, & Mʳˢ· Speirs at home, & concluding at Lady Riddells whose Levee was large & I staid long Mʳˢ· Riddell call'd on me before Dinner, came again to Tea & attend us to Moyes Lecture which on this Night was on Botany, I was rather disappointed in all points, a very large company, miserable walking both there & back tho such a step Mʳˢ· R. staid late

Thursday Jan: 14ᵗʰ·

Wet in the Morning, but became fair at Noon, & most extremely windy, even to a hurricane at Night; Mʳˢ· Bruce & Miss Bruce call'd on one & took me with them to visit Lady Rothes which was very pleasant we went afterwards to some Milliners shops on the Bridge. very busy in the evening making a fire screen.

Friday Jan: 15ᵗʰ·

Dry & mild but very windy during the course of the Day, & extremely wet at night, went into the Court of Session at 11 o'clock with Mʳˢ· Riddell Miss Sinclair & Col: Fullerton, where we continued 2 or 3 hours, being well entertain'd by Erskine & other pleaders, went afterwards to some shops & to visit Mʳˢ· Brown to Tea & Supper at Sir James Riddells, meeting Sʳ· James & Col: Colquhoun very merry after Supper

Saturday Jan: 16ᵗʰ·

Very wet in the Morning & tho it ceased to rain before Noon was damp & very uncomfortable all Day, Margret Brown made an early call here I call'd on Mʳˢ· Riddell & went together to Stranges dancing Practising where was a great crowd not much amused. the Boys drank Tea at Mʳ· Broughams. wrote to Mʳˢ· Pennington

Sunday Jan: 17ᵗʰ·

Most uncommonly mild, & tho rather damp was a very fine Day, but towards Night became very windy, went to both services at Sᵗ· Georges Chappel between visited Mʳˢ· Brown, Mʳˢ· Baillie of Polkemmet & Lady Sinclair happy & pleasant evening with the Boys

Monday Jan: 18ᵗʰ·

Fine in the Morning tho very windy, but at mid.day became showery, & so remain'd all Day, went out early to some shops, join'd Francis at the Dancing School, afterwards visited Lady Dukenfield Lady Grant, Mʳˢ· Fyffe, not one at home, most sure of Lᵈʸ· C: C: at all times came home quite blown away & then visited Mʳˢ· Hay went at 8 o'clock to Lady Riddells where we join'd a very large party, previous to going to the Queens Assembly at which was 850 persons collected & poor Compte D'Artois among the number, such very great heat & crowd took off much of the amusement at home between one & two.

Tuesday Jan: 19ᵗʰ·

A dry mild pleasant Day without sun call'd first on Lady Riddell on <u>some</u> <u>bussiness</u>, then visited Mʳˢ· Macdowall, Mʳˢ· Oliphant, Mʳˢ· Sands, Mʳˢ· Davies just come to Town, & Mʳˢ· Dalrymple, all at home, Miss Sinclair call'd on me before Dinner, a home evening full of employment.

Wensday Jan: 20ᵗʰ·

A dry & fine Day with much sunshine & great wind, quite a tempest at night I never went out being fully employ'd in preparations for our grand Ball which commenced at 8 o'clock, with Tea, the company consisted of 22 Ladies & 24 Gentlemen including our 4 noble selves, a most excellent party, 7 of the officers of the Windsor Foresters & 3 of their Ladies, tho the company was so large there was no crowd, the Music was excellent by the adITion of Mʳ· Sharp, much excellent dancing, plenty of Nequs[4] & friends, sandwiches &'c & 3 Card Tables the House not cleard till past two every one seem'd so much pleased that we could not fail at having pleased likewise; to have our endeavors so well approved

Thursday Jan: 21ˢᵗ·

Dry but very windy, went out at Noon to make some visits, those I found at home were Lady Rothes, Mʳˢ· Brown, & Mʳˢ· Hugh Robinson where there was a large circle, at 3 went to Madame Rosignolis to see Frank learn Cotilions not at home till past 4, so tired with the labors of the former evening I went to Bed at nine

---

4.   Nequs — Negus is the name of a drink made of port, mixed with hot water, spiced and sugared—similar to mulled wine.

Friday Jan: 22^d.

The finest Day ever seen at this time of Year being mild, no wind & much sunshine, so warm I sat with the window open & had scarce any fire, I declined going out expecting many complimentary visits[5] which took place 16 people calling at different times in the Morning, rec'd Letters from Miss Anne Snow & M^rs. Buxton, answerd hers directly being on so interesting a subject.

Saturday Jan: 23^d.

A dark Morning with a good deal of wind at Noon turn'd to rain; & such tempestuous wind it was quite alarming & at night blew so great a hurricane every creature was fearful of stirring out of their houses we went early with M^r. Carlan to introduce him to M^rs. Davies, she & Miss A. Baillie accompanied me to Madame Rosignolis practising, where I staid till past 4, & came home in a Chair with much sick of being blown over, the Principal Dined with us, & our Boys dined at Sir N. Dukenfields & had miserable coming home as he had going home rec'd a Letter from my Sister Travell.

Sunday Jan: 24th.

A wet & very boisterous Morning, dry & more calm at Noon & afternoon but very tempestuous again at night. I did not venture to Church in the Morning but went to S^t. Georges in the afternoon wrote to Miss Anne Snow.

Monday Jan: 25th.

After a most dreadful night of high wind, the Morning apeard very little better, the storm continuing almost as great as in the night accompanied by very frequent storms of rain & the air much colder my only visitors were Capt^ns. White & Bruce & M^rs. Trotter, went to Tea & supper with Lady Riddell, where was only Miss Bruce & M^r. M. Riddell, many many Rubbers at Cribbage

Tuesday Jan: 26th.

Dry early in the Morning, but soon became wet, & most disagreably stormy, so as quite to prevent my walking out, M^rs. Speirs & her Daughter & Principal Gordon our only visitors & the latter we detain'd to Dinner M^r. Witts & I went to drink Tea & Sup, quite in a friendly way with M^rs. Oliphant no one there but old M^rs. Macdowall, much whist playing very chearful & pleasant

Wensday Jan: 27th.

If possible a still worse day, the showers being more severe & the Wind more tempestuous so much so as to oblige me to go in a Chair to Lady Riddells Levee, where I met as usual a large & pleasant party. it growing less stormy I made some visits before I returnd home, went to the Play with Lady Riddell in her Box, Cumberlands last new Play of First Love in which M^rs.

---

5.   Ceremonial calls were part of the visiting, and visiting card etiquette. Ceremonial visits were made the day after a ball or within a day or two after a dinner party, and within a week of a small party. For this purpose it sufficed to simply leave a card.

Twiselton[6] had a principal part but her performance did little justice to the character, I was much pleased with the piece in general & it was well acted. Mr. Witts again spent the evening at Mrs. Oliphants.

Thursday Jan: 28th.

A happy change in the weather, being a universal clear fine Day, with constant sunshine. Mr. Baillie call'd early in his Coach to convey Mr. Witts & Principal Gordon, to Compte D'Artois Levee I went in the Coach also & visited Lady Dukenfield & Lady C: C: & He brought me back & left me at Mrs. Browns where I sat an hour then join'd Mr. Witts & we visited the Wilkinson family, Mrs. Baillie & Miss Sinclair. declined an evening engagement for the sake of enjoying the Boys at home. rec'd a letter fm. Miss Snow

Friday Jan: 29th.

A damp foggy Morning, which soon terminated in hard rain for some hours, I went early to Lady Riddells to settle some important points & sat a chearful hour or two with her & her pleasant Nephew the Col:, & afterwards another with Mrs. Brougham. we all 4 dined most pleasantly with Mrs. Davies, her own family the party, & her Son Warburtons birth Day the cause; all the full grown gentry went to the Play, a thin House, & the Wheel of Fortune wretchedly perform'd. Mrs. Twiselton a sad actress.

Saturday Jan: 30th.

Dry tho gloomy in the Morning but became very wet as usual at Noon; Mr. Witts out all Morning assisting Col: Riddell to see <u>sights</u>, I visited Lady Hunter Blair, Lady Betty Cunningham, Mrs. General Campbel & Mr. Riddell, all at home but the latter. we dined at Lady Riddells meeting Miss Macartney & Sir James Colquhoun, & in the evening to Cards & a cold supper came Mr. & Mrs. Baillie & 2 Miss Baillies, Mrs. & Miss Dalrymple, Col: Colquhoun & Mr. M. Riddell. staid late

Sunday Jan: 31st.

A dry & tolerably fine Day, cold clear air & some sunshine, went to both services at St. Georges Chappell between visited Lady Dumfries & Miss Crawford the latter only at home, much writing in the evening. wrote to my Sister Travell.

---

6. Charlotte Ann Frances Twisleton, née Wattell (±1770–1812). Charlotte was the daughter of John Wattell and niece of Sir John Stonehouse. She met Thomas James Twisleton (1770–1824), second son of Lord Saye and Sele when she was 18 and he 19, and a student at Westminster School; their mutual interest in amateur theatricals bringing them together. The young couple eloped to Scotland and married there 28 September 1788. They had no surviving children and eventually divorced. Francis Witts in later life became very friendly with the son of Thomas, Frederick Benjamin Twisleton (1799–1887), Rector of Broadwell and Adlestrop. In 1847 Frederick Benjamin succeeded as 16th Lord Saye & Sele. In the diary entry for 22 February 1848 Francis Witts he tells the family story: . . . *His father, Dr. Twisleton, Archd. of Ceylon, and a younger Brother of the Lord S. and S. of that day, was a very gay and dissipated young man. Even when a pupil at Westminster School he devoted himself to private theatricals, and at a very early age became entangled with a Miss Wattell a Stage heroine, as young and giddy as himself. Her he married, and poverty, dissention, and separation were the result of the ill conditioned union. She bare him no live child, and on their being parted, she went on the stage as a means of support, he prosecuting his studies at Oxford. At Edinburgh, as an actress, she became the mistress of one Stein, a merchant, who kept her until she had borne him a Son, and eventually separated from her. This connection enabled Mr. Twisleton to obtain a divorce; after which he married a Miss Ashe, the mother of the present Lord and his two brothers.*

Monday Feb: 1st.

Damp & foggy in the Morning, rather showery at Noon but became tolerably fine afterwards, Mr. Witts spent 7 hours at the Trial of the O'Neils I went to meet Francis at the Dancing School, afterwards made long visits to my invalid Friends Ldy. C: C: Ldy. Dukenfield, & Mrs. Brown; went in the evening to the new establish'd Card Assembly in George Street with Mrs. Baillie & Mrs. Davies a very pleasant meeting tho a great crowd home soon after twelve.

Tuesday Feb: 2d.

Much such another Morning, but terminated far worse, being wet at noon & very wet at night, Mr. Witts out most of the Morning with Col: Riddell He, Mr. Baillie, Sr. N. Dukenfield & Mr. Crauford Bevell were my only visitors, & just before it began raining I went to call on Miss Macartney & Mrs. Halkett Craigie both of whom I found at home obliged to come home in a Chair. after Tea went with Col: Riddell in a Hackney Coach to join Ldy. Riddell & another Ldy. at the Circus, better pleased in all respects than I by any means expected Horsemanship excellent & Pantomine very tolerable went home to a very chatty supper with her Ladyship & the Col: rec'd a Letter fm. Mrs. Granville

Wensday Feb: 3d.

A very wet disagreable Morning & indeed remain'd so till very late in the Day when it cleared up, it effectively prevented my stirring out even to Lady Riddells Levee, Mr. Witts there & he afterwards went w.h Mr. Baillie visiting to the Barracks, we both dined at Mr. Baillies, no stranger Lady but myself but several Gentlemen, play'd at Cassino & staid supper very pleasant

Thursday Feb: 4th.

Having been something of a Frost in the night, it was a universal bright fine Day, constant sun but very cold air, Went at 11 with Ldy. Riddell & her Col: in her Coach first to see the glass works at Leith, then kept on the Musselburgh road till the turn to the Barracks, where we made unsuccessful visits to all the Ladies there. the same to Ldy. Grant & a long one to Lady Dukenfield, from where we drove to Georges Square, where we made many more finding only Mrs. Douglass at home, did not return home till 4 well tired. went to Cards & Supper at Mrs. Fyffes an unconnected party of 15 but not unpleasant much whist & a very excellent Supper. rec'd a Letter from Mrs. Tracy.

Friday Feb: 5th.

Wet & comfortless early in the Day, & cold & very stormy the remainder I kept within all the Morning & had no interruption, but a visit from Lady Rothes who call'd in the evening in her Coach to take me to Lady Riddells where there was a smart pleasant party of 14 3 Card Tables & a cold supper. brought home again by Lady Rothes.

Saturday Feb: 6th.

Tolerably fine in the Morning, but became very showery at Noon spent the greater part of the Morning at Madame Rosignolis practising where there were great crowds sat wholly with Mrs. Brougham spent the evening quietly & comfortably at home.

Sunday Feb: 7th.

A very disagreable Day, being wet and stormy, & very cold, went to Morning service at St. Georges & evening at St. Andrews where Mr. Moodie was peculiarly edifying, between services made a long visit to Mrs. Brown & a short call on Lady Riddell Principal Gordon dined here & our near Neighbor Mrs. Hay drank Tea.

Monday Feb: 8th.

Wet early in the Morning, but clearing off I ventured down to the Dancing School early but was disappointed in meeting Francis, but visited Lady C: C: & did a good deal of bussiness at several shops, & ended by a long private visit to Lady Riddell, with whom I went to the Card Assembly at night, & a very pleasant party besides, it was full but not too full & very agreable play'd both at Whist & Cassino.

Tuesday Feb: 9th.

Wet & extremely wet the greater part of the Day & night, & very cold with frequent flights of hail & sleet & prodigious high wind, I had little inclination & less leisure to go out being very busy preparing for a grand rout I was to have in the evening, at which were collected 28 Ladies & 22 Gentlemen, mostly very smartly dress'd so the shew was splendid, 6 Card Tables in the Drawing Room, & a large round one in the Study everything went off well, & all seem'd to approve.

Wensday Feb: 10th.

Having been a frost in the night it was a dry cold day, but very pleasant being constant sunshine, Miss Browns call'd on me, to go to Lady Riddells where as usual we found a large circle, went from thence to make my first visit to Lady Forbes, very pleasant reception, made several other calls, finding only Lady Hunter Blair & Mrs. Brown at home. went to Cards & Supper at Lady Sinclairs a very genteel pleasant party of 8 Ladies & 11 Gentlemen not at home till a very late hour.

Thursday Feb: 11th.

Quite a disagreable Morning, being thick rain & fog for the general part, & at noon a smart shower of Snow which melted as it fell, but late I braved it all, & went to Lady C: C: having some pleasing things to tell her there I met Mrs. Charteris, on my return home attended Francis both at his French & Dancing class, at the latter much pleased by a well danced Cotillion went with the Boys to the Circus, & joind Lady Dukenfield & the Rookes party which was very numerous being all their children. much pleased with the Poney Race.

Friday Feb: 12th.

Wet early in the Morning, at Noon it came only in severe showers attended by most violent wind & at intervals sunshine & extreme dark clouds I never went out & Mr. Witts but little my guests Miss M. Oliphant, Mrs. Fullarton Miss Mackay & Miss Sinclair the Principal call'd in the evening before we went to Cards & Supper at Mrs. Dalrymples, rather a better party then hers usualy are 13 in number & a good supper very successful at Whist wrote to Miss L. Lee

Saturday Feb: 13[th.]

A cold stormy Day but tolerably dry having been something of a frost, M[rs.] Riddell call'd upon me before I could get out, when I only made a visit to the Baillies & then went to Stranges dancing practising where I join'd M[rs.] Dewar & was amused went to Cards & supper at M[rs.] Oliphants a droll hetrogeneous party of 15, several young people an attempt at reel dancing, very great luck at Whist rec'd a most melancholy Letter from M[r.] Burslem.

Sunday Feb: 14[th.]

A dry & therefore tolerably good Day, tho very cold, Francis accompanied me to M[r.] Sandfords chappel where I sat in M[rs.] Grants Seat between services visited M[rs.] Speirs, & M[rs.] Davies the latter not at home went to evening service at S[t.] Georges, evening spent as were proper at home with our Boys.

Monday Feb: 15[th.]

A dry & bright pleasant Morning but soon after mid.day became wet & very wet, I went early to meet Francis at the Dancing School then made visits to L[dy.] Dukenfield, Lady C: C: & M[rs.] Fyffe the latter not to be seen, did some shop bussiness & on my way home visited M[rs.] Brown, M[rs.] Riddell, & M[rs.] Brougham went to the Card Assembly with M[rs.] General Douglass Miss Douglass a most astonishing crowd far too much so to be quite pleasant.

Tuesday Feb: 16[th.]

Quite an unpleasant Day being a wetting fog or thick small rain the greater part of it, which took from me all idea of stirring out, my only guest in the Morning M[rs.] Brougham. M[r.] Witts dined wth M[r.] Grant of Kilgraston,[7] & the Principal drank Tea & spent the evening with me & the Boys. rec'd a Letter from Miss Anne Snow, & Miss Louisa Lee

Wensday Feb: 17[th.]

A very pleasant change in the weather being a clear dry air with much sun & some wind which made it fine dry walking. I first visited L[dy.] H. Blair & M[rs.] General Douglass both of whom I found at home then spent an hour in a large circle at Lady Riddells from whence I made several other visits finding only M[rs.] Baillie & M[rs.] Baillie of Polkemmet at home.[8] Miss Leslie Baillie drank Tea with us en famile. wrote to Miss Gorges.

Thursday Feb: 18[th.]

Not a very good day the air being thick & at times very moist, which made it very unpleasant walking, yet still I was obliged to go to some shops & ended my peregrinations by spending an hour at the Dancing School seeing many cottilions. went to Cards & Supper at Sir N.

---

7.   Francis Grant of Kilgraston (d. 1819). Francis was the second, but first surviving son of Patrick Grant (1708–1783), and Beatrix (1710–1780), daughter of Donald Grant of Inverlochy. He married Anne née Oliphant, daughter of Robert Oliphant of Rossie, Postmaster-General of Scotland. The family seat was Kilgraston House, Bridge of Earn, Perthshire.

8.   William Baillie (d. 1816), Lord Polkemmet, was the son of Thomas Baillie of Polkemmet and Isabel Walker. He married, first, 1768, Margaret Colquhoun (b. 1751), daughter of Sir James Colquhoun of Luss, 1st Baronet and Helen Gordon. He married, secondly, 1803, Janet Sinclair, daughter of George Sinclair. Janet was the sister of John Sinclair of Ulbster (1754–1835), 1st baronet.

Dukenfields a good party of 18 but still it was not lively yet we were not at home till between 1 & 2. wrote to M^rs. Granville

Friday Feb: 19th.
Quite a sad day of wind & rain from Morn to night no stirring out for me & my only visitor M^rs. Browning, the Principal came late in the evening to talk & backgammon. wrote to Miss B: Guydickens.

Saturday Feb: 20th.
A very tolerable day, dry with a mild air, I went to call on Lady Riddell to carry her to the Dancing School practising, where I eat sandwiches, spent 4 hours or near it among the gay young crew & with several friends; went to Cards & Supper at Lady Rothes a large party of 24 a great crowd in their House a cold supper to which 2 sets sat down rec'd a Letter f^m. Sis^r Travell

Sunday Feb: 21st.
Another mild & very pleasant Day went to S^t. Georges Chappel in the Morning & to evening service at Mr Sandfords who perform'd admirably, between made an unsuccessful visit to Lady Mary Murray & a long one to M^rs. Brown. Henry Brougham drank Tea here.

Monday Feb: 22^d.
Dry & rather pleasant, tho an easterly wind & the air thick went out at Noon & Mr Witts with me on a string of visits in the new Town, those we found at home, were M^rs. Campbell & Miss Graham Miss B: Mure, M^rs. Wilkinson, M^rs. Robinson Scott afterwards went to some shops on the Bridges. went to the Card Assembly in Lady Riddells party not quite so full as the Monday before but pleasant play'd a great deal at Whist. rec'd a Letter f^m. M^rs. Erskine

Tuesday Feb: 23^d.
A cold & rather comfortless Day, being a thick fog & strong east wind, yet I was out a good deal, visiting, first Lady Sinclair then M^rs. Brougham from thence to see the invalid Browns to some shops & ended by seeing Francis at the Cottilion. Tea Cards & Supper at Miss Bruces, a good party of 12.

Wensday Feb: 24th.
A very fine clear Day having been something of a frost which made it perfectly dry with much sun, Lady Dukenfield call'd early & we went together to Lady Riddells, where we found as usual a circle afterwards made several calls, finding only M^rs. Brown & Lady C: C: visible there we parted & I visited my way home, meeting only M^rs. Belsches at home who was very pleasant. went to the Windsor Foresters Play in L^dy. Riddells Box the Rivals & the spoil'd child, the House very full & wonderful good performance for this Theatre.

Thursday Feb: 25th.
Another most delightful clear fine Day, much sun & no wind, went out at 11 to attend Francis at the Dancing School, from thence went to Georges Square, where made many visits, those I

found at home were M^rs. Hamilton, M^rs. Craigie, & Miss Abercromby on my return again went to the Dancing School to see the Cottilion went to an early Tea at M^rs. Wilkinsons, meeting only M^r. Winthrop, an English student. at 8 went to a party at Lady Riddells of 16 very lively & pleasant several young people & Officers rec'd a Letter from Miss Snow.

Friday Feb: 26th.

A cold foggy Day but dry in general, I staid at home all Morning receiving visits at seperate times from Lady Hunter Blair, Lady Riddell, M^rs. Brougham & M^rs. Baillie, being my beloved Francis's birth day, he had three or 4 young friends to spend the evening with him after we had made Tea for them we went to Cards & Supper at M^rs. Macdowalls, a large party of 11 Gents & 7 Ladies very lively & pleasant. wrote to Sis^r. Travell

Saturday Feb: 27th.

Still colder & more unpleasant tho dry till quite <u>night, being</u> a strong easterly wind, went out at Noon on a train of visits, made but six finding all at home, went at ½ past 5 in Lady H: Blairs Chariot carrying two Misses with me, to Lady Dukenfields to a charming young Ball of 54 young people a nice & proper supper at an early hour & excellently well conducted in all points between 9 & 10 I join'd a large supper party at Captn. Browns 16 Ladies & 13 Gents 5 Cards Tables & an elegant supper not at home till very late.

Sunday Feb: 28th.

Much such another day, monstrously cold but dry, went to Morning service at S^t. Georges between both call'd on the Oliphants, had much interesting conversation with them & went a short airing with them on Leith road before we all went together to S^t. Andrews Church an excellent discourse from M^r. Moodie[9]

Monday Feb: 29th.

Showers of rain & sleet in the Morning but bright & fine the rest of the Day but very cold went at one o'clock with Lady H: Blair in her Chariot to make an unsuccessful call on Lady Dukenfield & another on Mrs Lockhart, made a long visit to the Browns & met many & on my way home call'd on Lady Rothes went to Tea & Supper quite en famille with M^rs. Oliphant meeting only M^r. M. Riddell much whist & conversation.

Tuesday March 1st.

A very similar day only the storms were slighter till quite evening when it became cruel rain went at 11 to meet Frank at the Dancing school from thence made a very long visit to L^dy. C:

---

9.   William Moodie (1759–1812). Moodie was a Scottish Minister, Moderator of the General Assembly of the Church of Scotland, philologist, and Professor of Hebrew (and Oriental Languages) at Edinburgh University. In 1787, he was asked by the Town Edinburgh to be Minister of St Andrew's Church in the fashionable New Town and he took up post on 25 October 1787. Six years later (1793) the post of Professor of Hebrew and Oriental Languages was added to his duties at the University, which he held in conjunction with his position at St Andrew's Church until he died. Several diary entries by Agnes refer to 'Mr L. Moodie', and it appears that this is a brother or a cousin to William. This assumption is more or less verified by Agnes's entry for 7 December 1794: '*much gratified by hearing excellent discourses from the two Mr. Moodie.*'

St Ninian's Row, between Leith Street and
Princes Street. An engraving by W. Forrest from
a painting by Daniel Wilson.

C: where M^r· Witts join'd me & we walk'd home over Calton Hill, view clear & delightful quite a home evening a great but very pleasant rarity.

Wensday March 2^d·

Dry but cold & unpleasant being a strong east wind consequently very thick atmosphere, went out at noon first visited Miss Sinclair then M^rs· Loch for the first time, afterwards attended L^dy· Riddells Levee for an hour then call'd on Lady Forbes, M^rs· Stewart & M^rs· Baillie, finding all the whole Clain[10] at home, & before Dinner, went into the old Town on bussiness, went to Tea & Supper at S^r· James Riddells quite en famile meeting M^r· Campbell, Major Melville & M^r· M. Riddell very ill success at Cribbage

Thursday March 3^d·

Frost & had been a fall of snow in the night which the thaw aided to melt away fast which made it intolerable bad morning, so I quietly staid at home the whole Day without seeing anyone Morn: or evening wrote to M^rs· Burslem a painful Letter[11]

Friday March 4th·

Quite a sharp frost but a clear fine Day being little wind & much sun, walk'd in the streets for exercise for an hour or two came home at noon to meet M^r· Sandford who staid two or three hours talking on interesting subjects to him, went in the evening to a stupid large party at M^rs· Speirs a terrible large proportion of females.

---

10. This is very difficult to read and may not be correct.
11. William Burslem (1746–1820). William Burslem was born at Market Drayton and educated at St John's College, Cambridge; Rector of Ightfield, Shropshire, 1774–1820. Rector of Hanbury, Worcestershire, 1780–1820. Married firstly, 1785, Ann Harvey (d. 1796) of Marston-upon-Dove, Derbyshire; secondly, 1798, a daughter of Rawson Aislabie. By his first marriage he had one son, William Justice Burslem (1787–1826). William Burslem was a close friend of Edward and Agnes Witts. He also performed the wedding ceremony for Francis Witts and Margaret Backhouse at Bath on 30 May 1808. This letter was in reply to William's letter to Agnes which she received on 13 February. The letters related to the death of Ann Burslem who was buried at Hanbury in 1796 and for whom there is a monument in the church.

Saturday March 5th.

Still frost & hard but in the early part of the Day much sun which made it pleasant, spent the greater part of the Morn: at the Dancing school practising where Frank made a grand exhibition went to Mrs. Stewarts to Cards & Supper an imense party of 16 Gentlemen & 14 Ladies much card playing, staid till a very late hour

Sunday March 6th.

Sharp frost but fine & pleasant being much sun went to St. Georges Chappel to both services between visited Mrs. Macdougall & Mrs. Brown Mrs. Davies & Miss A: Baillie drank Tea here quite in a friendly pleasant way & staid till 10 o'clock

Monday March 7th.

No change of weather, but cold & very disagreable, the air being thick & a strong propensity of flitting snow, went early to the Dancing School, from thence to Lady C: C:, afterwards to make some visits in & about Georges Square found no one at home but Miss Gordon with Lady H: Dalrymple, ended at the Browns. Mr. Witts dined at St. James Colquhouns a Gentleman party, I went to the Card Assembly with Mrs. Davies & Miss Graham pleasant enough play'd a great deal at Cassino.

Tuesday March 8th.

Weather still more unpleasant being a raw kind of cold & rather damp from frequent small flights of Snow, I never stirr'd from the fireside nor saw anyone. wrote to Miss Snow.

Wensday March 9th.

Disagreably cold & windy tho dry in the Daytime with thick easterly wind, at night snow & rain, went a string of visits besides Lady Riddells Levee those I found at home were Miss Mures & Miss Dalrymple went at night to a very splendid Ball at Mrs. Baillies where more than a 100 of the smart & gay were got together a prodigious handsome supper, & all in the old stile, not at home till near 4 in the Morning.

Thursday March 10th.

Quite a bitter cold Day, a dry east wind & a great deal of it, bustled hard to get in time to St. Andrews Church being Fast Day where we heard a most excellent Sermon from Mr. Moodie well suited to the occasion, made an unsuccessful visit to Mrs. Lockhart between services, heard a very fine Sermon from Mr. Sandford in the afternoon, Mr. Winthrop drank Tea here unexpectedly, & made a tired evening pass off very chearfully

Friday March 11th.

Very much the same kind of weather only not quite so cold, made my first visit in the Morn: to the Browns to see their Son just arrived, from thence made many more visits finding, Baillies, Mrs. Macdowall & Mrs. Sands only at home, went to Dine at the Browns quite en famille, much pleased with the new part of their family returnd home at seven o'clock to dress to go to Mrs. Fergussons Ball w.ch was both numerous & pleasant, 120 persons, play'd much & with success both at Whist & Cassino, a large cold supper attended at different times, not at home till near three

Saturday March 12th

Still the same gloomy cold weather & in the evening a little rain, sat waiting till one o'clock expecting Mr. Cooper who had arrived from England but then was obliged to accompany L^{dy.} Dukenfield, Mrs. Roche, & Mrs. Honeyman, to Stranges general practising where was a great crowd & much singing as well as Dancing, Mr. Witts dined with Mr. Cooper & a party of his Friends at his Hottel, & in the evening join'd me at a Supper party of 20, at Major Melvilles lively & pleasant enough tho many Strangers the Boys went to a party at L^{dy.} Hays.

Sunday March 13th

On the whole a very fine Day, dull & sombre in the Morning, but bright sun which waken'd finely after mid.day, Mr. Cooper breakfasted with us & afterwards carried us in a Chaise to Invereke to visit his old Friend & our new acquaintance Mrs. Browning, whom we found at home & very pleasant we also call'd on M^{r.} & Mrs. Charteris & returned home only to Dinner: Mrs. Lockhart drank Tea here & was exceedingly obliging & agreable; Mr. Cooper & Mr. Winthrop both call'd late in the evening.

Monday March 14th

Far from a pleasant Day tho the air was milder, but it was damp & much inclined to rain, & at night the wind was high even in a hurricane I went at 11 to join Francis at the Dancing school from thence sat an hour with good Lady C: C:, where Mr. Cooper & Mr. Witts pick'd me up in a Coach on their return from the Levee afterwards I paid several visits on the new Town, finding only Mrs. Wilkinson & Mrs. Bruce at home; went to Dinner at Sr. N. Dukenfields taking Mr. Cooper with us & where we met M^{r.} & Mrs. Browning, all went to the Card Assembly, where I play'd Whist with bad luck in Lady Rothes's party. almost blown away.

Tuesday March 15th

A dull unpleasant day, but dry till near afternoon when it became rainy & comfortless I never stird all Morning but rec'd visits from Lady Hailles & two of her young Ladies,[12] Lady Hamilton Dalrymple & Miss Gordon; Mrs. Phillips & Dr. Cooper in the evening went to a very smart Ball at Mrs. Davies's consisting of from 80 to 90 persons, a great many of them Gentlemen, 3 Card Tables a very handsome supper. not at home till very late wrote to Mrs. Erskine

Wensday March 16th

A dry but cold unpleasant day being a strong east wind, went to Lady Riddells Levee where was fewer than usual, from thence made a visit or two, & one to Dr. Cooper at his Hottel who was just going off in the Mail Coach, on my return home call'd on Mrs. Jones who was at

---

12. Lady Hailes was the second wife (and widow) of David Dalrymple, 3rd Baronet, Lord Hailes (1726–1792), Scottish advocate, judge and historian. His father, James Dalrymple, 2nd Baronet, of Hailes, Haddingtonshire, Auditor of the Exchequer in Scotland, was a grandson of James Dalrymple, 1st Viscount of Stair; and his mother, Lady Christian Hamilton, was a daughter of Thomas Hamilton, 6th Earl of Haddington. The eldest of sixteen children, he succeeded to his father's baronetcy upon his death in 1751. He had married first, 1763, Anne, daughter of Sir George Broun, Lord Coalston, a Lord of Session, by whom he had a daughter, Christian (d. 1838). He married secondly, 1770, Helen (d. 1799), daughter of James Fergusson, Baronet, of Kilkerran, Ayrshire, by whom he had another daughter, Jean (d.1803) who married her cousin, James Fergusson.

Sir James Grant (1738–1811) with his regiment, the Strathspey or Grant Fencibles. An etching by John Kay, 1798.

home, in the evening went to Cards & Supper at Sʳ Nathaniel Dukenfields the party Riddells, Rookes, Browns, & Melvilles, very pleasant & agreable.

Thursday March 17ᵗʰ·

A very fine Day, milder air & much sun, set out on a string of visits, those found at home were Mʳˢ· Stewart, Mʳˢ· Oliphant, Miss Dalrymple Hailes,[13] & Mʳˢ· Halkett Craigie, went to Tea & Supper at Mʳˢ· Oliphants meeting Lᵈʸ· Riddell, Mʳˢ· Macdowall & Col: Colquhoun. rec'd Letters from Mʳˢ· Pennington & my Sister Travell

Friday March 18ᵗʰ·

Another clear & very fine Day, but being busy at home did not go from home in the Morning rec'd visits from Mʳ· Baillie, Mʳ· J: Cuningham Mʳˢ· Sands & Miss Macdougall, poor George came home early from School with a feverish complaint but better before night. went to Dine at Sʳ James Grants a large party of 20 handsome Dinner & very pleasant, except coming home at 9 o'clock

Saturday March 19ᵗʰ·

Still good dry weather but cold George almost well but prudently confined, went early to Dancing school practising where I spent the whole morning, Francis dined & past the remainder

---

13.   This is presumably Jean Hailes.

of the Day at L^dy. H: Blairs. Bob: Brown Dining here, went to Cards & supper, at M^r. Com. Browns, a large party of 19 chiefly young people but nothing very pleasant excepting some good singing after supper.

Sunday March 20th.

No change in the weather being yet dry & cold, went to Morning service at S^t. Georges Chappel where a Stranger preach'd admirably between Services rec'd a long pleasant visit from M^rs. Belsches, went to evening service at the New Church principaly to attend L^dy. Dukenfield to hear D^r. Blair who brought me home in her Carriage Charlotte Stewart, & Georgianna Brown dined here

Monday March 21st.

An exceeding fine & pleasant Day, being dry, mild, with much sun, joind Francis at the Dancing School, visited Lady C: C, where M^r. W. came to me, & we walk'd over the Calton Hill, afterwards to the west end of Queen Street to learn the character of a Servant, concluding my Morning rambles with a long chatty call on Miss Sinclair, went to the Card Assembly with M^rs. Davies play'd much at Cassino in two sets.

Hospital of Our Lady, Paul's Work, Low Calton; a watercolour by Daniel Wilson. The access to Edinburgh by the great London road was inconvenient. To enter the city from the south, the route ran through narrow streets. In 1814 many buildings were swept away and an elegant arch, Regent Bridge, was thrown over the hollow, making the descent from Calton Hill into Princes Street easy and agreeable.

A detailed map from the time when the bridge was opened in 1819. All this happened after Agnes's time, and the walk to Calton Hill would have been more arduous. She would, however, have seen the above buildings—the orphanage hospital.

Tuesday March 22ᵈ·

Weather very similiar dry & pleasant but I did not go out having the rhumatism w.ᶜʰ caused a stiff neck &'c; my Morning visitors Miss Leslie Baillie[14] & Mʳˢ· Balfour, & to Tea came by appointmᵗ· Mʳˢ· Mure, Mʳ· & Miss Wilkinsons 4 in number & Mʳ· Winthrop their Mother prevented by illness, no cards but all conversation. odd & uncommon.

Wensday March 23ᵈ·

Still dry, but not so pleasant the air being thick & very little sun. was from 11 in the Mornᵍ· till ½ past 4 in the afternoon, at the Dancing school general practising, should have been too much tired but for sitting between Lᵈʸ· Dukenfield & Mʳˢ· Brougham met the former at Cards & Supper at Mʳ· Com: Browns a genteel party of 16, equal number of each sexes.

Thursday March 24ᵗʰ·

Rather a cold stormy day with frequent symptoms of rain tho none fell to speak on being kept off by severe westerly wind. I went to Morning Prayers at Sᵗ· Georges afterwards rec'd a

---

14. Lesley Baillie (1768–1843). Lesley was a daughter of Robert Baillie and May, née Reid. She was a granddaughter of Anna Cunninghame and John Reid, second son of the minister of the parish, their daughter being her mother. Through her mother she was related to Sir Robert Cunninghame of Auchenharvie. Lesley was born at Mayville, Stevenston, North Ayrshire and married, 1799 Robert Cumming of Logie, Morayshire. Her lasting fame derives from being Robert Burns's 'Bonnie Lesley', "*the most beautiful, elegant woman in the world*".

long visit at home from Lady Riddell. then went in search of Lodgings for the Dukenfields, & paid a visit or two finding only L^dy Rothes at home. pass'd the evening quietly at home. rec'd a Letter from Miss L Lee & wrote to my Sister Travell.

Friday March 25th

A most bitter cold Day, with a high & severe westerly wind which blew the dust about dreadfuly, a colder good Friday was seldom known went in Mrs Wilkinsons Coach with herself & family to the Cowgate Chappel to hear her Son preach who gave a very clever & suitable sermon. went to St Georges chappel to evening service. Peter Brougham drank Tea here. wrote to Mrs Whalley on her Marriage.[15]

Saturday March 26th

Rather a better day tho still very cold, but the wind was not quite so high, & there was some sun, went to Morning prayers, after which with L^dy Riddell visited Mrs General Campbell went home to pick up Mr W. intending to go to Georges Square but on the Bridge meeting L^dy Dukenfield she tempted me to go visiting with her into the new Town where we met L^dy Hailes, Mrs Davies & Mrs Dundas at home. I then accompanied her to see L^dy C: C: & walk'd home calling on Mrs Brown in my way; Cards & Supper at L^dy Sinclairs a party of 16, very pleasant but very late.

Sunday March 27th

A miserable cold & tempestuous day, wind so high it was with difficulty I could stand upon my Legs walking to Chappel, went to St Georges both Morning & evening, where Mr Cleeve was assisted by a stranger in a very large number of communicants evening I spent quietly & pleasantly rational with the Dear Boys

Monday March 28th

Still cold & sharp but not quite so severe, went again to Morning prayers at St Georges, walk'd afterwards to Georges Square where we only found at home Mrs Douglass, Mrs Clerk & Miss Robinsons, I went to the Card Assembly with Miss Sinclair, full of very genteel company I play'd at Cassino in a very lively party with success.

Tuesday March 29th

Again cold & rather stormy looking like rain but none fell till night, went early with Sr James & Lady Riddell in their Coach to Inveresk to visit Captn & Mrs Browning, who we found at home not so Mrs Gray at Musselburgh but Mrs Rooke & Mrs Longen at the Barracks, walk'd in the evening to an undress'd party at L^dy Riddells Mrs Baillie of Polkemmet & her Daughter Sr James Colquhoun & Mr M. Riddell the company

---

15. Mrs Whalley was Martha, née Tracy Travell (1764–1839), the niece of Agnes, being the eldest daughter of her brother, Ferdinando Tracy Travell. This was a second marriage for Martha, her first husband, John Buxton, having died in 1790. Her new husband William was considerably younger than herself. They had married 25 February 1796.

Wensday March 30th.

Very similiar weather dry & cold, made many visits besides Lady Riddells Levee, those I found at home were Miss Macartney Mrs. Campbell, Mrs. Oliphant & Mrs. Mure, came home early to dress before Dinner to be in time to go before six to Madame Rosignolis Ball went with Lady Dukenfield, joined by the other Ladies of the Windsor Forresters, a splendid Ball, & much delighted with Franks exhibition. at home near two

Thursday March 31st.

Much the same weather strong symptoms of rain but too cold to come down tho a little fell in the Morning, my first visit to see Mr. & Mrs. Grant who were just arrived, most agreably & pleasantly rec'd, afterewards visited the Spiers & Wilkinsons both at home; went to Tea Cards & supper at Lord Polkemmets, a droll party of 14 & much card playing.

Friday Ap: 1st.

A damp mild Morning with much fog, & at night severe rain, I staid at home all Morning very busy, & let no one in but Mrs. Brougham, whose company as ever I highly enjoyd went late to Cards & Supper at Mrs. Dalrymples, a large hetrogeneous party of 21, many Military of various discriptions, at home very late. rec'd a long pleasant Letter from Lady Elcho.

Saturday Ap. 2d.

A damp fog in the Morning, which produced an uncommon mild & fine Day when the sun had sufficient power to dispel it rain at night went at Noon to see Lady C: C: walk'd so far & back with Lady Riddell, made an unsuccessful call on Mrs. Phillips, & a long one on Mr. Brown, went to Cards & Supper at Mrs. General Campbells, an odd but not unpleasant party of 14, 2 whist Tables some reel Dancing & singing after Supper.

Sunday Ap: 3d.

Quite a disagreable day being throughout a strong wetting fog, & at night very hard rain went to both services at St. Georges Chappel Mr. Wilkinson preaching in the Morning & reading Prayers in the afternoon, a most excellent sermon which gave general satisfaction Mrs. Brougham sat with us for the sake of hearing Him: a quiet comfortable evening as usual on Sundays.

Monday Ap: 4th.

Another as unpleasant a day as the former if not more so, The fog being still thicker & more wetting, went at 12 o'clock to St. Georges Chappel with Mr. Witts to a collection of Choral Music perform'd there for the benifit of the Organist & others, nothing very extraordinary, & the company tho numerous not brilliant, return'd home directly after, went to the Card Assembly, My Husband also, where Miss Graham join'd me, play'd 2 rubbers in a pleasant party at Whist a great but genteel crowd Duc De Bourbon D'Angoleme &'c &'c there.[16] rec'd Letters from Ldy. Edwd. Bentinck & Miss Anne Snow.

---

16. Louis Antoine (1775–1844), duc'd Angoulême. Louise was the eldest son of Charles Philippe, comte d'Artois.

This etching by John Kay, entitled 'The Great and the Small,' was published in 1797. The Duc d'Angoulême, constantly attended the Saturday drills of the Royal Edinburgh Volunteers, whose uniform—blue with red facings—very much resembled that of the French national guards. The etching was meant to contrast the athletic Scotsman and the fragile French man, then a young man of 22, and of a somewhat feeble frame. Major-General Roger Aytoun was the eldest son of John Aytoun of Inchdairney, and of Isabella, daughter of Robert Lord Rollo. He was a man of remarkable stature, being upwards of six feet four inches in height, and broad and strong in proportion.

Tuesday Ap: 5ᵗʰ·

Still rather a thick gloomy sky but the air was dry, joind a very large & genteel party to see the Ventriloquist perform his wonders of changing & disposing his voice to various objects & parts of the room, from thence walk'd with Lady Riddell & Miss Askew to Georges Square, found Mʳˢ· Hamilton, Mʳˢ· Calderwood Denham only at home spent the evening quietly at home being tired & unwell the Boys went to Stranges Public for 2 or 3 hours.

Wensday Ap: 6ᵗʰ·

A most delightful Day mild & fine like summer, which let all the gay world on the move, at noon I made a long sidorant[17] at Lady Riddells meeting numbers, from thence walk'd with Miss Bruce in the streets & to see her House on Hill Street, not at home till Dinner time, went to a smart pleasant Ball at Lᵈʸ· Hailles's from 50 to 60 people very agreable & well conducted an elegant cold supper.

Thursday Ap: 7ᵗʰ·

A dry & tolerably fine Day but rather cold, & not being quite well I staid in the whole of the Morning, my only visitors Mʳ· & Mʳˢ· Grant, went to Tea Cards & Supper at Mʳˢ· Mures no one there but 6 of the Wilkinson family wrote to Mʳˢ· Pennington.

---

17. This makes no sense, but it is difficult to interpret what Agnes was trying to write. It could have been sidosant, in which case she may have been intending *soi disant* in the sense of a 'so-called' gathering, a pretence or pretentious gathering, a so-say gathering.

Friday Ap: 8ᵗʰ·

A pretty good Day being tolerably clear & late in the Day some sunshine, I made good use of it by being out many hours in the Morning first going to the Dancing School, then to Lady C: C: returning to the New Town visited the Browns in Sᵗ· James Square afterwards paid many more visits found only Lady Grant & Mʳˢ· Dundas at home on my return found Capᵗⁿ· & Mʳˢ· Browning & Miss M. Macfarlan, went to Tea & Supper at Mʳˢ· Wilkinsons no one but their own family but chearful & pleasant enough

Saturday Ap: 9ᵗʰ·

Quite a mild growing Morning, & at various parts of the Day heavy showers of rain, I went to the Dancing School practising, spending the whole Morning very pleasantly, sitting by Lady Dukenfield the whole time. the Boys dined in a large young party at Major Melvilles, & had a dance in the evening we went to Cards & Supper at Mʳˢ· Macdougalls a party of 12 as many Gents as Ladies rec'd Letters from Mʳˢ· Granville & Mʳˢ· Whalley. the first time.

Sunday Ap: 10ᵗʰ·

An unpleasant wet Morning, but became dry at mid.day, George was the only one who went to Morning Service, Mʳ· Witts went to evenᵍ· service to the High Church with Mʳ· Wilkinson the Boys & I to Sᵗ· Georges, Mʳ· & Mʳˢ· & 3 Miss Wilkinsons & a Mʳ· Stott with them drank Tea with us.

Monday Ap: 11ᵗʰ·

A tolerably fine Day being dry & not cold Mʳ· Witts went to the Levee with Mʳ· Wilkinson & to see other sights, I made several near visits finding only Lady Sinclair & Mʳˢ· Brougham at home, went to the Card Assembly in Lady Riddells party very full & agreable.

Tuesday Ap: 12ᵗʰ·

Quite a mild pleasant Day, being dry & warm without wind rec'd visits from Miss Graham & Miss Stewart Scott before we went with Miss Bruce to call on Lady Maxwell at Shrub Hall who we found at home & gave us a very obliging reception call'd on Mʳˢ· Brown in Sᵗ· James's

Potterrow, near St George's Square. An engraving by T. Stewart from a painting by Daniel Wilson.

Smollet's House, St John Street, Canongate. An engraving by T. Stewart from a painting by Daniel Wilson.

Square on our return went early to Madame Rosignolis Public, my party M^rs. Brougham, 2 Miss Wilkinsons & Miss C: Stewart join'd Lady Dukenfield & many others, an excellent meeting & my beloved Frank perform'd to the delight of all who were interested about him

Wensday Ap: 13th.

Very much the same kind of weather only not quite so mild being a strong wind went to Lady Riddells as usual, & made several other visits, those I found at home, were the Wilkinsons & M^rs. Major Sands went to the Play in M^rs. Baillies Box, arrived to & fro in M^rs. Davies Carriage, the Play the Suspicious Husband; in wch Johnson made but a very moderate figure in the character of Ranger. wrote to Miss A. Snow

Thursday Ap: 14th.

Still dry but not very pleasant the wind being high & the dust intolerable. went to call on my two invalid Friends in the Canongate, Lady Dukenfield & Lady C: C: the former confined to her Bed & <u>very</u> ill on my return did some necessary shopping bussiness. went in the evening to Lady Sinclairs, meeting some pleasant people but not so many as had been expected. rec'd a Letter from my Sister Travell.

Friday Ap: 15th.

No change in the weather being still dry & mild, Lady Riddell sat half an hour with me before I went out at Noon, call'd at Lady Sinclairs to visit her Sister M^rs. Fullarton lately arrived, made some other visits & did some little bussinesses finding no one at home but M^rs. Brown. went to Cards & supper at M^rs. Davies's a pleasant party of 30 not at home till very late

Saturday Ap: 16th.

A very fine mild day as usual, went late with Mrs. Davies when she sat for her Picture to Stewart, & went in her Chariot to call on poor Ldy. Dukenfield who I found a little better & in her Drawing room, on my return made two or three visits finding no one at home but Ldy. H. Blair the Boys Dukenfields dined here, we went to Tea Cards & Supper at Sr. James Riddells no one there but Miss Askew & Mr. M. Riddell

Sunday Ap: 17th.

Very much the same weather with rather more sunshine went to St. Georges Chappel in the Morning & St. Andrews in the evening, not much edified at either a Stranger perfoming but moderately at the latter, between services visited Mrs. Oliphant evening spent quiet as usual. rec'd a pleasant Letter from Miss Snow. wrote to Sisr. Travell

Monday Ap: 18th.

Again fine & dry continuing a most pleasant season, went early to meet Frank at the Dancing School afterwards air'd with Lady Dukenfield on the Queens Ferry road, visited Lady C: C: where Mr. Witts join'd me to walk home with me. my cold made me feel very stupid & unwell. no interruption to a quiet evening at home but a short visit from Mrs. Auchenlech wrote to Lady Edward Bentinck & read in a poor Novel

Tuesday Ap: 19th.

No change in the weather, my cold being worse than better I prudently staid at home from Morn. to night, my Morning visitors Lady Sinclair always agreable & Mrs. & Miss Dalrymples, evening quiet our own happy party. wrote to Miss Louisa Lee

Wensday Ap: 20th.

Such an uncommon hot fine Day there was seldom ever experienced at the time of the Year realy too hot to move about with comfort, made a great many visits besides attending Lady Riddells Levee, those I found at home were the Speirs family & the Baillies. walk'd again between Dinner & Tea to view the foundations digging of Mr. Sandfords intended Chappel &'c. Mr. W. began reading Martin

Thursday Ap: 21st.

Quite as hot, but not so pleasant a day the wind being in the east & very high which made the dust intolerable & added to the extreme heat but having made an appointment with Miss Bruce to accompany her to Georges Square on some visits we set forth at mid.day but came home almost baked. call'd on Mrs. Douglass, Mrs. Hamilton, & I on Miss Maria Craigie in the absence of her Mother & I finish'd by a visit to the Browns, too much over done to walk in the evening. rec'd a letter fm. Miss Forrest

Friday Ap: 22d.

Still extremely warm, but a much pleasanter day by the wind being not near so high staid within till three o'clock & for a wonder without one caller, then went to walk in Queen Street for an hour. Francis went early to a Ball at Mrs. Halkett Craigies, & me to a very smart pleasant

Sir James Hunter Blair (1741–1787). James was the second
son of James Hunter. He married, 1770, Jane, eldest daughter
of John Blair of Dunskey, Wigton. Despite having four
brothers, Elizabeth out-survived them all and she inherited
the family estate. James Hunter then assumed the extra name
Blair. Lady Elizabeth Hunter Blair was a quite a close friend
to Agnes Witts.

party & handsome supper at Lady Hunter Blairs, 10 middle aged, & as many very young
people, <u>walk'd</u> home between 1 & 2. wrote to M^rs. Granville

Saturday Ap: 23^d.

Another charming Day the wind being rather high made the dust intolerable, at night it
increased to a little Hurricane & brought on a fine shower of rain, I went out late to make
some visits those I found at home were M^rs. Campbell of Shervan & M^rs. Macdowell. the Boys
dined & were at a dance at M^r. Balfours, we spent the evening at M^rs. Spiers's a good party of
20 more agreable than usual.

Sunday Ap: 24th.

A bright pleasant day but not so warm the wind being in the North but happily the dust laid
went to S^t. Georges Chappel in the Morning & S^t. Andrews in the evening, where M^r. Moodie
was most peculiarly delightful, between services visited the Baillies & M^rs. Davies their cousins
being going to leave them. M^rs. Wilkinson brought her Sister M^rs. Young to introduce her &
to drink Tea. very pleasantly chatty.

Monday Ap: 25th.

An ascending fine & pleasant Day bright sun & charming clear air, I went to meet Francis
at the Dancing School then visited Lady Catherine & on my way home did a little shopping
&'c, when I returned met Lady Dukenfield who wanted to tell me her distress that S^r. Na^l.
was ill, dined at S^r. James Riddells, where we met three young Ladies, & three of the Windsor
Forresters & M^r. Riddell, went to the Card Assembly in the party which was a wretched bad
thing not more than 40 people & only two Card Tables. Hellen Wallis enter'd on her place

Tuesday Ap: 26[th.]

A still warmer Day the air being thicker & not so much of it we took a very long walk going over the Calton Hill to the Abbey, from thence to the Kings Park & back again, calling on the Dukenfields in the way, finding the Baronet not worse but under D[r.] Gregory's care; went to Drink Tea at M[rs.] Grants a Dull formal party, play'd 2 stupid rubbers at Whist & were at home before ten o'clock not over delighted

Wensday Ap: 27[th.]

Weather appearing to be rather on the change stormy air & gloomy sky & at night fleeting rain but not to continue, after being at the accustomed Levee as usual made several visits finding only M[rs.] Dalrymple & Miss Macdougall visible, went to Cards & Supper at Miss Abercrombys a very pleasant party of 8 Gentlemen & 7 Ladies. not at home till one.

KAY.

His Majestys Historiographer

Revd William Robertson DD (1721–1793). Author of *A History of America*, 1778. Robertson was the uncle of Eleanor Brougham, née Symes. It is likely that this association was the cause of Agnes picking up his book prior to her visit to the Broughams.

Thursday Ap: 28[th.]

A great change in the weather perhaps a useful one but certainly not a pleasant one, being gloomy in the Morning, wet at Noon & so it continued the rest of the Day & night. Col: Colquhoun my only Morning visitor, we went to Cards & Supper at M[rs.] Macdowalls, a party of 14 to me rather a new set but by no means an unpleasant one

Friday Ap: 29[th.]

Another dull dark Day looking like rain but very little fell in the course of it, I did not judge it fine enough to go out either Morning or evening being not very well. read & worked much M[r.] Witts in Robertsons America & I in the Rose of Raby[18] the Boys at an evening party at M[r.] Broughams.

Saturday Ap: 30[th.]

Again dark & lowering with pretty frequent small showers, & very cold, which gave me no sort of inclination to go out, the first Day of Francis's College vacation both classes ending on Friday they both dined & spent the evening in a large party at Lady H: Blairs, M[rs.] Davies made me a long visit in the Morning w.[ch] was the only interruption to another comfortable busy day

Sunday May 1[st.]

Very unlike a poetic May Day the wind being high & in the east of course extremely cold & the sky so

---

18. Agnes Musgrave, *Cicely; or the Rose of Raby*, a novel in 4 volumes, 1796.

lowering as to portend much rain tho little or none fell, went to St. Georges in the Morning, & St. Andrews to the evening service not highly gratified at either, between made some visits finding only Lady Sinclair at home went to Drink Tea with Mrs. Wilkinson in Hennikers Lodgings where she was removed to. Mrs. Young & Mr. Winthrop there also home early. the Boys paid their first visit to young Monseiur Polastron in the evening.[19]

Monday May 2^{d.}

Wet, cold & very disagreable the early part of the Day, but before noon became dry tho not pleasant, I was not very well therefore kept quite quiet all Morning, went to drink Tea in a friendly way at Sr. N. Dukenfields to congratulate him on his recovery no one there but Miss Sinclair who carried me in her Chaise at home by 10 o'clock playing 2 or three merry rubbers at Cassino previously.

Tuesday May 3^{d.}

A bright fine Day but cold out of the sun being a strong east wind, Miss Askew made us a visit before we sallied forth, went first to Mrs. Wilkinsons sale where was a great crowd afterwards visited Mrs. Davies, Mrs. Syme, & Mrs. Brown. went to Tea, Cards, & Supper at Lady Sinclairs, 9 Ladies & only Mr. Robinson & Mr. Witts but it was lively & pleasant as all Lady Sinclairs parties are.

Wensday May 4th.

Gloomy, dark & cold, with great signs of rain but none fell, attended Lady Riddells Levee whither Frank accompanied me, & besides I visited & found at home Lady Rothes, Mrs. Halkett Craigie & Mrs. Wilkinson, went to drink Tea at our next Door Neighbours Mrs. Hay & the Boys with us rec'd a Letter from Mrs. Browning & answer'd it.

Thursday May 5th.

Again rather sharp & cold but made pleasant by uninterrupted sunshine went over the Calton Hill accompanied by Mr. Witts & Frank into the Cannongate, to see Lady C: C: call'd on L^{dy.} D. but without success, went to the Abbey to survey the appointments putting up for Count D.Artois. went to Tea Cards & supper at Lady Riddells Boy & all a pretty large party tho in a free way, pleasantly enjoyed by the unexpected arrival of Sr. N. & Lady Dukenfield.

Friday May 6th.

Very much the same weather still cold easterly winds I never went out till to Dinner at Lord Dumfries's, a party of 12, none very smart or lively a very handsome Dinner & a very obliging reception but a dull thing altogether & home by the time it was dark.

Saturday May 7th.

No change of weather but pleasant from constant sunshine, my first call on Miss Craufurd, who I found tolerable & always agreable, then to Mrs. Brown, & afterwards on Mrs. Wilkinson

19. Young Monsieur Polastron was Louis de Polastron (1785–1804), the son of the Comte d'Artois' mistress, Marie Louise d'Esparbès de Lussan (1764–1804). She was a lady-in-waiting to Queen Marie Antoinette. She married Denis de Polastron (1758–1821).

with whom I went to be introduced to Lady Emilia Drummond.[20] went to Drink Tea with Mrs. Young meeting all the Wilkinson family.

Sunday May 8th.

Still miserably cold but dry & at times some sunshine, neither Mr. Witts or I went to church in the Morning having writing & other bussiness to do preparatory to receiving Mrs. Browning in the evening who was coming to stay with us two or three Days went to evening service at the Cowgate Chappel to hear Dr. Rudd preach his farewell sermon nothing famous return'd with L^{dy.} Dukenfield to Dine with them Boys & all, where besides meeting Mrs. Browning were Wiloubly Rooke[21] & little Count Polastron, we had a very lively pleasant Dinner & walk'd home as it was dark bringing Mrs. Browning in our hand.

Monday May 9th.

Again cold & windy, tho with a good deal of sunshine, rec'd visits from Sr. N. & Lady Dukenfield & Miss Abercromby & went with L^{dy.} D. in her Carriage to Raeburn & Stewarts the Printers & with Mrs. Browning to make an unsuccessful visit or two, Lady Riddell Count Polastron & his abbey[22] the young Dukenfiellds & two Broughams Drank Tea here, went afterwards to the Card Assembly which tho thin was remarkably lively & pleasant.

Tuesday May 10th.

Another very similiar Day only still more cold being less sun, rec'd several very early visitors some to wait on our agreable guest, got out soon after 12 going to the Dancing School to see Francis & others Dance went afterwards to some shops, & I concluded my walk, by making a long & interesting visit to Mrs. Davies, not at home till Dinner was on Table, Mrs. Browning & I went at seven to a large party at Lady Riddells, where I only staid two hours, leaving my friend & joining my Husband at a large party at Sr. William Forbes's 13 Ladies & 12 Gent, very agreable indeed

Wensday May 11th.

The wind being changed it was much milder, which brought on frequent gentle showers in the course of the forenoon more useful than pleasant to us, who had walk'd early into Georges Square while Mrs. B. visited some of her friends I visited mine but found only Mrs. Craigie at

---

20. Lady Emilia Drummond was a French émigré. She was the second daughter and (but sixth child) of James Drummond (1708–1766), who but for the attainder of his father, would have been the 3rd Duke of Melfort. James had married, 1755, at Lussan, Marie (b. 1728) daughter of François de Berenger, of St Paul-Trois-Châteaux. James had succeeded to the large estates of his mother, who had been the only daughter of Jean D'Audebert, Count of Lussan. Emilia's eldest brother James Louis, quasi 4th Duke had died in 1788, her next brother was Charles Edward, he put in a claim for the reversal of the attainder in 1803, but this was rejected in 1808; he died unmarried in Rome. The family finally achieved the reversal of the attainder in 1853.
21. Willoughby Rooke (1782–1869). Willoughby became Sir Henry Willoughby Rooke, a general in the army, and present at the battle of Waterloo. His elder brother, who became Lt-Col. John Charles Rooke, served in Egypt and Portugal and who died of wounds at San Jean de Luz, 1813. Both were sons of Charles Rooke (*see above*), who in 1794, with the blessing of the King had formed the Royal Windsor Forresters.
22. Agnes probably means Abbé. In pre-revolutionary France the title Abbé had been used for all young clergymen with or without consecration, and many became tutors.

home, glad to pick up a Hackney Coach to convey us in the dry to Lady Riddells where we join'd the gay circle & afterwards visited at M^r. Browns. M^rs. Browning quitted us at Dinner time to go to Major Melvilles, where we also went to Tea Cards & Supper a great party of 20, among them 5 of the Windsor Forresters.

Thursday May 12th.

Quite a stormy disagreable day strong appearance of rain wch fell however only in small flitting showers, but the wind so high it was miserable moving, I only went out to make 5 visits but not rec'd at any Principal Gordon Dined with us having call'd the Day before to notifie his arrival, most happy at his return & to see him look so well & in good spirits

Friday May 13th.

Wet early in the Morning, but soon clear'd off tho' it remain'd very stormy the whole of the Day so as not to tempt me to go out, my only Morning visitor S^r. N. Dukenfield, & Peter Brougham drank Tea here, amused & interested by the Novel of the Forresters.[23] wrote to Miss Snow.

Saturday May 14th.

Quite a pleasant Day the air being much milder, & at mid.day a good deal of sunshine went into the Cannongate to make visits found only Lady Dukenfield at home, who kept me to spend the rest of the day with her, our Husbands being to dine with Dr. Gregory, our Boys were added to our party, & a very pleasant social Day it proved, intersperced agreably with drinking Tea with good Lady C: C: who was highly pleased with her three Ladies walk'd home between 10 & 11.

Sunday May 15th.

Again dry & bright but an extreme cold wind which gave one little idea of its being Whitsunday, M^rs. Browning call'd on us to accompany us to S^t. Georges Chappel where we were being detained by a large number of communicants, between services visited M^rs. Campbell of Saddel, went again to S^t. Georges at evening service the Boys dined at Madame Polastrons, M^rs. Davies drank Tea here, & we went late to sup at Lady Riddells, meeting M^rs. Askew as well as her Daughter Miss MacFarlan & Principal Gordon. rec'd Letter from my Sister Travell

Monday May 16th.

Very much the same sort of weather warm in the sun & very cold out went early w^h. M^r. Witts to call on M^rs. Davies, & aid a conference on education, I afterwards made many visits those I found at home were Miss Speirs's, M^rs. Oliphant, M^rs. Brown S^t. James Square, & Miss Melvilles & M^rs. Browning, went to the Card Assembly which was full & very gay indeed rec'd a Letter from Miss Snow.

Tuesday May 17th.

A most disagreable day tho dry being such a high cold wind & the dust intolerable after having seen Frank dance at the School I spent a most comfortable hour with Lady Dukenfield

---

23. This was probably the novel by Ann Radcliffe (1764–1823), *The Romance of the Forest* (3 vols.) 1791.

in most friendly converse, & I did some bussiness on the Bridge on my return; when I came home found the good Principal intending to dine with us, & he staid till it was dark rec'd a Letter from Lady Edward Bentinck.

Wensday May 18th.

An uncommon warm fine Day tho still a thick & easterly wind & dust terribly troublesome went to Lady Riddell & a string of other visits those I found at home were Miss Macdonald, Lady Sinclair, Mrs. Baillie Pol. & Mrs. Brougham, the Boys drank Tea with the Wilkinson family & Mr. W. & I took a pleasant walk to Bernards Well &'c & when we came home found the good Principal who staid talking & playing at Backgammon till near bed time.

Thursday May 19th.

Very much the same kind of day only being more wind it was less pleasant, but I never went out the whole Day being very busy over looking everything preparatory to Catherines departure, admitted only Mr. Baillie to take leave Mrs. Wilkinson & 2 younger Daughters drank Tea here. wrote to Mrs. Whalley.

Friday May 20th.

A fine Day from having a great deal of sunshine but still the same cold wind remaind made a great many visits, those I found at home where Miss Bruce Mrs. Captn. Brown Mrs. Campbell of Shervan Mrs. Dewar & Mrs. Com: Brown, went to Tea Cards & Supper at Lady Riddells meeting Miss Bruce Mr. Riddell & Mr. M. Riddell great batteling at Cribbage. wrote to my Sisr. Travell.

Saturday May 21st.

Exactly the same weather great abundance of sun to make up for the cold wind made a first visit to Lady Dukenfield in their new Lodgings accompanied her Sons & my own to the Dancing School practising where I only staid a few minutes & visited Lady C: C: walk'd after Tea with the Boys nearly to Cotes Bridge found the Principal on our return who play'd at Backgammon till near eleven.

Sunday May 22d.

A less pleasant Day than many former ones being little or no sun & the wind in the same points, went to both services at St. Georges Chappel little gratified by Mr. Cleeves elocution on our return from Morning Service, found poor old Catherine had been sent to go aboard the Vessel,[24] well pleased to let her slip off in so easy a manner, visited the Wilkinsons in their new Lodgings between Churches. after Tea walk'd with the Boys to Cannon Mills &'c, & on my return sat an hour with Lady Dukenfield, to enquire after little Egerton who had got the Measles.

Monday May 23d.

A very fine Day upon the whole a mixture of sun & boisterous wind, but towards even temperate & very pleasant, at mid.day I went with Frank to the Dancing school where Principal Gordon

---

24. Catherine Newman had been a servant to the Witts family since April 1793, and had accompanied them from Gloucestershire.

gave us the meeting, & on my return home did some bussiness in shops, M^rs. Com: Brown dined with us the Principal likewise drank Tea & we all walk'd home with her & in Queen Street afterwards finishing the night with Back gammon.

Tuesday May 24th·

Such a very high wind that it was far from a pleasant Day, the dust being quite intolerable & towards evening such strong black clouds as indicated approaching rain I was only out in the Morning to visit Lady Dukenfield & her Nursery & to call on Miss MacFarlan, in the evening walk'd with Francis on the Calton Hill but it was far from being pleasant.

Wednesday May 25th·

Quite a charming warm clear Day the wind being turn'd westerly, & the dust happily laid by some refreshing rain that had fallen early in the Morning, attended Lady Riddells Levee, & among those people I found at home of several I call'd on were Miss Campbells of Fairfield, Miss S: Dundas M^rs. Wilkinson & M^rs. Com: Brown. spent the evening at Lady Riddells meeting Lady & Miss Sinclair, S^r. James Colonel, & Cap^tn. Colquhoun, & M^r. M. Riddell

Thursday May 26th·

A very unpleasant Day being an extreme high wind accompanied at times by small short showers, I never stirr'd out the whole Day busying myself in various employs, & our only visitor was Principal Gordon for a short time in the Morning wrote to Lady Elcho.

Friday May 27th·

Still a tremendous high wind but no rain & much sunshine, which tempted me to go out just to call on Lady Dukenfield, & then accompanied by M^r. W. we walk'd to the Abbey & its environs by way of shelter, visited Lady C: C: on my return where I was joind by L^dy. D. who brought me home in her carriage. spent the evening at Lady Riddells meeting M^rs. Mure M^r. & M^rs. Macdougall & a M^r. Duwall, S^r. James & Col: Colquhoun.

Saturday May 28th·

Another stormy & very disagreable Day, perpetual small showers & in the evening a very sharp one, rec'd visits from M^rs. Browning & Miss Campbell from Inveresk, & from M^r. Phillips & late went to call on M^rs. Wilkinson. spent the eveng. at M^rs. Mures dull & stupid enough, very cold & comfortless, Lady Riddell, M^rs. David Hume & a M^r. Campbell the only company. no grand entertainment.

Sunday May 29th·

Still very much the same weather high cold wind & perpetual showers in the evening very severe ones. M^r. Witts attended the Lord Commissioner thro the Day I did not go to church in the Morn: but went to evening service at S^t. Andrews where I carried Lady Dukenfield having previously paid her a visit, a miserable Stranger preacher M^r. Witts return'd home before Tea. rec'd a letter from Miss Anne Snow.

Monday May 30th.

Rain & pretty constant for the greater part of the Day, accompanied by strong wind & very cold for the time of year glad of a good fire & very happy not to feel it necessary to stir out of the house the whole Day. wrote to Mrs. Tracy Sandywell

Tuesday May 31st.

Again very stormy, with frequent cold showers, some severe of hail, Sr. N. & Lady Dukenfield, & the Principal my Morning guests, & I went with her Lady ship in her Chariot to the Barracks to enquire after Mrs. Rooke who was very ill, walk'd a little in the evening chiefly in the streets but it was too cold for pleasure, the Principal came in the even: for B. gammon

Wensday June 1st.

A much better Day than several former ones, being scarce any showers, the air more mild & much sun, my first visit to the Dukenfields the rest of the children sickening for the Measles, then to Lady Riddells as usual & afterwards found at home of those I visited Mrs. Macdowall, Mrs. General Douglass & Mrs. Com. Brown the Principal dined here, & Mrs. & 2 Miss Wilkinsons drank Tea here, & when the latter went away I went & sat 2 hours with poor Lady Dukenfield while the Gentlemen battled away at Backgammon.

Tuesday June 2d.

A very charming Day throughout, & so fine a evening as had not been known for this Year, Lady Riddell & Miss C: Scott were my Morning visitors, & late I went to see the Dukenfield Nursery who were going on tolerably, Mrs. Mure drank Tea here without desire or invitation but was pleasant enough, at her departure we went walking towards Bernards Well & its vicinity, found the Principal at our return home ready for Backgammon

Friday June 3d.

Not quite so pleasant a day, the air being colder as well as less sunshine, I went out early spent an hour & ½ at the dancing school attending both the Boys it being Georges commencement from there visited both Lady C: C: & Mrs. Fyffe the latter long & interesting, ended my career by calling on the Dukenfields who were all very indifferent indeed, went to Cards Tea & Supper at Lady Riddells, a party of 11 pleasanter than usual Sr. James & Lady Foules, Major & Miss Melville, Principal Gordon, Col: Colquhoun & Mr. Mrs. Riddell & Miss Plenderleith.

Saturday June 4th.

Another very fine clear Day well suited to the universal Royal rejoicing of the Day,[25] I went out with Husband & Sons to see the preparations at the Parliament House besides went to see Wilkinsons & Dukenfields, who I found in so very moderate a state, that I went again &

---

25. George III was born on 4 June 1738 in London, son of Frederick, Prince of Wales and Augusta of Saxe-Gotha. He became heir to the throne when his father died in 1751, succeeding his grandfather George II in 1760. He was the first Hanoverian monarch to use English as his first language. In 1761, George married Charlotte of Mecklenburg-Strelitz and they enjoyed a happy marriage, with 15 children.

spent the whole evening, & late induced Lady D. to take a walk in Queen Street &'c Mr Witts as usual went to drink the Kings health at the Parliament House.

Sunday June 5$^{th.}$

Just the same pleasant clear weather with much sunshine from Morn to night went to St Georges Chappel twice between services rec'd visits from Miss Campbells of Fairfield & Mr Bruce & Mr White, & visited Lady Dukenfield & her Nursery after Tea walk'd with the Boys to Georges Square & the Meadows very pleasant indeed.

Monday June 6$^{th.}$

No change in the weather till evening when it became cold & stormy & looking like rain went out at Noon to make some visits finding M$^{rs.}$ Young, M$^{rs.}$ Fraser Lovat, & M$^{rs.}$ Com: Brown at home, & look'd in on the Dukenfields Nursery & rec'd a visit from Mr D. Erskine before Dinner, after Tea walk'd with the Boys on Calton Hill, & sat a quar^r of an hour with Lady Dukenfield before we got home.

Tuesday June 7$^{th.}$

Cold & unpleasant in the Morning with frequent small showers which in the evening fell more materialy, I staid within all Morning receiving visits from M^r G: Fergusson & Miss Sinclair, went to Cards & Supper at Lady Sinclairs, meeting a pleasant lively party of 14 the greater proportion Gentlemen

George Fergusson, Lord Hermand (d. 1827). Fergusson was admitted advocate in 1765 and practised successfully at the bar for 34 years. On the death of Robert Macqueen of Braxfield in 1799 he was promoted to the bench and took the title Lord Hermand. An etching by John Kay, 1799.

Wensday June 8th.

Dry warm & fine, tho with a considerable deal of wind, my first call on Lady Dukenfield, with whom I found all her young ones able to quit their Beds, I then went to Lady Riddells from there to make other visits finding Miss Bruce of Stenhouse & Miss Graham & her Aunt home Mrs. Wilkinson & her invalid Daughter drank Tea here, Mr. Witts sat with me with Lady Dukenfield from 9 to 10.

Thursday June 10th.

Just the same weather rather showery looking in the Morning but bright in the evening, I went very early in the Day to the dancing school both Boys performing, visited Lady C: C: went to some shops, & on my return call'd both on the Dukenfields & on Mrs. Brougham, Principal Gordon dined here, & I went to the Play with Lady Riddell in her Balcony Box, where a large party were collected the performance very indifferent. rec'd a Letter from my Sister Travell

Friday June 10th.

A very mild & pleasant feeling Day, tho with strong clouds & propensity to rain & a sharp shower at Dinner time, made our first call on Lady Dukenfield, proceeding to Georges Square when among many visits we made found none at home but Miss Scott & Mr. H. Robinson afterwards call'd on Mrs. Brown St. James Square Mrs. Wilkinson for the last time. went to Tea Cards & Supper at Mrs. Macdowalls, a pleasant large party of three card Tables & a good Supper, but heard there with painful concern of poor Mrs. Penningtons Death

Saturday June 11th.

Rather a gloomy sky, with signs of rain but none fell till quite evening, rather full of bussiness all morning preparing for going to Captn. Brownings at Inveresk for 2 or 3 days, convey'd there by Lady Dukenfield, who with Sr. Nathl. Dined there as also Mr. Charteris Mr. Campbell, his Son & two Daughters & Mr. Steel play'd at Whist in the evening.

Sunday June 12th.

Dry & fine through the whole Day with some sun & a good deal of wind, went to the English Chappel at Musselburgh a very moderate performance, afterwards call'd on Mrs. Charteris, Capt. Hide dined & Supt, & Mr. Holah supt also. before Tea we walk'd again to Musselburgh & home by the Church yard at Inveresk where the view is very fine Lady Dalrymple & Daughter drank Tea. wrote to my Sisr. Travell

Witts Family Papers F192

1796

Monday June 13th.

Not a very pleasant Day being a very high wind which made the dust intolerable, no sunshine nor rain till quite evening, soon after breakfast we all walk'd down to Musselburgh to make the first visit to Mrs. Kearney, from thence Mr. W. & I walk'd to Stoney Bank to see Mrs. Graham where we made a very chearful visit as we did to Mrs. Charteris, & to the Miss Campbells of Ashenddon, Col: & Mr. Kearney, Col: Adeane, Lord Esgrave Miss Rae & Miss Jane Douglass dined, & the three former play'd'Cards & staid Supper. well pleased with my Cousins

Tuesday June 14th.

Very much the same kind of weather in the Day & again showery in the evening, Mrs. Browning was so kind as to bring us home in her carriage, by the way we made an unsuccessful call on Mrs. Rooke. Mrs. Erskine of Cambo & her Sis^{r.} Mrs. Smith came to me as soon as I got home after wch I went to call on Lady D. & Mrs. Brown. went to Tea, Cards & supper at Lady Riddells 2 Miss Cockburns, Miss Bruce of Stenhouse & the 3 Gentlemen Colquhouns. rec'd a Letter from Miss Neville.

Wensday June 15th.

A Dry Morning but a very showery Noon, such perpetual storms of hail & cold rain that it might almost be term'd perpetual, yet I kept visiting on from house to house after I had been at Lady Riddells Levee, finding only at home Mrs. Mure Mrs. Macdonald & Lady Sinclair, Mrs. Erskine, Mrs. Smith Anna Inglehart & Mr. Com: Brown drank Tea here

Thursday June 16th.

Quite dry the whole of the Day, but windy & not much like mid.summer. went early with Frank to the Dancing School & before Georges hour paid a comfortable visit to Lady C: C: afterwards visited Lady Dukenfield, Major & Miss Melvilles, & a long & very interesting visit to poor Mrs. Young, walk'd pleasantly with the Boys after Tea on Queen Street &'c &'c when we came home found the Principal. rec'd a Letter from Mrs. Parsons. wrote to Miss Anne Snow.

Mrs Smith—quite possibly not the same Mrs Smith—in the costume of 1795. An etching by John Kay.

Friday June 17th.

Very much the same gloomy stormy weather but the air warmer & in the afternoon some small showers. went at Noon into Georges Square, visited M^rs. D. Hamilton, Miss Cockburns & M^rs. Craigie, the 2 latter only at home. M^rs. Young & her Daughter drank Tea & M^rs. Hay call'd late in the evening to take leave. call'd on M^rs. General Campbell returning home from Georges Square & found her at home

Saturday June 18th.

A most uncommon high wind for the time of year, quite tempestuous, but dry the whole of the Day with almost constant sunshine. Col: & M^rs. Kearney & their three little Girls call'd on us & we accompanied them in their Coach to Bruntsfield Links to a grand field Day, of the Volunteers, the wind so high there was no getting out of the carriage. Principal Gordon dined here, & we adjourn'd to Tea, Cards, & Supper at Lady Riddells where was Miss Bruce, Major Melville & M^r. M. Riddell.

Sunday June 19th.

Again very windy & showery, some very sharp ones obliged to return from Morning service at S^t. Georges in a Chair went to the evening at S^t. Andrews a stranger preacher too damp & chilly to go out in the evening, when S^r. Nathaniel Dukenfield sat an hour or two with us, & was very pleasant. wrote to Lady Edward Bentinck.

Monday June 20th.

Wet early in the Morning & showery & very windy & cold till noon, & very unlike mid summer the whole of the Day I never stirrd out all Morning my only visitor Col: Kearney, we went to Dine at Sr James Riddells, to meet the Brownings & a pleasant small party, went to the Card Assembly my imediate party M^rs. Kearney & Miss Campbells of Fairfield it was pleasantly full & very agreable rec'd Letters from M^r. Burslem & Miss Snow.

Tuesday June 21st.

Dry but very little warmer or more pleasant, the air being thick & little sun the Principal call'd upon us very early, & accompanied me to the Dancing School to watch George & afterwards to call on Lady C: C: & M^r & M^rs. Brown on my return home rec'd visits from M^rs. Macqueen & Miss Cockburns & their Aunt. after Tea went to the Castle Hill to see the evening Parade of the Hopetown Fencibles, little amused but by the Music rec'd Letters from M^rs. Hyett & M^rs. Davies.

Wensday June 22d.

Had been much rain in the night, was dry but thick & gloomy, till afternoon when there again fell a considerable quantity of rain, went as usual to Lady Riddell, where there was realy quite a crowd assembled, on account of 2 Raffles that were then & there to be decided, from thence went to the Assembly Room to see M^r. Dundas's Dinner set out, & also into the kitchin to see it dress'd, made a few Visits finding only Lady Blair at home, the Principal came late & we finish'd the evening with a great deal of back gammon.

William Baillie (d. 1816), Lord Polkemmet, was the son of
Thomas Baillie of Polkemmet and Isabel Walker. He was
called to the bench in 1792. An etching by John Kay, 1799.

Thursday June 23ᵈ·

A pleasanter Day than some former ones, the wind not being so high or cold, Mr. Witts went
out early to take a long walk with into the Country with Principal Gordon, I staid within
all Morning receiving visits from Lady Foulis, Miss Bruce of Kinnard & Mrs. Brougham the
Principal dined & spent the evening here as did Sr. Nathaniel & Lady Dukenfield & Miss
Sinclair much conversation as well as Whist & back gammon.

Friday June 24th·

Again very unpleasant weather such a tempestuous wind it was quite a hurricane, with a gloomy
sky & strong appearance of rain, went at Noon to make some visits mostly unsuccessful &
walk'd in the Streets with Mr. Witts by way of exercise went to Tea, Cards & Supper at Lord
Polkemmets[1] a large party of 15 more Gentlemen than Ladies & pleasant enough

Saturday June 25th·

A stormy, & very disagreable Day scarce any rain but such a very high wind it blew quite
a tempest, I staid within all Morning, receiving visits from Mrs. Duff, Principal Gordon &

1.　William Baillie, Lord Polkemmet (±1736–1816). Baillie was the eldest son of Thomas Baillie (d. 1785), writer to the signet,
　　and his wife, Isobel Walker (d. 1777). Descended from an ancient Linlithgowshire family, he was educated for the bar
　　and was admitted as an advocate in 1758. Baillie served as sheriff-depute of Linlithgowshire for more than twenty years.
　　In 1793, as Lord Polkemmet, he was promoted to the bench and became a senator of the college of justice. He was said
　　to have owed his preferment to Lord Braxfield. A great favourite with Scottish lawyers, Baillie was liked for his good
　　humour and use of Scottish dialect. After listening to an over-long speech by Henry Erskine he was said to have reserved
　　his judgment to the following day, saying: 'I'll just mak'it play wimble-wamble in my wame o'er my toddy till the morrow'.

Captain Hide all at different times, went to Tea Cards & Supper at M^rs. Macdowalls, a very pleasant lively party of 15

Sunday June 26th.

Wet in the Morning, as well as being still very windy which kept me from going to Church in the Morning, went to evening service at M^r. Sandfords Chappel, before which paid some visits meeting only M^rs. Com. Brown at home, the three elder Dukenfields dined with us, the younger ones came to Tea as did 3 of the Broughams a fine young riotous party when near dark went to sit at home with S^r. Nathaniel & Lady Dukenfield.

Monday June 27th.

Neither so cold or so windy but not like midsummer, & in the afternoon a sharp shower went to meet George at the Dancing School, & to make a long call on Lady Catherine C: afterwards made two or three unsuccessful visits & survey'd Nixons Minatures, Lady Riddell sending me a Ticket for the Card Assembly I went without wishing or intending it being chaperon to the 4 Miss Douglas's, very thin but very genteel company. rec'd a Letter from Miss B. Guydickens

Tuesday June 28th.

Quite a summer Day, remarkably mild & pleasant, accompanied Lady Dukenfield to New Hailes & a string of unsuccessful visits at Inveresk not at home till ½ past four but ever happy in her Society, tho grieved it was her last Days stay in so near me, went to Tea, Cards & Supper at Lady Riddells a large, Drawing Room party of 15 M^r. & M^rs. Ridell from Mount Riddell there.

Wensday June 29th.

A continuance of fine weather tho realy rather too broiling hot, particularly at Lady R's Levee where an imense party was collected, at another Raffle, from thence as usual made some visits finding only M^rs. Halkett Craigie at home in the evening we had a large party at home to Tea, Cards & Lemonade 11 Ladies & 8 Gentlemen very lively & pleasant

Thursday June 30th.

Quite as hot if not more so in the Morning but rather cooler towards evening, having got three Tickets for the peers Election M^r. W. Frank & myself went down to the Abbey between 10 & 11 where we remain'd till past 2 highly amused with all we saw & heard, more particularly with Lord Lauderdales elocution,[2] taken from thence by Lady Riddell in her Coach shopping & visiting in the South Town, went to Cards & Supper at M^r. G: Fergussons, a party of 12 Lord Justice Clerk, M^rs. Macqueen &'c

---

2. After the Act of Union 1707 abolished the Parliament of Scotland, sixteen Scottish representative peers, all elected from among the peerage of Scotland, were chosen to sit for one parliament. After each dissolution of parliament, a new election of representative peers took place. One name put forward was for George, 14th Earl of Errol, an officer in the army. At the election of 30 June 1796, the earl of Lauderdale protested and petitioned the House of Lords against his return, on the ground that he was not the male descendant of the original earls, but, on the charter of 1666, his election and title were declared valid by the House of Lords 19 May 1797. He died 14 June 1798, aged 32. He had accompanied the expedition against Ostend the previous year. He was then labouring under the disease which ended his life, and was subject to occasional attacks of delirium, in one of which he is said to have disclosed the object of the expedition prematurely.

Friday July 1ˢᵗ·

If possible still hotter than ever from Morn to night I was nearly broil'd with walking to the South Bridge to some shops, went both to Dine & Sup at Lord Justice Clerks carried there by Lord Polkemmet, a party of 12 mostly Gentlemen very few remain'd in the evening but a family party but it was very pleasant. rec'd a Letter from Lady Dukenfield & Mʳˢ· Granville & wrote to the former.

Saturday July 2ᵈ·

Not so hot the wind being high & rather stormy, Mʳ· W. set off between 7 & 8 on a speculation to procure Lodgings at Dunbar at noon I went with Mʳˢ· Riddell &'c to the Review of the Volunteers in Bruntsfield Linx, & in the evening to the Play in Mʳˢ· Macqueens Box, very well entertain it being the first Night of Miss Wallis's performing who appeard both in Every one has his fault & Roxalunn in the Sultan,³ & we had a very pleasant Set in the Box

Sunday July 3ᵈ·

By no means a fine Day the wind being both high & cold, & at times small showers, I went with the Boys to Sᵗ· Georges Chappel, & from there went to make a long visit to Mʳˢ· Com: Brown, did not go to evening church but dress'd to dine at Sir James Riddells only their own family party excepting Miss MacFarlan, went to Drink Tea at Lord Stonefields with Mʳˢ· Browning carried there by Lady Riddell in her Coach, most politely rec'd by Mʳˢ· Campbell, walk'd home with Miss Macdonald who was there. rec'd a Letter from my Dear Husband vex'd he did not return.

Monday July 4ᵗʰ·

A dry & pretty fine Day, but wet in the evening, went at Noon with the Boys to the Dancing School, from thence to Lady C: C: & to some shops ending by calling in Sᵗ· James's Square, when I came home found Mʳ· Witts return'd well. went to Cards & Supper at Mʳ· Belsches a motley large party, singular but not unpleasant

Tuesday July 5ᵗʰ·

Very much the same kind of weather & showery again in the evening, at home & very busy all Morning packing up & preparing to send things away to Dunbar; rec'd no one but the Principal went to Tea, Cards & Supper at Mʳˢ· Macdonalds taken there & back by Lady Riddell in her Coach a droll party of 11 nothing very delightful.

---

3.   Tryphosa Jane Wallis (1774–1848). Tryphosa was born at Richmond, Yorkshire, where her maternal grandmother was associated with the management of the theatre. She appeared as a child in Dublin at the Smock Alley and Crow Street theatres with her parents. The family returned to England, where she continued performing, and after her mother's death in 1785 she was essentially adopted by Lord and Lady Loughborough (later earl and countess of Rosslyn). Through their influence she made her début at Covent Garden on 10 January 1789, as Sigismunda in James Thomson's *Tancred and Sigismunda*. She performed in both Bath and Bristol until 1794, and became a great favourite. On 4 March 1794 she delivered an effusive speech at a farewell benefit and was presented with a medallion from the ladies and gentlemen of Bath, as a 'small tribute to her private virtue and public merit'. From October 1794, she was engaged at Covent Garden, for three years at £18 a week. Her final performance at Covent Garden was on 22 May 1797. She then appeared for a short time at Newcastle and Edinburgh before marrying James Elijah Campbell of the 3rd regiment of the foot guards, at Gladsmuir, East Lothian. On her marriage she left the stage for a time.

Wensday July 6th.

Lowering in the Morning & became wet & very wet before Noon & so continued for several hours, but was chiefly dry in the evening tho very stormy, I went thro all the wet to Lady Riddells more to see poor Mr. Riddell who was alarmingly ill with a fever, afterwards sat a chearful hour with Mrs. Stewart on her recovery, after Tea went an airing with Lady Riddell to Dudinstone Francis with us.

Thursday July 7th.

A tolerable fine Day tho some showers fell, very busy preparing for our approach little Journey, went out at Noon to see Mrs. Brown Mrs. Brougham, & Lady C: C: & so many little Jobs very much distresst with the account of Mr. Riddells alarming situation, call'd on Miss Graham, & she late here in the evening on the melancholly subject. rec'd a letter from my Sister Travell.

Friday July 8th.

A bright & very fine Day throughout tho rather cold & stormy towards evening, after a bustling Morning till 10 o'clock we set forth in the Haddinton Fly Principal Gordon being with us to set off, my spirits a good deal agitated with receiving a very bad account of Mr. Riddell, the only passenger besides ourselves & Maid was a Dutch Officer, it is on the whole a very fine drive of 27 miles to Dunbar, the last 11 from Haddinton we came in a Post Chaise arriving at 5 o'clock glad enough to eat our cold Dinner Lady Dukenfield sitting by; we afterwards walk'd about for an hour or two much pleased with the Town & its environs, went to Bed early well tired with all the Labors of the Day

Saturday July 9th.

A dark gloomy Morning which turn'd out a very showery unpleasant Day & quite cold, very busy all Morning setting our house in order, visited by Mrs. Browning, returnd home with her to see her little habitation & call'd on a Mrs. Fall a very pleasant Woman to whom we had been recommended by Lady C: C: dined enfamile with Lady Dukenfield, when she went to Camp we return'd home to Tea, after, which walk'd with the Boys on the Pier to the Fort &'c. rec'd Letters from Mrs. Witts of Nibley, & Miss Graham with something a better account of poor Mr. Riddell

Sunday July 10th.

As miserably wet & stormy a Morn^{g.} as it had been a night, but fortunately it cleard off at Breakfast time, was dry tho very windy, till quite night when it was again quite showery, at 10 o'clock went in Sr. N. Ds Carriage to Camp where my Lady was before arrived, Lord Adam Gordon being on the ground the Troops of all three Regiments were drawn out for inspection after which a large party assembled in Sr. N. Ds Tent where a cold collation was prepared after which we visited all the Regiments & went into many of the Tents. I drank Tea with Mrs. Rooke in her very little Cottage, meeting Lady D. & Mrs. Browning & staid till near ten. Mr. Witts & the Boys walk'd in the meantime

Monday July 11th.

No rain of any consequence, but still cold & cloudy & towards evening extremely windy went between 7 & 8 to bathe in the Bath, where I plunged in with much intrepidity, my three Gents likewise bathed, I had such a succession of company all Morning I did little Lady Dukenfield, Mrs. Rooke Mrs. Kearney, Mr. Fall & Cap^{tn.} Ximenes,[4] S: D. dined & drank Tea here, after which as we were going to walk sprung upon one of the Miss Baillies who were travelling South with Mrs. G. Campbell who we visited for a few minutes & took her Niece to see the chief beauties around Dunbar. rec'd a Letter from Mrs. Savage & wrote to my Sister Travell Miss Graham & Miss M. Brown.

Tuesday July 12th.

No change for the better in the weather still lowering, windy & cold & late in the evening rain. Lady Dukenfield made an early & long call in the Morn^{g.} after which we all 4 walk'd accompanied by Saml. Dukenfield on the Back road towards the Camp, & looking into Mr. Claverings Place were by him politely invited in introduced to his Wife & taken to the top of the House to see the fine view,[5] all dined with Mrs. Browning, where to Tea came Major & Mrs. Belaces very agreable English people brought Mrs. B. home with us to eat cold Meat & chat.

Wensday July 13th.

Another bitter cold & stormy day with incessant showers tho not severe ones, but much rain had fallen in the night, I went to bathe with Mrs. Rooke & her Daughters as spectators, at noon went across the way to Lorimers Inn to visit Mrs. Belaces, & afterwards Lady Dukenfield, where Mrs. Browning calld for me in her Carriage to take me to visit Mrs. Kearney in her Cottage in the Fields & found her at home, M^{r.} W dined with Col: Rooke at the Mess, & Mrs. Browning again call'd on me in her Carriage to take me to the Camp where we survey'd much Military manouvring, & Drank Tea with Mrs. Kearney in the Colonels Tent, all pleasant but being so extremely cold. wrote to Mrs. Davies.

Thursday July 14th.

Very wet early in the Morning but soon cleard off & the wind being changed it was much warmer & there was much sunshine, I was prevented bathing also by having a very bad cold. at Noon L^{dy.} D. call'd on me to go with her over the way to introduce her to Mrs. Belices from thence we visited together at Mrs. Drysdales, Mr. Witts dined in Camp with Col: Kearney,[6] & I very pleasantly with Mrs. Rooke & her young people, after which we went down to Camp but were too much affraid of the damp to stay long but return'd to Tea & Syllabub at which Mr. Witts joind us. rec'd Letters from Mrs. Rycroft, Lady C: Charteris & Mrs. Wilkinson & wrote to Miss Louisa Lee.

---

4. Captain Morris (Moses) Ximenes (1762–1830). Ximenes was a member of the London Exchange, where he made a large fortune. In 1802 he was elected a warden of the Bevis Marks Synagogue, but declined to accept; and on being fined he resigned from the community and became converted to Christianity. He appears to have adopted a military career, and was known as Captain Ximenes; he was knighted, and became High Sheriff of Kent.

5. Colonel Henry Mord Clavering was commander of the 2nd Argyllshire Regiment, raised 25 October 1794, disbanded at Ayr, 24 July 1802. In 1805 he was listed as a Brigadier-General of the 98th Foot.

6. This appears to be James Kearney. His name does not show up in other records of the Fencible regiments and he may have been recruited into the Royal Windsor Forresters as an officer by Colonel Charles Rooke. The Fencible regiments were all disbanded by 1800 and he next appears as a Major in 12th Light Dragoons, 27 May 1802; followed by Major in 2nd Dragoon Guards, 1 June 1805 (on exchange from 12th Light Dragoons); served in Walcheren 1809; brevet Lieutenant-Colonel 25 July 1810; Lieutenant-Colonel 16 June 1814; commanded 2nd Dragoon Guards 1814 to 1830; brevet Colonel 12 August 1819.

Let Puppy's bark, and Asses bray,
Each Dog and Cur will have his day.

This print is one of Kay's retaliatory pieces. It appears that Alexander Campbell, offended at the etching of his brother the precentor, and having some skill in the art of drawing, produced, by way of revenge, a caricature of Kay—in which John Dow was represented as dragging him by the ear to the Town Guard. The caricature gave amusement to Mr Campbell's friends, among whom it was chiefly circulated. Kay retaliated by producing the *Medley of Musicians*, in which Mr Alexander Campbell, then organist in a chapel, appears with a hand-organ on his back—his brother of the Canongate Church is straining his vocal powers in the centre—Bailie Duff, to the right, is chanting it on the great Highland bagpipe—while behind, Meek, the blind Irish piper, and the city Fish-Horn Blower, are lending their 'sweet sounds'. The couplet is quoted from Samuel Butler's *Hudibras*: 'Let puppies bark and asses bray—Each dog and cur will have his day.'

Friday July 15th.

Quite a mild fine Day till Dinner time when the wind turn'd to the east & it became cold & gloomy my cold too indifferent to think of bathing, my Gents did, Lady Dukenfield made me a very early visit, Mr W & Francis went to the Court Martial, I had a visit from Mrs. Kearney, & walk'd for an hour with C: Dukenfield & George on the Pier &'c, Mrs. Browning call'd on me in the evening to take me to Camp to Drink Tea in Coll: Rookes Tent where was a large company assembled Sr James & Lady Stewart Lord Darlington[7] &'c &'c not at home till near 10. rec'd Letters from Anne Snow & Miss Graham & wrote to Mrs. Com: Brown.

---

7. William Harry Vane (1766–1842). Vane succeeded as 4th Earl of Darlington in 1792. In 1810 he successfully laid claim to the Pulteney Estate in Bath after the Countess of Bath died intestate in 1808. In 1827 he was created Marquess of Cleveland and was Bearer of the Third Sword at King William IV's coronation on 8 September 1831. In 1833 he was made Baron Raby, of Raby Castle in the County Palatine of Durham, and Duke of Cleveland. In 1839 he became a Knight of the Garter in 1839. He was present at the camp as commander of what had been the Durham Regiment of Fencible Cavalry, raised 19 April 1794, but appears to have been reformed as the Princess of Wales's Fencible Cavalry, 4 troops, 14 April 1795.

Saturday July 16th.

Wet, foggy & very disagreable in the Morning clear'd at Noon, was dry the rest of the day but very cold & windy in the evening, went directly after I had breakfasted with Mrs. Ord to see Mrs. Brownings Lodgings & visit her in the course of the Morning visited Lady D. & rec'd one from Mrs. Belices, all our family went to Tea in Sr. Nathaniels Tent a very large mixt company both came & return'd with Lady D. kept very late wrote to Lady Catherine Charteris.

Sunday July 17th.

A most uncommon high wind & at various parts of the Day small showers & in short a very unpleasant Day did not any of us go to church in the Morning but read the service at home, visited Mrs. Belices in her new Lodgings opposite, & as we were all walking to evening church with Lady Dukenfield met Lord Elcho's Coach, of course return'd with them w.h much joy to Lorrimers Inn for two hours where we held much interesting conversation, I drank Tea tetetete with Lady D. when our comfort was quite broke in upon by the arrival of a few Lines from Lady Riddell with the melancholly relation of Mr. Riddells death that Morning much <u>very</u> much hurt.[8] wrote to Lady Riddell & Miss Snow.

Monday July 18th.

A mild & very beautiful Morn a most happy change but it proved very transient, as at 4 o'clock it began raining which continued more or less all the evening but was gloomy hot, we all Bath'd & directly after breakfast I went & sat an hour with Mrs. Browning, Lady Hamilton, & Lady Suttie call'd on me, we went to dine with Sir James & Lady Stewart 2 miles off Mr. W. rode & I went with the Dukenfields the Rookes & their own family set being the whole of the party, supt also not at home till between 12 & 1 wrote to Lady Elcho.

Tuesday July 19th.

Mild air but very showery the greatest part of the Day & in the evening continued hard rain I never went out all Morning but rec'd many visitors Sr. Nathaniel & Lady Dukenfield at different times Mr. Clavering & Mrs. Macdonald & Mrs. Kearney & her little Girls; Frank went with the Dukenfields to a Ball at Sir James Halls & did not return home till near 4 in the Morning, we went to Tea & Supper at Mr. Falls no one there but Col: Cummier. wrote to Miss Graham

Wensday July 20th.

A very pleasant mild Day with a good deal of sunshine & clear air, but as usual it overcast in the evening & became violent hard rain at night Sr. Nathaniel, & Mr. Rooke our only Morning callers & at Noon I went to call on Lady Dukenfield, & Mrs. Rooke &, walk'd with the latter for two hours among the rocks &'c, went to Drink Tea & play at Whist at her Cottage a large agreable party of 12 or 14.

Thursday July 21st.

After a night of prodigious hard rain it was a very showery Morning, so perpetual at Noon & afternoon that it might almost be said constant rain the evening dry with a boisterous wind,

---

8.   Thomas Milles Riddell (1756–1796) of Larbert, Stirling, lord of the manor of Billockby in Norfolk.

we went at 10 o'clock with all the Rookes & Dukenfields accompanied by M^r. & M^rs. Fall to survey one of the Greenland Ships laden with the best part of 10 Whales, from thence we all went to look at M^rs. Fall's beautiful work,[9] call'd on M^rs. Browning & then home, M^r. W. spent the Day at the Court Martial & dining with S^r. Nathaniel at the Mess the Boys & I were a very happy trio & walk'd a great deal after Tea tho almost blown away rec'd a Letter from Lady C; C: & wrote to D^r. Pennington & Miss Betty Guydickens.

Friday July 22^d.

For the greater part of the Day dry with some sunshine tho rather cold & stormy, I only had Lady Stewart as a Morning caller, & went out only to sit half an hour with Lady Dukenfield, drank Tea with her, meeting M^rs. Rooke & M^rs. Browning quite a working party, ending by a rubber at Whist. rec'd a Letter from Miss Graham, & wrote to M^rs. Wilkinson.

Saturday July 23^d.

Very similiar weather, still cold & stormy & at times flying showers of rain, M^rs. Belice & M^rs. Browning here in the Morning, after which we 4 walk'd on the Pier rocks &'c, drank Tea Syllabub & fruit with M^rs. Rooke meeting M^rs. Browning &'c, call'd on L^dy. Dukenfield who was unwell in our way home rec'd a Letter from M^rs. Com: Brown.

Sunday July 24th.

Quite a wet Morning, & continued showery till mid.day & dry & fine afterwards. M^rs. Rooke call'd to take me to Church, where we sat in M^r. Falls Seat & were very well pleased with M^r. Caffre the Preacher I went with M^rs. R. to call on Lady Stewart who we found at home, on our return call'd on Lady D, M^r. W dining at Camp with Cap^tn. Browning, I dined with Col: & M^rs. Rooke, we drank Tea with Lady D. meeting M^r. & M^rs. Fall & M^rs. Browning.

Monday July 25th.

Tolerably fine in the Morning, very showery at Noon & quite hard rain in the afternoon, I got a fine Bathing, & at noon went with Lady Dukenfield in her phaeton first to M^rs. Hamiltons at Beld where we found no one at home, & being no ways intimidated by the drove thro' Dunbar again & went to M^r. Hays at Spot where we made a pleasant visit, their place being well worth seeing, the house 500 years old, built upon a rock, with a deep Moat all round, over which hangs a great deal of wood, the evening proving so very wet the Tea drinking party was in Col: Rookes House instead of his Tent, where was assembled L^dy. D. M^rs. Browning M^rs. Hay & 2 Miss Hays concluding by Cards.

---

9.   The East-Lothian and Merse Whale-Fishing Company was formed in 1752 by Charles and Robert Fall and Robert Melville. They had a fleet of five vessels employing over 200 whalers on the Greenland fisheries with additional side ventures of coal, salt, milling, Baltic timber, salmon fisheries. The partners remained based at Dunbar despite the west coast soaring above the east in trade. Even when the commercial banking and insurance industries began to take a more professional approach towards lending, the Falls were able to continue as before and Robert had married an heiress of the Coutts banking family. In 1788 the earl of Lauderdale bought many of the Dunbar assets and Robert, the last surviving cousin, retired and died in 1796. However, before then activity went on under his wife's name and land reclamation schemes, a spinning school and a textile factory at Belhaven continued until her death in the early part of the nineteenth century.

Tuesday July 26th.

Wet in the Morning, dry & pleasant at Noon very wet in the afternoon, & very lowering in the evening, I went to bathe at 11 & afterwards call'd on Lady D. went with her in the afternoon first to call on M^rs. Fall, & then to drink Tea with M^rs. Rooke in her Cottage, it being too damp for the Camp meeting L^dy. Stewart & M^rs. Kearney, play'd at Cassino & eat Syllabub & fruit the Gentlemen joining us late.

Wensday July 27th.

Quite a fine & very uncommon pleasant Day being wholly dry excepting a short shower at 3 o'clock, went with Lady Dukenfield in her Phaeton a most charming long airing in which we included visits to Lady Stewart & M^rs. Kearney finding only the latter at home, on my return call'd on M^rs. Belairs, we dined with M^rs. Rooke on Venison meeting Lady D. went to drink Tea at Camp in Col: Kearneys Tent a large Party. wrote to Lady Riddell.

Thursday July 28th.

Another very fine Day some rather lowering clouds at times, but no rain for a wonder I sat busy at work all Morning receiving visits from M^rs. Rooke & her Son[10] Major Belairs & M^rs. Browning went to dine at S^r. N. Dukenfields on Venison meeting Rookes, & to Tea & Supper at M^r. Falls, the young people of each family being there also. rec'd a Letter from Miss Snow.

Friday July 29th.

A thick misty Morning, which terminated in a fine Day till after Dinner when there was a sharp shower, & some trifling ones later in the evening call'd late on Lady D. & walk'd afterwards with the Boys part of the way to Camp with M^r. Witts as he was going to dine with the Perthshire Regiment before we return'd home drawn in to Major Belairs[11] tent Solon Goose taken by Ldy. D. to Tea in Lady Stewarts Tent where was a large & smart party, & fine desert after the Parade much press'd to Sup with Col: Adeane but waved it to return with Lady D. wrote to Lady C: C:

Saturday July 30th.

An extreme fine Morning & continued so till the evening when it alter'd much & became cold & stormy after breakfast I call'd on Lady D. & M^rs. Browning, eat cold Solon Goose with M^rs. Rooke, & then went on to see M^rs. Clavering at Winterfield, Miss Rookes & the three eldest Dukenfields drank Tea here & we walk'd in the Fields towards S^r. Peter Warrenders.[12]

Sunday July 31st.

No rain but by no means a pleasant Day being both cold & windy, Miss Rookes call'd on me to go to Morning Church, where we had an excellent discourse as well as in the afternoon,

---

10. Mrs Rooke was Elizabeth, née Dawson, of, Langcliffe Hall, Yorkshire. There were two sons; Henry Willoughby (1782–1869) and John Charles Rooke, who died of wounds in the Peninsular War.

11. Agnes Witts started by referring to the Major and his wife as being of the name 'Belice', but later changed to 'Belair'. No Major Belair has been discovered.

12. Agnes Witts means Sir *Patrick* Warrender (1731–1799); who succeeded as 3rd baronet in 1772. His family seat was Lochend, near Dunbar.

where I went again, M^r. Witts dined in Camp, I went in the afternoon & sat ½ an hour with Lady Dukenfield on her return home; after Tea walk'd with the Boys, & join'd M^rs. Ord & some others. wrote to M^rs. Granville & rec'd a Letter from Lady Elcho.

Monday Aug^st. 1st.

Quite a fine Day on the whole tho the wind was high & many clouds about, went early with M^rs. Ord in her Chaise, & M^r. Clavering, to Press Mannon to see a House offerd to her a most romantic old place 5 miles off, on our return visited Lady Darlington[13] which with more Lodging hunting in the Town, occupied the time till Dinner, went to drink Tea with M^rs. Rooke, meeting Lady Darl: Lady Duk: & M^rs. Browning very pleasant. on our return home found Principal Gordon arrived. rec'd a Letter from Lady Riddell.

Tuesday Aug^st. 2^d.

An intire dry day, with much sun as well as wind but pleasant enough till evening when it became quite cold, the Principal breakfasted with us I went a short airing with M^rs. Rooke in her open carriage & visited L^dy. Dukenfield & M^rs. Drysdale the Principal dined with, & we all drank Tea in Col: Kearneys Tent, M^rs. R. taking me & bringing me back in her Coach.

Wensday Aug^st. 3^d.

Very similiar weather hot sun but much cold wind, went at, Noon with Principal Gordon in a Chaise to Lord Elcho's at Brunston to be ready to attend them to the Haddington Ball of which my Lady was the Queen, had a comfortable family party at Dinner, & a very lively pleasant Ball of 65 persons many well known to me, did not return to Brunston till between 4 & 5 in the Morning bringing M^r. Charteris home with us a great additional pleasure

Thursday Aug^st. 4th.

Another dry but very flowing day with little or no sun, a very late breakfast collected us all very pleasantly together after which we stroll'd about & my Lady & I had much interesting conversation, in the evening late we return'd to Dunbar very happy in finding our good Boys quite well rec'd a Letter from my Sister Travell.

Friday Aug^st. 5th.

A gloomy Morning which terminated in a long & violent shower of rain before I could return from bathing & almost wetted me thro; it clear'd but was succeeded by a most tempestuous wind the whole night as well as day. I sat an hour with L^dy. Duk. & at noon arrived the Elcho family who paid us a short visit in their way to many others, I was much occupied all Day with reading the late Miss Burneys new Novel of Camilia,[14] in the evening walk'd with the Boys but it was very unpleasant. rec'd a Letter from Lady Catherine Charteris.

---

13. Katherine, née Powlett (1766–1807), 2nd daughter and coheir of Harry Powlett, 6th and last Duke of Bolton. Katherine married her cousin William Harry Vane in 1787.

14. *Camilla*, subtitled *A Picture of Youth*; a novel by Frances Burney, first published in 1796. An enormously popular eighteenth-century novel, *Camilla* is one of the first novels in the advancing spirit of romanticism.

Saturday Aug^{st.} 6th.

A dry but very unpleasant day being such a prodigeous high wind that it blew quite a tempest from Morn: to night, I never stirr'd out the whole day bur for a few minutes late in the evening Col: Adeane, M^{r.} & Mrs. Hyde, & Lady Darlington & her children my Morning visitors, & Lady Dukenfield sat two hours here after Tea relating her adventures at Archerfield.[15] deeply engaged in Camelia.

Sunday Aug^{st.} 7th.

Not much a better day being still very cold & windy; but more temperate towards evening I went to Church at both services where a stranger perform'd the service miserably between visited Mrs. Fall, went to Drink Tea in Col: Rookes Tent with a large party, carried there by Captain & Mrs. Hyde & supp'd in Col: Adeanes Tent with the three Ladies of the Cambridge Regiment & 8 Gentlemen very pleasant indeed.[16] quite dark return^{g.} home. rec'd a Letter from Miss Anne Snow.

Monday Aug^{st.} 8th.

Very stormy in the Morning & so continued more or less the whole of the day, with frequent hard showers or rain, Lady Dukenfield, Mrs. Browning, & Mrs. Kearney here in the Morning, & we went to drink Tea with Mrs. Rookes meeting L^{dy's} Darlington & Dukenfield, & play'd at Cassino.

Tuesday Aug^{st.} 9th.

A warm close Morning, & so it remain'd the greater part of the Day, tho with more wind but no rain, went with Mrs. Browning to make a Morning call at Brunston found only Lady Elcho & Kitty at home, I dined with Lady Dukenfield & her children Mr. Witts in Camp with Sr. Nathaniel but he join'd us at Tea we return'd home early & I wrote a Letter to my Sister Travell.

Wensday Aug^{st.} 10th.

A clear day, warm & very pleasant day, but the wind both changing & rising in the evening it was cold beyond belief for the time of year, Lady D. made an early visit, our own party of 4 walk'd to call on L^{dy.} Darlington who we did not find at home but Mrs. Clavering we were sure of, carried by Lady D to drink Tea with a large party in Col: Kearney's Tent, but it was dull & rather comfortless altogether

Thursday Aug^{st.} 11th.

Quite a charming summer Day throughout, warm but not hot, fine air but no wind, went out early with Lady D. in her Phaeton for a short drive in the fields & a call on Mrs. Kearney, walk'd & visited a little with Mr. W. afterwards drank Tea, play'd at Cassino, & supt at Captain Hydes, meeting Mrs. Browning & 2 or three officers.

---

15. Archerfield is a country house and estate approximately twelve miles north-east from Dunbar in the parish of Dirleton, East Lothian.
16. Colonel Robert Jones Adeane (d. 1823), the son of General James Whorwood Adeane (1740–1802). Adeane was Colonel of the Cambridgeshire Regiment; raised 25 April 1795; disbanded early 1800.

Friday Aug^{st.} 12th.

Another very similiar fine Day at last quite summer, at Noon made a short call on L^{dy.} Duk. then went an airing with Mrs. Hyde just to call on L^{dy.} Steuart who was not at home, & afterwards to view the Troops on the Sands, dined at Mr. Hays at Spott[17] taken by the Hydes a party of 18 sad large proportion of Ladies, not very lively at home by 10 o'clock.

Saturday Aug^{st.} 13th.

Just as fine a Day as the two former most pleasant not being too hot Sr. N. D. sat with us while we were at Breakfast, & Lady D. Mrs. Hyde & Mrs. Browning visited me in the Morning & we all went together to call on Mrs. Bellock, carried by L^{dy.} D. in the afternoon to drink Tea in <u>his</u> Tent a very large party 18 Ladies & Gentlemen innumerable a walk about the Camp between Tea & a Smart disert not at home till near 10. wrote to Lady Riddell & Mrs. Com: Brown.

Sunday Aug^{st.} 14th.

If possible a still finer Day, quite hot but not oppressive, went to Morning church, after which Lady D. call'd & Mrs. Browning made a very long visit, we went to drink Tea at Sr. James Stewarts to meet Lord & Lady Elcho who had dined there, taken there & brought back again in Sr. James's Chaise.

Monday Aug^{st.} 15th.

As fine a day as possible warm & clear but not oppressively hot soon after breakfast made visits to Mrs. Hyde, Mrs. Rooke & Lady Dukenfield & on my return rec'd a long one from Mrs. Kearney, dined & supt at Sr. James Stewarts meeting Mackenzies Brownings, & Hydes &'c going with the latter well enough.

Tuesday Aug^{st.} 16th.

Still as much fine summer weather as ever went out only in the Morning to call on Lady Duk. & Mrs. Browning & in the even^{g.} walk'd with the Boys to the Castle Rocks &'c & very late on our return sat an hour with M^{r.} & Mrs. Fall wrote to Lady C: Charteris

Wensday Aug^{st.} 17th.

One of the hottest day there had been at all, went out only to see Lady Duk. much oppress'd all day myself & very far from well Mrs. Hyde my only Morning visitor, at night went to a Ball at Frasers, a most excellent, & very good Meeting from 60 to 70 persons 24 of them officers Lord & Lady Elcho being there made it doubly pleasant came home at one. rec'd a Letter from Mrs. Davies.

Thursday Aug^{st.} 18th.

Rather the most broiling hot Day there had been, very little air & much sun, hardly possible to keep cool tho ever so quiet, call'd on Lady Duk. & Mrs. Browning, walk'd a little on the Pier with some Edinbro acquaintance, Mrs. Browning drank Tea & supt here play'd at Cassino with the Boys.

---

17. Spott is a small village on the eastern fringes of East Lothian just over two miles south-west of Dunbar. The Hays of Yester were related to the Earl of Tweeddale.

Friday Aug^{st.} 19th.

Again very hot rather oppressively so & appearing like a thunder storm approaching but it did not prove so, Lady Duk. made me a long early call in the Morning, & came again at 6 o'clock in the evening in the Phaeton to take me a drive, went 4 miles on the London road & back when she drank Tea with us & Sr Nathaniel join'd her, wrote to Miss Graham & Miss A: Snow.

Saturday Aug^{st.} 20th.

Much the same weather if possible still hotter & one of the finest evenings ever known Francis took a ride or <u>two</u> in the Morning on Captain Brownings Poney, all happiness, Mrs. Mackenzie & Mrs. Rook call'd on me in the Morning, I never stirr'd out between bathing & going with Sr N. & Lady Duk. to dine at Lord Elcho's, where we pass'd a very lively pleasant Day indeed, as much fun as ever was in any party not at home till between 1 & 2 in the Morning rec'd a Letter from Mrs. Whalley & wrote to Mrs. Hyde

Sunday Aug^{st.} 21st.

No great change in the weather equaly fine & hot till evening when it became a little lowering, & a transient shower fell, went to Morning Church, Lady Duk. took Mr W. & myself to dine in Sr Nathaniels Tent quite a domestic pleasant little Dinner, Sr James Hale, his little Boys & some other Gentlemen only to Tea at home as it became dark rec'd a Letter from Miss Graham.

Monday Aug^{st.} 22^{d.}

Another very fine Day tho with a strong wind, but a most peculiar fine clear evening at home quiet all the Morning, went at 2 o'clock after calling on Lady Dukenfield with Mrs. Browning in her Chaise to Camp, where I sat quietly reading in Cap^{tn.} Hydes Tent, till it was Dinner time in Col: Kearneys Tent, where we were a party of 12 very pleasant, walk'd about the Camp, & to the Parade till it was dark & drank Tea in Col: Adeanes Tent. rec'd a Letter from Miss Lee.

Tuesday Aug^{st.} 23^{d.}

Extremely hot very oppressively so from Morn to night, Lady Duk. here after breakfast I walk'd a little & went to see Lord Lauderdales strange House, Mrs. Rooke & Daughter made a long visit Father, Mother, & Sons dined with Mrs. Hyde, walk'd a little in the evening drank Tea & supp'd also to wch was added Cap^{tn.} Bellock, Col: Adeane & Cap^{tn.} Hyde wrote to Mrs. Erskine of Cambo.

Wensday Aug^{st.} 24th.

A fine pleasant Day without either sun or wind & not near so hot as some of the preceding Days, rec'd an early visit from Lady Duk: & M^{rs.} & Miss Wardlow passing thro, went a late airing with Lady Duk. visiting Miss Gilpins instead of Mrs. Fall at the Hill & brought home Sr Nathaniel from the Camp. went late to the Ball with the Bart & his Lady, not near so full a one as the week before but pleasant enough. wrote to Miss Graham.

Thursday Aug^{st.} 25th.

A prodigeous broiling hot Day, quite overcoming, ill suited to my many bustles packing & quitting Dunbar, accompanied by Lady Duk. made take leave calls on Mrs. Browning & M^{rs.}

Fall, & rec'd them from M^rs. Hyde & M^rs. Kearney & at 2 o'clock set out bag & baggage for Brunston stopping by the way for half an hour at M^r. Claverings met with a pleasant reception from our friends to whom was added at Dinner only two odd men; play'd at Cards in the evening till a late hour.

Friday Aug^st. 26th.

A rainey Morning & tho it clear'd in a degree was showery more or less till Dinner time & was a very fine evening, walk'd a little about the home premises & to Dinner arrived M^r. Nisbetts Family & the Duke of Rutland & three other Gents in his party,[18] some of them very pleasant & quite a lively agreable Day altogether a Fiddle as well as Cards in the evening. terrible late hours the worst

Saturday Aug^st. 27th.

Again very fine weather, tho the air was sharper but the sun brilliant, a late breakfast & much dawdling. afterwards till the Gentlemen all set out on a Tour to the Bas.[19] from whence they join'd us at a very late hour at Dinner at M^r. Nisbetts at Archerfield, a very handsome place a noble Sea view, but rather a want of shelter from scarcity of wood a charming house nobly furnish'd & most elegantly kept the entertainment quite in a high stile, not at home till one in the Morning.[20]

Sunday Aug^st. 28th.

Most charming weather still, so clear an air that tho the sun shone perpetualy it was not too hot, walk'd but little, sat chiefly with Miss Charteris who was not well, S^r. James Steuart & M^r. Trotter call'd in the Morning, M^r. Witts & George walk'd to Cap^tn. Brown's at Congalton, much free & very interesting conversation in the course of the day. rec'd a Letter from M^rs. Erskine of Cambo.

Monday Aug^st. 29th.

Quite a thick Morning, small rain or <u>Scotch</u> <u>Mist</u>, which you will, which tolerably cleard off at noon, the afternoon fine, & in the evening came on most suddenly a very uncommon thick wetting fog, Morning was spent very busily assisting to set our Friends all off for Edinbro' in their way into Fife but it suiting our engagements better to remain at Brunston for two or three Days they most kindly urged our remaining spent the rest of the Day most pleasantly tho quietly, & between Dinner & Tea walk'd to Stevenson, late Lady Sinclairs, now just taken by M^r. Sitwell who we found there, & very politely shew'd us the place, I found it very long walk, tho but for the fog it would have been most pleasant. wrote to Lady Dukenfield

---

18.   John Henry Manners (1778–1857); 5th Duke of Rutland. At this point in his life, the teenage duke had just taken his MA at Cambridge. He was presumably heading to Archerfield to stay with his cousin, Mrs Mary Nisbet.

19.   The Bass Rock, or simply The Bass, an island in the outer part of the Firth of Forth approximately 1.2 miles offshore, and 3.1 miles north-east of North Berwick.

20.   William Hamilton Nisbet (1747–1822); MP Haddingtonshire 1777–1780, East Grinstead 1790–1796 and Newport, Isle of Wight 1796–1800. Nisbet married, 1777, Mary née Manners, daughter of Lord Robert Manners. They had one child: Mary Nisbet (±1784–1855), married, 1799, Thomas Bruce, 7th Earl of Elgin; of 'Elgin Marbles' fame. They divorced 1808 and Mary married Robert Fergusson of Raith, and the couple settled at Archerfield.

Tuesday Aug^(st.) 30^(th.)

A most glorious & true summer Day very clear air & much sun & quite a fine evening, M^r. Witts rode imediately after breakfast to Congalton & N: Berwick House to settle our visits, Lady Dukenfield & three eldest children came at noon, & I persuaded her to stay Dinner, delighted to see her, but sorry to part with her very soon after when we took a walk till quite dark. rec'd Letters from Lady Dukenfield, M^(rs.) Tracy & my Sister Travell & wrote to M^(rs.) Rycroft.

Wensday Aug^(st.) 31^(st.)

Quite a pleasant Day tho neither so hot nor so much broiling sunshine, M^r. W. rode to Haddington on some errands, Cap^(tn.) & M^(rs.) Brown sat an hour with me, & between Dinner & Tea we walk'd to see both the House & Gardens at Gilmerton belonging to the unfortunate Kinloch family, the latter excellent but the former stands low & dull, as well as very damp.[21]

Thursday Sepr. 1^(st.)

Rather a dull cloudy Morning, & not very warm thro' the whole of the Day tho it kept dry busy all Morning packing &'c, to be ready for S^r H: H. Dalrymples[22] Coach which came to carry us to Dinner at North Berwick House a drive of 6 or 7 miles thro a varied & fine Corn Country, where we found Cap^(tn.) & M^(rs.) Brown besides a party of their own family circle of 8 or 10 very lively & pleasant, it is a handsome place the House standing on a fine eminence, which is large & well laid out, & handsomely furnish'd much card playing in the evening.

Friday Sepr. 2^(d.)

A fine Day on the whole excepting a sharp shower at breakfast time, a good deal of sun as well as wind, the party variously dispersed in the course of the Morning, M^r. Witts & I took a walk Lady Haddington & M^r. J. Dalrymple[23] & Miss Gascoigne made a Morning visit, a chearful Dinner & evening party.

Saturday Sepr. 3^(d.)

Quite a lowering Morning which very soon produced a serious wet Day, accompanied by much wind, fit for nothing but writing & reading interspersed with much conversation,

---

21. The 'unfortunate' Kinloch family at Gilmerton was headed by Alexander Kinloch (±1752–1813). His eldest brother had been Francis Kinloch, 6th Baronet (±1747–1795). Two months after he had succeeded to the title, Francis was murdered on the front stairs by his deranged brother Archibald whose health had declined after service in the West Indies. Archibald was not hanged after his trial but released into the care of his family, becoming *de jure* 7th Baronet. It was to prove a very controversial plea and which is known to be one of the earliest recorded defences on the grounds of insanity. He died in 1800 and Alexander then succeeded as 8th Baronet. He married, 1801, Isabella Stowe (b. ±1773).

22. Hew Hamilton-Dalrymple of Bargany (±1746–1800), 3rd Baronet. He married, ±1772, his cousin Janet Duff, daughter of William Duff of Crombie and Elizabeth Dalrymple. Hew Hamilton-Dalrymple had been MP for Haddingtonshire 1780–86 and was Auditor of the Exchequer in 1786. He changed his name from Dalrymple to Hamilton Dalrymple in 1796. His son, also named Hew Hamilton-Dalrymple (1774–1834), 4th Baronet, was MP for Haddingtonshire 1795–1800; Ayrshire 1803–07; 1811–18 and Haddington Burghs 1820–26.

23. John Dalrymple (±1776–1835). John was a cornet in the 28th dragoons 1795, lieutenant 1797, rising eventually to Major-General in 1819; MP for Haddington Burghs 1805–06; succeeded his brother Hew as 5th Baronet in 1834.

Lady Haddinton M[r.] J. Dalrymple Miss Gasgoigne, M[r.] & M[rs.] Charles Dalrymple[24] & M[rs.] G: Dalrymple[25] dined here making up a party of 20. wrote to my Sis[r.] Travell

Sunday Sep[r.] 4[th.]

A dry Day with much sun & wind the younger part of the family went to church at North Berwick I walk'd with S[r.] Hew among his improvements & accompanied him & L[dy.] Dumfries in her Coach to evening service where we previously visited M[r.] & M[rs.] C: Dalrymple, a large party of 20 again at Dinner, Major Eaton & Cap[tn.] Thackery from the Camp & 4 other Gentlemen wrote to Lady Duken.

Monday Sep[r.] 5[th.]

A most tremendous wind accompanied by such lowering clouds as portended rain by far too bad to permit our crossing the water into Fife which we had intended, S[r.] Hew, Miss Ailston M[r.] W. & I braved it & took a very long walk to one of S[r.] Hew's new Farms much pleased with the Country, no company at Dinner but extremely chearful & pleasant quite enfamille. wrote to Miss Forrest.

Tuesday Sep[r.] 6[th.]

Again a most stormy terrible Day, & in the Morning hard rain for several hours, which wholly put off even the smallest idea of our voyage, but was fine at noon & very fine in the afternoon, walk'd a little in the Garden before Dinner, to which were added besides the family party Col: & M[rs.] Kearney, who returnd to Dunbar before Supper a very chearful evening.

Wensday Sep[r.] 7[th.]

Tolerably fine early in the Morning but soon became so tremendously windy that again our Voyage was postponed, tho we were absolutely in the Coach to go to North Berwick to go aboard, walk'd a good deal with S[r.] Hew & his Son, <u>almost</u> blown away so doing, our party much reduced, by the departure of Lady Dumfries,[26] & M[r.] & Miss Gordon[27] but a very merry evening notwithstanding.

Thursday Sep[r.] 8[th.]

Still rather windy but so much a more temperate Day that we began to think we might attempt crossing the water, & went down to N. Berwick in the Coach at 11 o'clock, & went aboard

24. Charles Dalrymple (d. 1799). Charles was the son of Sir Robert Dalrymple of Castleton (d. 1734) and his second wife Anne Cunninghame (1706–1776); and was therefore uncle (or half-uncle) to Sir Hew Hamilton Dalrymple. He married (for a second time), 1769, Mary Dalrymple, née Douglas (d. 1799), the widow of Lieutenant Colin Campbell Dalrymple (1725–1767).

25. Colonel George Dalrymple (1757–1804). George was the son of Mary Dalrymple and Lieutenant Colin Campbell Dalrymple (1725–1767). He married, 1785, Martha Willett, née Miller (b. ±1758), off Mount Denison, Nova Scotia.

26. Anne Dalrymple-Crichton (±1738–1811), dowager Lady Dumfries, widow of William Dalrymple-Crichton (d. 1768), 5th Earl of Dumfries. Anne had married, 1769, a Scottish judge, Alexander Gordon (1739–1792), Lord Rockville, the youngest son of William Gordon, 2nd Earl of Aberdeen, but she appears to have retained the style of 'Lady Dumfries'. She was the daughter of William Duff and Elizabeth, daughter of Sir Robert Dalrymple, and therefore sister to Lady Hamilton Dalrymple.

27. Mr and Miss Gordon were children of Lady Dumfries and her second marriage to Alexander Gordon.

at 12 well assisted by good M^r C: Dalrymple, who was kindly anxious we should have every accomodation, at first the sea ran severely high & I was much alarm'd but our little vessel rode it well, & we perform'd our voyage well & very quickly, going over to Ansthruther which is 16 miles across in 10 minutes less than two hours, & the wind lowering & the weather becoming fine I should realy have enjoy'd it but for being so extremely sick that I could have no enjoyment, a moderately good Inn, afforded us a moderate Dinner from which I was refresh'd, & took a little walk afterwards to view the adjacent Country, which is in some measure similiar to East Lothien but not near so rich either in Corn land or Wood. at 5 o'clock arrived Mr Erskines Carriage, which convey'd us to Cambo House about 5 miles distant,[28] over a fine country commanding to the left a noble Sea view, our Friends rec'd us with the utmost cordiality, & we found with them a large circle of Dining company who soon went away excepting Mr Durham of Largo[29] & a Young Lady with him who staid all night, play'd a little at Whist and went early to Bed being nearly knock'd up. rec'd a Letter from Lady Elcho.

Friday Sepr 9$^{th.}$

A most prodigeous fine & hot Day rather oppressively so early in the Day but delightful towards evening, walk'd after breakfast down to the Sea but soon sent in by the heat, Mr Durham & his young Lady took their leave, a pleasant Day of quiet enjoyment with our worthy friends, walk'd to the Garden &'c before Tea & play'd a little at Whist. wrote to Lady Catherine Charteris

Saturday Sepr 10$^{th.}$

A fog in the Morning which in some degree return'd at various parts of the Day, & at night there was hard rain being rather unwell I walk'd very little the Gentlemen <u>all</u> rode out in the Morning, the Boys supremely happy in seeing a fine course & Frank in at the Death of a Hare. evening spent like the former

Sunday Sepr 11$^{th.}$

Quite a glorious clear hot Day very little like the season of the Year, went down with M$^{rs.}$ Erskine & Anna to see them Bathe after breakfast & walk'd a little again before Dinner to which came Mr Erskines Brother & his Wife & return'd after Tea their House being only 4 or 5 miles distant. in the even^g the Boys read one of Blairs Sermons. wrote to Lady Hamilton Lady Wedderburn, & M$^{rs.}$ Davies.

---

28. The Cambo estate had been sold to the Charteris family in 1759, who bought it for Francis Lord Elcho, who was then studying at St Andrews University. Thomas Erskine (±1745–1828), was British Consul at Gothenburg in 1775. He married, 1771, Anne, daughter of Adam Gordon of Ardoch. Ersksine had been a successful merchant in Sweden, and on returning to Scotland he re-purchased the Cambo estate and invested heavily in improving the estate, building picturesque Georgian estate farms, and carrying out extensive land drainage. He commissioned the architect Robert Balfour to remodel the house in 1795. In 1799 he succeeded his nephew, Charles Erskine, as 9th Earl of Kellie.

29. James Durham of Largo (1732–1808). Durham's most famous son was Admiral Sir Philip Charles Calderwood Henderson Durham, GCB (1763–1845). He saw service in the American Revolutionary War, French Revolutionary War and Napoleonic Wars and his service was lengthy, distinguished and at times controversial. Others children were James Durham (1754–1840), later General; Thomas Durham (1756–1815); Margaret Strange, née Durham (1760–1791) and William Durham (1764–1786). The family Durham of Calderwood maintained a house at George's Street, north side. They appear to be related to another of Agnes's acquaintances, Miss Cunningham Durham of No. 1 South Charlotte Street.

Monday Sepr 12th.

Another very delightful Day, clear air & fine sun Col: Moneypenny his Son & another Gentlemen call'd here early after which we all set off for St Andrews the 4 Ladies in the Chaise, & the 4 Gents on horseback, the distance 7 miles, roads good, & Country fine open corn land, with a grand view of the Ocean, the approach to the Town shews it off to great advantage it stands moderately high with a handsome Bay before it, it wears the vestige of great antiquity, & the principal things worthy observation in it are its ancient bricks which are very fine, its school & College is still in estimation, we met with great civilities from the Principal Dr Maccormick,[30] & several others, & were shew'd the churches & everything at all worthy of remark, but on the whole I thought it a dull & very melancholly spot. return'd home to a very late Dinner well tired with the labors of the Day.

Tuesday Sepr 13th.

A dull Morning which was succeeded by a very showery day, amounting almost to constant rain but the Day appear'd neither long nor tiresome from, much work & other employments, & pleasant free converse with a little whist in the evening. rec'd Letters from L.^{dy.} C: Charteris, Mrs. Granville & Miss A. Snow.

Wensday Sepr 14th.

Tolerably fine in the Morning, but afternoon became very stormy, accompanied by thick misty rain, which continued all Day, at Noon the Ladies in the Chaise & the Gents walk'd, went to survey the eastern most part of the County call'd Fifeness, a small promontery jutting out into the Sea with a small Villiage on it, a most dreary spot appearing quite like the end of the world, from thence to Balcomie a Seat belonging to the Marchioness of Titchfield standing high, & very exposed, & possessing little beauty or Merit but a very extensive Sea view the House is large, & old with a great number of ill chosen Pictures with little merit in them on our way home we stoppd at Warmiston to pay a visit to two old Miss Lindsays in Days of yore great friends of Lord Elchos. a Mr Lindsay dined here rec'd a most pleasing Letter from Lady Dukenfield & wrote to Mrs. Hyett.

Thursday Sepr 15th.

After a night of very hard rain it became a mild & very charming Day clear air & much bright sun I walk'd a little Mr W. & the Boys with Miss Stewart went to see Miss Lindsays, Mr Erskine dined at a Public meeting & M.^r & Mrs. Dewar & Daughter arrived quite late. wrote to Lady Dukenfield & Mrs. Grant.

Friday Sepr 16th.

Very wet early in the Morning, & tho it ceased raining, was a very stormy damp disagreable Day & quite oppressively hot, walk'd a little at Noon in Garden &'c, & Mr W., myself, Francis, Mr Erskine & Miss Stewart went to Dine at Col: Moneypennys at Pitmelly,[31] a very pleasant visit return'd home soon after Tea.

---

30. Dr Joseph McCormick (1733–1799), Principal of the United College, University of St Andrews.
31. Lt-Col. Alexander Monypenny of Pitmilly (1726–1801).

Saturday Sep.ʳ 17ᵗʰ·

Another stormy & very unpleasant Day with frequent showers went down with the bathers & were caught in hard shower coming back. no addition to our family circle which was very pleasant. wrote to Lord Tracy an interesting Letter.

Sunday Sep.ʳ 18ᵗʰ·

A very fine Day upon the whole much sun & wind, Mʳ· Erskine & Mʳ· Witts the only ones that went to Church, we walk'd, & had a sermon & Prayers, Mʳ· & Miss Moneypenny call'd & all but Mʳˢ· Erskine went to dine at Awdrie Mʳ· Nathan Erskines about 5 miles distant of a most execrable road, an old House but very fine situation & most glorious Sea view, not at home till quite dark.

Monday Sep.ʳ 19ᵗʰ·

Such an uncommon fine Day as much give delight to all the Gentlemen went a coursing Mʳˢ· Erskine & I took a long charming interesting walk by the Sea Side, a large party dined consisting of Dʳ· Mʳˢ· Mʳ· & Miss McCormick, Mʳ· Tyrell & Dʳ· Hill, who going away early we had as usual a pleasant evening of whist & conversation

Tuesday Sep.ʳ 20

A most sad reverse of weather being a constant succession of wind & rain from Morn: to night & very cold & damp also, excepting from lamenting the cold on the earth, I little cared about it as I found many employs in the Morning & much pleasant & sociable intercourse in the evening.

Wensday Sep.ʳ 21ˢᵗ·

If possible a still more inclement day the wind being higher, & the rain more severe, it absolutely blew quite a tempest, but in such pleasant society it little interrupted our comfort, a fiddle & little dance made the young people quite gay in the evening wrote to Miss Anne Snow & rec'd a Letter from Lᵈʸ· Wedderburn.

Thursday Sep.ʳ 22ᵈ·

A better day tho far from fine being still very stormy but little rain fell, but we felt glad we had been persuaded to put off our Journey were extremely glad to get an hours Walk after breakfast after having been shut up for two Days. Major & Mʳˢ· Dewar made their departure for Mʳ· Nathan Erskines

Friday Sep.ʳ 23ᵈ·

A tolerable fine Morning which improved into a very pleasant day & was perfectly dry from Morn to night, we bid adieu to Cambo & our very pleasant & worthy friends at mid.day with infinite regret & much gratitude for all their kindness & went to Sᵗ· Andrews in a most miserable hired Chaise from there on our arrival made some visits & walk'd about the Town till Dinner time drank Tea with Mʳ· & Mʳˢ· Maclean, & supp'd at Dʳ· McCormicks with a pleasant small party, very hospitable indeed.

Saturday Sep.ʳ 24ᵗʰ·

Quite a beautiful fine Morning which continued so till 2 o'clock when a thick misty rain came on

A later engraving of the Grassmarket and the Castle, by William Ballingall, 1877.

which lasted the whole of the evening & at night became very hard rain; we left St Andrews between 9 & 10, & went 10 miles to the Ferry at Woodhaven, thro a fine Country commanding Sea views, Corn land much Wood & many Gentlemens Seats. the Hill leading down to the Ferry presents a most glorious scenery, the Firth of Tay is three miles across to the Town of Dundee which is a beautiful object on the Waters edge, although I never saw a Scene I was more struck with, wind & Tide being in our favor we cross'd in a very comfortable Boat in 18 minutes Dundee is a very large Town, very populous, & of great Trade, Gordons Inn is a very good one where we made an excellent Dinner, during the preparation for it, we walk'd in many part of the Town; left it at 4 to go 9 miles to Sir J. Wedderburns at Balindean on the Perth Road, the evening proved so very bad, we could see but little of the fine rich country we pass'd thro, & did not arrive till quite dark, found a large company assembled a Lady Douglass & a Major & M$^{rs.}$ Duff being added to their own large family circle, met with a very pleasant reception saw reels danced & play at whist, rec'd a Letter from M$^{rs.}$ Grant.

Sunday Sepr 25$^{th.}$

As fine a day as possible more like mid:summer than Michs. constant warm sun & clear air after a very chearful social breakfast, L$^{dy.}$ Wedderburn Major Duff, Mr Witts & I went in the Coach the three Boys on Horseback, to see Mr Pattersons at Castle Huntley[32] about 4 miles

---

32. George Paterson (1734–1817). Paterson was born in Dundee and rose to the rank of surgeon in the army. He then became secretary to Sir John Lindsay who was appointed to enquire into the relations between the East India Company and the Nawab of the Arcot in 1769. He married the Anne Gray and bought Castle Huntly in Perthshire, which his wife's ancestors had built in 1452 and which for many years had been in the hands of the Strathmore family.

distant a very fine place a large old House in the Castle Stile, in high repair & well furnish'd, & commanding both an extensive & rich view from the top of the Castle as well as a fine command of the Tay. evening past very chearfully as well as agreably. wrote to Mrs. Erskine.

Monday Sepr. 26th.
Another equaly fine Day no interruption till quite evening when it became lowering & a little rain at Noon walk'd with J. Wedderburn, & G: Brown, to the very top of the Hill behind the House, & survey'd a most noble view of the River & Castle, to Dinner came M^{r.} & Mrs. Patterson & family, Lord Rollo & Mr. Oliphant of Rossie, & a Cap^{tn.} Wedderburn the three last staid all night a very chearful pleasant Day. wrote to Lady Elcho & Mrs. Grant.

Tuesday Sepr. 27th.
If possible still finer weather than ever, most charming for the remaining harvest I walk'd a little after breakfast, we dined at Mrs. Alluns at Errol about 7 miles off at least Sr. John my Lady & Miss J. Wedderburn & ourselves, a Sweet country we had to pass thro' the greater part of the way on the road to Perth, a fine situated place very near to the River a handsome entertainment but very singular family return'd home by the bright light of the stars.

Wensday Sepr. 28th.
Just the same delightful fine weather if possible still more like summer, a quiet home Morning, but went to Dine at Mr. Patisons, Boys & all, no one there but the two families but that made a very considerable large party. return'd home before supper time by the same brilliant light as the former evening. wrote to Miss Louisa Lee

Thursday Sepr. 29th.
As fine in the Morning but became a little cloudy, & lowering, at Noon which brought on a very small shower, after which it was fine again, after breakfast left our very pleasant friends at Balindean with much regret having spent our time so very pleasantly, went to Perth 14 miles of a very fine Country the same continuance of rich corse land, the approach to the Town I ever think pleasing stoppd an hour there, walk'd to survey the Barracks then set out for Mr. Grants

A distant view of Perth and the bridge and river approach. An early nineteenth-century engraving.

at Kilgraston 4 miles distant, it is a very moderate place & sad old House, met with a very kind reception, Mr Johnston only with them, but Mrs Oliphant & her Daughter arrived in the evening having dined out, much mirth & whist playing, rec'd a Letter from Lady Dukenfield.

Friday Sepr 30th

Rather a cloudy dull Day without either much sun or wind but quite dry, Miss Oliphant, Mr Grant, Mr W. & I took a very long walk about His own Woods & greenhouses, wch by the by are not very beautiful less so than much of the adjacent country, no additional company, but the evening pass'd very chearfuly.

Saturday Octr 1st

Much the same weather, a little cold & stormy with now & then faint gleams of sunshine, Mr Witts & Sons attended by Mr Johnston walk'd to pay visits at the ossie[33] & Newton, Mrs Oliphant & I went in her Chaise to Perth on Some errands, fortunately the Dukenfield family were arrived just before & I had much pleasure in seeing in seeing them. Mrs O. & Daughter dined at Lady Elizabeth Moncriefs

Sunday Octr 2^d

Dry but not very pleasant weather being rather cold & stormy, went to church in the Chaise at the Bridge of Erne, where we were detain'd a great while by a most elaborate preacher who gave us two distinct sermons, after Church Miss Oliphant & I went to call both at Rossie at Newton, found the family at home at the latter & made a very pleasant visit evening very sombre & yet argumentative

Monday Octr 3^d

A finer Day on the whole with a little sunshine we left Kilgraston soon after breakfast Mr Oliphant calling first & went to Walnefields Inn at Perth, to see the Dukenfields with whom we spent the whole Day very pleasantly rec'd a Letter f^m Mrs Erskine

Tuesday Octr. 4th

A disagreable damp foggy Morning wch too soon produced a thorough wet Day, with a very close warm air, not pleasant to be quite confined after a very chearful breakfast, with our friends they all set off for Lord Balgonies & we in vain tried to take a walk, rec'd visits in the Morning from Sr John Wedderburn, Mr Grant & Mr Oliphant of Conde, had a good Dinner & a quiet evening. wrote to Lady C: Charteris, Mrs Rooke, & my Sister Travell.

Wensday Octr 5th

A most happy change in the weather being a bright & uncommon fine Day from Morn: to

---

33. Clach Ossian (Ossian's Stone). This is a glacial erratic in a field off the road through The Sma' Glen. It was reputed to be the grave of the Bard Ossian. When it was moved out of the way by General Wade's road builders 'with much effort' it is said a cavity 2 feet square was found under it. This contained ashes, scraps of bone and bits of burned heather. The contents were removed with great ceremony by the local Highlanders and reburied in Glen Almond.

34. Alexander Leslie (1749–1820), Lord Balgonie. Deputy Lieutenant of Fife, 1794; Lt. Col. Fife Milita, 1798. He married, 1784, Jane, née Thornton (1757–1818). He succeeded in 1802 as 9th Earl of Leven,

night left Perth at 11 o'clock to follow our friends the Dukenfields to Lord Balgonies,[34] as we pass'd over the Bridge of Erne amused by the sight of the Hunt, went for three miles on the Kinross road, then struck off to the left over the Abernethy Hills, which we continued ascending far upwards of four miles over a very dreary wild Country tho the views below into the Corse of Gouric were rich & beautiful, pass'd thro Falkland a very miserable old Town nothing worthy of remark in it, but the views of its fine old Castle, from thence to the New Inn the Country rather finer the vale being rich & fertile where we were very happy to arrive after a tedious stage of 18 miles wch took us up 5 hours, a good Dinner soon refresh'd us & we set out again to go 4 miles farther to Balgonie thro a rich & pleasant Country, & arrived there as it was dark meeting with a very polite reception & besides our old Friends, there was a Mr Fyers & Miss Ruthneves staying in the House, it is an extreme old one in the Castle stile but by no means uncomfortable & the situation very pleasant the River Leven running close to the House & many fine old Trees gracing its banks.

Thursday Octr 6th.

Another very fine Morning at Noon a very severe Shower, which sent the Gentlemen home dripping from a ride they had taken to Weymss Castle the Ladies all walk'd in the Garden & woods, & work'd very socially & pleasantly, & Cards in the evening. much pleased by the fine shew of young people amounting to a round Dozen, & forming quite a flight of steps. 3 Neighbouring Clergymen dined here

Friday Octr 7th.

Much such another Day, & at the same hour another Shower tho not so violent a one at mid. Day the Dukenfield family went for a night to Weymss Castle, the Gentlemen rode & Lady Balgonie & I took a long & very pleasant walk exploring views & Country, Miss Ruthneves being likewise gone our party was much reduced but very pleasant & we play'd a lively game at Cribage at night.

Saturday Octr 8th.

As fine a day as possible for the time of year constant sunshine & mild air, the Gentlemen as usual took a long ride & my Lady & I our walk to the Viliage of Milton & its pleasant environs, the Dukenfields return'd to Dinner, to which also came Col: David Leslie,[35] my Lords Brother & Mr Balfour the former remaining all night a very chearful evening.

Sunday Octr 9th.

A dark gloomy Morning which before Noon produced rain & it became a wet very wet Day the whole party young as well as old excepting Lady D. who was not well went to Church at the Viliage of Markinch, where we had a very long Sermon from a very young Man. Mr Fyers went away early in the Morning & there was only our own party the whole Day

---

35. David Leslie (±1754–1838). David was the son of David Leslie, 8th Earl of Leven and Wilhelmina Nisbet. He married, 1787, Rebecca Gillies, daughter of Reverend John Gillies. David Leslie was an army officer and rose to the rank of general.

Monday Oct^r *10*th

After a frosty night it was a very clear fine Morning with constant sunshine, but a high wind a general dispersion took place of the whole party the Dukenfields returning to Perth Col: Leslie to Melville & ourselves to Edinburgh, but none quitted Balgonie till 12 & one, when we bid adieu to our courteous friends with grateful regret; the stage to Kinghorne is 12 miles of a very stoney unpleasant road, the Country varied & the Sea views fine the Town of Kirkcaldy very tedious to pass thro', being a mile & half in length but a very beggarly looking place, were surprized when we got to Kinghorne, to be sent on a quarter of a mile to the New Inn close on the Shore, where the people were only gone to reside that very Day of course everything in sad confusion

Tuesday Oct^r *11*th

Quite a cold stormy Morning with short flying showers, but not lasting, & early in the day clear'd off to be dry & fine left Kinghorne between 8 & 9 in the passage Vessel for Edinburgh which is well appoint'd & in which were at least 50 Persons aboard, the distance across to Leith is 7 miles which we were more than a hour & ½ performing the wind & tide xxx both against us but it would have been by no means unpleasant but for the extreme cold which we could not wonder at, when we saw many of the Hills coverd with snow, a Coach from Leith brought us & our baggage to our own house by 11 o'clock after I had turn'd myself round went out to make some needful visits those I found at home were M^{rs}· Brown & M^{rs}· Young, Miss Brown sat two or three hours with us in the evening. rec'd Letters from Lady Riddell, Miss Snow, M^{rs}· Wilkinson, my Sis^r· Travell, M^r· Clavering & D^r· Pennington.

Wensday Oct^r *12*th

Had been very wet in the night & continued so till between 8 & 9 when it became very fine & remain'd so the whole Day with much sun which made it quite dry, Cap^{tn}· & M^{rs}· Browning made us an early visit at Noon we sallied forth on various bussinesses, & to call on Lady C: Charteris who rejoiced to see us, not at home till near Dinner time. wrote to M^{rs}· Whalley.

Thursday Oct^r· *13*th

A dry & pretty good day with much sunshine went out to make several visits unsuccessful in all but M^{rs}· Brown, the Principal here all the evening much chat wrote to Lady Balgonie & M^r· Clavering.

Friday Oct^r· *14*th

Wet in showers the greater part of the Morning but dry & fine the rest of the day, very busy all Morn: in a variety of employs, went to Dine at M^r· Browns, rather a motley crew of 12 but by no means unpleasant, when we left them accompanied by the Principal we went to sit an hour or two with Lord & Lady Elcho &'c at Walkers Hottel. rec'd a Letter from B. Guydickens

Saturday Oct^r· *15*th

Damp in the Morning, but fine & very fine afterwards & the evening particularly clear & Moonlight went at Noon to Walkers Hotel to call on the Elchos & walk'd with them the greater part of the Morning to shops & to visit Lady Catherine, & ended my Morning walk by calling on M^rs. Browning went to Dine at Fortunes Tavern with the Elchos the Boys also to Tea all very merry & joyous wrote to M^rs. Grant & Lady Dukenfield.

Sunday Octr. 16th.

Fine both Day & night tho rather sharp & cold, went to Morning Church at S^t. Georges, M^r. Witts having a bad cold never stirr'd out the whole Day, visited M^rs. Mure & others after Church, Lady Elcho & Daughter & M^r. Com: Brown here, & I walk'd & visited with the ladies till near Dinner time, went to Tea with my Friends at Walkers Hotel, a very large party of both French & English

Monday Octr. 17th.

A clear & very fine Day tho with a cold air went out at twelve o'clock & did not return till three making some few unsuccessful visits, doing some little matters of bussiness, & taking leave & seeing the Elcho's set off the most melancholly & unpleasant of all bussiness Cap^tn. & M^rs. Browning drank Tea & play'd a chearful game at Cassino here. wrote to M^rs. Riddell, the first time

Tuesday Octr. 18th.

Wet in the Morning, & damp & showery the remainder of the day tho sometimes the sun shone I never stirr'd out the whole Day M^rs. Young call'd here she came again in the evening to Tea as did Principal Gordon.

Wensday Octr. 19th.

An exceeding fine mild day with perpetual sunshine, my first Morning call to comfort Lady C: C: for the loss of her friends, then to make an unsuccessful call on M^rs. Longan, after walk'd a little about the Abbey on my return home visited M^rs. Brown for an hour or more went to Tea & supper at Cap^tn. Brownings, where we met Col: Hearne a merry game at Whist & chearful evening. rec'd Letters from M^rs. Rooke & M^rs. Davies.

Thursday Octr. 20th.

Wet in the Morning, & damp & rather showery the remainder, which determined me not to put my nose out of Doors but rec'd many visitors in the Morning such as Lady Hailes & some of her Misses, Miss Melvilles M^rs. Major Sands & the 2 Miss Browns. much work in the evening & wrote to Miss Anne Snow. rec'd Letters from Lady Balgonie, Lady Dukenfield & M^rs. Grant.

Friday Octr. 21st.

Again Wet in the Morning, but the Wind becoming high tho very mild it kept off the rain till evening; went out to make some visits those I found at home were M^rs. Wardlaw & M^rs. Browning walk'd after on the bridges on some errands again a quiet evening writing to Lady Dukenfield & M^rs. Erskine.

Saturday Octr. 22^d.

By no means a pleasant Day being a very high damp wind, I never went out nor had any Morn^g. caller but Lord Elcho for a few minutes before Dinner the Principal dined with us & M^r. H. Brougham came to Tea. wrote to M^rs. Granville

Sunday Octr. 23^{d.}

Quite a brilliant fine Morning which before Noon became very stormy & many heavy fell in the course of the Day. Lord Elcho breakfasted with us before he returnd to the Country, went to Morning service at St. Andrews where Mr. Moodie pleased as ever, afterwards call'd on Mrs. Browning as did Mrs. Wardlaw on me before I went to evening service at St. Georges. wrote to Lady Edwd. Bentinck.

Monday Octr. 24th.

A pretty sharp frost which produced a clear & very fine Day tho certainly very cold well suited to my appointment with Mrs. Browning to walk with her & our Gentlemen to make visits in Georges Square, where I only found Miss Arlston & Miss Scotts at home of the many I made, on our return call'd on Mrs. Brown & on Miss Melvilles where we were more successful dined at Cap^{tn.} Brownings, meeting the Melvilles, M^{r.} & Mrs. M. Buchannan, & Miss Arlston very chearful & pleasant, play'd at Whist & supp'd also rec'd a Letter from my Sis^{r.} Travell

Tuesday Octr. 25th.

Still frosty but not quite so pleasant a day being less sun. went out at Noon to do various little shopping bussinesses, call'd on Lady C: C: & on Mrs. Fyffe, both pleasant because friendly, a quiet home much reading in Ned Evans[36] a very good new Novel wrote to Lady Elcho

Wensday Octr. 26th.

An exceeding fine but sharp cold Day Lord Balgonie made an early visit & took Mr. Witts with him a long progress, during which I paid 10 visits, finding only Lady Balgonie, Mrs. H. Robinson & Mrs. Jones at home, Cap^{tn.} & Mrs. Browning, & Mr. M. Riddell drank Tea here & play'd a lively game at Whist wrote to Mrs. Grant.

Thursday Octr. 27th.

Still dry & frosty but not so pleasant a day being a thick fog which never went well off we went to pay our Marriage Visit to D^{r.} & Mrs. Gregory which went off vastly well peep'd in upon fair Lady C: C: call'd unsuccessfully on Mrs. Phillips more so on Mrs. Brown, the Principal dined & drank Tea with us. wrote to Lady Dukenfield about Tutors.

Friday Octr. 28th.

Very much the same kind of weather thick & gloomy but dry, Mr. Witts walk'd to Leith with the Principal I never stirrd out all day rec'd visits from M^{rs.} & Miss Douglass & Mr. Laird. wrote to Mr. Burslem

Saturday Octr. 29th.

Another foggy day still dry but very cold & unpleasant, went at Noon to call on Mrs. Browning,

---

36. *The History of Ned Evans*, by Elizabeth Hervey, 1796. Ned Evans is a rags-to-riches hero, whose early existence in poverty in Wales is dramatically changed when he saves the beautiful Lady Cecilia Rivers from an assault and is invited to Ireland by her father. After spending time with the great and the good of Irish society, Evans travels to America where his fortunes once more reverse and he is captured and enslaved by American Indians, before escaping back to Ireland.

who we found at home & very chearful, afterwards on M^rs. & Miss Macdonald who we likewise found at home too cold to wish to walk farther. M^r. Laird drank Tea here. wrote to my Sister Travell.

Sunday Octr. 30th.

A bright pleasant looking day but an extreme cold wind, went to S^t. Georges to both Services & between calld on M^rs. Brougham, my first visit from an odd circumstance since my return home, on M^rs. Browning before Dinner. a comfortable home evening as usual.

Monday Octr. 31st.

Extremely cold & windy again tho with much sun my first call on Lady Balgonie, then on Lady C: C: from whence I went to see George at the Dancing school, did some errands on the bridge &'c, visited M^r. Brown only at home in the evening treating the Boys to play at Whist the first time.

Tuesday Novr. 1st.

Weather most suitable to the Day, being a thick foggy Morning which proved an intire wet succeeding Day, M^r. W. out on many calls I never stirrd nor saw anyone the whole Day but did much & wrote to D^r. Pennington

Wensday Novr. 2^d.

Something a better day, but still damp & foggy which did not induce me to go from the fireside, M^rs. Browning here for two or three hours in the Morning & M^rs. Brougham call'd very pleasantly. rec'd a Letter f^m. M^rs. Grant.

Thursday Novr. 3^d.

An unpleasant Day, being cold & stormy with frequent hard showers of rain, I ventured to call on poor M^rs. Young & M^rs. Browning & with her Cap^m. Browning went to visit at Com: Browns where were long detain'd by stress of weather & in our way home were shewn the Excice Office. drank Tea, play'd at Cassino, & supt at Cap^m. Brownings rec'd a Letter from M^rs. Wilkinson, Lady Elcho & Lord Edwd. Bentinck

Friday Novr. 4th.

Another very damp disagreable Day & very stormy which kept me by the fireside the whole of it M^rs. Young & Principal Gordon drank Tea here wrote to M^rs. Wilkinson much about her Sister.

Saturday Novr. 5th.

Tolerably dry & fine but very very cold. first call'd on M^rs. Browning about a Nursery Maid afterwards made many visits finding only Lady Wedderburn & M^rs. General Douglass at home, a pleasant chearful evening at home as ever with the dear good Boys.

Sunday Novr. 6th.

A wet & very unpromising Morning, wch rather improved, but was windy & very showery the whole of the day, tho contrived to go twice to Church at S^t. Georges without much wet, staid the Sacrament where M^r. Lawson assisted; a general communion all over the Town being the Preaching week. call'd on M^rs. Browning before Dinner.

Monday Nov. 7th.

A bright clear Morning, which proved very transient as it alterd before Noon, & became wet between one & two, just allow'd me to visit M.rs. Grant & M.rs. Young, the Principal dined, & the moment we expected M.rs. Browning also came the account she was brought to Bed of a Son the moment I had dined went in a Chair to see after her. young D.r. Duncan & M.r. Henry Brougham drank Tea here.

Tuesday Nov. 8th.

Having been quite a sharp hoar frost in the Night it was a bright clear Morning, which very soon became quite as much the reverse, being miserably wet the greater part of the Day & Night; nevertheless rec'd visits from M.rs. Gregory, M.rs. Phillips & Sir John Wedderburne, went to Tea Cards & Supper at Miss Bruce's meeting only 2 Ladies by no means a dull evening, a vast deal of Whist playing Frank went to attend Playfairs mathematical Class

Wensday Nov. 9th

Damp & thick in the Morning, & tho it became more dry was never clear so I never stirr'd out but work'd hard & much amused with attending to the Pavilion a Novel written by M.rs. Crespigney,[37] Cap.tn. Browning & Miss Campbell of Fairfield my visitors.

Thursday Nov. 10th.

Very much the same kind of weather thick & dry, went out rather early on a long train of visits in the Neighbourhood, actualy made 14, finding only at home 8 of the families, drank Tea at M.r. Jones's very sombre indeed, no one else being there. heartily glad to <u>return</u> home.

Friday Nov. 11th.

Just a Similiar Day by no means cold rather wetting in the evening, went out to some shops visited Lady C: C: for a long season, as likewise M.rs. Brown, Principal Gordon drank Tea here. rec'd a Letter from M.rs. Erskine, by M.r. Erskine.

Saturday Nov. 12th.

Another thick sombre Day but dry till towards evening when it was wet, staid at home all Morning, & rec'd visits from M.r. Erskine & Major Melville went to Dinner & supper at M.rs. Mures meeting M.rs. Fraser Lovatt, Miss P. Elphinston & Miss Graham an odd but not unpleasant visit. much Whist & Cassino wrote to M.rs. Davies.

Sunday Nov. 13th.

Again damp & foggy but no rain went to S.t. Georges Chappel in the Morning, afterwards visited M.rs. Browning & her Nursery for the first time went to hear M.r. Moodie at S.t. Andrews in the afternoon evening spent as usual. wrote to Lady Dukenfield.

Monday Nov. 14th.

No kind of change in the weather quite as foggy as ever but quite dry, rec'd visits from Lady Wedderburne & M.rs. Bruce of Kinloch before I set out on my walks accompanied the latter to

---

37. *The Pavilion, A Novel*, by Mary Champion de Crespigny, 1796.

see an Invalid Friend on M^rs. Youngs account who I afterwards call'd on & made two other unsuccessful visits merry evening with the Dear Boys, & finished the Pavilion well pleased with it.

Tuesday Novr. 15th.

A dark lowering Morning, which produced a wet uncomfortable Day, no going out for me & saw no one but Cap^tn. Browning who sat an hour here in the Morning, much employment & great comfort in the Boys

Wensday Novr. 16th.

Very much the same kind of weather only accompanied with a severe wind, the Day spent very much the same in a variety of useful employs among the rest wrote to Lady Edward Bentinck.

Thursday Novr. 17th.

A happy change in the weather being a little frosty, which produced a clearer air & some sunshine, out several hours making visits, 4 only of them successful, evening comfortable as ever. rec'd Letters from S^r. N. Dukenfield & Miss Louisa Lee

Friday Novr. 18th.

A perilous Day of wind & rain from Morn to night, most wonderfuly dark, yet my young Men ran about from Class to Class as if summer & sunshine. rec'd long & pleasant visits in the Morning from Captain Hyde & Captain Browning.

Saturday Novr. 19th.

Quite a tremendous Day of rain hail sleet & wind without cessation till Dinner time when we were engaged to Dine at M^r. Fyffes a sort of wedding Feast for D^r. & M^rs. Gregory, sat down 18 to a very handsome entertainment, & very pleasant everybody being well acquainted with each other at home soon after 9.

Sunday Novr. 20th.

Almost as bad a day storms of Snow instead of rain but not to lye, all the forenoon which kept me from Church, & damp fog in the afternoon, before even^g. service at S^t. Georges call'd on M^rs. Browning. rec'd Letters from Lady Riddell, M^rs. Wilkinson, Miss Snow & my Sister Travell wrote to Lady Riddell.

Monday Novr. 21st.

Having been a little frost in the night the air was clearer, & the streets more dry which made me attempt a walk into the Canongate to see Lady C: C: did some bussiness in the old Town & sat ½ an hour with M^rs. Browning, & a little while with M^rs. Young before I got home. in the evening amused by D^r. Mores new publication of Edward.[38] rec'd a pleasing but melancholly Letter from M^rs. Riddell.

---

38. John Moore (1729–1802), physician and writer. Moore's second novel, *Edward: Various Views of Human Nature, Taken from Life and Manners, Chiefly in England*, finally appeared in two volumes in 1796 and was intended to appease those who suspected that he could not draw the manners of a virtuous man. John Moore was the father of General Sir John Moore (1761–1809), of Corunna fame.

Tuesday Nov.ʳ 22.ᵈ

Quite a horrid disagreable Day being a most tremendous thick fog, & most bitterly cold, Mᵣ Witts having a cold we both kept the fireside warm & had no interruption to pursuing our book Edward with great avidity, but a long visit from Principal Gordon in the Morning. rec'd a long & pleasant Letter from Mʳˢ· Granville & wrote to Sᵣ· N. Dukenfield.

Wensday Nov.ʳ 23.ᵈ

Again foggy & some rain also as disagreable a day as possible tho the air more mild, no kind of interruption to our fireside employments but a visit from Mʳˢ· Balfour before Dinner. much reading in Edward & wrote to my Sister Travell.

Witts Family Papers F193

1796

Thursday Novr 24th.

Another very dismal Day of thick Fog & rain which made the streets wretched; of course no temptation to stir from the fireside. our only visitor the Principal for a short time in the Morning. finished reading Edward well pleased with it on the whole rec'd a Letter from L^{dy.} Edwd. Bentinck wrote to Miss Snow

Friday Novr 25th.

No kind of change in the weather, flying mists or small rain the greater part of the Day. Mr. Witts ventured out a little while I kept my station at the fireside & workt hard no one calling. wrote to Mrs. Savage

Saturday Novr 26th.

A more clear dry air arising from something of a frost, truly happy to set my foot ever more out of Doors, went several visits in the new Town, finding Mrs. Dalrymple, Lady Forbes, Mrs. Duff Mrs. Halkett Craigie, Major Melville & Mrs. Browning at home at Tea Principal Gordon brought a Mr. Campbell a friend of his with 2 young Sons to introduce them to ours an odd short visit.

Sunday Novr 27th.

Quite a bright clear Morning but changed at Noon to such an intense thick fog as was quite uncommon & lasted till it was dark, went to St. Georges chappel to Morning service where Mr. Lawson preached spent the time between services with Mrs. Brown & went with their family to Mr. Sandfords chappel where we were well pleased. rec'd a Letter from S^{r.} N: D:

Monday Novr 28th.

Having been a frost in the night was clear & dry & charming walking tho very cold, went out early to make visits in Georges, & Brown Squares &'c, of all that I made only found 6 at home went to Tea Cards & supper at Mr. Grants a pretty good party of 15 but not very lively & gay.

Tuesday Novr 29th.

Again frosty & cold in the Morning, but at Noon turn'd milder, & a very hard shower of rain fell after visiting Mrs. Young, & doing some bussiness in the old Town I call'd on Lady C: C: where I was very glad to meet Mr. George Wood & brought home in his Chariot. evening quiet & comfortable as usual.

Brown Square from the Society. An engraving by W. Forrest from a painting by Daniel Wilson.

Wensday Nov.ʳ 30ᵗʰ·

A most uncommon hard frost for one night accompanied by such a tremendous high North wind that it was piercing cold, I made 6 visits in the Morning, finding Mʳˢ· Oliphant, Mʳˢ· G: Douglass & Mʳˢ· Robinson at home, I went to Drink Tea with Mʳˢ· Browning, meeting Miss J: Melville & Miss Macdonald.

Thursday Dec.ʳ 1ˢᵗ·

Quite as cold & hard a frost as before but rather a thick air, I did not feel inclined to stir from the fireside & received in the Morning Sʳ James Colquhoun & Mʳˢ· & Miss Moneypenny to Dinner Principal Gordon & to Tea, Major, Mʳˢ· & Miss Dewar, delighted with receiving a long Letter from Lady Dukenfield & Miss Anne Snow & wrote to Miss Elizabeth Guydickens

Friday Dec.ʳ 2ᵈ·

Another frosty Morning, but at Noon a gentle thaw came on, & at night hard rain with severe wind was happy by an early hours visit from Sʳ Nathaniel Dukenfield in his way to England, at Noon sat an hour with Mʳˢ· Browning, & another with Mʳˢ· Brown meeting several people, went to Cards & Supper at Mʳ· Balfours, a large party of 8 Ladies & 10 Gentlemen pleasant enough, home very late.

Saturday Dec.ʳ 3ᵈ·

A severe Day of rain, hail, & wind, quite confining from Morn to night, amused by hearing Mʳ· Campbells wonderful travels over Land to the East indias, & work'd hard the Boys spent the evening with the young Campbells Sons, to the above.

Sunday Decr. 4th.

As hard a frost, & as severely cold as could well be borne went to S^t. Georges Chappel to both services between visited M^rs. Brougham, & before Dinner M^rs. Browning, George drank Tea with his friend Deans rec'd a Letter from Lady Dukenfield, & wrote to Her.

Monday Decr. 5th.

A most dreadful Day having been a considerable fall of Snow in the night, accompanied by a Severe wind which yet continued, & likewise freezing so hard all Day the streets were slippery like glass, happy when my Dear Boys came safe home from their several Classes, saw no one all Day but Cap^tn. Browning no kind of inclination to attend the first Card Assembly tho so near as Bernards Rooms.

Tuesday Decr. 6th.

Still very sharp frost, but being no wind & some sun it was not so piercing cold which tempted me to venture out under the escort of my Husband to visit Lady Rothes, M^rs. Campbell of Balimore & M^rs. Deans, as well as others I did not find at home drank Tea with Cap^tn & M^rs. Browning she very far from well so home quite early.

Wensday Decr. 7th.

Quite a miserable Day of thick fog & rain wch produced a temporary thaw but froze very hard again at night quite as cold as ever, saw no creature but Cap^tn. Browning, entertaind with having Charlotte Smiths new Novel of Marchmont.[1] rec'd a Letter from Lady Dukenfield & wrote to L^dy. Bentinck

Thursday Decr. 8th.

Still a sharp frost, but being no wind & some sun was a better Day than several of the former ones, but I had no inclination to go out but rec'd visits from M^rs. D. Erskine, M^rs. & Miss Dalrymple & Miss M. Brown. wrote to Lord Tracy & M^rs. Wilkinson.

Friday Decr. 9th.

Another frosty day tho somewhat inclined to thaw at mid-day but not very bad walking, made several visits those at home, M^rs. Dundas, M^rs. Mure, M^rs. Bence, M^rs. Stewart & M^rs. Young, Principal Gordon drank Tea here began reading Nature & Art.[2]

Saturday Decr. 10th.

A thick looking Morning which produced a confirm'd thaw thro the Day & hard rain at Night, saw no company all Morn: but did much usefull bussiness Frank dined at M^r. Balfours, & George drank Tea at M^r. Broughams, M^r. W & I drank Tea & supt at Commissioner Browns.

---

1. *Marchmont*, by Charlotte Smith, first published 1796 in 4 volumes.
2. *Nature and Art*, by Elizabeth Inchbald, first published 1796. The story explores the opposition between the upbringing and actions of Henry Norwynne, an unspoiled 'child of nature' who has been reared without books on an African island, and the corrupt conduct of his aristocratic older cousin, William.

Back of the White Horse Close,
Canongate. An engraving by W. Forrest
from a painting by Daniel Wilson.

Sunday Decr 11th.

A more unpleasant Day than even many former ones, a slow cold thaw still continuing, with now & then trifling showers which made it shocking walking & a frost again at night, I only went to service in the Morning to St Andrews where I was not much edified by the new assistant Mr Clarke, Mrs Browning call'd to take leave before Dinner, Young James Riddell dined here & James Deans drank Tea rec'd an <u>interesting</u> Letter from Lady Dukenfield, which I answerd, & rec'd one from my Sister Travell, & wrote to Mrs Granville.

Monday Decr 12th.

Frosty but not sharp, the air mild & the streets dirty, however ventured down into the Canongate to make 5 visits finding none at home but Mrs Fyffe, & poor Lady C: C: who was rejoiced to see me once more after a fortnights absence on my return before Dinner rec'd a first visit from Mrs Deans, & Mr Brougham here for a short time in the evening.

Tuesday Decr 13th.

Had been a severe Frost in the night & was a bright fine Day, Mr Witts walk'd down to Leith, & during his absence I rec'd visits from Lady Rothes & Miss Maitland, Captain & Miss Halkett, Mrs Hay, & Cap.^tn Hyde & Mr Hollah. wrote to Mrs Riddell

Wensday Decr 14th.

A thick fog & most gloomy sky which very early in the Day produced a rapid thaw but at night as usual it froze again, neither Mr Witts or myself quitted the fireside nor saw a Creature, & not much entertain'd by the reading of Marchmont. wrote to Miss Louisa Lee.

Thursday Decr 15th.

Another almost equaly gloomy Day the weather appearing quite undecided, except when some trifling Showers of snow fell our quiet no otherwise interrupted but a long call from Sr N. Dukenfield who arrived from England the night before. wrote to Mrs Erskine.

Friday Dec.ʳ 16ᵗʰ·

Another very gloomy Day in point of weather being fog, rain & cold thaw, no chance of even wishing to stir down stairs, of course saw no creature but Sʳ· N. Dukenfield, for a few minutes early in the Day who brought his little Catherine to shew me before he carried her to Perᵗʰ· wrote to my Sisʳ· Travell.

Saturday Dec.ʳ 17ᵗʰ·

A wet damp day, but freezing again at night, another Day of confinement even to Mʳ· W. without any other interruption than a late Morning call from Miss E: Campbell of Fairfield. Francis in the evening at Mʳ· Broughams rec'd a Letter from Lᵈʸ· Dukenfˡᵈ·

Sunday Dec.ʳ 18ᵗʰ·

A very severe frost which render'd the streets completely Dry & clean, a tolerable clear air & some sun but it was intensely cold, went to both services at Sᵗ· Georges Chappel where as now pretty constantly Mʳ· Lawson assisted. between services visited old Mʳˢ· Macdowall just returnd to Town & walk'd in Princes Street with Miss Macdonald meeting a large part of the World.

Monday Dec.ʳ 19ᵗʰ·

Frost again & hard in the Morn: but changed at mid.day to fog & thaw & at night a little rain I made 4 visits all at home Lady Hunter Blair, Mʳˢ· Campbell of Balimore, Lady Rothes & Maria Brown her Mother being ill in Bed, made the excuse of a little head to break my engagement with Miss Campbells of Fairfield to go to the Card Assembly not feeling up it, much happier with my own Gentlemen at home

Tuesday Dec.ʳ 20ᵗʰ·

A very hard frost, but rather a gloomy looking day tho quite dry I never went out nor Mʳ· Witts hardly at all, neither had we any callers, began reading Lock on the human understanding.[3] wrote to Miss A: Snow

Wensday Dec.ʳ 21ˢᵗ·

Quite as sharp a frost & very cold, but with some sun w.ᶜʰ made it pleasanter, the Principal call'd here for a great wonder before we went our walk w.ᶜʰ was into the old Town on a variety of bussinesses & before I came home made a long visit to Mʳˢ· Brougham Miss Macdonald drank Tea.

Thursday Dec.ʳ 22ᵈ·

A piercing cold Day more so than any of the former ones tho dry & pretty good walking which tempted me to venture alone to make 10 visits in the New Town finding only 4 at home went to Cards & Supper at Major Dewars, an odd hetrogenious party mostly strangers to us but being odd was rather amusing rec'd Letters from Lady Edward Bentinck & Mʳˢ· Erskine

---

3. John Locke (1632–1704). Locke's *Essay Concerning Human Understanding* had been first published in 1689 and had always remained in print. Not a light book, it seems an unusual subject for Agnes to read.

Friday Decr. 23.^{d.}

Another quite as severe a day tho with rather more Sun, went to St. Georges Chappel where Mr. Lawson gave a Sermon & Mr. Cleeve read prayers without returning home walk'd to Brown's & Georges Square, made seven visits finding 3 only at home shopp'd on the bridges, & sat an hour with Mrs. Brown on our return home. wrote to Mrs. Charteris.

Saturday Decr. 24.th.

No kind of change in the weather frost as hard & cold as severe, I gave myself a holiday & staid at home seeing no Creature the whole Day but the Principal for a short time in the evening. rec'd a Letter from Mrs. Davies, & wrote to Lady Dukenfield.

Sunday Decr. 25.th.

Few Christmas Days ever known more cold, or a harder frost but some sunshine, went wrapp'd up as well as could divine, to both services at St. Georges chappel very large congregations & a wonderful number of communicants between churches call'd on the Rooke Family who came to Town the Night before

Monday Decr. 26.th.

Severely cold as ever with snow storms at intervals & a very searching wind, quite sufficient to deter me from going out, my Morning callers Miss M. Brown & Mrs. Sandford, went to drink Tea with Col. & Mrs. Rooke play'd at Cassino & talk'd more. rec'd a Letter from Mrs. Browning & wrote to Miss Neville.

Tuesday Decr. 27.th.

A very bitter cold Day, with continued hard frost, & very severe wind, not any one of our own family stirr'd out of the House, but George to school & saw no one but Cap.^{tn.} Colquhoun. rec'd a letter from Mrs. Wilkinson & wrote to Mrs. Browning.

Wensday Decr. 28.th.

Quite a tremendous Morning of most violent wind & hard snow which lay for some hours but a thaw coming on in the evening, it soon melted away saw no Creature, nor rec'd any Letters quite a blank Day but for much reading working & talking.

Thursday Decr. 29.th.

Happily a continued Thaw in the shape of a fog & sometimes rain, & tho some wind, it was mild & warm in comparison, yet to me confining from the extreme dirt of the Streets wch kept all visitors from me also. wrote to Mrs. Witts Nibley House

Friday Decr. 30.th.

Quite a mild thaw, which turn'd after mid.day to hard rain, as warm as it had been cold, & most miserably dirty in the Streets yet I call'd on Mrs. Rooke Mrs. Wardlaw, & Mrs. Young where I was long detain'd by the rain & came home through it at last.

Saturday Decr 31st

An uncommon mild open Day without either sun or much wind, very pleasant being out of Doors except from the extreme dirt tried both very sufficiently by walking much first to see Lady C: C: where met Mrs Fyffe, made unsuccessful visits to Mrs Gregory & Mrs Phillips, & to Mrs Brown from whence walk'd the length of Princes Street to call on Mrs Macdonald; drank Tea at Col: Rookes less agreable from Mrs Rookes being very indifferent. the Dear Boys very happy by being at a Ball at Lady Janet Dundas's rec'd Letters from Mrs Browning & my Sis^r Travell.

Rec'd 117 Letters
wrote 118 Letters

1797

Sunday Jan: 1st

The new year open'd with peculiar gloomy weather having been much rain in the night small rain or mist the greater part of the Day & in the evening continued hard rain, went to Morning Service at St Andrews a serious Sermon suitable to the Day from a Young Stranger, one less good on the same subject from Mr Cleeve in the evening at St Georges chappel.

Monday Jan: 2^d

Thick fog & rain the greater part of the Day wholly confining, M^rs & Miss Oliphant here in the Morning evening as usual. rec'd Letters from Lady Dukenfield & Mrs Charteris & wrote to Mrs Browning

Tuesday Jan 3^d

Quite a fine Winter Day mild yet clear air & some sunshine, but the streets moderately dirty yet ventured to brave it & walk to the South Town on some bussiness & calls found Lord & Lady Balgonie at home in Leven House meeting many & various People wrote to Lady Dukenfield.

Wensday Jan: 4th

Such a thick fog in the Morning that all even near objects were in a manner invisible, this at noon turn'd to small rain which in the evening became hard rain no moving for me rec'd visits from Mrs Hay & Margaret Brown. went to a large & smart Party at Mrs Com. Browns 18 Ladies & as many Gentlemen so many of them young people that there was more dancing than Cards refreshment well regulated but no supper home at near one.

Thursday Jan 5th

A very similar Day equaly damp & disagreable but not so much hard rain, but quite as confining, Col. Rooke & his Son & Mr MacFarlan our only visitors much working & reading began reading Plain Sense a Justly good Novel.[4]

---

4. *Plain Sense*, by Frances Margaretta Jacson (1754–1842); first published 1795.

The Scottish Patriot.

John Sinclair (1754–1835), 1st Baronet of Ulbster and Thurso Castle.

Friday Jan: 6ᵗʰ·

No sort of change in the weather quite as moist & damp from the air as on the earth, I never went out of the House & Mʳ Witts very little & for a wonder saw not a Creature the whole of the Day. rec'd a Letter from Lady Dukenfield & wrote to my Sister Travell.

Saturday Jan 7ᵗʰ·

Still a thick gloomy atmosphere, but the air was more dry, of course the streets cleaner which tempted me to make several necessary visits but met with no one at home but Mʳˢ· Young & the Brown family, drank Tea & play'd Cards at Col: Rookes, Mʳ· W. went to sup at Mʳ· MacFarlans in the hope of meeting Compte Purgstall[5] but disappointed. Frank at Mʳ· Broughams. wrote to Lady Dukenfield.

Sunday Jan: 8ᵗʰ·

Very much the same kind of day the air being more clear made it pleasanter, went to Sᵗ· Andrews Church in the Morning, & Sᵗ· Georges chappel in the evening, not much pleased with

---

5. Wenzel Johann Gottfried Count von Purgstall (1773–1812). Purgstall was born in Graz and educated at Graz and Jena where he gathered around himself other young like-minded intellectuals of Germany. After finishing his studies the young count moved to Scotland, where he then met his future wife, Baroness Anna Cranstown. Upon his return to Austria von Purgstall volunteered to go into state service, and soon his house in Viennese suburb became a meeting point of all highly educated and patriotically inclined men. In 1807 the count became the province-councillor of his native Graz and partook in preparation for Struggle for Liberation of 1809.

Mᵣ Clarkes Oratory, better with Mᵣ Fenwick who preach'd for Mᵣ Cleeve, between churches visited Mʳˢ Dundas, Lady Sinclair,[6] & Mʳˢ Speirs, the two latter at home & just come to Town, before Dinner visited Mʳˢ Langan at Col: Rookes

Monday Jan: 9ᵗʰ

Certainly a fine winter Day, being dry tho rather a thick air, made good use of it by visiting Mʳˢ Longan Lady C: C:& ending with the Browns where as ever met a large circle evening as usual quiet & happy at home enjoying the Dear Boys wrote to Mʳˢ Wilkinson

Tuesday Jan: 10ᵗʰ

A hoar frost & thick fog w.ᶜʰ occasioned somewhat of a Rhyme, the fog never well went off & it was rather a cold comfortless Day, for our expedition to the Queens Ferry to meet little Katherine Dukenfield, who Mʳˢ Page brought from Perth to meet us, stopp'd an hour to bait the Horses, therefore did not return long before Dinner, & our little guest went to Lady Blairs before Tea. rec'd a Letter from Lᵈʸ Duk:

Wensday Jan: 11ᵗʰ

A terrible cold, windy Day certainly frosty being quite dry, I calld early at Lady Blairs to carry Caᵗʰ Dukenfield some visits first to Mʳˢ Rooke, who lent us her Chaise in which we went to some shops with Miss Rookes & afterwards to call on Lady Balgonie & also Lady C: C: when I had deposited my young charge at her home I went to drink Tea at Mʳˢ Rookes to meet old Mʳˢ Dundas, Mᵣ W. being confined at home with a swell'd face, I lost my Money at Cards but got a good supper & spent a chearful Morning.

Thursday Jan: 12ᵗʰ

Equally cold & severe tho not much of a frost sent to early by Lady H: Blairs say little Catherine was so ill, it was unfit for her to be sent to school, I went to her House early to meet Dᵣ Gregory & found her very ill of a fever, staid there all Day only just coming home to Dinner sadly alarm'd but highly pleased with the attention shewn by the worthy family wrote to Lady Duk:

Friday Jan: 13ᵗʰ

Very much the same weather in the Morning, but at Noon changed to very hard rain with considerable wind, before it came on I went to Lady Blairs & staid there the whole Morning, the Dear Child much better, went again in the evening accompanied by Mᵣ Witts to a large but rather hetrogenous Supper Party wrote again to Lady Dukenfield.

Saturday Jan: 14ᵗʰ

A sharp frost & bitterly cold the wind being high & in a severe corner I went to make a string of charitable visits, finding only my Nursery at Lady Blairs at home, & Mʳˢ Young went to

---

6.   Lady Sinclair features extensively in Agnes Witts' diaries. It seems likely that she was Diana Jane Elizabeth née Macdonald, daughter of Alexander, 1st Baron Macdonald. She married, 1788, John Sinclair (1754–1835), 1st Baronet of Ulbster and Thurso Castle, Caithness as his second wife. John Sinclair was MP for Caithness, President of the Board of Agriculture 1793–98, 1806–14; Privy Councillor 1810; cashier of excise (Scotland) 1811–30. Colonel of the Rothesay and Caithness fencibles 1794; Lt.-Col. and Commandant of the Caithness volunteers 1803, Col. 1803.

Dine at D[r.] Gregorys, a party of 12 the Brown family apart very agreable & pleasant, call'd on Ldy: C: C: before I came home. James Riddell dining with our Boys.

Sunday Jan: 15[th.]

Quite a charming Winter Day being a moderate frost, no wind, little fog, & much sun; went to S[t.] Georges Chappel to both services, between went to Lady H: Blairs & to call on M[rs.] Sym, the Principal drank Tea & staid late rec'd a letter from Lady Dukenfield & answer'd it

Monday Jan: 16[th.]

Very much the same kind of Day only the air not quite so clear, rec'd an early visit from Count Purgstall to gather German instructions afterwards went on bussiness into the old Town visited M[rs.] Fyffe, Lady C: C: & M[rs.] Longan the two latter only at home, on our return visited M[rs.] Brown & old M[rs.] Dundas on M[rs.] Longans affairs & travails. rec'd a Letter from M[rs.] Erskine.

Tuesday Jan: 17[th.]

Very little frost but dry tho rather foggy, which the sun vainly endeavor'd to dispel at Noon made several Morning calls those I found at home were Lady Blair, Miss Campbell, & Miss Graham, Miss MacFarlan, & Miss Melvilles, & after my return home had a visit from Maria Brown. The Principal dined here & staid late at Backgammon rec'd a Letter from M[rs.] Browning.

Wensday Jan: 18[th.]

The same mild damp weather & very dirty w.[ch] being rather unwell determined me not to go out, rec'd visits from Lady Cathcart[7] & M[rs.] Laurenson & wrote to M[rs.] Davies & M[rs.] Browning

Thursday Jan: 19[th.]

A most uncommon warm Day for the season, still very damp & dirty but I went to see the young Nursery at Lady Hunter Blairs, to call on M[rs.] Young & on M[rs.] Dundas of Dundas all of whom at home; went to Dine at M[r.] Grants at Kilgraston a small very pleasant party supt also & play'd at Vingtun very chearful. rec'd a Letter from Miss L. Lee

Friday Jan: 20[th.]

Still equaly warm & damp, but a better day being some wind & sun but I did not go out, but rec'd visits from a M[rs.] & Miss Campbell of Stonefield & Miss Mure, went to Cards, & Supper at M[rs.] Dundas's of Dundas a party of 10, nothing very lively or pleasant walk'd home wrote to Lady Edward Bentinck.

Saturday Jan: 21[st.]

A very disagreable Day of high wind & small fleeting showers, a quiet intire home Day no

---

7.   Elizabeth Schaw Cathcart, née Elliot (d. 1847), was the wife of William Schaw Cathcart (1755–1843), who had succeeded as 1st Lord Cathcart in 1776. He became 1st Viscount in 1807 and 1st Earl in 1814. He had served in the American Revolutionary War and had married Elizabeth, the daughter and coheir of Andrew Elliot of Greenwalls, Co. Roxburgh, in New York in 1779, when Elliot was Lieutenant-Governor. Lord Cathcart distinguished himself at the Battle of Buren, 8 January 1795 and was in command of troops that left Germany in December of that year. He was Lord Lieutenant of Co. Clackmannan, 1794–1803; and Vice Admiral of Scotland from 1795 until his death.

sort of interruption but a pleasant long visit from Isabela Graham. Frank at Mr Broughams.

Sunday Jan: 22^d

Weather still worse the wind blowing quite a tempest & many severe showers, got with difficulty to St Andrews Church in the Morning, w.^h less to St Georges chappel, where Mr Lawson pleased us far better than Mr Clarke had done. rec'd a Letter from Mrs Wilkinson & wrote to Mrs Erskine

Monday Jan: 23^d

Severe wind & rain in the Morning but dry the rest of the Day tho not fine enough to go out Lord & Lady Balgonie here agreably in the Morning Katherine Dukenfield made the first visit here also rec'd Letters from Mrs Wilkinson again, Mrs Browning Miss Anne Snow & L^dy Dukenfield answerd the latter.

Tuesday Jan. 24th

Dry, & cold, & so very high wind it was far from pleasant walking, yet I made 12 visits in the new Town those I found at home were Lady Forbes, Mrs Macdowall, Mrs Stewart & Mrs Brown a quiet home evening & wrote to Miss Snow.

Wensday Jan: 25th

Not even so good a day as yesterday, the wind more tempestuous & cold & at night quite a hurricane, yet I was obliged to go into the old Town to several shops, also call'd on L^dy C: C:, tired to death on my return, in the evening rec'd a visit from Sr N. & his Son Lloyd just come to Town,[8] declined returning to supper with him at Lady Hunter Blairs. visited Mrs Young in the Morning before we went into the old Town

Thursday Jan: 26th

Quite a tremendous stormy day with a little small rain towards evening it blew a perfect hurricane, Sr N. D. made an early visit here & carried Mr W. with him to many different visits, Mrs Fyffe my only Morning caller. wrote to Lady Riddell

Friday Jan: 27th

Fine early in the Day but soon the wind became even higher than the former Day was so dreadful it was hardly possible to keep one's feet yet I ventured to make 9 visits in the New Town. those I found at home were Lady Blair, Mrs Campbell Mrs. Robinson Scott Lady Sinclair, & Mrs Baillie went to Cards & Supper at Lady Rothes a party of 30 very pleasant home late. rec'd a Letter from Sis^r Travell

Saturday Jan: 28th

A clear fine Day with much sun & little wind till quite evening when it again blew hard, out again on the never ending task of visiting made seven found 5 at home, Katherine Duk. dined here & three Broughams drank Tea. rec'd a Letter from Mrs Rooke & wrote to Mr Bates.

---

8. Nathaniel Dukinfield (1746–1824), 5th baronet, a family friend of the Wittses. John Lloyd Dukinfield (1785–1836), succeeded as 6th baronet.

Sunday Jan: 29th.

Again a most severe & dreadful wind accompanied in the evening by prodigeous hard rain Mr. Witts & George only went to Morning Service I went to the evening at St. Andrews, & from thence went to a friendly family Dinner at Mrs. Speirs's where we met only Mr. Grant & the 2 Mr. Dunlops very chearful & pleasant came home with 4 Men about my chair for safety wrote to Mrs. Wilkinson & my Sisr. Travell

Monday Jan: 30th.

Quite as severe a wind if not more so with frequent showers & hard rain again at night in spite of all I fulfill'd my intention of taking Kath. Duk. to school at Musselburgh, accompanied by Margret Brown, went afterwards to Inveresk where I made an interesting visit to Mr. & Mrs. Charteris & call'd likewise on Mrs. Graham. rec'd a Letter from Mrs. Hyett[9] & wrote to Lady Dukenfield.

Tuesday Jan: 31st.

Very much the same weather almost equaly stormy & disagreable, no temptation to go out & saw no one in the Morning but old Mrs. Dundas Tea Cards & Supper at Mrs. Macdowalls a party of 14 pleasant enough except having very bad luck at Whist wrote to Louisa Lee.

Wensday Feb: 1st.

Another horrid stormy Day, wind so violent as to be quite alarming, my spirits much agitated with that & several other circumstances; Relieved & amused by going in the evening to a very pleasant party at Mr. G. Fergussons of 26 more Gentlemen than Ladies a pleasant cold Supper in the Drawing room very lively & agreable with much singing. wrote to Lord Elcho.

Thursday Feb: 2d.

Unceasing Wind & that dreadful, but it was quite dry with constant sunshine which tempted to brave all the hurricane, call'd first on Mr. & Mrs. Charteris who were come to Town with their Bairns to xxx under inoculation then into the old Town on some shopping a long visit in St. James Square, & another still more so to Mrs. Campbell of Balimore, Mrs. Young drank Tea here Mr. Witts went to a private Supper at Lady Sinclairs & I to the Assembly with Lady Rothes who directed, a very full one & a very select good set of company not at home till two in the Morning. rec'd a letter fm. Mrs. Riddell

Friday Feb: 3d.

Still most dreadfully stormy & after mid.day accompanied by such frequent showers there was no stirring out, & in the evening uncommon hard rain, the Principal dined here & we went to a large pleasant party at Lady Hailes near 40, 2 Card Tables & a smart Dance, excellent cold collation not at home till three wrote to Mrs. Browning

---

9. Mrs Hyett—a frequent correspondent with Agnes—was Sarah Hyett, née Adams (1746–1804), who had been a friend and correspondent of Samuel Johnson. She was married to Benjamin Hyett (1741–1810). Benjamin was the son of Nicholas Hyett who had inherited the Painswick, Gloucestershire estate. The Hyetts were on friendly terms with Agnes and Edward Witts. They died childless.

Saturday Feb: 4ᵗʰ·

A very happy change in the weather being perfectly calm & mild, clear air & constant sunshine which tempted me to be out three hours in the forenoon making many visits of which I found 5 at home Mʳˢ· Hay & Mʳˢ· Young & her little Girl drank Tea here much talk on many subjects.

Sunday Feb: 5ᵗʰ·

Again mild & without any wind but a thick misty air which made it close & unpleasant went to Morning Service at Sᵗ· Georges evening at Sᵗ· Andrews, between went to enquire of the Misses Melvilles the poor Major having died very suddenly in the night much shocked by it,[10] & to see Mʳˢ· Young who was taken ill. evening as usual wrote to Mʳˢ· Rooke.

Monday Feb: 6ᵗʰ·

Quite a charming Day being mild & without wind, made good use of it by being out on my Legs till I was tired to death, first to see Mʳˢ· Young who continued very ill, then into the South Town to see Lady Hamilton & several in & about Georges Square but found none at home but Miss Abercrombie went afterwards to see Lady C: C: & when I returned to the new Town to see her great & little Nephew the Principal here in the evening. went again to Mʳˢ· Youngs before Tea rec'd Letters from Lady Dukenfield & Mʳ· Bate

Tuesday Feb: 7ᵗʰ·

A very similiar Day quite pleasant I was out a great deal in the Morning, but chiefly shopping xxxxxxxxx &'c & with Mʳˢ· Young as usual quiet evening. rec'd a pleasant Letter from Mʳˢ· Granville

Wensday Feb: 8ᵗʰ·

The same mild pleasant weather without either much sun or wind, out a good deal in the Morning making visits those I found at home were the Charteris's, Mʳˢ· Brougham just return'd from Carlise, & Mʳˢ· Brown, where we likewise play'd Cards & Supt quite in a free way meeting the Bishop of Rhodes[11] & Mʳ· Erskine of Cambo,[12] Charlotte Stewart & Anna having call'd in the Morning to announce their arrival & bring me a Letter from Mʳˢ· Erskine

---

10. Major John Melville of Cairnie. The Melville family lived in Princes Street and throughout the diary there are frequent references by Agnes to the Major and his daughters. One daughter, the youngest, can be identified as Mary. She married James Home Rigg Esq. of Moreton, July 1808.

11. Vincenzo Labini (1735–1807). Labini was an Italian archbishop who served as Bishop of Malta from 1780 to 1807; he was also titular Archbishop of Rhodes from 3 March 1797. It appears that Agnes was anticipating the event.

12. Erskine of Cambo is one of the unnamed younger sons of David Erskine (d. 1769) 3rd baronet Erskine of Cambo who would have been in the company of the bishop. He was closely related to Charles Erskine (1739–1811), an Italian-Scottish papal diplomat and cardinal who was the son of Colin Erskine, youngest son to Alexander Erskine of Cambo and maternal grandson of Alexander Erskine, 3rd Earl of Kellie, by his marriage to Agatha Gigli of the noble family of Gigli of Anagni. He was educated by Cardinal Henry, Duke of York, [*of the Jacobite branch*] at the Scots College, Rome, and was afterwards a successful advocate, becoming a Doctor of Laws in 1770. In October 1793, Erskine was sent as papal envoy to Great Britain. By his tact Erskine established good relations with the Court of St James and the ministry, diminished the dissensions among Catholics, and avoided stirring up any anti-Catholic demonstration against himself. During his stay in London the pope named him a full auditor, and in 1795 gave him additional powers as envoy extraordinary. Whether the cardinal travelled north to Edinburgh is not clear. From the diary entry of 22 September 1796 this particular person was Mr Nathan Erskine, but as he is frequently in the company of Principal Gordon, the Catholic connections are clear.

Thursday Feb: 9th.

No kind of change in the weather only rather colder, still under the necessity of making several visits chiefly to the sick & ill so of course several at home, the Principal spent the evening here very brisk at Back Gammon.

Friday Feb: 10th.

Again a most pleasant dry day walk'd by myself into the old Town to the Miss Makers Lady C: C: &'c tired myself sadly, the principal here for a short time in the evening.

Saturday Feb: 11th.

A much colder Day with strong appearance of falling weather, but only trifling small showers fell before Dinner, M^r. W & Frank accompanied me to Charlotte Square to call on Miss Campbell, survey'd M^r. Sandfords Chappel, made a visit or two besides, one to M^rs. Young & M^rs. Charteris where I staid long the little Girls being far from well.

Sunday Feb: 12th.

Very much the same kind of weather which early in the afternoon turn'd to very hard rain which continued all the evening, went to both services at S^t. Georges Chappel, great difficulty to get home from the rain. between churches attempted a visit to poor Miss Melville, made a very feeling one to M^rs. Riddell at her Mothers who was just come to Town & to the Charteris's as well as some others in the evening wrote to Lady Dukenfield.

Monday Feb: 13th.

Hard rain in the Morning which went off soon, & was a bright clear day, but rain at night again I was neither disposed to go out or receive any Morning Company, but went to Drink Tea & sup at M^r. Campbells of Balimore no one there but M^rs. General Campbell & M^rs. Riddell, play'd at Cribbage.

Tuesday Feb: 14th.

Quite a severe cold Day & with some sunshine, but the wind was high & sharp which gave me no courage to go out, my only visitors M^rs. Dalrymple & her Daughters, went to Dine at M^r. Robertsons Scotts a very genteel party of 14, we only staid supper a very conversible family party wrote to M^rs. Erskine of Cambo.

Wensday Feb: 15th.

Not quite so cold a day but still very severe but being dry I venturd to make many visits in the new Town finding nearly half at home went to Cards & Supper at M^r. Fyffes, a mixed & not very lively party. began reading the Italian Romance.[13]

Thursday Feb: 16th.

Very much the same kind of dry sharp weather, went at Noon accompanied by M^r. Robertson

---

13. *The Italian, or the Confessional of the Black Penitents* (1797). Ann Radcliffe, née, Ward (1764–1823). This was the last book Radcliffe published during her lifetime.

Scott & my Husband up to the Tower of the High Church to see the manner in which the Chimes were play'd very curious, the view from the top of the Church fine, the way up fatiguing but easy from thence went to see the Panorama or view of the burning of the Ship Boyne,[14] admirable well painted, went afterwards to some Shops which kept me out till past 4 & tired me to Dea[th.]

Friday Feb: 17[th.]

A clear fine Day tho rather cold w.[ch] made me fearful of going out having much Rhumatism very busy & saw no one till we went to dine at M[r.] Charteris's, meeting M[r.] & M[rs.] Hamilton & a M[r.] Gordon came home between 8 & 9 & pursued the Italian romance with great vigor

Saturday Feb: 18[th.]

A most uncommon fine clear Day with much warm sun w.[ch] was uninterrupted, went to Martins the Painter to see M[rs.] Charteris set for her Picture afterwards to call on M[rs.] Grant & then with M[rs.] Charteris for a short time to Stranges practising James Riddell dined here & I drank Tea with Mrs. Young.

Sunday Feb: 19[th.]

Still dry fine weather but a good deal colder went to both Services at S[t.] Georges Chappel between visited poor Miss Melvilles, the first time admitted & walk'd in Princes Street. Anna Inglehart dined & Peter Brougham drank Tea. rec'd a Letter from Captain Browning & answer'd it & wrote to M[r.] Bate.

Monday Feb: 20[th.]

Another most delightful fine day such a mild air quite like summer, out a great deal chiefly making visits many unsuccessful ones went to the Card Assembly with M[rs.] Oliphant & Miss Hellen Speirs very full & realy very agreable rec'd a Letter from Miss Snow.

Tuesday Feb: 21[st.]

Something of a frost which made the air colder or else an equally fine Day, made so much use of it that I was out between 4 & 5 hours, old Town, South Town & Cannongate came home tired to death could do little but attend to the Italian Romance w.[ch] however did not much like

Wensday Feb 22[d.]

Still dry & fine, but much colder than several former Days, remained at home all Day receiving in the Morning a visit from M[rs.] Robinson Scott & a very long interesting one from Col: Colquhoun

---

14. HMS *Boyne* caught fire and blew up on 1 May 1795 at Spithead. She was lying at anchor while the Royal Marines of the vessel were practising firing exercises. It is supposed that the funnel of the wardroom stove, which passed through the decks, set fire to papers in the Admiral's cabin. The fire was only discovered when flames burst through the poop, by which time it was too late to do anything. The fire spread rapidly and she was aflame from one end to the other within half an hour. Most of the crew were rescued, but there were eleven fatalities. Later in the day, the fire burnt the cables and *Boyne* drifted eastward till she grounded on the east end of the Spit, opposite Southsea Castle. There she blew up soon after. The painting Agnes Witts refers to was a panorama, a popular theme at the time, a circular or semi-circular large format representation of the subject.

Nisbet of Dirleton's House, Canongate. An engraving
by T. Stewart from a painting by Daniel Wilson.

Thursday Feb: 23ᵈ·

A most delightful Day, dry, warm & without any wind, out a great while in the Morning
making many visits in the New Town finding many at home went to Cards & Supper at Mʳˢ·
Oliphant a large party of 24, many smart thou not at home till quite late rec'd a Letter from
Lady Dukenfield

Friday Feb: 24ᵗʰ·

No change in the weather still dry & fine made 4 friendly visits in the Morning all at home
Mʳˢ· Young, Mʳˢ· Campbell of Balimore, Mʳˢ· Syme, & Mʳˢ· Brown the Principal dined here, &
staid late playing at his favorite back gammon.

Saturday Feb: 25ᵗʰ·

If possible a still finer Day than many former ones, yet having a bad cold I thought it more
prudent to stay within & for a wonder had no visitors Frank drank Tea at Mʳ· Broughams
much entertained with having the Children of the Abbey.[15]

---

15. *The Children of the Abbey*, a novel by the Irish romantic novelist Regina Maria Roche (1764–1845). It first appeared
in 1796, in London in 4 volumes, and related the tale of Amanda and Oscar Fitzalan, two young people in love who
are robbed of their rightful inheritance by a forged will.

Sunday Feb: 26th.

The same charming dry weather but rather colder & my cold being very indifferent I did not go to Church in the Morning but in the evening to St Georges where Mr Cleeve pourd forth an invectic Sermon, wch were likewise done in all the Churches some in a very masterly stile, as also a solemn admonition from the Presbytery, went before Church to see Mrs Young, Miss Stewart & Miss Inglehart dined & drank Tea here wrote to Miss Anne Snow. my Dear Franks birth day wrote to Mrs Erskine

Monday Feb: 27th.

Fine weather still, made much use of it by walking from the Merchants Hospital where went to speak about plain work down the back way to the Abbey, visited Mrs Dugald Stewart agreably, & went to make a take leave visit to poor Mrs Young who was going the next Day, went to the Play, the Fashionable Loves orderd by Lady Hailes, sat in the stage Box next as Matron to Lady Rothes's party in her absence not much amused, & an empty house excepting the Boxes.

Tuesday Feb: 28th.

Having been a frost in the night the air was keen, but equaly fine as any of the former Days visited Lady Rothes, Mrs Fyffe, Lady C: C: Mrs Gregory & Mrs Brown all at home, went to Tea Cards & supper at Lady Rothes's a large mixd but very pleasant party rec'd a Letter from Lady Riddell

Wensday March 1st.

Still the same very fine weather but a frosty air, but I staid within, my only visitors Miss Macdonald & Miss Campbell of Arhaddan & Mr Bushly Maitland, much amused by the Children of the Abbey

Thursday March 2d.

The wind being high & turn'd to the east it was a severe day tho with much sun, yet I went to the South Town to make visits, meeting Mrs Craigie & Miss Alston only at home, a quiet home evening as usual rec'd a Letter from Mrs Rooke & wrote to Mrs Granville

Friday March 3d.

The same continuation of dry cold no temptation to go out the Rhumatism in my head being very indifferent, rec'd visits from Miss Scott of Gala Mrs & Miss Campbell of Stonefield, & Miss Campbell of Fairfield, evening much amused by the children of the Abbey rec'd the pleasure of a Letter from Mrs Erskines own hand a happy proof of her amendment.

Saturday Mar: 4th.

Quite as severe a day if not more so, wind extremely high & due east no moving out of Doors for me again & my only visitor Lady Sinclair rec'd a Letter from my Sister Travell.

Sunday Mar: 5th.

Equally as cold & disagreable with strong inclination to snow & rain, which latterly fell severely after evening church, went to Morning Service at St Georges, evening at St Andrews between visited M^rs. Brougham & M^rs. Hay at night wrote to Lady Dukenfield rec'd Letters from M^rs. Davies & M^rs. Browning

Monday Mar: 6th.

A very unpleasant Day, fog attended by flights of snow & sleet in the forenoon which sent me home dripping from visiting M^rs. Brown & at Miss Drysdales School went to Dinner at M^r. Bxxxxx's a large party pleasant because meeting Lady Rothes went to a pleasant card assembly with the party & return'd back to Supper not at home till between 2 & 3

Tuesday Mar: 7th.

Again dry but rather cold & stormy which gave me no temptation to go out, & had no visitors but M^rs. & Miss Churchill, a quiet pleasant evening making an end of the Children of the Abbey with wch we were much pleased. wrote to M^rs. Browning

Wensday Mar: 8th.

Quite a fine pleasant Day the air being much milder than many former ones made 10 visits in the New Town finding 8 at home, went to Cards & Supper at M^r. Campbells the Receiver Generals a large smart party very agreable. rec'd a Letter from M^rs. Young on her Journey from Preston.

Thursday Mar: 9th.

As usual dry & fine, but the frost being sharp & the air easterly & keen was very cold, being the general Fast Day, the whole early part of the Day was spent in going to the High Church, a most famous sermon from M^r. Greenfield in the Morning, & a very good one from M^r. Moodie in the afternoon both to most crowded audiences between services, visited Lady C: C: & walk'd about, went to Tea, <u>conversation</u> & supper at Lady Sinclairs, a pleasant party of eight

Friday Mar: 10th.

Tho a prodigeous night fine Morning early, it turn'd out a bad Day & a worse night being storms of snow, rain hail & wind, & severely cold, being obliged to go into the world on Some errands, I finish'd by making a long call on M^rs. Brown, went to Cards & Supper at Lady Cathcarts a party of near 30 lively & amusing enough much music & singing. rec'd a Letter from M^rs. Wilkinson.

Saturday Mar: 11th.

Still dry, but so severely cold I staid within & saw not a creature the whole Morning, went to Cards & Supper at Lady Hunter Blairs a smart party of 30 equal number of each sex & many young & gay. The Boys went to a dance at M^r. Christies of Dure. rec'd a Letter from M^r. Bate.

Sunday Mar: 12th.

Quite cold if not more so with some showers of hail & sleet which soon dried went to S^t. Georges chappel to both services between visited Lady Cathcart & Miss MacFarlan only the Caths. at home. rec'd a letter form Miss Louisa Lee & wrote to Lady Riddell.

Monday Mar: 13^(th.)

A sharp hoar frost, but a charming fine day being no wind & constant sun being out 2 or 3 hours walking I came home tired to death, making several calls in Georges Square & its Neighbourhood as well as in the new Town a quiet home evening. rec'd Letters from Miss Betty Guydickens & M^r. Burslem.

Tuesday Mar: 14^(th.)

Just such another clear fine Day with never failing sun, but my rhumatism was so indifferent I had no wish to go out, & saw no one in the Morning but Miss Wedderburns & Miss Brown, went to Cards & supper at Lady Rothes's a sober little party. rec'd a Letter from my Sister Travell, answer'd it & wrote to M^r. Bate.

Wensday Mar: 15^(th.)

Another most glorious Day, which tempted me to be long out going first to see Lady C: C: & look around by the Abbey, & back Leith road to see M^(rs.) Brown S^t. James's Square a quiet home evening.

Thursday Mar: 16^(th.)

Not quite such fine weather being dark & cold, with signs of falling weather, but little came I staid within the whole Day seeing no one but the Principal who was here both Morning & evening rec'd a Letter from M^(rs.) Browning answer'd it & wrote to M^(rs.) Davies & Miss Louisa Lee.

Friday Mar: 17^(th.)

Another cold gloomy day but yet dry out a good while in the forenoon, making seven visits in the New Town for a wonder all at home, a home evening rec'd a Letter from Lady Dukenfield.

Saturday Mar: 18^(th.)

A bright & very fine from Morn to night tho very cold, went out no more in the forenoon than for an hour or two to Stranges general practising whither I was accompanied by M^(rs.) Brougham, dined with M^(rs.) General Campbell, quite en famille but hearty, went to Cards & Supper at Sir Hew Hamiltons a pleasant party but terribly late. Frank at the Georges Square young Assembly George at M^(rs.) Dundas's of Dundas.

Sunday Mar: 19^(th.)

Quite a sharp frost, but warm & fine from unremitting sunshine, went to Church both times at S^t. Georges chappel, taking with me in the Morning Miss Graham M^(rs.) G: Campbells Friend, between services visited M^r. Maitland & Lady Rothes & walk'd in Princes Street. Charlotte Stewart & Norma Inglehart dined here

Monday Mar: 20^(th.)

Fine but cold. M^r. Witts walk'd to Leith &'c I staid at home & rec'd visits from Lord & Lady Balgonie M^(rs.) Fyffe, Miss Moneypenny, & Miss Baillie, went to Tea Cards & supper at M^(rs.) Campbells of Balimore a pleasant, easy, but small early party walk'd home wrote to M^(rs.) Tracy

Ancient Signal Tower, Tolbooth Wynd, Leith. An engraving by W. Forrest from a painting by Daniel Wilson.

Tuesday Mar: 21ˢᵗ·

Gloomy cold, being east wind & thick air found it very unpleasant walking to see Lady C: C: who was low & poorly, visited likewise Mʳˢ· Brown & Mʳ· Maitland, went early to Stranges Ball,[16] very full & amusing staid till nine o'clock when we went to Cards & Supper at Mʳˢ· Macdowalls, a very great party expected but from disappointments there was but few, & it was dull & late.

Wensday Mar: 22ᵈ·

A miserable gloomy cold Day with continued east wind & a great deal of it, which neither tempted me out or any one to come here, went to drink Tea at Lady Rothes, by way of playing at whist with & amusing poor Mʳ· Maitland no one there excepting their own family & the Marquess of Tweedale,[17] left them at 9 o'clock to go to a Supper party at Mʳˢ· Dalrymples, 9 Ladies & as many Gentlemen more agreable than usual wrote to Mʳˢ· Erskine

---

16. Ayrshire-born David Strange was a dancing master, Todricks's Wynd. He appears to have branched out in later years to the extent of giving demonstrations and putting on balls. One of his pupils included the scientifically minded Mary Somerville, who described him in her memoirs: '*He was exactly like a figure on the stage; tall and thin, he wore a powdered wig, with cannons at the ears, and a pigtail. Ruffles at the breast and wrists, white waistcoat, black or velvet shorts, white silk stockings, large silver buckles and a pale blue coat completed his costume. He had a little fiddle on which he played, called a kit. … Every Sunday afternoon all the scholars, both boys and girls, met to practise in the public assembly rooms … We used to always go in full evening dress. We learnt the minuet de la cour, reels and country dances.*'

17. George Hay (1753–1804). George succeeded as 7th Marquess and 8th Earl of Tweeddale in 1787 on the death of his 1st cousin once removed, and namesake. Hay married, 1785, Hannah Charlotte (d. 1804), fourth daughter of James Maitland, 7th Earl of Lauderdale. He was earlier an officer in the naval service of the HEIC and was Lord Lieutenant of Haddington 1795–1804. In 1802 he and his wife went to France for the benefit of his health. They were detained by Napoleon and imprisoned at Verdun where they both died two years later.

Thursday Mar: 23ᵈ·

A cold sombre Day in all points the weather being dark & gloomy, & we neither went out or saw anybody the whole Day, but were fully employ'd

Friday Mar: 24ᵗʰ·

Rather a milder air but equally gloomy, walk'd into the old Town on some bussiness afterwards into the New, survey'd Mᵗ· Sandfords new building chappel,[18] made three visits finding only Lady & Miss Sinclair at home with whom I sat a chearful hour rec'd a Letter from Lady Edward Bentinck.

Saturday Mar: 25ᵗʰ·

Had been a wet night, & was wet till noon & very stormy cold, & gloomy the remainder of the day, saw not a Creature but the Principal for a few moments in the forenoon a take leave call wrote to Mʳˢ· Hyett. James Riddell dined & drank Tea.

Sunday Mar: 26ᵗʰ·

Dry in the Morning but at noon became very stormy, with severe showers of rain & hail, very unsuitable to going backwards & forwards to church at both services at Sᵗ· Georges between made 3 visits finding only Lady Rothes at home the Boys drank Tea with Mʳˢ· Campbell of Balimore.

Monday Mar: 27ᵗʰ·

More or less a wet Day from Morn to night consequently never went out nor saw any one but a Lady for the character of Hellen, very full of employment & heard much of Woodland Cottage[19] with which not much charm'd wrote to Mʳˢ· Wilkinson.

Tuesday Mar: 28ᵗʰ·

A dry cold gloomy Day made several visits in the forenoon finding only Miss Campbell of Shervan & Mʳˢ· Brown at home evening as usual.

Wensday Mar: 29ᵗʰ·

Wet dark & gloomy, no temptation to go out, tho weather improved after mid.day, my only visitors Miss B. Mure work'd much in the Morning while attending to Eloise Montblanc[20] a good Novel, went to Cards & supper at Miss Bruars of Stenhouse, a large party intended but

---

18. Daniel Sandford (1766–1830), founder of the Charlotte Chapel congregation, was the first Bishop of the reunited Scottish Episcopal Diocese of Edinburgh. His chief importance to ecclesiastical history is in his role in reunifying and restoring the fortunes of the Episcopal Church, but he was also a significant figure in Regency Edinburgh, particularly in his contribution to education. He was born in Dublin, but after his father's death his mother took the family to Bath. He studied at Christ Church, Oxford, and was curate of Hanworth in Middlesex before moving to Edinburgh. When Sandford first moved to Edinburgh he stayed in Brown's Square (now replaced by Chambers Street), but by 1793 he lived at 5 Hanover Street. In 1797, the year Charlotte Chapel was opened, he moved to 3 North Castle Street.

19. *Woodland Cottage*, a new novel in two volumes was published in 1796 by Hookham and Carpenter. Most novels, although ostensibly anonymous, had known authors. The authorship of this work remains unknown.

20. *Eloise de Montblanc*, a new novel in four volumes, London: William Lane at the Minerva Press, 1796; also anonymous.

from disappointments dwindled to only 10 but it was lively & pleasant enough rec'd a Letter from M^rs. Browning.

Thursday Mar: 30th.

Quite a warm charming Day mild air & constant sun, made much use of it, by visiting in Brown & Georges Square & afterwards in the new Town, Tea Cards & Supper at Lady Rothes's, meeting M^rs. Macdowall & M^r. D. Erskine for a short time poor M^r. Maitland very indifferent. rec'd a Letter f^m. M^rs. Erskine

Friday Mar: 31st.

Very suitable weather to the Season being very showery producing an equal show of sun & clouds I did not go out in the Morning, but had a large Levee M^rs. G. Campbell & her Lady Miss Graham M^rs. Machas & her two Daughters, M^rs. Brougham, & M^rs. Grant went to a Ball at Miss Drysdales our whole family party, a most excellent one more than 150 people at, very genteel company, & most admirably well conducted not at home till three in the Morning

Saturday April 1st.

Dry & cold tho fine, being a very sharp high wind, went out at Noon to make some visits finding very few at home, concluding at M^rs. Browns Lady Mary Lindsay here before I went out went in the evening in the usual stile to Lady Rothes's very chearful M^r. M. being better, L^dy. Hailes & 2 of her Ladies there & M^r. D. Erskine.

THE REV^D. "PATRIOT.

Revd Dr Thomas Hardie (d. 1798). In 1788 Dr Hardie was elected to the Professorship of Ecclesiastical History in the University of Edinburgh. An etching by John Kay.

Sunday Ap: 2ᵈ·

Cold & showery tho very trifling ones & soon dry again went to Morning service at Sᵗ· Andrews & heard a most excellent sermon from Mʳ· Hardie to evening at Sᵗ· Georges, between made a visit of ceremony to Miss Drysdale, & walk'd in Princes Street Mʳˢ· Campbell of Balimore & Miss Graham drank Tea here, much pleasant conversation.

Monday Ap: 3ᵈ·

An extreme cold unpleasant Day the wind being due east, & much of it, but was dry till after Dinner when there was rain for some hours. went to see Lady C: C: with whom finding other visitors I did not stay long before I went home visited Mʳˢ· Macdowall & Lady Rothes, the Boys were taken by Mʳˢ· Christie in her Coach to a Ball at Lord Balgonies we went to Cards & supper at Mʳˢ· Speirs's a mix'd party of 14 Ladies & 8 Gentlemen well enough.

Tuesday Ap: 4ᵗʰ·

Wet & very wet in the Morning but when it became fair at noon was neither warm or pleasant enough to tempt me to go our, nor any one to call on me, went to Tea Cards & Supper at Mʳ· J. Campbells a very pleasant party of 10 in the back parlour, excellent entertainment & hearty welcome wrote to Miss Anne Snow.

Wensday Ap: 5ᵗʰ·

Again wet in the Morning & cold & showery all the Day, & the wind still in the same unpleasant corner, I never went out all Day nor saw any one but Miss Carnegie for half an hour work'd much & heard Leluco read.

Thursday Ap: 6ᵗʰ·

Quite a similiar day in point of weather, staying within, & all my employments Mʳ· Witts little out, my only guest my new acquaintance Mʳˢ· Stewart of Hanover Street

Friday Ap: 7ᵗʰ·

Still wet & stormy equaly confining saw no one but Captain Rooke & a <u>nameless</u> officer of the Windsor Forrestors with him, I was very far from well all the evening. rec'd a charming long Letter from Lady Dukenfield, wrote to Lᵈʸ· E: Bentinck

The next day being taken very ill & a miscarriage the consequence I was confined to my Bed & room for a week & sufferd very considerably, attended by Dʳ· Stewart & Mʳ· Manderston by whose skill & care aided by divine assistance I gradually mended my Dear Husband & Sons the most kind & tender of Nurses during my confinement saw a few intimate Friends. the weather continued cold, wet & stormy till the 13ᵗʰ & was then mild & fine during that week rec'd 2 Letters from Mʳˢ· Whalley, 1 from my Sister Travell, Miss B. Guydickens & Mʳˢ· Wilkinson

Saturday Ap: 15ᵗʰ·

A Mild & very fine looking Day but grew cloudy towards evening, ventured down into the drawing room for the first time but was very weak & indifferent, Miss Maitland & her Brother & Mʳˢ· Fyffe & her Daughter call'd in the evening. wrote to Lady Dukenfield.

Sunday Ap: 16th.

An unpleasant change in the weather being again cold & very wet in the Morning, & showery the remainder of the Day tho fine in the evening Mr. Witts & the Boys much at St. Georges chapel being Easter Day, Mrs. Speirs & one of her Daughters call'd on me in the Morning & Charlotte Stewart in the evening.

Monday Ap: 17th.

Wet in the Morning, dry at mid.day & a severe shower again in the evening I was but very indifferent all Day, Mrs. Macdonald, Col: Riddell & Miss Stewart & Anna here in the Morning, & Mrs. Brown for an hour in the evening.

Tuesday Ap: 18th.

Very much the same kind of weather fine & showery alternately, I was better, therefore not fatigued by a large circle of Morning callers, such as Mrs. Douglass & Daughter, Miss Graham, Miss Bruce, Mrs. Dundas, Miss Bruce of Stenhouse, & Ldy. H. Blair rec'd a Letter from Ldy. Dukenfield & wrote to Miss Guydickens

Wensday Ap: 19th.

A fine Day upon the whole dark clouds & sun alternately but the wind in the east. Miss M. MacFarlan & Mrs. Hay my only callers, before I went out in a Chair for air, went as far as Lord Morays where I stove to suck in the reviving air on my return call'd on Mrs. Speirs & Mrs. Macdonald, also on Lady Rothes who was out, Maria Brown here for an hour or two in the evening Mr. Witts at a Supper at Mrs. Speirs's.[21]

Thursday Ap: 20th.

Still an east wind but being little of it & much warm sun, it was a glorious day, & I employ'd it, Mrs. Speirs calling to take me on an airing which did me much good, drank Tea with our next neighbour Mrs. Hay. rec'd a Letter from Lord Elcho wrote to Mrs. Rooke

Friday Ap: 21st.

An extreme cold windy Day with some flying showers, & being easterly I did not venture out; rec'd visits from Mrs. General Campbell Miss MacFarlan, & a most pleasant one from Mrs. Gregory, went to Cards & Supper at Lord Polkemmets a large & agreable party. wrote to my Sisr. Travell

---

21.   Mary Speirs (±1735–1818) was the second wife and widow of Alexander Speirs of Elderslie (1714–1782), and daughter of Peter Buchanan of Silverbank and Auchentorlie. Her eldest son, Archibald (1758–1832), inherited the Elderslie estate and her second son, Peter (1761–1829) was an eminent Glasgow merchant in tobacco, etc., and built a large cotton spinning mill marking the entry of Fintry into the world of industry. Mary appears to have had a country home near Dunmore Park, between Falkirk and Stirling, apparently, according to Agnes Witts, very close to the banks of the River Forth. The Witts family had visited there back on 23 September 1794. Her Edinburgh town house was 59 George Street. They seem to be associated with, or related to the Mure family. There were at least four daughters, and from the diaries we know that two of them were named Helen and Grace. Agnes initially spelt the name as 'Spiers', but later changed to 'Speirs'.

Saturday Ap: 22ᵈ·

Much such another cold disagreable Day never stirr'd from the fireside, nor saw any one, the Boys drank Tea with Miss Graham to meet Riddell. rec'd Letters from Mʳˢ· Granville & Miss Lee & wrote to Lady Dukenfield.

Sunday Ap: 23ᵈ·

Weather better tho still cold, much sun & a westerly wind, went to both services at Sᵗ· Georges between made a long visit to Mʳˢ· Brown, before Dinner to Lady Rothes & poor old Mʳ· Maitland, Anna Inglehart drank Tea here. wrote to Mʳˢ· Erskine

Monday Ap: 24ᵗʰ·

The wind being westerly it was a mild pleasant Day, tho without much sun, I made some visits near at hand those I found at home, were Mʳˢ· Dundas of Dundas, Mʳˢ· Campbell of Fairfield Mʳˢ· Halkett Craigie & Mʳˢ· Syme, went to drink Tea at Miss MacFarlans, meeting many strangers, at nine went to a large party at Mʳ· Commissioner Browns pleasant enough.

Tuesday Ap: 25ᵗʰ·

Dry & tolerably pleasant, but being little sun not warm, went out late merely to take a walk survey'd Mʳ· Sandfords Chappel & walk'd in the environs took another walk before Tea Francis accompanying

Wensday Ap: 26ᵗʰ·

A cold uncomfortable day with frequent showers of hail & rain but dry in the evening staid at home all Morning & rec'd visits from Lᵈʸ· Hailes & 2 of her Misses, Mʳˢ· Dundas, & Principal Gordon just return'd to Town, again walk'd before Tea very cold rec'd a Letter from Lady Dukenfield.

Thursday Ap: 27ᵗʰ·

Had been a wet night, was a gloomy Morning, but turn'd out a beautiful bright Day with little wind & much sun, made many visits in the new Town, finding at home Lᵈʸ· Rothes, Mʳˢ· Sands, Mʳˢ· Macdowall Mʳˢ· Mure & Mʳˢ· Stewart, drank Tea at Mʳˢ· Hays meeting Mʳˢ· & Miss Oliphant, Cards & Supper at Lᵈʸ· Sinclairs a party of 22 an equal number of each sex much amusement from the Maclouds being there, beat Madame 3 rubbers at Whist <u>nice</u> fun.

Friday Ap: 28ᵗʰ·

Quite a cold disagreable Day, with strong east wind & frequent severe storms of hail & rain fit for nothing but to stay at home & be much employ'd saw not a Creature

Saturday Ap: 29ᵗʰ·

A most happy reverse of weather being a warm & delightful fine day & I was fully employ'd from Morn: to night, made many visits in the forenoon, those I found at home were Mʳˢ· Robinson Scott, Miss Campbell of Shervan, Mʳˢ· Dundas, & Mʳˢ· Brown J: Riddell dined here & I went with the Boys to the Play the cure for the heart ache[22] much entertain'd left them

---

22. *A Cure for the Heart Ache* (1797); by Thomas Morton (1764–1838). This five-act comedy was first performed at Covent Garden, 10 January 1797.

to enjoy the Farce by themselves going to Cards & Supper at M^rs. Oliphants a party of 16, mostly Ladies. home very late.

Sunday Ap: 30th.

Rather a cold stormy day but fine I accompanied M^rs. Duff to M^r. Sandfords chappel in the Morning & sat in her Seat, went to S^t. Georges to evening service, between rec'd visits from Lord Balgonie & M^r. Blane, & visited M^rs. Brougham Miss Stewart & Anna dined here & went away so early, that we walk'd in Queen Street, & calling on Lady Rothes, staid to drink Tea with her & poor M^r. Maitland who we thought better. wrote to M^rs. Whalley.

Monday May 1st.

Dry & tolerably fine excepting a very severe hail storm at three o'clock, I made good use of the Morning, by making visits & shopping on the bridge found only M^rs. Fyffe, D^r. Gregory, & L^dy. C: C: at home came back in a Coach my spirits much shocket by seeing in the papers the death of poor M^rs. Rycroft[23] wrote to her poor Father on the painful event & rec'd a Letter from M^rs. Wilkinson.

Tuesday May 2^d.

A cold comfortless day with many showers & in the evening quite wet, I never went out, nor saw any one till the Principal came to Dinner & Miss MacFarlan to tea, play'd at Whist with great success. wrote to Lord Elcho.

Wensday May 3^d.

A mixture of sunshine, wind, & very severe showers of hail & rain, & those frequently but it dried so quick, that having much bussiness at Shops I ventured into the old Town & contrived not to get very wet, a stay at home evening. wrote to Lady Dukenfield & M^rs. Charteris.

Thursday May 4th.

Rather lowering in the Morning but turn'd out warm & very fine till the afternoon when it became wet & very wet, being the Fast Day previous to the preachings it was a holiday to both Boys. M^r. W. & I walk'd to Bernards Well before Dinner. James Riddell drank Tea here. rec'd Letters, from M^rs. Tracy, M^rs. Davies & my Sister Travell, which sadly revived my grief for our poor Niece Rycroft. wrote to M^rs. Tracy.

Friday May 5th.

Such a very showery Day, & some so very violent that it might be deem'd almost an intire wet day, I was far from well therefore had not a wish to stir out nor saw a creature. wrote to M^rs. Riddell

---

23. Jane Rycroft (1765–1797) was Agnes's niece, the second daughter of Agnes's brother Ferdinando Tracy Travell (1740–1809) and Martha, née Rollinson (1741–1780). Jane had married, first, William Naper (1749–1791), a connection of Lord Sherborne; she married secondly, 1794, Henry Rycroft, Knight Harbinger to the king. See the diary entries for 31 May and 17 June 1794.

Saturday May 6th.

Tolerably fine till near Dinner time when there was again heavy showers of hail & rain nay some snow visible, walk'd for a little while at Noon, afterwards rec'd visits from Miss Wedderburn Miss Brown & Principal Gordon.

Sunday May 7th.

For a great wonder a day without any rain some threatening clouds, but a sharp north wind disipated them, went to Church to both services at St. Georges chapel between walk'd in Princes Street & made an unsuccessful call on Mrs. Brown. went into Mourning for my poor Niece wrote to Sisr. Travell

Monday May 8th.

Still cold stormy disagreable weather went out late just to take a walk in the streets & came back both starved & tired, went to Tea Cards & Supper at Mrs. Oliphants a small party Lady Ramsay there Miss Speirs's & Mrs. Dunlop walk'd there & home.

Tuesday May 9th.

Weather still worse wind being in the east & very high & some showers, tho some sunshine I never had a wish of stirring from the fireside not saw anyone, work'd much & wrote to Mrs. Wilkinson

Wensday May 10th.

Wind higher & cold more severe so much so as difficult to keep warm close to the fire again a home Day without one interruption to work & reading.

Thursday May 11th.

No change for the better in the weather but rather the contrary, being equally cold & stormy, with frequent hard showers & at night continued rain a Morning of work & reading without any interruption drank Tea, & supt at Mrs. Speirs an easy party of 14 but alas! chiefly women. rec'd a Letter from Mrs. Wilkinson & wrote to Mrs. Granville

Friday May 12th.

Rather more promising weather in the Morning but turn'd to rain at Noon & was very gloomy in the evening, again confined from all air & exercise. Mr. Witts dined at Mr. Blairs & join'd me in the evening at a party at Mrs. Bruces of Kinloch where he was the only Man to 10 Ladies dull, tedious & late.

Saturday May 13th.

Wet & lowering in the Morning, but at mid.day clear'd & was dry & pleasant the rest of the day, with a milder air, fortunate for our promised excursion to Inverick for which place we set with Principal Gordon at 12, by the way stopp'd for ½ an hour to see C: Dukenfield at the school at Musselburgh, found Mr. & Mrs. Charteris pleasantly glad to see us, Mr. Graham & Dr. Stewart dined there & we return'd home at 10 o'clock having pass'd a pleasant Day.

Sunday May 14^(th.)

A fine & warm Morning, which early changed to wet & stormy, w.^(ch) became almost uninterrupted rain went to S^t. Georges chapel in the Morning & S^t. Andrews in the afternoon, some difficulty to get home dry from the latter & in a chair from the former.

Monday May 15^(th.)

A warmer Day tho still east wind but dry excepting a shower at mid.day, a bustling day from packing with one servant & taking another spent 2 or 3 hours before Dinner in M^r. Sandfords new chapel chusing a seat for M^(rs.) Davies a great crowd & confusion. wrote to M^(rs.) Davies.

Tuesday May 16^(th.)

Weather fine than many former Days mild air & dry till evening when it became wet & very wet tired myself dreadfuly, with visiting Miss Melvilles till past four, the Principal dined & M^(rs.) & Miss Macdowall drank Tea & play'd at Whist.

Wensday May 17^(th.)

Dry & pleasant in the Morning but at 12 o'clock became wet & showery & so continued more or less the whole of the day which made it quite stay at home & saw no one work'd much; & was greatly entertain'd with having Bertrands private Memoirs of the French revolution.[24] wrote to M^(rs.) Charteris

Thursday May 18^(th.)

Very much the same day as the former, being fine early, & very showery till evening when it was again fine, within all Morn: no callers but M^(rs.) Hay & Principal Gordon to take leave being going to England walk'd in the evening in Queen Street &^c. rec'd a Letter from Lady Dukenfield.

Friday May 19^(th.)

Quite a fine summer day being wholly dry, & very warm tho a strong west wind I made several visits in the new Town meeting with five at home, staid within all evening

Saturday May 20^(th.)

A pretty good day, with a few showers but trifling, at home all Morning without any callers Anna Inglehart dined here & James Riddell drank Tea walk'd a little in the Streets after Tea & was caught in the rain. wrote to Lady Dukenfield undated M^(rs.) Charteris

Sunday May 21^(st.)

Dry & fine excepting being being <u>most</u> disagreably windy, M^r. Witts went to Church twice & dined with the Lord Commissioner the Boys & myself to both services to S^t. Georges chapel by way of a final take leave, between, visited Lady Janet Dundas as on the death of her poor

---

24. Bertrand; *Private Memoirs Relative to the last year of the Reign of Lewis XVI, Late King of France*, published London, 3 volumes, 1797.

Brother[25] & Lady Hunter Blair, Mother & Sons dined at Mr Browns no one there but Miss Dalrymples Mr Witts join'd us at Tea. rec'd Letters from my Bro^r Ferdinand, my Sister Travell & Miss E. Guydickens

Monday May 22^d

Again grown very cold & rather stormy but little or no rain fell but the wind being turn'd to the east I had much rhumatism in my head & never stirr'd out the whole day nor saw a creature. wrote to Mrs Wilkinson & Miss Snow.

Tuesday May 23^d

A fine Day tho rather gloomily hot by being a thick air & little sun set forth to make visits those I found at home Mrs Speirs, Mrs Mackay & Mrs John Campbell went very early to the Concert in order to get good Seats as the crowd was expected to be so great to hear Giornovichi[26] play, & great indeed it was 500 being supposed to be present, & 200 turned away from the Door, the heat quite overcoming, I went with Mrs Douglass & her party.

Dugald Stewart (1753–1828). A portrait by Henry Raeburn. Stewart was professor of mathematics at the University of Edinburgh (1747–1772) and in 1785 succeeded Ferguson in the chair of moral philosophy. Young men were attracted by his reputation from England, Europe and America.

25. Lady Janet Dundas (1720–1805) lived at 16 George's Street in 1797, presumably having moved from Queen Street. She was the daughter of Charles Maitland, 6th Earl of Lauderdale and Lady Elizabeth Ogilvy; and the widow of Thomas Dundas of Fingask (d. 1786) whom she had married in 1744. Lady Janet and Thomas had six children: Bethia (d. 1770); Margaret Bruce (d. 1774); Janet, married James Deans; Mary (1754–1785), married James Bruce of Kinnaird; Maj.-Gen. Thomas Dundas of Fingask (1750–1794) and Charles Dundas, 1st and last Baron Amesbury (1751–1832). The brother who Lady Janet was mourning was Patrick Maitland (1734–1797) who had died two days before.
26. Ivan Mane Jarnović (1747–1804), often known in Italian as Giovanni Mane Giornovichi, was a virtuoso violinist-composer of the eighteenth century whose family was of possibly Ragusan (today Croatian) origin. He performed in almost all major centres including Paris, Berlin, Warsaw, St Petersburg, Vienna, Stockholm, Basle, London, Dublin, amongst others. He was an acquaintance of Joseph Haydn, with whom he shared concert programmes in London.

Wensday May 24th.

Quite a true warm summer Day & a most pleasant evening, I sat quietly at home all Morn. & rec'd visits from Col: Prendyard, Mrs. Cleeve & to our surprize Principal Gordon, who never went his purposed Journey to England, he dined & drank Tea with us, & we walk'd afterwards on a crowded Mall in Queen St.

Thursday May 25th.

Another very hot summer Day, but not so pleasant the wind being quite tempestuous till evening when it was very fine, I staid within all Morning, saw no one but Mrs. & Mrs. Stewart, walk'd after Tea with the Boys to Drumshew27 & on Queen Street. wrote to Miss Louisa Lee.

Friday May 26th.

Hot in the Morning but at noon became stormy & frequent showers fell in the course of the day, which prevented my going out at all, saw no one but Mr. Blane work'd & read much.

Saturday May 27th.

Again a most tremendous wind but little or no rain, I did not go out in the Morning but rec'd visits from Miss Bruce of Stenhouse Mrs. & Miss Campbell & Principal Gordon again to take leave before he took his passage for England after Tea made visits to Mrs. Fyffe & Lady C: Charteris.

---

27. Drumsheugh Gardens.

Witts Family Papers F194

1797

Sunday May 28th.

A wet & consequently disagreable Morning, & tho it clear'd in some degree before Noon was very cloudy & showery the remainder of the day, yet we managed to get tolerably well to & from Mr Sandfords new Chapel (Charlotte Chapel) where he perform'd admirably & his dedacatory prayer excellent between services visited M^rs. Rudyard & M^rs. Skene found only the former at home Mr P. Brougham[1] drank Tea with us. rec'd a Letter from Lady Dukenfield & wrote to my Sis^r Travell

Monday May 29th.

Quite a true summer day at least till after noon when it became cold & lowering, & was showery in the evening, made nine visits in the new Town those I found at home were M^rs. David Erskine, M^rs. Brougham, M^rs. Halkett Craigie, & M^rs. Bruce of Kinloch began <u>hearing</u> Family Secret.[2]

Tuesday May 30th.

Rather cold & stormy, tho but little if any rain fell, my Morning visitors were M^rs. & Miss Skene, Miss Macdonald, Lady Sinclair & Mr Law, walk'd after Tea with Mr Witts & Francis to Bernards Well &'c wrote to Lady Dukenfield.

---

1. Peter Brougham (1781–1800). Peter was the third son of Henry Brougham (1742–1810) and Eleanor (Eleanora) (*c.* 1750–1839), née Symes. Eleanor was the niece of Dr William Robertson, the historian and principal of Edinburgh University and a relation of William Adam (1751–1839). Peter's eldest brother, Henry (1778–1868), 1st Baron Brougham and Vaux became Lord Chancellor of Great Britain. As a young lawyer in Scotland Henry helped to found the *Edinburgh Review* in 1802 and contributed many articles to it. Peter died a tragic death as a teenager in 1800. Agnes's son, Francis, also a great diarist narrates the tale in his diary entry for 24 June 1830. He had been in the House of Commons, listening to the Lord Chancellor, Henry Brougham, giving an address to the House, and reminisces on his youthful days in Edinburgh: *The third of the family was my contemporary & intimate, Peter, a youth of very superior talents: like his elder brothers, he was brought up at the High School of Edinburgh, where & in the Junior classes of the College, I was his sworn friend & brother, the Pylades & Orestes of the Rector's Class. He had a talent not unequal, I apprehend, to that of Henry; but he was early cut off, ere it was developed: destined for the military service in India, he was on his voyage thither, when a quarrel arose, about nothing, between him & a young naval officer serving on board the Indiaman, in which he sailed; (he was a brother of Lady Wemyss;) the young men had been intimate, but an imaginary affront was to be revenged; when the ship came to anchor off the coast of Brazil, they fought, Brougham was wounded in the thigh, carried on board the vessel, and his antagonist put under arrest on shore; there was every prospect of the wound soon healing; but a new catastrophe was at hand. The ship, the Queen, took fire; in the confusion, the wounded youth had been forgotten; but he crawled from his hammock & took refuge in the rigging. There was one, however, who was not unmindful of him; his former intimate & late antagonist: he saw from the shore the flames gaining head, he thought of Brougham's helpless state, he broke his arrest, hurried off with a boat, arrived in time to rescue him from his perils, conveyed him on shore; but the hurry, the alarm, the exposure, had been too much for the poor youth's weakened frame, & a few days fever terminated his short career....*
2. Mr Pratt, pseudonym for Samuel Jackson (1749–1814), *Family Secrets, Literary and Domestic*, 1797.

Wensday May 31ˢᵗ·

Quite cold & unpleasant from high wind & flying showers, Frank & I sympathized with each other from pains in our head & face, Mʳˢ· Thomson here in the Morning, & Mʳˢ· Hay & Mʳ· Sandford in the evening, the former, to take leave, the latter on much Chapel bussiness & conversation—

Thursday June 1ˢᵗ·

Dry but far from a pleasant Day being an extreme high wind & so cold a one that the sun lost its power, not out in the Morning, Miss Melvilles call'd here, repented sorely walking out after Tea being nearly starved & brought on the pain in my face, in the hope of shelter walk'd to Bernards Well &'c, but in vain.

Friday June 2ᵈ·

Very much the same weather only not quite so cold or windy yet I thought it best to keep the house, Mʳˢ· Rudyard & Mʳ· Erskine of Cambo here in the Morning, & Miss Drysdale, Misses Stewart & Inglehart drank Tea. rec'd a Letter from Mʳˢ· Erskine.

Saturday June 3ᵈ·

Still disagreably cold & windy, went to Chapel, where Mʳ· Sandford gave us a most excellent Sermon, afterwards made a long visit to Mʳˢ· Brown St. James's Square & in the evening attempted to walk, but it was so miserably cold, glad to come home early.

Sunday June 4ᵗʰ·

No better weather almost blown away going to & from Charlotte Chapel where we were long detain'd by numerous communicants, walk'd in the evening in Queen Street much crowded.

Monday June 5ᵗʰ·

Quite a fine Day throughout warm w.ʰ little or no wind a great comfort, & very fortunate for the appearance & rejoicing of the Day, went with my Sons to Miss Drysdales house in Sᵗ· Andrews Square to see the Regiments drawn up previous to their going to Leith Links for a grand exhibition a fine sight walk'd with Sons in the absence of their Father who was gone to the Parliament house to drink the Kings health to Bernard Well &'c. rec'd Letter from Miss A. Snow

Tuesday June 6ᵗʰ·

An unpleasant Day being such a severe wind that made the dust quite intolerable till some flying showers in the afternoon laid it. went to Chapel from thence visited Mʳˢ· Mure, Mʳˢ· Oliphant, Miss Jane Dundas & Mʳˢ· Brown, went to Tea & Supper at Mʳˢ· Oliphants, Lᵈʸ· & Miss Sinclair the only party alltogether very odd & terribly late home. rec'd Letter fᵐ· Lᵈʸ· Dukenfield

Wensday June 7ᵗʰ·

Better weather tho still cold & windy but much sun, a long chatty call from Miss Graham my only company in the Morning, went to Tea & Supper at Mʳˢ· Speirs's, a small party but pleasant enough much card playing home in tolerable time wrote to Miss Anne Snow.

Thursday June 8th.

Dry & tolerably fine through the day late in the evening gloomy, with a trifling shower Col: Rooke made an early call, my only visitor after Tea with the Boys went to see Lady C: C: afterwards walk'd in the environs of the Abbey, wrote to M$^{rs.}$ Browning

Friday June 9th.

A warm & very fine Day tho with an easterly wind, quiet at home again in the Morn: & rec'd M$^{rs.}$ Clerke, & M$^{rs.}$ & Miss Moneypenny after Tea walk'd to the Calton Hill to see the Artillery fire & perform many manovres where a great crowd was assembled on the occasion

Saturday June 10th.

Bright & fine from Morn: to night but being still an easterly wind not too hot for a wonder walk'd to Georges Square made several visits those I found at home were M$^{rs.}$ Craigie & M$^{rs.}$ Douglass Charlotte Stewart & Anna dined with us, & accompanied us in our evening walk to Queen Street &'c &'c.

Sunday June 11th.

Still an easterly wind, but in the Morn: it was as oppressively hot & close as in the evening it was cold & disagreable, went to Charlotte Chapel to both services a prodigeous fine Sermon in the evening on the subject of the Day, between services call'd on M$^{rs.}$ Macdowal, after Tea went to M$^{r.}$ Browns for an hour or two.

Monday June 12th.

Very hard continued rain till quite the afternoon when it became dry but not clear, of course no interruptions to Morning employments, went to Tea and supper at M$^{rs.}$ Macdonalds to be introduced to her Son a little party nothing very brilliant rec'd Letters from Lady Riddell & my Sister Travell.

Tuesday June 13th.

Not a pleasant Day being a cold east wind with scarce any Sun, & having much rhumatism I had no wish to go out in the Morning, Miss Hellen Speirs & M$^{r.}$ & M$^{rs.}$ Campbell of Fairfield call'd, Miss Abercromby drank Tea with us & going away early we walk'd in the streets & near environs of the Town.

Wensday June 14th.

A worse rather than a better Day & a thick wetting fog coming on in the evening, I never stir'd out of the House the whole day, my only visitors were Charlotte Stewart & Anna Inglehart to take leave, & M$^{r.}$ M. Riddell. wrote to M$^{r.}$ Burslem

Thursday June 15th.

Very far from a good day being wet early in the Morning, gloomy all day, & a wetting mist again late in the evening, at home all Morn without seeing a Creature in the evening merely walk'd down to see Lady C: C: to wish her joy of the good tidings contain'd in a Letter I had rec'd from Lady Elcho. wrote to M$^{rs.}$ Erskine

Friday June 16^(th.)

Dry, but dull & cold with continued east wind, went early to the Court of Session accompanied by Miss Bruce of Stenhouse M^(r.) W. & Frank, to hear M^(r.) Erskine[3] plead in the Nisbet Cause[4] which he did most ably for more than three Hours, seldom more entertain'd & the Court crowded call'd at Com: Browns on our return home. walk'd late in the evening in the Streets. rec'd a Letter from Miss Neville & wrote to Lady Dukenfield.

Saturday June 17^(th.)

No change in the weather excepting being rather warmer, tho the same thick unpleasant air continued, visited M^(rs.) Dugald Stewart & M^(rs.) Gregory both at home & very pleasant, also L^(dy.) C: C: again in the hope of meeting M^(r.) Charteris, who at last was not well enough to come into Town, in the evening walk'd by sufferance in M^(rs.) Scotts place at Bellevue. rec'd a Letter from M^(rs.) Davies.

Sunday June 18^(th.)

An unpleasant Day tho dry, being cold & very windy, the Boys only went to Chapel in the Morn: staying at home to write Letters, we all went to the evening service, D^(r.) Willich drank Tea here & gave us much German information, Miss Melvilles call'd & we walk'd late in Queen Street among a smart groupe wrote to Lady Elcho & Lady Edward Bentinck.

Monday June 19^(th.)

Wet & very wet the greater part of the Morning, & so damp & cold in the evening I had no relish for going out, & saw no one but Miss Bruce of Stenhouse, work'd much & heard much reading in Wilberforces Christianity[5] & wrote to my Sis^(r.) Travell

Tuesday June 20^(th.)

A fine bright Day from constant sunshine but a cold east wind, went very early to the Court of Session with Miss Bruce, to hear the decision in the Nisbet cause, which went in favor of the Baronet almost to universal satisfaction, a long visit to Col & M^(rs.) Moneypenny almost fill'd up the Morn after Tea made a short visit to M^(rs.) Macdonald & a longer to M^(r.) & M^(rs.) Brown S^(t.) James's Square rec'd a Letter from M^(rs.) Young.

Wensday June 21^(st.)

Seldom so bitterly cold on this day, much east wind & no sun, happy to sit by a good fire the whole Day, Miss Macdonald & Miss Grace Speirs the only interruption to much work & reading.

---

3.   Thomas Erskine (1750–1823), 1st Baron Erskine. Thomas Erskine, the Lord Chancellor, was born in Edinburgh, the youngest son of Henry David Erskine, 10th earl of Buchan.
4.   John Nisbet (d. 1827), 8th baronet. John married, November 1797, Maria, née Alston, an American actress, the daughter of William Alston of South Carolina, and thereafter lived much of his time in the United States. They separated in 1820 and John Nisbet moved to Italy and died at Naples in 1827. The Court of Session case has not been investigated.
5.   William Wilberforce (1759–1833); *A Practical View of the Prevailing Religious System of Professed Christians, in the Middle and Higher Classes in this Country, Contrasted with Real Christianity*, London: T. Caddell, 1797.

Thursday June 22ᵈ·

A very similiar Day not at all better, but I could no longer submit to be shut up, but was out 2 or 3 hours in the Morning, chiefly shoping in the old Town & visiting Lady C: C: glad to spend the evening by the fireside.

Friday June 23ᵈ·

Much the same gloomy cold weather, & late in the evening it became very wet, Miss Bruce of Stenhouse my only Morning caller, she & Miss Margret MacFarlan accompanied us soon after Dinner in a walk to call on poor Mʳˢ· Macdougal at Leith, not finding her at home we came back tired, disappointed & rather wet, kept the Ladies to take a late Tea with us

Saturday June 24ᵗʰ·

Wet early in the Day but dry & pretty fine the remainder much working & reading in the Morning, James Riddell dined here he & Peter Brougham accompanied us in a walk after Tea to Bernards Well &'c

Sunday June 25ᵗʰ·

A fine Day from constant sunshine & clear air, but cold wind being still in the east which produced a gloomy sky in the evening & a trifling shower of rain between services at Charlotte Chappel where we went both times, rec'd a visit from Miss Bruce of Kennaird, & paid one to Lᵈʸ· Sinclair of Muchele⁶ in the evening attempted a visit to Lady H. Blair, more successful in one to Miss Melvilles where I sat an hour or two wrote to Mʳˢ· Charteris.

Monday June 26ᵗʰ·

Much such another clear fine Day only the evening proved very fine & much warmer went over the Bridge in the Morning to pay some Bills, visited Lady Betty Cunningham & Mʳˢ· Brown after Tea went to sit an hour or two with Mʳˢ· R. Scott. the Boys most happy receiving a Box of Classical Books from England by Sea to Leith

Tuesday June 27ᵗʰ·

Fine & pleasant in spite of continued east wind, did not move all Morning & saw no one but Mʳˢ· Bruce of Kinloch, went to Cards & Supper at Miss Bruce's of Stenhouse a mixt party of 14, but not unpleasant. wrote to congratulate Mʳˢ· Browne

Wensday June 28ᵗʰ·

Dry & tolerably fine early in the Day but at Noon changed to very showery, & in the afternoon prodigeous hard ones, no one here in the Morning but Mʳ· Skene, much employ'd by traficking with a Broker went to Cards & Supper at Miss MacFarlans six Ladies & as many Gentlemen chearful & lively enough

---

6. Lady Sinclair of Murkle, 26 George's Street. Mary Sinclair, née Blair (d. 1818). Mary was the daughter of William Blair of that Ilk. She married John Sinclair of Murkle, 6th Bt., son of Robert Sinclair and Isabella Ker. They had one son, Robert Sinclair of Murkle, 7th Bt. (1763–1795).

Above left: Three Legal Devotees. Andrew Nicol, Mary Walker, and John Skene. Andrew Nicol (see below); Mary Walker was an intolerable pest about Parliament House. Insane, the object of her legal solicitude was the recovery of a sum of money which she conceived to be due to her from the Magistrates of Edinburgh. John Skene was a flax-dresser, but this trade was a matter of secondary consideration, as through some form of insanity he conceived he was commissioned to hold two situations of the highest importance in the country—Superintendent of the Court of Session, and of the General Assembly. He worked nearly all night at the dressing of flax—only retiring to rest for an hour or two towards morning. He then rose, and, having arrayed himself in the clerical style represented in the print, proceeded to the Parliament House. He believed his presence actually necessary to the proper dispatch of business, and continued his extraordinary exertions session after session.

Above right: Andrew Nicol was a linen weaver. Some misunderstanding having arisen between him and a neighbour about the situation or boundary of a dunghill, nothing less could adjust matters than an appeal to a court of law. Andrew seems to have been successful in the inferior courts ; but his opponent, having a longer purse, carried the case to the Court of Session, and by one expedient or other, protracted a decision until he compelled poor Andrew to be incarcerated for debt. The whole affair was certainly a satire on judicial proceedings; but it took such possession of the simpleton's mind as to engross all his attention, and week after week he travelled from Kinross to Edinburgh to inquire about the progress of his law-suit. Kay relates that when the print was published in 1802, no fewer than 116 subscribers were obtained among the gentlemen of the legal profession.

Thursday June 29th.

Wet in the Morning, dry at Noon & very fine in the evening a home & uninterrupted Morning M^r. Law drank Tea here & we all 4 accompanied him a little on his way home to Lauriston. rec'd Letters from M^rs. Erskine & M^rs. Granville & wrote to M^rs. Davies.

Friday June 30th.

Quite a warm & very delightful Day from Morn to night perfect summer, out in the Morning making several visits, but found only M^rs. Edmonstone, Miss Dirorns, & M^rs. Brown at home

Mr Witts in court in the Morning witnessing Lord Kelly being locked to his estate,[7] dined also with Mr Erskine & a large party on the occasion at Fortnums Tavern Mrs Rooke call'd after Tea accompanied her in her Coach, to make several calls & sat with her till near dark.

Saturday July 1.st

Very unexpectedly after so glorious a preceding evening it was almost an intire wet Day till quite evening & sometime extreme hard rain, of course no moving, nor saw any one till after Tea when Mr Rooke call'd to say their Coach should convey us to spend an hour or two with his Ladies which it did. rec'd Letters from L.^dy Dukenfield & Miss Anne Snow, & wrote to Mrs Young

Sunday July 2.^d

A bright fine Morning but by Noon a severe shower came on which obliged me to return from Charlotte Chappel in a Chair, but was dry enough to walk there to evening service, & got home again pretty dry between the storms wch were very severe during the whole of the Day. Mr Law both dined & drank Tea here.

Monday July 3.^d

Very hard rain early in the Day but tho it soon became dry it was a cold comfortless Day with a high wind, Mrs Rooke & her three Misses were here in the Morning, as also Mrs Gregory, went to Cards & Supper at Mrs Mure's as usual a party of 9 Ladies & only 2 Gentlemen but chearful enough. lost 20 pennies at Cassino rec'd Letter f.^m Mrs Charteris

Tuesday July 4.th

A fine pleasant Day upon the whole extremely windy till afternoon, but more temperate afterwards, rec'd a long visit from Mrs Campbell of Stonefield[8] & a Niece of the same name, after Tea went first to call on L.^dy C: C: & then walk'd to the Abbey & its environs & was not at home till near ten o clock - wrote to Miss Elizabeth Guydickens

Wensday July 5.th

Quite an indifferent Day being wet & gloomy, too much so to go out or see any one even Mr Witts never stird work'd & read much & wrote to Mrs Erskine.

Thursday July 6.th

Fine & promising in the Morning but at noon such violent showers that it might be almost term'd perpetual, went first to call on Mrs Brown on her return from Dalkirk, then to the South Town in the hope of making a string of visits, but soon check'd by the violence of the rain, & detain'd for near an hour at Mrs D. Hamiltons tho she was not at home for shelter & obliged at last to come home in a Chair Col: & Mrs Clitherow here in the evening, being come into Town from Sunderland most happy to see them rec'd a Letter from Mrs Hyett

---

7. Charles Erskine, 8th Earl of Kellie (±1764–1799). Charles succeeded to the earldom following the death of his cousin, Archibald Erskine (1736–1797). Charles died unmarried two years later.
8. Elizabeth née Anstruther (1766–1839), married, 1787, Col. Colin Campbell, younger of Stonefield (b. 1761).

Friday July 7th.

Dry & rather gloomy hot till Dinner time when it again became as wet as usual for the remainder of the Day, Mr. W. myself & <u>Francis</u> went to Breakfast with the Clitherow party at Drumbreakes[9] & stroled about with them the whole Morning, till after a merry <u>Luncheon</u> together they set off for Sunderland a very lively pleasant Morning. much interested in the evening by the last Vol: of family Secrets.

Saturday July 8th.

No rain all Day, but such a gloomy thick air that it was oppressively hot, tho with very little sun, Mrs. Macqueen my only visitor, Mr. Witts & I went to the Play in Mrs. Campbells Box to see Bannister in the Will,[10] highly entertained & a very crowded House rec'd a Letter from Mrs. Riddell & wrote Miss A. Snow

Sunday July 9th.

Rather showery in the Morn: but very trivial ones, fine afterwards & peculiarly pleasant in the evening, Mr. W. only at Chapel in the Morn. before I went to evening service call'd on Mrs. Mure, walk'd till late in Queen Street a crowded Mall. rec'd a Letter from my Sisr. Travell & wrote to Lady Dukenfield.

Monday July 10th.

A fine quite warm Day from Morn to Night, rather oppressively so, which kept me quiet in the forenoon receiving only a chatty visit from <u>Aunt</u> Jenny Dundas, went to Drink Tea with Miss Abercrombie meeting Lady Salton[11] & Miss Fraser & Miss Mackenzie made a unsuccessful call on Mrs. Brown, on my return wrote to my Sister Travell

Tuesday July 11th.

Quite a disagreable Day, in point of weather, being hot thick air with frequent fleeting showers but of no consequence, rec'd an early visit from Sr. N. Dukenfield & his two eldest sons, afterwards walk'd to the Cowgate after bargains visited Lady C: C: & tried to do the same to Mrs. Gregory, our two young friends dined with us & accompanied Frank & myself to the Play to see Bannister in his capital part of Fainwell in a bold stroke for a Wife wonderfully well entertained.[12]

---

9.   Drumsheugh Gardens. Agnes clearly has a problem with understanding this name.

10. Mr Bannister is presumably the famous actor, John Bannister (1760–1836), but the play being referred to as *The Will*, is confusing. According to *A Biographical Dictionary of Actors, Actresses, Musicians, Dancers, Managers & Other Stage Personnel in London, 1660–1800* the play being performed at the Theatre Royal Edinburgh on Saturday 8 July 1797 was Thomas Moreton's, *The Way to get Married*, a comedy in five acts, with serious situations. This was first produced at Covent Garden 23 January 1796, performed 41 times, and became a stock piece for the theatre. On this night, 8 July 1797, Tryphosa Jane Wallis appeared as the character Julia Faulkner.

11. Eleanor [Helen] Fraser, née Gordon, Lady Saltoun (1730–1800), daughter of John Gordon of Kinellar. Eleanor had married George Fraser, 13th Lord Saltoun of Abernethy (1720–1781). Presumably Miss Fraser was Eleanora Fraser (d. 1821).

12. Susanna Centlivre (±1667–1723). *A Bold Stroke for a Wife'* was a satirical play of 1717. The plot expresses the author's unabashed support of the Whig Party: she criticises the Tories, religious hypocrisy, and the greed of capitalism. Colonel Fainwell is the leading character in this play.

Mansion of George 1st Marquis of Huntly, Bakehouse Close, Cowgate. An engraving by W. Forrest from a painting by Daniel Wilson.

Wensday July 12$^{th.}$

A pleasant day in point of weather, no rain, little wind or sun, S$^{r.}$ N. Dukenfield here for an hour or two in the Morning, when M$^{rs.}$ Edmondstone call'd at 6 o'clock went with the Bart & Miss Blair to Bruntsfield Links to the inspection of the 2$^{d.}$ Battalion of the Duke of Buccluechs Reg$^{t.}$ of Volunteers, & the colors presented by the Dutchess, returnd to Lady Blairs at 9 who regaled us well with Tea &'c to refresh us after our fatigue. rec'd a Letter from L$^{dy.}$ Dukenfield

Thursday July 13$^{th.}$

Quite a close hot day, with a very disagreable thick air & in the evening very oppressive M$^{r.}$ & M$^{rs.}$ Moneypenny here in the Morning a take leave call, after Tea, M$^{r.}$ Witts, Frank & self, walk'd to Wherriston &'c, a fine walk, not at home till near dark rec'd a Letter from Lady Edward Bentinck.

Friday July 14$^{th.}$

A fine, but oppressively hot Day universal sunshine till evening when the thickness of the air was distressing to be out in, out for three hours in the forenoon shopping & visiting M$^{rs.}$ Brown; after Tea went out late in Queen Street &'c some thunder

Saturday July 15$^{th.}$

Very hard rain in the Morning, but cleared at Noon, & was clear & fine the remainder of the Day, at home all Morning without any callers in the evening call'd on Lady C: C: & return'd home over the Calton Hill

A view from Calton Hill. An engraving by George Cook from a painting by J. M. W. Turner. The new Regent Bridge is visible, something that would *not* have been familiar to the Witts family as they descended the hill.

Sunday July 16th.

One of the finest summer Days that could be only too hot to move much with comfort went to both services at Charlotte Chappel, between made a long, tho first visit to Lady Campbell, in the evening walk'd in the most crowded set of company I ever saw in Queen Street.

Monday July 17th.

A severe storm of Thunder & violent rain early in the Morning, dry by mid.day tho still windy & rather chilly in the evening at home all Morning without any interruption but Mrs. Brougham, after Tea walk'd our whole party round the base of the Castle & home by the Lothian road. rec'd Letters from Dr. Pennington & Miss L. Lee, wrote to Ldy. Dukenfield, & Mrs. Charteris.

Tuesday July 18th.

Small rain in the Morning, but tho it became dry, it was very stormy the rest of the Day & not being well in my stomach I never went out, neither saw any one. much entertained by hearing Smiths Moral sentiments.[13] wrote to Mrs. Granville.

---

13.   Adam Smith (1723–1790). *The Theory of Moral Sentiments*, 1759.

Wensday July 19th.

Fine & dry in the Morning, but became very showery at mid.day & so remaind more or less the greater part of the Day, at home all Morning & saw no one but Miss C: Scott after Tea walk'd only to Charlotte Chapel to give directions for lining the Pew kept there by a shower rec'd a Letter from Mrs. Davies & wrote to Mrs. Riddell.

Thursday July 20th.

Fine but extremely windy which made it unpleasant a violent shower from three to four accompanied with Thunder, went out in the forenoon to make several visits, those I found at home were Mrs. Campbell of Fairfield, Mrs. Syme & Mrs. Campbell of Saddel, where I was detain an hour or more from stress of weather, walk'd in the evening to Georges Square & home thro the old Town & over the Mound, call'd at Lady Sinclairs on some bussiness, who detained us to a chearful conversable Supper with her & her Daughter rec'd Letters from Mrs. Wilkinson, Mrs. Young & Miss Snow.

Friday July 21st.

Very wet early in the Day but tho it became dry it was gloomy & by no means pleasant the rest of the day, neither went our or saw anyone the whole of the Morning, after Tea Mr. W. Frank & I walk'd over the Calton Hill to the Abbey & about it.

Saturday July 22d.

Fine in the Morning but at mid.day became so violently wet there was no stirring out tho prepared for it, very happy to hear of Lady Riddells being come to Town, James Riddell drank Tea here much working & reading occupied the Day. rec'd a Letter from Miss Maitland.

Sunday July 23d.

Dry in the Morning but before church time was wet, & more or less so till afternoon, went to St. Andrews Church in the Morning & Charlotte chapel in afternoon between visited Ldy. Riddell, most happy to meet, went to Dine Boys & all at Mr. Com: Browns, Mrs. & Miss Mure there only went with the latter to the Quakers Meeting at the Circus for an hour not much edified. home by dark

Monday July 24th.

A fine day without any rain but much wind & some sun, the first Day of the Races but the Town appeard very little enliven'd by them, went to make my long intended visit to Miss Campbell at Newington found them at home & Mr. Macdonald walk'd home with us, went to Tea & Supper at Lady Riddells, Lady Sinclair & Mr. M. Riddell there much as usual

Tuesday July 25th.

A thick lowering Morn: which turn'd out a fine Day & perculiarly clear evening tho rather cold went out late to make an unsuccessful visit to Mrs. Macvicar, made one likewise to Mrs. Thomson walk'd with Sr. James & Lady Riddell in Queen Street &'c, before Tea where Mr. Witts & Miss Bruce of Kinnaird join'd us, much Cribbage & chearful conversation. wrote to Mrs. Wilkinson.

Wensday July 26[th.]

A fine Day tho an east wind, & in the evening extremely hot & close, a home quiet Morn with much working, & attending to Smiths Moral Sentiments no interruption, walk'd after Tea with Lady Riddell & the 2 Miss MacFarlans in M[rs.] Scotts Grounds, a sweet Haymaking Scene. rec'd a Letter from Lady Dukenfield.

Thursday July 27[th.]

A thick gloomy shire which at many periods of the day produced small rain & in the evening was very cold, M[r.] Witts went to the Race I staid solus at home writing, drank Tea & supt at Lady Riddells meeting only Miss Orde wrote to Lady Elcho & L[dy.] Ed:[d] Bentinck

Friday July 28[th.]

Quite a gloomy disagreable Day very thick air with frequent small misty rain so truly unpleasant that even M[r.] Witts never stirr'd out any more than myself, nor of course did we see any one, but full of many employments among others wrote a long Letter to D[r.] Pennington.

Saturday July 29[th.]

Extreme hard rain till mid.day when it ceased, but remain'd a very gloomy disagreable day thro'out & very damp, another sombre Morning without any interruption, James Riddell dined here & we all walk'd in the Streets in the evening wrote to Lady Dukenfield.

Sunday July 30[th.]

After a most tremendous night of the most severe rain I ever heard, it was nearly as violent a day of rain accompanied by sharp east wind, only went to evening service at Charlotte Chapel & that in a Chair. Peter Brougham drank Tea here. wrote to M[rs.] Davies.

Monday July 31[st.]

Continued hard rain till after breakfast, clear & fine till between 3 & 4 when there were a most severe shower or two but dry & fine in the evening, made rather a long call on M[rs.] Macdowall then into the old Town on several bussinesses among others to suit my eyes with a pair of Spectacles, walk'd late in Queen Street in evening with M[r.] M. Riddell.

Tuesday Aug[st.] 1[st.]

Quite a gaudy Morn: which as often produced rain even before mid.day, & the showers were very perpetual till quite evening, M[r.] Sandford here for an hour or two on several bussinesses, Miss Campbell of Patricks Square afterwards, walk'd late in Princes's Street &'c.

Wensday Aug[st.] 2[d.]

A more intire day & consequently fine Day than most former ones we had been accustomed to made good use of it by visiting M[rs.] Fyffe, M[rs.] Gregory, & Lady C: C: & found all at home likewise did some bussinesses on the Bridges, went to Tea Cards, & Supper at L[dy.] Sinclairs no one there but D[r.] & M[rs.] Walker, but chatty enough.

Thursday Aug^(st.) 3^(d.)

Dry & shewey in the Morning but before I could get out which I much wanted to do, it became wet in such violent & frequent showers that it might almost be call'd perpetual till quite evening, saw no one till Miss Drysdale & C: Stewart call'd here after Tea & accompanied us in our Street walk. damp & unpleasant

Friday Aug^(st.) 4^(th.)

Rather a cloudy Day, but upon the whole dry & pleasant made good use of it, by walking to Patricks Square to visit Miss Campbell did several pieces of bussiness on the Bridge coming home, made as unsuccessful visit to L^(dy.) B. Cunningham,[14] & one to M^(rs.) McGee, M^(r.) Sandford drank Tea with us & staid two or three hours much to our satisfaction. rec'd a letter from M^(rs.) Young & answer'd it.

Saturday Aug^(st.) 5^(th.)

A most tremendous high wind, accompanied by some flying showers, but no rain of any consequence a busy Morning, of one thing or other, a visit from Miss Melvilles, & another from L^(dy.) H: Blair, to walk down with us to her quar^(ts.) at Leith to dine, no one but Lord Binny, & Miss Macleod except their own family, walk'd up again before dark; chearful & pleasant enough.

Sunday Aug^(st.) 6^(th.)

Again very windy but happily quite dry & much sunshine, went to both services at Charlotte Chapel between visited M^(rs.) Brougham, when to my utter astonishment <u>He</u> made his appearance in an easy manner,[15] M^(rs.) B. went with me to Chapel Charlotte Stewart dined with us & walk'd with us in Queen Street.

Monday Aug^(st.) 7^(th.)

A dull gloomy warm Day, but dry till three o'clock when hard rain came on for two or three hours, went out in the forenoon to make several visits those I found at home, were M^(rs.) Cunningham M^(rs.) Rudyard, M^(rs.) Dirom & M^(rs.) Duff & M^(rs.) Edmondston a home evening. rec'd Letters from M^(rs.) Brown and M^(rs.) Musson the latter little expected.

Tuesday Aug^(st.) 8^(th.)

Quite a similiar day to the former one, being dry & gloomy in the Morning & wet in the afternoon, I went out late for a walk, merely to carry a Letter to the post office, M^(rs.) Cunningham here first, no stirring in the evening. wrote to my Sis^(r.) Travell.

---

14. Lady Betty (Elizabeth) Cunningham (d. 1804), of 9 St Andrew's Square and Coates House. Betty was the younger sister of James, Earl of Glencairn. Lady Betty lived with her mother, the Dowager Countess; she never married. It was to Lady Cunningham that Burns wrote from Ellisland on 22 January 1789, indicating his poetic plans, and he sent her his first sent a copy of his 'Lament for James, Earl of Glencairn', on her brother's death. In the accompanying letter, undated, he wrote: *If, among my children, I shall have a son that has a hear, he shall hand it down to his child as a family honor, and a family debt, that my dearest existence I owe to the noble house of Glencairn.* When the 1793 edition of his Poems appeared, Burns sent a copy to Lady Cunningham with this note: *But for the generous patronage of the late James, Earl of Glencairn to the Author, these volumes had never been. In memory of the obligations he conferred on me; and in gratitude to your Ladyship for your goodness, do me the honor to accept these volumes.*

15. Eleanor married Henry Brougham (1742–1810) in May 1777. It seems that relations between Eleanor and Henry were strained. Agnes Witts and Eleanor maintained a friendship until Agnes's death in 1825.

Wensday Aug^st. 9th.

Wet in the Morning, stormy & wet in showers the chief of the day but dry in the evening.
being engaged to dine at M^r. Campbells at Mayfield close to the Leith Battery, we ventured
to sally forth Francis with us in a hackney Coach as far as Leith a very chearful pleasant Day
tho no one but their own family. walk'd home by Bonnington the young Ladies part of the
way with us. George join'd us at Tea Time

Thursday Aug^st. 10th.

Severe wind, but very little if any rain not tempting enough for me to go out, neither saw anyone
till I went to Tea Cards & Supper at Sir James Riddells as they return'd the night before, no
one there but M^r. M. Riddell much fighting at Cribbage rec'd Letters from Lady Dukenfield
& my Sis^r. Travell, & wrote to Miss Snow

Friday Aug^st. 11th.

Quite a fine warm day not even the pretence of rain till quite evening & then very trifling a
bustling Morn: preparing George for the High School examination whither his Father & Bro^r.
attended him, & where he was happily adjudged Lux of his Class great joy I went out early &
never return'd till 4 o'clock making several visits first in the new Town, afterwards L^dy. C.C &
others in that quarter to several shops, & ending by trying on a Gown at Miss Waddells, on
my return found an invitation as well as the Boys, (their Father dining with the Major Nales)
to dine at S^r. James Riddells to meet M^rs. Riddell, supt also M^r. M. Riddell again.

Saturday Aug^st. 12th.

A fine but very windy Morning a shower at Noon & very fine in the afternoon, very busy all
Morning at various things before all Dining at Sir James Riddells again, call'd for ½ an hour
on M^rs. Riddell at her Mothers House, supt also no company but their own family party.

Sunday Aug^st. 13th.

Lowering but mild & fine & in the afternoon some misty showers, went twice to Charlotte
Chapel, a sad difference between M^r. Sandford & his substitute, between services visited L^dy.
R. Bruce, M^rs. Riddell & M^rs. Bruce of Kinloch only the two latter at home, S^r. J: Riddell here
for an hour or two in the afternoon in confidential conversation, M^rs. Mure drop'd in to Tea
& when near dark walk'd a little in Queen Street. wrote to M^rs. Dundas.

Monday Aug^st. 14th.

Quite a fine warm day, tho at times cloudy & at night small rain but short, at home all Morning
till three when I went out to some shops, Sir J Riddell here again on the same business, & the
pleasant M^r. Arbuthnot, went to Tea Cards & Supper with L^dy. Riddell meeting Lady Campbell,
M^rs. Riddell & Miss MacFarlan

Tuesday Aug^st. 15th.

Quite a dry warm & pleasant Day tho with a good deal of wind, M^r. Witts & George down at Leith,
Francis accompanying me on various shopping bussiness, rec'd visits from M^rs. Riddell & M^rs. Duff
after my return, spent the evening as usual at S^r. James's M^rs. Riddell & M^r. M. Riddell only there

Wensday Aug^(st.) 16^(th.)

Another very fine Day begining to be very full of bussiness against our approaching departure the Boys be also packing & spending most of the Morning on a Leith expedition, M^(rs.) Brougham, M^(r.) Laird, & Lady Riddell here she went with us into the old Town where I visited Lady C: C: & M^(rs.) Gregory & her nice Boy, Tea Cards & elegant Supper at Lady Campbells meeting the Riddell Family & Miss MacFarlans

Thursday Aug^(st.) 17^(th.)

A hot & perfect summer Day from Morn to night, so much engaged all Day with pack^(g.) & giving orders I admitted no one but M^(r.) Com: Brown went in the evening as usual to Lady Riddells, Miss Bruce & M^(r.) M. Riddell there only M^(rs.) Riddell gone

Friday Aug^(st.) 18^(th.)

A brilliant Morning, which was however very temporary as at 12 violent rain came on & continued uninterrupted the whole Day, very busy all Morn preparing for our departure M^(r.) D. Erskine call'd on us from an error, the Chaise never came till three o'clock which from losing our road, prevented our reaching M^(rs.) Dundas's at Dundas Castle[16] till past 5, the rain pouring like torrents all the way, found a large family party at Dinner, S^(r.) William & Miss Sterling, M^(rs.) Brown, & a M^(rs.) & Miss Edmonstone, a very chearful pleasant evening with 2 Card Tables for a short time. Dundas Castle is 11 miles from Edinbro, a very short distance from the Queens Ferry, is situated on a considerable eminence, of course commands a fine view of the Firth &'c the old Castle a perfect ruin stands close to the habitable House, which is old & very indifferent one rec'd a Letter from M^(rs.) Buxton, & wrote to Lady Dukenfield, M^(rs.) Erskine & M^(rs.) Riddell.

Saturday Aug^(st.) 19^(th.)

Tho a lowering Morn: it turn'd out a tolerable fine Day with only a very trifling shower or 2, took a fine walk about the premises, which are very fine, & capable of much improvement, some Morning callers, & M^(rs.) Graham of Airth & her Daughter, & M^(r.) Seton came to Dinner, M^(rs.) Edmonstone & her Daughter going away, play'd at Cassino with shocking luck rec'd Letters from M^(rs.) Wilkinson & Miss Betty Guydickens.

Sunday Aug^(st.) 20^(th.)

A lowering Morning, & not very bright any part of the Day, but quite dry & very pleasant, M^(rs.) Dundas, M^(rs.) Graham, & myself took a delightful airing to Lord Roseberrys at Barnbeugle a charming place about three miles distant w.^(ch) commands a beautiful view of the Firth & is very highly cultivated & well wooded, from thence we went to M^(r.) David Dundas's at

---

16.   Mrs Dundas was Christian (d. 1832), 2nd daughter of William Stirling, 2nd baronet of Ardoch and Mary, daughter of Charles Erskine, 1st baronet of Alvah. Christian had married, 1784, George Dundas, 23rd Dundas of Dundas. George had been a captain in the service of the HEIC, and commander of the *Winterton*, East Indiaman, and died when that vessel had foundered off the coast of Madagascar, 22 August 1792. When George had departed from Edinburgh he had left Christian pregnant, and the son, James (1793–1881) was born on 14 January 1793, becoming chief on his birth as 24th Dundas of Dundas. He sold Dundas Castle 1875.

Duddingstone[17] where M[rs.] Dundas's youngest children were staying[18] return'd home only time enough to Dress for Dinner to receive Cap[tn.] & M[rs.] Maitland & Miss Gibson from Clifton Hall,[19] a very pleasant chatty evening rec'd an <u>interesting</u> Letter from M[rs.] Davies

Monday Aug[st.] 21[st.]

A gloomy Morning with some Small showers but none of consequence, & it proved a mild fine travelling day, as we left Dundas after breakfast taking Hopetoun House on our road to Lenlithgow a fine situation commanding an extensive view of the Firth but not so pleasing a one as Barnbeugle the house an imense pile of building but we had neither leisure or inclination to go into it indeed found we had no time to spare, changed Horses at Lenlithgow but did not reach Mount Riddell[20] till ½ past four found M[rs.] Robinson & Miss Mackenzie there, play'd at Cassino in the evening.

Tuesday Aug[st.] 22[d.]

Quite a fine day upon the whole, for tho there was not much sun, there was little wind, & scarce any showers & those most trifling, walk'd about the premises a good deal in the Morning, M[rs.] Speirs & 2 of her Daughters here in the forenoon. cards again in the evening. rec'd a Letter from Lady Dukenfield.

Wensday Aug[st.] 23[d.]

So truly a warm fine Day we have been little accustome'd to this summer, perfectly bright & clear from Morn: to night, walk'd at Noon with Miss Robinson by the Canal side & a long round; General & M[rs.] Maxwell & her Mother M[rs.] Wilson dined here.[21] rec'd a Letter from Miss Anne Snow & wrote to M[rs.] Davies.

Thursday Aug[st.] 24[th.]

A gloomy Morning w.[ch] produced a very wet Noon & afternoon, no one ventured out but George who was unwilling to be disappointed of a promised ride, from work, conversation, playing with the bairns & Cards the day was not long. rec'd Letters from Lady Dukenfield & M[rs.] Browning.

---

17. The Dundas family at Duddingston were not closely related to Dundas of Dundas. As for the name 'David', Agnes appears to have made a mistake as David was in fact the eldest son. The head of the family was John Hamilton Dundas (1745–1820), eldest son of Agnes Dundas and Gabriel Hamilton. John married Grizel Hamilton (d. 1822) daughter of John Hamilton of Barns. There were ten children from this marriage of which the eldest was David Dundas Hamilton (1783–1805). John Hamilton Dundas was Vice Lieutenant of the county of Linlithgow.
18. Apart from James Dundas of Dundas, there were three daughters: Christian (b. 1785; Maria (b. 1787) and Anne (b. 1791).
19. Alexander Charles Maitland (1755–1848); succeeded as 2nd baronet, 1820. He was the son of General Alexander Maitland, 1st baronet and Penelope Madan. He married, 1785, Helen Gibson-Wright, daughter of Alexander Gibson-Wright of Cliftonhall and Kersie and Margaret, née Gibson.
20. Now named Larbert House, in Larbert, north-west of Falkirk; the house in 1797 was called Mount Riddell and was built in 1790 for James Riddell (1728–1796), 1st baronet of Ardnamurchan and Sunart. It was remodelled in 1822 for the later owner, Sir Gilbert Stirling. The resident in 1797 was James's widow, Sarah (1731–1817), a close friend of Edward and Agnes Witts.
21. Major-General William Maxwell (1754–1837); succeeded as 7th Baronet Maxwell of Calderwood, 1829. He married, 1792, Isabella, daughter and heiress of Henry Wilson of Newbottle, County Durham. He fought in the American Revolutionary War and was taken prisoner after the Battle of Saratoga.

A view of the Old Town from Princes Street, an aquatint by J. Carr and A. Kay, *c.* 1814.

Almost the opposite view, the North Bridge and Calton Hill from the mound, an aquatint by Sir John Carr, 1809.

Friday Aug^{st.} 25th.

A perfect contract in point of weather being as fine a Day as possible from Morn to night, Mr. Witts took advantage of it by taking a ride to Stirling to see Sr. N. Dukenfield who was arrived there with 2 Troops of the W. Forresters, in expectation of riots we walk'd & talk'd, evening as usual, rec'd a Letter from Mrs. Erskine & wrote to Lady Dukenfield.

Saturday Aug^{st.} 26th.

A stormy blustery Day but without rain till quite evening, when small rain came on walk'd a little in the Morning, went to dine at General Maxwells at Park Hill three miles from Falkirk a fine situated small place,[22] no other company, did not return home till dark.

Sunday Aug^{st.} 27th.

Not a very pleasant Day being cold & stormy tho scarce any rain fell but the wind was quite tempestuous, I never stirr'd out the whole Day there being no Church service at Larbert, wrote

22. Parkhill House, Polmont. The house and estate was acquired in 1788 by James Cheape of Sauchie who seems to have changed its name from Parkend to Park Place and six years later to Parkhill. Cheape had started building the house around 1790, after which Major-General William Maxwell either bought or rented the property.

& conversed much. rec'd Letters from Lady Dukenfield & my Sis.^r Travell, & wrote to Lady Riddell & Miss Louisa Lee

Monday Aug.st 28th.

a brilliant & fine a Day as we had been little used to quite oppressively hot, much walking & riding by both young & old & no less conversation being our last Day at Mount Riddell.

Tuesday Aug.st 29th.

A lowering Morn: wch alas produced a very contrary Day to the former, being hard rain thro the Day after 12 o'clock, very unlucky for our short Journey of 6 miles to Mrs. Grahams at Airth[23] who rec'd us with the utmost hospitality & had invited Mrs. Speirs & her Daughter to meet us; the house is very old but some rooms good & all neat & in repair, a chearful pleasant evening playd at Cribbage with much success

Wensday Aug.st 30th.

Wet & very wet again after quite the Morning & so distressingly close & hot as was very uncommon, impossible to stir out of doors, hardly to mount to the top of the house to see the prospect but survey'd all the House, went to dine at Mrs. Speirs meeting a large party to the number of 16, agreable enough, but glad to return to a great party at Cribbage.

Thursday Aug.st 31st.

Somewhat a better day being without rain, tho, still stormy with a mixture of sun & clouds but certainly fine on the whole, fortunate for our movement which took place after breakfast, quitting our agreable acquaintance with grateful regret, going 10 miles to Stirling an intire vale road & not very good, but thro a fine country never a mile from the Firth much great Satisfaction in meeting with Sr Nathaniel & L.^{dy.} Dukenfield walk'd a little before dining with them & the officers at the mess a chatty evening.

Friday Sepr 1st.

One of the most intire & distressing wet Days I ever saw, no cessation of rain from Morn to night & that very violent much interesting conversation with my aimable Friend, & chearful meals at the Mess rec'd Letters from Mrs. Riddell & Mr. Bate & wrote to my Sister Travell.

Saturday Sepr 2^{d.}

A most happy change in all our prospects in weather particularly being a universal fine Day & the brightest night I ever saw, fortunately an order came for the Troops to return to Perth, so after we had walk'd to the Castle & round the walks, M.^{r.} W & myself accompanied L.^{dy.} Dukenfield in her Carriage her Maid going with the Boys in ours 21 miles to Crieff of a fine Country in general, but bad roads & hilly, & we had pass'd it before, here we dined & did

---

23. Ann Graham, née Stirling was the daughter of Henry Stirling of Ardoch, 3rd Baronet. She had married, 1760, William Graham (1730–1790), 2nd Graham of Airth and they had seven sons and seven daughters. When Agnes Witts refers to Miss Graham it is not clear which Miss Graham she refers to, whether it is a daughter of this Ann Graham of Airth or the Grahams of Fintry.

not reach Perth 17 miles farther till between 9 & 10 & took a poor abode at Wakefields Inn.

Sunday Sepr 3.^{d.}

Another fine Day excepting a scarce but short shower at Noon. went to the English chapel the service perform'd while a new one is building in the Guildhall, an odd place, strange Clergyman & very mix'd congregation accompanied Mrs. Rooke home to the Barracks & she took me in her Coach to L.^{dy.} Dukenfields where I spent the remainder of the Day Mr. Witts & the Boys coming to Dinner return'd to our sleeping quarters early & wrote to Mrs. Riddell.

Monday Sepr 4.th.

A cloudy but dry & rather pleasant day, at Noon went with Mrs. Rooke in her Phaeton to call at Mr. Grants at Kilgraston[24] a very pleasant drive & very friendly reception, dined with Col: & Mrs. Rooke & supt also Sr N. & Lady Dukenfield being added to our party in the evening, a chearful party at Cribbage & a very agreable day altogether.

Tuesday Sepr 5.th.

A dry Morning, but looking very gloomy & at noon quite hurricane of wind which produced most extreme violent rain, the whole of the evening accompanied by severe wind. after breakfasting & preparing for our departure, went to sit 2 or 3 hours with Lady Dukenfield the chaise calling to take me up, to go to Mr. Grants at Kilgraston, where we found a Dr. Finley & Miss Craigie added to themselves, a chatty pleasant evening in spite of storms & tempests. wrote to Mrs. Robertson Scott.

Wensday Sepr 6.th.

A bright fine Day, much sun & wind but no rain, but so extremely wet & dirty, could walk very little, sat very comfortably to work in the Morning, & the evening was spent in the same chearful way

Thursday Sepr 7.th.

A mild fine Morning but before noon became cloudy which produced heavy rain for the rest of the Day wch made our Day pass very similiar to the former one the Gentlemen rode to Mr. Oliphants at Newton

Friday Sepr 8.th.

Quite a shewey Morning having been something of a slight frost, but changed at noon to cloudy, & in the afternoon again to severe rain, left Kilgraston at nine & went to breakfast at Sir N. Dukenfiellds at Perth while the horses baited, set out directly after for Cupar in Angus 13 miles of a good road, & in general pleasant cultivated country, particularly the last 3 miles Cupar is rather a miserable looking Town, where we only staid to change horses & eat bread & cheese, & proceeded on to Forfar 19 miles farther the first half of the way or more rather a dull country & very bad road, but all mended when we came within view of Glames

---

24. Francis Grant (d. 1819), of Kilgraston. Francis married, Anne, eldest daughter of Robert Oliphant of Rossie.

Castle, Lord Strathmores excepting the weather as it then perfectly pour'd & the sky as thick as possible, yet we could not resist driving up to the house to see the outside of that noble edifice, & its adjacent fine woods, modern plantations, & rich pasturage the Castle standing in a noble large Park highly pleased with it 5 miles farther to Forfar of a good hard road.

Saturday Sep.' 9th.

Rather a stormy doubtful looking Morn: but happily it so improved that it turn'd out a bright fine Day tho extreme cold for the time of year, & much to our astonishment to see the Grampian Hills cover'd with Snow, left Forfar after Breakfast going 12 miles to Brechine of a fine level road & then a pleasant newly cultivated country tho originally the soil wet & bad, Brechine stands well, & is rather a clean well built small Town, at the entrance is Brechine Castle a seat of M.' Maules, after changing Horses we went 8 miles farther to Montrose, over a much better cultivated country commanding fine views of the River Eske which fills a Loch close to the Town, many handsome Gentlemens Seats & much corn land; Montrose stands well on rather an elevated situation about a mile distant from the Sea, is a well built neat Town, & the Inn good, tho mean in its appearance, we walk'd both before & after Dinner, & in the evening rec'd a visit from M.' & M.'s Renny.[25] rec'd Letters from M.'s Davies & Miss Anne Snow & answer'd it.

Sunday Sep.' 10th.

A most remarkable clear fine Day constant sunshine but a cold air, went to Breakfast at M.' Rennys with them & their 12 children, & accompanied them to the English Chapel, which is a handsome building standing on the Linx, a large genteel congregation & a good preacher, left Montrose imediately after Church & came 10 miles on the Aberdeen road to M.' Robertson Scotts at Benholme,[26] a most singular place situated on the edge of a deep woody glen, the adjacent country rather barren, & distant about a mile from the Sea found a large party besides their own family, M.'s Craigie her Son & Daughter, Miss Carnegie & Miss Scott.

Monday Sep.' 11th.

A dull gloomy looking day with much wind & no sun, but no rain till quite night, walk'd a little about the premises, Sir David & Lady Carnegie came to Dinner & staid all night a very pleasant chearful even.' of music, cards, & reel dancing. wrote to Lady C: Charteris.

Tuesday Sep.' 12th.

Very stormy in the Morning, which before noon produced such violent & incessant rain that even the Gentlemen could not stir out, but prevail'd to have a Whist party before Dinner a merry varied evening as usual

---

25. James Renny (1736?–1826?), of Montrose.
26. George Robertson married the heiress Isabelle Scott of Benholme and Hedderwick and adopted the name of Scott. Their son, Hercules James Robertson (1795–1874) became a Scottish judge, and was appointed a Lord of Session assuming the judicial title Lord Benholme, after his mother's family seat.

Wensday Sepr. 13th.

Very near if not quite as wet & tempestuous a day, but much chearfulness within made the disappointment of not going out the less much reading, working writing in the Morning, Music, Cards & dancing in the evening. wrote to M^rs. Erskine & M^rs. Whalley.

Thursday Sepr. 14th.

Tho rather a lowering looking Morning it gradualy became a most charming fine Day, which from being such a rarity was doubly valuable; all but M^rs. Robertson set forth on an expedition to Den Finela some in, others on the Carriage & the rest on horseback the distance about 4 miles on the Moutron road, the Den is very woody & deep & the Waterfall of about 60 feet high from being rapid was well worth seeing, we survey'd both sides of the Den with much labor & slippery walk & afterwards went to see M^r. Brands at Lauriston about a mile farther, another Den, but dress'd in a very good stile with a large house & very handsome approach & Porters Lodge, return'd home just in time to dress for Dinner well tired, yet still the evening was as much varied with music singing & Dancing which kept us up till a late hour.

Friday Sepr. 15th.

Not so good a day, but tolerably dry & fine excepting a shower at noon, left Benholme soon after breakfast, stop'd at Montrose to change Horses, & proceeded on to Sir David Carnegies at Kinnaird 7 miles farther stopping for a few minutes by the way at M^rs. Ogilvies but did not get out of the Carriage, met with a most obliging reception from the baronet[27] & his Lady with whom we had our former favorable opinion confirm'd a large & prodigeous handsome house, to which their establishment & mode of living is answerable, 5 or 6 Gentlemen besides three of their Daughters made a party of 14 at Dinner which was handsome & desert elegant, much music & singing as well as dancing with the young people & a little Whist rec'd a Letter from Lady Riddell.

Saturday Sepr. 16th.

A dull gloomy Morning but happily remain'd dry till two o'clock when it became wet & so continued the rest of the evening, did not leave Kinnaird till that time the variety of things to see & admire fully occupied it, took a drive thro' the woods & by the side of the River Eske myself with Lady C. in her little low carriage the Gentlemen following after in the Coach, on our return partook of a nice cold collation which enabled us to go on to Aberborthick 13 miles of not very good or pretty country, & nothing very striking to remark, till we came within sight of the noble ruins so well known & so much admired, the beauty of wch however is much lessen'd by the disagreable red colour of the stone, of which the Town which is large & straggling is also built, the Inn tho to outside appearance bad turn'd out neat & comfortable. the Town stands close of the Sea on a little elevation, & there is a small Fort & harbour a comfortable Dinner & even^g. & wrote to Lady Dukenfield.

---

27. David Carnegie (1753–1805), 4th baronet Carnegie of Kinnaird. He succeeded to the baronetcy in 1765 and built the mansion now called Kinnaird Castle. He was MP Montrose Burghs 1784–1790 and Forfarshire 1796–1805. He married, 1783, Agnes Murray (1764–1860), daughter of Andrew Elliot (1728–1797), of Greenwells, County Roxburgh. Elliot had been appointed Lieutenant-Governor of the Province of New York. In 1783 he was part of the delegation that met with George Washington. He was the acting governor from April 1783 to November. Elliot left for Scotland in December 1783.

Sunday Sepr 17.th

A cloudy Morning which however produced a dry & most beautiful bright Day, the Boys went early to explore the ruins, it was too wet & damp & I was too unwell to attempt it, left Aberborthick between 9 & 10 to go to Dundee a stage of 17 miles of moderately good roads but injured by the late heavy rains, the road runs very near to the Sea the whole of the way, & is very prettily varied by Gentlemens Seats, fine corn land, some wood & many plantations, the approach to the Town of Dundee quite enchanting, close to the Firth of Tay, got some Soupe & cold Meat at the Inn, & got about to cross, but we had a most tedious passage of near an hour & ½, for want of both wind & tide, forced to tack from side to side & with some difficulty landed at last at Woodhaven where a grand pair of Horses carried us 11 miles to St Andrews just as it was dark, where we got a most wretched Dinner supper, after which M.^r & Mrs Maclean sat ½ an hour.

Monday Sepr 18.th

Showery very early in the Morning but became extremely fine till mid.day, when it was again showery & so continued all the evening, went to Breakfast at Mr Macleans, where we found a most excellent one & some friends staying in the house with them, call'd at Dr McCormicks, & walk'd with Mrs Macleans among the ruins &'c till we set out for Cambo where we met a most animated & friendly reception from Mrs Erskine tho my Letter never arrived till after myself, Mr Erskine out but he return'd to Tea as did Mrs Thomas, Miss Hall & Miss Stewart who had been dining out rec'd a Letter from Lady Catherine Charteris.

Tuesday Sepr 19.th

Very heavy showers at intervals all the former part of the Day, but mild & pleasant enough between to tempt me to walk a little, but soon sent back in a hurry, the comfort of our Day much interrupted by Mrs Erskines being so unwell as never to be in company after Dinner to which Dr Thomas arrived a Singular character. a little whist in the evening.

Wensday Sepr 20.th

Quite a miserable Day of almost perpetual rain, which made me extremely happy to take to fires, no possibility of stirring out, Mrs Erskine too indifferent to come out of her room, I work'd much & heard Mr W. read in the German Play of the Robbers[28] much pleased with it, whist as ever in the evening. wrote to Lady Riddell.

Thursday Sepr 21.st

On the whole more tolerable weather being mostly dry, a shower at mid.day accompanied by Thunder, walk'd with the Ladies to their bathing & round the home circuit. Mr Erskine the whole of the Day at Kelly. wrote to Mrs Brown

Friday Sepr 22.^d

Rather lowering in the Morning but turn'd out a bright & charming fine Day, the Gentlemen bathed, conversed, & visited at Col: Moneypennys, we walk'd, & in the evening play'd at

---

28. *The Robbers* (*Die Räuber*) is the first drama by Friedrich Schiller. The play was published in 1781 and premiered on 13 January 1782 in Mannheim.

Commerce with the young people, Dr Melville & Mr Adamson from St Andrews dined here. wrote to Mrs Davies

Saturday Sepr 23^d

Quite a stormy disagreable Day, but little rain fell, till quite evening when it came in torrents, Dr Thomas & his party went in the Morning to see the wonders of St Andrews, Mr Erskine & Fran^s conversed, & Mr W. & I walk'd for an hour on the long sands, Mrs Erskine a good deal better in the even^g came a Mr Rolland²⁹ a Nephew of Mr Erskines rec'd Letters from Mrs Riddell & Miss Snow.

Sunday Sepr 24th

A doubtful looking Morning after a night of severe rain but turn'd out a brilliant fine Day such a rarity as was highly to be prized, went to the English Chapel at Crail to hear Dr Thomas preach who performd extremely well, a strange looking place & very small congregation, walk'd part of the way home, the Thomas party went for the night to Awdrie. wrote to Mrs Riddell

Monday Sepr 25th

Another charming Day constant sunshine & fine air so beneficial for the harvest, was upon the Sands for two hours, just accompanying my Gentlemen to their bathing & then the ladies, tired myself sadly, & was quite ill in the evening. wrote to Mrs Wilkinson.

Tuesday Sepr 26th

If possible a still finer Day less wind & warmer, went again to the Sands with the Ladies to bathe George went a coursing, Mr Witts & Frank visited at Col: Moneypennys³⁰ & bathed as they return'd the two Mrs Moneypennys & Mr Travel dined here a chearful addition.

Wensday Sepr 27th

A dry & pleasant feeling Day tho rather gloomy in appearance but no rain fell, D^r & Mrs Thomas & their party went away early, Mr Erskine dined at Crail, I went with my Gentlemen to walk at Noon after they had bathed. rec'd Letters from Lady Dukenfield & Mrs Brown, & wrote to the latter & my Sister Travell.

Thursday Sepr 28th

Another very similiar day, but after mid.day some sun which made it pleasant I accompanied my Gentlemen to the Sea, & walk'd on the Sands, Mr Rolland went away; & to Dinner came Col Dewar & M^r & Mrs James Dewar but went away in the evening rec'd Letters from Lady Dukenfield, Mrs Granville my Sister Travell & Mr Burslem.

Friday Sepr 29th

Still dry but not so fine as some former Days, looking threatening & being rather cold, yet as

---

29. Peter Rolland was a captain in the service of the HEIC and died some time before 1835. His daughters adopted the surname Erskine. Presumably Peter Rolland had married one of the sisters of Thomas Erskine (±1745–1828).

30. Lieutenant-Colonel Alexander Monypenny of Pitmilly (1726–1801). The Monypenny family of Pitmilly were related to the Dundas family of Duddingstone.

usual I went with <u>my</u> <u>family</u> to the Sea, no interruption to a quiet day, a little whist at night. wrote to Lady Dukenfield

Saturday Sepr 30.th

A unpromising Morning with a small shower or two, but clear'd up at Noon & was a fine Day, but a very thick fog in the evening, walk'd in the forenoon, & all went to dine at Col: Moneypennys excepting Mrs. Erskine sat down 13 to Dinner, tho only one Gentleman excepting the two families very easy & pleasant at home by 9 o'clock.

Sunday Octr 1.st

Quite a thick fog which cleard off before Noon & was a close warm day tho not a bright one, walk'd to Kings Barns to Church where Dr. Adamson from St. Andrews performd the service extremely well, on the way home visited M^{r.} & Miss Jeffrey at Cambo Farm, all this knock'd me up, & I was low & very unwell all the evening not the better for knowing it to be the last likely to be ever pass'd in the society of our aimable friend

Monday Octr 2.^d

A stormy Morning, but no rain till mid.day which continued more or less the whole of the day & sadly interfered with the pleasure of passing thro a new Country which the greater of the way to Largo was, left Cambo at 11 with agitated feelings, stopt for half an hour at Crail, to visit Miss Lindsays, & passing thro Ansthruther, Petherween &'c making 17 miles to Largo, the road lying mostly thro corn fields varied by several Gentlemens Seat, the country mends as you draw near to Largo, which is a handsome place, situated finely commanding an extensive view of the Firth which is here form'd into a very considerable Bay, rec'd a very polite reception from Mr. Durham,[31] his Niece Miss Nairne & Miss Gibson a chearful evening with Cassino.

Tuesday Octr 3.^d

A bright fine Morning, but becoming cloudy at Noon, produced some showers, but dry again in the evening left Largo after breakfast, & tho the stage to Kinghorn was only 15 miles we were 4 hours going it so bad & hilly were the roads, & tho a country much boast'd of we were disappointed in it when we got to Kinghorn found that neither wind or Tide would serve for crossing in a large Boat & was affraid to go in a pinnance, therefore quietly resolved to pass the night at the New Inn at the waters edge which we had found very comfortable last year.

Wensday Octr 4.th

A universal brilliant fine Day, without a cloud & quite warm, most fortunate for our voyage which was tedious even to 4 hours, but not disagreable the weather was so fine, got home just at 4, got a cold scrambling Dinner & glad to go early to rest.

Thursday Octr 5.th

Just as bright & fine a Day tired myself compleatly first with resettling & then with visiting,

---

31. James Calderwood Durham (1732–1808); 5th of Largo and Polton.

Lady C: C: & M^rs. Gregory, unsuccessfuly M^rs. Brown, & meeting M^rs. Rooke & her Daughters walk'd with them to the South Town Tea Cards & Supper at Lady Riddells who had call'd in the Morning, meeting 4 other Ladies. rec'd a Letter from Miss Anne Snow.

Friday Octr. 6th.

Still dry, but rather cold & lowering, I did not go out, but rec'd visits from Lady Sinclair, M^r. Brown & his Daughter Margaret & Miss Campbell, went again to Lady Riddells in the evening, meeting Lady Campbell Miss MacFarlan & Sir William Hart an odd but very entertaining companion.[32] wrote to M^rs. Erskine & Miss Snow.

Saturday Octr. 7th.

A bright fine Day, tho rather a cold east wind, made several visits in the new Town, finding at home M^rs. Sandford, M^rs. General Campbell & M^rs. Brown, went to Tea Cards & Supper meeting Lady Sinclair, Lady Campbell, M^rs. Rooke & Col: Taylor

Sunday Octr. 8th.

Quite a cold unpleasant Day tho dry went to both services at Charlotte Chapel, between made some visits went to Tea & Supper at Lady Riddells, Boys also to meet S^r. William Hart & converse of Foreign affairs, very entertaining & instructive

Monday Octr. 9th.

Yet dry & pleasanter than the former day went early with M^rs. Rooke & Miss Graham to the Court of Justiciary to hear the Trial of the Eccles Militia rioters so well entertain'd that we staid there till was four,[33] went to Tea at M^rs. Rooks no one there. rec'd Letters from M^rs. Davies & M^rs. Riddell.

---

32. William Neville Hart (1741–1804). Hart was a banker, politician and diplomat. He was an interesting character and it is not surprising that the Witts boys found him fascinating. His mother was the under-housekeeper or Mistress of the King's Household, a position she was to hold for more than fifty years. His father held various positions at Court including that of Gentleman Usher to King George II. Hart had married twice and was an MP. After leaving Parliament in 1774, Hart travelled extensively on the Continent, France, Italy, Germany and the northern courts. He went to Poland where he became Chamberlain to Stanislaus Augustus Poniatowski, the last king of Poland. On 27 December 1794, Hart was created knight of the Order of Saint Stanislaus. King Stanislaus also conferred on him the Order of the White Eagle. On 23 October 1804, Hart died at Inveraray Castle, a property owned by the Duke of Argyll.

33. In January 1797 Government agents uncovered plans for a general uprising in Scotland and the establishment of a Scottish Republic. Scottish republicans were in close contact with the United Irishmen. Nine prominent Scotsmen, including progressive members of Parliament and several Scottish peers, were named as members of the 'Provisional Government of the Scottish Republic'. The president of this government was a young Scottish lawyer, Thomas Muir. Muir had already been sentenced to fourteen years transportation to the penal colony at Botany Bay but had made a daring escape in an American warship and made his way to France where he had been honoured as the first non-Frenchman to be made a citizen of the republic.

This book is not the place to detail the Scottish republican ideals, but there were numerous serious disturbances, and this trial is but one example of the outcome. The Government needed to be rid of the 'United Scotsmen' leadership, a number of whom had been arrested for involvement with the Militia riots. The first of the Militia Trials was held on 9 October 1797. Lord Braxfield, the 'hanging judge'—a friend of Edward and Agnes Witts—sentenced three men and a woman from Eccles, Berwickshire, to 14 years transportation to Botany Bay. Edward and Agnes met the judge socially just three day later and undoubtedly the conversation turned to the subject of the trial.

Illustrious Martyr in the glorious cause
Of truth, of freedom, and of equal laws.

Thomas Muir (1765–1798). Muir was sentenced to transportation for 14 years, but from Sydney he escaped on board a ship to the United States, and eventually found his way to France, via Cadiz, Spain. He died at Chantilly near Paris, 27 September 1798.

Tuesday Oct.r 10th.

Again dry but being an easterly wind was cold & not pleasant, went at Noon with Husband & Frank to some shops in the old Town, & afterwards to make some visits in Georges Square, a Mr. Armstrong an Irish Student recommended by Mr. Baillie drank Tea with us afterwards wrote to Mrs. Davies & Mrs. Riddell. Mrs. Brougham here before Dinner

Wensday Oct.r 11th.

Very much the same weather cold & windy, Mr. Witts out all Morning assisting Mr. Armstrong, rec'd visits from Lady Riddell & Miss Graham & late walk'd with Frank on the Leith Walk & call'd on Mrs. Brown. wrote to Ldy. Dukenfield

Thursday Oct.r 12th.

Dry but very cold with much wind in the forenoon visited Lady Riddell, Mrs. Brougham & Lady B. Cunningham all at home, went to Tea Cards & Supper at Lady Riddells meeting the Lord Justice Clerk & Mrs. Macqueen Lady Campbell & Miss Graham. rec'd a Letter fm. Mrs. Erskine

Friday Oct.r 13th.

A gloomy Morning which before the day was far spent produced a wet cold & disagreable day, of course I staid at home all Morn: & had no interruptions, went to Tea Cards & Supper at Lady Campbells meeting only Lady Riddell & Miss Graham.

Saturday Oct.r 14th.

Bright & fine with a cold wind walk'd to call on Lady C: C: who was the only one of several

Revd James Struthers (1770–1807), Minister of the Relief
Chapel, College Street. An etching by John Kay.

friends I call'd on in that quarter of the Town M^r· Witts dined at M^r· Grants, James Riddell
& Eva Chalmers dined with the Boys & I. Tea Cards and Supper at M^rs· Rookes, meeting
only Lady Riddell

Sunday Oct^r· 15th·
Very cold & stormy, tho but very little rain but strong appearance of it, went accompanied
by Miss Graham to hear M^r· Struthers Preach in the Circus,[34] a great & wonderful Orator
she went with me to evening service at Charlotte Chapel where M^r· Sandfords mild elocution
was more satisfactory, between services made 2 or 3 visits no one at home but Lady Sinclair.
M^r· Armstrong dined here. rec'd Letters from Lady Dukenfield & my Sister Travell & wrote
to M^rs· Davies.

Monday Oct^r· 16th·
Quite a stormy suspicious looking Morning which at Noon terminated in extreme hard rain
with little or no cessation till quite late at night, went at ten with M^rs· Rooke & Miss Sinclair
to the Court of Justiciary to hear the trial of the Bath gate rioters in which Lord Polkemmet
was a principal evidence staid in Court nearly 7 hours but not highly amused M^r· Witts &
Frank remaining in Court I dined with M^rs· Rooke, & before we went to Lady Riddells in the
evening, drove round the Town to view the illuminations, in honor of Admiral Duncans defeat

---

34. Presumably St Stephen's Church in the Circus.

Adam Duncan, Viscount Duncan (1731–1804). An etching by John Kay.

of the Dutch Fleet on which occasion great rejoicings had been made all day.[35] S[r.] Will[m.] Hart & Col Taylor at Lady Riddells very lively & pleasant rec'd a Letter from M[rs.] Davies

Tuesday Oct[r.] 17[th.]

A bright chearful looking Day tho cold & windy, extreme hard rain again at night staid at home all Day receiving visits in the Morn: from M[rs.] Phillips, Miss Bruce of Kinnaird & Adair Craigie, & in the evening we had a party to Tea & Cards of Ladies Riddell, Sinclair, & Campbell, M[rs.] Rooke & Daughter, Miss Graham, Miss Sinclair, S[r.] W. Hart Col: Taylor & Son & M[r.] Armstrong. rec'd a Letter from Miss L. Lee, & wrote to M[rs.] Duncan[36] & M[rs.] Davies

35. The Battle of Camperdown, 11 October 1797. In 1795, the Dutch Republic had been overrun by the army of the French Republic and had been reorganised into the Batavian Republic. In early 1797 the Dutch fleet was ordered to reinforce the French at Brest. The rendezvous never occurred; the French and Dutch had failed to capitalise on the Spithead and Nore mutinies that paralysed the Royal Navy during the spring of 1797. In October 1797 Vice-Admiral Jan De Winter conducted a raid into the North Sea. When the Dutch fleet returned to the Dutch coast on 11 October, Admiral Adam Duncan was waiting, and intercepted De Winter off the coastal village of Camperduin. Attacking the Dutch line of battle in two loose groups, Duncan's ships broke through at the rear and van and were subsequently engaged by Dutch frigates lined up on the other side. The battle split into two separate fights, one to south, where the more numerous British overwhelmed the Dutch rear, and one to the north, where a more evenly matched exchange centred on the battling flagships. As the Dutch fleet attempted to reach shallower waters in an effort to escape the British attack, the British leeward division joined the windward combat and eventually forced the surrender of the Dutch flagship *Vrijheid* and ten other ships.

36. Admiral and Mrs Duncan were acquaintances of Edward and Agnes Witts.

Wensday Octr 18th.

Very wet in the Morning, showery all Day, accompanied with excessive wind, & extreme hard rain also at night, never stirr'd out or saw any one wrote to Mrs. Granville

Thursday Octr 19th.

A dry & universaly fine Day, tho cold, I made good all of it in the Morning by making many visits in the new Town those I found at home were Lady Blair, Forbes, & Riddell, Mrs. Mure, Mrs. Skenes, & Mrs. M. Sands, a pleasant home evening. rec'd a Letter from Lady Elcho & wrote to my Sister Travell.

Friday Octr 20th.

An uncommon cold disagreable thick Morn: being a strong east wind, & before Dinner turn'd to rain & in the evening became quite tremendous with high wind & violent rain, sat an hour in the forenoon with Mrs. Rooke & likewise with Mrs. Brown, Tea Cards & Supper at Miss Bruces of Kinnaird no one there but Lady Riddell & Miss Jenny Bruce

Saturday Octr 21st.

No change for the better in the weather being storms & tempests more or less the whole of the Morning, & even still worse in the evening, Mr Armstrong here in the Morning, Tea Cards & Supper at Lady Sinclairs a large mix'd Company & very late as usual rec'd a Letter from Mrs. Davies & answerd it

Sunday Octr 22^{d.}

Wet as usual in the Morning, but cleard at Noon & was a tolerable fine evening, went to Morning service at St. Andrews & evening at Charlotte Chapel charming Sermon from Mr. Moodie & no less so from Mr. Sandford between services rec'd a visit from Mrs. Rooke & walk'd in Princes Street. rec'd a Letter from Miss Duncan & wrote to Mrs. Musson.

Monday Octr 23^{d.}

Wet & damp in the Morning dryer afterwards but not fine, so I had no temptation of go out neither saw any one but was full of home bussinesses & in the evening play'd at Cribbage with the Boys rec'd a Letter from Mrs. Savage & wrote to Mrs. Erskine

Tuesday Octr 24th.

A very lowering Morning, which at Noon became very wet for several hours, but ceased in the evening, no interruption to a very quiet working Morning but an <u>unexpected</u> visit from Col: & Mrs. Callander Tea Cards & Supper quite en' famille at Mrs. Rookes

Wensday Octr 25th.

One of the most tempestuous & dreadful wet days from Morn: to night I ever saw, wind in the east & as cold as possible no interruptions to many employs. rec'd a Letter from Mrs. Davies, & wrote to Miss Betty Guydickens. forgot to note that on Tuesday I had my first french Lesson from Mr. Drummond

Thursday Octr 26th.

A cold stormy Day but in general dry made an early call on Lady Riddell, & another on L^{dy.} Sinclair with Mrs. Rooke, who carried me in her Coach to Musselburgh to see Miss Dukenfield, a pleasant chatty drive both there & back, went to Tea Cards & supper at Lady Riddells, meeting Lady Campbell & Miss MacFarlan.

Friday Octr 27th.

Sharp clear frost with constant sunshine, rec'd an early call from Lady Riddell, made several calls in the Canongate & walk'd about the Abbey, found no one at home but Lady C: C: till I came to Mrs. Browns. evening again spent at Lady Riddells no one there but Mrs. Rooke, Sir James invisible wrote to Lady Dukenfield.

Saturday Octr 28th.

Another frosty, bright Day, made many visits in the New Town finding only Mrs. Dalrymple Miss Campbell & Miss MacFarlan at home, met crowds in the streets & walk'd in Princes Street with Mrs. Rooke a home evening wrote to Mrs. Davies.

Sunday Octr 29th.

Quite as sharp a frost, & most extremely cold quite piercing, went to Charlottes Chapel to both Services between walk'd in Princes Street for the Sun, & call'd twice on Lady Riddell Sir James being much worse. Mr. Armstrong dined with us, & Mr. Tyrrel drank Tea soon after which Mr. Witts & I went to Lady Riddells to sup where we met Sir James Colquhoun, Sir William Hart & Mr. Gibson. very dismal & awkward

Monday Octr 30th.

Again a sharp frost, & most extremely cold from being an east wind & little sun, rec'd visits from Miss Abercrombie, Miss Scott & M^{r.} & Miss Campbell after which went to make enquiries after Sir James Riddell call'd on Lady Campbell, Miss Campbell & Miss Graham at home in the evening. rec'd a Letter from Miss Anne Snow.

Tuesday Octr 31st.

No change in the weather equally dry & cold, Mr. Sandford here in the Morning before we set out on our walks, sat an hour with Lady Riddell Sr. James a little better walk'd to the Bridge on some bussiness, call'd on Mrs. Rooke & Lady Campbell, after Dinner call'd on by Mrs. Riddell in consequence of whose being come into Town. we made a late visit to Lady Riddell spent the evening with Mrs. Rooke

Wensday Novr 1st.

Fine & bright in the Morning, but the wind changing at Noon, it became both cloudy & stormy, & in the evening quite tempestuous, Mrs. Riddell breakfasted here, & we afterwards went to visit Lady Riddell, after which we walk'd to Georges Square; where I made several calls but found no one at home but Mrs. Douglas Cavers, returnd back in Sir James's Chaise, & before dinner rec'd a pleasant visit from Mrs. Stewart & Mrs. Macdowall Grant. Mrs. Riddell here for 2 or 3 hours late in the evening. rec'd a letter from Mrs. Erskine

Thursday Novr 2^d.

Frost gone, & of course a damp disagreable day, & at times small rain, summoned very early in the Day to poor Lady Riddell, by Sir James's death, which took place at 11 o'clock.[37] staid there all the Morning, writing Cards & Letters, went there again after Tea to the same employments, & staid till between 11 & 12 suping with Mr John Riddell & Mr Gibson

Friday Novr 3^d.

Again open mild weather, but very stormy at Noon with some short showers, but dry & cold in the evening, went at 11 again to Lady Riddells, to meet Sir William Forbes & Mr Charles Hope to be present at the opening of some important papers, there the whole Morning, brought Mrs Riddell & her Son home to dinner spent the evening with the Rookes very chearfully the Col: being return'd to them. rec'd a Letter from L.^dy Dukenfield

Saturday Novr 4th.

A most uncommon mild & brilliant fine day for the season of the year in the sun quite hot made an early & unsuccessful call on Lady Riddell as still she would not see me, walk'd about a good deal & made a long visit to Mrs Brown. Mr W. Frank & myself went to Dine at Mr Campbells at Newington a party of 11 the most agreable of whom were a Cap.^tn & Mrs Duggan of the Norfolk Light Dragoons. George dined at Col: Rookes. rec'd a Letter from Mrs Davies.

Sunday Novr 5th.

A sadly different day, being a thick wetting fog the greater part of the day & hard rain in the evening, did not go to Chapel in the Morning but accompanied Miss Rookes in their Coach to evening service at Charlotte Chapel. Col: Rooke here between services. rec'd a letter from Mrs Musson, & answer'd it.

Monday Novr 6th.

Quite a mild day, but not very pleasant being a thick foggy air, & extremely dirty in the old Town where I went to visit Lady C: C: & Mrs Fyffe, Mrs Riddell & Mr Jardine here in the evening

Tuesday Novr 7th.

Very much the same sort of weather, only the fog going off better it was pleasanter & in the country clear & warm, at noon went in Col: Rookes Coach accompanied by Frank to visit Mrs Charteris at Inveresk By the way made an unsuccessful visit to Mrs Duggan at the Barracks, call'd on Catherine Dukenfield, & sat an hour or two very pleasantly with my Cousin & her sweet bairns, Mr Witts in my absence present at the opening of Sir James Riddells Will, Mrs Riddell here for an hour after Dinner; went in the evening to a large mixt party of 30, at Commissioner Browns, odd & not very pleasant.

Wensday Novr 8th.

Another day of the same kind in the sun both dry & warm, went to make my first visit to Lady

---

37. Lady Riddell's stepson, Thomas Milles Riddell (1756–1796) of Larbert, Stirling, 'lord of the manor of Billockby in Norfolk' had died 17 July 1796. His son, James Milles Riddell (1787–1861), succeeded as 2nd baronet.

Riddell, a trying bussiness but found her better than I expected from thence went to make a like melancholy call on M$^{rs.}$ Rooke on the death of her Sister. wrote to Lady Dukenfield. M$^{r.}$ Gibson dined & spent the even$^{g.}$ here.

Thursday Nov$^{r.}$ 9$^{th.}$

A continuation of the same mild foggy weather, at times the sun got the better of the mist went imediately after breakfast to call on M$^{rs.}$ Riddell who was leaving Town, Miss MacFarlan call'd here before M$^{r.}$ Witts & I went with Miss Rookes in their Coach to survey D$^{r.}$ Chapmans School at Libberton much pleased with the drive to & fro & with the situation but nothing else went to Tea & Supper with Lady Riddell no one there but no want of conversation

Friday Nov$^{r.}$ 10$^{th.}$

Again foggy but very fine in the sun went early with Miss Rookes in their Coach shopping afterwards sat some time with M$^{rs.}$ Rookes & made such long visits to M$^{rs.}$ Speirs & Miss Graham that I was not at home till Dinner time. went to a strange supper party at M$^{rs.}$ Mures scarce anybody there—rec'd a Letter from my Sister Travell.

Saturday Nov$^{r.}$ 11$^{th.}$

A frost having been in the night it was a colder but not much clearer air, but much drier walking all the family went to prayers & sermon at Charlotte Chapel, afterwards visited M$^{rs.}$ Campbell of Balimore, M$^{rs.}$ Robertson Scott, & M$^{rs.}$ Brown, Tea & supper at Lady Riddells meeting a Miss Maxwell just come to stay with her & M$^{r.}$ Gibson before visited M$^{rs.}$ Hay.

Sunday Nov$^{r.}$ 12$^{th.}$

Another very similiar day but after mid.day the fog became still thicker being the Communion at Charlotte Chapel, most of the forenoon was spent there, M$^{r.}$ Gibson assisted M$^{r.}$ Sandford & preach'd for him in the evening service very well. wrote to M$^{rs.}$ Browning. rec'd a Letter from M$^{rs.}$ Young

Monday Nov$^{r.}$ 13$^{th.}$

Tolerably fine early in the day, but at noon became as usual foggy & cold, went to the S Bridge on some errands accompanied by Francis, & afterwards visited M$^{rs.}$ Gregory & Lady C: C: drank Tea & supt very chearfuly at Col: Rookes.

Tuesday Nov$^{r.}$ 14$^{th.}$

Very stormy & at times showers & a damp west wind, at home all Morn without any interruption, Tea & Supper at Lady Riddells no one there but Miss Maxwell. wrote to M$^{rs.}$ Davies.

Wensday Nov$^{r.}$ 15$^{th.}$

Quite an unpleasant day with high wind rain & storms of Sleet so of course no temptation to stir out & no interruption the whole Day to many employs but an agreable one, an hours visit from M$^{r.}$ Robert Arbuthnot. wrote to my Sister Travell

Thursday Novr 16th.

Not much a better day, excepting being dry, for it was still cold & windy, & having had a cold I gladly kept the house receiving in the Morning visits from Miss Sinclair, Miss Anne Scott, & Captains Duggan & Matthews. wrote to Mrs. Young.

Friday Novr 17th.

Rather a more promising Morning, but grew cold & very windy at Noon yet I went out & made many visits, finding at home, Mrs. Sandford Mrs. Halkett Craigie, Mrs. Baillie & Miss Melvilles, as ever a fully occupied evening at home

Saturday Novr 18th.

Another very cold but dry frosty day I gladly sat all Morning by the fireside & saw no one but Mr. Gibson. drank Tea & supt at Col: Rookes, two of the Miss Melvilles there also rec'd Letters from Mrs. Wilkinson & Miss Snow.

Sunday Novr 19th.

A sharp frost & most bitterly cold but changed after dark to rain. went to Charlotte Chapel to both services, carried by Mrs. Rooke to the evening which was uncommonly crowded between made three visits, finding only Mrs. Speirs &'c at home. wrote to Mrs. Erskine & Miss Anne Snow.

Monday Novr 20th.

Quite a change in the feel of the weather being again very mild, tho with a considerable damp wind & of course very dirty, yet I ventured to go to see Lady C: C: & made a long visit to Mrs. Brown on my return chearful home evening rec'd a Letter from Mr. Parrier & wrote to Mrs. Riddell

Tuesday Novr 21st.

Frost again, & being a sharp wind & no sun was very cold & not clear having the use of Lady Riddells Carriage Horses, I went attended by Mr. Witts, & visited Mrs. Duggan & Mrs. Matthews at the Barracks, & proceeded on to Lady Hailer's where we found an empty house. a home evening.

Wensday Novr 22^{d.}

Quite a tremendous Morning of wind & rain, but happily <u>clear'd</u> at Noon & was a bright fine afternoon with strong indications of frost. Mr. W. & I set off at two o'clock with Lady Riddells horses & a borrow'd P. Chaise, to go to Dine at Col: Callanders at Preston Hall[38] found nobody there but Sir Alexander Purvis[39] & his Family sumpetous shew & entertainment but no real amusement or satisfaction whist in the evening. rec'd a Letter f^{m.} L^{dy.} Duken.

---

38. John Callender (1739–1812), of Westerton, Stirling and Preston Hall, Edinburgh. John was the first surviving son of Alexander Callander of Westerton. He married, 1786, Margaret, daughter of John Romer of Cherwick, Northumberland; widow of Bridges Kearney. John Callender had had an Army career, ending as lieutenant-colonel of the 29th Dragoons, but his career ended before the onset of the American Revolutionary War. He was MP for Berwick-upon-Tweed, 1795–1802 and 1806–1807. He was created 1st baronet, 1798.
39. Alexander Purves (1739–1812), of Purves Hall and of Eccles, Berwickshire, 5th baronet. He married first, 1766, Catherine née Le Blanc, she died 1772. He married secondly, 1775, Mary, daughter of Sir James Home of Manderston. Alexander Purves was an officer in the Army, retiring in 1781 as major in the 18th Foot.

Thursday Novr. 23^d.

A very severe frost for one night & tho extremely cold must be deem'd a very fine winter Day from clear air & constant sunshine left Preston Hall after Breakfast & went thro the Duke of Buccleughs Park & grounds at Dalkeith to Inveresk, where we sat half an hour with M^rs. Charteris, stoppt at both Schools at Musselburgh & came home with <u>pleasure</u> between 3 & 4

Friday Novr. 24th.

Another very severe Night of frost & continued freezing hard all day tho from sunshine very pleasant walking, walk'd to the South Town on some visits, but found none at home but M^rs. Campbell of Stonefield, & Lady Campbell on my return dined at Col: Rookes meeting Col: & M^rs. Burgoyne supt also our own party. rec'd a Letter f^m. M^rs. Riddell

Saturday Novr. 25th.

Still a hard frost, but being a thick foggy air was a very disagreable day & bitterly cold scarce ever stirr'd from the fireside & saw no one but M^rs. Rooke for half an hour in the Morning rec'd a Letter from M^rs. Graham & wrote to L^dy. Dukenfield

Sunday Novr. 26th.

Had been a considerable fall of Snow in the night, which was turn'd to hard rain in the Morning, & continued so more or less all day we none of us went to Chapel in the Morning <u>but all</u> in the evening, before wch I went to see Katharine Dukenfield at Col: Rookes, M^r. Armstong dined here. wrote a short Letter to M^rs. Whalley.

Monday Novr. 27th.

A most unpleasant Day of universal thick fog & frequently hard rain, a total impediment to all movement, & <u>foreign</u> society, M^r. Witts all the forenoon at the Court Martial of the Durham rangers[40] much work reading & many pleasant &'c &'c –

Tuesday Novr. 28th.

Another quick change to extreme hard frost & intense cold, made many visits in the new Town, those I found at home were M^rs. Campbell of Balimore M^rs. Speirs, M^rs. Burgogne, M^rs. Rooke who was ill & M^rs. Brown, went to Tea & Supper at M^r. Browns quite en'familleé no one there, rather trite.

Wensday Novr. 29th.

Tho an extreme hard frost yet a pleasant day from there being much sun & little wind I made

---

40. This is something of a mystery, but it may be related to the Fifeshire Fencibles, a militia raised by Colonel James Durham of Largo. This was raised on 20 October 1794 and disbanded at Kilkenny, Ireland, 11 April 1803. The curious and discreditable action on the part of the authorities in Ireland in relation to William Orr—who was executed—may be part of this strange affair. Ostensibly William Orr had been arrested for administering the oath of the United Irishmen to two members of Fifeshire Fencibles—Hugh Wheatley and John Lindsay. The matter is too complex and too detailed to be gone into here but in 1797 there was a high degree of paranoia among the authorities resulting from the turmoil cocktail of the mutinies at Spithead and the Nore, the French invasion of Fishguard and the on-going troubles in Ireland.

good use of it, by going to see Lady C: C: &'c on my return home made a late but very long call on M^rs. Brougham, early in the Day visited M^rs. Rooke & Miss Drysdale

Thursday Novr. 30th.

Quite a tremendous bad day of Snow & wind without much interruption, & coming in Storms it was at times so dark it was aweful fit for nothing but a variety of home employs much entertain'd by Robisons Book on True Masonry[41] went to Tea & Supper at Lady Riddells, the first time for near a fortnight no one there but Miss Maxwell, the first people admitted.

Friday Decr. 1st.

Another very direful day, but happily both snow & frost were going fast, from frequent hard rain in the course of the day, but compleatly confining to the House, no interruption to incessant working & reading but visits in the Morning from Col: Orde M^r. Campbell of Arhaddan,[42] & M^r. Jardine.

Saturday Decr. 2nd.

A damp foggy day, but with little rain & at night frosty, borrow'd Lady Riddells horses in order to make visits at many distant parts of the Town in which M^r. W. accompanied me, found only Miss Mackenzie, M^rs. Rudyard, & Lady Riddell at home. rec'd Letters from M^rs. Granville & Miss A: Snow.

Sunday Decr. 3rd.

Quite a hard frost, but a very pleasant day from much sun & the absence of wind went to both services at Charlotte Chapel between visited Lady Riddell with the Boys, Lady Sinclair, & M^rs. Rooke, M^r. Tyrell dined here & Messrs. Armstrong & H. Brougham drank Tea. rec'd a Letter from M^rs. Wilkinson

Monday Decr. 4th.

Again frosty & a tolerable good day tho without sun & rather a thick air but in the evening most dismaly changed to first snow & afterwards more violent rain, went in the Morning to several shops in the old Town, & ended by making M^rs. Brown a long visit, Tea & Supper at Lady Riddells, no one there but herself & Miss Maxwell rec'd a Letter from M^rs. Erskine.

---

41. John Robison FRSE (1739–1805). Robison was a physicist and mathematician; he was also professor of philosophy at the University of Edinburgh. He was appointed as the first General Secretary to the Royal Society of Edinburgh and also worked with James Watt on an early steam car. Following the French Revolution, Robison became disenchanted with elements of the Enlightenment. In 1797 he published *Proofs of a Conspiracy against all the Religions and Governments of Europe, carried on in the secret meetings of Freemasons, Illuminati and Reading Societies*—alleging clandestine intrigue by the Illuminati and Freemasons. The secret agent monk Alexander Horn provided much of the material for Robison's allegations. French priest Abbé Barruel independently developed similar views that the Illuminati had infiltrated Continental Freemasonry, leading to the excesses of the French Revolution.
42. Mr Campbell of Arhaddan is not known and no such place has been identified. Agnes Witts may have meant Auchmedden, but no obvious Campbell has been identified there.

Tuesday Dec.ʳ 5ᵗʰ.

Quite an unpleasant Day from a thick damp fog, & in the evening rain with violent wind saw no Creature the whole day, but in expectation all Morning of Mʳ. C: Hope. wrote to Mʳˢ. Wilkinson

Wensday Dec.ʳ 6ᵗʰ.

A drier day from being a little frosty but not much pleasanter being severely cold & very tempestuous, had a long pleasant visit from Mʳˢ. Brougham in the Morning the only person we Saw Tea & Supper at Mʳˢ. Speirs's quite a female party excepting Mʳ. Witts. wrote to Miss Louisa Lee.

Thursday Dec.ʳ 7ᵗʰ.

Severe frost, but being no wind or fog & some sun it was very pleasant moving & I made good use of it, visiting Lady Riddell Ldy. C: C: Mʳˢ. Orde, & Mʳˢ. Macdonald besides bussiness in the old Town. drank Tea & play'd at Cassino at Col: Rookes a party quatre. rec'd a Letter from Miss Anne Snow with an alarming acco.ᵗ of her Nᵂ. Robert

Friday Dec.ʳ 8ᵗʰ.

A dark gloomy Morning which soon produced a wet & very wet day, till quite night, of course I never moved all Morn: from the fireside, & saw only Mʳˢ. Macqueen who sat an hour with me Tea & Supper at Lady Riddells, no one there excepting the two Ladies, but Mʳ. Gibson. wrote to Miss Anne Snow.

Saturday Dec.ʳ 9ᵗʰ.

As usual an alternate frost, which produced a clear air & some sunshine, but cold, & very dirty walking, went out early & made 8 visits finding only Lady Riddell, Mʳˢ. Campbell of Balimore[43] & Miss Graham & afterwards went an airing with Mʳˢ. Rooke to Leith, & its environs. Frank dined at Lord Polkemmets. rec'd Letters from Lᵈʸ. Dukenfield & my Sister.

Henry Home, Lord Kames; Hugo Arnot; James Burnett, Lord Monboddo. An etching by John Kay. Hugo Arnot (1749–1786) was the author of *The History of Edinburgh*, 1779. A second edition was published in 1817 which contained the excellent map by Robert Scott.

Sunday Decr. 10th.

A most wretched wet & damp day, some of the showers snow, & most bitterly cold, went to St. Andrews Church in the Morning a most excellent Sermon from a young Stranger, between services visited Mrs. Hay, went with Miss Rooks in their Coach to Charlotte Chapel in the evening, great Crowds went to Tea & supper at Lady Riddells to meet Mrs. Riddell & her Children rec'd Letters from my Bro^{r.} Ferdinand & Miss Snow & wrote to my Sister Travell.

Monday Decr. 11th.

As usual a reverse in the weather being a severe frost, but clear & fine with much sun, call'd upon very early by Mrs. Macqueen to go with her to the Court of Justiciary to hear the trial of the Lanarkshire Rioteers,[44] which did not end till 12 o'clock at night I staid the whole only returning for an hour with Mrs. Macqueen to eat Mutton chops at her House, much entertain'd but greatly fatigued by heat & crowd so great that my poor Husband was obliged to go home fainting at 9 o'clock

Tuesday Decr. 12th.

As usual an alternate Day damp & uncomfortable enough, indeed I was too much tired to wish to stir from the fireside, had a long interesting visit from Mrs. David Erskine & a call from young Mackenzie. a comfortable home evening.

Wensday Decr. 13th.

Neither Frost or thaw, but a tolerable day over head mild & clear but miserably dirty walking however I made 9 visits in the New Town those I found at home were Mrs. Edmonstone, Mrs. Mackay, Mrs. Allan & Mrs. Wardlaw, Tea Cassino & a boil'd Fowel at Col: Rookes very lively & pleasant

Thursday Decr. 14th.

A damp unpleasant Day without positive rain, I did not go out in the Morning, but rec'd visits from M^{rs.} & Miss Speirs's & Mrs. Wardlaw, went to Cards & supper at Mrs. Macdonalds, a party of 12 but not very lively or gay. wrote to my B^{r.} Ferdinand.

---

43. The Campbells of Ballimore are complex. Mungo Nutter Campbell of Ballimore (1785–1862) provides a possible clue. Campbell was the eleventh child of Alexander Campbell, the collector of customs at Port Glasgow. He matriculated at the University of Glasgow in 1799. In 1809 Campbell married his cousin Helen, daughter of the founder of the West Indies merchants John Campbell Snr & Co. He became a partner in his father-in-law's firm and eventually its principal. In 1811 Campbell inherited the estate of Dellingburn. He purchased Belvidere in 1813 and sold it seven years later, around the time he acquired Ballimore on Loch Fyne. Mungo Nutter Campbell's father, Alexander, had married, 1766, Susanna Campbell, daughter of Alexander Campbell and Helen Campbell. If the acquiring of Ballimore was through inheritance, then the Mrs Campbell of Ballimore *may* have been Susanna. Another link adding credence to this supposition is the fact that Mungo Nutter Campbell had a photograph taken of himself by T. & R. Annan & Sons, Photographers. In the National Gallery of Scotland, Edinburgh, there is a photograph of Mrs Campbell of Ballimore also by T. & R. Annan & Sons, Photographers. This leads to the conclusion that the family retained an Edinburgh base.

44. The riots in Lanarkshire in October 1797 were by anti-militia rioters. Their actions were not prompted by disaffection as such or by disinclination to fight, but the method of recruitment. Instead of by volunteering or conscription by ballot, press gangs roamed the streets and forcibly detained men to serve. Following the Royal Navy mutinies at Spithead and the Nore, these were worrying times for the governing classes who feared contagion from Revolutionary France.

Friday Dec.r 15th.

Wet & very wet the greatest part of the day so much so that even Mr. Witts never went out till we went to Tea, Cards, & supper at Lady Riddells meeting Lady Campbell & Sir James Colquhoun.

Saturday Dec.r 16th.

dry tho lowering in the Morn which produced much rain both after noon & night, rec'd a long & agreable visit from Mr. S. Fergusson my only visitor, the young Men dined at Mrs. Campbells of Balimore, & we went to a Tea & Card party at Col: Rookes, where 23 men assembled all <u>choice</u> <u>spirits</u>.[45] wrote to Mrs. Erskine.

Sunday Dec.r 17th.

Dry tho cold & foggy went to both services at Charlotte Chapel, between visited Miss Grace Speirs & Miss Bruce of Stenhouse without returning home, Mr. Campbell of Balimore, Mrs. Riddell & her 5 eldest Children drank Tea here. wrote to Lady Dukenfield.

Monday Dec.r 18th.

A cold stormy day with but little rain till the evening, when it was quite tempestuous I did not go out in the Morning but rec'd visits from Mrs. Duggan & Mrs. Mathews & Mr. Armstrong, went to Tea Cards & Supper at Mrs. Campbells of Balimore not a very large party nor very lively.

Tuesday Dec.r 19th.

Again windy & rather wet in the Morning but happily cleard early, for all the various movements the day suggested, being a general thanksgiving for the several Naval victorys,[46] I went in the Morning to St. Andrews, & heard a fine pointed Sermon from Mr. Moodie, & a still more striking one from Mr. Sandford in the evening, between services made 2 or 3 visits finding only Mrs. General Douglass at home, Tea, Cards & Supper at Col: Rookes to meet the Bride & Bridegroom, Mr. & Mrs. Cecil, Miss Drummon & Miss Murray.

Wensday Dec.r 20th.

Bright & promising in the Morning but soon became too showery & disagreable for me to think of going out, but rec'd visits from Lady Ramsay Mrs. Macvicar & Miss Campbell & Miss Robertson went to spend the evening at Lady Riddells meeting Lady Campbell & Miss MacFarlan.

Thursday Dec.r 21st.

Having been a little frost in the night it was a tolerable fine clear Day tho miserable dirty walkg. yet I try'd it much by first making visits in the new Town & then over the Bridge into

---

45. The expression of 'choice spirits' seems to have been coined by an anonymous book published in 1774: *The Wit's Miscellany, or a companion for the choice spirits; consisting of a great variety of odd and uncommon epigrams, facetious drolleries, whimsical mottos (translated, imitated), etc.*

46. The Battle of Cape St Vincent had taken place earlier in the year, 14 February 1797, when Admiral Sir John Jervis defeated a larger Spanish fleet under Admiral Don José de Córdoba y Ramos near Cape St Vincent, Portugal. More recently, the Battle of Camperdown was a major naval action fought on 11 October 1797, between a Royal Navy fleet under Admiral Adam Duncan and a Dutch Navy fleet under Vice-Admiral Jan de Winter. The battle resulted in a complete victory for the British who captured eleven Dutch ships without loss of any of their own.

some shops, again at Lady Riddells, meeting Lady Sinclair M^rs. Riddell & M^r. Gibson, rec'd a Letter from M^rs. Davies.

Friday Decr. 22^d.

A miserable wet & foggy Day so dark it was gloomy, saw no one in the Morning but M^r. & M^rs. Cecil, M^rs. Brown dined here & M^rs. Hay also drank Tea. rec'd a Letter from M^rs. Wilkinson & wrote to M^rs. Davies

Saturday Decr. 23^d.

Dry tho still rather foggy & extremely dark & gloomy, no walking for me, but rec'd visits from M^rs. Cunningham, Miss Nairne & Miss Drysdale spent the evening at Lady Riddells meeting Col: & M^rs. Rooke & Sir James Colquhoun recd a Letter f^m. Louisa Lee

Sunday Decr. 24th.

Dry, cold, & very windy, went to both services at Charlotte Chapel, between visited M^rs. Campbell of Balimore M^rs. Riddell &'c, & made one or two other visits without finding any one at home, a comfortable quiet evening at home. rec'd Letters from Lady Dukenfield & M^rs. Erskine wrote to Lady Elcho & M^rs. Wilkinson.

Monday Decr. 25th.

Dry & tolerably fine tho very windy, in the Morning, changed at Noon to be damp & very thick & in the afternoon was wet & quite tempestuous, spent many hours in Charlotte Chapel from the number of Communicants, time only between services to call at L^dy. Riddells to carry Miss Maxwell to evening service. M^r. Armstrong & Eva Chalmers dined here.

Tuesday Decr. 26th.

Stormy, & rather wet & at night wind tremendously high, I neither went out or rec'd any visitors, spent the evening at Lady Riddells no one there but M^r. Gibson. wrote to Lady Grey & L^dy. Dukenfield.

Wensday Decr. 27th.

A better Day than several former ones, being dry & not windy & a little sun, made good use of it, by just visiting M^rs. Rooke & M^rs. Brown & afterwards Lady C: C: & did some bussiness on the Bridge evening again spent at L^dy. Riddells Miss MacFarlan

Thursday Decr. 28th.

Dry but dreadfully windy I went to Prayers at Charlotte Chappel & afterwards made many visits finding at home M^rs. Dixon, Lady Forbes, Miss Hays Lady Sinclair, & M^rs. Rooke, Tea, Cards & supper at Lord Justice Clerks not a large party but pleas^t

Friday Decr. 29th.

Again most tremendously windy & very damp, no temptation to stir out nor saw any one but Sir William Hart who call'd before Dinner, went to Tea at Lady Riddells meeting a larger party than usual, & from thence went to Cards & Supper at M^rs. Stewarts a party of 18.

Saturday Decr. 30th.

Rather a better day being dry & not very windy, but at night both wet & windy to a great degree, went on several bussinesses into the old Town attended by Frank, Tea, Cards & supper with M^rs. Rooke, meeting Lord Justice Clerk & M^rs. Macqueen.

Sunday Decr. 31st.

Quite dry, but very disagreable from the severity of the wind, went to both services at Charlotte Chapel between made a long visit to M^rs. Brougham, brought M^r. Gibson home to Dinner.

Rec'd 159 Letters
wrote 152 Letters

1798

Monday Jan: 1st.

Tho cold a tolerable day for the opening of the new Year, went to Charlotte Chapel to Morning prayers, & calling on Lady Riddell afterwards was taken a short airing by her, Miss MacFarlan of the party likewise on my return call'd on M^rs. Rooke spent the evening at Lady Riddells, meeting Miss MacFarlan, M^r. Gibson & M^r. J. Riddell

Tuesday Jan: 2^d.

Having been a sharp frost in the night, it was both dry & clear, & being little wind & some sun was a very fine winter day, made great use of it by making many visits in the South Town finding only M^rs. Douglass Cavers, Miss Robertsons & Miss Macdonald at home, much enjoyment in a home evening, so great a rarity. rec'd Letters from Miss E. Guydickens & my Sis^r. Travell & wrote to M^rs. Charteris

Wensday Jan: 3^d.

Still a sharp frost, & very similiar day to the former only not so much sun, I did not go out but rec'd a visit from M^rs. General Campbell Tea Cards & supper at Lady Riddells meeting Lord Justice Clerk, & M^rs. Macqueen, Lady Campbell & M^rs. Rooke very chearfull & pleasant. wrote to Lady Hunter Blair & M^rs. Granville.

Thursday Jan: 4th.

A most dreadful day of rain & wind for some hours in the forenoon it blew quite a hurricane, saw no one in the Morning but M^r. Gibson who came to take leave, went to Tea Cards & supper at M^rs. Rookes to meet Sir N. & Lady Dukenfield who had arrived to Dinner of course a pleasant even^g.

Friday Jan: 5th.

In all respects as bad if not a worse day the wind being as high, & some of the showers being snow it was bitterly cold no stirring all Morning nor saw any one, went to dine at M^rs. Rookes to meet the good Bart: & his aimable Wife, & in the evening & to supper we were join'd by

Lord Justice Clerk & M^rs. Macqueen. sorry to bid adieu to our good friends who were going South the next Morning.

Saturday Jan: 6th.

A much better day than many former ones, being a hard frost, with little wind, made good use of it, by visiting L^dy. C: C: & M^rs. Fyffe, both at home but not M^rs. Gregory, shopt on the Bridge & ended by a long visit to M^rs. Brown. spent the evening at Lady Riddells with L^dy. Campbell & Sr J. Colquhoun

Sunday Jan: 7th.

Increased frost tho quite dry in spite of some fog, at Charlotte Chapel in the Morning, afterw^ds. visited M^rs. Baillie & M^rs. Davies arrived the night before, & went with Lady Campbell to evening Service at the Circus to hear Mr Struthers,[47] wonderfuly great but not pleasing, call'd on M^rs. Rooke before we came home to Dinner. wrote to my Sister Travell.

Monday Jan: 8th.

Continued hard frost but tho cold was far from being unpleasant being no wind, went at Noon to introduce M^r. Young to M^rs. Davies, made many visits afterwards those I found at home were Lady Grant, Miss Campbell & Miss Graham & Miss Grace Speirs, went to Drink Tea with M^rs. Rooke previous to going with her & a party to the Card Assembly in Bernards Room which tho not numerous was very pleasant, Mr Witts spent the evening at Lady Riddells

Tuesday Jan: 9th.

Still hard frost & most cutting cold went on several bussinesses in the old Town, & made am unsuccessful one to M^rs. J. Dundas & a Long & pleasant one to M^rs. D. Erskine spent the evening at Lady Riddells meeting Lady Campbell, M^rs. Rooke & Miss Bruce of Stenhouse.

Wensday Jan: 10th.

A thick gloomy sky in the Morn^g. which produced a ground thaw at Noon, & violent hard rain at night at home the whole of the Day receiving visits in the Morning from M^rs. & Miss Brisbane, M^rs. Stewart, M^rs. Fergusson, M^rs. Macdowall Grant, Miss Campbell, & Miss Macdonald, a pleasant evening full of employs wrote to M^rs. Erskine.

Thursday Jan: 11th.

A most severe day of violent wind & hard rain, which occasioned an uninterrupted Morning of much bussiness, went to Tea, Cards & Supper at Lady Riddells meeting Lady Campbell & Sir James Colquhoun

---

47. The Relief Church (or Presbytery of Relief) was a Scottish Presbyterian denomination founded in 1761. The Circus of Edinburgh had been for some time used by the Relief Secession while their chapel was being rebuilt. During this interval the preaching of their minister, the Revd Thomas Struthers attracted much attention, and the novelty of the place, as well as his eloquence, had drawn around him out of all classes of the community.

Friday Jan: 12th·

A tolerable fine Day neither rain or frost but having much of a cold I kept house in the Morning & rec'd visits from Mr· & Mrs· Baillie & Miss Baillies Mrs· Davies, & Mrs· & Miss M. Rooke, went to Tea, Cards and supper at Miss Abercrombies, a pleasant party of 13 wrote to Miss Snow.

Saturday Jan: 13th·

Weather still better being yet dry & clear without frost having appointed Mrs· Davies for a long private conversation did not go out but afterwards rec'd visits from Mrs· Balfour, Mr· Phillips, Miss Maxwell & Mrs· & Miss Allan went to Cards & Supper at Mr· George Fergusson's a very pleasant party of 22 elegant cold supper & four card Tables.

Sunday Jan: 14th·

Quite a damp disagreable stormy day, wind so high it was scarce possible to keep ones feet, yet I walk'd both times to Charlotte Chapel brought back by Mr· Baillies Coach, between services made 3 visits finding only Mrs· Baillie of Polkemmet at home, & rec'd visits from Mrs· & Miss Rooks & Miss Allan. rec'd a Letter from Miss Blair.

Monday Jan: 15th·

Day being a little frosty in the Morning foggy & damp at noon, & extremely wet at night, went early with Mrs· Rooke to the Court of Justiciary to be present at Carnesons trial, but disappointed by its being put off, afterwards made 2 or 3 visits finding Lady Riddell & Miss Fergusson at home, went to Tea at Mrs· Rookes to meet Captains Duggan & Mathews & their Ladies, & all went together to the Card Assembly which was full & agreable. rec'd a Letter from Mrs· Whalley

Tuesday Jan: 16th·

Damp & disagreable tho no rain, went by appointment at mid.day to Mrs· Davies on School bussiness, visited Mrs· Henry Scott, Miss Drysdale & a long one to Mrs· Brown, spent the evening at Lady Riddells meeting Lady Dalhousie, Miss MacFarlan & Sir James Colquhoun

Wensday Jan: 17th·

Still dry tho foggy till afternoon when rain came on, went with Mrs· Rooke & Miss Baillies again to the Court on the same trial but again disappointed one panel being fled & the other bail'd sat afterwards with Mrs· Rooke & visited Miss Bruce & Mrs· J. Campbell, dined & supt at Mr· Baillies no one there scarcely but there own family

Thursday Jan: 18th·

Quite a dreadful & continued bad day of wind & violent rain from Morn to night without cessation saw no one the whole Morning, went to Lady Riddells to spend the evening meeting Mrs· Rooke & Miss Mary 2 Miss MacFarlans, Miss R. Bruce & Sir J. Colquhoun. rec'd a Letter from Mr· Charteris.

Friday Jan: 19th·

Dry, mild & not unpleasant went with Lady Riddell in her Coach an airing accompanied by Miss Maxwell & Miss M. MacFarlan on the Queens Ferry road several miles. went to Tea

Cards & Supper at Lady Campbells, a mixt but pleasant party of 14 rec'd rather a melancholy Letter from Miss Anne Snow

Saturday Jan: 20ᵗʰ·

A very similiar Day only clearer & still more pleasant, went visiting with Mʳˢ· Rooke in her Coach first to Lady C: C: then to Hawke Hill to see Miss Wedderburne, their Aunt Mʳˢ· Johnson only visible on our return visited Lady Sinclair & Mʳˢ· Dundas. spent the evening at Lady Riddells no one there but Sʳ J. Colquhoun

Sunday Jan: 21ˢᵗ·

Quite a tempestuous day & at noon a very severe shower of rain which unfortunately came on, on our return from Morning service at Charlotte Chapel, luckily clear'd up to return again in the afternoon, having previously made a visit to the Speirs; Mʳ· Sandford even more eloquent than usual; wrote to Lady Dukenfield.

Monday Jan: 22ᵈ·

Rather wet early in the Morning accompanied by most violent high wind which continued unabated till the evening, precluding even the power of stirring out in the Morning, or seeing any one. Mʳ· Witts dined w.ʰ Mʳ· Blane, & I with Lady Riddell meeting 4 other Ladies & to Tea 4 more, went to the Card assembly with Mʳˢ· Rooke & Miss Maxwell full & pleasant.

Tuesday Jan: 23ᵈ·

Dry & clear but still with considerable wind, went into the old Town on several bussinesses & made some visits finding only Mʳˢ· Brown in James Square at home, for a great treat spent the evening at home

Witts Family Papers F195

1798

Jan: 24th Wensday

Fine in the Morning but before mid day it became both wet & windy, neither went out or saw any one in the Morning but Miss J: Wedderburne spent the evening at Lady Riddells meeting Miss Graham & Miss MacFarlan.

Thursday Jan: 25th.

Having been a little frost, it produced an uncommon fine day, being constant sunshine & no wind made much use of it being out 3 or 4 hours chiefly in making visits in the new Town finding 7 families at home, spent the evening again at Lady Riddells, Lady Campbell, Mrs. Macdowall, Mrs. Rooke Miss MacFarlan & Sir J; Colquhoun the party.

Friday Jan: 26th.

No rain till quite evening, but a high & disagreably damp wind, went out early to call on Mrs. Davies to go to the Coachmakers about Trunks, before I went with Mrs. Rooke to visit Mrs. Duggan & Mrs. Mathews at the Barracks, at home in the evening & not very well

James Peddie, (1759–1845). Minister of the Associated Congregation, Bristo Street. An etching by John Kay.

Saturday Jan: 27th.

Dry excepting two or three trifling showers but very stormy & cold, out the whole Morning with Mrs. Davies, looking for houses & various sorts of furniture, spent the evening at Lady Riddells no one there but Sr. J. Colquhoun & Son

Sunday Jan: 28th.

No rain till quite night when it was severe accompanied by tremendous wind which indeed was dreadful all day, went in the Coach with Mrs. Davies &'c to both services & back to Charlotte chapel & between drove to the Cannongate when I visited Lady C: C:

Monday Jan: 29th.

A most wretched stormy day violent wind & some little rain on the whole a comfortless day & I was far from well which made me resist all intreaties to go the Card Assembly, saw no one but Mr. Baillie, rec'd a Letter from Mrs. Erskine

Tuesday Jan: 30th.

Better weather early in the Day, but at mid.day turn'd severely cold & horribly windy at night awefuly so, visited Lady Sinclair, Mrs. Sandford & Mrs. Rooke all at home & went into the old Town on bussiness spent the evening at Lady Riddells meeting Lord Justice Clerke & Mrs. Macqueen & several others

Wensday Jan: 31st.

A most shocking day from Morn to night of wind & snow chiefly in storms but very severe of course neither stirr'd out or saw any one till we went to Lord Stonefields to Dinner,[1] no creature but themselves & to Tea Mrs. Macqueen, Mr. Durham & Miss Nairne, brought home before supper & after many rubbers at Whist in their Carriage

Thursday Feb: 1st.

A very similiar day, only not quite so bad from the wind bot being so violent the showers of snow shorter, & some sun at intervals, quite confining much work & reading & George at a dance at Mrs. Deans.

Friday Feb: 2^{d.}

Frost gone, disagreable thick fog & sometimes rain yet I had several Morning callers such as Mrs. Oliphant, Mrs. Brown, Lady Hailes & Miss Dalrymple Cards & Supper at Mrs. Fyffes a large chearful party.

---

1.   John Campbell of Stonefield (d. 1801), better known as Lord Stonefield, was a prominent Scottish lawyer. The Ramsay portrait, regarded as one of the artist's finest, is notable for the assertive gaze of the sitter and the exquisite rendering of the intricate costume. It was painted in 1749, the year before Campbell's marriage to Lady Grace Stuart, daughter of the 2nd Earl of Bute, and the year after he was admitted to the Faculty of Advocates. He was appointed Lord of Session in 1762 and sat for 39 years on the bench until his death in 1801.

John Campbell of Stonefield (d. 1801). An etching by
John Kay, 1799.

Saturday Feb: 3^{d.}

A most dreadful stormy day both of wind & rain of course no going out in the Morning nor
any company to receive, spent the evening at Lady Riddells no one there but Miss Bruce of
Kinnaird & Sir James & Col: Colquhoun. rec'd a Letter from my Sis[r.] Travell.

Sunday Feb: 4th.

Having been something of a frost, it was clear, calm, & pleasant went to both services at
Charlotte Chapel between made some visits finding only Miss MacFarlan & Miss Campbell
of Shervan at home. M[rs.] Hay & her Niece drank Tea here. wrote to my Sister Travell.

Monday Feb: 5th.

Dry & calm but not very pleasant being a thick air from east wind, made some visits finding
M[rs.] Rooke, M[rs.] Macdonald, & M[rs.] Brown at home. M[r.] Witts spent the evening at Lady
Riddells, & I went to a very crowded Card Assembly accompanied by Miss Baillie.

Tuesday Feb: 6th.

Quite a dry & fine mild day without either rain or frost not going out in the Morning I rec'd
visits from M[rs.] Davies & Miss S. Baillie, Col: Rooke & Miss Abercrombie spent the evening
at Lady Riddells, meeting only M[rs.] Macqueen & Miss Ord

Wensday Feb: 7th.

Another very mild pleasant Day made several visits in the New Town, finding at home M[rs.]
Baillie Pol,[2] M[rs.] Sands, M[rs.] Stewart, M[rs.] Macdowal & M[rs.] Thomson, went to the Play with

---

2.   Margaret Baillie, née Colquhoun, of Polkemmet.

Military Promenade. This famous etching by John Kay, 1795, shows some of the fashionable citizens—male and female—who made the Edinburgh Volunteers part of Edinburgh society. The promenade is led by General Francis Dundas. The next military character, in the centre with the volunteer cap and feather is Agnes's acquaintance Mr Henry Jardine. Behind him is Robert Dundas. The full-length figure with the military hat and veil—which he wore in ridicule of the ladies—represents the eccentric Captain Hay, or the 'Daft Captain' as he was usually styled. The last military character is the Earl of Eglinton. The ladies attired in military uniform are the Miss Maxwells; see note 27, diary F190.

M^rs. Rooke much entertained by the Heir at Law,[3] supt at L^dy. Riddells, meeting L^dy. Campbell, M^rs. D. & M^r. & M^rs. Jardine

Thursday Feb: 8th.

A continuance of the same dry & mild weather, made good use of it, by walking to Georges Square &'c making visits those I found at home were M^rs. Baillie, &'c, M^rs. Craigie, M^rs. Hamilton & Miss Moneypenny a home evening a pleasing rarity rec'd a Letter from Lady Dukenfield.

Friday Feb: 9th.

Quite as fine weather being still dry went into the old Town on Several businesses, & walk'd on the Castle Hill, visited M^rs. Hamilton in Ramsay Garden without success, but found M^rs. Rooke at home on my return.

Saturday Feb: 10th.

A sad day of most violent wind & very frequent rain, an intire interruption to all Morning going out or company, but not to bussiness spent the evening at Lady Riddells, meeting M^rs.

---

3. *The Heir at Law*, 1797, by George Colman (the younger) (1762–1836).

Fraser Lovat, Miss MacFarlan, Miss Bruce Sir James Colquhoun & M^r. McCloed. rec'd a Letter from Miss Snow.

Sunday Feb: 11th.

As great a wind, quite a hurricane but being little or no rain, tho a very damp wind I went to both services to Charlotte Chapel, between services made several visits finding Mrs. Campbell of Balimore & Mrs. Macdowall at home. wrote to Miss Anne Snow.

Monday Feb: 12th.

Still very tempestuous but dry & much sunshine, went with Lady Riddell an airing, as well as walk in the Kings Park almost blown away Tea Cards & Supper at Lord Polkemmets a Social pleasant party, but not large.

Tuesday Feb: 13th.

Quite a mild fine Day, rather inclined to be stormy but very pleasant, went to Musselburgh with Mrs. Rooke, to see the little Dukenfields at their seperate schools, spent the evening at Lady Riddells, Mrs. Macqueen Mrs. Campbell Stonefeld, Mrs. Carre, Col & Mrs. Rooke

Wensday Feb: 14th.

A stormy disagreable Morning which produced a wet afternoon, Mrs. Davies sat 2 or 3 hours with me on interesting conversation, we dined at M^r. Baillies a party of 16, Col: & Mrs. Rooke & several Gentlemen, play'd at Cards & home between 10 & 11

Thursday Feb: 15th.

A bright cold day inclined to be frosty & at noon a severe shower of snow, hail, & rain, Miss Grace Baillie my only visitor, Tea Cards & Supper at Col: Rookes, an agreable small party, of genteel people

Friday Feb: 16th.

Had been a sharp fall of snow in the night & was very lowering in the Morning, but at Noon clear'd up to be bright & fine, very fortunate for the great military appearance throughout the Town in honor of Lord Duncan, went with Mrs. Rooke to Georges Square, & saw the first part of the shew from Mrs. Carres house, then went into Princes Street to Col: Rookes where as well as many others we survey'd the remaining glories of the procession, dined, drank Tea, & supt with Mrs. Rooke

Saturday Feb: 17th.

Quite a wretched Day of Snow & wind, good for nothing but being quiet all Morn. which got thro' much bussiness, & heard Lewis's new Play of the Castle Spectre[4] spent the evening at Lady Riddells, the two Miss Bruces, Miss Graham & Sir James Colquhoun, & Mr. & Miss Hamilton Bangour for an hour or two. rec'd a Letter from Mrs. Granville

---

4. *Castle Spectre*, 1797, by Matthew Gregory Lewis (1775–1818).

Sunday Feb: 18ᵗʰ·

A severe frost which returnd the snow on the ground, but from much sun & little wind it was pleasant enough, went to both services at Charlotte Chapel, between made some visits finding only the Speirs at home, Mʳ· Gibson dined here & spent the whole evening in much <u>talk</u>

Monday Feb: 19ᵗʰ·

Another frosty day, but pleasant tho cold, being little wind & much sun, & not very bad walking, went first with Frank to see him cut capers at the step masters, visited Lady C: C: Mʳˢ· Gregory, Mʳˢ· Brown, & Mʳˢ· Rooke all at home went to a small party at Lady Riddells for two hours before going to the Card Assembly with Mʳˢ· Rooke not very full but pleasant enough.

Tuesday Feb: 20ᵗʰ·

Frost going very unpleasant yet I air'd with Lady Riddell accompanied by Mʳˢ· Fraser Lovat & Miss R. Bruce to Leith & on the Musselburgh road, rec'd a visit from Mʳˢ· Brougham on my return, went to the Play in Mʳˢ· Baillies Box, the Wheel of Fortune ill acted & the House shamefuly thin when considered the profits were to be appropriated to Government. miserably cold.

Wensday Feb: 21ˢᵗ·

A clear bright day having been a trifling frost, but slippery bad walking, went to Charlotte Chapel being Ash: Wednesday 2 hours & ½ there with a long service & fine sermon, had only time to visit Lady Buchan before dressing to dine at Lord Stonefields taken to Georges Square in Col: Rookes Coach who were there also a pleasant party of 9 & 2 others to Tea & Cards supt at Lady Riddells, no one there but Miss MacFarlan

Thursday Feb: 22ᵈ·

A miserable day of snow, rain & thaw quite confining, till we went to spend the evening at Lady Riddells, meeting Lady Campbell, Mʳˢ· Fraser, Miss Graham, Mʳˢ· Macdonald, Miss Bruce & Sir James Colquhoun

Friday Feb: 23ᵈ·

A little frost, but a fine day with much sun but dreadful bad walking, went to Morning Prayers to a very thin congregation afterwards made a long visit to Mʳˢ· Sandford one to Mʳˢ· Campbell of Balimore, & one to Mʳˢ· Brougham again at Lᵈʸ Riddells a very small party

Saturday Feb: 24ᵗʰ·

Frost in the Morning, thaw at Noon & wet at night staid at home all Morn. saw no one but Mʳˢ· Rooke as usual at Lady Riddells, meeting both the Miss Bruces Miss MacFarlan & Sir James Colquhoun wrote to Mʳˢ· Erskine

Sunday Feb: 25ᵗʰ·

Frost in the Morning, & thaw afterwards which made the streets such dreadful walking it was a Sea of mud, yet went to Charlotte Chapel twice, in the evening in the Baillie Coach, between services visited Lady H Blair & Mʳˢ· Baillie Mʳ· Gibson dined here.

Monday Feb: 26th.

A tolerable fine dry day, but still very moderate walking, made an unsuccessful call on M^rs. D. Erskine, a long visit to M^rs. Brown & another to M^rs. Davies, went to the Play in the even^g. accompanied by Francis as a birthday treat, sat in M^rs. Rookes Box house very full, the road to ruin[5] being bespoke by Lord Duncan late home

Tuesday Feb: 27th.

A mild & very fine Day being much sunshine & little wind, & being much better walking I ventured to Georges Square to make several visits those I found at home were M^rs. Murray of Abercaithie, M^rs. Clerk, M^rs. Hamilton, & Lady Lelius Macqueen,[6] no interruption to a quiet home evening but an hours conversation with M^rs. Young. wrote to M^rs. Charteris

Wensday Feb: 28th.

Frost quite gone, but a cold stormy disagreable day, much wind & no sun went to Morning Prayers with M^rs. Baillie in her Coach, afterwards visited M^rs. Grant M^rs. Fergusson & M^rs. Stewart all at home, went to Dine with M^rs. Mure 9 Ladies to two Gentlemen, stupid enough, went away early to Cards & Supper at Lord Justice Clerks, taken by Col: & M^rs. Rooke a small chearful party. rec'd a Letter f^m. M^rs. Browning

Thursday Mar: 1st.

An uncommon mild fine Day quite like Spring & became dry, sat ½ an hour with Col: Moneypenny & as long with Lady C: C: a home evening, rec'd Letters from M^rs. Erskine M^rs. Wilkinson & my Sister Travell.

Friday Mar: 2d.

Another mild fine Day but not so pleasant being a thick damp air, went to Morning prayers from thence, made many visits but only found M^rs. Davies & M^rs. Brougham at home spent the evening at Lady Riddells, meeting Miss Orde, Miss MacFarlan & Sir James Colquhoun

Saturday Mar: 3d.

Much the same kind of mild weather only more wind I staid at home all Morning my only visitors M^rs. Baillie & M^rs. Davies spent the evening again at Lady Riddells M^rs. Campbell of Balimore, Miss Bruce of Kennaird & her Niece, & Sir James Colquhoun <u>again</u>, wrote to M^rs. Granville.

---

5.   *The Road to Ruin* (1792), Thomas Holcroft (1745–1809).

6.   This Looks like 'Lelius' and it is repeated on 22 March 1798. Lady Macqueen had married Lord Braxfield (Lord Justice Clerk, Robert Macqueen) in 1792. Lord Braxfield's first wife died in 1791 and his final years were enlivened by his second marriage in 1792 to Elizabeth (d. 1820), daughter of Robert Ord, chief baron of exchequer. He wooed her in inimitable fashion: '*Lizzy, I am looking out for a wife, and I thought you just the person that would suit me. Let me have your answer, off or on, the morn, and nae mair aboot it*'. In her he seems to have met his match. When his butler resigned on the grounds that he could no longer stand her continual scolding, Braxfield retorted: '*Lord! ye've little to complain o'; ye may be thankfu' ye're no married to her*'. They had no children. Agnes Witts usually refer to Mrs Macqueen, so it is unclear why this sudden change is introduced. It may have been a nickname conferred on his wife by Lord Braxfield in an allusion to the Elizabethan *New Arcadia*. In the 1580s Sir Henry Lee was known as 'Lelius' and he was Queen Elizabeth's champion at the tilts. Lord Braxfield was undoubtedly a well-read man. Agnes presumably felt close enough to the MacQueens to join in on the family bonhomie.

Sunday Mar: 4th.

A damp unpleasant Morning which terminated in hard rain at Noon, & very showery all the afternoon at Charlotte Chapel at both services convey'd to & from by Mrs. Rooke & Mrs. Baillie a quiet evening as usual. wrote to my Sister Travell

Monday Mar: 5th.

Again damp in the Morning dry & fine all the day, & wet late in the evening went to some shops on the Bridge made a long visit to Mrs. Brown where I met numbers & walk'd in the new Town. went to a crowded Card Assembly with M^{rs.} & Miss Rooke & Miss Murrays, Mr. Witts at Lady Riddells wrote to Mrs. Whalley.

Tuesday Mar: 6th.

An intire dry & tolerably fine Day, I staid within all Morning without letting any one in dined at Col: Rookes, meeting Col: Bristowe & Mr. Bruce & to Tea & Cards the party was increased to 17, at nine o'clock we & some others went to Mrs. Baillies Ball a very smart thing more than a 100 people, very handsome supper not at home till between 3 & 4.

Wensday Mar: 7th.

A mild but cloudy Morn; which after mid.day turn'd to wet & damp, but became dry again, rose late so did little in the Morning but visit Lady C: C: spent the evening at Lady Riddells meeting Rookes, Lady Sinclair Lady Campbell & Miss Bruce

Thursday Mar: 8th.

No rain, but a stormy damp, & windy day being the general Fast, spent great part of the forenoon in Charlotte Chapel a fine Sermon in the evening to a most crowded congregation.

Friday Mar: 9th.

An unpleasant day being a cold thick easterly wind & in the evening severe rain went to Morning prayers at Charlotte Chapel, from thence by Mrs. Rooke to make visits at the Barracks, Georges Square &'c, met her & several more at Lady Riddells in the evening.

Saturday Mar: 10th.

The rain that had fallen in Town, was snow in the country to cover all the adjacent hills, & tho the day was bright & dry was cold & frosty, accompanied Mrs. Rooke to the two schools at Musselburgh to see the young Dukenfields spent a strange evening at Mrs. Oliphants a hetrogenious party of more than 20 late & not very pleasant.

Sunday Mar: 11th.

A pretty sharp frost, but fine from constant warm sun, twice at Charlotte Chapel as usual, Mr. Sandford gave a peculiar fine sermon between services made 4 visits those I found at home were Mrs. Campbell of Balimore & Mrs. General Campbell. a home even^{g.}

Monday Mar: 12th.

Again frost with a pretty sharp wind staid at home all Morning receiving visits from M^{rs.}

Campbell of Balimore, Miss Graham & Miss Mackenzie drank Tea with our next Door Neighbour M^rs· Hay a chatty visit two Ladies being there

Tuesday Mar: 13th·

Very much the same kind of weather very cold wind & constant bright sun went an airing with Lady Riddell & Miss Maxwell on the Libberton & Dalkeith roads very pleasant. spent the evening at Lady Riddells meeting Miss Ord, Miss Bruce Kennaird & M^r· Gibson.

Wensday Mar: 14th·

Dry & frosty but rather cold & stormy went to Morning prayers, disagreable domestic disarrangements, busy in hunting after a servant in Nellys place, who was married in the evening after only a few hours knowledge to us visited M^rs· Rooke & M^rs· Davies both at home.

Thursday Mar: 15th·

Frost gone very unpleasant day of frequent showers of hail & rain which became constant at night, at home all Morn hired a Servant, went to Tea Cards & Supper at Lady Riddells meeting Col: & M^rs· Rooke M^rs· Macdowall & Miss Bruce imidiately after supper went with the Rookes to a very good assembly conducted by M^r· General Douglass not at home till between two & three

Friday Mar: 16th·

A most true March Day being perpetual storms & some very violent ones of hail & rain carried to Chapel by M^rs· Baillie &'c & afterwards drove about with them to make some unsuccessful visits at home early, a home evening much fatigued. rec'd a Letter from M^rs· Erskine

Saturday Mar: 17th·

Wet in the Morning very cold & stormy all Day & wet at night went with M^rs· Rooke for two hours to Stranges general practising & afterwards visited Lady Brehan, went to the Castle Spectre in M^rs· Macqueens Box very much entertain'd indeed.

Sunday Mar: 18th·

Weather quite as bad incessant storms of hail, yet continued to get both times to Chapel brought back each time by friends, between services visited M^rs· Riddell at her Mothers just come to Town.

Monday Mar: 19th·

The same unvaried stormy weather yet braved it to make long visits to Lady C: C: & M^rs· Brown, went to the Card Assembly Miss Baillie of Polkemmet with me, not full & miserable bad company play'd at Whist with M^rs· Oliphant rec'd a Letter from M^rs· Charteris.

Tuesday Mar: 20th·

Tolerably fine early, but at mid.day began such incessant storms of snow & hail, as to be almost perpetual, rec'd visits from M^rs· J: D: Thomson & Miss Davison, spent the even^g· at Lady Riddells, meeting M^rs· Rooke, Miss Bruce of Kennaird Miss Graham & Sir James Colquhoun wrote to Miss A. Snow

Wensday Mar: 21ˢᵗ·

A tolerable bright fine Day after a fall of snow in the night that remained for some hours on the ground carried to prayers by Mʳˢ· Baillie & afterwards to Georges Square to make some visits found only Mʳˢ· Macqueen at home, afterwards visited Mʳˢ· Brown, Mʳˢ· Rooke Mʳˢ· Davies, & Mʳˢ· Riddell, spent the evening at Lady Riddells meeting only Lady Campbell & Miss Bruce.

Thursday Mar: 22ᵈ·

Quite a stormy uncomfortable day being a mixture of Snow & hail but dry in the evening rec'd visits from Lady Lelius Macqueen & Mʳˢ· Riddell went to the Assembly Mʳˢ· Rooke being the Lady Directoress carried a long train of Misses with me an excellent Assembly not at home till between 2 & 3 in the Morning.

Friday Mar: 23ᵈ·

Cold & stormy as usual but pretty dry, after going to Morning prayers, visited much in the New Town finding at home Mʳˢ· Grant, Mʳˢ· Dirom &'c, Mʳˢ· Craigie, Mʳˢ· Baillie Polkemmet went to Cards & Supper at Sir Willᵐ· Forbes a large & very agreable party the larger number Gentlemen as late returning home as the preceding evening. transpose the events of this Mornᵍ· with those of Wednesday a mistake having been made in the relation of them

Saturday Mar: 24ᵗʰ·

A much milder & consequently a far more pleasant Day accompanied Lady Riddell & Miss Graham in an airing to Leith &'c, dined at Mʳ· Browns to meet Lady Wedderburne went again to the Castle Spectre in Mʳˢ· Baillies Box a very crowded House. Mʳ· Witts at Lᵈʸ· Riddells

Sunday Mar: 25ᵗʰ·

In spite of an east wind a very uncommon mild fine Day constant sunshine as usual both times at Charlotte Chapel between made 4 visits finding only Miss Campbell of Shervan at home. wrote to Mrs. Charteris.

Monday Mar: 26ᵗʰ·

A disagreable cold stormy day, w.ᶜʰ prevented even the wich of going out & saw no one but Mʳˢ· & Miss Stewart in the Morning & went to a small party at Lady Riddells in the evening

Tuesday Mar: 27ᵗʰ·

Dry & tolerably fine tho not pleasant, made good use of the Morning by going to Several Shops in the old Town, & made several visits in the South Town, those I found at home were Miss Moneypenny & Mʳˢ· Carre; went again to Lady Riddells, meeting Lord Justice Clerk & Mʳˢ· Macqueen Col: & Mʳˢ· Rooke, Miss Graham &'c.

Wensday Mar: 28ᵗʰ·

A fine Morning, & indeed Day but for a severe shower at Noon, which caught us at Church, brought home by Mʳˢ· Rooke, when dry made visits to Mʳ· John Campbell, Lady H: Blair & Mʳˢ· Davies, Tea Cards & Supper at Col: Rookes a very pleasant party of 12.

Thursday Mar: 29th.

Cold day, disagreable east wind Mrs. Brougham, & Miss Rookes here before I went to call on Mrs. Rookes to see her poor sick little Boy with whom I had been the day before spent the evening at Lady Riddells, meeting Lady Campbell & Miss MacFarlan & L^{dy.} Augusta Clanercy for a short time.

Friday Mar: 30th.

Quite a disagreable day being very frequent showers of snow & sleet, carried to Morning prayers by Mrs. Baillie, afterwards went with L^{dy.} Riddell in her Coach visited L^{dy.} C: C: Mrs. Phillips & Mrs. Border's Nursery, again in the evening at Lady Riddells, where was Miss Bruce & both the Miss MacFarlans. rec'd a Letter from Louisa Lee.

Saturday Mar: 31st.

Cold extreme cold strong east wind & much appearance of snow coming staid at home all Morning & saw no one but Miss Dalrymple went as usual to Lady Riddells a party of 10, L^{dy.} Buchan, Mrs. Macdowall Mrs. Stewart, Miss Bruce of Stenhouse & Miss MacFarlan. rec'd a Letter from my Sister

Sunday April 1st.

Extreme cold for the day, flying showers of snow in the Morning, at Charlotte Chapel at both services between visited Mrs. Bordes & Mrs. Davies her three eldest Boys drank Tea here wrote to my Sister

Monday Ap: 2^{d.}

A boisterous cold & showery day wch held out no temptation to me to go out in the Morn^{g.} & admitted no one our <u>whole</u> family dined very pleasantly rather a select party at Mrs. Macdowalls supt also with some additions.

Tuesday Ap: 3^{d.}

A gloomy Morn: which produced a violent shower at Noon, & it remain'd showery more or less the whole of the day, carried to church & brought back by Mrs. Baillie. spent the evening at Col: Rookes, a tolerable pleasant party form'd chiefly for the purpose of playing at Quadrille rec'd a Letter from Miss Anne Snow

Wensday Ap: 4th.

Another dull Morning, rain again at Noon which continued thro the day accompanied by most violent wind quite a hurricane brought back from Morning prayers by Mrs. Rooke visited Mrs. Bordes &'c spent the evening again at Col: Rookes in the hope of meeting Sr. N. & Lady Dukenfield who never arrived beat most sadly at Cassino

Thursday Ap: [day number blank]

For a wonder a day without rain & a good deal of sun, but a very distressing high wind, went to Prayers as usual with Mrs. Baillie afterwards visited Miss Campbell & Miss Graham, Mrs. Campbell of Balimore, & Mrs. Brougham, Miss Muswell drank Tea here by way of take leave visit, & Sr. N. Dukenfield & his children were added to the party.

Edinburgh from the Calton Hill, a painting by Alexander Nasmyth featuring the bridewell and the prison.

A similar view brought in nearer focus; a painting by J. M. W. Turner, 1804.

Friday Ap: 6th.

Very wet in the Morning, & continued showery the whole of the day attended by strong wind went to Morning service in a chair kindly assisted by friends carriages afterwards, between services visited by Lady Dukenfield & Mr. Baillie much rejoiced to see the former & to see her looking well the evening spent at home suitably to the seriousness of the day

Saturday Ap: 7th.

Happily quite dry, with much wind as well as sun, but certainly a fine Day, after Morning Prayers, accompanied Lady Dukenfield & her Children to Musselburgh in her carriage; spent the evening at Col: Rookes meeting the Baronet & his Lady & Mrs. Brown walk'd there & home.

Sunday Ap: 8th.

Severe high wind both Morning and evening, but the day was bright, very fine & the sun quite warm, spent many hours in Chapel, <u>doubly</u> interested by attending my beloved Frank for the first time to the Altar.[7] evening pass'd I hope as it ought, after such a ceremony.

Monday Ap: 9th.

A wonderful hot fine day for the season, went to Morning prayers afterwards with the Baillie family visited L^{dy.} Sinclair, & then went & eat cold meat with Lady Riddell. afterwards <u>broil'd</u> into the old Town on some necessary bussiness, went to the Card Assembly which was genteel & pleasant with L^{dy.} Dukenfield & Mrs. Rooke.

Tuesday Ap: 10th.

Another very oppressive hot Day, went to prayers at Charlotte Chapel, & from thence accompanied Mrs. Davies to make visits return'd home with me for an hour. both dined & supt at Lady Riddells a <u>sober</u> party of 8 or 9 pleasant enough but for extreme heat.

Wensday Ap: 11th.

Another extreme hot Day kept quite quiet all the Morning excepting going to sit with Lady Dukenfield for an hour or two, met her & Sir N. at Dinner at Col: Rookes, went with them & the young people of the three families to the Theatre to see Eliston in the Mountaineers[8] on the whole much entertaind, but enervated with heat

Thursday Ap: 12th.

Quite as hot as ever all Day but cooler in the evening, obliged to go into the old Town on many bussinesses, visited Miss Dalrymple & on my return poor Lady D, confined by a sprained ancle. spent the evening at Lady Riddells a chearful party of 9, very late Card playing.

---

7. Francis Witts was now fifteen years old. He was born 26 February 1783.
8. Robert William Elliston (1774–1831). Elliston was an actor and later became a theatre manager. *The Mountaineers* was a play by George Coleman, first performed at the Haymarket Theatre, London, on 3 August 1793. Elliston played Octavian, and this was a famous part for him. In 1798 Elliston was still very much at the beginning of his theatrical career.

Friday Ap: 13ᵗʰ·

Still very hot in the sun, & much of it but a cool east wind, went out only to call on Mʳˢ· Davies & sit an hour or two with poor Lady Dukenfield for the last time as she was going next Morning, a painful parting probably for so long a time. went in the evening to a <u>very</u> large party at Miss Bruces of Stenhouse odd but pleasant rec'd a comfortable Letter from Mʳˢ· Erskine.

Saturday Ap: 14ᵗʰ·

Weather somewhat changed, being dark & lowering in the Morning, a severe shower at Noon dry but cold in the evening went a <u>Town</u> airing with Lady Riddell visited Lady C: C: for half an hour spent the evening at Lady Riddells her Ladyship so ill she was obliged to go to Bed before Supper, Miss Ord, Miss Bruce Kennaird & Miss MacFarlan there

Sunday Ap: 15ᵗʰ·

A damp doubtful looking Morning, & a most violent shower at Noon dry at night but extremely cold, at Chapel both Services convey'd to & fro by kind friends after Dinner visited Lady Riddell in her bed tho better, & drank Tea with Miss Ord, very chatty home before it was dark.

Monday Ap: 16ᵗʰ·

A day of uninterrupted rain from Morn to night of course quite confining & much home bussiness transacted besides writing to Miss Louisa Lee.

Tuesday Ap: 17ᵗʰ·

A bright & very fine Day after the Storm made much use of it by first going to see Lᵈʸ· Riddell who was got into her Dressing Room afterwards went into the old Town on several errands & look'd at many Lodging. after Tea went out again on the same pursuit. rec'd a Letter from Miss Snow & wrote to my Broʳ· Ferdinand.

Wensday Ap: 18ᵗʰ·

Another as pleasant a day being bright & fine, rec'd a long visit from Mʳ· H. Brougham before I went out to visit Mʳˢ· Rooke & Mʳˢ· Brown & transact more bussiness in the old Town, spent the evening at Lady Riddells meeting Lady Campbell & Miss Bruce Kennaird

Thursday Ap: 19ᵗʰ·

Quite a universal wet Day from Morn to night, which occasioned much stay at home bussiness to be transacted spent the evening at Col: Rookes a pleasant chearful party of 12.

Friday Ap: 20ᵗʰ·

A charming change in the weather being as universal a fine Day bright sun & no wind very fortunate for our expedition to Dalkeith to see Capᵗⁿ· & Mʳˢ· Lee of the Shropshire Militia taking Major & Mʳˢ· Bordes with us in Lady Riddells Coach went to see her Ladyship after Dinner drank Tea with her & returnd home to Dress to go to a party at Mʳˢ· Com: Browns odd but pleasant evenᵍ·

Saturday Ap: 21st.

Clear & fine in the Morning but wet in the afternoon, much engaged all the forenoon with an Auctioneer looking over our furniture, spent the evening at Lady Riddells meeting Lady Campbell, Lady Sinclair, Mrs. Rooke & Mrs. Mure.

Sunday Ap: 22d.

A damp Morning but tolerably fine the rest of the day tho rather cold at Charlotte Chapel both services a peculiar fine Sermon from Mr. Sandford between visited Mrs. Baillie &'c & Miss Ord drank Tea & supt at Lady Riddells meeting Lady Colquhoun & Miss MacFarlan.

Monday Ap: 23d.

A most beautiful fine Day throughout, rec'd visits from Miss Sinclair, Captn. & Mrs. Lee, Mr. & Miss Rooke, Mrs. Bordes, afterwards went out Lodging hunting to see Raeburns Pictures & to call again upon Miss Ord, spent the evening again at Lady Riddells rather a large party rec'd a Letter from Lady Dukenfield.

Tuesday Ap: 24th.

Similiar fine weather tho with an Easterly wind, made visits to Mrs. Bordes & Mrs. Rooke, & then went in Lady Riddells Coach to Leith, to call on Mr. Oliphant converse with him & some Merchants relative to our passage to Hamburgh & went into a Trading Vessel, return by the Cannongate to visit Lady C: C: again spent the evening at Lady Riddells meeting Ladies Campbell, Sinclair, & Ramsay, Miss Sinclair Miss Bruce & Col: Colquhoun.

Wensday Ap: 25th.

No change of weather, out 3 or 4 hours in the Morning on various necessary bussinesses in the old Town, Major & Mrs. Bordes drank Tea here previous to their departure.

Thursday Ap: 26th.

Still dry but without sun & so windy as to make the dust quite disagreable, made several visits in the new Town those at home were Mrs. Baillie &'c, Mrs. Sandford & Mrs. Brougham spent the evening at Lady Riddell a large mixt set.

Friday Ap: 27th.

Quite a fine warm day with much sun & clear air went out late in the forenoon to accompany Lady Campbell to see Raeburns & Danloux Pictures[9] went Lodging hunting, & ended with visiting Mrs. Mackenzie, went to Lady Riddells as usual in the evening to meet Mr. & Mrs. Baillie & Mrs. Davies Mrs. Askew & Mrs. Riddell there also.

---

9. Sir Henry Raeburn (1756–1823) was a Scottish portrait painter and Scotland's first significant portrait painter since the Union to remain based in Scotland. He served as Portrait Painter to King George IV in Scotland. Henri-Pierre Danloux (1753–1809) was a French painter. He emigrated to London in 1792 thereby escaping the French Revolution. It is interesting that this exhibition in Edinburgh should feature these two as the controversy relating to the famous painting of the Reverend Robert Walker Skating on Duddingston Loch, better known by its shorter title *The Skating Minister,* is an oil painting in dispute between these two men. The official attribution is to Sir Henry Raeburn but some experts believe it to be the work of Danloux.

Saturday Ap: 28ᵗʰ·

A still finer day than many former ones tho an east wind, went out early to attend Mʳˢ· Davies to visit Mʳˢ· Brougham from whence went into the old Town on bussinesses, & Georges Square to make visits, found Mʳˢ· Renny Mʳˢ· Douglass Cavers & Miss Abercrombie at home at home in the evening a pleasant rarity.

Sunday Ap: 29ᵗʰ·

A cold disagreable day from being a severe east wind, went as usual to both services at Charlotte Chapel between visited Mʳˢ· Dirom, Mʳˢ· Macdowal, & Mʳˢ· Riddell, Mʳˢ· Davies & her four sons drank Tea here. rec'd Letters from Mʳˢ· Rooke & My Brother Ferdinand & wrote to Lᵈʸ· Dukenfield.

Monday Ap: 30ᵗʰ·

An extreme cold unpleasant Day being dark & gloomy & continued east wind, a stay at home Morning without any interruption Tea Cards & supper at Mʳ· John Campbells, a mixt party of 18. wrote to my Brother Ferdinand.

Tuesday May 1ˢᵗ·

In point of weather very unlike the day being thick & lowering & at times misty yet ventured to the South Town, principaly to visit Mʳˢ· Macqueen & enquire after the Justice did some bussiness in the old Town. spent the evenᵍ· at Lady Riddells a pleasant party of 8. Our young Men at a Dance at Mʳˢ· Campbells Duntroon rec'd a Letter from Miss Anne Snow

Wensday May 2ᵈ·

A fine dry, but cold day, quite busy all Morning with beginning preparations for moving went late to Cards & Supper at Mʳˢ· Macdowals a chearful pleasant party of 10. wrote to Mʳˢ· Rooke

Tuesday May 3ᵈ·

Quite a similiar day in point of weather, as well as in various employs all Morning Tea Cards & Supper at Mʳ· Baillies Queen Street an odd mixt set of Company.

Friday May 4ᵗʰ·

A bright & very pleasant Day in spite of continued east wind, went into the old Town on several necessary bussinesses, & visited Mʳ· Erskine of Cambo just returned from London dined & Supt at Lady Riddells meeting Mʳˢ· Riddell & 2 Children in the evening added to the party Miss Bruce of Stenhouse & our young Men. rec'd a Letter from Lady Dukenfield.

Saturday May 5ᵗʰ·

A Wet Morning, but fine evening as busy as possible all Morning with moving preparations, spent the evening chearfuly at Lady Riddells meeting Mʳˢ· Macdowall, Mʳˢ· Fraser Lovatt & Miss Bruce of Kennaird

Sunday May 6ᵗʰ·

A bright & very fine day, tho cold with continued east wind, did not go to Chapel in the

Morning, but to evening Service, in the afternoon Mr W. & calling on Miss Ord staid to drink Tea, home early & wrote to my Sister Travell.

Monday May 7$^{th.}$

Another similiar Day, work'd as hard as possible all Morn: with continued packing sat an hour with Lady Campbell, before going to spend the evening with Lady Riddell where was a party of seven or eight intimates.

Tuesday May 8$^{th.}$

Still bright fine weather but so very much hurried in quitting our poor favorite Mansion that I could little enjoy that or anything else, accomplished all tolerably. & got into our Lodgings in South St Andrews Street to a late Tea finding them pleasant & comfortable rec'd a Letter from Miss B. Guydickens.

Wensday May 9$^{th.}$

A cloudy but dry Morning, & very bright afternoon, went early back to Hanover Street to arrange things for the Sale, on return busy in setting Lodgings in order went late to Cards & Supper at Lady Sinclairs, a large party, many Gentlemen but sadly late.

Thursday May 10$^{th.}$

A shewey Morning, but became at noon rainy & most violently so all the eveng. & night, unlucky for our <u>Roupe</u> at home quietly all Morning dined & supt at Mr Baillies chiefly to meet Mr Sandford only 3 or 4 others besides their own family. much agreable conversation in wch our friend shone. rec'd Letters from M$^{rs.}$ Musson M$^{rs.}$ Granville, & my Sis^r Travell very long expected.

Friday May 11$^{th.}$

A gloomy Morn: which produced a cold showery Day & a very wet night, went out with Lady Riddell in her Coach, to make unsuccessful visits in Georges Square also to call on Lady C: C:, spent the evening with L$^{dy.}$ Riddell at her new Lodgings in Drysdales Hotel, Miss MacFarlan only there Mr Witts supt at Miss Bruces of Stenhouse. rec'd a Letter from Miss Snow. wrote to Miss Anne Snow & M$^{rs.}$ Erskine.

Saturday May 12$^{th.}$

Another showery day, between whiles pleasant enough, & fine in the evening; Lady Sinclair call'd in the Morning after which I visited Lady R. & M$^{rs.}$ Brown caught in a shower. aird in the afternoon with Lady R. accompanied by M$^{rs.}$ Fraser & Miss Bruce, went to Musselburgh & call'd on the young Dukenfields, drank Tea & play'd at Whist after our return Mr Witts being added to the party.

Sunday May 13$^{th.}$

Wind turn'd to the east dark & gloomy strong inclination to rain tho little fell, both services at Charlotte Chapel, between visited M$^{rs.}$ Grant, Miss Ord & M$^{rs.}$ Baillie. cold unpleasant evening quiet at home. wrote to Miss B. Guydickens

Monday May 14th·

An extreme cold disagreable Day strong east wind & frequent small showers, after calling on Lady Riddell went to our late house on some bussiness & made an unsuccessful call or two afterwards Tea, Cards & Supper & Frans· also at Mrs· Com: Browns meeting Mr· Mrs· & Miss Fyffe, & Mr· Graham rather sombre

Tuesday May 15th·

A dry & very pleasant day, I was only out from 3 to 4 going to our old house & a little stroll, rec'd visits from Mrs· Brougham Mrs· Davies & her Sister Clemantine, & Mrs· Campbell of Stonefield, went an airing for an hour with Lady Riddell previous to our spending the evening at Lady Sinclairs, meeting a party of 10 well known friends. rec'd a Letter from Mrs· Rooke.

Wensday May 16th·

Quite a peculiar pleasant fine Day without interruption, well suited to an expedition I took with Lady Riddell accompanied by Lady Sinclair & Mrs· Fraser Lovatt to see Sir George Clerks at Pencuik 12 miles distant,[10] & Mr· Lockharts at Dryden 6 miles distant on our return dined singularly but chearfuly at an ale house at Penicuik, the drive great part of it romantic & beautiful, & the place out of Doors very uncommon & pretty, the House large & handsome in its Architecture, but not good within being divided into small rooms & ill furnish'd, Dryden is a large handsome house standing low & rather dull the grounds fine but want modern improvement did not return to Town till 10 o'clock, staid with Lady R till 11 sending over for Mr· Witts wrote to Ldy· Dukenfield.

Thursday May 17th·

Wet & very wet till after mid.day & very showery the remainder & very cold from frequent hailstorms a much engaged Morning, uninterrupted but by a visit from Miss MacFarlan, Tea, Cards & Supper at Miss Bruces of Stenhouse a party of 12, taken by Lady Riddell in her Coach for whom it was made. recd a Letter from my Sister Travell & wrote to Mrs· Tracy

Friday May 18th·

Quite a cold disagreable day with very high wind & a mixture of sunshine & small showers went out at Noon to make visits found Miss Campbell of Shervan, Mrs· Speirs, Mrs· Dalrymple & Mrs· Brown at home Mr· W. dined with Lord Balgonie as he is Commissioner for his Father Lord Leven Mrs· Davies call'd here before I went in the evening to take a Town airing with Ldy· Riddell, & finishing by going with her to a party of 12 at Miss MacFarlans rather a thick business Tea Cards & Supper.

---

10.   George Clerk (1787–1867), 6th baronet. George succeeded his uncle, John Clerk (d. 1798) as a minor. Penicuik House was built in 1761 by Sir James Clerk, the 4th Laird of Penicuik and 3rd Baronet. Clerk had travelled widely, especially in Italy, and had studied Italian architecture. The house was a great meeting point for figures of Enlightenment Edinburgh, who came to see the collection of paintings, including a noted ceiling painting of Ossian's Hall, by Alexander Runciman. The interior was gutted by fire in 1899, but formerly had many fine rooms. Now a roofless shell, it is constructed of ashlar, it has a central hexastyle portico with two-way stair, piano nobile, basement and Palladian windows. At the time of writing (2015) is currently undergoing a major restoration.

Saturday May 19th.

Dry with constant sunshine, but by no means a pleasant Day, being a prodigeous high wind & dust intolerable, which kept me within all Morning rec'd visits from Mrs. Brown & Georgiana, & Mrs. Fyffe & her two Daughters, went to Tea Cards & supper at Mr. Baillies meeting only their newly arrived English friends Mr. & Miss Hatton very chearful rec'd a Letter from Miss L. Lee wrote to Mrs. Granville

Sunday May 20th.

An exceeding fine clear day, after having calld on Lady Riddell went to St. Georges Chapel in her Seat, between services made an unsuccessful call on Lady Balgonie, went with Lady R. to Charlotte Chapel a peculiar fine sermon from Mr. Sandford, Mr. Witts dined publicly with Lord Balgonie, we <u>all</u> 4 drank Tea by Lady C: Cs bedside on our return sat an hour or two with Lady Riddell who had a large conversation circle chiefly of the Colquhoun Family & Lady Arbuthnot.

Monday 21st.

An uncommon bright fine day, went out early in the Coach with Lady Riddell, first to call on Lady Hailes at New Hailes a very pleasant visit, then to Musselburgh on other calls returning by Leith & ending by visiting Mr. & Mrs. Cleeve Mr. Witts all the day attending the Lord Commissioner Tea Cards & supper at Mr. Baillies very agreable to meet Lady Riddell a party of 15.

Tuesday May 22d.

Not so pleasant a day being a thick close air with no Sun, rec'd visits from Lady Sinclair & Lord Balgonie, before I went out to visit Mrs. Turin, Mrs. Hay & Mrs. Brougham on my return found Mrs. Davies who staid till Dinner time. went with Lady R. to Cards & supper at Mrs. Mures a miserable dull party of 9 or 10.

Wensday May 23d.

A fine & prodigeous hot Day being clear air & broiling sun perfect summer, obliged to go out on bussiness into the old Town, came back quite roasted, taken to dine at Lord Stonefields by Lady Riddell a very pleasant small party, an agreable Englishman one, Lord Webb Seymour[11] sat an hour with Lady Riddell on our return.

Thursday May 24th.

Another quite as hot a day as any of the preceding, went out at Noon to meet Mrs. Dubie at her new house to look over some of her new furniture, afterwards visited Miss Ord & Mrs. Brown the only ones at home of several call'd upon Mrs. Campbell of Stonefield here for an hour in the evening before we went to Tea, Cards & Supper at Mrs. Oliphants, a party of 21 when not half the number were expected extremely unpleasant.

---

11. Lord Webb John Seymour (1777–1819). John Seymour was the fourth son of Webb Seymour, 10th Duke of Somerset (1718–1793), who had married, 1769, Anna Maria (Mary Anne) Bonnell (d. 1802), daughter of John Bonnell, of Stanton Harcourt, Oxfordshire.

Friday May 25th.

Not the least change in the weather as clear & sultry as ever at Noon call'd on Lady Riddell & dawdled a little about with her went to Tea, Cards & Supper at Mrs. Macdowals a very chearful, pleasant party of 14.

Saturday May 26th.

If possible still hotter than ever being a thick sultry air, went to Prayers & Sermon at Charlotte Chapel, went imediately on my return in a Hackney Coach to Lord Stonefields George w.^h me to take an early Dinner & accompany Mrs. Campbell to the Colonels house at Inveresk calling at Musselburgh for the Dukenfields & others from the schools, to drink Tea, & revel in Country air & scenery, return'd to Town at nine & join'd Mr. Witts at Lady Riddells where we pass'd the remainder of the evening.

Sunday May 27th.

Such an intense hot day as was seldom ever felt at any time of the Year so oppressive as scarce to be borne, at Charlotte Chapel, most of the forenoon as being Whit Sunday there was many communicants, Mrs. Davies here for an hour after Tea, walk'd with her &'c in Queen Street before we went to Supper at Miss MacFarlans to meet Lady Riddell, where was likewise Lord & Lady Arbuthnot & Mrs. Fraser.

Monday May 28th.

Hard rain for 2 or 3 hours in the Morning, afterwards clear & fine but changed to quite a sharp air at home all Morn. rec'd visits from Mrs. Mure & Miss Speirs, call'd on Lady Riddell for a few moments before Mr. W. Frank & I went to Cards & Supper at Miss Abercrombies a young very pleasant little party, walk'd both there & back. wrote to Miss Snow & Mrs. Rooke.

Tuesday May 29th.

A very fine pleasant day tho the wind in the east but constant sunshine sat an hour with Lady Riddell, painful because my last visit to her, sat as long very pleasantly with Lady Forbes; walk'd a <u>family</u> party in the evening to Georges Square & the meadows. Mrs. Brown & Margaret here for ½ an hour on our return. rec'd a Letter f^{m.} B. Guydickens

Wensday May 30th.

Quite a fine day in spite of continued east wind at home all the Morning agitated both by pain & pleasure, in seeing poor Lady Riddell set out of England, & receiving a most elegant proof of Mrs. Davies grateful esteem, Mr. Witts at Leith in the Morning, walk'd in the evening all 4 in Queen Street & its environs wrote to my Brother Ferdinand.

Thursday May 31st.

Continued fine weather still warmer than the former Day went at Noon to Georges Square sat an hour with Mrs. Macqueen, & as long a one with Mrs. Carre did some bussiness in the old Town & came home so tired I staid within the remainder of the day. wrote to my Sister Travell

Friday June 1ˢᵗ

Still hot & dry, but not very pleasant from being still an east wind, which caused the air to be thick & oppressive, at home all Morn, had the pleasure of a long visit from Mʳˢ Brougham, & a short one from Mʳˢ Speirs & Miss Helen. went all 4 of us to drink Tea with Mʳ & Miss Campbells at Newington, went in a Hackney Coach to the toll & walk'd back. rec'd a Letter from my Sister Travell

Saturday June 2ᵈ

A fine cooling shower in the Morn. & another short one at mid.day, which caught us & long third one stay on a visit to Mʳˢ Fyffe, call'd also on Lady C: C: & Mʳˢ Brown, late in the evening walk'd with the Boys to Bernards Well Queen St. &'c

Sunday June 3ᵈ

Quite an unpleasant Day being an extreme high wind which made the dust fly <u>intolerably</u>, & strong inclination to rain in the eveng mild & pleasant went to Charlotte Chapel to both services, between visited Mʳˢ Macdowal, walk'd late in Queen Street. wrote to Mʳˢ Wilkinson

Monday June 4ᵗʰ

Dry but another unpleasant Day from continued wind & dust, being the Kings <u>birth</u>day, there was much <u>noisy</u> rejoicing in the street & in Sᵗ Andrews Square all the Volunteer troops drawn forth as last year, our windows commanding so fine a view we had many collected for the spectacle. I never stirr'd out the whole day Mʳ Witts & Frank drinking the Kings health at the parliament House in the evening. wrote Mʳˢ Hyett

Tuesday June 5ᵗʰ

A very pleasant day being bright & clear & with less wind but in the evening an English shower or Scotch mist, made several calls in the new Town those I found at home were Mʳˢ Baillie &'c, Miss Campbell of Shervan & Miss Ord, Miss Campbells from Newington drank Tea with us. wrote to Mʳˢ Erskine

Wensday June 6ᵗʰ

An uncommon fine hot Day so delightful a day is not often seen, Mʳ Witts at Leith &'c, my only Morning visitor was Sir John Wedderburne extremely pleasant, went late to call on Mʳˢ Brown after Tea walk'd to Brown & Georges Square & a little in the Meadows.

Thursday June 7ᵗʰ

Just such another fine warm day staid myself by making several visits those I found at home were Mʳˢ Baillie, Mʳˢ Davies Miss Sinclair & Lady Ramsay to hot & to tired to go out in the evening. wrote to Mʳˢ Savage

Friday June 8ᵗʰ

No kind of change in the weather prudently staid within all Morn: & rec'd visits from Mʳˢ Macdowal, Miss M. Brown, & Sir Willᵐ Ramsay, & Miss Mures after Tea, before we went to walk on the Leith Walk & afterwards in Queen Street. rec'd a Letter from Miss Snow.

Saturday June 9th.

As hot & fine weather as ever if not more so, George confined from school by a little feverish complaint, after making a call or two in the new Town went over the bridge & did some shop bussiness, & to Georges Square to sit an hour with Mrs. Campbell of Stonefield, Cards & Supper at Mrs. Com: Browns, an odd mixt party as usual of Scotch English & French. rec'd Letters from Ldy. Dukenfield & Mrs. Rooke

Sunday June 10th.

Still dry but more wind & less sun than many former Days at Charlotte Chapel both services, before Morning rec'd a visit from Lady Wedderburne & between visited the Bride Mrs. Dalrymple & Mrs. Syme Mrs. Davies & Miss Hatton drank Tea with us, & old Mrs. Auchenlecks call'd for ½ an hour. walk'd for a short time with our Ladies in Queen Street, George still confined.

Monday June 11th.

An extreme hot day from perpetual broiling sun, wch made me keep house till quite <u>night</u> but rec'd many visitors Lady Forbes &'c, Mr. & Mrs. Fyffe Miss Scotts, & Mr. Sandford & Mr. Doremont, & after Tea Mrs. Mathews, when she went Mr. W. Frank & I went to see Lady C: C: returnd over the Calton Hill & sat ½ an hour with Mrs. Brown; George still far from well. rec'd Letters from my Br. Ferdinand & Mrs. Wilkinson

Tuesday June 12th.

Quite a similiar day equaly hot as any of the former, at home all Morning nursing George who was but moderate, Mrs. & Miss Baillies of Polkemmet my only visitors, went to Cards & Supper late at Sir William Ramsays, a pleasant genteel party of near 20. Mr. Witts at Leith in the Morning.

Wensday June 13th.

No change in the weather tho a little lowering in the Morning, George not well yet & poor Frank rather failing with headache & feverish symptoms, I went out for a short time at Noon

The ancient Council House, Coal Hill, Leith. An engraving by T. Stewart from a painting by Daniel Wilson.

visiting M^rs. Mackenzie & M^rs. Brown, late in the evening M^r. W. & I left our nursery & walk'd on the Calton Hill. rec'd a pleasant Letter from L^dy. Riddell.

Thursday June 14th.

Weather if possible more oppressively hot than ever, not a possibility of keeping cool even by perfect quiet. rec'd visits from M^rs. Brown & M^rs. Brougham, Boys both better, went to Tea, Cards & Supper at M^r. Fyffes, an easy chearful young party walk'd home. wrote to Lady Riddell

Friday June 15th.

Still extremely fine & much pleasantter from being quite so intensely hot ventured out in the forenoon to call on Lady Cathcart & Miss Graham both of whom I found at home. M^r. Witts & I drank Tea with M^rs. Erskine in a quiet free way much rational conversation walk'd afterwards in Queen Street rec'd a Letter from M^rs. Rooke & wrote to L^dy. Dukenfield.

Saturday June 16th.

Again most dreadfully hot, never went out nor saw any one till we all 4 (the Boys being got nearly well) went to dine with M^rs. Davies in a pleasant family way, walk'd in the evening in Queen Street till it was late.

Sunday June 17th.

Most oppressively hot again in the Morning, more temperate at Noon, & lowering in the evening with an uncommon thick fog, went to both services at Charlotte Chapel, between visited the Speirs family, & M^r. Davies whom I accompanied to make a first visit to M^rs. Sandford, spent the even^g. at home Miss MacFarlan here for an hour late. rec'd a Letter from M^rs. Erskine.

Monday June 18th.

Fine but not very hot in the Morning a heavy thunder shower at mid.day which M^r. Witts happily escaped on his return from Leith very fine in the evening tho again rather hot, walk'd after Tea to Georges Square & sat ½ an hour with M^rs. Macqueen on our return sat an hour with M^rs. Davies

Tuesday June 19th.

Mild rain early in the Morning which soon cleard off & was a cool & very pleasant Day spent the greater part of the Morning with M^rs. Brougham taking my work late visited Miss Ord, only out for an hour in the evening in Queen Street, eager to return home to my poor Frank who had sufferd dreadfully with the tooth ache. wrote to M^rs. Musson.

Wensday June 20th.

Wet early in the Morning, became dry for a few hours, but after mid.day was wet & very wet the rest of the day, of course saw no one but work'd hard & endeavor to amuse poor Frank who sufferd much from the pain in his face.

Thursday June 21st.

Intirely wet from Morning to night with hardly any interruption, a perfect domestic day again, but happily my Nursery was much better which enlivened the whole party. rec'd a Letter from M^rs. Granville.

Friday June 22^d.

Quite dry but still gloomy sky & rather oppressive M^r. Witts at Leith, & I ventured by myself into the old Town on several bussinesses, Frank being not yet well enough to leave the house, on my return rec'd visits from M^rs. Gregory, & M^r. M. Riddell walk'd in the evening & George with us a Town circuit

Saturday June 23^d.

A charming day, being dry & clear with some sun, did not go out in the Morning nor saw anyone but M^r. Jones, & M^r. David Leslie just arrived from an English school. M^r. Witts & I drank Tea with Lady C: C: walk'd afterwards in Kings Park &'c & home by the Calton Hill.

Sunday June 24th.

An extreme hot Day, tho with considerable wind quite oppressive till the evening went to the Tolbooth Church in Sr James Colquhouns seat to hear the much talk'd of M^r. Simeon by no means pleased either with his matter or manner much more so by our own quiet preacher in the evening at Charlotte Chapel, M^r. Leslie dined & drank Tea, walk'd a little late, in Queen Street rec'd a Letter from my Sister & answerd it.

Monday June 25th.

A moist Morning, but turn'd out a hot fine Day with a good deal of wind M^r. Witts at Leith in the Morning, & Miss Macdonald my only visitor M^rs. Davies, Miss Hatton, & M^rs. D. Erskine drank Tea here, & Lady Cathcart call'd for ½ an hour walk'd late in Queen Street. wrote to Miss Snow & Miss Coxwell an enquiry after M^rs. Tracy.

Tuesday June 26th.

A cloudy Morning which became almost an uninterrupted wet Day tho never very hard rain of course never stirr'd out nor saw anyone

Wensday June 27th.

Very hot & sultry, rather a gloomy sky but no rain fell, & an uncommon pleasant evening, M^r. Witts at Leith but first accompanied poor Frank to have a tooth drawn wch at last failed tho gave him great pain, I made 8 visits in the new Town finding Miss MacFarlan, Miss Melvilles & M^rs. Davies at home walk'd with her & Miss Hatton after Tea on the Calton Hill.

Thursday June 28th.

Wet in the Morning & gloomy the rest of the day with now & then trivial showers at home all the Morning without seeing any one, between Dinner & Tea went with M^r. W. & Frank to Dicksons Chapel in New Street to hear M^r. Simeon preach less pleased with him even than on Sunday came home to Tea & walk'd in Queen Street till ten o'clock very hot & close wrote to M^r. Burslem a Letter long owed.

Revd David Dickson (1754–1820), Minister of the New North Church, Edinburgh. An etching by John Kay, 1797.

Friday June 29th

A dull Morning, which became wet before mid.day, but dry again in the evening, neither went out nor saw any one in the Morning, walk'd only a <u>street</u> walk in the evening. rec'd a Letter from Mrs. Hyett & wrote to Mrs. Browning.

Saturday June 30th

Fine till after the middle of the day when it turn'd out showery & some very strong ones, in one of which detain'd on a visit to Mrs. Macqueen made two other unsuccessful calls in Georges Square & did some bussinesses on the Bridge staid at home all the evening Frank visiting at Leith.

Sunday July 1st

Hot & close with frequent threatening showers but none of any consequence fell, not being quite well my three Gentlemen went to Chapel in the Morning without me before evening Service I made a long visit to Miss Ord drank Tea at Lord Polkemmets a large young party & walk'd in Queen Str.

Monday July 2d

Such perpetual showers all the forenoon & some very violent that it might be call'd almost constant rain, not out in the Morning & saw only Lady Sinclair dined all four at Mrs. Davies's meeting a Captain & Mrs. Lewis, Mr. & Mrs. Sandford & old Mr. White exceedingly pleasant from much conversation, play'd a rubber at Whist not at home till between 10 & 11 when it was fine dry walking.

Tuesday July 3d

A gloomy hot day but little if any rain fell, Mr. Witts & George at Leith, I staid within all Morning & rec'd take leave visits from Captn. & Mrs. Mathews & Mrs. Campbell of Stonefield, all going to the South; Cards & supper at Mrs. Davies's a pleasant but <u>very</u> late party of 20, much singing from Miss Patons

Wensday July 4th

Quite similiar weather extremely hot & late in the evening small rain almost tired to death with walking to Georges Square to see Mrs. Campbell, before they went visited likewise Mrs. Lowis & Mrs. Hamilton & did some bussiness, on the Bridge. went to the Play with Mrs. Davies &'c, to see Mr. & Mrs. Knight in the road to ruin.

Thursday July 5th

A fine day tho rather gloomy, with considerable wind, & after Dinner a hard shower but dry afterwards I was at home all Morning & saw no one Mr. Witts in the Court of Session hearing pleadings on the Bargany cause, after Tea walk'd the Town walk. wrote to Mrs. Erskine call'd on Miss Graham

Friday July 6th.

Fine in the Morning but very showery the rest of the day & some of them very severe ones accompanied M^{r.} & Mrs. Sandford to the Court of Session to hear Mr. Erskine speak for more than three hours sat comfortably but not so well amused as expected walk'd in the streets late in the evening.

Saturday July 7th.

A hot tho windy Morning, wet in the afternoon, but dry again in the evening, Mr. Witts at Leith & I rec'd visits from M^{rs.} G: Fergusson Miss MacFarlan & Henry Brougham, walk'd in the streets as usual when it became dry. rec'd a Letter from Miss Coxwell

Sunday July 8th.

Quite a fine Day without either rain wind & too much sun, being ill with a complaint in my stomach did not go to Chapel in the Morning but foolishly going in the afternoon, was brought home faintly in a Chair & sufferd much for the time. Mrs. Davies & Miss Hatton drank Tea here & I was well enough to walk with them in Queen Street. wrote to Mrs. Tracy.

Monday July 9th.

A fine dry day tho rather windy not going out I rec'd visits from Miss Davidsons, Cap^{tn.} & Mrs. Lowis, & Mrs. Brougham, Tea & Supper at Lady H. Blairs, scarce any one there but her own family walk'd with her to Bernards Well.

Tuesday July 10th.

Another fine day Mr. Witts on his usual bussiness at Leith, Frank accompanied me to visit L^{dy.} C: C: & some other calls in the Cannongate going over the Calton Hill, walk'd in the evening towards Belveine fortunately joining Mrs. Brougham & her Daughter returning from a walk.

Wensday July 11th.

Very much the same weather only a trivial shower or two at Noon, as usual at home all Morning, but saw no one but the two Miss Hays, walk'd in the evening on the Queens Ferry road Queens Street &'c. wrote to Mrs. Rooke

Thursday July 12th.

A clear fine Day with hot sun tho cool wind & a sharp shower in the evening, Mrs. Davies call'd early & we made a visit together & afterwards went all over Mr. Blanes House, I then visited Mrs. Macdowal & Mrs. Brougham, went to Tea Cards & Supper at Mrs. Macdowals, 10 Women to one Man, a good supper & chearful enough tho I lost my money at all games I play'd.

Friday July 13th.

A fine Day with hot sun tho cold wind Mr. Witts as often at Leith, I at home & received visits from Mrs. David Erskine & Miss Bruce of Kennard, walk'd in the evening wth the Boys by the

Lothian road to Bruntsfield Links Georges Square &'c. M^r. Sandford here in the afternoon. rec'd a Letter from Miss Forrest

Saturday July 14th.

A showery Morning, but soon came on most violent showers accompanied by Thunder & continued more or less the whole of the day, wch of course was stay at home & alone.

Sunday July 15th.

Quite as bad if not a more showery day till the evening when it became dry but not pleasant, too bad for me to go to chapel in the Morning & obliged to go in a chair to evening Service from whence we went to dine at M^r. Sandfords to meet M^r. & Miss Doorman from Hamburgh both informing & agreable. walk'd home by Queen S^t. wrote to Miss Forrest on Mrs. Wyndhams match

Monday July 16th.

Very wet & showery accompanied with some Thunder till mid.day when it became dry & fine, call'd on M^r. & Miss Doorman at their Hotel & afterwards made 5 visits in the new Town finding all at home, walk'd street walks in the evening & made a personal enquiry after L^{dy.} H. Blair & sat ½ an hour with Miss Campbell of Shervan. rec'd two Letters from my Sis^r. Travell

Tuesday July 17th.

A remarkable fine day neither too hot, or much wind or sun at home all Morning & saw no one but Miss MacFarlan dined & Frank with us at Mrs. Davies to meet M^r. Fraser & M^r. Christison Miss H. Speirs & Miss Oliphant drank Tea ended one visit by walking in Queen Street. rec'd Letter from L^{dy.} Riddell, L^{dy.} Dukenfield, & Mrs. Erskine & wrote to Mrs. Granville

Wensday July 18th.

Cloudy in the Morning & indeed much of the day with considerable wind & in the evening some showers, Frank breakfasted with Mrs. Oliphant at Leith, I made visits in the new Town, finding Mrs. Mure, Miss Ord, & L^{dy.} B. Cunningham at home a stay at home evening. wrote to my Sis^r. Travell

Thursday July 19th.

Quite a pleasant day neither wet, hot, or windy, M^r. Witts at Leith absolutely taking our passage in the George & Mary Cap^{tn.} Hog, Frank walk'd with me to visit Mrs. Macqueen & Mrs. Davidson after Tea visited Mrs. Graham of Airth at Mrs. David Erskines, Mrs. Bell at L^{dy.} H: Blairs & Miss Campbell of Sherwar, & walk'd in Queens S^t. till it was dark. rec'd a Letter from Mrs. Whalley.

Friday July 20th.

An intire wet day excepting 3 or 4 hours at mid.day & in the evening extremely hard rain fir for nothing but home employments wrote to Mrs. Browne.

Saturday July 21ˢᵗ·

Dry & bright in the Morning but very windy & during the course of the day perpetual hard showers w.ᶜʰ made all going out impossible & Mʳ· Witts had a very bad cold, bussied ourselves with beginning to pack up.

Sunday July 22ᵈ·

Still stormy but the showers were trifling & less frequent which allow'd me to go both times to Chapel, between services Mʳ· Oliphant call'd on us from Leith & put us in a hurry by his ideas of the speedy departure of the Hamburgh Ships; Dʳ· Duncan drank Tea with us, & much entertain'd & inform'd us Mʳˢ· Davies & Miss Hatton call'd on me to walk in Queen Street where it was pleasant.

Monday July 23ᵈ·

Quite a fine Day without any rain but rather cloudy in the evening, Frank Breakfasted at Leith & we learnt with some precision we were to sail on the 2ᵈ· of August Mʳ· Witts accompanied me to visit Lady C: C: & Mʳˢ· Brown just return'd from Fife, in the evening call'd on Mʳˢ· Davies & walk'd with her & Miss Hatton

Tuesday July 24ᵗʰ·

Another day with only a very little rain early in the Morning & extremely fine afterwards much engaged in packing all Morn M. Brown call'd before Dinner to ask us to Tea to meet Dʳ· & Mʳˢ· Thomas. walk'd a little in Queen Stʳ· afterwards. rec'd a most affecting Letter from Dʳ· Pennington, wrote to Lady Grey, Miss Snow, & Miss Lee.

Wensday July 25ᵗʰ·

Tho an east wind a fine Day with hot Sun till afternoon when it became cloudy & small showers fell, made 11 visits in the new Town finding 7 at home, after Tea made three more in my Queen Street walk finding only Miss Campbell of Shervan at home. wrote to Lord Edward Bentinck.

Thursday July 26ᵗʰ·

Rather showery in the forenoon but clear & fine in the evening, busy all the Morning in a variety of preparatory bussiness therefore saw no one after Tea, made 4 visits finding only Miss Mackay at home, & afterwards sat an hour with Mʳˢ· Davies who was much out of spirits on her poor Cousins death. wrote to Lady Dukenfield.

Friday July 27ᵗʰ·

A fine dry day not out all Morning being much engaged in packing, & saw no one, but Mʳ· Oliphant from Leith, went to Drink Tea with Miss Ord, & afterwards to sup with Mʳˢ· Oliphant a stupid small party. wrote to Lady Riddell

Dr Andrew Duncan (1744–1828). In 1789 Dr Duncan was elected to the Professorship of the Theory of Medicine in the University of Edinburgh. An etching by John Kay, 1797.

Saturday July 28th.

A cloudy Morning & in the course of the forenoon several flitting showers fell yet I paid no attention but walk'd to Georges Square to make visits finding only Mrs. Douglass Cavers & Mrs. Lowis at home, the Boys dined at Mr. Campbells at Newington, Mrs. Davies & Miss Hatton drank Tea here & when they left us, we went to a large mixt party at Mrs. Com. Browns pleasant enough.

Sunday July 29th.

An intire fine Day, went to both services at Charlotte Chapel, between visited Lady Forbes & Lady Sinclair both at home. little Doorman dined with us & we drank Tea with Mrs. Davies. rec'd a letter from Miss Forrest.

Monday July 30th.

Wet & stormy in the Morning & rather showery all the forenoon, the Boys breakfasted with Mrs. Douglass Cavers, between the showers I contrived to make several visits finding Ldy. Blair, Mrs. Sandford, Miss Hays, Mrs. Davies & Lady B. Cunningham at home, went late in the evening to sit an hour with poor Lady C: C: rec'd a Letter from Miss Snow & wrote to my Sister Travell

Tuesday July 31st.

A most wretched day of wind & rain quite a tempest, most unfortunate for the Races w.ch begun the day before, the Morning spent in packing, all of us dined with Mrs. Davies, poor Miss Hatton confined to her Bed with a little fever just dry enough to walk home. interested by reading Clèrys new publication.

Wensday Augst. 1st.

Weather dry but not pleasant being a thick gloomy east wind, I again made visits finding Mrs. Mackenzie, Mr. D. Erskine, Mrs. Davies & Mrs. Brown at home, all of us dined at Lady Sinclairs a family party not very gay on my return home sat ½ an hour w.th Miss Campbell rec'd a Letter from Mrs. Rooke.

Thursday Augst. 2d.

Dry tho cloudy early in the Morning but soon most violent showers came on, & wet till Dinner time, Mr. Witts out on many bussinesses & poor Frank at Leith convoy Hunting I recd a visit from Sir John Callandar & made a long interesting one to Mrs. Brougham much affected with parting from her, after Tea made visits to Ldy. H. Blair & Mrs. Davies to enquire after Miss Hatton wrote to Mrs. Erskine.

Friday Augst. 3d.

Another showery & very disagreable Day being little dry but for 3 or 4 hours & then gloomy, extremely busy all Morning with in packing, made a last visit to Miss MacFarlan, & dined in a family way at Mr. Com: Browns he being returnd from London, call'd late in the evening on Mr. & Mrs. Sandford, & supt at Lady H. Blairs in a most friendly way. rec'd a Letter from Lady Dukenfield.

The harbour at Leith.

Saturday Aug^{st.} *4*^{th.}

Dismaly wet early in the Morning, a sad prospect for our final pack & departure, but happily cleard off before the Coach was loaded to go down to Leith, much fatigued, & a good deal agitated, made a last call on Dear Mrs. Davies, & also on poor Lady C: C: on our way to Leith grieving parting both. took up our abode at Blackbulls Tavern at Leith, sad confusion being the end of the Races, very glad to obtain a Bed in a private house Cap^{tn.} Hog not advising us to go on board till Morning Mr. Witts absent from us all the evening going in a Boat to the vessel to see the Carriage safely deposited. rec'd a Letter from my Sister Travell.

Sunday Aug^{st.} *5*^{th.}

A very promising Day, both of sun & wind which improved hourly, between 11 & 12 went in a small boat with the Cap^{tn.} & 2 Gentlemen passengers, to the George & Mary which lay in the roads & about an hour after set sail the wind so favourable that we were nearly out of sight of land the next Morning, our accomodations realy tolerable, & our provisions good, & Mr. Ryan an uncommon pleasant companion for the three first days I sufferd much from incessant sickness but afterwards stand it well. Francis writing a minute Journal, I shall only say we landed at Hamburgh on Monday evening the 13th. having been much pleased with our sail up the Elbe accompanied Mr. Ryan to his Hotel l'Copenhagen accomodations bad enough glad to go to our repose early.

Appendix 1

The Witts Family

The Witts family originated in the Netherlands, probably under the name de Witt (or de Witts). Two brothers—Edward and Thomas—settled in England at Aldbourne in Wiltshire, possibly as protestant exiles from the Spanish enforcement of Catholicism. The date is unknown, but most immigrants to England were from the southern Netherlands and the main period of migration was after the commencement of the eighty years' war in 1568. They may have been weavers or had other skills within the textile industry and joined many others of their countrymen settling in the woollen cloth industry areas of the west of England.

Edward flourished, but Thomas became poor. The parish register for the Civil War period is missing—having been removed to St Omer in France for 'safe-keeping' and never having been returned and so early references to Edward and Thomas are unavailable. The first documentary evidence is for the marriage of Edward Witts of Aldbourne to Joane Hinton (Jane Fenton?) in 1649. Their son Edward (1650-1715), also of Aldbourne, married (secondly) Miriam Adams. Their son Edward (1676-1736) married Sarah Broome of Witney in 1701 and they presumably made their main home at Witney, while also maintaining strong links with Aldbourne.

The Broome family was one of distinction in the Witney area and the marriage alliance would have been deemed a good one. Sarah's father Richard was the last of the male line in that branch and so presumably some of the Broome family wealth devolved to Edward and Sarah.

Of the seven children, our interest is in the fourth born, Broome Witts (1713-1768). Broome married Apphia Anthony in 1741 and they settled in Chipping Norton, Oxfordshire, where Broome became a prominent member of society. He was a successful woolstapler and carried on his business in Chipping Norton and at Friday Street in London, sharing out his time between the two establishments and residing at both. He was also the Receiver General of taxes for Oxfordshire. Apphia died in 1760 and Broome followed her in 1768 after an attack of smallpox. Broome may not have been the originator of this business, for it appears that a business of linen drapers operating under the name of Witts & Porter had been active in Friday Street as early as 1740. Broome could have originated the business in his twenties but it is more likely that it commenced under his father Edward following his move from Aldbourne to Witney.

The business continued at Friday Street following Broome's death and the tenancy was held by widow Witts. This is probably the widow of Edward who had died in 1754. She seems to have been assisted by her son Broome (another Broome, nephew to Broome of Chipping Norton) and eventually also by her grandson Broome P. Witts—the line of the Witney Witts.

The Witney Witts

It seems from the above that the brothers Edward and Broome were quite close and were in business together continuing to develop their father's business. The eldest brother, Edward, made his base in Witney and almost certainly maintained strong contacts with the 'Aldbourne Witts.' Like his brother Broome, Edward became prominent in his town. He was twice bailiff and had a shop and warehouse adjoining the town hall, rented Farm Mills, and was a general dealer, chapman and wool dealer. All of the family at this time appear to have been strong Quakers:

25 August 1828
The family of the Witts's was originally a dissenting family: B. P. Witts's branch is still; my Grandfather went both to Church & meeting, but had his children baptized in the Church of England, to which all his descendants have adhered.

Edward died in 1754, presumably leaving the business to his wife and son. This son Broome, together with his first cousin, also named Broome (*see* pedigree above—Broome Witts, 1744-1827) then married two sisters bearing the surname London. 'Chipping Norton' Broome married the youngest, Amelia London; 'Witney' Broome married the eldest, Elizabeth. 'Witney' Broome and his bride then moved to new suburbs near to Camberwell, setting up the branch of the 'Witney Witts' that we might refer to as the 'Champion Hill Witts'.

At a period between the 1770s and 1790s the business changed with the emphasis being placed on silk instead of wool. The major centre of silk manufacture was at Spitalfields, little more than a fifteen minute walk from Friday Street. By the 1790s the driving force of the business was the grandson—Broome Philips Witts—and he was wealthy enough at the turn of the century to buy a spacious house in Brunswick Square. In 1794 he was in partnership as Witts & Rowley at 21 Friday Street—silk weavers & muslin warehouse. In 1799 he appears to have been by himself and took the enterprising decision of employing George Courtauld, to convert a flour mill in Pebmarsh, Essex into a silk mill to utilise the water power. George was born in 1761 and apprenticed to the silk trade in 1775. After setting up a throwsting mill in Spitalfields, unsuccessfully, he went to America. He seems to have travelled back and forth several times before accepting the commission from Broome P. Witts. As manager he was paid £350 a year, plus a house and five acres of land. In 1809 he left B. P. Witts's employment and opened up his own mill nearby in Braintree—thus started the mighty Courtaulds Textiles empire. This Braintree mill was soon being run by his American born son, Samuel and the Courtaulds business developed speedily from this point. Other Spitalfield manufacturers seemed to have followed and silk manufacture soon became centred around Essex and Suffolk. At its height in the 1850s the industry employed 6,500 workers.

The Chipping Norton Witts.

As mentioned above, Broome Witts married Apphia Anthony in 1741. Of their nine children it is known that George and Anthony died in infancy. The five main siblings of Edward Witts were Apphia (1743-1840), Broome (1744-1827), Sarah (1745-1834), Richard (1747-1815) and John (1751-1816)—all of whom appear in the diaries of Agnes and Francis Witts. A sixth surviving sibling—Alice (1742-1800)—fleetingly appears in Agnes's diary entry for Wednesday 13 May 1789: '—*Very hot & windy, went soon after Breakfast taking Lady Lyttelton with us to see Mrs. Williams in her retreat at Rotherhithe....*' And that is the last that is heard of her.

The eldest male sibling, Broome, took no interest in the family business. He married Amelia London and settled at Nibley House, North Nibley, Gloucestershire as a gentleman farmer at sometime around 1793, in fact Edward and Agnes accompanied him on viewings of the property when he was considering it. He was a churchman, but Amelia retained her nonconformist views and attended Rowland Hill's tabernacle in Wotton-under-Edge. Soon after 1802 the house and estate was sold by the Smythe family and Broome managed to buy himself out of the tenancy. He then moved to Cookham near Maidenhead where he bought an attractive estate adjoining the banks of the Thames named 'The Retreat'. He and Amelia lived here on the Berkshire side of the river for a number of years, and later bought a villa on the opposite site of river, named Cookham Grove, living there until his death in 1827. There were no children of the marriage. They were well-respected in the area and considered rather more than gentry.

Following Edward Witts' business failure there was some friction in the family when the support expected from his elder brother was not forthcoming. Letters from Edward to his sister, Lady Lyttelton, describe the bad feeling:

My Brother Broome, came yesterday to me, by my desire: but his Visit turned out the very reverse, of what I expected. & whatever feeling you discoverd in his mind on the occasions, that arose when you was at Nibley— it was all evaporated before he came under my Roof: as instead of Sympathy or compassion —, he seemed to regret that our settled income was so secured, as to prevent him the effect of Bankruptcy. in truth that is all we have left; & tho' I asked him to be a Trustee to my Affairs, he said very calmly, he was so little of a Man of bussiness that he hardly ever choze to put pen to paper. — His contempt of the World, from having restored a once broken fortune, ought not to have appeard in a House of distress— & is totally the reverse of Richard, who tho he has lately raised Money to assist me has sent a Letter worthy of a Brother & a friend in Affiction.

This letter, written in March 1793 from Rodborough seems to indicate that bankruptcy might be avoided—but it was not to be and eventually all was sold expect for certain items allowed by the commissioner. What benefit Broome might have gained from Edward's eventual bankruptcy is not clear. The discord did not last, and on 29 August 1794 Broome visited and stayed with Edward and Agnes in Edinburgh while on business there. A further eight years on and friendly terms were firmly restored. Edward, Agnes and the two boys stayed with Broome and Amelia at Nibley House between November 1800 and January 1801. During this period, a serious effort was being made to send Frank to Oxford, and Broome offered £25 per year as his contribution to the plan.

In later years Francis (Frank) was to enjoy considerable inheritance from his uncle; a large part of the family path back to prosperity.

Interesting family information comes from a Francis Witts's diary extract:

Wednesday 14 November 1827
... we received the melancholy information of the death of my Uncle. It was conveyed to me in a letter from Mr Edward Witts of Champion Hill, nephew to my Aunt, and our distant cousin, who was at Cookham Grove, when the event happened about eight o clock on Sunday evening ... I

have no distinct grounds of conjecturing, what may be the provisions of my uncle's will; doubtless, his widow will enjoy all for her life, and the disposal of her own considerable fortune after her death; but my uncle leaves a paternal estate in the city of London, besides other landed & personal property, all in his own disposal. I am the immediate heir, as the son of his next brother, & now become by my Uncle's decease the head of the Chipping Norton branch of the Witts family, as Mr Witts of Brunswick Square is of that branch, which was the older and settled at Witney. I am inclined to think, my uncle has considered me as his representative; a little time will shew: should it not be so, thanks be to GOD for the competence, I already enjoy through his money.

Francis went to the funeral and was at the reading of the will afterwards:

… I was made residuary legatee: What such residue may be I cannot form any judgment, but I should not think above £2000 or £3000.

Apphia, Lady Lyttelton

The eldest of the Chipping Norton Witts's was the most famous of the brood. Apphia had been engaged to her cousin, Richard Witts, and after three years of exchanging letters, she sailed to India in 1769 to marry him, only to find on her arrival that he had died. They had not seen each other since he departed for India in 1763, when she was just a seventeen-year-old girl. Within a matter of months she found a husband—someone a little older with a distinguished career behind him, for Colonel Joseph Peach had been in the army since 1746 and had fought in the Canada campaign of 1754-55. He was present at the successful attack at the Heights of Abraham in Quebec in 1759 where he was wounded and where General Wolfe was killed. In the late 1760s he found himself in India as Governor of Calcutta and was on hand to comfort the young lady who had expected to meet her fiancé. They married in 1770, but the union was short-lived, for within six months Joseph Peach was also dead and Apphia returned to England a rich young widow. With her new found wealth and a decided taste for rural life in splendid surroundings she bought the Leasowes near Hagley, once the residence of the poet Shenstone. The grounds at Leasowes had been the glory and the downfall of Shenstone. He was the first to use the French term 'Ferme Ornée' — it exactly expressed the character of his grounds. It was not long before word of Apphia Peach's fortune of £28,000 reached the ears of her neighbour, Thomas Lord Lyttelton. Although he could be charming, Thomas already had a formidable reputation as a profligate, a gambler and a rake. Quite how Apphia was taken in by him is a mystery, but in a whirlwind romance—seemingly cynical on his part and sincere on hers—the couple gained the blessing of George, 1st Lord Lyttelton (the good lord Lyttelton, Thomas's father) and married on 26 June 1772. William Combe, the author of *Dr Syntax* described Lyttelton in scathing terms in his *Diaboliad*, dedicated 'To the worst man in His Majesty's Dominions,' introducing him with his satellite cousin, Captain Ayscough:

> Is there a guilty deed I have not done,
> What say you, Coz? The Captain's answer 'None.'
> Have I not acted every villain's part?

> Have I not broke a noble parent's heart?
> Do I not daily boast how I've betrayed
> The tender widow and the virtuous maid?
> By deeds of ill have I not seemd to live?
> The Captain gave a bold affirmative.

That Thomas was a man of great capabilities was clear enough. His outstanding abilities were attested by Chatham, Burke and by Shelburne, and yet these gifts were lent towards misdoings. The elder Lord Lyttelton said there was a streak of madness in his son's character which might exempt his misdoings from punishment in the next world. Charles James Fox called him 'a very bad man—downright wicked.' Horace Walpole in his *Last Journals*, August 1773, writes that his 'natural parts' were better than his father's, but that his 'detestable character was devoid of every principle and sentiment that became a man [that his] ingratitude, profligacy, extravagance, and want of honour and decency seemed to aim at nothing but afflicting his father, shocking mankind, and disgracing himself.'

The marriage lasted only eight months. In February 1773 a separation was agreed upon and Tom went off to live with a mistress and their illegitimate child. Lord Lyttelton senior championed his daughter-in-law's cause and seems to have been very close to her. The Queen told Lord Lyttelton that 'she had made a new acquaintance with a relative of his which gave her pleasure, as Mrs. Lyttelton had a universal good character.' The pair—father-in-law and Apphia seemed to have got on remarkably well and the London season suited them both, with the elderly lord at his brightest for years and Apphia also enjoying herself. Unfortunately his protection did not last long, for he died on 22 August 1773.

Even more unfortunate for Apphia were the rumours that circulated in London about her relationship with her father-in-law. A novel which appeared in 1775 under the title *The Correspondents, An Original Novel* was rumoured around Town to have been genuine letters between Apphia and her father-in-law. Horace Walpole believed it to be true, but it is almost certainly a forgery, although it did give Apphia celebrity status for a good while. Fanny Burney— the author of the gothic novel *Evelina*, writing in 1782 tells of a party at which she met Mrs Boscawen, Mrs Chapone, Hannah More, Mrs Carter, Mrs Baker, Mr Wraxall, General Paoli, Mrs Garrick, Sir Joshua Reynolds and 'all the belles esprits.' She adds:

> I was also gratqified by meeting with the lady of the late young Lord Lyttelton, who was made very celebrated by the book called the *Correspondents*, which was asserted to be written by her and the old Lord Lyttelton, but proves to be an impertinent forgery. She is still pretty, though a little passée, and very elegant and pleasing in her manners.

This extract shows that Apphia was at the heart of society and interestingly many of these people became long-standing friends as young Frank Witts witnessed eighteen years later:

13 May 1800
We all met & dined at Lady Lytteltons . . . Lady Lytteltons universal kindness was extreme I assisted as Landlord, & she behaved to me with the greatest affection: in a kind aunt some little eccentricities may be forgiven. We returned home after dinner & prepared to attend a party there at 8 o'clock.

I cannot say, it was any thing very charming, but I was highly delighted by the kind & friendly manner, in which Principal Gordon met us. General Paoli was also there. We were introduced to Mr Boldero the Banker. We supped there, & returned after midnight.

Although the book was shown to be a forgery, mud sticks, and to this day copies of *The Correspondents* in libraries carry the legend 'said to be based on correspondence between George, Lord Lyttelton and Mrs Apphia Peach'.

Apphia's estranged husband developed a parliamentary career on the side of the Tories (partially explaining Fox's bitter statements) and much is written about him—but nowhere near as much as was later written on his dramatic end. Dr Johnson put it this way:

Sir, it is the most extraordinary thing that has happened in my day—I heard it with my own ears from his uncle, Lord Westcote. I am so glad to have every evidence of the spiritual world that I am willing to believe it.

Johnson's friend, Dr William Adams replied, 'You have evidence enough—good evidence, which needs no support.' Dr Johnson growled out, 'I like to have more!' Thus the Doctor was willing to believe what it suited him to believe, even though he had the tale at third or fourth hand; for Lord Westcote was not with the wicked Lord Lyttelton at the time of his death, on 27 November 1779. Dr Johnson's observations were made on 12 June 1784. Lord Westcote was Thomas Lyttelton's uncle and his report—presumably as he gave it to Johnson was as follows:

On Thursday the 25th of November, 1779, Thomas Lord Lyttelton, when he came to breakfast, declared to Mrs. Flood, wife of Frederick Flood Esq. of the Kingdom of Ireland, and to the three Miss Amphletts (who were lodged in his house in Hill Street, London, where he then also was) that he had had an extraordinary dream the Night before. He said he thought he was in a room which a Bird flew into, which appearance was suddenly changed into that of a Woman dressed in white, who bade him prepare to die, to which he answered 'I hope not soon, not in two months.' She replied: 'Yes, in three days.' He said he did not much regard it because he could in some measure account for it, for that a few days before he had been with Mrs. Dawson when a Robin Redbreast flew into her room.

When he had dressed himself that day to go to the House of Lords, he said he thought he did not look as if he was likely to die. In the Evening of the following Day, being Friday, he told the eldest Miss Amphlett, that she look'd melancholy; but, said he 'You are foolish and fearfull, I have lived two Days and God willing I will live out the third: On the morning of Saturday he told the same ladies that he was very well, and believ'd he *shou'd bilk the Ghost*. Some hours afterwards he went with them, Mr Fortescue and Captain Wolseley, to Pitt Place at Epsom; withdrew to his bedchamber soon after eleven o'clock at night, talked cheerfully to his servant, and particularly inquir'd of him what care had been taken to provide good Rolls for his breakfast the Next Morning; step'd into bed with his waistcoat on, and as his servant was pulling it off, put, his hand to his side, sank back, and immediately expired without a groan.

The many reports about the death of the Wicked Lord Littleton are numerous and interesting but this is not the place to narrate them. What precisely Apphia did following the death of her estranged husband is not known. Nor do we know what happened to her £28,000 but we may surmise that her husband squandered it. A flashback in the diaries provides some information:

Tuesday 31 July 1827

At the expiration of two hours & twenty minutes we arrived at Peachfield lodge, for such is the name, which my good Aunt has at last given to her singular abode; a name recalling to her memory her earlier matrimonial connection, the more auspicious of the two, that which subsisted between herself, and a respectable Colonel Peach, of the East India Company's service, much her Senior in years, who paid his addresses to her in that distant clime, whither she had gone to fulfil an engagement with a cousin, an Edward Witts, in the company's service, but who had died previously to her arrival at Madras. Death soon removed the worthy colonel, and his young widow, a sincere mourner, returned to her native land with twenty thousand pounds, which he had left her, and many romantic ideas. She in an evil hour accepted the addresses of the profligate, selfish, unprincipled M.r Lyttelton; he deserted her, she took refuge in the protection of his excellent Father, who then lived. The solid good of her Indian thousands was commuted for a settlement of £1000 per ann. on the Hagley Property.

On Frank Witts' first visit to London in 1801 he had the opportunity of visiting his aunt on many occasions, and the cultured literary and social scene enjoyed by his aunt was evident in his reference to a 'blue stocking party':

21 May 1801

Returning home with Lady Lyttelton & Miss Eycott, we called upon Miss Forrest, I afterwards dined with her Ladyship. In the Evening I again repaired there & met chiefly a blue stocking party; blind Dr Moyne, the two Grecian Historians, Gillies & Mitford, Mrs. Goodenough, Miss Fords, Miss Guydickens's, &c. I had much conversation with the latter, as also with Dr. Gillies & a very agreable young man, Mr. Holford.—After seeing Miss Ford home, I repaired to our lodgings.

The social life of Lady Lyttelton continued the following week with another soirée:

Wednesday 27 May

In the Evening to a party at Lady Lyttelton's, which was musical; The Harp, Grand Piano Forte & voice; the chief performers were, Miss Hadsley, Miss Bowles, Miss Canning, Miss Kearney, the Misses Halifax, Miss Stanhope, le Compte de Montmorency &c. Among the Company I particularly remarked le Duc de Montpensier, Mr. & Mrs. Kearney, the Miss Guydickens, Mr. Wood, Mrs. Goodenough, Mrs. Canning &c.

This gathering was prestigious. The duc was the younger son of Louis Phillipe who became King of France in 1830. Mrs. Canning was probably the first cousin of the Miss Guydickens, the mother of George Canning the future prime minister.

By 1808, Lady Lyttelton was finding the expense of a London establishment too great and hints at economy were being made:

Monday 22 February 1808—17 Berkley Street, Portman Square.

Arrived at 10 o clock in Piccadilly, & after breakfasting with Wm. Headley at Hatchett's, came to my Aunt Lady Lyttletons, whom I found economising but not comfortably.

By 1802 we find Lady Lyttelton back in a rural idyll, but not at such a grand extent at Leasowes. Instead she settled for the fashionable but modest setting of Great Malvern in Worcestershire. A flashback gives the year: *9 May 1825 ... having resided in the parish three & twenty years.* It may be presumed that the expense of the Berkeley Street house proved too much and sometime after 1808 she must have decided to give up London and have Malvern as her only base.

It seems that Apphia had the same enthusiasm for life as her brother Edward and the word 'romance' is used on several occasions. Earnestness, enthusiasm—with a comprehensive mind and considerable range of information. A vivid and vital woman—even if, in Frank's words—slight eccentricity exists. As we shall see from the following passage, Frank chooses a delightful euphemism to describe the workings of her mind when he says 'her ideas rarely flow in the same current as those of the generality of the world...'

Monday 9 May 1825
My Aunt's house is in the valley beneath the village of Great Malvern, from which its distance may be a mile & half, being on the verge of a common, part of the ancient Malvern chase, now known by the name of Barnards Green. It is a new erection of her Ladyship, who, though an octogenarian, is a person of most active mind: her ideas rarely flow in the same current as those of the generality of the world, and her taste in building is as peculiar as in other respects. Hence we see two very enjoyable, lofty & spacious sitting rooms appended to a nest of cottage parlours, diminutive sleeping rooms, or rather closets, and comical contrivances in the way of offices, passages & staircases; The whole covering no inconsiderable portion of a garden, which is yet in its infancy. This place, still without a name, my Aunt has been preparing as a city of refuge, when her lease should cease of Pickham Grove, another cottage on the same common, not many hundred yards distant, which she has occupied for many years, having resided in the parish three & twenty years.

Francis did his best to keep up the connections and seems to have seen his aunt about once a year during this period. His snobbishness about titled connections seems to come out in this following extract relating to a rare visit from his aunt:

Wednesday 24 September 1828
We received this evening, to pass a day or two with us, my aunt Lady Lyttelton, who with wonderful energy had accepted of an invitation to Stanway from Lady Elcho, and had arrived there on Saturday last. We had written to intreat her to prolong her journey hither, if it were only for a day or two, and begged her to bring her friend and companion at Stanway, Lady Juliana Annesley, half sister to Earl Mount-norris, sister to Lady John Somerset, &c. This elegant young woman, a connection of the Lyttelton family, is a frequent and favoured guest at Peachfield Lodge; but being very acceptable to the circle at Stanway she was detained there, & could not accept our invitation. I thought my Aunt stouter than when I parted from her in the summer at Malvern.

In reading the diary one cannot help but be struck by the sense of vultures in waiting. Almost certainly there was sense of family and concern, but equally the younger generations of the family being in attendance could really only have justified their existence there, for as long as they did, in a sense of expectation—and almost certainly the same was true of Francis, although delicacy forbade any mention of the degree of expectation. Apphia, Lady Lyttelton, kept them all waiting, but at last she gave in to nature:

Sunday 12 April 1840

In the afternoon a messenger arrived from Malvern dispatched by Captain Witts with a letter to announce to me the decease of our aged Aunt, Lady Lyttelton, which took place about 4 o cl. P.M. yesterday. Her release must be considered a happy one, as relates both to herself and others, for she had been so long decaying in bodily strength, and in the powers of her mind, that she was reduced to the most helpless state of second childhood. My cousin urges me to set out immediately for Peachfield Lodge, feeling that nothing can be done as to the funeral or other arrangements till my arrival …

Francis was not disappointed. His aunt left the bulk of her estate to Edward, Francis's son. The effort had been worthwhile. Francis most certainly had a very high regard for his aunt, he found her amusing, cultivated, but equally he found her eccentric to a high degree. She came from the generation that separated the raw eighteenth century from the extreme politeness of the later part of the century. She was well-connected, had natural intelligence and mixed in a very interesting set of people. She had been presented at court and had caught the attention of the Queen, she mixed with the literati of the age and through a book wrongly attributed to her, she had become an overnight celebrity. All-in-all Apphia was an amazing woman living at an amazing time.

The Tracy and Travell Pedigree

Agnes was descended from John Tracy, 3rd Viscount Tracy of Rathcoole. Her mother, Anne Tracy (1701-1763), married John Travell (1699-1762), of Swerford House, Oxfordshire. John was from a wealthy mercantile family with business in London.

At the time of the Edinburgh diaries, Agnes had four living siblings. There were two unmarried sisters living in Cheltenham; Anne (1738-1826) and Catherine (1742-1804). Agnes's eldest brother, Francis (1728-1801), lived at Swerford, but Agnes had little contact with him. Her younger brother, Ferdinando, remained much closer, probably through the fact that they were nearer in age. Ferdinando Tracy Travell (1740-1808) was a widower and rector of Upper Slaughter, Gloucestershire; he had two grown and married daughters, Martha (1764-1839) and Jane (1765-1797). Agnes was close to both of her nieces and Jane features in the Edinburgh diaries.

Despite the closeness of Agnes to Ferdinando there were often fractious letters and these recur throughout the Edinburgh years. Whether or not Ferdinando approved of the move to Edinburgh is not clear, but Agnes frequently refers to letters from her brother in her daily diary entries. Despite the acerbic views being aired back and forth, Ferdinando proved to be a strong support and following the family's return from Denmark in 1801 he provided about one third of the cost of sending Francis to Oxford.

A much fuller history of the Witts and Travell families can be found in *The Nomad: The Complete Diary of a Cotswold Parson*, volume 1, 2008. ISBN 978-1-84868-000-5.

Letters from Edward and Agnes Witts
From Bownham House and Edinburgh and Elsewhere

Bownham House 21. March 1793

Dear Lady Lyttelton

I am much obliged to you—for all the kind expressions in your Letter of the 17th: & take an early opportunity to answer it: as the Crisis of our Journey, I hope is not far distant: for when a Plan is once formed, the sooner it is accomplishd in all respects the better. but you seem not to understand that the Education of our Boys—under our own Eyes, as well under our Roof, is absolutely necessary to our reduced income, & for which Motive, we move to Scotland where oeconomy & Education, go hand in hand.—The Charter House & Merchants Taylors, must therefore give way to the necessity, the deprivation of Trade, makes necessary, tho it will allow us the society we should have lost; & the opportunity of watching their morals & principles; which our new Situation will afford; I hope, & repay us, for the Exile, we pursue on such well founded motives. We have not yet fixed what Servant attends my wife, one English one is absolutely necessary; & *Lord & Lady Elcho last week dedicated part of 3 days to a full Consideration & plan for our removal, Situation & Reception in Scotland whenever we go. . & nobody can be better informed in all Respects than they are.* My Brother Broome, came yesterday to me, by my desire: but his Visit turned out the very reverse, of what I expected. & whatever feeling you discoverd in his mind on the occasions, that arose when you was at Nibley—it was all evaporated before he came under my Roof: as instead of Sympathy or compassion—, he seemed to regret that our settled income was so secured, as to prevent him the effect of Bankruptcy. in truth that is all we have left; & tho' I asked him to be a Trustee to my Affairs, he said very calmly, he was so little of a Man of bussiness that he hardly ever choze to put pen to paper.—His contempt of the World, from having restored a once broken fortune, ought not to have appeard in a House of distress—& is totally the reverse of Richard, who tho he has lately raised Money to assist me has sent a Letter worthy of a Brother & a friend in Affiction. Molly the Boys Servt is the person we wish to take with us & Kitty has had several offers thro' my Wife: but at present is not informed of them: when she is you shall hear. My two Sisters from Cheltenham come us tomorrow & probably stay till we go—We therefore shall not have an opportunity of seeing the party of Nibley again, & indeed parting Scenes without congenial feelings, are better avoided—the Settlement my Brother, had the hardness to tell my Wife to her face, was too much for her—perhaps you are a stranger to. it is £2500 of my personalty & my Estate at Chip Norton which now produces—about £110.—in all perhaps £210. besides the Annuity for my Life of ye D. of Malbro', which if my Brother had had the happiness of being a Father; he would not think too much for their maintainance & Education, so far different am I in that respect, that any bounty will be thankfully received by me; to extend that Education ,beyond the narrow limits I am now engaging in—I confess I am much hurt, wounded minds as ours are, XXX ill bear oppressive Treatment. My Wife presses her kind Regards to those of your affectionate

Friend & Brother
Edwd: Witts.

Calwich June 14th. (1793)

My Dear Lady Lyttelton

Your Letter Rivy witht date either of time or place left me in ignorance concerning it, otherwise than that I had sincere pleasure in hearing that you thought yourself better for your residence near the Seaside & I heartily wish the benifit you have rec'd may prove lucky; when I rec'd your Letter, Mr. Witts had left me here with our good & kind friends, while he went into Oxfordshire, in the vain hope of concluding his unfortunate affairs in some measure to his satisfaction, but the very harsh & cruel treatment we continue to meet with leaves us little hope of a speedy, or happy conclusion, & has so much depress'd my spirits that I have had no power to attend to any thing, & as the principal cause that you required an early answer from me, were of such small consequence I make no apology for remaining to this time silent to you; in regard to the pictures you alude to, no space of time can ever make me indifferent to the memory of my once very Dear friend Mrs. Sabine, & should as little have thought of leaving behind me, my most favorite possession as that, but I now little know what or whether I have any possession now left me; as in a most barbarous & unheard of manner, all our property which we had packe'd up before we left Bownham House, under the eye & permission of an official Man, empowerd by the Comissioners to superintend our removal & sent them up to London in readiness to be put on board a vessel for Scotland have been for the last week unpacke'd & ransacke'd by one of the Assigne's by orders from the commissioners under the false idea we had removed more than we were allow'd, how it will all end I know not, but I have little doubt we shall unfairly be the sufferers as in no one instance have circumstances turn'd out in a favorable manner for us. by this stroke which on every account is such a severe trial I confess my self quite overcome, for after having taken the utmost pains to act with the strictest propriety & uprightness to be so accused, & to have every thing belonging to me in the hands of such rapacious enimies was a blow I was little prepared for: this detention of course breakes into all our schemes, as we leave this place on the 17th. & intended in a quiet easy manner to have proceeded on to Scotland in the hope of finding out a secluded situation where if possible we might be at rest, & free from the shafts of ill fortune; but till this iniquitous bussiness is finish'd, we must not go so far distant, have therefore determined to halt on the road for 10 Days or a fortnight at a cheap Sea Bathing place in Lancashire till our fate is decided; my health & spirits being dashed (?) that without some aid I am little able to enco/unter/ (hole in letter) the various difficulties I have to struggle with one who has not suffer'd in a similiar manner can form any idea, to which the very small assistance XX have met with except from my own Brothers & Sisters & Neices & the very hospitable friends are XXX now & have been so long with, has not a little (con)tributed (lost hole) to encrease, till cruel experience has taught me the contrary, I thought that to be unfortunate was a certain claim to compassion from those who term themselves friends but we have found it otherwise, our sole trust is in the Almighty who I doubt not will give us equal power to our inclination, "to strive for, & protect our beloved Boys; I feel his powerful goodness in permittng yr. beloved Brother to enjoy perfect health & strength whenever you are so kind to wish to write to us be so good to enclose it, under cover to the Right Hon'ble Lord Edward Bentinch Michelefield Green Watford Herts who having kindly offer'd to be a constant passport to all my Letters, will ever know where to address me, this is such a convenience I cannot be enough grateful for, tho poor Dear Man he laments this is the only good he is able to do us.

Your Brother Joins me in wishing every good & comfort may await you; I am with sincerty your affectionate but much afflicted Sister

A: Witts.

Edinburgh 28th Octb. 1793

My Dear Lady Lyttelton

You may render me a very essential Service, if you will allow me to trouble Mr. Du Val to, go to my my Brother Richards in Harley St., & to Mr. W.in Friday Street, & if he fails of success there to Mr. Daniel his Solicitor, to Enquire where he is at present, or has been for the last two Months; as I have had no answer to three Letters I have wrote to him of great importance to my Comfort at present, & am indeed very much distressed by his Silence—the fact is he has in his hands about £50—of my Son's Money, given to them at Sundry times by their Several Relations, which we find it necessary now to employ in their Service as well the £100—you have so generously adopted. & in the full confidence that it would arise as soon as called for, I have purchased £40—at least of Furniture here on their Acct & want their Money to repay it: & to 3 Letters wrote the 17th. of Augt.—ye 17th. of Sep. & the 8th. of Octb. he has given me no answer whatever. Mr. Witts of Friday Street can inform Mr Du Val where Mr. Daniel lives, who hears from him frequently, & I should be obliged to him to say to Mr. Witts in Friday Street, that a Letter from him would be very acceptable, especialy if he has seen lately my Brother Richards Son which he often does—I have the satisfaction of saying that our future plans here are likely to be much more to our satisfaction: by having agreed for a very commodious & well Situated House, in the new end of the Town, in North Hanover Street with a Western Aspect, that will give us the warmest Climate this Town affords; it is what is called an upper flat— with two floors of 4 Rooms on each—the price is £400: one of which according to yr kind Letter, I have promised to pay at Lady day: As the money from Swerford Park is not yet, come in, till when we shall have the space between Lady day & Witsuntide for completing the purchase & taking possession—. & till when indeed we are obliged to rent Furniture at the exhorbitant expence of £15 or 18£ p Cent.—for to avoid which, I have stretched all my confined powers, to buy a few necessaries: & the money my Brother witholds is at present very distressing to me.—a Letter also from Mr. Wapshott, mention's Mrs. Betts is pretty well, but very low; as my Brothers had not remitted her the Annuity she expected in June, when you sent the £7. 10/- I hope by this time they have relived her Anxieties.—In a former Letter of yours, you expressed a Wish from Mr. Sabine for his Mothers picture—which arrived here with the rest of our Baggage.—& you may inform him that there is an English Clergymans Son here, who is a very good Miniature Painter: his price is £2. 2/- & if Mr. Sabine wishes to have either a Copy or the original, I could get it done here & sent up to him by some secure hand,—but we should be sorry not to have, a memorial ourselves, of the poor sufferer, whose agonies in her last Visit to us; as well as the pleasures, we had before enjoyd in her better days, can never be eradicated from our

Minds.—Mr. Cleve the father of the young Painter is the most celebrated Reader & Preacher, in the English Chapells in this place: which at present are 5 in number, but Mr. Clive is so great a favorite & popular, that a subscription of £2200. has been made by his Friends to build him a New Chapell, in the New Town, & a House for his Residence adjoining to it; it is a most perfect, & beautifull piece of Gothic Work, an Octagon—with Galleries which admits Six hundred Persons—& as it will be very near to our intended residence, we have secured a pew for our Family in it, on the 17th. of Novb. it will be opened for Service—his preaching is nearer to Dr. Horseley's both in clearness, & voice, than any one I have heard—& his XXXXX XXXX a very masterly stile—indeed, he at first XXXXX for the education of his family; was an English Tutor, of XXXXX celebrity—his Chapell is called St. Georges Chapell & more Episcopal, than any of the others; who deviate in some few points for our Service—but not material ones—he is the only Clergyman in Scotland of our Church who wears a Surplice—He has besides a small living in England—you would be very much pleased with the decency of the Services here in all Aspects: in the Establishment, Dr. Blair & a few more are very eminent as preachers—but the other part of their Service is by no means, so long, or attended to, I mean the prayers, as in the Chapells in London, or any of the best stile of dissenting congregations in England.—& you be shocked to hear, that tho' the parade of their funerals much exceeds, any one in England—the Corpse is only followed to the Grave, by Men, who are all in Weeper Mourning—even the Coachmen & Bearers—yet there is no Service whatever nor a Clergiman attending—a few friends see the remains closed to the Top of ye Grave & the last Sod put on with a Spade: at which instant every one of the attendants, pull off their Hatts—make a Bow to the Grave & return to their Houses.—there is seldom less than 20, & more frequently from 50 to 80—Attendants. I have the satisfaction to say we are all pretty well & hope this will find you so, & Miss Stone if she is with you: accept our kind Regards & believe me

Yr: Affectionate Bror Edwd:. Witts.

Edinburgh 26th: April 1795.

My Dear Lady Lyttelton

I feel so much by Experience how gratifying it is, to enquire personally after distant Friends, that I take this oportunity of introducing to you the Bearer—whose Name is Bancroft; who came here last Autumn, to go thro' a Course of Lectures with the Medical professors of this University after having finished his Education at Cambridge, & taken the degree's necessary for practice. He came so well Reccomended in all respects to the professors, as well as people of consequence that he very soon got into the very best Society here, & has been so happy as contribute much to the Comfort of our Circle in particular; as well as many agreable parties to which he has been introduced thro' our means.—He has lived much abroad, & for some time was Secretary to Mr. Walpole at Munich, & is perhaps as polished a young man, as the Scotch Ladies have seen for some time.—He can give you a very correct Account, of the estimation he holds the professional Men here, as well as the Society we are engaged in: & is so good as to have promised me from his Correspondents in Germany, the best information he can procure, to facilitate a plan we have in view at a distant period, if possible to Spend two or three years on the Continent, probably when Francis has gone thro' all the Classical, Learning of this University; which he enters upon in October next.—& the period, when he may return back again; to Study professionally—he is now but twelve years old, & before Eighteen, a professional Study would be improper, therefore we have two or three years in the Interval to enlarge their minds, & give them perhaps the addition of the living Languages, & a larger intercourse of Men & things—Mr: Bancroft will explain more of our plan, He assures me by experience that as we have found this place certainly one third cheaper than any part of England to reside in; we shall find the Continent, one third cheaper, even than this.—I shall probably before you receive this send you a welcome to your London House, & an answer to your last Letter. I have the satisfaction to say we are at present in very good health, tho my wife has undergone in the severity of the early part of the year a severe confinement, by a Miscarriage, which as you may judge; required great care and attention to recruit (?). Mr Bancrofts Father, was a Medical & Political Friend & attendant with Dr. Franklin during his residence in Paris—& has publishd many Chimical & professional Works which are highly spoken of; he took his degrees in Scotland reccomended by Dr. Jos. Banks & many litterary Men: & is now Resident in London—with—his family—Accept kind Regards & be so good as to mention us, as gratefull to all who think us worthy of their Enquiries—you (will) (lost text) soon hear again from your Affectionate Brother & Sincere Friend

Edwd: Witts

Edinburgh 16th Feby: 1796 .

My Dear Lady Lyttelton

I take up a large Sheet of Paper to fill up as any occurrences worth relating arise in my Mind; but chiefly to express my Gratitude to you for the pains & trouble you have had, especially in corresponndencies, on matters of bussiness, which I well know to be very unpleasant, in point of Subject,—as well as employment.—your Letter of the 16th Jany, came to my hands a post or two after a very improper Letter from my Brother Richard—to whom, as well as my Brother Broome, I wrote on the same day as I did to you, on the Sale of ye Life Estate—juding it, a duty to my Sons, as well as myself to make no distinction—in—the Application to my Family on that Sale. My Bror. Richd.s Letter thro' Mr. B.P. Witts of Friday Street—begins thus—"Dear Bror. Mr. B. P. Witts forwarded to me your Letter to him, & also a Copy of Mr. Wapshotts, concerning the purchase of the Revirsion which the Assignees have to dispose of and as you wish it may be bought by one of your Family I have sent Mr. Wapshott word, I would buy it & wait his Answer."—this reply puts you also in possession of the motive that induced Mr. B. W—to make that Offer: but, as he has not informed me, if he purchased it out of his own purse, or from the £50—he detained from my Sons as a Trutee—which I requested of him, if no other person in my family acceded to it,—It still remains, whether the omen of this purchase, arises from Generosity, or Justice due to the Boys—in his opinion in placing part of their Money in that Matter.—I am equally obliged & gratefull for your kind Intentions, however the affair concludes, and am extremly sorry for the multiplied trouble of writing it has given you—If Miss Stone in her french Correspondence with her Cousin at Eversheds could get Mr. R. Witt's real intentions, in this purchase, by a Message from you on that Subject; I should be much obliged to her for the trouble of ye enquirey: as till I know those Intentions, I delay to answer his Letter—which finishes in a very unworthy & unjust attack on Mr. B. P. Witts—for the kind & usefull Services he has rendered me in repeated Instances of kindness & Attention since I left England—I hope too, the Visit my Sister Stone & her Daughter paid at Eversheds has obliterated from Mr. R. W—the Sentiments he entertained of Mr. Stone & interference with Mrs. Grubb, which was nearly of ye same complexion, as his present resentment to Mr. B W. of Friday Street.—I had hoped that three years absence, would have softened the high tone he assumes in his last Letter to me: but it requires a strong mind to hear with propriety the great emancipation, he now feels from the Trustees of his Sons Estates, which has long harrassed his Mind; & of which no one rejoices more than I do, for I am clear he, as well as all his family were basely used. I agree with you in the goodness of Heart of the young Heir.—but from the unfortunate mode of Education, he has hitherto gone thro', I hardly think he has Strength of Understanding sufficient to impell him, for the ensuing three year's to finish, what the Variety of Masters, & the Severity of the Trutees have left undone— and a Sage Mentor, on entering into the World, would be, a very valuable acquisition, whether he travells in his own Country or out of it. He has shown no propensity to Vice of any kind—& therefore might more easily be led into the best Course of Manly Studies & Employments, independant of Litterature, but I fear he has a natural Idleness, as well as but little Inclination to Exercise, which is absolutely necessary to form great part of the Enjoyments of Life. I know you have the kindest Intentions in mentioning repeatedly your opinion of my Wifes Brother—whose principles I never doubted, but whose Conduct in Life has in many respects been as erroneous, as perhaps ever fell to a Man in his Situation-: & which,—with regard to his treatment of my wife, since our Seperation in the essential points of Brotherly Love & kindness, is as unpardonable, as any I have ever met in the Course of my acquaintance in the different Stages of Life I have gone thro'—for it is not the money that he has expended for her use, or my Sons, if it was tenfold what it is—could excuse the constant severity of Temper, & want of Compassion—that he has evinced from the begining—which no other Person whatever in, or out of our family Conections has equalled.—perhaps you have already heard from Mrs. A. Travell of the intended match (or perhaps it is by this time completed)—of Mrs. Buxton, his Daughter, to the eldest Son of Mr. Whalley an old fellow Collegian of y are still to live on with her Father who makes no objection to this Match— which compleats the fourth in his family—all equally surprising to their friends and Relations.—His Piety & principles, will be his security hereafter: but his prudence or Judgment, have been far from infallible.—I thank you for your kind mention of my Sons, who continue in excellent health growing tall & Stout.—they are employed most hours in the Day in various occupations, & this time especially now the Town is filled with all Ranks & Classes of people is so full of incidents, and Events, that the Hours out of Study are never for any time Vacant & from the intercourse our Journey in the Summer gave us in many families, they are become great favorites—& indeed models to many of their College & School fellows—at least their Parents point them out as such.—they have some private Friends, & associates, but not many—as they have only the afternoons, but what are filled up with bussiness of some kind or other.—perhaps if you were to Converse with them, you would discover, the Scotch Idiom, but considering their using the Accent allways in their Classes, they have kept the English Pronounciation much more pure than our friends here expected.—but indeed we have now in Edinburgh a pretty large English Party—and the Windsor Forresters have been universally received in all the best families, & conduct themselves much to the Satisfaction of every body—some pleasant Men too from the Cambrige Cavallry are very well received, & add altogether so much to the brilliancy of the Assemblies, that an undrest Ball on Mondays—is added this year—to the Dress Ball on Thursdays; which used to be the only one; in this Town, tho' the South Town has a very good Room—& a Ball on Tuesdays—which with private Balls—(which the Scotch have a Rage for) generally fills up every day except Sundays—& sometimes 3 or 4 on a night. We indeed felt it absolutely necessary to return in some small degree, the unbounded Civilities & kindness we have experiend from our Introductions, this year.—and calculating from the Families who have invited us to eat & drink in their Houses, (excluding those who are only morning Visitors)—we found the number so large, that in Janyary, we gave a Ball & Sandwich's—to half the Party which really amounted to 47. Persons—& on the 9th. of this Month, we gave an English—Rouhd—the first that has ever been attempted in Edinburgh to 60 more invited—but 50—actualy came. consisting chiefly of Heads of Families & Matrons—the Windsor Forresters were at the First—& some of them at the last.—they both luckily gave very great satisfaction, & by the kindness of Lady Riddell & other Friends, we were splendidly furnished with every thing, we wanted for our accomodation, as well as Servants.—the Expence of both, was very small, especially as we had a very fine Gentleman Musician to add to our fiddle, whose Daughter was at the Ball, & his greatest Delight is in that department,—This mode of return we found much easier & Cheaper than a number of smaller Parties—& gave infinitely more satisfaction . till next year we shall no occasion for such exertions, finding as we do the gradual decrease of English friendships & connections, it is our Duty as well as enjoyment to make friends here for our Boys, who have six or Seven years still, to employ in preparing them to enter in to the World, but it remains in the womb of fate, how to employ that period, & to wait for the Events as they arise.—Dr. Bancroft has assumed his Diplomatic title, in the way he wished for by being appointed Physician to the Army, thro' the Interest of Lord Grenville—it not only gives him actual pay of half a Ginnea a day, but may probably promote his gratification still more by going abroad with the Troops—no situation is more likely to ensure fame & fortune in that time: as they have no difficulties to strugle with, to get employment as other men of that Profession have.—Our Friend Dr. Pennington is finishing his studies in London this Winter & I believes means to go & settle at Nottingham, XXXXX his old Friends. The serious people of this place begin to be better satisfied with our little French Court at Holyrood House.—about a fortnight ago, Monsieur's Son the Duc D'Angueleme came with the rest of the party, which consists of 13—persons besides Domestic Servants.—His Allowance is fixed at twelve thousand Pounds a year, & the State Officers contract with the Several Trademen;—for everything & send the Bills up to the Exchequer for payment. so that it is the fault of the Tradesmen themselves, if they suffer them to create Debts: & they all begin to be aware of the advantage the Town has, by so large a Sum of the Public Money—being spent among them, instead of remitted to London. For the first month Monsieur had a Levee twice a Week, to receive the Compliments of all the Official Men in the Country as well as the Country Gentelmen & indeed every one who were in the habit of visiting the Commander in Cheif Lord Adam Gordon. but as the Crowd is now over it is to continue regularly every Monday—& is generally a Circle of from 30 to 40.—Duc DAngulemé his Son arrived about a fortnight ago, & has been not only introduced in public—but to private Assemblies—as well as Some of the Suite—who accept of dining Visits—but the Prince & his Son, alone neither receive nor pay dining Visits anywhere.—The old Suit of Apartments belonging the Royal Family, are preparing for their residence: at present they occupy Lord Adam Gordons, & Lord Bredalbane Apartments, under the same Roof.—at the Queens Ball on the Birth day—Lord Adam G—& all his Staff introduced Monsieur to the Whole Assembly—the Dutchess of Buccleugh presiding as Directoress as they are here call Lady Patroness's.—there were near 900 in the Room, who were astonished at the Ease & Elegance of the Count & his Suite in so numerous a party of Strangers—indeed they are in general, very little accustomishd to the high bred persons—as their own Nobility & Gentry except those who belong to the English Court are at least half a Century behind in Courtly Etiquette—there is a Countess Polignac, (whose Husband is with Louis the 18th. at Verona (?), who with a Son about 11 year old & another Lady, have taken a House near the Pallace, but does not yet appear elsewhere. the Son is attending Francis's French Master, a Mr. Drummond—to learn English, & we were fortunate enough to bring down an English Grammar of Bishop Louth's—for his use.—I hope you will have much satisfaction in Mrs. M Hamss—that will make amends for the repeated inconveniencies you have experiend in your London House—tho' the Scotch Reel was not so serious, as the loss of the Linen Chest last year, yet imprudencies of that Sort generally lead to bad consequences.—I wish you could be here on the 26th: of this month & see Francis dance a Scotch Reel at Lady Dukinfields Ball, which is on the Wedding Day of Sr. h (?) & her Ladyship)—my wife has this morning been arranging the party of young Gentlemen & Ladies—none exceeding the Age of Francis—& the great point is—to select the best Charactered Boys for which purpose as well as many others, my wife is frequently Consulted.—The Situation of poor Lady Clive is less painfull to her Friends, as well as herself by the tranquillity of mind she declines in, & considering the nature of the disorder—the least painfull in all respects.—The mildness of the Season here keeps pace with yours in England, nor is the Season at present unhealthy, tho' we have had a great deal of wet Weather—but accompanied by some strong Northern Blast's—that in a degree has purified the Air.—the Consequence of the Season is propitious to the poor, as fuel & Fish are in plenty. This Town is unusualy full this year, & as a proof 5 or 6 large Houses from 2000£ to £3500—have sold within the 6 Months last past that had been on Sale for the two last years.—& to the astonishment of the inhabitants, the Hotells are now as full of English Travellers & Visitors as in the Summer Season.—my wife & myself perfectly reccolect Lord Sackville & Home at old Drayton which we visited once in our return from Oundle, in the Late Lords Time.—The present Lords attachment to Mrs. Rigby continues very Constant. The Hairense I well remember, with the feasts & Tournaments of Chilvalry—I fear this Letter will tire you as much in reading—as your kind pacquet did in writing—but if it finds you—& all your Neighbourhood at the Sands in as good Health as it leaves Us—it will be a great gratification to hear of it from any hand to—your Faithfull & Affect Brother EW.

Edinburgh 31st. March 1797

My Dear Lady Lyttelton

Early in February last, I wrote you a very interesting Letter, & early in this month Mr Witts of Friday Street sent me word he had communicated to you the substance of our Alarms, in this part of the world—under the awfull appearances, & events that have lately occurred & tho the mere safety of this Kingdom, as well as of England on the subject of the Invasion is subsided—the interior of it, & this Town—in particular—is in—so anxious a State from the difficulties in—money matters, that I must beg your answer to the Letter I wrote you in Februay; & also that you will inform me if you have had any communication with the family at Eversheds, or if they are in Town. as I wrote to him at the same time, & have received no answer.—as if I have no other mode of alleviating the embarrassments we are under, I must sink part of our own Income to procure it.—Had the war been at an End we could with ease & Comfort have proceeded to fullfill our plan on the Continent.—this Spring, where we have should have been able to retrench, & make our Income—answer our expences—but even the dearness of provisions & accumulating Taxes & Burthens is every day encreasing here, & to change our Situation is impossible, as we have I fear less reason to expect Sir James & Lady Riddell down—now, than earlier in the year, I shall write to Mr. Witts in Friday Street to let him know, a Mr. Gilchrist who is a large dealer with him, goes to London on Monday next, & has promised me to bring down with his purchases in London, anything that Mr. Witts may request him to take.—Which could be a good way of sending the Books you kindly mentioned in your last Letter. I hope you have escaped the Influenza we hear so much of from our London Correspondence, & the bad Effects of your Fog, & East Winds—the Winter here, has been remarkably mild & ye. Spring forward. the Equinoxtional Winds were but transcient, & we have lately had some mild Showers, which was much wanted.—excepting Slight Colds, we have been perfectly well, Tho the Society for the last three months; has been, to one half of the Town beyond the bounds of moderation or prudence, the other half, have been in proportion holding back as much as possible—we are among the last Set.—& have in general been engaged but two or three times in a week in private parties, & avoided all publick ones—I wish you may have been able to have seen much of Lady Riddell as she expressed much pleasure in the introduction, & by her own Account, but time has passed very far from her usual comforts.—Sir James has I fear embarrassed himself, by buying in, an Estate he went up to sell,—& tho they had a good large House ready furnished, & untenanted, by selling the furniture first, they have driven themselves into dissagreable Lodgings—& I hear have not be able to dispose of the Lease of the House as he intended—as Lord Edwd. Bentinck still continues his good Offices to us, I hope you will soon avail yourself of his Passport XXXXXX give me great pleasure to hear it brings me XXXXX Xllegence that you have passed the Winter XXXX your Retirement in the parsonage with Health & Satisfaction — accept our united kind & affectionate Regards—& believe me Yours very Sincerely

Edwd. Witts.

This Winter we have reading over to our Sons a very large Quantity of Old Letters from the year 1768.—from their old Connections—on, both sides, to open to their minds, now very capable of forming a Jugement—the Terms we formerly lived upon.—. & to explain the various changes & vicissitudes that occur in the Course of thirty Years—to the world we have lived in, & the parties we have associated most with.—

Edinburgh 10th: July 1797

My Dear Lady Lyttelton

I thank you Sincerely for your Letter of the 23 June, which has unravelled much of the mistery, & many of my fears, from the Contents of your last Letters.—how my Letter came to be lost, written in Februay I cannot guess, unless from the direction of the Cover, which I think was frankd by Captn Hamilton Dabrymple, & I reccolect rather obscure—in looking over my file of Letters I find I sent you inclosed the Letter of the Principal of Glasgow College, for Dr. Glass's insiption, with my sincere regret at not being able to avail myself of any part of that Establishment for my Sons.—I think now if Mr B P Witts, woud request Mr Fredrich Whalley to examine the dead Letters as they are called in the Post Office lying to be owned (for want of decyphering) it may yet be obtained, unless it failed, between Berkeley Street & Wansted.—as I have never yet had one Letter miscarry without being accounted for.—your kind enclosure of three Guineas come safe—& I have returned you in this the unsigned note according to your request—but as to the acknowledgment or Receipt from the Warfe man for the Box, it did not come in your last Letter I mean that of of the 30th. of May, which has led, to all the Dilemna about the Box which is at last arrived safe, & proves a very gratifying & acceptable present to my Sons, as it will not only be a foundation for the future Library of both, but is peculiary desirable, as the smaller edition's of the Classic's are exactly suited to travell with us on the Continent, & the Amsterdam Editions of which they chiefly consist, are in great estimation. the delay of their arrival was not owing to your Care—as your own direction, was quite proper & sufficient—but somebody afterwards with a Brush wrote a large Direction on the Box to me at Leith—in course it lay in the Cellar of the Shipmaster for near two Months, before he discoverd me in the directory of Edinburg—& sent a porter up with it.—'twas Col: Rookes note you inclosed to me, instead of the Warfe Man. or else I should have discovered it on its arrival.—for your satisfaction George shall copy Lord Elcho Letter—to Mr. Travell, which has miscarried—which will explain the whole transaction—.—Mr. Travell answer was precisely this—"I am desired by my Brother & Sisters to say that their Incomes are much too short", to "allow of any diminution of them"— nor can any of us approve of being "securities upon a contingency which might affect our Representatives at a Remote Period."—the Question asked by Lord Elcho, was only ten Pound appeas, (?) between the Party of 4 Brothers & Sisters—to 3 of whom—my Wife & my Sons are the legal Representatives— Lord Elcho s observation on it was, that such an answer admitted no Comment—& at the only meeting his Lordship had with Mr. Travel in Town.—he made the matter still more extraordinary in his Estimation, but not venturing to mention a syllable of the bussiness,—to the 4. the Expence would have been 2.. 10/- each, 'till my Sons come of Age—which was the object he asked, & which in consequence of the refusal of my wife's Family, I resolved for reasons I have before given you to apply to mine—the necessity of this application is not so much to relieve past occurrences, as to provide for next 4 years—& as I have not succeeded in our family application: I have obtained it here from a very kind & excellent Man—Mr. Erskine of Cumbo—in whose House we were hospitably entertained last year & where we shall again revisit in the two months vacation that the School allows to George.—Lord Elchos wish was to prevent us sinking our own Income for the £200: which after all, is not sunk, but that it is absolutely necessary to prepare that Sum beforhand when we go to the Continent, in case of any Contingencies—and in settling all our affairs here next May, I hope & trust I shall accomplish my wishes—in the mean time my Dear Sister you may do me a very sincere kind office if you would apply to my Brother Richard seriously to return the £50 & the Int. due to my Sons for to assist us in the plan we have formed which he has no right either in honesty or Justice to detain from them any longer as it is consists entirely of the accumulated Guineas & half Guineas collected from their Relations—& can never be so well disposed of as in the finishing of their Education—I am very glad to gather from your Letter that no individual distress—more than the Times have occasioned the pressures you complain of.—certainly in our small Scale, we feel them less—as we have no Luxuries that come under the great Taxes—& thank God in the plan proposed for the next 4 years we shall be wholly exempt from all Taxes: The price of Butchers meat is now our greatest grievance.—I own I by no means feel the very severe apprehension's either for publich or private affairs—& the wisdom & steadiness of Government have certainly removed allready great part of ye danger by keeping under the dissafected part of the Kingdom's—by the two Treason Bills—& by their proper Exertion in the last Mutiny—which has in the end done more good than harm, as it has called out the powers of the Army as well as their principles to the view of the world at large, & left no hope's to ye Dissafected Insurgents—I am very glad to have now heard the certainty of the Situation of my Nephew John which exceedes my Expectations, as at his time of Life to be a 2d Lieutt. in a 74 Gun Sun, if he has health & Luck must ultimately bring early in Life to a very reputable Station in the Navy—& it is a never failing truth, that no situation in Life, is so likely to succeed as when it meet's the mind of the Object—even in the outset—of this I can speak from experience—I had two Letters from Mr. Sabine one on the Road & another the day of the marriage.—I have answered it fully, & expressed just what I feel, that no match could be happier if his Daughter is satisfied, as so worthy & active, as well as rich a Man, may be essentially usefull to the rest of the family. Mrs. Hyatt sent us a very long & interresting Acct. of our Connections by the same post as your last, & mentions the state of Mr. Browne from the variety of Climate to be like most others who have so engaged—& adds that unfortunately he looks, as much older than he is, & Mrs. Browne does younger.—but expresses her entire Satisfaction in the match. She likewise adds (after a discription of her encreased size, as a fat & Joly Lady, near twelve Stone in Weight—who used to be called by Dr. Kennicott Slim Sal). that Lady Lyttelton has stood still for the last twenty years, & looks in as good Health & Spirits, as in any period of her memory.—on looking over the Letter again, I will repeat her own words "Lady Lyttelton too, is grown rather fat, looks remarkably well & not a day older than she did 20 years ago"—I generaly think that a third person is a much better judge, than parties concerned, but notwithstanding as you must be the best judge of the present state of your Health, why should any circumstances make you omit a Visit to Cheltenham to ensure you so great a blessing, especially as you have so many friends within the Circle of that Journey—I am still more desirous to urge it, as it may give you a reccolection of a Plan I once before suggested, when you are 100 miles nearer to this place, to make a party with my Sisters to come & winter with us—& by that means have one interview of my family in our destined 10 years seperation -: if we mutualy live so long. if you & Mrs. Travells would let your ready furnished Homes for the time—you are absent, I will answer for it you will save Money by the Journey & perhaps pass as chearfull a winter, independant of family Connections. as well as seeing a number of old acquaintance on both sides whom we know in this Kingdom—One Coach would bring you all, & honest Jn o Lucas whom I have neglected to mention in my last Letter is capable of being as usefull a Servant in any description as any Man in his Condition I ever saw in my Life—I have tried him all description's—& and have no reason to think that misfortunes would lessen his worth or exertions, & I could prepare a ready furnished House at a little Notice: & relieve you from any of impositions or difficulties that strangers are liable to: perhaps it may be the only opportunity you may have of seeing either, seeing us or our Sons: for 10 years is a formidable period in all our Lives.—tho' I am by no means a Croker, & have many blessings now around me, & hope long to enjoy them: Mrs. Hyatt speaks like you & many others of the dreadfull Situation & appearances of the times in London: but concludes by mentioning how wonderfull it was, that no wise & serious persons were so much alarmed in the Country, & and all of them looking sanguinely, that the times would mend.—in truth—the worst news comes first to ye knowledge of ye Capital: & there is so great a bulk of wicked & mischeifeous people there to sound alarms—& as many more to encrease them: that all at a distance from that Volcano of Alarm, receive the impression's with more Caution; & having more time for reflection, than the multitude in London, are less liable to the impositions & prejudices that are dissemminated.—just at the period of Mr. Brownes Marriage, a Letter from Lady Elcho to my wife announced the offer of Lord Grey to Miss Charlotte, the Eldest Daughter, of Lord Elcho. you may suppose this match gives the utmost Joy to all the family as the Stamford Family, is not only more emminent for Rank & Riches than wisdom & Morality. his Lordship is Col: of a Militia Regiment, & now at Newcastle. the match will take place in about six weeks. & we have some hopes of seeing them afterwards in Scotland, if his Regiment remains in the North. the first Marriage of a family (especialy of 4 Daugts.) is a lucky omen for the rest.—Lord Elcho is by time in London to receive his Son, who is languishing under a Cruel illness from a fall from his Horse two years ago, which returned again—in October last so violent that he is unable to move either in a Carriage or on Horseback: & a Government Yatch from hence was procured to take him to London by Sea & he embarked last Wednesday—to get the best advice London will afford. His Wife has lately given him—another Son: & she is now nursing it & therefore does not go up with him—he is a very estimable private Character & I hope to God the London Surgeons & Physicians may be more successfull than those of Edinburgh & enable him to attend in comfort & Ease his lovely Sister to the Altar when she enter into the Splendid establishment she well deserves.—Principal Gorden is now on a Visit to Lord Bute—I am sorry you did not see him. if he remains in England he will probably return here again in the Autumn. I know Dr. Taylor personally & by Character—if he does not succeed with our Nephew. I guess he has too much of the Grandfather in his Stuborn Mind—we have every reason to expect Sir Jms. & Lady Riddell in the course of the week. they do not stop at Buxton as they intended.—You will forgive this long Detail—I hope this will find you quiety settled in your Parsonage & have leasure to arrange the Plan I have proposed—which would be a source of great pleasure to Yr. Affect. Bror EW. accept the Gratitude of My Son's & the kind Regards of Mrs. Witts.

Edinburgh—17th Novr. 1797—

My Dear Lady Lyttelton—

I was not at all surprised, but much gratified, to receive your Letter from Cheltenham—& think you have acted very judiciously, by giving the Waters so fair a trial as you may be enabled to do by making it your Winter Rresidence. there cannot be a warmer, or a pleasanter Situation as the walks near the Town are suited to every Season & from ye well known experience of many pleasant & happy periods I have passed in my Life in that town & its Neighbourhood; I knew no Small Town better suited to a winters retirement. I hope the Waters will have the full effect you expect from them: & perhaps if they establish your Health at this period—it may add many future years of Comforts & Enjoyments. I shall direct this Letter to Cheltenham, as your headQuarters, which will not probably be more than—one Stage or two from the idea you give me of your intended Visits & Movements. Mrs. Travell as yourselves are the best judges of the practicalility of an interview with us, before the month of May, when we have no reason to delay or German Tour— especially as a peace has taken place in the Empire—but in any Case, our first years destination would have been very totally out of the reach or sound of Warlike allarms—you will be sorry to hear that we many Reasons to regret the loss of poor Sir James Riddell—whose Health has continued to decline ever since he returned to Scotland. & you the State of Suffering he was under in London last year—however that Journey was in many senses very propitious, as he had an opportunity of settling many essential matters of business that would otherwise have been very uncomfortable perhaps to Lady Riddell. The confidence he has placed in me since his return to Scotland, on an unhappy dispute with his Sons Widdow Mrs. Riddell—& in the Education of his Grandson—has taken up a great deal of our time & thoughts, & we were eventually very usefull as mediators altho' the conduct of Mrs. R—was so imprudent—that in the last hours, he had not fortitutude to suffer her to appear—or to see him—& she must long regrett the imprudence, of refusing the advice of her friends & especially of ourselves, to forbear any applications on bussiness, to a man visibly on the verge of Eternity—he died on the 2d. Novr.—having only been confined to his Bedchamber 3 or 4 days or indeed out of society, as he came & sat with us in our Evening Visits; tho' from his disorder, he could sit at Table, or eat but in private from the weakness of his Stomach, which refused all animal food for many months except in the Shape of Soups—or soft Potted meat's in this State, his Servant one morning found him in very alarming Shivering fit, and proper medical assistants came in, but the next night— an internal postume, broke, & he voided an immense burthen of Bile in the most fetid state—which for a short time seemed to relieve him: but the consequent weakness & debility, & indeed the Exausted Nature brought on the last moments evidently without pain, or of much suffering, & probably not aware of his own danger. he had only Returned ten days from Buxton, which, he was allways in the habit of going to in former bilious attacks—& it is probably those Waters prevented the Crisis, while he staid there, & afforded him more Ease—but on his return, & every day since, His faculties visibly declined.—this Event is a very serious loss to us, as if he had lived he meant to have sent his Grandson under my Care for the 4 years we may be absent as he as well as every one else were conscious how improper & unsafe it would be to leave him under the Mothers Care, who by indulgence already has bought the Boy into a very improper train of Mind: & tho she is excluded from the Guardianship—it remains doubtfull if the Trustees & Guardians will carry into excution the intentions of his Grandfather. he had some time before his death, insisted on her corresponding thro' me, on the Subject of his Education:—& we happily succeeding in making both the Parties satisfied with the measures we pursued—Lady Riddell & all the other friends of the Day, are as conscious as his Grandfather was of the necessity of removing him from the Mother, especialy now he is come into his Title, & liable to all the low insinuaitions of the dependants about him: as well as the improper partiality & indulgence of his Mother. As soon however as the Trustees begin on the subject of the Guardianship—proper Steps will be taken with the most serious & well informed of those that act (for Sir James has named 20 Trustees & Guardians in his will) to make them acquainted with the real Intention of the Testator—Lady Riddell has a clear Jointure of £1800—a year—& all the Plate Linen China Jewels & Furniture, as well as Carriages—for her Life without any Inventory—but what she herself may give up to ye Trustees.—she has besides near £4000—in her own disposal. She means to reside here till we quit the place in May next.—& in future to reside in Bath. which is best suited to her present time of Life, & will give her in the general XXXXX of that place an opportunity of meeting with most of her old friends, & getting on in her own stile of small parties every Evening instead of crowded assemblies—her whole Conduct on his Event is judicious & proper: & as she never once enterd into any of the troublesome disputes Mrs. Riddell created, she pay her the most proper attention while she remains in the Country. Sir Jamess Body is taken up to Yarmouth, to be buried by his first wife, who made a solemn request to him, in her last hours to that purpose.—it creates a great Expence, but the Trustees on investigating his papers found his Conduct with respect to his affairs so honourable to all parties—that no single difficulty was made to all his arrangements.—so much we have lived in the family, & the kindness & uniform respect & affection he always shewed to all our Circle, will allways make me remember him with gratitude—& is the only appology I can give for the detail I have given.—you mention that the German Plan may probably be retarded by

the want of a peace—but in fact the late Peace in the Empire, is very favorable to our plan—&
procures us an assylym from the heavy Taxes & burthens of this Country—I cannot contract my
Circle as you can—for the two Boys are become young Men: but till they fully prepared to stand
on their own Ground I shall loose no opportunity of enabling them to do it in the best manner I
can. I am sure you will find Thos. Lucas very honest, & I am equally sure I find as usefull in both
the Capacities, you employ him as any Servt. I ever had. & hope he will continue long in your
Service. Catherine Newman had too much indulgence in our Service for 18 years to make her likely
to suit many placces—I did not expect she would long remain with you. I have lately met with
some Gentlemen who were witness to a very very serious offer of Marriage from Mr. Lee Steere at
Harrowgate to a Miss Daniel, the Daughter of rich (?) east Indian, who with his Wife & Son &
two daughters Mr. Steere followed from York Races where he recived as he said the first Shot thro'
his Heart—from Miss Daniel—The Mother a very vulgar odd Woman was very sanguine for the
Match—but the Father gave his Daughter her Choice, & he was refused—& in consequence left
Harrowgate, but with a determination to visit the family again in Harley Street, where they live as
well as himself. Mr. Taite a Man very eminent in the Law here & Membr. of Parlt. told me he
consulted him on the bussiness, & that he gave him very cautious advice, to know the family a
little longer before he made his proposals—but his ardor was too great—& in an short absence
Mr. Tait was on a visit he made his proposals & was refused, Mr. Tait said his Conduct was in no
degree improper, except a little dashing about his Curricle & Horses—& that he opened to him
his fortune & view in Life, confessing he knew very little of the world & wished for a private
life—he asked him if he knew his Uncle & Aunt in Endinburg & spoke frequently of them—but
to his great surprise never mentioned having either Father Mother, Brother or Sister to any one of
the Party at Harrogate.—I have written an Acct. of this transaction to his Father, as I thought it
right he showd know it: but it a sad proof of his stubborn Rebellion against his father in not asking
his Consent on so material a point. the young Lady was a prodigeous fine Singer in the Italian Stile,
nor very pretty but a genteel & Elegant figure. I belive they have a place in Yorkshire, as well as
their House in Harley, & were a great entertainment to the Company in the House, as the old Lady
to the distress of the young ones was perpetually ordering them to sing to any of the Gentlemen
who desired it—they were said to be very rich. I have not heard much of the Book you mention
Maurice's History of Liderton. our present Reading is Mr. Gisborn Duty of Men of all Profession
and a 8°. vol: of the Duties of Women—But as my wife is now taking some general Lesson in the
French Language & we find many preparations for our departure—as well as many usefull
Employments for our friends—this winter will not afford us so much reading as former ones—tho
we never open our doors to any one before one o Clock which gives us a long morning.—you may
probably have seen in the papers that Col: Montague Burgogne, who is now residing here with his
family, has had the great misfortune to loose his only Son by the Croop—all the first Physicians
were calld in but nothing could save the poor Child—he was I believe about 8 Yrs. old—to add to
their great private distress, the Col himself is to be tried by a Court Martial which begins on Monday
next in the Castle, for 38—Charges made against him by some infamous noncommissiond officers
in the Regt. abt. the forage—which altho' it may be got over most probably to his Credit, yet in
the present State of his Mind as well as Mrs. Burgogne's, it must be very dissagreeable, especialy
as it may last a long time to investigate. I met him in in the Court of Sessions some time ago & had
a good deal of Conversation with him, but did not introduce myself—but Mrs. Rooke who with
the Col: & his family are now in Endinburgh for the Winter meant to have made a party to meet

them: as my wife was very well acquainted with him; Col: Rooke is one of the Court Martial. Poor Mrs. Rooke has sufferd much by the loss of a Sister at Liverpool, last week who had long been in a very melancholy state from a parralictic Affection. so that between the two Houses of Mourning my wife has been propetualy employed in kind offices & attentions—I am glad to glad to hear from my Bror. John in Sepr. that he has frequent Letters from LXXXXX who went out with Lord Hugh Symour, to join Lord Vincent fleet—he says he is in XXXXX & Spirits—& his pay raissed a Shilling a day & some other deductions taken of makes his pay now nearly 5/- a day & is also entitled to £30 prize money—fortunately their Ship was not of the unfortunate Teneriffe Party which sufferd so much, tho' he says the Crew growled much they were not sent.—I find also he was equally fortunate in leaving Plymouth a fortnight before the Mutiny began, I hope to God the poor fellow may continue to receive the same protection from Providence, & his father will have less Reason to regret the Choice he made for himself Indeed from all the Events in the Course of this War, the Navy will find that experience will restore all the old Maxims, & that all our future Energies must depend in their protection for their is hardly Soil in Europe besides our own that is safe in point of principles to venture an Army upon without risque of rebellion & outrage. Mrs. Travell has sent us word, you are hesitating between Cheltenham & Clifton for your winter Residence—either of them are pleasant & afford good Society in a small scale in the Winter — The University Classes are just begun & Francis fully employd in Mathematicks—& French, Greek & German Languages—besides being an Assistant in the French to his Mother who take three Lesson a week from a Master, & in our own intercourse at home, she comes on much beyond our Expectation—but steadyness & perseverence will generally overcome large as well as small difficulties. That George may have time—to finish his Latin Classic's well & acquire french, he does not begin Greek till he goes to Leipsic—where he will plunge at once into Greek & German—except a few first principles Francis may initiate him in all our View are now concentord on that plan, & we have some very good advisers here who give us all usefull information.—Pray let me know in your next Letter where Mrs. Williams is—I thought I heard she & her Husband had settled at Taunton in Devonshire—but some late Letter mentioned she was at Miss Wheates at Glympton. When have you seen her? & in what state of Health of Mind or Body is she?—as I have heard no particulars since I saw her in her Hut in the Garden when I hardly thought she would live to this time—but probably that was a peculiar time, & she may still keep pace with his six Brothers & Sisters—who to say the truth in point of Health & abilities—are under no small obligations of Gratitude to Providence for the Blessings they still enjoy.—As you have no chance of seeing my Bror. Richard before we quit the Kingdom I shall say no more on the subject, than that if he reflects with horror at his Sons conduct to him—what right has he to expect the esteem or respect of his Nephews— when he can condescend to deprive them in the only time of their Lives when the Money is essential, to accelerate & add to their future prosperity—even the Donations of their earliest friends—the principal & Interst of that Money would enable us to purchase the Carriage we are preparing to embark with without putting us to the necessity of sinking more of our Income to further the plan we adopt.—If he had taken his Sons to his Bosom, as I have done, & made them his friends in Confidence, as well as affection, he would not probably have felt the Sting he now does—he need not add another , to it, by his harshness & Cruelty to my Sons—We are all well, thank God & happy—& for them as well as myself I sign myself yours most affectionately

E Witts

This following letter was sent from Lord Elcho in London to Ferdinando Tracy Travell at Upper Slaughter. It did not have desired effect and no loan was forthcoming from Ferdinando or his brother and sisters. However, in late 1801 or early 1802 he relented to a degree by funding Francis to perhaps about one third of the cost of his studies and accommodation at Oxford.

Portland Place 10 Decr. 1797

My dear Sir.

It will most probably appear to you rather surprising on my part, addressing you on the subject which I am going to do in this Letter: but from my near connection with your family, & the very flattering & most friendly manner I have ever been received by it; I am induced to hope that my venturing to offer an opinion & to solicit your consideration as well as the other branches of yr family of the circumstances I shall now mention will not be taken in any shape amiss by you or them. In the conversation I had with you yesterday, I told you how much I was pleased with the manner in which your Sister and Mr Witts had conducted themselves since they retir'd to Scotland & the very great & necessary pains they have taken in the education of their Children. I am further convinced that both from the report of others & from what I saw they have taken great pains to live within their small income. But I have reason to believe & permit me to say I am not surprised at it, they have run a little short, & yet not much in near 4 years they have been there. The whole I fancy within a £100 but even this in their situation without any resource is a serious sum. I am well aware of the former kindness of their friends & how much has been done for them: but at the period of life their Sons now are & the very strict attention they really have paid to keep things within bounds I must say I could wish a small effort was made to enable them to pursue their very well digested plan. Two hundred Pounds now would be putting them above the world for the remainder of the period of their Son's Education. I heartily wish I was so circumstanced, as to be a contributer to their happiness in this instance but alas I have not the means. I do not pretend to say that any of their friends have but such a sum might be borrowed upon the Credit of the family & the interest for a few years paid among their friends till the young men could repay the principal & in this way it would not affect them much. I should fain hope that what I have stated will not be taken amiss, I really mean to serve & I most fully assure you that I had no commission from either your sister or her husband. He did explain to me that he wished he could find means to raise £100 & asked my advice about it but he never hinted to me the smallest expectations from his friends & I am now induced to suggest this to you from a hope that by the figure these young men are likely to make in life such a timely exertion would be amply repaid in solid comfort to the family. I have no more to add on this subject only to request your forgiveness & that of your Brothers & Sisters for presuming of offer my opinion which nothing but a sincere good wish for the prosperity of every one connected with you would have induced me to do.

I am yr afte Elcho